T0181051

Communications
in Computer and Information Science   **1675**

More information about this series at https://link.springer.com/bookseries/7899

Teresa Guarda · Filipe Portela ·
Maria Fernanda Augusto (Eds.)

Advanced Research in Technologies, Information, Innovation and Sustainability

Second International Conference, ARTIIS 2022
Santiago de Compostela, Spain, September 12–15, 2022
Revised Selected Papers, Part I

 Springer

Editors
Teresa Guarda 🄳
Universidad Estatal Península de Santa
La Libertad, Ecuador

Filipe Portela 🄳
University of Minho
Guimarães, Portugal

Maria Fernanda Augusto 🄳
BITrum Research Group
Leon, Spain

ISSN 1865-0929   ISSN 1865-0937 (electronic)
Communications in Computer and Information Science
ISBN 978-3-031-20318-3   ISBN 978-3-031-20319-0 (eBook)
https://doi.org/10.1007/978-3-031-20319-0

This Springer imprint is published by the registered company Springer Nature Switzerland AG
The registered company address is: Gewerbestrasse 11, 6330 Cham, Switzerland

Preface

The need for a greener and more digital world leads academia, governments, industry, and citizens to look for emerging, sustainable, intelligent solutions and trends.

These new solutions and ideas must promote communication and ubiquitous computing between society agents, i.e., citizens, industry, organizations, networked machines and physical objects, and provide a promising vision of the future, integrating the real world of knowledge agents and things with the virtual world of information. The emerging approaches under study or development can address several dimensions with a technological focus like information, innovation, and sustainability and topics such as computing solutions, data intelligence, ethics, security, privacy, and sustainability.

The change observed in society modifies the landscape of human activity, particularly regarding knowledge acquisition and production, offering new possibilities and challenges that need to be explored, assessed, and disseminated.

To expose and disseminate such information, ARTIIS arose. ARTIIS is an international forum for researchers and practitioners to present and discuss the most recent innovations, trends, results, experiences, and concerns from the varying perspectives of technology, information, innovation, and sustainability. This book is split into two volumes and contains a selection of papers accepted for presentation and discussion at the second International Conference on Advanced Research in Technologies, Information, Innovation and Sustainability (ARTIIS 2022) and its workshops. ARTIIS 2022 received 191 contributions from authors in 37 countries worldwide. The acceptance rate was 37.69%, with the program comprising 72 regular papers.

The first volume of the book contains all the papers on the topics of Computing Solutions and Data Intelligence:

- Computing Solutions addresses the development of applications and platforms involving computing and related to some area of knowledge or society. It includes papers on networks, pervasive computing, gamification, and software engineering.
- Data Intelligence focuses on data (e.g., text, images) acquisition and processing using smart techniques or tools. It includes papers on computing intelligence, artificial intelligence, data science, and computer vision.

The second volume collates all papers relating to Sustainability or Ethics, Security, and Privacy:

- Ethics, Security, and Privacy focuses on a more strict and secure area of information systems where the end-user is the main concern. Vulnerabilities, data privacy, and cybersecurity are the main subjects of this topic.
- Sustainability explores a new type of computing which is more, green, connected, efficient, and sustainable. Subjects like immersive technology, smart cities, and sustainable infrastructure are part of this topic.

ARTIIS 2022 had the support of the CIST Research and Innovation Center of the Universidad Estatal Peninsula de Santa Elena, Ecuador, and the Algoritmi Research Center of Minho University, Portugal. It was realized in a hybrid format, taking place both face-to-face and virtually at Xunta Cultura y Educación Secretaría Xeral de Política Lingüística, Santiago de Compostela, Spain, during September 12–15, 2022.

The Program Committee was composed of a multidisciplinary group of more than 175 experts from 29 countries, with the responsibility for evaluating, in a double-blind review process, the papers received for each of the main themes proposed for the conference and special sessions. Each paper was reviewed by at least 3 Program Committee members and final acceptance decisions were made by the Program Committee chairs.

The papers accepted to ARTIIS 2022 are published in this volume in Springer's Communications in Computer and Information Science (CCIS) series. It is indexed in DBLP, Google Scholar, EI-Compendex, SCImago, and Scopus. CCIS volumes are also submitted for inclusion in ISI Proceedings.

Besides the main conference, ARTIIS 2022 hosted 12 special sessions:

- ACMaSDA 2022 - Applications of Computational Mathematics to Simulation and Data Analysis
- CICITE 2022 - Challenges and the Impact of Communication and Information Technologies on Education
- CICT 2022 - Cybersecurity in Information and Communication Technologies
- ET-AI 2022 - Emergent Technologies and Artificial Intelligence
- GAT 2022 - 2nd Workshop on Gamification Application and Technologies
- IHEDIE 2022 - Inclusive Higher Education and Disruptive Innovation in Education International Workshop
- ISHMC 2022 - Intelligent Systems for Health and Medical Care
- IWEBTM 2022 - International Workshop on Economics, Business and Technology Management
- IWET 2022 - International Workshop on Electronic and Telecommunications
- RTNT 2022 - Emerging Technologies to Revitalize Tourism
- SMARTTIS 2022 - Smart Tourism and Information Systems
- TechDiComM 2022 - Technological Strategies on Digital Communication and Marketing

We acknowledge those who contributed to this book: authors, organizing chairs, steering committee members, Program Committee members, and special sessions chairs. We sincerely appreciate their involvement and support that were crucial for the success of the ARTIIS 2022.

The success of this second edition gives us a lot of confidence to continue the work. So, we hope to see you at the third edition in 2023.

September 2022   Teresa Guarda
                                                         Filipe Portela
                                              Maria Fernanda Augusto

Organization

Honorary Chair

Brij Bhooshan Gupta   NIT Kurukshetra, India

General Chairs

Teresa Guarda   Universidad Estatal Peninsula de Santa Elena, Ecuador

Filipe Portela   University of Minho, Portugal

Program Committee Chairs

Teresa Guarda   Universidad Estatal Peninsula de Santa Elena, Ecuador

Filipe Portela   University of Minho, Portugal

Maria Fernanda Augusto   BITrum Research Group, Leon, Spain

Organizing Chairs

Maria Fernanda Augusto   BITrum Research Group, Spain

José Manuel Neira   Federación de Asociaciones para la Movilidad Europea, Spain

Jorge Oliveira e Sá   Universidade do Minho, Portugal

José Maria Diaz   Universidad a Distancia de Madrid, Spain

Steering Committee

Andrei Tchernykh   CICESE Research Center, Mexico

Beatriz De La Iglesia   University of East Anglia, UK

Bruno Sousa   University of Coimbra, Portugal

Enrique Carrera   Universidad de las Fuerzas Armadas ESPE, Ecuador

Ricardo Vardasca   ISLA Santarem, Portugal

Wolfgang Hofkirchner   Technische Universität Wien, Austria

Workshops Chairs

Abrar Ullah   Heriot-Watt University Dubai, UAE
Teresa Guarda   Universidad Estatal Peninsula de Santa Elena,
                                   Ecuador

Special Sessions Chairs

Alanis, Arnulfo   Tijuana Institute of Technology, Mexico
Almeida, Sofia   European University of Lisbon, Portugal
Augusto, Maria Fernanda   Universidad Estatal Peninsula de Santa Elena,
                                   Ecuador
Balsa, Carlos   Polytechnic Institute of Bragança, Portugal
Baltazar Flores, Rosario   Technological Institute of León, Mexico
Calderón Pineda, Fausto   Universidad Estatal Península de Santa Elena,
                                   Ecuador
Chuquimarca, Luis   Universidad Estatal Península de Santa Elena,
                                   Ecuador
Gama, Sílvio   University of Porto, Portugal
Garzozi-Pincay, René Faruk   Universidad Estatal Península de Santa Elena,
                                   Ecuador
Guarda, Teresa   Universidad Estatal Península de Santa Elena,
                                   Ecuador
Guivarch, Ronan   University of Toulouse, France
Lopes, Isabel   Polytechnic Institute of Bragança, Portugal
Mota Pinto, Filipe   Polytechnic Institute of Leiria, Portugal
Ninahualpa, Geovanni   Armed Forces University, Ecuador
Pinto, Mario   Polytechnic Institute of Porto, Portugal
Pombo, Nuno   University of Beira Interior, Portugal
Portela, Filipe   University of Minho, Portugal
Queirós, Ricardo   Polytechnic Institute of Porto, Portugal
Ribeiro, Isabel   Polytechnic Institute of Bragança, Portugal
Rivero Pino, Ramon   Universidad Estatal Península de Santa Elena,
                                   Ecuador
Silva, Bruno   University of Beira Interior, Portugal
Sousa, Bruno   University of Coimbra, Portugal

ARTIIS Program Committee

Abreu, Maria José   University of Minho, Portugal
Alanis, Arnulfo   Tijuana Institute of Technology, Mexico
Aljuboori, Abbas   Al Zahra College for Women, Oman
Almeida, Sofia   European University of Lisbon, Portugal

Álvarez Rodríguez, Francisco	Autonomous University of Aguascalientes, Mexico
Andrade, António	Universidade Católica Portuguesa, Portugal
Araújo, Silvia	University of Minho, Portugal
Augusto, Maria Fernanda	Universidad Estatal Peninsula de Santa Elena, Ecuador
Azevedo, Ana	Polytechnic Institute of Porto, Portugal
Bacca Acosta, Jorge Luis	University of Girona, Spain
Baczynski, Michal	University of Silesia in Katowice, Poland
Balsa, Carlos	Polytechnic Institute of Bragança, Portugal
Baras, Karolina	University of Madeira, Portugal
Biloborodova, Tetiana	Volodymyr Dahl East Ukrainian National University, Ukraine
Braghin, Chiara	University of Milan, Italy
Bravo-Agapito, Javier	Complutense University of Madrid, Spain
Cano-Olivos, Patricia	Universidad Popular Autónoma del Estado de Puebla, Mexico
Carrera, Enrique V.	Armed Forces University, Ecuador
Casillas Martín, Sonia	University of Salamanca, Spain
Castro Silva, Daniel	University of Porto, Portugal
Ciumasu, Ioan	University of Versailles Saint-Quentin-en-Yvelines, France
Costa, Ângelo	University of Minho, Portugal
Dourado, Antonio	University of Coimbra, Portugal
Dutta, Kamlesh	National Institute of Technology Hamirpur, India
Falkman, Göran	University of Skövde, Sweden
Fatahi Valilai, Omid	Jacobs University Bremen, Germany
Fernandes, António	Polytechnic Institute of Bragança, Portugal
Gago, Pedro	Polytechnic Institute of Leiria, Portugal
Garcia Clemente, Felix	University of Murcia, Spain
Gatica, Gustavo	Andrés Bello National University, Chile
Gohar, Neelam	Shaheed Benazir Bhutto Women University, Pakistan
Gomes de Oliveira, Gabriel	State University of Campinas, Brazil
Gomes, Luis	University of the Azores, Portugal
Gomes, Raphael	Federal University of Goiás, Brazil
González Briones, Alfonso	University of Salamanca, Spain
Guarda, Teresa	Universidad Estatal Península de Santa Elena, Ecuador
Guerra, Helia	University of the Azores, Portugal
Gupta, Nishu	Chandigarh University, India
Härer, Felix	University of Fribourg, Switzerland
Hornink, Gabriel	Federal University of Alfenas, Brazil

Hossian, Alejandro	National Technological University, Argentina
Ilarri, Sergio	University of Zaragoza, Spain
Kirsch-Pinheiro, Manuele	Pantheon-Sorbonne University, France
Latorre-Biel, Juan-Ignacio	Public University of Navarre, Spain
Laurent, Anne	University of Montpellier, France
León, Marcelo	Guayaquil Business Technological University, Ecuador
Lopes, Frederico	Federal University of Rio Grande do Norte , Brazil
Lopes, Isabel	Polytechnic Institute of Bragança, Portugal
Lopez, Josue	CETYS University, Mexico
Lopezosa, Carlos	University of Barcelona, Spain
Lucena Jr., Vicente	Federal University of Amazonas, Brazil
Machado, José	University of Minho, Portugal
Marques, Bertil P.	Polytechnic Institute of Porto, Portugal
Maskeliunas, Rytis	Kaunas University of Technology, Lithuania
Matos, Luis	University of Minho, Portugal
Mazon, Luis	Universidad Estatal Península de Santa Elena, Ecuador
Méndez Reboredo, José Ramón	University of Vigo, Spain
Messina, Fabrizio	University of Catania, Italy
Mishra, Pankaj	Pantnagar University, India
Mota Pinto, Filipe	Polytechnic Institute of Leiria, Portugal
Mura, Ivan	Duke Kunshan University, China
Oliveira e Sá, Jorge	University of Minho, Portugal
Oliveira, Pedro	Polytechnic Institute of Bragança, Portugal
Panagiotakis, Spyros	Hellenic Mediterranean University, Greece
Peixoto, Hugo	University of Minho, Portugal
Pinto, Mario	Polytechnic Institute of Porto, Portugal
Pombo, Nuno	University of Beira Interior, Portugal
Portela, Filipe	University of Minho, Portugal
Queirós, Ricardo	Polytechnic Institute of Porto, Portugal
Quintela, Helder	Polytechnic Institute of Cávado and Ave, Portugal
Ribeiro, Isabel	Polytechnic Institute of Bragança, Portugal
Rodriguez, Alejandro	Polytechnic University of Madrid, Spain
Rufino, José	Polytechnic Institute of Braganca, Portugal
Rusu, Eugen	"Dunarea de Jos" University of Galati, Romania
Scherer, Rafal	Częstochowa University of Technology, Poland
Schütz, Christoph	Johannes Kepler University Linz, Austria
Semaan, Felipe	Fluminense Federal University, Brazil
Simões, Alberto	Polytechnic Institute of Cávado and Ave, Portugal
Sousa, Bruno	University of Coimbra, Portugal

Stalidis, George	Alexander Technological Educational Institute of Thessaloniki, Greece
Stavrakis, Modestos	University of the Aegean, Greece
Swacha, Jakub	University of Szczecin, Poland
Tchernykh, Andrei	Ensenada Center for Scientific Research and Higher Education, Mexico
Utz, Wilfrid	OMiLAB, Germany
Van Der Haar, Dustin	University of Johannesburg, South Africa
Vardasca, Ricardo	ISLA Santarem, Portugal
Vicente, Henrique	University of Évora, Portugal
Villao, Datzania	Universidad Estatal Península de Santa Elena, Ecuador
Vito, Domenico	Polytechnic University of Milan, Italy
Winter, Johannes	National Academy of Science and Engineering, Germany
Younas, Muhammad	Oxford Brookes University, UK

Special Sessions Program Committee

Aguiar, Jose	Polytechnic Institute of Bragança, Portugal
Aguirre, Luis Eduardo	Ecuadorian Air Force, Ecuador
Alanis, Arnulfo	Tijuana Institute of Technology, Mexico
Almeida, Sofia	European University of Lisbon, Portugal
Alves, Carlos	Federal Center for Technological Education of Rio Janeiro, Brazil
Andrade, Roberto	National Polytechnic School, Ecuador
Balsa, Carlos	Polytechnic Institute of Bragança, Portugal
Baltazar Flores, Rosario	Leon Institute of Technology, Mexico
Barriga Andrade, Jhonattan Javier	National Polytechnic School, Ecuador
Borovac Zekan, Senka	University of Split, Croatia
Branco, Frederico	University of Trás-os-Montes and Alto Douro, Portugal
Calderón Pineda, Fausto	Universidad Estatal Península de Santa Elena, Ecuador
Campos, Ana Cláudia	University of Algarve, Portugal
Castellanos, Omar	Universidad Estatal Península de Santa Elena, Ecuador
Chertovskih, Roman	University of Porto, Portugal
Chuquimarca, Luis	Universidad Estatal Península de Santa Elena, Ecuador
Cobos Alvarado, Edgar Fabián	Universidad Estatal Península de Santa Elena, Ecuador
Contreras, Sergio Octavio	Universidad De La Salle Bajío, Mexico

Correia, Ricardo	Polytechnic Institute of Bragança, Portugal
Cunha, Carlos R.	Polytechnic Institute of Bragança, Portugal
Diaz, Estrella	University of Castilla-La Mancha, Spain
Diaz, Paul	Armed Forces University, Ecuador
Fajardo, Marcelo	Escuela Superior Politecnica del Litoral, Ecuador
Felizardo, Virginie	University of Beira Interior, Portugal
Fernandes, António	Polytechnic Institute of Bragança, Portugal
Fernandes, Paula Odete	Polytechnic Institute of Bragança, Portugal
Fonseca, Xavier	Polytechnic Institute of Porto, Portugal
Gama, Sílvio	University of Porto, Portugal
Garzozi Pincay, Yamel Sofia	Universidad Tecnológica Equinoccial, Ecuador
Garzozi-Pincay, René Faruk	Universidad Estatal Península de Santa Elena, Ecuador
Gaxiola Vega, Luis	Autonomous University of Baja California, Mexico
González, Nelia	Universidad de Especialidades Espíritu Santo, Ecuador
González, Nelia Josefina	Milagro State University, Ecuador
Grinberga-Zalite, Gunta	Latvia University of Life Sciences and Technologies, Latvia
Groma, Linda	Latvia University of Life Sciences and Technologies, Latvia
Guarda, Teresa	Universidad Estatal Península de Santa Elena, Ecuador
Guivarch, Ronan	University of Toulouse, France
Hernandez Leal, Fabiola	Tijuana Institute of Technology, Mexico
Hernández, Patricia	Technical University of Cotopaxi, Ecuador
Jurado Reyes, Pedro Omar	Universidad Católica de Santiago de Guayaquil, Ecuador
Lopes, Isabel	Polytechnic Institute of Bragança, Portugal
Magdaleno Palencia, Jose Sergio	Tijuana Institute of Technology, Mexico
Magnere, Milton	Alas3 Ingeniería Limitada, Chile
Maridueña Arroyave, Milton	University of Guayaquil, Ecuador
Marques, Bertil P.	Polytechnic Institute of Porto, Portugal
Márquez, Bogart Yail	Tijuana Institute of Technology, Mexico
Martinez, Rosa Maria	University of Almería, Spain
Mazon, Luis	Universidad Estatal Península de Santa Elena, Ecuador
Mesquita, Susana	Aveiro University, Portugal
Messina Scolaro, María del Carmen	University of the Republic, Uruguay
Montella, Raffaele	University of Chicago, USA
Moreno Brieva, Fernando Javier	King Juan Carlos University, Spain

Moreno, David	Polytechnic School of Chimborazo, Ecuador
Muyulema-Allaica, Carina Alexandra	CAAPTES Asesorías Y Consultoria En Proyectos, Ecuador
Muyulema-Allaica, Juan Carlos	Universidad Estatal Península de Santa Elena, Ecuador
Ninahualpa, Geovanni	Armed Forces University, Ecuador
Orrala, Néstor	Universidad Estatal Península de Santa Elena, Ecuador
Palacios, Marcela	Instituto Tecnológico Superior de Purísima del Rincón, Mexico
Paparella, Francesco	New York University Abu Dhabi, UAE
Pedrosa, Isabel	University of Coimbra, Portugal
Peñafiel, Carlos	Universidad Nacional de Chimborazo, Ecuador
Piloto, Paulo	Polytechnic Institute of Braganca, Portugal
Pirela, Alonso	Universidad Estatal Península de Santa Elena, Ecuador
Pombo, Nuno	University of Beira Interior, Portugal
Pucha-Medina, Paola Martina	University of Cantabria, Ecuador
Quezada Cisnero, Maria	Tijuana Institute of Technology, Mexico
R. Souza Pereira, Leonice	University of Beira Interior, Portugal
Ramires, Ana	European University of Lisbon, Portugal
Ramirez, Margarita Ramirez	Autonomous University of Baja California, Mexico
Ramos, Celia	University of the Algarve, Portugal
Reis, Rosa	Polytechnic Institute of Porto, Portugal
Renteria, Leonardo	Universidad Autónoma de Chiapas, Ecuador
Ribeiro, Isabel	Polytechnic Institute of Bragança, Portugal
Rivera, Oscar	National Autonomous University of Mexico, Mexico
Rocha, Cristian Javier	University of Seville, Spain
Rodriguez, Rosalba	Armed Forces University, Ecuador
Romero Rodríguez, Wendoly	Instituto Tecnológico Superior de Guanajuato, Mexico
Rubio, Yoshio	Center for Research and Development of Digital Technology, Mexico
Rufino, José	Polytechnic Institute of Braganca, Portugal
Ruiz, Ulises	National Institute of Astrophysics, Optics and Electronics, Mexico
San Andrés Laz, Esthela	Technical University of Manabi, Ecuador
Sangurima, Miguel	Universidad Católica Andrés Bello, Ecuador
Seabra, Claudia	University of Coimbra, Portugal
Silva Sánchez, Marianella	Universidad Estatal Península de Santa Elena, Ecuador

Silva Sprock, Antonio	Central University of Venezuela, Venezuela
Silva, Bruno	University of Beira Interior, Portugal
Swacha, Jakub	University of Szczecin, Poland
Temperini, Marco	Sapienza University of Rome, Italy
Tomalá, José Xavier	Universidad Estatal Península de Santa Elena, Ecuador
Tutivén, Christian	Escuela Superior Politecnica del Litoral, Ecuador
Vaca-Cardenas, Leticia	Technical University of Manabi, Ecuador
Vasconcelos, Paulo	University of Porto, Portugal
Vieira, Luís	University of Porto, Portugal
Vrellis, Ioannis	University of Ioannina, Greece
Wembe, Boris	University of Toulouse, France
Yoo, Sang Guun	National Polytechnic School, Ecuador
Zacarias, Henriques	University of Beira Interior, Portugal
Zambrano, Marcelo	Universidad Técnica del Norte, Ecuador

Sponsors

Universidad Estatal Peninsula de Santa Elena, Ecuador
Universidade do Minho, Portugal
Universidad a Distancia de Madrid, Spain
Xunta de Galicia, Spain
Compostela Group of Universities

Contents – Part I

Data Intelligence

Contents – Part II

Ethics, Security, and Privacy

Computing Solutions

Self-training of Manufacturing Operators Using Finger-Tracking Wearable Technologies

Angel Dacal-Nieto[1]([✉])[iD], Breogán Raña[1], Juan Moreno-Rodríguez[2],
Juan José Areal[2], and Víctor Alonso-Ramos[1]

[1] CTAG - Centro Tecnológico de Automoción de Galicia,
Pol. Ind. A Granxa, 36475 O Porriño, Spain
`angel.dacal@ctag.com`
[2] PCAE - Peugeot Citroën Automóviles España (Stellantis),
Rúa Citroën 3–5, 36210 Vigo, Spain

Abstract. The process of training a manufacturing operator is usually long and complex, involving time, resources, and expert trainers. This paper proposes a new approach to train novice workers using wearable technologies. The solution is formed by hardware elements (finger-tracking gloves), and a software platform which records the performance of an expert manufacturing operator, and where a novice operator can learn and self-compare with the expert. This new solution 1) does not require the continuous presence of a trainer, 2) makes the factory autonomous to generate its own learning content, 3) allows a quantifiable and objective readiness measure of the novice operator, and overall 4) means a complementary and more effective and faster learning method. The solution has been validated as a proof of concept at the Stellantis Vigo factory in Spain, with positive reviews from their workers. This new approach can be applicable in many fields, especially when dealing with tasks requiring high manual dexterity.

Keywords: Wearable · Finger tracking · Sensorized gloves · Learning techniques

1 Introduction

A manufacturing operator whose training has not been effective can cause different problems in a factory, such as delays, lack of performance, and affectation to the overall production. That is why training new manufacturing employees is a process in which the companies invest many time and resources, up to 1.300$ per employee in the pre-pandemic 2019 [1]. Thus, it is crucial to search for new means and methods to make it as quick and efficient as possible.

In recent years there have been some innovations in terms of worker training tools, with the incorporation of new technologies in the industrial sector [2]. However, nowadays the core of the industrial teaching is still based on traditional

T. Guarda et al. (Eds.): ARTIIS 2022, CCIS 1675, pp. 3–15, 2022.
https://doi.org/10.1007/978-3-031-20319-0_1

techniques such as video visualization, reading documentation, and non-objective assessment. These methods are not very accurate; on the one hand it is difficult to transfer the know-how in some specific operations, and on the other hand it is complex to verify in an objective manner that the knowledge has been properly assimilated.

A group of innovative tools proposed in the last years concerns Virtual Reality (VR) and Augmented Reality (AR) [3]. Although immersive and useful, these techniques do not usually allow the factory to be fully autonomous, especially concerning the creation of models and the programming of actions in these environment. This is relevant, not only because this means an extra expense to outsource, but also because of the changing nature of manufacturing business, which requires the content to be kept up to date with very high frequency.

In this context, this paper proposes a new solution to allow a self-training approach, by using wearable technologies (finger-tracking gloves) and a software platform. This tool allows to preserve and exploit the operators know-how in a more efficient way, since the data about the movements of both fingers and wrists will be stored in the application. The learning operator can visualize this and other complementary content, practice, and eventually self-assess, thus obtaining a quantifiable objective measure of readiness to a specific workplace. Additionally, the platform allows the factory to be autonomous regarding the content creation, since it is the operators themselves which generate data.

This research has been conducted under a proof-of-concept framework with the Stellantis group, in its factory located in Vigo, Spain. Several workers have tested the tool, by performing real tasks such as cable connections, tube assembly and mounting doors.

In this paper, Sect. 2 will present background and related technologies. In Sect. 3 the architecture and rest of technology aspects will be commented. Section 4 will present the main results and applications. Finally, Sect. 5 will summarize the conclusions and next steps.

2   Background

There are several technologies related with learning for manufacturing operators that have been proposed and evaluated in the last years. This section will highlight some of them.

The most classical approach is the usage of videos, description of the texts and observation of senior operators. The subjective perception of a trainer is what triggers the introduction of the novice operator in line. In some cases, some innovations, such as voice guidance [4] or gamification techniques [5] have been followed, as complement of these rigid principles. This approach, although limited and non-quantifiable, is still the rule in most of factories in the world.

Extended Reality techniques have been recently introduced as a support tool for teaching in factories. In this line, some systems have used Virtual Reality to recreate the workplace and its procedures, so that a novice operator can interact with it in controlled conditions and prepare for the real workplace [6]. Augmented

Reality is another technology to support learning, in this case based on the projection of content over a real scene using some wearable devices in form of goggles [7]. The operators can learn the procedures by observing and interacting with these projections, eventually becoming able to reproduce the workplace [8]. In other cases, computer-based simulation environments have been used to train operators, sometimes using complex reproductions of the workplace [9]. However, these techniques do not allow an easy creation content by the personnel in the factory. They usually need an expensive and outsourced creation of models, scenarios and programming behaviours. The autonomy of the factory is, thus, insufficient.

A complementary approach for teaching in factories could be based on registering the movements and actions of a senior operator during the execution of a workplace, and the comparison of this expert execution with the execution of a novice operator. In this body tracking line, there are several technologies related. Inertial Measurement Units (IMUs) are well-known wearable devices that can capture the movements of the human body, for different applications such as ergonomics or detection of human intention [10]. However, this equipment only provides a limited degree of accuracy, and especially the hands get out of this detection. Machine Vision is also a very robust technology to capture human pose, in this case without any wearable device [11]. However, machine vision suffers from occlusions, and again the accuracy in the hands is limited.

A new approach is based on the usage of sensorized gloves which allow a fine finger-tracking of a human hand. Finger tracking and wrist tracking were born mostly focused for video games industry, and navigation through augmented scenarios [12], as well as registration of hand postures for multiple purposes such as training of robotic systems [13] and Human-Computer interaction [14].

There are current models available in the market with different features, mainly the degrees of freedom, their interoperability capabilities, connectivity, and haptic feedback [15]. As an example, the Fig. 1 shows the models from Manus [16] and Mace Virtual Labs [17]. There are dozens of options nowadays, such as the device from Magos [18].

While the finger tracking is usually performed by these models, the tracking of the wrist is usually done by an additional attachable device, such as the Vive Tracker [19]. This is basic to register where the hands move and are placed with respect to the body, and each other.

The finger-wrist tracking approach allows an autonomous creation of content, is wearable, do not suffer so much from occlusions, and enables the calculation of a quantifiable degree of readiness of the novice operator. This will be the basis for this paper, to be explained in the next sections.

3   Development

3.1   Architecture

The self-assessment solution is composed by software and hardware components. The user wears the finger-tracking gloves (Manus Prime X gloves in our case [16]),

Fig. 1. Left: Manus Prime X Haptic Glove. Right: Mace Virtual Labs Bebop

with the associated wrist tracking devices attached (HTC vive track in our case [19]). The gloves are connected to the Manus software platform, called Manus Core, where everything related with the configuration of the finger tracking technology is done. The HTC Vive trackers are connected to Steam VR [20] where the wrist tracking technology is configured. The Manus Core integrates the two technologies (finger and wrist tracking), since it is compatible with Steam VR. The whole hardware set costs less than 10.000€.

The main application obtains data from three sources of information: 1) the data from the gloves (finger and wrist trackers, through REST API), 2) the information stored in the database (users, operations, videos saved, etc.), and 3) a camera able to record the worker while obtaining tracking information.

The user interface is created in Unity. Alternatively, some parts of the application can be also visualized through an Android-based wearable device, such as the augmented reality glasses Real Wear HMT-1 [21]. There is an APK application in execution in the glasses, connected to the main application through a WiFi network.

This architecture can be seen in Fig. 2.

3.2 Workflow

The application can be explained as the next sequential workflow:

1. An administrator user can create other users, workplaces, operations and the factory hierarchy.
2. An expert user can record the workplace activity, wearing the gloves, and being recorded by a camera.
3. A novice user can visualize the expert content, both hands and video.
4. The novice user can self-assess to a workplace, wearing the gloves, obtaining a quantifiable measure of the readiness to perform in that specific workplace.

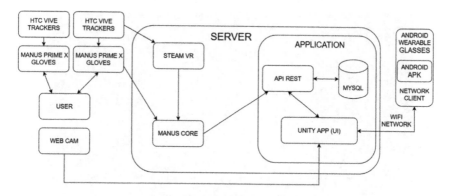

Fig. 2. Architecture diagram

5. An administrator can check a polyvalence matrix including the readiness level of each operator for each workplace in the system.

These five main steps from the workflow will be detailed in the next sections, and is drafted in Fig. 3.

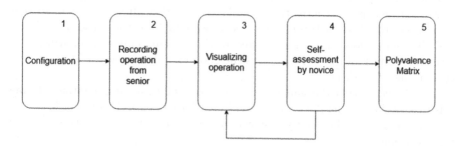

Fig. 3. Workflow of the solution

3.3 Configuration

There are two main roles defined in the application: the operators and the administrators. The administrators can define workplaces, following the complex hierarchy of an automotive plant, in which there are different levels for the division, unit, etc. Additionally, every workplace is divided into operations, which are the atomic actions within a workplaces. This makes sense, since an automotive workplace can have from 1 to 3 min of cycle time, generally speaking, and comparing long operations is not convenient, both for the system and for the novice operators, as it will be commented.

An example of these configuration functionalities is shown in Fig. 4.

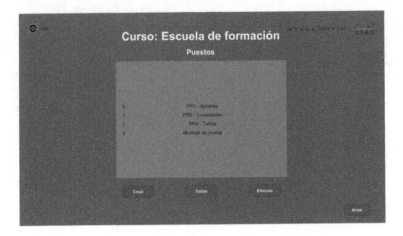

Fig. 4. Configuration functionalities

3.4   Recording Operation from Senior

This phase aims to safeguard the know-how of a senior operator. It involves that a senior operator of a workplace, either in the manufacturing line, or in a controlled scenario, executes the workplace, operation after operation, so that it gets registered, both through the recorded data from the sensorized gloves, and through a video camera connected to the system. This register will act as a the benchmark of the workplace, as the good execution to learn from for next generations of workers.

It is expected that the senior operator is assisted by an administrator during this task, although the data and content creation are entirely automatic.

An example of this activity is shown in Fig. 5, where the system is registering the execution.

3.5   Visualizing Operation

After recording how a workplace must be performed, the next step involves showing this information to the novice operators that need to learn how to execute it.

This task is intended to be performed autonomously by the novice operators, as many times as required, without the product or tools correspondent to the workplace. Two main methods have been defined for this purpose: 1) using a computer, so that both the hand movements and the video can be watched (Fig. 6), or 2) using the augmented reality device, to visualize only the hand content (Fig. 7).

While the first method has been shown to be more convenient in general, the second one allows to focus in the movements of the actual hands while keeping the senior movements in the AR device. It is important to note that the glasses are not using augmented reality, but just the projection of the recorded hands.

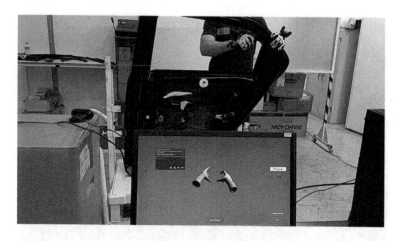

Fig. 5. Recording from senior operator

In any case, the objective of the novice operator is to match the movements of the senior operator for each operation, because that would mean that the dexterous actions have been learned, as a very relevant part of the learning of the workplace actions.

3.6　Self-assessment by Novice

It is expected that, after visualizing the content of a workplace, a novice operator wants to self-assess and check if the learning process has been successful. Again, this step is intended to be performed autonomously by the novice operator, but in this case using the tools, parts or products related to the workplace, in a teaching not-in-line environment.

The system can compare two recordings of an operation, such as the ones coming from senior and novice, and score how similar the movements were, thus obtaining a quantifiable measure of this similarity. A recording from the gloves and trackers come in a JSON file, composed by the xyz positions of 8 degrees of freedom in the fingers (in this particular Manus model) and one additional for the wrist, for each hand, in a sampling frequency 50 Hz.

Each instant of the execution, defined by these 3 data for each 9 degrees of freedom, is compared, obtaining a number between 0 (no similarity) and 100 (perfect similarity). This comparison is an Euclidean distance measure, based on how far the novice measures are from the senior, for each of the 9 degrees of freedom.

The total similarity measure is the average measure for each of the measurement instants, throughout the operation time. The total operation time is the senior time, which means that all the measures from the novice exceeding this time, are ignored.

This method will be improved in the future, taking into account more accurate techniques, such as machine learning, since currently two very similar

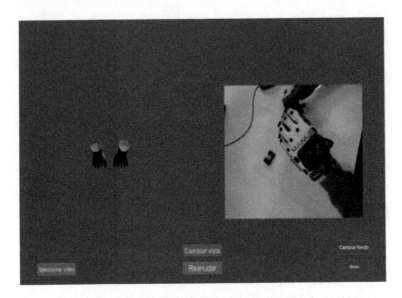

Fig. 6. Visualization using computer

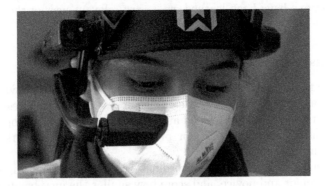

Fig. 7. Visualization using AR glasses

executions, slightly de-synchronized, are measured as very different. As it has been previously indicated, it is recommendable that the operations to compare are as short as possible. This way, the chances for the novice operator of de-synchronizing from the senior execution, are lower.

As it can be seen in Fig. 8, the novice operator can see his/her gloves in real time, and the pre-recorded gloves of the senior operator behind. This combined visualization during the assessment aims to help the novice operator to match the senior movements.

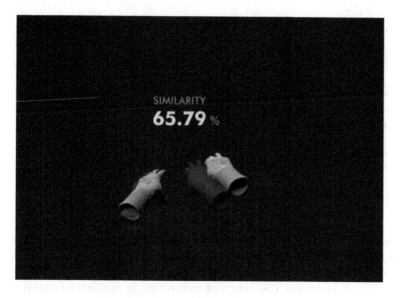

Fig. 8. Self-assessment process

3.7   Polyvalence Matrix

The self-assessment results are registered in the system, so that the administrator users can check the best performance for each operator and operation. This generates the so-called polyvalence matrix, a typical concept in automotive industry, in which the level of knowledge of each operator for each workplace, can be seen.

The improvement with respect to the traditional polyvalence matrices, is that this solution includes the objective and quantifiable measurements obtained during the self-assessment. This will allow the factory to make better decisions based on these data, about how and when to deploy the operators through the workplaces.

4   Results

4.1   Evaluation

The system has been evaluated as a proof-of-concept in the Stellantis factory at Vigo (Spain), one of the most productive in the group.

Four main dexterous workplaces have been tested by 10 operators, related with 1) assembly of electric connectors, 2) assembly of plastic tubes, 3) screwing using automatic machines, and finally 4) assembly of door components, which can be seen in Fig. 9, and aimed to fit door rubbers before the assembly of the glass in the door. These operations have been chosen thinking on the dexterity and usage of the fingers of the operators in specific complex ways.

Fig. 9. Evaluation in Stellantis

In general, the application received favourable feedback from the operators, with high potential, although they agree that the similarity measure needs to be improved.

The factory considers the new tool interesting in applications related with rubber assembly, plastic assembly, interior component placement, connections, wiring placements, assembly and disassembly of complex parts in engines, maintenance, among others. These are not only exclusive of the automotive sector, but also from others such as aerospace, metal, and manufacturing in general. An example can be seen in Fig. 10.

Fig. 10. Application fields for the tool: precision mechanical assembly

4.2 Impact

The potential improvement and impact of the tool is more qualitative than quantitative, since it is born as a complementary method to be used in collaboration with other approaches.

The tool should decrease the need of a trainer observing the operators, so that it is expected some economic saving in this line, since the tool acts as a traditional test. Additionally, it removes some subjectivity from the process.

The tool allows to save this valuable know-how from the senior operators, that is not usually stored. We can estimate here that, if the senior operator leaves the company, this tool can save training time, and thus money, during the process of teaching new operators, avoiding that the new operators have to figure out how the movements were made.

And finally, the method does not require the assistance of external partners to create content, since it is created automatically by the system. This makes it economically more sustainable.

5 Conclusions

In this paper, we have presented a new method to train manufacturing operators, based on the usage of finger-tracking wearable gloves as a way to register and compare the execution of a workplace. The flow of 1) registering movements from a senior operator, 2) visualizing this knowledge, 3) auto-assessment by the junior operator, and 4) creation of a polyvalence matrix, is the core of the idea. A software platform, using commercial hardware devices, has been developed and tested as a proof-of-concept in a Stellantis factory in Spain.

This new method is especially addressed for manual operations in which the dexterity is relevant and important. There are examples in the automotive, aeronautic, or agrofood industries that fit in this category. This solution is born as a complementary tool to others already existing, in order to fill this group of dexterity-based workplaces.

Following, a list of the most relevant advantages is shown:

- Less time of a teacher or supervisor is necessary during the training period. The self-assessment aims to reduce the necessity of a trainer in the whole learning sequence.
- Portable and wearable devices allow the system to be used in line, or in a teaching room. This way they can register in real conditions.
- The factory is autonomous to create new content without the need for IT or AR/VR experts. The collection of an operation is the creation of content itself. There is no need of outsourcing the creation of models or scenarios.
- The expert know-how is saved in a very accurate manner, complementing video content.
- A new objective KPI is introduced in the learning process, as a readiness measure to start working in the line.

The current solution will be improved in the future, in a series of actions in order to make it more robust and adequate for the factory usage in more sectors:

- The similarity algorithm will be updated, using machine learning techniques. This should improve the accuracy when the executions de-synchronize. Additionally, to limit the de-synchronization, the execution speed will be customized, so that the junior operators can start learning with lower speed, until they are ready to test a real manufacturing speed.
- The visualization of the generated content will be optimized to be used with a Virtual Reality device. This should improve the current visualization via AR and computer.
- Switching the execution of the application from a local instance to a cloud-based system. This would allow to centralize the data collection and apply updates for every user.
- More finger-tracking gloves models will be supported, to allow a better compatibility with the market.
- The validation of the solution will be performed on a bigger sample of operators, including more complete surveys regarding its usability and effectiveness, creating a control group of operators using the traditional method, and measuring the performance of both groups to assess the learning improvement.

Acknowledgements. The authors want to acknowledge the contribution of the project "Facendo 4.0" and respectively to the agency GAIN from the Xunta de Galicia regional government of Spain, for its funding.

References

1. State of the Industry report. Associacion for Talent Development ATD. www.td. org/soir2019 Accessed 4 Oct 2019
2. Hulla, M., Hammer, M., Karre, H., Ramsauer, C.: A case study based digitalization training for learning factories. Procedia manuf. **31**, 169–174 (2019)
3. Naranjo, J.E., Sanchez, D.G., Robalino-Lopez, A., Robalino-Lopez, P., Alarcon-Ortiz, A., Garcia, M.V.: A scoping review on virtual reality-based industrial training. Appl. Sci. **10**, 8224 (2020)
4. Longo, F., Nicoletti, L., Padovano, A.: Smart operators in industry 4.0: a human-centered approach to enhance operators' capabilities and competencies within the new smart factory context. Comput. Industr. Eng. **113**, 144–159 (2017)
5. Liu, M., Huang, Y., Zhang, D.: Gamification's impact on manufacturing: Enhancing job motivation, satisfaction and operational performance with smartphone-based gamified job design. Hum. Factors Ergonomics Manuf. Serv. Industr. **28**(1), 38–51 (2018)
6. Monetti, F.M., de Giorgio, A., Yu, H., Maffei, A., Romero, M.: An experimental study of the impact of virtual reality training on manufacturing operators on industrial robotic tasks. Procedia CIRP **106**, 33–38 (2022)
7. Eder, M., Hulla, M., Mast, F., Ramsauer, C.: On the application of augmented reality in a learning factory working environment. Procedia Manuf. **45**, 7–12 (2020)
8. Holm, M., Danielsson, O., Syberfeldt, A., Moore, P., Wang, L.: Adaptive instructions to novice shop-floor operators using Augmented Reality. J. Industr. Prod. Eng. **34**(5), 362–374 (2017)

9. Knoke, B., Thoben, K.D.: Training simulators for manufacturing processes: literature review and systematisation of applicability factors. Comput. Appl. Eng. Educ. **29**(5), 1191–1207 (2021)
10. Malleson, C., Gilbert, A., Trumble, M., Collomosse, J., Hilton, A., Volino, M.: Real-time full-body motion capture from video and IMUs. In 2017 International Conference on 3D Vision (3DV), 449–457 IEEE (2017)
11. Cao, Z., Simon, T., Wei, S. E., Sheikh, Y.: Realtime multi-person 2D pose estimation using part affinity fields. In Proceedings of the IEEE Conference on Computer Vision and Pattern Recognition, 7291–7299 (2017)
12. Dorfmuller-Ulhaas, K., Schmalstieg, D.: Finger tracking for interaction in augmented environments. In Proceedings IEEE and ACM International Symposium on Augmented Reality, pp. 55–64 IEEE (2001)
13. Dacal-Nieto, A., et al.: TRAINMAN-MAGOS: capture of dexterous assembly manufacturing know-how as a new efficient approach to support robotic automation. Procedia Comput. Sci. **200**, 101–110 (2022)
14. Shah, K. N., Rathod, K. R., Agravat, S. J.: A survey on human computer interaction mechanism using finger tracking. arXiv preprint arXiv:1402.0693 (2014)
15. Zhu, M., Sun, Z., Zhang, Z., Shi, Q., He, T., Liu, H., Lee, C.: Haptic-feedback smart glove as a creative human-machine interface (HMI) for virtual/augmented reality applications. Sci. Adv. 6(19), eaaz8693 (2020)
16. Manus Homepage. www.manus-meta.com/. Accessed May 2022
17. Mace Virtual Labs Homepage. www.macevl.com/. Accessed May 2022
18. Magos Homepage. www.themagos.com/. Accessed May 2022
19. Vive Homepage. www.vive.com/. Accessed May 2022
20. Steam VR Homepage. www.steamvr.com/. Accessed May 2022
21. Realwear Homepage. www.realwear.com/. Accessed May 2022

GraphQL or REST for Mobile Applications?

Antonio Quiña-Mera[1,2]([⊠]) [iD], José María García[3] [iD], Pablo Fernández[3] [iD],
Paúl Vega-Molina[4], and Antonio Ruiz-Cortés[3] [iD]

[1] Universidad Técnica del Norte. FICA Faculty. eCIER Research Group,
Av. 17 de Julio 5-21, Ibarra, Ecuador
`aquina@utn.edu.ec`
[2] SCORE Lab. Universidad de Sevilla, Av. Reina Mercedes s/n, 41012 Sevilla, Spain
[3] SCORE Lab. I3US Institute. Universidad de Sevilla, Av. Reina Mercedes s/n,
41012 Sevilla, Spain
`{josemgarcia,pablofm,aruiz}@us.es`
[4] Universidad de las Fuerzas Armadas ESPE, Sangolquí, Ecuador
`spvega1@espe.edu.ec`

Abstract. Currently, GraphQL has emerged as a query language for developing web APIs that propose to improve several data access problems of RESTful APIs. The present paper aims to study the effects on software quality of APIs developed with REST and GraphQL architectures consumed from mobile applications. For this, we design a computational experiment that compares the quality characteristic "performance efficiency" of mobile application consumption to three APIs; one GraphQL API and two REST APIs (one exposes complex queries on several endpoints, the other exposes complex queries on a single endpoint). The results show that the software quality of the API developed with GraphQL architecture is higher than that developed with REST architecture.

Keywords: GraphQL API · REST API · Quality evaluation · Mobile application

1 Introduction

Today, Microservice Architecture (MSA) is a trend to develop reliable and efficient applications that overcome technical and functional deficiencies such as redundancy, recovery, and scalability. The MSA consists of small applications (microservices) with a single responsibility (functional, non-functional, or cross-cutting requirements) that can be deployed, scaled, and tested independently [2,25]. Microservices communicate over the HTTP(s) protocol via lightweight mechanisms that commonly use the *REpresentational State Transfer* (REST) architectural style to build *Application Programming Interfaces* (APIs). REST has been rapidly accepted in the industry since its emergence in 2000 [29]. However, it has shown some problems, such as *query complexity*, requiring multiple

T. Guarda et al. (Eds.): ARTIIS 2022, CCIS 1675, pp. 16–30, 2022.
https://doi.org/10.1007/978-3-031-20319-0_2

HTTP requests to obtain multiple resources. In addition, *over-fetching* occurs when a request returns more data than necessary; and *under-fetching* occurs when an API resource does not return enough information, thus requiring additional requests [18,28].

In this sense, in 2015, GraphQL emerged as an alternative to solve several reported problems of REST [24]; the application of this paradigm in software development has had a growing interest in academia, and industry [21,28]. Therefore, we have observed that several studies compare various quality characteristics between REST and GraphQL; however, we found that no study compares these paradigms in the context of consumption from mobile applications. For this reason, we defined the following research question for this study:

- **RQ**: What effect do the development architectures of APIs consumed from mobile applications have on software quality?

To answer the research question presented, we propose to conduct a computational experiment that compares the software quality of the REST and GraphQL architectures in the development of APIs consumed from a mobile application.

The rest of the document is: Sect. 2 shows the theoretical foundation of REST, GraphQL, and software quality characteristics. Section 3 shows the configuration of the computational experiment. Section 4 shows the execution of the experimental design proposed in the Sect. 3. Section 5 displays the experiment results. Section 6 shows the threats to the validity of the experiment. Section 7 shows a discussion of the results with related work. Finally, Sect. 8 shows the conclusions of the study and future work.

2 Theoretical Foundation

REST (REpresentational State Transfer) is an architectural style for distributed hypermedia systems [6]; based on the HTTP standard for the development of web services, specifically for the development of REST APIs or also known as RESTful APIs [17,19]. The main design criteria of the REST architecture are i) all things on the Internet are abstracted as resources. ii) Each resource corresponds to a URI (unique resource identifier). iii) Standard actions such as GET, POST, PUT, DELETE, and HEAD of the HTTP protocol are used for the operation of resources. iv) The resource identifier will not change when applying multiple operations; what changes is the operator. v) Operations do not have status [8].

GraphQL is a query language, and execution engine for describing capabilities and data model requirements for client-server applications [24]. To implement GraphQL application servers (*API GraphQL*), it is not necessary to use a specific programming language or persistence mechanism. Instead, GraphQL encodes the capabilities of the type-system-based data model using a uniform language that responds to the following design principles: product-centric, hierarchical, strong typing, client-specified queries, and introspective. The primary operations of GraphQL are queries, mutations, and data subscriptions [5,24].

The **Software Quality Characteristics** for this study are based on the ISO/IEC 25010 standards that establish a model with characteristics and sub-characteristics to measure the software's internal, external, and use quality [10]. In addition, the ISO/IEC 25023 standard establishes measures, including measurement functions associated with the quality characteristics in the software product quality model [11].

The **Experiment (or controlled experiment)** in software engineering is an empirical investigation that manipulates a factor or variable of the studied environment. Therefore, the researcher needs laboratories to study practitioners' problems and develop and evolve solutions from experimentation [30]. Because experimentation addresses the context of the problem presented in Sect. 1 and is the most commonly used strategy in software engineering [7], we will apply it to this study.

3   Experimental Setting

3.1   Goal Definition

We define the objective of the experiment using the Goal Question Metric (GQM) Approach [1], considering the following:

- **Analyze** the software development process
- **for the purpose** to compare the performance efficiency of software architectures on mobile devices
- **with respect** to software quality
- **from the point of view** of the researcher
- **in the context** of a computational laboratory.

3.2   Factors and Treatments

The factor under study is the software architecture, specifically in developing APIs that mobile applications will consume. The *treatments* applied to this factor are:

- GraphQL architecture for API development.
- REST architecture for API development (considered as the control level).

We will compare the performance efficiency of these architectures consumed by a mobile application.

3.3   Variables

The *Independent variable* is the "Software architecture for API development", applied with two treatments: GraphQL architecture and REST architecture. We operationalize this variable by developing three APIs: a GraphQL API, a REST API that exposes composite queries on separate endpoints, and another

REST API that exposes composite queries on a single endpoint (similar to the GraphQL API).

The *dependent variable* is "Software Quality", which we operationalize using the "Performance efficiency" characteristic of the external software quality according to ISO/IEC 25010 [10]. Performance efficiency is the evaluation of performance concerning the number of resources used under stated conditions [10]. Below, we detail the metrics chosen to quantify the dependent variable:

- *Average response time*, is the time it takes to complete a job or an asynchronous process [11]. The measurement function is:

$$X = \sum_{I=1}^{n} (B_I - A_I)/n \qquad (1)$$

  where A_I is the time to start job I; B_I is the operation time to perform the tasks at observation I; and n is the number of observations [11].
- *Transaction processing capacity*, ask the question: How many transactions can be processed per unit of time? [11]. The calculation function is:

$$X = A/B \qquad (2)$$

  where A is the number of transactions completed during the observation time; B is the observation duration [11].

3.4   Hypothesis

In this section, we posed the following hypotheses based on the research question **RQ**:

- H_0 *(Null Hypothesis)*: There is no difference in the software quality effects of APIs developed with the GraphQL architecture and consumed by a mobile application.
- H_1 *(Alternative Hypothesis 1)*: There is a difference in the software quality effects of APIs developed with GraphQL architecture and consumed by a mobile application. The quality of software produced by GraphQL architectures is higher than that of REST architecture.
- H_2 *(Alternative Hypothesis 2)*: There is a difference in the software quality effects of APIs developed with GraphQL architecture and consumed by a mobile application. The quality of software produced by GraphQL architectures is lower than that of REST architecture.

3.5   Design

In this experiment, we design a computational laboratory to establish the necessary conditions to compare the performance efficiency between the GraphQL architecture and the REST architecture. Where we set up three experimental tasks that will implement common data queries and mutation scenarios (four use cases), the first task consists of exposing a GraphQL API. The second task involves exposing a REST API with several endpoints for complex queries. Finally, the third task involves exposing a REST API with one endpoint for complex queries. We define three data query use cases with different levels of complexity, and one data insertion use case, which will be executed three times with varying amounts of records.

The three tasks will be consumed by a mobile application, which will measure with the different metrics established in Sect. 3.3 the efficiency of the software quality performance of the GraphQL and REST architectures. Table 1 shows the design of the experiment.

Table 1. Experiment Design

Use cases	Repetitions	GraphQL architecture	REST architecture	REST single endpoint architecture
Use case 1	3	1, 100, 1.000, 10.000, 30.000, 50.000 (records)		
Use case 2	3	1, 100, 1.000, 10.000, 30.000, 50.000 (records)		
Use case 3	3	1, 100, 1.000, 10.000, 30.000, 50.000 (records)		
Use case 4	3	5 - 10 - 20 - 30 (seconds)		

3.6 Use Cases

The first three use cases describe data query requirements, and the fourth describes data insertion according to the data structure chosen for the study, which is described below:

Use Case 1: Activities execution: consult the execution of activities performed by employees.
– Query complexity level: 1
– Fields:
  • ConsumptionTimes: detail, EndDate, StartDate, activity, customer_id, pre-invoice_id, project_id, type_id

Use Case 2: Activities in detail: query the detail of the employees' activities.
– Query complexity level: 2
– Fields:
  • Activity: activity_id, detail, status, priority
  • Project: project_id, detail, request_id, company_id
  • Pre-invoice: prefinvoice_id, detail, amount, customer_id

Use Case 3: Solution Tasks: query the solution tasks performed in the employees' activities.
– Query complexity level: 3
– Fields:
  • Activity: activity_id, detail, status, priority
  • Project: project_id, detail, request_id, company_id
  • Pre-invoice: prefinvoice_id, detail, amount, customer_id

- Distributor: consumer_id, detail
- Rate: type_id, detail, concept

Use Case 4: Activity execution: is the time of the execution of the activities planned for the employees.

- Mutation: data insertion.
- Fields
  - ConsumptionTimes: detail, EndDate, StartDate, activity, customer_id, pre-invoice_id, project_id, type_id.

3.7 Experimental Tasks

In this section, we describe and design the experimental tasks of the computational laboratory according to the treatments (see Sect. 3.2), variables (see Sect. 3.3), design (see Sect. 3.5), and use cases (see Sect. 3.6) defined for this empirical study.

Experimental Task 1: GraphQL API. This task aims to implement the use cases defined in the Sect. 3.6 in a GraphQL API, which a mobile application will then consume.

Experimental Task 2: REST API. This task aims to implement the use cases defined in Sect. 3.6 in a REST API, exposing each data access resource at different endpoints (normal behavior in REST APIs).

Experimental Task 3: API REST Queries Single Endpoint. This task aims to implement the use cases defined in Sect. 3.6 in a REST API that exposes in an endpoint the compound queries described in the use cases (behavior similar to GraphQL APIs).

In this sense, we complement the computational lab architecture by developing a mobile client application that consumes the APIs described in the experimental tasks. Figure 1 shows the architecture of the experimental lab.

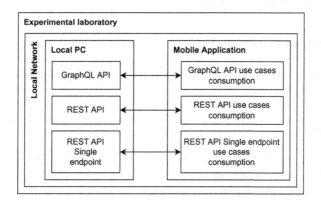

Fig. 1. Experimental laboratory architecture

3.8 Instrumentation

The following is a description of the instrumentation of the computational laboratory used in the experiment:

Local-PC specifications, is a computer that has the following characteristics:
- Operating System: Windows 10 Pro 64-bit
- Processor: Intel (R) Core (TM) i7-5500U CPU @ 2.40GHz
- Memory: RAM 8 GB
- Internet connection of 75 MB bandwidth.

Mobile device specifications, is a cell phone with the following features:
- Brand: Huawei P30 lite
- Model: MAR-LX3A
- Operating System: Android version 10
- Processor: Hisilicon Kirin 710
- RAM: 4GB
- Storage: 128GB
- Resolution: 2312×1080

Development environment, consists of the following applications and technologies:
- Integrated development environment: Visual Studio Code v1.62
- Programming language: JavaScript
- JavaScript runtime environment: NodeJS v14.17.5
- Client application npm libraries: React Native 16.8.6, react-apollo 2.5.5
- GraphQL API npm libraries: graphql v15.5.0, graphql-server-express v1.4.1, graphql-import v1.0.2, y graphql-tools v7.0.5, cors 2.8.5
- REST API npm libraries: graphql v15.5.0, graphql-server-express v1.4.1, graphql-import v1.0.2, y graphql-tools v7.0.5, cors 2.8.5

Data collection and analysis, consists of the following applications:
- Microsoft Excel 365
- R Studio Desktop 0.99.903.

4 Experiment Execution

The experiment was run in Octuber 2020, using the experimental setting proposed in Sect. 3.

4.1 Sample

The sample data repository belongs to a technology company in the city of Latacunga - Ecuador, which has the adequate amount of data to run the experiment according to the design exposed in Sect. 3.5.

4.2   Preparation

We started the preparation of the computational lab by verifying the connection to the enterprise database with the GraphQL, REST, and REST single endpoint APIs deployed on a Local PC. Next, we confirmed the connection and operation of the experimental tasks described in Sect. 3.7 from the mobile application to each exposed APIs. Finally, after verifying the operation of the experimental environment, we ran the experiment according to the design established in Sect. 3.5.

4.3   Data Collection

We collected the results, on the one hand, the response times after the execution of use cases 1, 2, and 3 performed from the mobile application; on the other hand, and the number of transactions after the execution of use case 4. In each run of the use cases, the mobile application printed the results on screen, which we copied and recorded in a Microsoft Excel 365 file.

5   Results

In this section, we present the results obtained from the execution of the experiment (Sect. 4.3); the statistical analysis of the metrics of average response time and transaction processing capacity of the quality sub-characteristic performance efficiency; and a summary of the effects on the software quality of the APIs developed with the GraphQL and REST architectures consumed by a mobile application.

5.1   Average Response Time

After analyzing the results of the average response times obtained by executing cases 1, 2, and 3 of the experiment designed in Table 1, we observe that the response times of the GraphQL API are approximately *fourteen* times lower than the times of the REST API, and API REST Sigle Endpoint, as shown in Fig. 2.

Statistical Analysis of Average Response Time. First, we analyze for each level of query complexity the degree of linear relationship that the APIs have, for which we use Pearson's correlation matrices, as shown in Fig. 3. Where we highlight the following correlation values that are located between -1 and +1, level 1 of query complexity shows that API REST Single Endpoint and API REST have a positive linear correlation of 0.718. At level 2, API REST Single Endpoint and API GraphQL positively correlate to 0.754. Finally, at level 3, API GraphQL and API REST Single Endpoint have a positive linear correlation of 0.580, while API REST has a similar positive correlation of 0.583.

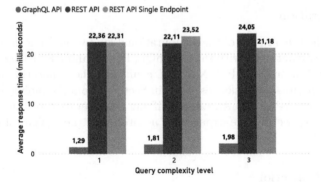

Fig. 2. Average response time by query complexity level

		Query complexity level: 1			Query complexity level: 2			Query complexity level: 3		
		RASP	RAPI	GAPI	RASP	RAPI	GAPI	RASP	RAPI	GAPI
RASP	PEA	1	,718**	0,363	1	,560**	,754**	1	,709**	,580*
	SIG		0,001	0,139		0,16	,000		0,001	0,12
	N	18	18	18	18	18	18	18	18	18
RAPI	PEA	,718**	1	0,161	,560**	1	0,436	,709**	1	,583*
	SIG	0,001		0,524	0,16		0,071	0,001		0,11
	N	18	18	18	18	18	18	18	18	18
GAPI	PEA	0,363	0,161	1	,754**	0,436	1	,580*	,583*	1
	SIG	0,139	0,524		,000	0,071		0,12	0,11	
	N	18	18	18	18	18	18	18	18	18

Legends:

PEA. Pearson correlation   GAPI. GraphQL API

SIG. Significant (bilateral)   **. Correlation is significant at the 0.01 level (bilateral).

RASP. REST API Single Endpoint   *. Correlation is significant at the 0.05 level (bilateral).

RAPI. REST API

Fig. 3. Average response time correlation

After performing the correlation matrix, we apply the Wilks' Lambda statistic as a discriminant analysis that allows us to visualize if there are significant differences or not between the groups of results of the average response time of the application of the different architectures of the APIs in the experiment. Table 2 shows the test of group means.

In table 2, we observe that the significance level (SIG) of the GraphQL API is 0.004, being the lowest, which concludes that there are differences between the groups and that the GraphQL API has a significant advantage over the others.

5.2 Transaction Processing Capacity

In this section, we analyze the results of the transaction processing capacity obtained when executing use case 4 of the experiment designed in Table 1. GraphQL has the highest processing capacity, reaching up to three times more

Table 2. Average response time group means test

	Wilks' Lambda	F	Gl1	Gl2	SIG
API REST single endpoint	,976	,622	,2	51	,541
API REST	,986	,371	,2	51	,692
API GraphQL	,808	6,049	,2	51	,004

mutations than the REST API and API REST Single Endpoint, as shown in Fig. 4.

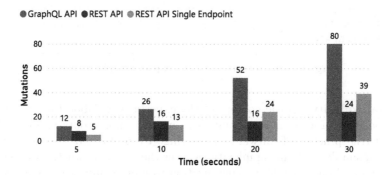

Fig. 4. Transaction processing capacity by time

Statistical Analysis of Average Response Time. Again we analyze the degree of linear relationship that APIs have with Pearson correlation matrices, as shown in Fig. 5. In addition, we highlight the positive linear correlation value of 0.999 of the GraphQL API with the REST Single Endpoint API, showing an advantage of GraphQL with the other architectures.

6   Threats to Validity

In this section, we establish a set of situations, factors, weaknesses, and limitations that threaten the validity of the experiment results [30].

Internal Validity. We developed the experimental laboratory, the APIs REST Single Endpoint, REST, GraphQL, and the mobile application to contribute to the internal validity using the SCRUM agile development framework. Where we performed an iterative-incremental follow-up and technical support to the requirements exposed in the tasks and design of the experiment; finally, we executed acceptance tests of the implemented use cases.

		RASP	RAPI	GAPI
RASP	PEA	1	0,942	,999**
	SIG		0,058	0,001
	N	4	4	4
RAPI	PEA	0,942	1	0,926
	SIG	0,058		0,074
	N	4	4	4
GAPI	PEA	,999**	0,926	1
	SIG	0,001	0,074	
	N	4	4	4

Legends:

PEA. Pearson correlation   GAPI. GraphQL API

SIG. Significant (bilateral)   **. Correlation is significant at the 0.01 level (bilateral).

RASP. REST API Single Endpoint   *. Correlation is significant at the 0.05 level (bilateral).

RAPI. REST API

Fig. 5. Transaction processing capacity correlation

External Validity. In the context of the experimental laboratory, we used a data repository of a technology company, thus obtaining a data approach from the industrial practice of software engineering. We performed the experimental tasks with simple-medium complexity to cover the common practice of querying and inserting data. Therefore, generalization to more complex tasks is limited; however, since these are basic data manipulation tasks, it is a starting point for exploring the behavior of this type of study in complex systems.

Construct Validity. We developed the constructs for the experiment execution phase to automate the performance efficiency metrics in each use case and establish the impact on the study's dependent variable. We defined the constructs consensually among the experimenters and validated them with acceptance tests.

Conclusion Validity. In this section, to mitigate the threats, the study's conclusions were supported by a statistical analysis of the results of the experiment.

7 Discussion and Related Work

For this section, we conducted a short literature review in search of studies that compare REST and GraphQL architectures. For the search, we used popular databases in software engineering: ACM Digital Library[1], Springer-Link[2], IEEE Xplore Library[3], Scopus[4], and DBLP[5]. We found 14 studies:

---

[1] See https://dl.acm.org.

[2] See https://link.springer.com.

[3] See https://ieeexplore.ieee.org.

[4] See https://www.scopus.com/.

[5] See https://dblp.org.

[3, 4, 8, 9, 12–16, 20, 22, 23, 26, 27]. After analyzing the earlier studies, we highlight the comparisons made between architecture characteristics, usability, complex query structure, interoperability, data transfer effectiveness, flexibility, and response time (most frequently). Where studies generally compare GraphQL APIs vs. REST APIs, but no study makes a comparison using a mobile client. Therefore, we note that our study is unprecedented in this area and can contribute interesting results to the body of knowledge about GraphQL. In addition, our results agree with most of the results of the analyzed studies.

8 Conclusions and Future Work

8.1 Conclusions

This article studies the effects on software quality of APIs developed with the REST and GraphQL architectures that are consumed from mobile applications; therefore, we pose the research question What effects do the development architectures of APIs consume from mobile applications have on software quality? We answer the posed question by designing and executing a computational experiment that compares the software quality of three APIs that a mobile client consumes. In this regard, on the one hand, we build one API with GraphQL architecture and two APIs with REST architecture, one of them exposes complex queries on several endpoints, and the other REST API exposes complex queries on a single endpoint. Nevertheless, on the other hand, the quality of the software is represented by the characteristic "Performance efficiency," which we operationalize with the metrics of average response time and Transaction processing capacity.

The result of the experiment indicates that both the average response time and Transaction processing capacity of the GraphQL API have better performance efficiency than the APIs developed with the REST architecture. Therefore, statistically, alternative hypothesis 1 is accepted. We conclude that there is a difference in the effects of software quality of the APIs developed with the GraphQL architecture and consumed by a mobile application. Therefore, GraphQL architectures' software quality is higher than REST architectures.

8.2 Future Work

We encourage the scientific community to conduct similar studies where mobile applications consume GraphQL, REST, and hybrid architectures between REST and GraphQL. Similarly, we promote the study of which technologies are the most efficient for developing efficient backend and frontend using REST and GraphQL architectures.

References

1. Basili, V.R.: Software modeling and measurement: the goal/question/metric paradigm. University of Maryland, Tech. rep. (1994)
2. Baškarada, S., Nguyen, V., Koronios, A.: Architecting microservices: practical opportunities and challenges. J. Comput. Inf. Syst. **60**(5), 1–9 (2018)
3. Brito, G., Mombach, T., Valente, M.T.: Migrating to GraphQL: a practical assessment. In: SANER 2019 - Proceedings of the 2019 IEEE 26th International Conference on Software Analysis, Evolution, and Reengineering, pp. 140–150. IEEE, Hangzhou (2019). https://doi.org/10.1109/SANER.2019.8667986, https://ieeexplore.ieee.org/abstract/document/8667986/
4. Brito, G., Valente, M.T.: REST vs GraphQL: a controlled experiment. In: Proceedings - IEEE 17th International Conference on Software Architecture, ICSA 2020, pp. 81–91. Institute of Electrical and Electronics Engineers Inc., Salvador (2020). https://doi.org/10.1109/ICSA47634.2020.00016
5. Facebook, I.: GraphQL — A query language for your API (2016). https://graphql.org/
6. Fielding, R.T., Taylor, R.N.: Principled design of the modern web architecture. ACM Trans. Internet Technol. (TOIT) **2**(2), 115–150 (2002)
7. Guevara-Vega, C., Bernardez, B., Duran, A., Quiña-Mera, A., Cruz, M., Ruiz-Cortes, A.: Empirical strategies in software engineering research: a literature survey. In: 2nd International Conference on Information Systems and Software Technologies, ICI2ST 2021. pp. 120–127 (2021). https://doi.org/10.1109/ICI2ST51859.2021.00025
8. Guo, Y., Deng, F., Yang, X.: Design and implementation of real-time management system architecture based on GraphQL. In: 2018 2nd Annual International Conference on Cloud Technology and Communication Engineering, CTCE 2018, vol. 466, p. 9. Institute of Physics Publishing, Nanjing (2018). https://doi.org/10.1088/1757-899X/466/1/012015, https://stacks.iop.org/1757-899X/466/i=1/a=012015?key=crossref.aea9adb1d7f75507f4831f4bca08dc61
9. Hartina, D.A., Lawi, A., Enrico Panggabean, L.: Performance Analysis of GraphQL and RESTful in SIM LP2M of the Hasanuddin University. In: The 2nd East Indonesia Conference on Computer and Information Technology (EIConCIT) 2018. pp. 237–240. Institute of Electrical and Electronics Engineers Inc., Indonesia (2018). https://doi.org/10.1109/EIConCIT.2018.8878524, https://ieeexplore.ieee.org/abstract/document/8878524/
10. ISO/IEC: NTE INEN-ISO/IEC 25010. International organization for standardization, Geneva, Switzerland, 1 edn. (2015)
11. ISO/IEC: ISO/IEC 25023:2016 Systems and software engineering - Systems and software Quality Requirements and Evaluation (SQuaRE) - Measurement of system and software product quality, vol. 1. International organization for standardization, Geneva, Switzerland, 1 edn. (2016)
12. Khan, R., Mian, A.N.: Sustainable IoT sensing applications development through GraphQL-based abstraction layer. Electronics (Switzerland) **9**(4), 23 (2020). https://doi.org/10.3390/electronics9040564
13. Kozhevnikov, V., Shergalis, D.: Migrating from REST to GraphQL having long-term supported clients. Theor. Appl. Sci. 93(February), 180–185 (2001). https://dx.doi.org/10.15863/TAS.2021.01.93.31

14. Lee, E., Kwon, K., Yun, J.: Performance Measurement of GraphQL API in Home ESS Data Server. In: 2020 International Conference on Information and Communication Technology Convergence (ICTC), vol. 2020-Octob, pp. 1929–1931. IEEE, Jeju (2020). https://doi.org/10.1109/ICTC49870.2020.9289569

15. Mukhiya, S., Rabbi, F., Pun, V., Rutle, A., Lamo, Y.: A GraphQL approach to healthcare information exchange with HL7 FHIR. In: The 9th International Conference on Current and Future Trends of Information and The 9th International Conference on Current and Future Trends of Information and Communication Technologies in Healthcare (ICTH 2019) Communication Technologies in Healthcare, vol. 160, pp. 338–345. Elsevier B.V., Coimbra (2019). https://doi.org/10.1016/j.procs.2019.11.082.

16. Nogatz, F., Seipel, D.: Implementing GraphQL as a query language for deductive databases in SWI-Prolog using DCGs, quasi quotations, and dicts. In: 30th Workshop on (Constraint) Logic Programming, WLP 2016 and 29th Workshop on (Constraint) Logic Programming, WLP 2015, vol. 234, pp. 42–56. Open Publishing Association, Leipzig (2017). https://doi.org/10.4204/EPTCS.234.4

17. Pautasso, C.: RESTful web services: principles, patterns, emerging technologies. In: Web Services Foundations, pp. 31–51. Springer, New York (2014). https://doi.org/10.1007/978-1-4614-7518-7_2

18. Quiña-Mera, A., Fernández-Montes, P., García, J., Bastidas, E., Ruiz-Cortés, A.: Quality in use evaluation of a GraphQL implementation. In: 16th Multidisciplinary International Congress on Science and Technology, CIT 2021. vol. 405 LNNS, pp. 15–27 (2022). https://doi.org/10.1007/978-3-030-96043-8_2

19. Richardson, L., Amundsen, M., Amundsen, M., Ruby, S.: RESTful Web APIs: Services for a Changing World. O'Reilly Media, Inc., California, USA (2013)

20. Sayago Heredia, J., Flores-García, E., Solano, A.R.: Comparative analysis between standards oriented to web services: SOAP, REST and GraphQL. In: Botto-Tobar, M., Zambrano Vizuete, M., Torres-Carrión, P., Montes León, S., Pizarro Vásquez, G., Durakovic, B. (eds.) ICAT 2019. CCIS, vol. 1193, pp. 286–300. Springer, Cham (2020). https://doi.org/10.1007/978-3-030-42517-3_22

21. Seifer, P., Härtel, J., Leinberger, M., Lämmel, R., Staab, S.: Empirical study on the usage of graph query languages in open source Java projects. In: SLE 2019 - Proceedings of the 12th ACM SIGPLAN International Conference on Software Language Engineering, co-located with SPLASH 2019, pp. 152–166. Association for Computing Machinery Inc, Athens (2019). https://doi.org/10.1145/3357766.3359541

22. Singh, A., Jeyanthi, N.: MVP Architecture model with single endpoint access for displaying COVID 19 patients information dynamically. In: Proceedings - 2020 12th International Conference on Computational Intelligence and Communication Networks, CICN 2020, pp. 471–476. IEEE, Bhimtal (2020). https://doi.org/10.1109/CICN49253.2020.9242573, https://ieeexplore.ieee.org/abstract/document/9242573

23. Susrama, G., Diyasa, M., Budiwitjaksono, G.S., Amarul, H., Ade, I.: Comparative analysis of rest and GraphQL technology on Nodejs-Based API development. In: 5th International Seminar of Research Month 2020, vol. 2021, pp. 43–52. Nusantara Science and Technology Proceedings, Zoom/Live Streaming Youtube (2021)

24. The GraphQL Foundation: GraphQL (2018). https://graphql.github.io/graphql-spec/June2018/

25. Thönes, J.: Microservices. IEEE Softw. **32**, 4 (2015). https://doi.org/10.1109/MS.2015.11

26. Vazquez-Ingelmo, A., Cruz-Benito, J., García-Penalvo, F.: Improving the OEEU's data-driven technological ecosystem's interoperability with GraphQL. In: 5th International Conference on Technological Ecosystem for Enhancing Multiculturality, TEEM 2017, vol. Part F1322, p. 8. Association for Computing Machinery, Cadiz (2017). https://doi.org/10.1145/3144826.3145437
27. Vesić, M., Kojić, N.: Comparative analysis of web application performance in case of using REST versus GraphQL. In: Fourth International Scientific Conference ITEMA 2020, pp. 1–9. Edekom Balkan, ONLINE-Virtual (2020). https://doi.org/10.1163/156854293X00151
28. Vogel, M., Weber, S., Zirpins, C.: Experiences on migrating RESTful web services to GraphQL. In: Braubach, L., et al. (eds.) ICSOC 2017. LNCS, vol. 10797, pp. 283–295. Springer, Cham (2018). https://doi.org/10.1007/978-3-319-91764-1_23
29. Wang, S., Keivanloo, I., Zou, Y.: How do developers react to RESTful API evolution? Lecture Notes in Computer Science (including subseries Lecture Notes in Artificial Intelligence and Lecture Notes in Bioinformatics) **8831**, 245–259 (2014)
30. Wohlin, C., Runeson, P., Höst, M., Ohlsson, M.C., Regnell, B., Wesslén, A.: Experimentation in Software Engineering. Springer, Berlin, Heidelberg, 1 edn. (2012). https://doi.org/10.1007/978-3-642-29044-2, https://www.springer.com/la/book/9783642290435

Projections and Predictive Analysis of *Tenebrio Molitor* Production Using Simulation Technique

Pablo Guzman[1] (ID), Jocelyn Monsalve[1], Daniel Morillo-Torres[2] (ID),
Gonzalo Aguila[1(✉)] (ID), and Gustavo Gatica[1] (ID)

[1] Faculty of Engineering - CIS, Universidad Andres Bello, Antonio Varas 880, Providencia,
Santiago de Chile, Chile
{gonzalo.aguila,ggatica}@unab.cl
[2] Faculty of Engineering, Pontificia Universidad Javeriana de Cali, Cali, Colombia

Abstract. Complex system operations must be mimicked or replicated, and simulations are conducted to predict their behavior. Herein, a discrete event simulation is presented to analyze *Tenebrio molitor* production using the SIMIO software, which allows the verification and validation of a mathematical model proposed, where temperature, luminosity, and humidity are controlled via simulation. Operation parameters such as the percentages of trays used for reproduction, the maximum capacity of the farm, the minimum weight of a tray for production, and the life cycle of the *Tenebrio molitor* are considered for the simulation. According to the results, 24 scenarios are evaluated to determine *Tenebrio molitor* production. The optimal scenario was where the farm had a maximum capacity of 1700 trays. It started with 100 trays, in which 5% were allocated for reproduction, considering that the scenario began with 100 trays; this number is considerably less than the number of trays used in scenarios 10 and 11, which start with 500 trays. The analysis of the proposed production of *Tenebrio molitor* shows that simulation can be used to control the estimated production.

Keywords: Simulation · Tenebrio molitor · Industrial application

1 Introduction

Recently, there has been an increase in the world population, which has increased the demand for animal protein sources as food. The literature reports high costs for the food processing industry in addition to its environmental impact. Therefore, there is an interest in finding alternatives to replace conventional protein sources, particularly entomophagy (Jansson 2015; World Population Prospects - Population Division - United Nations 2019; Avendaño et al. 2020).

Entomophagy is the consumption of insects by humans, a custom rooted in some native people. It provides a nutritional alternative to the biological value of the percentage of protein, and its components include vitamins, minerals, and polyunsaturated fatty acids. Its production presents numerous advantages, such as resistance to climatic changes, a low volume space required, and a low environmental impact (Medrano Vega 2019; Garcés Lopez 2021; Castiblanco and Rojas 2022).

T. Guarda et al. (Eds.): ARTIIS 2022, CCIS 1675, pp. 31–43, 2022.
https://doi.org/10.1007/978-3-031-20319-0_3

According to the Food and Agriculture Organization (FAO) of the United Nations, more than 1900 species of edible insects are consumed worldwide. The most consumed insects are Coleoptera (31%), Lepidoptera (18%), and Hymenoptera (14%). They are followed by grasshoppers, locusts, and crickets (13%); cicadas, leafhopper fulgoromorpha, mealybugs, and bedbugs (hemiptera) (10%); and termites (isoptera) (3%), dragonflies (odonates) (3%), flies (diptera) (2%), and other species (5%) (Van Huis et al. 2013; FAO 2018).

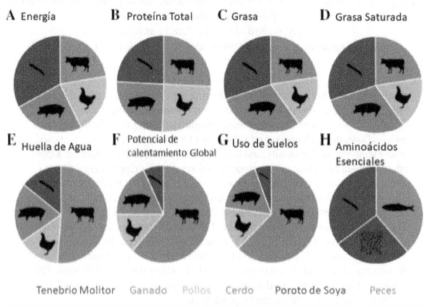

Nomenclature / Translation	
A = Energy	*Tenebrio molitor* = Mealworm
B = Total protein	Ganado = Livestock
C = Fat	Pollos = Poultry
D = Saturated fat	Cerdo = Pork
E = Water footprint	Poroto de soya = Soybean
F = Global warming potential	Peces = Fish
G = Land use	
H = Essential amino acids	

Fig. 1. Comparison of different nutritional and environmental parameters in different food sources. Obtained from (Van Huis et al. 2013).

Figure 1 shows a comparison of different nutritional parameters of *Tenebrio molitor* (only *Tenebrio* from here on) with different farm animal sources in terms of nutritional values (A–D) per 100 g, (E) water footprint per consumable ton, (F) global warming potential per 1 kg of consumable portion, (G) soil use per 1 kg of consumable portion, and (H) amount of essential amino acids obtained from conventional protein/food sources.

The literature demonstrates the benefits of consuming insects; however, not all countries have regulations to standardize human consumption (entomophagy), as in Chile.

The European Food Safety Authority has conducted several analyses and in 2021 indicating that *Tenebrio* is suitable for human consumption and commercialization; hence, the interest in identifying parameters, productive ranges, and a controlled environment for *Tenebrio* production has increased (Turck et al. 2021; Ravagli Castillo 2021).

Currently, there is a deficit in larval culture production owing to the lack of industrialization of the process (Hurtado 2019). Therefore, the following section defines the working methodology to develop a simulation experiment because it can determine the feasibility of using simulation to perform informed decision-making of a production process.

2 Methodology

The applied methodology considers nine stages combining mathematical and logical aspects. During the first stage, the problem is defined and the study to be performed is planned. The second stage involves data collection, which is the most important stage to generate a simulation model. In the third stage, the mathematical model is formulated. During the fourth stage, the model is constructed and verified. In the fifth stage, the model is tested. During the sixth stage, the model is verified using the simulation software; the validation must be performed at different times of this methodology. In the seventh stage, simulation experiments are designed, while in the eighth stage, the experiments are executed. Finally, during the ninth stage, the results are analyzed (Barceló 1996; Law and Law 2008; Cambar and Ocampo 2012).

An outline of the methodology is presented in Fig. 2, where the above mentioned stages are depicted.

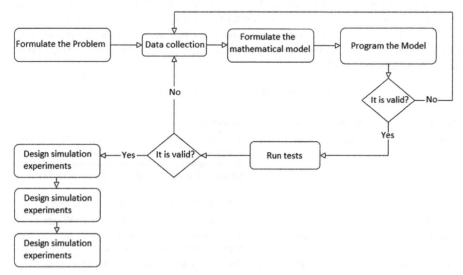

Fig. 2. Flowchart created using the data from the book "Simulación de sistemas discretos" in Spanish ("Simulation of discrete systems") by Jaime Barceló (1996).

Model validation is one of the main steps to confirm if the model adequately represents the system under study, thus validating the inductions and extrapolations regarding the behavior of the system based on the model (Barceló 1996).

3   Problem Statement and Study Planning

This study focuses on analyzing the process of producing *Tenebrio* using simulation techniques. For this purpose, it is necessary to model the life process of *Tenebrio*, to model the feeding and operational processes, and to identify different scenarios and optimizing its production.

When analyzing the process, the main entity (tray) is identified to contain a certain amount of mealworm that must go through two processes in parallel before going to production. These processes are the *Tenebrio* life cycle and the operational aspects of the production plant (inspection, cleaning and feeding). Both the processes are modeled via a discrete simulation.

It is worth mentioning that a limitation of this research corresponds to the lack of information found in the literature on this industrialization process of producing mealworm. Therefore, secondary data is used, and experts' opinions in this field were used to adjust the simulation model in this research. If historical data on this process were available, it would be possible to have a clearer and safer notion of the distributions and results obtained.

4   Data Collection

References and studies conducted in Mexico were used to obtain the data related to the *Tenebrio*. Thus, we were able to collect data to determine the times corresponding to the life cycle, mortality rates, and recommended feeding and reproduction percentages of the *Tenebrio*. Table 1 presents the data used in this model (Damborsky et al. 1999; Sarmiento-Hernández 2018).

Table 1. Initial data of the simulation model.

Variable	Number	Unit	Description
Size_tray	2000	cm^2	Trays of 2000 cm^2 area are considered. It is necessary to define this value for estimating the number of *Tenebrio* per tray and thus for conducting calculations regarding feeding, weight, and reproduction of the *Tenebrio*
Eggs_min	85	Eggs	A female beetle can lay a minimum of 85 eggs
Eggs_max	580	Eggs	A female beetle can lay a maximum of 580 eggs
Tenebrioxcm2_min	0.94	*Tenebrio*/cm^2	The minimum number of *Tenebrio* that can approximately fit in a tray per cm^2
Tenebrioxcm2_max	1.8	*Tenebrio*/cm^2	The approximate maximum number of *Tenebrio* that can fit in a tray per cm^2
Flour_per_tray	0.06–0.1	kg	Range of flour to feed 1000 *Tenebrio*
Tubers_per_tray	0.006–0.01	kg	Range of tubers to feed 1000 *Tenebrio*

In addition, the size of the trays and the number of larval *Tenebrio* per cm^2 are considered for simulation. Thus, it is possible to calculate the number of mealworms in each tray and determine the quantity of food required per tray because the proportion is indicated for 1000 *Tenebrio*.

The life cycle of the *Tenebrio* is ~6 months, i.e., ~125 days (see Fig. 3). The time elapsed in each stage varies; in some cases it is only a few days, while in others it is in months. Therefore, to enter the data into the simulation model must be used with the same time unit (weeks) as presented in Table 2.

Table 2. Life cycle duration and mortality rate of *Tenebrio*.

Stage	Expression	Units
Egg_larva	Random.Uniform (0.5714, 2.1429)	Weeks
Larva_pupa	Random.Uniform (8.6964, 13.0446)	Weeks
Pupa_imago	Random.Uniform (2.8571, 4.3482)	Weeks
Mating	Random.Uniform (2.1429, 13.0446)	Weeks
Mortality_rate_1	50	%
Mortality_rate_2	11	%

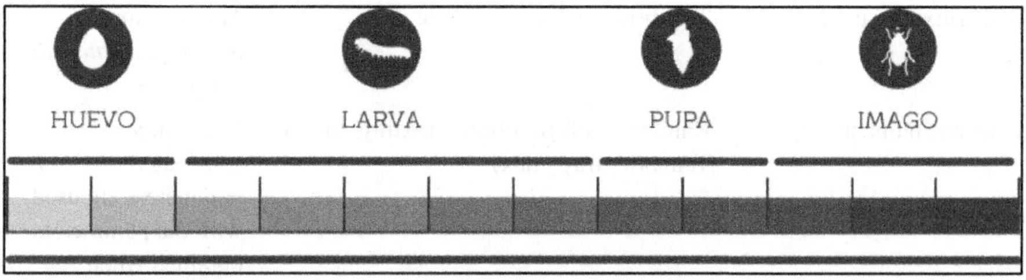

Nomenclature / Translation
HUEVO = EGG
LARVA = LARVA
PUPA = PUPA
IMAGO = IMAGO

Fig. 3. *Tenebrio* life cycle ("*Tenebrio molitor*-Gusano de La Harina" in Spanish (*Tenebrio molitor*-the flour worm), Proteinsecta, n.d.).

A complex aspect of the simulation is the data related to the operational part because the process is not industrialized. Therefore, we sought an expert judgment from a biologist who has been dedicated to the production and commercialization of mealworm in Mexico for 7 years. In addition, data regarding the duration time of the processes within the farm, inspection, cleaning, and feeding are obtained.

5   Formulation of the Mathematical Model

New variables can be obtained and entered into the simulation model using the data collected. These variables, function in the simulation, and their respective description are shown in Table 3.

Table 3. Dependent variables of the simulation model.

Variable	Expression/function in the simulation	Description
Eggs_number	Random/uniform (Eggs_min or Eggs_max)	Uniformly distributed parameters are used with the parameters obtained when calculating the minimum and maximum number of eggs that can be laid by a female *Tenebrio*
Tenebrioxtray_min	Tenebrioxcm2_min × Size_tray	The minimum number of *Tenebrio* per tray
Tenebrioxtray_max	Tenebrioxcm2_max × Size_tray	The maximum number of *Tenebrio* per tray
Tenebrio_numberxtray	Random/uniform (Tenebrioxtray_min or Tenebrioxtray_max)	Uniformly distributed parameters are used with the parameters obtained when calculating the minimum and maximum number of *Tenebrio* per tray (depending on the size of the tray, cm^2)
Trays_reproduction	Math. Round (((Tenebrio_numberxtray/2) × Eggs_number)/Tenebrio_numberxtray)	This formula was used to calculate the number of new trays entering the system after the breeding process
Food_rate_min	Tenebrioxtray_min /1000	Minimum food rate per tray is divided into 1000 because the proportion of food given is per 1000 *Tenebrio*

(continued)

Table 3. (*continued*)

Variable	Expression/function in the simulation	Description
Food_rate_max	Tenebrioxtray_max /1000	Maximum food rate per tray is divided by 1000 because the proportion of food given is per 1000 *Tenebrio*
Food_rate	Random/uniform (Food_rate_min or Food_rate_max)	After obtaining the minimum and maximum food rates, the values are entered as parameters and evaluated with a uniform distribution
Months_until_production	Number of months until reaching the maximum number of trays in the system	It will take the value of the months elapsed until the maximum number of trays in the system is reached

6 Construction and Verification of the Simulation Model

The SIMIO software is used for simulation, which is specialized in simulation and 3D animation in process flows for discrete events. It is based on a mixed approach that combines objects and procedures to generate behavioral models of logistic, industrial, and service systems (Simio - Software Simulación de Procesos Logísticos n.d.).

When implementing the model, preliminary tests are conducted to find the best way to represent the required system. For this reason, the model was simplified since it should only contain the level of detail required by the study's objectives to evaluate the data that was considered most relevant (Barceló 1996).

The main entity is the mealworms tray, in which, the mealworms must go through their life cycle along with the production process. Therefore, a process was introduced in the simulation as seen in Fig. 4, called "COPY_GENERATED_ENTITIES," which is activated when the entity "Tray_A" goes through the "Egg_larva" stage, creating an entity "Tray_B" to represent that while the mealworms undergo their life cycle, the larvae (after hatching) must be fed, inspected, and their trays should be cleaned periodically.

As can see in Fig. 5, the "start_production" process is activated when, after having repeated the life cycle of the *Tenebrio*, the maximum number of trays in the system is achieved, allowing a certain percentage of trays to be used for production and not all for reproduction, as was being done before of process activation.

38   P. Guzman et al.

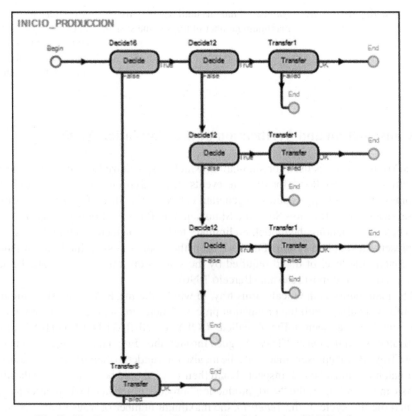

Fig. 4. *Tenebrio* tray process simulation using SIMIO software.

Figure 6 shows that the "production" process is activated every time an entity "Tray_B" leaves the servers where it is fed and evaluates if the weight of the *Tenebrio* is suitable to go into production or if it should be maintained in the feeding cycle.

Fig. 5. The "start_production" process simulation using SIMIO software.

Figure 7 shows the complete model and highlights "Combiner1" because it is essential to complete the production. When the conditions corresponding to the life cycle are

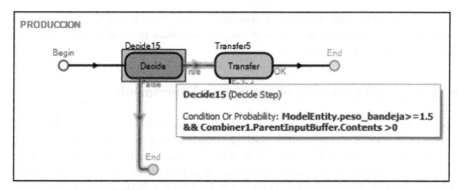

Fig. 6. The "production" process simulation using SIMIO software.

fulfilled and the tray reaches the minimum weight of 1.5 kg, the entities "Tray_A" and "Tray_B" are joined and thus represent the time elapsed and the feeding, cleaning, and inspection processes for *Tenebrio*.

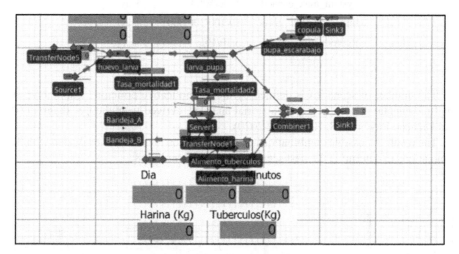

Fig. 7. Simulation of model using SIMIO software.

7   Model Test Runs and Validation

The initial results of the simulated model showed that the production was below expectation; therefore, meetings are held with the expert to validate and adjust the model. According to the expert judgment, "When we just started, we only dedicated ourselves to the reproduction of mealworms for a year and a half; after this time, we already had a stable production to begin sales" (I. Marquez, personal communication, September 15, 2021). The above is important because in the model production is realized in the larval stage. The model specified the maximum number of trays to be available, and production would only start when that number was reached; to reduce the waiting time, 100% of the trays were used for reproduction.

8   Design and Execution of Simulation Experiments

After making the final adjustments to the model, we began to evaluate the scenarios to be simulated. First, the variables that could directly influence the results were identified. The variables affecting the scenarios would be the maximum capacity of trays in the system, the number of trays with which the simulation would begin, and the percentage of trays required for reproduction (Guerrero Hernández and Henriques Librantz 2014).

The values between which the scenarios will be evaluated are described in Table 4.

Table 4. Variables referenced in the model.

Reference variable	Value per scenario	Unit
System_max_capacity	1700/5000	Trays
Initial_number _trays	10/100/300/500	Trays
Reproduction_rate	5/10/40	%

The number of scenarios is defined by the multiplicative principle, also known as the fundamental principle of combinatorial analysis, derived from the tree diagram (R and Pacheco Reyes 2008; Hernández 2020).

The result of possible combinations was 24 scenarios, which were evaluated with 30 replications to determine the best scenarios, as shown in Fig. 8.

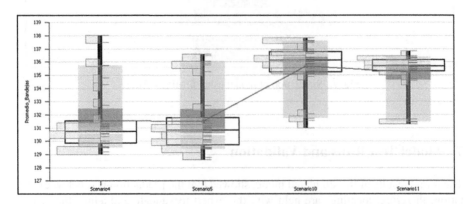

Fig. 8. Simulation results (average_trays) of model using SIMIO software.

9   Analysis of Results

Table 5 shows the four scenarios selected (4, 5, 10 and 11) from the 24 scenarios, presenting the shortest time to start production. The production is considered to start when the maximum number of trays exists in the system and 100% of them are used for reproduction.

Scenarios 4 and 5 start with 100 trays and a reproduction percentage of 5% and 10%, respectively.

Scenarios 10 and 11 start with 500 trays and a reproduction percentage of 5% and 10%, respectively.

Approximately 20–30% of the food is assimilated and contributes to its weight, while the other 70% is waste (which can also be marketed as fertilizer).

Table 5. Final results of the assays.

Result	Scenarios with the shortest time to start production			
	4	5	10	11
Months elapsed to start production	5.2	5.2	4.9	4.9
Monthly average of *Tenebrio* production (expressed in kg)	274.6	274.4	297.2	296.2
Monthly average of flour used for feeding (expressed in kg)	1797.4	1795.6	2166	2164.4
Monthly average of tubers used for feeding (expressed in kg)	561.4	560.4	683.4	682.7

10   Conclusion

This study shows that the estimation of the *Tenebrio molitor* production in an insect farm where temperature, luminosity and humidity are controlled is possible via simulation.

It was possible to analyze the operative variables such as the percentages of trays used for reproduction, the maximum capacity of the farm, and the minimum weight of a tray for the production. In addition, the durations of each stage of the life cycle of the *Tenebrio molitor* are considered.

The objectives of achieving a simulation model to determine the estimated production and the feed required and minimize the time to start a stable production were achieved. The optimal scenario was where the farm had a maximum capacity of 1700 trays. It started with 100 trays, in which 5% were allocated for reproduction, considering that the scenario began with 100 trays; this number is considerably less than the number of trays used in scenarios 10 and 11 that start with 500 trays.

In brief, the simulation is feasible for this type of production and can be further improved.

Acknowledgements. The authors are grateful for financing this work with funds from the internal project DI-12-20/REG, and thank Crimson Interactive Pvt. Ltd. (Enago) (https://www.enago.com/es/) for their assistance in manuscript translation and editing.

References

Avendaño, C., Sánchez, M., Valenzuela, C.: Insects: an alternative for animal and human feeding. Revista Chilena de Nutricion **47**(6), 1029–1037 (2020). https://doi.org/10.4067/S0717-751820 20000601029

Barceló, J.: Libro-simulacion de sistemas discretos (1996)

Castiblanco Rodriguez, S.T., Rojas Sarmiento, D.A.: (2022). https://universidadean.edu.co/invest igacion/grupos-de-investigacion

Damborsky, M.P., Andrigo-Ybran, T., Bar, M.E., Oscherov, E.: Ciclo_de_Vida_de_Tenebrio_molitor _Coleoptera_Teneb (1999)

FAO: La contribución de los insectos a la seguridad alimentaria, los medios de vida y el medio ambiente. Fao, pp. 1–4 (2018). http://www.fao.org/edible-insects/en/

Garcés Lopez, C.E.: Cristina Estefanía Garcés López Ingeniería en Alimentos Cristina Estefanía Garcés López (2021)

Guerrero Hernández, M.A., Henriques Librantz, A.F.: Simulación de eventos discretos de la cadena logística de exportación de commodities. Ingeniare. Revista Chilena de Ingeniería **22**(2), 257–262 (2014). https://doi.org/10.4067/S0718-33052014000200011

Hernández, R.: Técnicas de Conteo en la Probabilidad (2020)

Hurtado, C.: Desarrollo de un sistema de ambiente controlado para la producción y cría de Tenebrio Molitor y Zophoba Morio **20**, 124 (2019)

Jansson, A.: Insects as Food – Something for the Future? (2015)

Law, A.M., Law, A.M.: Proceedings of the 2008 Winter Simulation Conference S. J. Mason, R. R. Hill, L. Mönch, O. Rose, T. Jefferson, J. W. Fowler eds., pp. 39–47 (2008)

Medrano Vega, L.C.: Larvas de gusano de harina (Tenebrio molitor) como alternativa proteica en la alimentación animal, pp. 1–44 (2019). https://repository.unad.edu.co/bitstream/handle/10596/28001/lcmedranov.pdf?sequence=1&isAllowed=y

Pavon Cambar, A.E., Ocampo, J.: Integrando la Metodologia DMAIC de Seis Sigma con la Simulacion de Eventos Discretos en Flexsim (2012)

R, B.R., Pacheco Reyes, G.: Probabilidad y estadística-Samuel Fuenlabrada de la Vega Trucíos-3ED Related papers BECU LIBRO ALUMNO MAT EMAT ICA (2008)

Ravagli Castillo, A.C.: Prospección de los Insectos Comestibles como Fuente de Proteína Animal para el Consumo. Prospect for Edible Insects as a Source of Animal, pp. 1–28

Sarmiento-Hernández, A.P.: Establecimiento e implementación de un protocolo de cría de gusano de harina Tenebrio molitor (Coleoptera: Tenebrionidae), como apoyo al programa de conservación de la rana venenosa dorada Phyllobates terribilis (Anura: Dendrobatidae) en el Bioparque Waka. Universidad Nacional Abierta y a Distancia UNAD, 51 (2018). https://repository.unad.edu.co/handle/10596/17749

Simio – Software simulación de procesos logísticos: (n.d.). https://www.simio-simulacion.es/.Accessed 6 May 2022

Tenebrio Molitor- Gusano de la harina» Proteinsecta. (n.d.). https://proteinsecta.es/tenebrio-mol itor-gusano-de-la-harina/. Accessed 20 May 2022

Turck, D., et al.: Safety of dried yellow mealworm (Tenebrio molitor larva) as a novel food pursuant to Regulation (EU) 2015/2283. EFSA J. **19**(1), 1–29 (2021). https://doi.org/10.2903/j.efsa.2021.6343

Van Huis, A., Van Itterbeeck, J., Klunder, H., et al.: Edible insects: future prospects for food and feed security. In: Food and Agriculture Organization of the United Nations, vol. 97, no. 18 (2013). https://library.wur.nl/WebQuery/wurpubs/fulltext/258042

World Population Prospects - Population Division - United Nations (2019). https://population.un.org/wpp/Graphs/Probabilistic/POP/TOT/900

Automatic Recognition System for Traffic Signs in Ecuador Based on Faster R-CNN with ZFNet

David Zabala-Blanco[1], Milton Aldás[2], Wilson Román[3], Joselyn Gallegos[4], and Marco Flores-Calero[3,4(✉)]

[1] Department of Computer Science and Industry, Universidad Católica del Maule, Talca, Chile
dzabala@ucm.cl
[2] Grupo de investigación COESVI, Facultad de Ingeniería Civil y Mecánica, Universidad Técnica de Ambato campus Huachi, Av. Los Chasquis y Calle Río Payamino, Ambato, Tungurahua, Ecuador
mr.aldas@uta.edu.ec
[3] Universidad de las Fuerzas Armadas-ESPE, Av. Gral. Rumiñahui, s/n, PBX 171-5-231B, Sangolquí, Pichincha, Ecuador
{wmroman,mjflores}@espe.edu.ec
[4] Department of Intelligent Systems, I&H Tech, Latacunga, Cotopaxi, Ecuador

Abstract. This research presents an application of the Deep Learning technology in the development of an automatic system detection of traffic signs of Ecuador. The development of this work has been divided into two parts, i) in first a database was built with regulatory and preventive traffic signs, taken in urban environments from several cities in Ecuador. The dataset consists of 52 classes, collected in the various lighting environments (dawn, day, sunset and cloudy) from 6 am to 7 pm, in various localities of Ecuador, ii) then, an object detector based on Faster-RCNN with ZF-Net was implemented as a detection/recognition module. The entire experimental part was developed on the ViiA technology platform, which consists of a vehicle for the implementation of driving assistance systems using Computer Vision and Artificial Intelligence, in real road driving conditions.

Keywords: Deep learning · Traffic accidents · Traffic signs · Ecuador · Faster R-CNN · ZF-Net · Computer vision

1 Introduction

Traffic signs are bright colored and easy to understand signs that are found on urban and rural road infrastructure, as well as on highways. They were designed to regulate traffic, avoid accidents, and provide useful information for road users (drivers and pedestrians). World Health Organization (WHO) statistics indicate that traffic accidents are among the twenty leading causes of death worldwide, with 2.4% of deaths, the most common reasons being lack of concentration at the wheel or speeding reasons [28]. Precisely, the risk of an adult pedestrian dying

© The Author(s), under exclusive license to Springer Nature Switzerland AG 2022
T. Guarda et al. (Eds.): ARTIIS 2022, CCIS 1675, pp. 44–57, 2022.
https://doi.org/10.1007/978-3-031-20319-0_4

after being run over by a car is less than 20% at 50 km/h, and around 60% if the speed is near 80 km/h.

In Ecuador, in 2015, 13.75% of all traffic accidents happened at road intersections, meaning 8.14% of deaths were from this cause [2]. In regard to speed, it is known that 13.7% of accidents during 2017 were because of speeding [1]. This places the country at 74 worldwide [19]. Considering this problem, advanced driver-assistance systems (ADAS) have gained more importance, with the purpose of developing increasingly safer cars [8,27]; so they can automatically warn the driver of current traffic restrictions of the roads where they are driving, therefore significantly contributing to the prevention and reduction of road accidents.

Current ADAS are far from perfect because they work under limited conditions. They, particularly, do not correctly operate under the following conditions: bad weather conditions which reduce visibility (rain, snow, excessive sun exposure, and air pollution), if the windshield before the camera is dirty (with mud splashes, frost, snow, or covered with some adhesive), or if it is cracked or corrupted, if the camera fails to function, if there is obsolete or defective mapping, if there are hidden traffic signs, that do not conform to road regulations, or that are damaged or deformed [17,30]. Additionally, one of the main restrictions is that set by the country; each state has its own set of traffic signs [15], which is why ADAS must be extremely specialized for the country where it will be functioning.

Therefore, this research focuses in presenting an ADAS expert in the detection and identification of regulatory and preventive signs in Ecuador. Modern techniques for computer vision (CV) and deep learning (DL) have been used for its implementation with the goal of covering most of the difficulties presented in driving during the particular conditions mentioned before.

1.1 Gaps and Contributions of the Paper

The research gap and objective are:

- The relevant gap is that there is no significant research with traffic signs from developing countries.
- The main objective of this work is to build a system to detect traffic signs from Ecuador, which is a developing country.

The missed theoretical and practitioners contributions, our limitations, and the future research are:

- The most important missing contribution corresponds to the development of traffic sign detection systems in developing countries, because in these places accident rates are high.
- The main missing practical contribution is the construction of traffic signal databases of developing countries.
- One of the main limitations of this proposed is the number of traffic sign classes, because they only consider a subset of preventive and regulatory signs.
- In the future, the number of traffic signs will be increased and new specialized object detectors will be developed for traffic signs.

1.2   Organization of the Paper

This document is organized as follows: the second section presents previous works on traffic-sign recognition; the third section describes a new advanced driver-assistance system for Ecuadorian signs of regulatory and preventive nature. Implementation is based on the use of modern technology such as deep learning, along with traditional image processing techniques and computer vision. The following section shows the experimental results under real driving conditions during the day, as well as a database with traffic signs from Ecuador. Lastly, the last section is devoted for conclusions and future works.

2   State of the Art

To date, developing ADAS is a topic that is open to research, given its inherent difficulty of moving through real driving environments where there are abrupt and unexpected changes on the road's conditions (animal or pedestrian crossing), infrastructure (roadblock due to landslides or maintanence), and environmental conditions (rain, fog, or excessive sun exposure). Inevitably, these inherent factors, along with some human errors, can generate traffic accidents with catastrophic consequences [8,17,30].

On the other hand, increasing the computing power has made it possible for deep learning techniques to flourish and create solutions in different engineering fields. Particularly in developing ADAS specialized in traffic signs. Furthermore, the development of smart and autonomous cars has promoted building ADAS to perceive information from the driving surroundings [23].

Deep learning techniques are successful because of its capacity to learn and infer without needing previous specialized knowledge, materializing into a Convolutional Neural Network (CNN) as a fundamental axis of classification. Many architectures for detection and recognition of traffic signs have sprung from this [3], the most quoted ones among them are the following: CNN [7,9,10,14,24], R-CNN (Regions with Convolutional Neural Network) [26], RBFNN (Radial Basis Function Neural Network), FCN (Fully Convolutional Network), Faster R-CNN [34], YOLO-V2 (You Only Look Once), YOLO-V3 [16,31], and SSD (Single Shot Multibox Detector) [3,32]. For the moment, there is strong evidence that techniques based on a Faster R-CNN show better results, generating an average mAP of 93.24% [3].

Countries around the world are adapting their signs to Vienna Convention on Road Traffic. However, this is a process that happens slowly or not at all, which is why many signs have certain differences and others, simply, do not exist. A clear example of this is shown in Fig. 1, where the STOP and GIVE WAY traffic signs have a similar shape but a different content in Ecuador [7], Germany [25], and China [11], respectively. Therefore, it was necessary to construct the database used in this work.

In contrast to the high rates of road accident, there are few traffic sign databases of developing countries and, therefore, limited research; most studies correspond to developed countries; from them, the German databases GTSRB and GTSDB [3,21], Chinese databases Tsinghua-Tencent [24,32] and Chinese

Fig. 1. Differences between the STOP and GIVE WAY traffic signs in Ecuador, Germany, and China; in this order by column.

Traffic Signs [11], the USA's LISA [15], the Swedish's STSD [10], and the Malayan database used by Mohd-Isa et al. [16], or Lau et al. [14], have received considerable attention and are constantly cited in many works. More recently, there is the work of Flores-Calero et al. [7], who have constructed and used traffic-sign databases of Ecuador to implement the first proposal in this field.

3   System Description

The diagram for the development of this system is presented in Fig. 2, where we take an image input that then is passed through a deep learning structure to obtain output metrics which allow to trace and recognize Ecuador's regulatory and preventive traffic signs.

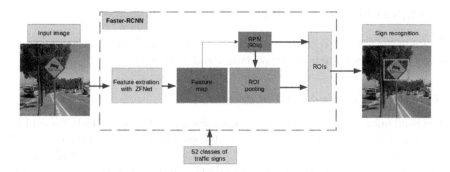

Fig. 2. Proposed diagram for traffic sign detection and recognition using deep learning: Regulatory and preventive signs in Ecuador.

3.1 Faster R-CNN Architecture Based on ZFNet

In recent years, with the fast development of deep learning, CNN are replacing traditional methods of object classification (generating characteristics plus classification algorithm). Based on this, deep-learning-based object detection algorithms are gaining ground because of the superior results they show. Faster R-CNN is a proposal for efficient object detection, where two networks called RPN (Regional Proposal Method) and Fast R-CNN work efficiently [20].

Regarding RPN, this is a convolutional neuronal network that is completely connected, and which can simultaneously predict objects' ROIs and their score.

The proposed regions are generated by the sliding-window method, as it is glided over the characteristics map from the last convolutional layer. This way, the RPN can locate multiple regions proposed by each glide. It locates the center of the anchors, which correspond to the generated ROIs in different scales and width/height ratio (AR, aspect ratio), over each position of the characteristics map.

Fast R-CNN is an object detector which combines classification and location. It receives an image and a set of proposed regions, generated by the RPN, as input. In the first phase the network processes the whole image with various layers of convolution and pooling to create a characteristics map. Then, a fixed size characteristics vector from each proposed region is extracted, and it moves to a fully connected (FC) layer for classification, using a soft-max function. Many proposals can be used to generate the characteristics map, such as AlexNet, LeNet, ZF-Net, etc.

On the other hand, ZFNet is a deep learning architecture based on AlexNet, and it was the winning proposal of the 2013 ILSVRC classification and detection challenge [33]. This network is composed of five convolutional layers, two pooling layers, followed by two FC layers, and finally, a soft-max layer. The pooling layers are located after the first and second convolutional layer, respectively.

4   Experimental Results

The main goal of this section is to present the results of the mentioned system, respect to database, metrics of evaluation and training process.

4.1 Ecuador Traffic-Sign Database

The visual information to develop this work was provided by the I&H Technology company. The videos, along with the traffic-sign images, were taken from different cities in Ecuador, among them: Quito, Latacunga, Salcedo, Ambato, and Sangolquí; on the visible spectrum, between the hours of 6 A.M. and 7 P.M., in 4 different lighting environments: sunrise, daytime, nighttime, and cloudy, according to the hours of the day. Regarding the capture distance, they were shot at a distance ranging from 5 to 40 m in front of the vehicle.

The color images are of standard size and have 960×1280 pixel resolution. Subsequently, the real regions (ROIs), where the traffic signs are, were labelled by hand; reaching a total of 37, 500 ROIs, divided into 52 classes, of which 28 correspond to regulatory ones, and the remaining ones are preventive. Many examples are shown in Fig. 3, where the regulatory signs are the ones with the biggest differences between countries. Additionally, the number of images per each class can be seen in Fig. 4, where the number of cases are evidently not homogenous. This is mainly because there are signs which appear with a higher frequency than others.

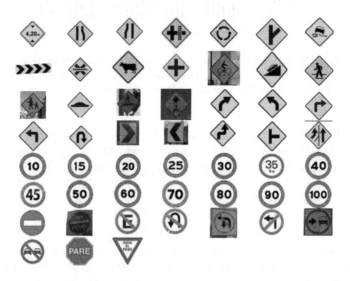

Fig. 3. Examples of regulatory and preventive traffic signs in Ecuador, divided in 52 classes. The four rows are regulatory, and the rest are preventive.

For storage and labelling, we followed the format established in the famous GTSRB and GTSDB datasets [25].

4.2   Evaluation Metrics

The first metric used to measure the quality of this proposal is the miss rate (MR) versus false positive per image (FPPI) [4], given by equations (1) and (2), respectively.

$$MR = \frac{FN}{TP + FN} \tag{1}$$

$$FPPI = \frac{FP}{\text{Number of images}} \tag{2}$$

where TP, FP, and FN are the true positives, the false positives, and the false negatives, respectively. Furthermore, to evaluate the performance of this proposal we used the mAP (mean Average Precision) metric, which was proposed

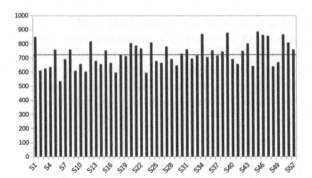

Fig. 4. Number of Ecuadorian traffic signs, divided into regulatory (red) and preventive (yellow), according to Fig. 3 notation. The name of the class is on the X axis, and the frequency of the signs is on the Y axis. (Color figure online)

in the 2010 PASCAL VOC challenge [5]. An object is considered as a correct detection (TP) if the IoU index is greater than the given threshold, on the contrary it is considered a wrong detection (FP). This value is between 0 and 1.

$$IoU = \frac{B_{gt} \cap B_p}{B_{gt} \cup B_p} \tag{3}$$

On the equation (3), B_{gt} is the true region, labelled manually, and B_p is the predicted region, meaning it is generated by the detection algorithm. In practice, the ROIs that represented by B_{gt} and B_p are formed by four values (x, y, w, h); where (x, y) is the upper left position, w is the width and h is the height. Figure 5 illustrates this diagram and its geometric representation.

Fig. 5. B_{gt} and B_p ROIs representation, and an illustration of equation (3) to calculate the IoU index.

Given the rigor needed to detect traffic signs, the threshold for the IoU was set at 0.5.

4.3   Model Training

Firstly, to share certain convolutional layers between RPN and Fast R-CNN networks, the training procedure composed by four steps [20] was followed. The steps were: a) training the RPN independently; b) training the Fast R-CNN detection network separately using the regions generated in the previous step; c) using the network in step b) to initialize the RPN and to just share the layers that were adjusted in the joint training of the two networks; d) finally, keeping the convolutional layers fixed, only adjusting the layers that are completely connected to the Fast R-CNN network.

Additionally, to improve training, the database was increased by using data augmentation techniques, to strengthen the model's sturdiness in terms of the different sizes and shapes, as well as avoiding over adjustment of the settings. All the images from the training set were randomly chosen according to the following rules: a) using the original image; b) taking a random region from the original image and naming it "subimage," thereupon, resizing the subimage to [0.5, 1] size and the width/height ratio to [0.5, 2]; c) reflecting the chance of the original image; and d) randomly trimming the original image [6, 22].

After that, to train the deep learning model, the database was divided into three sets with 70%, 15%, and 15% for the training, validation, and test phases, respectively.

The following settings shown in Table 1 were the ones used for the training stage, and are the ones required by Caffe library [29]. The weights were initialized with the previously trained ZFNet model and finite tuning with the ADAM optimization algorithm [13], which is used to reduce the time taken to train the model.

Table 1. Training parameters of ZFNet architecture.

Parameters	Value
Learning Rate (Base Lr)	0.001
Momentum	0.9
Weight decay	0.0005
Lr Policy	Step
Images per batch	100
Gamma	0.10

The equipment used for the training and testing consists of a computer with an 18.04 Ubuntu operating system, with a core 17-7700 core at 3.60 GHz with an 8 GB RAM, and graphic card, and a GPU with a memory of 12 GB. C++ language with the Caffe library was used to develop the software, along with an extension for Python [12].

5   Results Analysis

Results of the proposal based on the Faster R-CNN with ZFNet, on the database of signs from Ecuador are shown in Table 2, divided into regulatory and preventive. The mean Average Precision (mAP) is of 95.34%, which is one of the best results found in the state of the art.

Table 2. Results of mAP with the Faster R-CNN model with ZFNet of Ecuador's traffic signs.

Sign class	mAP value (%)
Regulatory	96.90
Preventive	94.28
Total	95.34

The MR (miss rate) versus FPPI (False Positive Per Image) curve, in log-log scale, is shown in Fig. 6, which shows how competitive the proposal is in the state of the art, compared to the Flores-Calero et al. [7] proposal.

5.1   Time Processing and Inference Time

Table 3 shows the calculation time of the final system, meaning the inference stage. These values are the average of the rendering of 37500 images.

Table 3. Calculation times for each of the modules in the total system.

Module	Time (ms)
Capture	2.00
Detection	101.00
Visualisation	0.70
Total	103.7

Also, it is clear that it processes 9, 64 frames per second, proving that we obtained a device which works in almost real-time.

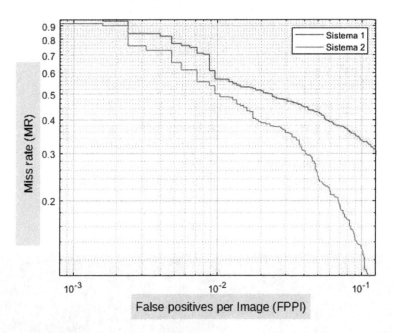

Fig. 6. MR versus FPPI curve. System 1 is [7]'s proposal and System 2 refers to the current work.

5.2 Perception and Processing System

The prototype (software + hardware) is shown in Fig. 7, the same which is comprised by a webcam camera and a processing card (1), as well as a display screen (2), and a 12 DC volts inverter with 120 AC volts, which is directly connected to the vehicle's battery.

The device stated in (1) has the following dimensions: $20 \times 6, 5 \times 4$ centimeters for length, width, and depth, respectively. The processing card is a Jetson Nano [18] gpu which has the characteristics written in Table 4. Also, this card is suitable for developing inference in deep learning models.

With this design we were able to obtain a portable device that does not interfere with daily driving activities. When it was tested on the road, the system was placed on the windshield of the ViiA experimental platform, as shown in Fig. 7, behind the rearview mirror.

Lastly, Fig. 8 depicts various examples of results generated by this proposal, in several real lighting and driving conditions on the road.

Table 4. Jetson Nano [18] GPU characteristics.

Parameters	Characteristics
Architecture	Maxwell
SM	1
CUDA cores per SM	128
CPU	4 core ARM
Memory	4 GB 64-bit LPDDR4
Bandwidth	25.6
Storage	16 GB eMMC 5.1 Flash
Power	5 W/10 W

Fig. 7. Detection system for traffic signs in Ecuador. This prototype was installed on the windshield, right behind the rearview mirror, of the experimental ViiA vehicle from I&H Technologies.

Fig. 8. Detection and recognition of traffic signs in Ecuador results. Preventive signs (a, b, c) and regulatory signs (d, e, f) under several lighting environments, with complex backgrounds in several locations.

6   Conclusions and Future Work

This research presented a prototype based on computer vision and deep learning for detection and recognition of traffic signs in Ecuador. At the moment, this device is specialized in regulatory and preventive signs, and is easy to install on the windshield of any vehicle.

Two strategies were used in this work to improve performance: i) constructing a database with Ecuador's traffic signs; ii) increasing the database using data augmentation techniques; iii) integrating the Faster R-CNN architecture with ZFNet for traffic sign detection.

Regarding the database, it contains regulatory and preventive signs under different lighting conditions, in a 6 A.M. to 7 P.M. range, including the signs' exact position and type. To measure the proposal's performance, we used the mAP index, which globally reaches a 95, 34%, a value which is one of the most competitive ones in the state of the art.

In the future, the database's size will be increased for each of the types of signs. In doing so, we expect to cover two relevant aspects: the first, will be to present a world reference database in the field of traffic sign detection, and secondly, fine tune the weights of the neuronal network which comprises the artificial intelligence. Finally, training new models for comparision.

Acknowledgment. This work was supported by I&H Tech, through the direct funding, the electronic equipment, the database and the vehicle for the development of the experiments. Also, we thank the reviewers and editor for their helpful comments.

Author contributions. All the authors have contributed to the development of the work, each one from their expertise.

Conflict of Interest. The authors declare that there is no conflict of interest.

References

1. Agencia Nacional de Tránsito del Ecuador. Siniestros Junio 2017 (2018)
2. Agencia Nacional de Tránsito del Ecuador. Estadísticas de siniestros de tránsito (2021)
3. Arcos-García, A., Alvarez-García, J., Soria-Morillo, L.: Evaluation of deep neural networks for traffic sign detection systems. Neurocomputing **316**, 332–344 (2018)
4. Dollar, P., Wojek, C., Schiele, B., Perona, P.: Pedestrian detection: a benchmark. IEEE Trans. Pattern Anal. Mach. Intell. **34**, 743–761 (2012)
5. Everingham, M., Van-Gool, L., Williams, C.K.I., Winn, J., Zisserman, A.: The PASCAL visual object classes (VOC) challenge. Int. J. Comput. Vis. **2**, 303–338 (2010). https://doi.org/10.1007/s11263-009-0275-4
6. Fawzi, A., Samulowitz, H., Turaga, D., Frossard, P.: Adaptive data augmentation for image classification. In 2016 IEEE International Conference on Image Processing (ICIP) (2016)
7. Flores-Calero, M., et al.: Ecuadorian traffic sign detection through color information and a convolutional neural network. IEEE ANDESCON, pp. 1–6 (2020)
8. Hagl, M., Kouabenan, D.R.: Safe on the road - Does advanced driver assistance systems use affect road risk perception? Transp. Res. Part F: Traffic Psychol. Behav. **73**, 488–498 (2020)
9. He, H., Hui, L., Gu, W.: Transferring digit classifier's features to a traffic sign detector. In: International Conference on Progress in Informatics and Computing (PIC) (2017)
10. Hu, Y., Zhang, C., Zhou, D., Wang, X., Bai, X., Liu, W.: Traffic sign detection and recognition using fully convolutional network guided proposals. Neurocomputing **214**, 758–766 (2016)
11. Huang, L.L: Chinese Traffic Sign Database TSDD
12. Jia, Y., et al.: Caffe: convolutional architecture for fast feature embedding. Int. J. Comput. Vis. 675–678 (2014)
13. Kingma, D.P., Ba, J.: Adam: a method for stochastic optimization. CoRR, abs/1412.6980 (2015)
14. Lau, M.M., Lim, K.H., Gopalai, A.A.: Malaysia traffic sign recognition with convolutional neural network. Int. J. Comput. Vis., 1006–1010 (2015)

15. Mogelmose, A., Liu, D., Trivedi, M.M.: Detection of U.S. Traffic Signs. IEEE Trans. Intell. Transp. Syst. **16**(6), 3116–3125 (2015)
16. Mohd-Isa, W.-N., Abdullah, M.-S., Sarzil, M., Abdullah, J., Ali, A., Hashim, N.: Detection of Malaysian traffic signs via modified YOLOv3 algorithm. Int. J. Comput. Vis. (2020)
17. Nguyen, B.T., Shim, J., Kim, J.K.: Fast traffic sign detection under challenging conditions. Int. J. Comput. Vis. **1**, 749–752 (2014)
18. NVIDIA. Jetson Nano (2021)
19. World Health Rankings. Road traffic accidents (2017)
20. Shaoqing, R., Kaiming, H., Ross, G., Sun, J.: Towards real-time object detection with region proposal networks, Faster R-CNN (2015)
21. Salti, S., Petrelli, A., Tombari, F., Fioraio, N., DiStefano, L.: Traffic sign detection via interest region extraction. Pattern Recogn. **48**, 1039–1049 (2015)
22. Shorten, C., Khoshgoftaar, T.M.: A survey on image data augmentation for deep learning. J. Big Data **6**(60), 303–338 (2019)
23. Sirbu, M.-A., Baiasu, A., Bogdan, R., Bogdan, R., Vida, M.: Smart traffic sign detection on autonomous car (2018)
24. Song, S., Que, Z., Hou, J., Sen, D., Song, Y.: An efficient convolutional neural network for small traffic sign detection. J. Syst. Archit. **97**, 269–277 (2019)
25. Stallkamp, J., Schlipsing, M., Salmen, J., Igel, C.: The german traffic sign recognition benchmark: a multi-class classification competition. In: IEEE International Joint Conference on Neural Networks, pp. 1453–1460 (2011)
26. Tabernik, D., Skocaj, D.: Deep learning for large-scale traffic-sign detection and recognition. IEEE Trans. Intell. Transp. Syst. **21**(4), 1427–1440 (2020)
27. World Health Organization WHO. Control de la velocidad (2017)
28. World Health Organization WHO. Accidentes de tránsito (2018)
29. XM and MTR. Berkeley AI Research (BAIR)/The Berkeley Vision, Learning Center (BVLC), and community contributors. Caffe library (2016)
30. Yang, T., Long, X., Sangaiah, A.K., Zheng, Z., Tong, C.: Deep detection network for real-life traffic sign in vehicular networks. Computer Networks (2018)
31. Yang, W., Zhang, W.: Real-time traffic signs detection based on YOLO network model. International Conference on Cyber-Enabled Distributed Computing and Knowledge Discovery (CyberC) (2020)
32. You, S., Bi, Q., Ji, Y., Liu, S., Feng, Y., Fei, W.: Traffic sign detection method based on improved SSD. Artif. Intell. Decision Support Syst. **11**(10), 475 (2020)
33. Zeiler, M.D., Fergus, R.: Visualizing and understanding convolutional networks CoRR, abs/1311.2901 (2013)
34. Zuo, Z., Yu, K., Zhou, Q., Wang, X., Li, T.: Traffic signs detection based on faster R-CNN. In: IEEE 37th International Conference on Distributed Computing Systems Workshops (2017)

VGG11 Parkinson's Disease Detection Based on Voice Attributes

Lucas Salvador Bernardo[(✉)] and Robertas Damaševičius

Kaunas University of Technology, K. Donelaičio St. 73, 44249 Kaunas, Lithuania
`lucas.salvador@ktu.edu`, `robertas.damasevicius@ktu.lt`

Abstract. Parkinson disease is the second most world widespread neural impairment. It affects approximately 2 to 3% of world's population with age over 65 years. Part of Parkinson's disease progress happens due the loss of cells in a brain region called *Substantia Nigra* (SN). Nerve cells in this region are responsible for improving the control of movements and coordination. The loss of such cells results in the emerge of the motor symptoms characteristic of the disease. However, motor symptoms appear when brain cells are already damaged, while oppositely voice impairments appear before the brain cells are being affected. This study aims to recognize Parkinson disease using 22 attributes, extracted from 195 voice records, being 147 from Parkinson disease patients and 48 from healthy individuals. The data is passed through a series of pre-processing steps, being them: balancing, where we applied a Synthetic Minority Oversampling Technique (SMOTE) to make the number of data per class equal, training and test segmentation, where the data was divided in 30% for testing and 70% for training, scaling, the data into intervals of 0 to 1, amplification, step where the values are converted into intervals from 0 to 100 and image generation, converting the numerical dataset into an image dataset. Later, the resulted image dataset was used to train a Visual Geometry Group 11 (VGG11) Convolutional Neural Network (CNN). The proposed solution achieved 93.1% accuracy, 92.31% f1-score, 96% recall, 88.89% precision on testing dataset, displaying a good performance when compared with other explored solutions.

Keywords: VGG11 · Parkinson · Voice

1 First Section

Parkinson's disease (PD) is the most prevalent form of neural disease that causes motor impairments such as rigidity, slowness, and tremor [1]. It is believed that the disease affects 2–3% of global population older than 65 years [2]. The disease is associated to the lack of dopaminergic neurons in a brain region called *Substantia Nigra* (SN) [3], although what triggers the process is yet not completely known [4]. Nerve cells in the SN region are responsible for improving the control over movements and coordination. The loss of neuron cells in SN regions results

T. Guarda et al. (Eds.): ARTIIS 2022, CCIS 1675, pp. 58–70, 2022.
https://doi.org/10.1007/978-3-031-20319-0_5

in the emergence of the motor symptoms characteristic of the disease which manifest itself, e.g., in cramped handwriting [5] or freezing gait [6]. However motor symptoms appear when brain cells are already damaged, while oppositely voice impairments appear before the brain cells are affected [7]. Despite the technological and PD comprehension advances, there is no specific test able to obtain the diagnosis of the disease. The process of detection of PD is made by a neurologist based on the patient's medical history, a set neurological and physical laboratory tests and a review of the patient's characteristic symptoms [8].

With the advance on the field of artificial intelligence (AI), the usage of technology for the automated detection of many of the human's diseases was made possible, which also includes a better understanding of the characteristics of PD [9,10]. Nowadays, many solutions are developed each year aiming to identify Parkinson's disease based on computer assisted approaches. Most of those, are based in powerful computational tools such as Convolutional Neural Networks (CNN), Machine Learning (ML), Deep Learning (DL).

Human's voice offers a wide amount of motor characteristics of human activity [11]. In view of that, recent studies have highlighted that approximately 90% of PD patients have had vocal disturbances [12], these disturbances are usually related to dysfunctions of the orofacial muscles involved in speech [13].

In view of the voice impairments, characteristic of 90% cases of PD [12], this study aims to apply a series of computational methods that includes Synthetic Minority Oversampling (SMOTE), and Visual Geometry Group 11 (VGG11) CNN to recognize PD using images generated from human speech features. To achieve such task, this study used a voice dataset [14], randomly selected, that consists of 195 data samples, including 147 data samples collected from PD patients, and 47 data samples collected from healthy individuals. Due the unbalanced characteristic of the applied data-set, the values, made of 22 attributes extracted from voice records, passed through a normalizing process by applying a maximum minimum algorithm, which converted the values to range of 0 to 1. The resulted data-set from normalizing process, was then scaled, by applying a SMOTE algorithm, this resulted in a total of 294 data, by expanding the minimum class, healthy, from 48 to 147. The values then were amplified by multiplying the scaled data by a constant C, chosen randomly. Later, the values were used for generating images following a logical process of construction, better explained further in this work, to then be submitted to the chosen CNN algorithm.

The innovations and contributions of this paper are:

- Development of a new image dataset by converting voice data into images.
- Application of new techniques (VGG11 deep learning model) to detect PD based on a public dataset;

The structure of this work was made as follows: In Sect. 2, works related to the addressed solution are analyzed. In Sect. 3, a theoretical foundation is displayed for easier understanding of the proposed method. Section 4 approaches the methodology used in this work. In Sect. 5, the results are presented, and in Sect. 6 the conclusions are and future works are shown.

2 Related Works

Due to its good performance on classifying images, CNNs have been vastly applied in image recognition fields [15]. Its applications are present in the most diversified fields, such as cyber-security, medicine, autonomous devices, etc. In view of the performance presented by such method when applied to medical problems, many works have been developed to obtain the diagnosis of many of the human's conditions. In this section, some works that approach the usage of CNN for detecting human's conditions based on voice attributes are presented. For example, in [16] a method for detecting Huntington's disease is proposed based on digitized voice signals from patients and healthy individuals, collected from records of reading poems in Lithuanian language. The data were collected based on 186 speech exams from 24 volunteers. The proposed solution achieved over 99% accuracy.

Bidirectional Long Short-Term Memory (BiLSTM) neural network and Wavelet Scattering Transform with Support Vector Machine (WST-SVM) classifier were used by [17] to detect speech impairments with patients on early stages of central nervous system disorders (CNSD). The proposed solution used 339 voice samples collected from 15 subjects, from which 7 presented early staged CNSD (1 Parkinson, 1 post stroke, 1 cerebral palsy, 3 Huntington, 1 early dementia) and 8 healthy individuals. The voice attributes were collected from voice records of Neural Impairment Test Suite (NITS) mobile app. The study obtained an accuracy of 94.50% with BiLSTM and 96.3% with WST-SVM.

The study [18] presented a model able to evaluate cognitive and motor deficits for individuals with symptoms of central nervous system (CNS) disorders, mild cognitive impairment (MCI), Parkinson's disease (PD), Huntington's disease (HD), and dementia. The data was collected using an mobile device running Android operational system, able to track cognitive, hand tremor, energy expenditure, and speech features of the individuals. The solution counted with 238 features collected from 16 tasks performed by the individuals and obtained in its best result and accuracy of 96.12%.

In [19] a model of decision support system for speech processing is proposed based on analysis of the speech signals. The data was then processed by composed mathematical transform with bio-inspired algorithm and spiking neural network to detect the presence of voice impairments. The method presented a final accuracy of 87.2%.

[20] developed a voice pathology detection tool based on Deep Learning, to achieve it, a pre-trained CNN was applied to a dataset of voice pathology in order to maximize the system accuracy. The proposed methods were tested using a Saarbrücken voice database (SVD). As a result, the system obtained 95.41% accuracy having also obtained 94.22%, F1-Score, and 96.13% for and Recall.

The work of [21] proposed a multiclass-pathologic voice classification using a multileveled textural feature extraction with iterative feature selector. The proposed system aimed to detect three diseases, being them: Frontal Resection, Cordectomy and Spastic Dysphonia. As a result, the proposed method obtained 80.93% in the worst case.

[22] proposed am approach to detect PD, based on vowels with sustained phonation applied to a ResNet model. A spectrum was calculated from the audio records which were used as images for the Convolutional Neural Network. The proposed solution was composed by 100 individuals data, being 50 of them Parkinson patients and 50 healthy subjects. Each subject was recorded 3 times. The proposed solution obtained above 90% accuracy.

[23] presented a solution for detection PD using of CNN. The proposed solution was applied in Magnetic Resonance Imaging (MRI) of Parkinson's disease patients and healthy individuals. The proposed method obtained 3–9% improvement when compared to other works developed with similar approach.

The work presented in [24] used voice records to diagnosis PD by applying DCNN. From the voices attributes spectral features are extracted from the sustained phoneme 'a'. The work obtained accuracy of 75.7%.

Goyal et al. [25] adopted a combination of Resonance based Sparse Signal Decomposition (RSSD) with Time-Frequency (T-F) algorithm and a Convolution Neural Network (CNN). The proposed hybrid approach discriminated PD and healthy subjects with an accuracy of 99.37%.

[26] adopted Variational Autoencoders (VAE) as a feature extractor and filter-based Relief and Fisher Score feature selection models. The classification was performed using multi-kernel Support Vector Machines (SVM) classifier trained with deep feature representations. The solution obtained an accuracy of 91.60%.

[27] developed a CNN in two stages, which included data pre-processing and fine-tuning based transfer learning steps. The solution reached an accuracy of 89.75% on the mPower Voice database.

[28] adopted time-frequency matrix (TFM) representation of voice characteristics and TFM decomposition using non-negative matrix factorization (NMF) for feature extraction. The approach achieved an average classification accuracy of 92% in PD patient and healthy speaker recognition on sustained vowel phonations and isolated words from the PC-GITA corpus.

[29] proposed a deep dual-side learning ensemble model that employed a deep network (an embedded stack group sparse auto encoder) to perform deep feature learning. Next, deep features were fused with speech features by using L1 regularization feature selection, thus constructing hybrid feature data. The data was sampled using an iterative mean clustering algorithm and hierarchical sample spaces were constructed based on a deep sample learning algorithm. Finally, the classification models were fused into a classification ensemble model using a weighted fusion mechanism. The mean accuracy of the proposed algorithm reaches 98.4% and 99.6% accuracy on two benchmark datasets.

3   Theoretical Foundation

In this section, a junction of necessary knowledge to the understanding of this work is built, presenting the theories behind the ideas and tools used for the development of the proposed solution.

3.1 Data Oversampling

Problems related to imbalanced classification, are often found in countless applications [30]. To overcome problems in which imbalanced classes may cause a trouble, techniques such as the Synthetic Minority over-sampling Technique (SMOTE), Fig. 1.

The process of generating data for balance the imbalanced class, consist on generating data for the minority class using a K-nearest neighbors (K-NN) approach. Differently from previous oversampling solution K-NN-base, where for any minority class, the synthetic values are randomly created directing to its k-nearest neighbors, SMOTE assigns weights to each neighbor direction. Smaller weights are assigned for positions that can produce over generalization [31].

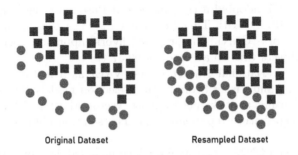

Original Dataset   Resampled Dataset

Fig. 1. Demonstration of an unbalanced data being balanced using SMOTE.

3.2 Feature Scaling

Features scaling is a relatively new technique, that allows fast scaling of input data instances to x time its size, preserving the characteristics of the data [32]. In other words, the process of scaling consists in putting the features values in the same range, doing so, no variable is dominant over other. The scaling approach is advantageous, once it can be re-used on different types of datasets, not being necessary to manually insert the data attributes.

There are many scaling techniques, varying from the mathematical principal in which they are based in, as example it is possible to highlight:

– Standardization Also called Z-score normalization. In this approach, the z-score of each value is calculated and used to replace the original value. The mathematical definition of such method, can be seeing at Eq. 1. Where σ is the variance and $\overline{x}$ represents the mean.

$$x' = \frac{x - \overline{x}}{\sigma} \tag{1}$$

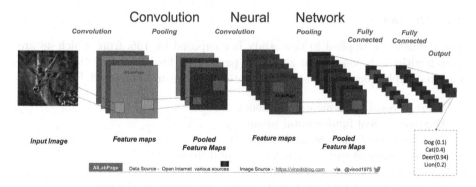

Fig. 2. Convolutional neural network structure Source: Adapted from [35]

- Min-Max Scaling Also referred as Normalization, this method scales the input feature in ranges of 0 to 1, mathematically this method can be represente by Eq. 2.

$$x' = \frac{x - min(x)}{max(x) - min(x)} \qquad (2)$$

- Binarizing Consists in a process of threshold the matrix like input array.

3.3   Convolutional Neural Network

Deep Neural Network, Fig. 2, is refereed to as Artificial Neural Networks (ANN) with multiple layers. Named due the mathematical linear operations between matrices, convolution. CNN layers include: Convolutional layer, non-linearity layer, pooling layer and fully-connected layer [33]. The deep architecture of CNN allows the extraction of a vast set of discriminating features at vast range of abstraction [34].

4   Methodology

This section will approach the computational, experimental and mathematical concepts used for the development of this work. The structural workflow of the proposed solution can be seeing in Fig. 3.

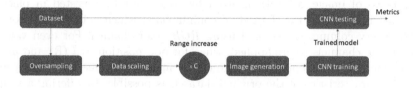

Fig. 3. Solution workflow

4.1   Dataset

The dataset [14] applied in this study is composed by 195, from which 48 are from healthy individuals that agreed to participate for its construction and 147 Parkinson volunteers. The data have a total of 22 features extracted, being them:

- Average vocal fundamental frequency
- Maximum vocal fundamental frequency
- Minimum vocal fundamental frequency
- Five measures of variation in fundamental frequency
- Six measures of variation in amplitude
- Two measures of ratio of noise to tonal components in the voice
- Two nonlinear dynamical complexity measures
- Signal fractal scaling exponent
- Three nonlinear measures of fundamental frequency variation

To ensure the data has an homogeneous distribution, it was submitted to an oversampling process, approached in the following section.

4.2   Oversampling

To balanced the dataset, a SMOTE algorithm was applied, once it offers an easy and fast implementation. The algorithm was supplied with 42 seeds to the random number generator. The result balanced dataset, was later scaled aiming to avoid possible huge data gaps. This process is better explained in the following section.

4.3   Data Scaling

The output from the SMOTE algorithm ranged the dataset attributes in the interval of $[-7.96, 592.03]$, to reduce this gap among the values, a *Minmax* algorithm was applied to the data, resulting in new values belonging to $[0, 1]$. To easier the further data visualisation, the dataset values were later dilated, by multiplying them by a randomly chosen constant $C = 100$.

4.4   Image Generation

The process of image generation, given by Algorithm 1, consisted in placing the 22 attributes from the dataset in column bars, which values went from 0 to 100. Every column was colored using RGB color channel. For even values, red and blue channels where applied, when for odd position, *red* (R) and *green* (G) channels, while keeping blue channel at maximum value 255, preserving as much characteristics of the original dataset as possible, by offering a visual demonstration of it.

Algorithm 1. Image generation

Input: Dataset
Output: Images
  for $i \leftarrow 0$ to $len(Dataset.Rows)$ **do**
    for $j \leftarrow 0$ to $len(Dataset[i].Colunms)$ **do**
      $BarSize \leftarrow Dataset[i].Coulunms[j]$
      $Red \leftarrow 0$
      $Green \leftarrow 0$
      $Blue \leftarrow 255$
      if j is even **then**
        $Red \leftarrow 255 * Dataset[i].Coulunms[j]$
      else if j is odd **then**
        $Green \leftarrow 255 * Dataset[i].Coulunms[j]$
      end if
      $PlaceOnImage(Red, Green, Blue, BarSize)$
    end for
  end for

The output images from Algorithm 1, presented in Fig. 4, were used as a new dataset to be for training and testing the selected CNN approach.

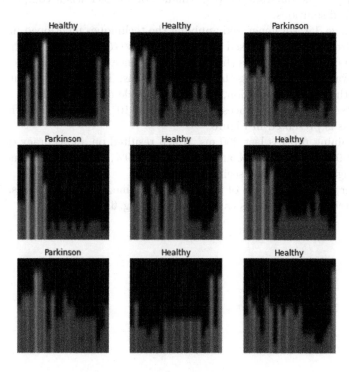

Fig. 4. Python code for image generation

4.5   CNN

After generating the images, the result image dataset was then divided into training and testing, resulting in 70% of data for training and 30% of data for testing. To compare the efficiency of the proposed solution, it was trained and tested using 3 different types of CNN approaches, *ResNet, VGG11* and *MobileNet*.

5   Results

The Python 3 script, developed for this solutions, was executed in a Colab GPU, with 13 GB RAM on a Linux - Ubuntu 18.04.3 LTS operational system. The generated image dataset was submitted to three CNN models, *VGG11, MobileNet* and *ResNet.* The trainning process for all three solutions was performed using 16 epochs, being this the value in which no improvement in the model's training was noticed. To maximize the performance of the models, the learning cycle of there were extracted, what limited the leraning process to the interval of 10^{-1} to 10^{0}.

The comparative results of the three CNN models are presented in Table 1, which displays the outstanding performance of VGG11 when compared to the other applied solutions.

The image dataset generated applying the techniques mentioned in previews chapters, from which, were used for training the *VGG11* model. For the training process, the number of epochs chosen was made once no improvement on model's accuracy was observed, being the value 16 epochs. To obtain maximum performance of the proposed solution, the learning cycle of the model was extracted, what limited the learning process to the interval 10^{-1} to 10^{0}, the learning curve by stop loss is presented in Figure.

The training process last 200 ms, which resulted on an accuracy of 93.10%, f1 score of 92.31%, recall 96% and precision 88.89%, the values obtained during the training process, can be seeing in Fig. 5.

To offer a graphical view of the metrics obtained from the results, the confusion matrix was plotted, as can be seeing in Fig. 6.

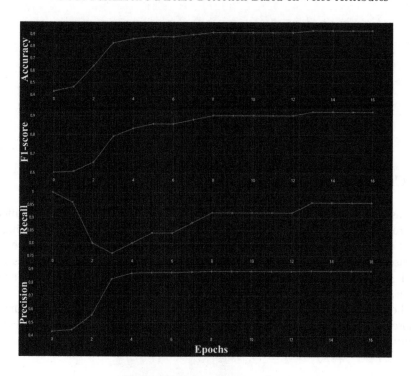

Fig. 5. Training process values

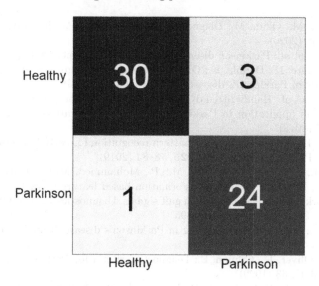

Fig. 6. Confusion matrix for the proposed solution

Table 1. Training results for the 3 testes approaches

Results	VGG11	MobileNet	ResNet
F1-Score	0.9231	0.8530	0.8979
Recall	0.9600	1.0000	0.8800
Precission	0.8889	0.7436	0.9166
Accuracy	0.9310	0.7436	0.9137

6   Conclusion

Parkinson's disease (PD) is the second most prevalent neural impairment, affecting around 50–150 from every 100,000 individuals. With the rapidly aging of global population, it is expected that the numbers of cases of the disease will increase drastically in the future. Once there are no known cure for the disease, it calls for a early diagnosis aiming to improve the life quality of those who suffer with it.

The solution proposed here showed itself as a viable solution to be further explored to obtain a faster and non-invasive to detect PD, allowing so a better quality of life to those who's lives are affected with it.

References

1. Armstrong, M., Okun, M.: Diagnosis and treatment of Parkinson disease. JAMA **323**(6), 548 (2020)
2. Poewe, W., et al.: Parkinson disease. Nat. Rev. Dis. Primers **3**(1) (2017)
3. Trist, B., Hare, D., Double, K.: Oxidative stress in the aging substantia nigra and the etiology of Parkinson's disease. Aging Cell **18**(6) (2019)
4. Pereira, C., et al.: Handwritten dynamics assessment through convolutional neural networks: an application to Parkinson's disease identification. Artif. Intell. Med. **87**, 67–77 (2018)
5. Bernardo, L., et al.: Handwritten pattern recognition for early Parkinson's disease diagnosis. Pattern Recogn. Lett. **125**, 78–84 (2019)
6. Priya, S.J., Rani, A.J., Subathra, M.S.P., Mohammed, M.A., Damaševičius, R., Ubendran, N.: Local pattern transformation based feature extraction for recognition of Parkinson's disease based on gait signals. Diagnostics **11**(8) (2021). https://doi.org/10.3390/diagnostics11081395
7. Tjaden, K.: Speech and swallowing in Parkinson's disease. Top. Geriatr. Rehabil. **24**(2), 115–126 (2008)
8. Gelb, D., Oliver, E., Gilman, S.: Diagnostic criteria for Parkinson disease. Arch. Neurol. **56**(1), 33 (1999)
9. Espay, A., et al.: Technology in Parkinson's disease: challenges and opportunities. Mov. Disord. **31**(9), 1272–1282 (2016)
10. Dash, S., Abraham, A., Luhach, A.K., Mizera-Pietraszko, J., Rodrigues, J.J.P.C.: Hybrid chaotic firefly decision making model for Parkinson's disease diagnosis. Int. J. Distrib. Sens. Netw. **16**(1) (2020). https://doi.org/10.1177/1550147719895210

11. Jain, A., et al.: Voice analysis to differentiate the dopaminergic response in people with Parkinson's disease. Frontiers Hum. Neurosci. **15** (2021)
12. Zhang, T., Zhang, Y., Sun, H., Shan, H.: Parkinson disease detection using energy direction features based on EMD from voice signal. Biocybernetics Biomed. Eng. **41**(1), 127–141 (2021)
13. Lechien, J., Blecic, S., Ghosez, Y., Huet, K., Harmegnies, B., Saussez, S.: Voice quality and orofacial strength as outcome of levodopa effectiveness in patients with early idiopathic parkinson disease: a preliminary report. J. Voice **33**(5), 716–720 (2019)
14. Little, M., McSharry, P., Roberts, S., Costello, D., Moroz, I.: Exploiting nonlinear recurrence and fractal scaling properties for voice disorder detection. Biomed. Eng. Online **6**(1), 23 (2007)
15. Wang, Y., Li, Y., Song, Y., Rong, X.: The influence of the activation function in a convolution neural network model of facial expression recognition. Appl. Sci. **10**(5), 1897 (2020)
16. Guimaraes, M.T., et al.: An optimized approach to Huntington's disease detecting via audio signals processing with dimensionality reduction. In: Proceedings of the International Joint Conference on Neural Networks (2020). https://doi.org/10.1109/IJCNN48605.2020.9206773
17. Lauraitis, A., Maskeliunas, R., Damaševičius, R., Krilavičius, T.: Detection of speech impairments using cepstrum, auditory spectrogram and wavelet time scattering domain features. IEEE Access **8**, 96162–96172 (2020). https://doi.org/10.1109/ACCESS.2020.2995737
18. Lauraitis, A., Maskeliūnas, R., Damaševičius, R., Krilavičius, T.: A mobile application for smart computer-aided self-administered testing of cognition, speech, and motor impairment. Sensors **20**(11) (2020). https://doi.org/10.3390/s20113236
19. Połap, D., Woźniak, M., Damaševičius, R., Maskeliūnas, R.: Bio-inspired voice evaluation mechanism. Appl. Soft Comput. J. **80**, 342–357 (2019). https://doi.org/10.1016/j.asoc.2019.04.006
20. Mohammed, M., et al.: Voice pathology detection and classification using convolutional neural network model. Appl. Sci. **10**(11), 3723 (2020)
21. Tuncer, T., Dogan, S., Ozyurt, F., Belhaouari, S., Bensmail, H.: Novel multi center and threshold ternary pattern based method for disease detection method using voice. IEEE Access **8**, 84532–84540 (2020)
22. Wodzinski, M., Skalski, A., Hemmerling, D., Orozco-Arroyave, J., Noth, E.: Deep learning approach to Parkinson's disease detection using voice recordings and convolutional neural network dedicated to image classification. In: 2019 41st Annual International Conference of the IEEE Engineering in Medicine and Biology Society (EMBC) (2019)
23. Shah, P., Zeb, A., Shafi, U., Zaidi, S., Shah, M.: Detection of Parkinson disease in brain MRI using convolutional neural network. In: 2018 24th International Conference on Automation and Computing (ICAC) (2018)
24. Khojasteh, P., Viswanathan, R., Aliahmad, B., Ragnav, S., Zham, P., Kumar, D.: Parkinson's disease diagnosis based on multivariate deep features of speech signal. In: 2018 IEEE Life Sciences Conference (LSC) (2018)
25. Goyal, J., Khandnor, P., Aseri, T.C.: A hybrid approach for Parkinson's disease diagnosis with resonance and time-frequency based features from speech signals. Exp. Syst. Appl. **182** (2021). https://doi.org/10.1016/j.eswa.2021.115283

26. Gunduz, H.: An efficient dimensionality reduction method using filter-based feature selection and variational autoencoders on Parkinson's disease classification. Biomed. Sig. Process. Control **66** (2021). https://doi.org/10.1016/j.bspc.2021.102452
27. Karaman, O., Çakın, H., Alhudhaif, A., Polat, K.: Robust automated Parkinson disease detection based on voice signals with transfer learning. Exp. Syst. Appl. **178** (2021). https://doi.org/10.1016/j.eswa.2021.115013
28. Karan, B., Sahu, S.S., Orozco-Arroyave, J.R., Mahto, K.: Non-negative matrix factorization-based time-frequency feature extraction of voice signal for Parkinson's disease prediction. Comput. Speech Lang. **69** (2021). https://doi.org/10.1016/j.csl.2021.101216
29. Ma, J., et al.: Deep dual-side learning ensemble model for Parkinson speech recognition. Biomed. Sig. Process. Control **69** (2021). https://doi.org/10.1016/j.bspc.2021.102849
30. Elreedy, D., Atiya, A.: A comprehensive analysis of synthetic minority oversampling technique (SMOTE) for handling class imbalance. Inf. Sci. **505**, 32–64 (2019)
31. Zhu, T., Lin, Y., Liu, Y.: Synthetic minority oversampling technique for multiclass imbalance problems. Pattern Recogn. **72**, 327–340 (2017)
32. Lanti, D., Xiao, G., Calvanese, D.: VIG: data scaling for OBDA benchmarks. Semant. Web **10**(2), 413–433 (2019)
33. Albawi, S., Mohammed, T., Al-Zawi, S.: Understanding of a convolutional neural network. 2017 International Conference on Engineering and Technology (ICET) (2017)
34. Tajbakhsh, N., et al.: Convolutional neural networks for medical image analysis: full training or fine tuning? IEEE Trans. Med. Imaging **35**(5), 1299–1312 (2016)
35. Sharma, V.: Deep Learning – Introduction to Convolutional Neural Networks — Vinod Sharma's Blog. Accessed 27 July 2021

RELAPP: A New Portable Electronic Rheometer for the Analysis of Viscoelastic Materials Based on Artificial Intelligence

Toni Monleón-Getino[1,2,3]([✉]), Joaquin Justel-Pizarro[1,2], and Angeles Sahuquillo[4] [iD]

[1] Section of Statistics, Department of Genetics, Microbiology and Statistics, University of Barcelona, 08028 Barcelona, Spain
amonleong@ub.edu
[2] BIOS3 Research Group in Statistics, Bioinformatics and Data Science, Barcelona, Spain
[3] GRBIO, Research Group in Biostatistics and Bioinformatics, Barcelona, Spain
[4] Laboratory for the Preparation of Quality Control Materials (Mat Control), Chemical Engineering and Analytical Chemistry Department, University of Barcelona, 08028 Barcelona, Spain
angels.sahuquillo@ub.edu

Abstract. RELAPP is an electromechanical device able to measure the elasticity, extensibility, tenacity and strength of flour doughs and other viscoelastic materials and can be easily adapted by artificial intelligence methods for the analysis of other parameters. Its working principle is based on applying a specific deformation on the sample and observing the dynamic response, which allows the physical properties of the material to be computed and measured. To control and visualize the measurement process, a software application was designed that performs the automatic readout of the electronic system. The resulting device, called "RELAPP", is configurable, portable, low cost and easy-to-use. Seven machine learning regression algorithms were applied to predict the target parameters from 1600 tests carried out in the laboratory. Correlation and validation studies of different kinds of flour samples using the new device and a standard Chopin Alveograph® allowed an accurate determination of the viscoelastic parameters of the analyzed dough with low prediction error (MAE, RMSE). Notably, the software uses an optimized XBoost algorithm to predict the range of values for the tenacity (T), extensibility (EX) and strength (S) of the sample and applies a geometrical method to compute its elasticity using the 3d axis information during the measurement.

Keywords: Machine learning · Material analysis · Wheat · Dough flour · Rheology · Validation

1 Introduction

1.1 Testing Viscoelastic Materials

Fluids are substances that deform when subjected to shear or pressure forces, and tend to take the shape of the container. The most interesting and complex are viscoelastic

T. Guarda et al. (Eds.): ARTIIS 2022, CCIS 1675, pp. 71–83, 2022.
https://doi.org/10.1007/978-3-031-20319-0_6

72   T. Monleón-Getino et al.

fluids, due to their thickness and elastic behavior, which allows the original state to be recovered when the shear force ceases. When bread or pasta doughs are kneaded or stretched, they show resistance (viscosity) and tend to retract and shrink (elasticity). In fluid mechanics, viscoelasticity is described by Maxwell elements, represented by a series of springs (elastic components) and pistons (resistant viscous elements). When subjected to weak pressure, a viscoelastic material is slightly deformed and can return to its original shape, whereas applying more force overcomes the resistance and produces elongation.

To evaluate the quality of viscoelastic materials (such as doughs made from flour, rubber, latex, foams, soft plastics, agar-agar, and others), different characteristics are considered, among which the most important are the rheological properties (elasticity, viscosity, extensibility and plasticity). As mentioned, elasticity is defined by how a material springs back to its original shape after deformation, whereas viscosity is the resistance to flow, and extensibility is the ability to stretch without breaking. Finally, the property of plasticity is defined as the propensity of a solid material to undergo permanent deformation under load. The present research is focused on the measurement of viscoelasticity of flour doughs [1, 2], which determines their processing conditions and final application (see Fig. 1).

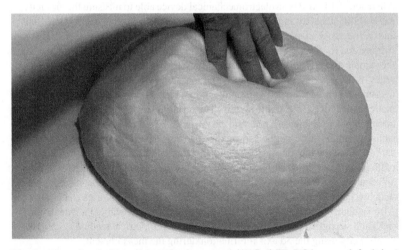

Fig. 1. Flour dough (From https://i.ytimg.com/vi/t4Cy6-7FoBQ/maxresdefault.jpg)

1.2 Rheology of Viscoelastic Materials

As wheat is highly variable in its physicochemical characteristics, different wheat flours are mixed to achieve the desired qualities. According to its category of "strength", each type of flour is allocated to the manufacture of different products, such as bread, pastries, and pasta. The classification is done by measuring the rheological properties (elasticity, extensibility, tenacity and stretch) of the flour dough.

Fig. 2. Top left: Chopin Alveograph® (with Alveolab®). Top right: Brabender Farinograph®. Bottom left: Buhler Amylograph-E®. Bottom right: National Manufacturing Mixograph® (images taken from the internet).

To evaluate the rheological properties of dough, experimental methods are widely used in industrial settings, as they provide precise and accurate results. Equipment currently used in analytical laboratories in large milling facilities includes the Brabender Farinograph®, Chopin Alveograph®, Extensograph®, Mixograph®, and Amylograph® [1, 2]. However, these instruments are costly and delicate, requiring specialized personnel for their operation (see Fig. 2). Other drawbacks include the need for intercalibration methods to detect bias, the bulky and non-portable nature of the equipment, and a lengthy measurement process. Moreover, these systems cannot evaluate all types of flours (e.g., whole meal flours, mixed flours, etc.) or perform continuous analysis. The need to supply an increasingly exacting market with new food products requires the application of more modern and efficient quality control techniques [1, 2], such as those based on artificial intelligence (AI). Specifically, machine learning (ML) has been used for this development. ML is a branch of AI that allows machines to learn without being expressly programmed to do so. An essential skill to make systems capable of identifying patterns in data to make predictions.

1.3 Objectives and Challenges

Currently there is no system available that allows in-field evaluation (outside the laboratory) of viscoelastic properties of flour doughs quickly and cheaply. To address this lack, we developed an electronic-computer application based on electronic sensors and mathematics/statistics from the field of ML capable of measuring elasticity and other rheological variables of industrial interest.

2 Material and Methods

2.1 Electromechanical Device RELAPP

An electromechanical device was developed (see Fig. 3) to measure the elasticity of flour doughs from their behavior when a mechanical force is applied and released. A software application ("App Rheometer") was designed to perform the controlling and automatic readout of the electronic system. The resulting device, called "RELAPP", constitutes a configurable, portable, low cost and easy-to-use rheometer for the measurement of viscoelastic properties of flour doughs.

Fig. 3. RELAPP device developed to measure properties of viscoelastic materials

By observing the dynamic response after the applied pressure is released, the physical properties of the sample can be computed and measured. The device can provide 3D elasticity values (using geometrical procedures) in a few seconds, as well as predict accurate rheological values of extensibility, tenacity and stretch using an ML-based model. If the user performs several replicates, the developed software can also calculate the coefficient of variation for each parameter, which is an estimate of the variability and repeatability of the measurement.

We used an experimental sample set with known real rheological values (obtained using a Chopin Alveograph® [3]) to build a suitable data model for parameter prediction. A patent for RELAPP is currently pending.

2.2 Experimental Data

Correlation studies were carried out on samples of different kinds of flour, comparing the data obtained with RELAPP and a Chopin Alveograph®. The predictive regression model developed from the deformation data captured by the RELAPP sensor was adapted accordingly and the accuracy of the measured viscoelastic parameters could be estimated. The alveograph values of P, L, and W [3] were obtained for all the analysed flour samples (assuming their equivalence to the RELAPP measurements of tenacity (T), extensibility (EX) and strength (S), respectively).

Experimental data produced by RELAPP collected over one year were used 1) to build a predictive model of rheological parameters, 2) to validate the accuracy of the device and 3) to assess the repeatability of the method. The sources of data were a) Spanish Proficiency Testing for the Analysis of Cereals (Circuito Español de Cereales – CEC) and b) a routine quality control laboratory of a flour company. A total of 1600 flour dough samples were collected and analyzed using RELAPP, providing experience and knowledge of the method. Part of the samples were used to verify the device and the repeatability of the method.

The dimension of the RELAPP output is [n, 4], where "n" equals the total time of analysis (number of step times), and the 4 columns are related to the 3 linear accelerations (in each step time) followed by another column containing the measurement time. The matrix was then resized using the bilinear method that provides our target dimensions.

During the experiments and measurements with RELAPP, an *ad hoc* protocol was developed in the Mat Control Laboratory for the preparation of flour dough samples using a kitchen mixer, whereas the flour company used the procedure recommended by the Chopin Alveograph® manufacturers [3]. Another procedure for wholewheat flour is pending validation.

2.3 Data Models

Regression analysis is used to model the relationship between a scalar response (e.g., dependent variables, rheological parameters) and one or more explanatory variables (often called predictors, covariates, independent variables or features, or in this case the RELAPP response) [4]. If there is only one explanatory variable, the process is called simple linear regression, and if more than one, multiple regression. The results of regression analysis are continuous or real values. Commonly used regression algorithms include linear regression (see Fig. 4), support vector machines, and boosting [5].

The objective of multiple regression analysis [6, 7] is to use independent variables with known values (i.e., the measurements obtained using RELAPP in matrix form) to predict the value of a single dependent value (i.e., a rheological parameter such as tenacity). Each predictor value is weighed, the weights denoting their relative contribution to the overall prediction. Multiple linear regression fits the function:

$$y = \beta_0 + \sum_{j=1}^{p} \beta_j x_j \tag{1}$$

where x_1, x_2, ..., x_p are the p predictor features, y the response features, and β_0, β_1, ..., βp the model $p + 1$ parameters under the constraint:

$$RSS = \sum_{i=1}^{n} y_i - (\beta_0 + \sum_{j=1}^{p} \beta_j x_j) \qquad (2)$$

to minimize the residual sum of squares (RSS) over the training data. The model parameters try to minimize the discrepancy between the real and expected data (according to the model) for the training data. Depending on the regression method [6], the algorithm used to predict y can change. In the case of linear multiple regression (the gold standard model), the point estimate solution of $\hat{\beta}$ in (2) is to use the ordinary least squares (OLS) method known as normal equations:

$$\hat{\beta} = (X'X)^{-1}X'Y \qquad (3)$$

There are several metrics involved in regression, such as root-mean-squared error (RMSE) and mean average error (MAE). RMSE is the square root of mean squared error (MSE). MAE is the absolute sum of actual and predicted differences, but as it lacks mathematical rigor, it is rarely used compared to other metrics [8].

When using methods based on ML, it is very common to divide the data sets into training sets (to train the models) and test sets (to evaluate the accuracy of the models and validate them). When it comes to training models, two major problems may be encountered: overfitting and underfitting [7]. Overfitting happens when the model performs well on the training set but not so well on unseen (test) data; underfitting occurs when it fails to perform well on both the training and test set. To avoid overfitting of the data, regularization is implemented, especially when there is a large variance between training and test set performance. Among the available regularization techniques are lasso and ridge [7].

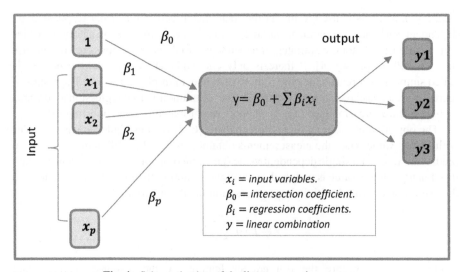

Fig. 4. Schematization of the linear regression process.

In the present study, a set of machine learning regression models [5, 6] were used to predict rheological parameters using the data matrices obtained in the experiments. This approach allowed us to obtain predicted parameters (tenacity, extensibility, stench) that were similar to the real values (i.e., those obtained previously by the Chopin Alveograph®, although other types of rheometer parameters could be used) [1].

We carried out extensive prior research on different types of regression models potentially suitable for our purposes [5]. After consulting various studies and carrying out tests, the following seven regression models were selected:

- Linear Regression: a type of linear model [7] considered to be the most basic predictive algorithm and the most used (the gold standard; see (1), (2) and Fig. 4).
- Lasso (least absolute shrinkage and selection operator) Regression: also referred to as the penalized regression method, this technique performs L1 regularization using shrinkage and feature selection [7].
- Ridge Regression: also referred to as L2 Regularization, this method puts a constraint on the coefficients by introducing a penalty factor. However, unlike lasso regression, which considers the magnitude of the coefficients, ridge regression is based on their squared values [7].
- Random Forest Regression: an ensemble technique that uses multiple decision trees.
- Support Vector Machine (SVM): a supervised learning algorithm used to predict discrete values. The idea is to find the best hyperplane with the maximum number of points.
- Tree Regression: a predictive model that uses a set of binary rules to calculate the predicted continuous valued outputs.
- XGBoost (Extreme Gradient Boosting): an optimization of Gradient Boosting, this ensemble method combines multiple weak models, as do decision trees.

For the construction and optimization of predictive models and data analysis, Python and R software were used.

3 Results and Discussion

3.1 RELAPP Validation

A prototype of this electromechanical device was validated in both laboratory and industrial settings. The validation of RELAPP (its application, characteristics, precision, capabilities, repeatability, and software) was carried out at the Mat Control Laboratory using the quality control samples obtained from the Spanish Proficiency Testing for the Analysis of Cereals (Circuito Español de Cereales – CEC), an annually organized event with the participation of expert laboratories in the field. The samples had variable characteristics and very well-established alveograph parameter values (Chopin Alveograph®). Measurements covering the entire linear range of possible values were incorporated to reduce prediction errors.

Validation was also carried out in the quality control laboratory of a flour company, which expressed interest in the device after an *in-situ* demonstration of its operation. After the personnel were trained in its usage, the prototype and a computer with the

RELAPP control software (see Fig. 5) were temporarily installed for validation using the real rheological measurements. During these tests, the staff operating the prototype showed a strong predisposition to collaborate with the research group. The tenacity and extensibility values provided by the device closely approximate the alveograph data. RELAPP may be useful for evaluating wholemeal flours and flours containing additives that cannot be measured with the Chopin Alveograph®.

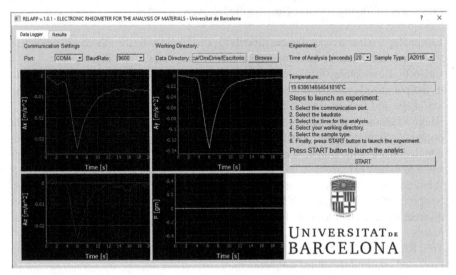

Fig. 5. Measuring flour dough deformation using RELAPP control software. The screen of the results obtained in a sample of wheat flour dough is presented.

3.2 Predictive Regression Models and Accuracy Validation

A variety of models were created using different techniques for each variable (EX, T, S), working with 1588 samples (a few samples were discarded as outliers). On the one hand, linear regression models were tested, with (lasso and ridge) and without regularization. Finally, regression models were developed using SVM, decision tree, random forest and XGBoost. The results were obtained by training using 5-fold cross validation for 100 iterations, except for XGBoost and random forest, for which 10 iterations were calculated. To select the hyperparameters of the models, an exhaustive grid search was carried out, except in the case of XGBoost and random forest, for which a random grid search was used (computing time >140 h).

The XGBoost model was found to produce the best results (minimum MAE) (see Table 1), alongside the SVM model in the case of parameter L.

Table 1. Accuracy of the different regression models and rheological parameters used. For the validation of the model, the mean average error (MAE) was used.

Model	Rheological parameter predicted	MAE
Linear Regression	T/P	28.5633
Ridge	T/P	27.1162
Lasso	T/P	27.5274
XGBoost	T/P	20.7995
SVM	T/P	23.2460
Tree Regression	T/P	28.6386
Random Forest Regression	T/P	27.5926
Linear Regression	S/W	94.8059
Ridge	S/W	94.8278
Lasso	S/W	92.1925
XGBoost	S/W	69.2972
SVM	S/W	84.8828
Tree Regression	S/W	98.1132
Random Forest Regression	S/W	95.9968
Linear Regression	EX/L	18.0964
Ridge	EX/L	15.5280
Lasso	EX/L	15.4142
XGBoost	EX/L	13.6578
SVM	EX/L	13.2936
Tree Regression	EX/L	16.0608
Random Forest Regression	EX/L	15.5761

T/P :Tenacity, S/W: Strength, EX/L: Extensibility

Using the hyperparameters obtained from the grid (results summarized in Table 1), the selected Xboost model was adjusted again to validate the results with 10-fold cross validation for 100 iterations. Figure 6 presents the results of the iterative validation (RMSE, MAE) usually performed in an iterative machine learning process. The statistical median and percentiles 5 and 95 are represented in each plot. It can be seen that the MAE and RMSE obtained are randomly distributed (Gaussian process or white noise). The

Table 2. Metrics used to validate the accuracy of the Xboost model for the principal rheological variables used: Tenacity (T), Extensibility (EX) and Strength (S). Several metrics are involved in regression such as root-mean-squared error (RMSE) and mean average error (MAE). The mean and standard deviation (Std) are presented for all iterations computed during the validation process.

Variable	Mean (MAE)	Std (MAE)	Mean (RMSE)	Std (RMSE)
Tenacity (P)	20.10934	1.59188	29.63114	2.59058
Strength (W)	66.64663	4.01085	86.57402	4.79032
Extensibility (L)	13.27630	1.01917	19.36928	1.48992

mean and standard deviation errors were used to obtain the mean accuracy of the selected model (Xboost) for each rheological parameter (see Table 2).

Table 2 shows the accuracy of the selected Xboost model used to fit the rheological parameters (T/P, EX/L, S/W), revealing a good approximation between real and predicted values (low MAE and RMSE). The distance between the real (actual) and predicted data is low (see Fig. 7). MAE and RMSE are smaller for P and L and medium for W, but their distribution ranges are also larger for W (90–500) than for L (50–160) and P (30–180). We believe that this approximation is sufficient for the practical application of the developed technology.

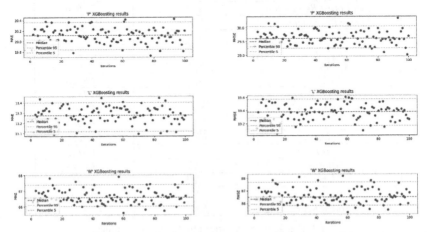

Fig. 6. Iterative process of validation computed 100 times using random training and test sets for the XBoost model (best accuracy) and each rheological parameter (T/P, EX/L, S/W). MAE plots (left) and RMSE plots (right) are depicted. The statistical median and percentiles 5 and 95 are represented in each plot.

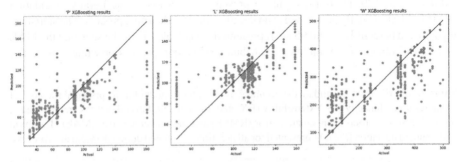

Fig. 7. Real versus predicted (actual) values for each rheological parameter (T/P, EX/L, S/W) obtained during the validation. Each point represents a prediction in the test set.

Finally, the RELAPP project also includes a complete software application, developed at the University of Barcelona and based on previous projects [9, 10], for the analysis of laboratory results and quality control data (saturability of viscoelastic parameters, equivalence tests, repeatability, outliers, non-inferiority test). This software objectively detects outlier values in the experiments and indicates the tolerance of parameters to certain experimental conditions (e.g., the effect of adding water to a flour dough during kneading on EX, S and T). It also verifies if the parameters are different or equivalent [11] to the reference values according to a particular protocol (see Fig. 8).

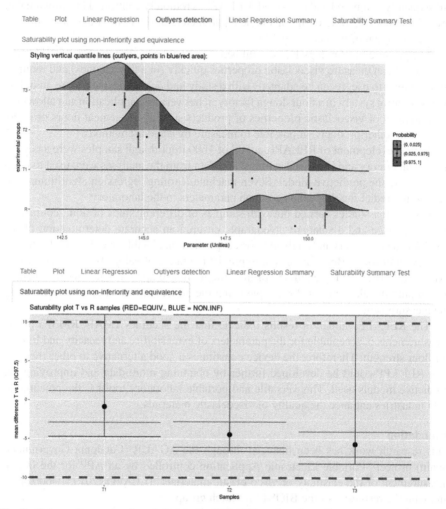

Fig. 8. Extra software developed during the RELAPP project that allows a complete analysis of data provided by RELAPP in the laboratory and quality control (saturability of viscoelastic parameters, equivalence tests, repeatability, outliers, non-inferiority test). (See in http://biost3. bio.ub.edu:3838/saturability/)

RELAPP can be adapted (with a study and *ad hoc* adaptation) to online quality control in a flour dough factory. It allows the fast and efficient measurement of viscoelastic properties of products such as wholemeal flours or flours mixed with other products.

4 Conclusions

A portable, configurable, low-cost device (RELAPP) has been developed to measure the viscoelasticity of cereal flour doughs and other related materials (e.g., plastics or latex). Its working principle is based on observing the dynamic response of a sample after the release of an applied mechanical pressure. The physical properties of the sample are subsequently computed and measured. RELAPP is remotely controlled by software that provides a quick reading of the rheological parameters of the flour dough, and allows a rapid assessment of the cereal quality.

The proposed technology has several benefits. The device is compact, portable, and low cost; it can measure viscoelastic properties quickly (in a few seconds) and requires little training to use; it can be adapted (with a study and *ad hoc* adaptation) to an online quality control system in a flour dough factory; it has versatile application and allows the measurement of viscoelastic properties of products such as wholemeal flours or flours mixed with other products, impossible to measure by standard methods.

In the development of RELAPP, a total of 1600 flour dough samples were analyzed in both laboratory and industrial settings, and data from the analyses were used to build and validate the predictive model. Seven machine learning regression algorithms were applied to predict rheological alveograph parameters in the laboratory.

Correlation studies carried out with samples of different kinds of flour, comparing the new device and a standard alveograph, ensured an accurate determination of the rheological parameters and enabled a correct prediction. Notably, the RELAPP software uses an optimized XBoost algorithm to predict the range of values for the tenacity (T), extensibility (EX) and strength (S) of the sample. It also applies a geometrical method to compute the elasticity of the sample using the 3d axis information obtained during the measurement.

The RELAPP validation results indicate that the accuracy (MAE, RMSE) of the measurements is acceptable for the parameters of extensibility and tenacity and limited for flour strength. Therefore, the device constitutes a good alternative to other rheometers. RELAPP could be developed further by obtaining more data and improving the predictive models used. This versatile and portable laboratory tool has the potential to help industries enhance the quality of viscoelastic materials.

Foundation
This research work has been financed through the AGAUR (Catalonia Government, Spain) project "Portable Electronic Application controlled by an APP for the in situ measurement of the elasticity of visco-elastic materials" (LLAVOR2019, ID6002445) and with the resources of the BIOST[3] research group.

Acknowledgments. We would like to thank María Serra, María De Más, Gina Roig and Jordi Ylla from YLLA 1878 SL for carrying out the tests with RELAPP and all their help and support; to Xavier Sánchez and Inés Marsà, technicians at Laboratory for the Preparation of Quality Control Materials (Mat Control) for having participated in the validation of the device and all the work carried out. Also, to Alexandre Vila who was part of the project. Finally, to Eva Martin and Miquel Sureda from the Bosh Gimpera Foundation of the University of Barcelona for their help and guidance in the project.

References

1. Monleón-Getino, T., Gordún, E.: Estudio del índice de elasticidad y mínimo de 1ª derivada alveográfica. Molinería y panadería **93**(1056), 66–74 (1998)
2. Monleón-Getino, T., Collado Fernández, M.: Calidad industrial del trigo y la harina. Técnicas de control estadístico de procesos y software. Alimentación equipos y tecnología **238**, 32–35 (2008)
3. Dubois, M., Dubat, A., Launay, B.: AlveoConsistograph Handbook. American Association of Cereal Chemists (2008)
4. Garcia-Garín, O., et al.: Automatic detection and quantification of floating marine macro-litter in aerial images: introducing a novel deep learning approach connected to a web application in R. Environ. Pollut. **273**, 116490 (2021)
5. Jiang, H.: Machine Learning Fundamentals A Concise Introduction, p. 67–76. Cambridge University Press, Cambridge (2021)
6. Deisenroth, M.P., Faisal, A.A.: Mathematics for Machine Learning. Cambridge University Press, Cambridge (2020)
7. DataCamp. Lasso and Ridge Regression Tutorial. Electronic document. https://www.datacamp.com/tutorial/tutorial-lasso-ridge-regression. Accessed 19 June 2022
8. Borja-Robalino, R., Monleón-Getino, A., Rodellar, J.: Estandarización de métricas de rendimiento para clasificadores Machine y Deep Learning. Revista Ibérica de Sistemas e Tecnologias de Informação, 184–196 (2020)
9. Stela, B., Monleon-Getino, A.: Facilitating the Automatic characterisation, classification and description of biological images with the VisionBioShape package for R. Open Access Libr. J. **3**(e3108), 1–16 (2016)
10. Monleón-Getino, T., Cambra-Sánchez, J.: APP API-STAT. Una aplicación para dispositivos móviles para el cálculo del nivel de infestación por varroa (Varroa destructor) en el campo. Vida apícola: revista de apicultura 200, 38–46 (2016)
11. Ocaña, J., Monleón-Getino, T., Merino, V., Peris, D., Soler, L.: Statistical methods for quality equivalence of topical products. 0.5 Mg/g Betamethasone Ointment as a Case-Study. Pharmaceutics **12**(4), 318 (2020)

How to Assess Business Technologies and Systems - A Global Approach with a Case Study

Beatriz Lobo[1] and Filipe Portela[1,2]([⊠])

[1] Algoritmi Research Centre, Universidade do Minho, Guimarães, Portugal
a80279@alunos.uminho.pt, cfp@dsi.uminho.pt
[2] IOTech – Innovation on Technology, Trofa, Porto, Portugal

Abstract. The role of technology is becoming increasingly significant in the growth and efficiency of businesses. Used in various industries, Technology Assessment consists of monitoring technologies and their relationship to their environment, thus contributing to the survival of companies in competitive markets. Technology Assessment will help identify existential problems and clarify them but will not solve them. The Technology Assessment Model reflects the everyday experiences of acquiring or using technology, as well as the perceived needs of the user. The focus of this paper is to create a global technology assessment model by studying the Technology Assessment Model 3 model. The questionnaire template is composed of seven sections. As a case study of the model created, the ioAttend platform was used. The sample questionnaire was adapted to the platform and collected responses with ioAttend users to understand their evaluation. It was concluded that users (acceptance average higher than 4) are more satisfied than administrators (acceptance average close to 4) for the four constructs evaluated. Kendall's Tau has a coefficient between −1 and 1, and its analysis revealed that most questions are either unrelated to each other (Tau coefficient equal to 0) or have an almost perfect relationship (coefficient close to 1).

Keywords: Technology assessment · Technology acceptance model · ioAttend

1 Introduction

Today, technology has become essential in organizations and businesses. The role of technology is becoming increasingly significant in the growth and efficiency of businesses [1]. Technologies play a critical role in the ability of companies to compete with other organizations. Selecting the right technologies can create remarkable competitive advantages and in the process of selecting them, several characteristics need to be explicitly considered [2]. Used in various industries, Technology Assessment (TA) consists of monitoring technologies and their relationship in their environment, thus contributing to the survival of companies in competitive markets. TA will help identify existential problems and clarify them, but will not solve them [3]. Thus, TA performed prior to technology adoption reduces the risk of ineffective investment decisions and keeps systems and technologies in check [1, 4].

T. Guarda et al. (Eds.): ARTIIS 2022, CCIS 1675, pp. 84–100, 2022.
https://doi.org/10.1007/978-3-031-20319-0_7

As Information Technology (IT) adoption has received considerable attention in the last decade, technology acceptance models have emerged [5]. The Technology Assessment Model (TAM) is the most widely used technology acceptance model [6]. This is not a descriptive model, meaning that it does not provide a diagnostic capability for specific failures in technology, but it is intended to assess and predict the acceptability of technology [7]. TAM reflects the everyday experiences of acquiring or using technology, as well as the perceived needs of the user [8, 9].

The focus of this paper is to create a global technology assessment model by studying the TAM 3 model, an evolution of the TAM model. As a case study of the model created, the ioAttend platform was used. The sample questionnaire was adapted to the platform and collected responses with ioAttend users to understand their evaluation. This platform was developed by the technological startup IOTech with the objective of facilitating the scheduling of attendance and events. Subsequently, with the results obtained in the questionnaires, a study of the same is carried out through indicators, for the purpose of demonstrating the results.

This article is divided into seven sections. The first section gives an introduction of the paper. The second presents the background and contextualizes the concepts discussed. Then, the third section represents the tools and methods used. The fourth section contemplates the global model of the questionnaire. The case study is presented in the fifth section. Then, in the sixth section, the results are discussed. Finally, in the seventh section, the conclusions are made.

2   Background

This section presents the crucial concepts for the development of this work, such as technology assessment, its importance in industry and organizations, the Technology Acceptance Model methodology, and finally a brief presentation of the ioAttend platform that will serve as the basis for the application of this study.

2.1 Technology Assessment

Mendes and Melo [3] state that a technology is the integrated set of knowledge, techniques, tools, and work procedures. Technologies that are considered new are used to replace procedures previously used by the organization. Due to the impacts that can be caused by a new technology in an organization, it is necessary to conduct a previous analysis. The purpose of TA in companies is to provide broad and objective information about the potential consequences of actions related to technological development. Its purpose is to find and point out more appropriate intervention alternatives in the development of technologies, due essentially to the concern with the effects, not only the planned ones such as cost/benefit, but particularly those that are not expected [3]. Through TA, companies can understand its compatibility for the use of a given technology, thus allowing the adoption of an action plan to prevent and reduce technology gaps [10]. According to Hamzeh and Xu [2], in the last years, transforming industries is being used advanced technologies (e.g. IOT, AI, Big Data). Identifying the best technology from a set of possible alternatives is the problem of technology selection. Thus,

TA performed prior to technology adoption reduces the risk of ineffective investment decisions and keeps systems and technologies in check [1, 4]. In addition to helping companies effectively identify strategic and operational gaps, enterprise TA also paves the way for companies to explore new concepts and ideas. By helping companies identify opportunities that leverage their interests, AT becomes central to driving the overall performance and efficiency of organizations [1].

2.2 Technology Acceptance Model

To develop a reliable model that could predict user attitudes toward the use and actual use and acceptance of any specific technology, Davis adapted the Theory of Reasoned Action (TRA) and Theory of Planned Behavior (TPB) theories and proposed the TAM [11]. However, the author made two main changes to the TRA and TPB models. First, he did not consider the subjective norm in predicting an actual behavior and only considered a person's attitude toward it. Second, he identified two primary factors that influenced an individual's intention to use a new technology: Perceived Usefulness (PU) and Perceived Ease of Use (PEOU) [5, 6, 11–13]. These considered the main determinants of attitude toward a technology, which in turn predicts the behavioral intention to use and ultimately the actual use of the system [8]. In TAM, PU refers to the degree to which a user believes that using a particular system will help improve their job performance, while PEOU refers to the degree to which a person believes that using a particular system will not entail effort [5, 6, 12].

Later, to complete the model by incorporating the antecedents of the original TAM, Venkatesh and Bala developed 2008 a model of the determinants of PEOU, TAM 3, to enable understanding of the role of interventions in technology adoption. TAM 3 comprises four constructs: PEOU, PU, Behavioral Intention (BI) and Usage Behavior (UB). The UB represents the actual use of the system by the individual. TAM 3 allows for a richer analysis of the relationship between users and technologies and stands out for including personal variables, thus allowing for a more human analysis, with the user being the determinant actor in the decision of whether to use a technology [13].

2.3 ioAttend

The application ioAttend was developed by IOTech, for IOS and Android. The ioAttend is an intelligent system capable of recording attendance at events, activities, in class, or at work, quickly and securely. The platform's main goal is to simplify the process of attendance booking and space management through a simple click, using triple authentication. The main functionalities of ioAttend are event management, user management, group management, space management, and saving user history. Organizations will be able to manage their events, their employees, and the spaces available for attendance registration quickly and digitally, avoiding the use of paper and the maintenance of electronic systems.

Based on IOTech's personal and professional experience, problems have been detected at the level of agenda and event management and thus, ioAttend emerges as an intuitive, simple, and easy-to-use solution that solves all the problems detected and presents new features that streamline the user's agenda management.

ioAttend can be used by two types of people: users and administrators. The tools available and the type of use vary according to the type of each user.

3   Material and Methods

This research aims to design a global questionnaire model based on TAM 3 methodology to evaluate several types of technology. TAM 3 was chosen because of experience with this approach and previous work [14, 15].

As a scientific research methodology to guide this work, Case Study (CS) was chosen. CS is an ideal methodology when a holistic and in-depth investigation is required [16]. It often uses qualitative data, collected from actual events, and aims to clarify, investigate, or report on current phenomena introduced in its own context [17]. Following the first stage of the methodology, the research design was made, the objective was outlined, which in this case is the realization of a global questionnaire model, and all the necessary information was collected. In the second phase, the model questionnaire was put into practice and developed. In the third phase, the model was adapted to the platform used as an example, the ioAttend, where through this questionnaire all the necessary data was collected to achieve the study objective. These were disseminated in chats with current employees of the IOTech startup as well as former employees. In the last phase, the data collected through the questionnaire was analyzed and a discussion and conclusion of the results were drawn up.

To develop this work, the tools described below were used:

– mSurvey: a platform developed by IOTech for conducting questionnaires;
– Microsoft Excel: this program was used to analyze the results obtained in the questionnaires;
– Paleontological Statistics (PAST): is a data analyzer software and was used for the Kendall's Tau analysis.

4   Global Assessment Model

For better organization of the questionnaire template, it has been divided into seven sections:

1. Level of Experience in the Technological Area;
2. Interface;
3. Operational Characteristics;
4. Technical Characteristics;
5. Behavioral Characteristics;
6. Relevance of the Platform;
7. Evaluate whether platform usage can be advantageous.

There are three possible response types: scaled, multiple-choice, or open-ended. The first section is made up of option response and aims to get to know the user better. From the second to the sixth section the answers are scaled responses and are dedicated to exploring the platform and understanding the user's desire to use it. In turn, the seventh and last section is open-ended and allows the respondent to suggest and report positive or negative aspects of the platform.

In regards to the scaled questions, the Likert Scale [18] was applied, ranging from one to five. This scale enables a level of agreement that the short or long-scale options do not, which also allows to obtain little dispersion in the results, with two negative values and other two positive values, and a neutral value [19].

The five levels stipulated for the scale were:

1. Totally disagree;
2. Disagree;
3. Neither agree nor disagree;
4. Agree;
5. Totally agree.

To get a better perception of the level of concentration and veracity of the answers, screening questions should be placed in the middle of the sections, thus ensuring that the questionnaires were answered responsibly by the respondent. An example of a screening question is "One + Three".

If the platform being evaluated contains more than one type of user (e.g. user, administrator) a different questionnaire should be created per user type. In case the questions are the same, there should be a question about the type of user the respondent is. This question can be for example put in Sect. 1.

To evaluate the functional and technical characteristics of the platform, it was necessary to understand the user's behavior towards the technology as well as their level of use. Thus, the questionnaires were based on the TAM 3 constructs, which are PU, PEOU, BI, and UB. The Delphi methodology was also used so that the questionnaires could be formulated with quality and rigor.

The questions with open answers do not enter into the analysis according to the TAM 3 constructs, as well as some questions with option answers since these only serve to obtain more data and feedback for analysis of the respondents. That said, some questions in Sect. 1 and all questions in Sect. 7 are not included in the TAM 3 analysis and they are presented below this text, and then the remaining sections of the questionnaire template will be presented in a matrix with the TAM 3 constructs. The questions with response options are presented with the appropriate examples of options.

1. Level of experience in the technological area

   1.1. In what business sector do you work? (e.g. Education, Technology, Other sectors)
   1.2. What is your role in the company? (e.g. Administrative, Consultant, Other)
   1.3. What is your position in the company? (e.g. CEO, Team Manager, Other)
   1.4. What is your experience in the technological area?
   1.5. What type of device do you usually use to access digital information (news, e-mail, reports, others)? (e.g. Cell phone, Tablet, Computer, Other)

1.6. What operating system do you currently use? (e.g. Windows, Android, iOS, Linux, Others)

1.7. On average, how often do you use technological devices per day? (e.g. Less than 2 h/day, Between 2 to 4 h/day, More than 4 h/day)

1.8. Type of User? (e.g. Full autonomy, Rarely needs technical support, Regularly needs technical support)

1.9. Do you use the computer mainly for? (e.g. Personal production application, Handle/consult administrative information, Handle/hide management information)

1.10. What device did you use to test the platform? (e.g. Laptop computer, Mobile Phone, Tablet, Other)

1.11. List the technical characteristics of this device.

2. Please evaluate if it is advantageous to use the platform

7.1. Why do you use the platform?

7.2. Positive aspects of the platform?

7.3. Negative aspects of the platform?

7.4. Suggestions to make the platform more advantageous.

To get a sense of user behavior it is necessary to map the questions with the TAM 3 constructs. Each question can evaluate more than one construct. Table 1 shows some possibilities for mapping. For example, the question "What is your experience in the technological area?" corresponds to the construct PU, PEOU and UB.

Table 1. Matrix between the questions and the TAM 3 constructs.

Questions	PU	PEOU	BI	UB
1. Level of experience in the technological area				
What is your experience in the technological area?	x	x		x
What type of device do you usually use to consult digital information (news, e-mail, reports, others)?		x		x
What operating system do you currently use?		x		x
On average, how often do you use technological devices per day?		x		x
Type of user?	x			x
What do you use the computer mainly for?	x	x	x	x
Which device did you use to test the application?		x		x
2. User interface				

(*continued*)

Table 1. (*continued*)

Questions	PU	PEOU	BI	UB
Do you consider the login page intuitive?		x		
Do you find it intuitive to change language on the platform?	x	x		
Is the application's interface adequate to the functions to be performed?		x	x	
Is the application design intuitive?		x		
Do you consider the navigation bar intuitive?		x		
Do you find it intuitive to log off the platform?		x		
Do you find the support area intuitive?		x		
Do you find intuitive to log out?		x		
3. Operational characteristics				
Do you consider the application easy and intuitive to use?		x		x
Do you consider that using the app doesn't require much mental effort?		x		
4. Technical characteristics				
Do you consider that access to the platform is fast?	x			x
Do you consider that access to the application is secure?	x			x
Do you consider that technical support is efficient?				x
Do you consider interoperability to be efficient?				x
5. Behavioral characteristics				
Does the platform motivate your use?				x
Do you use the application preferably for?				x
6. Relevance of the platform by the user				
Do you consider that the application brings direct or indirect benefits to users?	x		x	x
Do you consider that the app has been important in the digital evolution of your company?			x	x

To put the global model into practice, you need to adapt it to the technology you want to evaluate and create specific questions. Using a general application as an example, some additional questions in Sect. 3 referring to operational features are: "Do you consider that the application improves the performance of data recording?" and "Do you consider that the application allows greater control of data recording?". In Sect. 6 (User Relevance of the platform) it is also possible to add more questions, such as "Do you believe that using the platform influences the speed in the way data recording is done?" and "Do you consider that those who have a need to do data recording should use the platform?".

In this study and as a proof of concept of this global model the ioAttend application was used and will be put into practice in the case study. The case study helps to understand what kind of information and indicators can be obtained with this model.

5 Case Study

As a case study, the ioAttend application was used, where the global questionnaire was adapted to its needs. Two questionnaires were prepared to cover all types of users of the ioAttend platform, these being end-users and administrators. The administrators' questionnaire contains 58 questions and the users' questionnaire contains 51.

The questionnaires were shared with ioAttend users, which makes the respondents experts on the platform, thus not requiring many answers for the study to be credible. A total of 37 responses were obtained, where 51.35% correspond to the number of responses from administrators and 48.65% from users.

To obtain a more reliable and coherent analysis of the results, this analysis was initialized by excluding the answers of respondents who missed the screening question. The screening question was "One + Three" where the correct answer is the value 4. Answers with the value 1, 2, 3, or 5 are considered wrong, thus removing the questionnaires that contain these values in this question from the data analysis. 8 questionnaires were eliminated, which corresponds to 21.62% of the total number of answers acquired, 4 of which were for administrators and the rest for users. Thus, a new total of 29 responses were obtained for analysis of the results, corresponding to 51.72% of the number of responses obtained by administrators and 48.28% by users.

The data were automatically exported from the mSurvey platform to Excel format. After being exported and observed, the statistical data was created. Table 2 presents the technology experience of the respondents. For example, in the question "In what business sector do you work?" the most chosen answer option was "Technology" by both administrators and users, with 87% and 72% respectively.

To study the data, an overall analysis was performed of the questionnaire and per TAM 3 construct. Two types of analysis were performed: univariate statistical analysis and correlation coefficient (Kendall's Tau).

Table 2. Level of experience in Information Technology.

Questions	Answer	Admin	User
In what business sector do you work?	Technology	87%	72%
	Other Sectors	6%	7%
	Wholesale and retail trade	7%	7%
	Telecommunications	0%	7%
	Human health and social support activities	0%	7%
On average, how much time do you use technological devices per day?	More than 4 h/day	87%	71%
	Between 2 to 4 h/day	13%	29%
User type?	Total Autonomy	73%	79%
	Rarely needs technical support (less than 3 times/month)	20%	14%
	Regularly needs technical support	7%	7%
Do you use the computer mainly for?	Handle/Consult management information	34%	29%
	Personal production application (e-mail, word processing, spreadsheet)	53%	71%
	Handle/Consult administrative information	13%	0%
What device did you use to test the platform?	Laptop computer	47%	29%
	Cell phone	33%	64%
	Hybrid computer	7%	0%
	Fixed computer	13%	7%

5.1 Univariate Statistical Analysis

The univariate analysis covers the minimum (Min), maximum (Max), sum (Sum), mean (Mean), mode (Mode), standard deviation (SD), variance (Var), and median (Med).

Univariate Statistical Analysis per Respondent
To summarize the statistical analysis per respondent, the answers from users and administrators were grouped together. The Media of the sum of the questions is 155.862 which indicates that they responded with high values to the questions. The average response of respondents is 4.054 which means that they are satisfied with the platform. The mode of response is 5, equivalent to an "I totally agree". The standard deviation is 0.595, which is not very high but shows that there is a slight dispersion in the responses among respondents. The average of the variance shows that the value of each set is not far from the average value since it has a value of 0,455. The Median is the center value of a data set, being in this analysis 4. In general, respondents are satisfied with ioAttend. You can see this analysis in Table 3.

Table 3. Global univariate statistical analysis per respondent.

Avarage Sum	Mean	Mode	Avarage SD	Avarage Var	Med
155,862	4,054	5	0,595	0,455	4

Univariate Statistical Analysis per Question

In Tables 4 it is possible to observe the univariate analysis per question of the questionnaire conducted to users. By analyzing the Table 4 it is possible to understand that the average of the answers per question has a value of 4, equivalent to 30,41% of the answers. In almost all questions, at least one respondent, was evaluated with 2 or 3 a question. Only the questions in Sect. 7 were evaluated with the minimum value of 1. All questions were evaluated at least once with the value 5. Question 2.2 "Do you find it intuitive to change the language on the platform?" was the question with the lowest standard deviation, being 0,61. The mode of this questionnaire was the value 5.

Questions 2.2 "Do you find it intuitive to change the language in the platform?", 2.5 "Do you find the navigation bar intuitive?" and 2.6 "Do you find it intuitive how to visualize an event?" present the best results statistically with the highest response averages, these being higher than 4 and with the lowest standard deviation, this being well below 1. The mode of response to these questions is 5. This shows that users are satisfied with the topic addressed in these questions. In turn, questions 1.4 "What is your experience in the technological area?", 6.4 "Do you think the application has been important in the digital evolution of your company?" and 7.2 "View locations?" have the lowest response means, below 4, and a high standard deviation, higher than 1. The mode of response is 5.

Table 4. Univariate statistical analysis per question (user)

Question	Min	Max	Sum	Mean	Mode	SD	Var	Med
1.4	2	5	53	3,786	4	1,013	1,104	4,00
2.1	2	5	62	4,429	5	0,904	0,879	5,00
2.2	3	5	65	4,643	5	0,610	0,401	5,00
2.3	3	5	61	4,357	5	0,718	0,555	4,50
2.4	2	5	63	4,500	5	0,824	0,731	5,00
2.5	3	5	64	4,571	5	0,623	0,418	5,00
2.6	3	5	64	4,571	5	0,623	0,418	5,00
2.7	3	5	62	4,429	5	0,728	0,571	5,00
2.8	2	5	59	4,214	5	0,860	0,797	4,00
2.9	3	5	58	4,143	4	0,742	0,593	4,00

(*continued*)

Table 4. (*continued*)

Question	Min	Max	Sum	Mean	Mode	SD	Var	Med
2.10	2	5	60	4,286	5	1,030	1,143	5,00
2.11	2	5	60	4,286	5	0,881	0,835	4,50
2.12	3	5	60	4,286	5	0,700	0,527	4,00
2.13	2	5	58	4,143	5	0,915	0,901	4,00
2.14	3	5	61	4,357	5	0,811	0,709	5,00
2.15	2	5	64	4,571	5	0,904	0,879	5,00
3.1	3	5	61	4,357	5	0,718	0,555	4,50
3.2	2	5	61	4,357	5	0,895	0,863	5,00
3.3	3	5	63	4,500	5	0,732	0,577	5,00
3.4	3	5	58	4,143	4	0,742	0,593	4,00
3.6	2	5	59	4,214	5	0,939	0,951	4,50
3.7	2	5	61	4,357	5	0,972	1,016	5,00
3.8	2	5	60	4,286	5	0,958	0,989	5,00
4.1	3	5	59	4,214	5	0,773	0,643	4,00
4.2	3	5	63	4,500	5	0,627	0,423	5,00
4.3	3	5	59	4,214	5	0,860	0,797	4,50
4.4	3	5	57	4,071	4	0,703	0,533	4,00
5.1	2	5	58	4,143	5	1,059	1,209	4,50
6.1	2	5	59	4,214	5	0,939	0,951	4,50
6.2	2	5	57	4,071	5	1,100	1,302	4,50
6.3	2	5	59	4,214	5	0,939	0,951	4,50
6.4	2	5	52	3,714	4	1,097	1,297	4,00
7.1	1	5	56	4,000	5	1,134	1,385	4,00
7.2	1	5	55	3,929	5	1,334	1,918	4,00
7.3	1	5	57	4,071	5	1,223	1,610	4,50

The same results can be obtained for the administrators' questionnaires. The analysis allows us to conclude that the average of the answers per question corresponds to the values 3 and 4. 23,97% of administrators attributed the values 3 and 25,71% the value 4 in their answers to the questionnaire. In almost all questions, at least one respondent rated a question with 1 or 2. All questions were evaluated at least once with a value of 5. The mode of this questionnaire, the most frequently answered value, was value 5.

Questions 2.1 "Do you consider the login page intuitive?", 2.14 "Do you consider it intuitive to log out of the platform?" and 7.1.2 "Do you select the start and end date?" show the best results statistically with the highest response means, these being higher than 4 and with the lowest standard deviation, this being less than 1 or very close to 1. The mode of response to these questions is 5. This shows that administrators are satisfied with the topic addressed in these questions. In turn, questions 3.3 "Do you consider that the platform improves event management?", 3.6 "Do you consider that the platform allows mitigating situations of heavy workload?" and 6.4 "Do you consider that the platform has been important in the digital evolution of your company?" have the lowest response averages, close to 3, and a high standard deviation, greater than 1. The mode of response is 4, 3, and 3 respectively.

Analysis by Construct
Previously, the questions were divided by their corresponding constructs, these being four: PU, PEOU, BI, and UB. The statistical analysis of each construct will be performed for administrators and users per question.

Kendall Tau was used to measure the degree of agreement between two ordinal variables. The Tau correlation coefficient returns a value from −1 to 1, where 0 means the two variables are independent, 1 represents a perfect relationship, and −1 corresponds to perfect disagreement [20]. Several analyses were performed among which were the mean and standard deviation for each of the constructs per question and Kendall's Tau per construct per question. Next, some of the analyses performed will be presented. The analyses will be presented in more detail in an extended version of this article. The statistical analysis regarding the users' PU construct can be found in Fig. 1 and it is possible to verify that the average of answers in users is approximately 4.

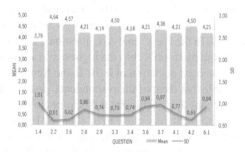

Fig. 1. Analysis of Mean and Standard Deviation of the PU construct (User)

Table 5 shows Kendall's Tau statistical analysis referring to the BI construct per administrator question. Most correlations have a Tau coefficient equal to or close to 0, which means that the questions are not related.

Table 5. BI Kendall's Tau administrator

	2.3	2.4	3.3	6.1	6.2	6.3	6.4
2.3		0,01	0,00	0,00	0,00	0,00	0,00
2.4	0,47		0,00	0,01	0,00	0,02	0,00
3.3	0,77	0,60		0,00	0,00	0,01	0,00
6.1	0,68	0,50	0,70		0,00	0,00	0,00
6.2	0,65	0,57	0,86	0,83		0,01	0,00
6.3	0,71	0,46	0,51	0,71	0,50		
6.4	0,82	0,57	0,78	0,77	0,76	0,70	

Regarding the UB construct, its analysis per question of users is shown in Fig. 2. This presents respondent response averages between 3 and 4.

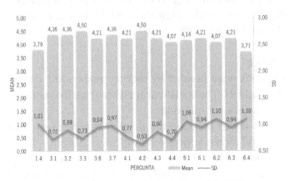

Fig. 2. Analysis of Mean and Standard Deviation of the UB construct (User)

6 Discussion of Results

When analyzing the construct PU, it is noteworthy the presence of some standard deviation in the answers of both respondents, approximately 1.00 per question, which refers to dispersion in the answers. In the users' analysis, question 2.2, "Do you find it intuitive to change the language on the platform?", has the highest average of 4.64, and is also the question with the lowest standard deviation of 0.61. In the Kendall's Tau analysis of the PU construct, it is noticeable that most of the respondents' answers to the questions are unrelated to each other since the Tau coefficient is 0 or very close to it. Some correlations of the questions show a coefficient very close to or equal to 1 which indicates that they are related to each other. The correlation of the administrators' answers to questions 1.4. "What is your experience in the technology area?" and 2.9. "Do you find the functionality of editing an event intuitive?" shows a Tau coefficient of 1 which indicates a perfect relationship. In turn, there are negative coefficients thus demonstrating that there is a small disagreement between the questions. The correlation of the administrators' questions 3.7. "Do you consider that the platform allows greater control of the various tasks?" and 1.4. is the one that presents the most negative coefficient being −0.45.

Analyzing the PEOU construct by question, it was concluded that the average of the respondents' answers is approximately 4. The users' answers to questions 2.2. "Do you consider it intuitive to change language in the platform?", 2.5. "Do you consider the navigation bar intuitive?", 2.6. "Do you consider it intuitive how to view an event?" and 2.15. "Do you consider it intuitive to log out?" are the ones with the highest average of 4.6. In turn, the lowest average is 3.6 and belongs to question 7.3.2. "Add external users or import via CSV?" of the administrators. As for the standard deviation, it has a value very close to 1, which demonstrates the existence of some dispersion in the answers of the respondents. The results of the Kendall's Tau correlation coefficient of the administrators of the PEOU construct show that most of the questions are not related since the coefficient is very close to or equal to 0. Regarding the coefficients close to

1, it is visible the presence of some and even two correlations where the coefficient is equal to 1 (1.4. "What is your experience in the technological area?" and 2.9. "Do you consider intuitive the functionality to edit an event?", and 1.4. And 2.14. "Do you consider intuitive to log off in the platform?") which shows a perfect relationship between the answers to these questions. The Tau coefficient equal to or greater than 0.80 is underlined to facilitate the reading of the table. In this analysis it is also verified the presence of negative coefficients which indicates a disagreement between the answers, being the correlation between question 7.1.3. "Select the type of event and your options?" and 1.4. With the highest negative coefficient of −0.47.

The analysis of the BI construct per question reveals that the respondents' average response is approximately 4 and the users' questions 2.4. "Is the application design intuitive?" and 3.3. "Do you consider that the application improves presence marking performance?" have the highest average of 4.50. The standard deviation is high, indicating a discrepancy in the respondents' answers. The question with the lowest standard deviation is question 2.3 "Is the application interface suitable for the functions to be performed?" with a value of 0.72. Table 5 presented before shows Kendall's Tau statistical analysis referring to the BI construct per administrator question. The correlation of questions 6.2 "Do you think those who deal with event management should use the platform?" and 3.3 "Do you think the platform improves event management?" has the closest coefficient to 1, being 0.86, thus showing that they are related. There are no values below 0 which show that there are no questions with answers in disagreement. The analysis concerning the user is very similar to this one.

Regarding the UB construct, its analysis per question of users is shown in Fig. 2. The users' questions 3.3 "Do you think the application improves the performance of presence marking?" and 4.2 "Do you think that access to the application is safe?" have the highest average of 4.50. Question 4.2. "Do you consider that access to the application is secure?" of the users shows the lowest standard deviation of 0.63. Overall, the questions show some standard deviation, this being very close to or greater than 1, which reveals a dispersion among the respondents' answers. According to Kendall's Tau, half of the correlations between the questions that make up the respondents' UB construct show a coefficient very close to or equal to 0, which reveals that they do not have a relationship. In the other half negative coefficients or coefficients higher than 0 are visible. No coefficients equal to −1 or 1 are found, which means that there are no disagreements or perfect relationships between the questions. The correlation with the most negative coefficient, −0.45, is between the administrators' question 3.7. "Do you consider that the platform allows greater control of the various tasks?" and 1.4. "What is your experience in the technological area?". In turn, the correlation with the highest coefficient is between the users' questions 1.4. "What is your experience in the technological area?" and 6.2. "Do you consider that those who need to mark presence in an event should use the platform?" and has a value of 0.94, which demonstrates a high relationship between the questions.

To summarize, Table 6 shows the 3 questions with the highest average and these all belong to Sect. 2 "User Interface" of the user questionnaire.

In Table 7 are the 3 questions with the lowest average, and these belong to the administrator's questionnaire. Two questions belong to Sect. 3 "Operational characteristics" and the other to Sect. 6 "Relevance of the platform by the administrator".

Table 6. The 3 questions with the highest average.

Questions	Mean
2.2. How intuitive do you find it to change the language on the platform?	4,643
2.5. Do you find the navigation bar intuitive?	4,571
2.6. Do you find it intuitive how to visualize an event?	4,571

Table 7. The 3 questions with the lowest average

Questions	Mean
3.3. Do you think the platform improves event management?	3,533
3.6. Do you consider that the platform allows you to mitigate high workload situations?	3,400
6.4. Do you consider that the platform has been important in the digital evolution of your company?	3,400

In Table 8 below it is possible to obtain a general perception of the average and mode of each construct, both for the administrator and the user. It is visible that the users are more satisfied with the platform than the administrators, but in a general way both accept the use of ioAttend.

Table 8. Global analysis for each construct

Constructs	Administrator		User	
	Mean	Mode	Mean	Mode
PU	3,812	5	4,292	5
PEOU	3,936	5	4,295	5
BI	3,714	5	4,224	5
UB	3,638	5	4,195	5

7 Conclusions

The development of this article aimed to create a model questionnaire according to the Technology Acceptance Model (TAM 3) to evaluate the acceptance of a technology by its users. The model questionnaire consists of 7 sections (Level of Experience in the Technological Area, Interface, Operational Characteristics, Technical Characteristics, Behavioral Characteristics, Relevance of the Platform, and Evaluate if it is advantageous to use the platform) to analyze the platform and the user's perception of it.

As a practical case, the ioAttend application was used, where the questionnaire was adapted to it and the necessary statistical analysis of the data obtained was performed. It was possible to conclude from the statistical analyses and Kendall's Tau that both users are satisfied with using ioAttend. However, it is visible that users (acceptance average of 4,252) are more satisfied than administrators (acceptance average of 3,775) for the four constructs evaluated (Perceived Usefulness, Perceived Ease of Use, Behavioral Intention, and Use Behavior). This indicates that improvements need to be made to the platform for them to feel more motivated and to continue using it. The PEOU construct was the one that got a better evaluation having the highest average responses in both the administrator (3,926) and the user (4,295). The question in which there was more agreement among the respondents was 2.2. "How intuitive do you find it to change the language on the platform?" with the lowest standard deviation of 0,610 in the users' questionnaire.

In the future, the results will be used to improve the system, mitigate some reported problems, and add new features. After that, a new round of questionnaires will be carried out to understand if there was any improvement for users at the level of TAM 3 constructs.

Acknowledgements. This work has been supported by IOTECH and FCT – Fundação para a Ciência e Tecnologia within the R&D Units Project Scope: UIDB/00319/2020.

References

1. Belle, C.: What Is Technology Assessment and Why Is It Important For Businesses? https://www.myasbn.com/small-business/technology/what-is-technology-assessment-and-why-is-it-important-for-businesses/. Accessed 01 Mar 2021
2. Hamzeh, R., Xu, X.: Technology selection methods and applications in manufacturing: a review from 1990 to 2017. Comput. Ind. Eng. **138**, 106123 (2019). https://doi.org/10.1016/j.cie.2019.106123
3. Mendes, M.L.S., de Melo, D.R.A.: Avaliação Tecnológica: Uma Proposta Metodológica. Rev. Adm. Contemp. **21**, 569–584 (2017)
4. Enginess: How to Conduct a Technology Assessment: A Four-Step Guide. https://www.enginess.io/insights/how-to-conduct-technology-assessment
5. Ma, Q., Liu, L.: The Technology acceptance model. In: Advanced Topics in End User Computing, Vol. 4 (2011). https://doi.org/10.4018/9781591404743.ch006.ch000
6. Sagnier, C., Loup-Escande, E., Lourdeaux, D., Thouvenin, I., Valléry, G.: User acceptance of virtual reality: an extended technology acceptance model. Int. J. Hum. Comput. Interact. **36**, 993–1007 (2020). https://doi.org/10.1080/10447318.2019.1708612
7. Masrom, M.: Technology acceptance model and E-learning. In: 12th International Conference on Education, pp. 21–24 (2007)
8. Regan, M., Horberry, T.S.A.: Driver Acceptance of New Technology (2013)
9. Aguiar, J., et al.: Pervasive information systems to intensive care medicine: technology acceptance model. In: ICEIS 2013 - Proceedings of the 15th International Conference on Enterprise Information Systems, vol. 1, pp. 177–184 (2013). https://doi.org/10.5220/0004441001770184
10. Oztemel, E., Ozel, S.: Technological competency assessment. Int. J. Serv. (2019). https://doi.org/10.1504/IJSTM.2019.098206
11. Marangunić, N., Granić, A.: Technology acceptance model: a literature review from 1986 to 2013. Univ. Access Inf. Soc. **14**(1), 81–95 (2014). https://doi.org/10.1007/s10209-014-0348-1

12. Elshafey, A., Saar, C.C., Aminudin, E.B., Gheisari, M., Usmani, A.: Technology acceptance model for augmented reality and building information modeling integration in the construction industry. J. Inf. Technol. Constr. **25**, 161–172 (2020). https://doi.org/10.36680/j.itcon.202 0.010

13. da Cunha Silva de Brito, J.V., Ramos, A.S.M.: Limitações dos Modelos de Aceitação da Tecnologia: um Ensaio sob uma Perspectiva Crítica. Gestão. Org. **17**, 210–220 (2019). https://doi.org/10.21714/1679-18272019v17esp.p210-220

14. Portela, F.: Improving pervasive decision support system in critical care using TAM. In: 8th International Conference on Current and Future Trends of Information and Communication Technologies in Healthcare (ICTH 2018), vol. 0 (2018)

15. Portela, F., Aguiar, J., Santos, M.F., Silva, Á., Rua, F.: Pervasive intelligent decision support system – technology acceptance in intensive care units. In: Rocha, Á., Correia, A., Wilson, T., Stroetmann, K. (eds.) Advances in Information Systems and Technologies. AISC, vol. 206, pp. 279–292. Springer, Heidelberg (2013). https://doi.org/10.1007/978-3-642-36981-0_27

16. Johansson, R.: On case study methodology. Open House Int. **32**, 48–54 (2007). https://doi.org/10.1108/OHI-03-2007-B0006

17. Branski, R.M., Franco, R.A., Lima Júnior, O.: Métodologia de estudo de casos aplicada à logística. In: Conference on XXIV ANPET, pp. 1–12 (2010)

18. Likert, R.: A technique for the measurement of attitudes. https://psycnet.apa.org/record/1933-01885-001. Accessed 30 May 2022

19. Matas, A.: Diseño del formato de escalas tipo Likert: Un estado de la cuestión. Revista Electrónica de Investigación Educativa **20**, 38–47 (2018). https://doi.org/10.24320/REDIE.2018.20.1.1347

20. Brossart, D.F., Laird, V.C., Armstrong, T.W.: Interpreting Kendall's Tau and Tau-U for single-case experimental designs. Cogent Psychol. **5**, 1–26 (2018). https://doi.org/10.1080/23311908.2018.1518687

Parametric Graph Project - Using LEGO Gears for Drawing Curves

Attila Körei[1]([✉])[iD] and Szilvia Szilágyi[2][iD]

[1] Department of Applied Mathematics, University of Miskolc,
Institute of Mathematics, Miskolc, Hungary
matka@uni-miskolc.hu
[2] Department of Analysis, University of Miskolc, Institute of Mathematics,
Miskolc, Hungary
matszisz@uni-miskolc.hu
http://www.uni-miskolc.hu/~matka, http://www.uni-miskolc.hu/~matszisz

Abstract. The parametric equations of plane curves are studied by all engineering and computer science students in the first semester of mathematical analysis course. Managing objects containing a parameter is usually difficult for students, so we developed a game-based learning program for parametric equations of curves, because active teaching methods provide strong support in motivating Generation Z students. In the Parametric Graph Project, we use the principle of operation of Spiropraphs, however, the curves are plotted using LEGO gears. In this paper, we summarize the results of this teaching experiment.

Keywords: Parametric equations for plane curves · Roulettes · Dynamic geometry software · LEGO gears

1 Introduction

Nowadays, game-based learning (GBL) is gaining ground thanks, among other things, to the fact that Generation Z students, who are growing up in a rapidly developing world, are less and less receptive to frontal teaching methods. Higher education is also changing to meet student needs. Therefore, emphasis shall increasingly shift towards learning in small group, in a playful way. Research has shown that game-based learning has a place in higher education as well, since it helps university students to acquire the needed skills. Compared to traditional teaching methods and tools, games provide a familiar, safe environment that makes learning a relaxed experience rather than a stressful one. Games are also great motivational tools [4,6,9,10,16]. Games used in technical higher education predominantly require info-communication tools. We believe that it is

This publication/research has been supported by the New Széchenyi Plan and Next Generation EU program through the project RRF-2.3.1-21-2022-00013, titled "National Laboratory for Social Innovation".

important to invent games that require more traditional, physical objects that can be used in a targeted way to learn a specific subject [7]. In doing so, we must not forget games and toys that are already available in the market. There are many games and toys that can be integrated into the teaching process with almost no changes. The use of LEGO bricks for educational purposes is not a new idea. For decades, the developers of LEGO Education system and other researchers have been working on programs and ideas that are excellent ways to promote playful learning on each level of education [2, 11, 12]. LEGO toys are extremely popular and widespread. With a few exceptions, engineering students possess their own LEGO Technic sets and almost all LEGO Technic boxes contain gears. Therefore, we believe that it is only logical to use LEGO gears for modelling the topic of parametric curves. To draw different curves, you need gears with different diameters and tooth pitches. In this project we used seven different LEGO gears and two racks.

During the first semester analysis course we define and model plane curves in several ways. In the first step we study curves as the graphs of functions or equations involving variables x and y of Cartesian system. Many plane curves fail the so-called vertical line test, so the points of the curve cannot be described as a graph of the function of the variable x. Because of this, in the second step we introduce another way to describe a curve by expressing both coordinates as functions of a third variable t. This variable t is called the parameter of the curve.

What does the parameter mean in mathematics in general? Shortly a parameter is a quantity which changes the characteristics of a system. The distinction between variables and parameters was described by Bard in [1] as follows: *We refer to the relations which supposedly describe a certain physical situation, as a model. Typically, a model consists of one or more equations. The quantities appearing in the equations we classify into variables and parameters. The distinction between these is not always clear cut, and it frequently depends on the context in which the variables appear. Usually a model is designed to explain the relationships that exist among quantities which can be measured independently in an experiment; these are the variables of the model. To formulate these relationships, however, one frequently introduces "constants" which stand for inherent properties of nature (or of the materials and equipment used in a given experiment). These are the parameters.* Obviously, we encounter parameters in many mathematical problems. In teaching mathematics at universities, we deal with many problems given by concrete data. However, a problem can be generalised by replacing one or more pieces of data with a letter expression, i.e. a parameter. The resulting problems often reveal relationships that are difficult to discover when solving problems with concrete data. There are also problems which originally do not contain a parameter, but it is useful to introduce one and solve the problem using a parametric equation.

Managing parameters is very important, but our experience shows that students are finding it increasingly difficult to work with them. An important task of education is to have the students be able to handle expressions, relations and equations containing a parameter. Given that, in addition to the theoretical part, practical experience also plays an important role in the learning process. This year we introduced a game-based learning experiment called Parametric Graph Project (PGP) to the students of the University of Miskolc. In the first part of the project, we drew several notable parametric curves with LEGO gears on graph paper applying the mechanism of Spirograph, and wrote the parametric equations for the curves based on the data measured and calculated using the characteristics of LEGO parts. The correctness of the equations was checked using the Desmos graphing calculator in the second phase of the project. Desmos also gave us the opportunity to investigate how the properties of the curves change when the parameter values are manipulated. In the last phase of PGP, students worked independently. They had to answer questions in the form of an online questionnaire. The questions were related to a family of parametric curves that contained three real parameters in addition to the changing parameter t.

In this paper we present our Parametric Graph Project and its results. After the introductory section, we summarize the basic concepts related to parametric curves and define roulettes, the family of graphs on which we focus. In the third chapter, the three phases of the project are described, and in the last chapter some concluding remarks are made.

2   Parametric Curves

In the rectangular coordinate system there are different ways to define a plane curve. Sometimes the curve is determined as a single function of one variable and we can use the explicit equations $y = f(x)$ or $x = g(y)$. If the explicit expression of the variables is not possible or convenient the curve can be defined by the implicit equation $F(x, y) = 0$ by some kind of relation between x and y. If F is a polynomial, then the curves given in the form $F(x, y) = 0$ are called algebraic curves and the degree of F is called the degree of the curve. For example the conic sections (parabola, hyperbola, ellipse) are algebraic curves of degree two. These curves can be obtained by intersecting a cone with a plane that does not go through the vertex of the cone or they can be defined as geometric location of points satisfying certain properties. Another way to define a curve, which is very common situation in physics and engineering problems, is to describe the trajectory of a moving point. For example, if a particle is moving in the plane with an initial velocity and experiencing a free-fall acceleration, it displays projectile motion. The easiest way to deal with this motion is to analyze it in each directions separately, and give the coordinates of the moving point by different functions, but both its x-coordinate and y-coordinate should depend on the same variable, for example of time. This process is called parametrization, the result of which is the system of parametric equations of the plane curve. More precisely, if x and y are continuous functions of t on an interval $I = [t_1, t_2]$ of real numbers, then the equations

$$x = x(t) \quad \text{and} \quad y = y(t), \quad t_1 \le t \le t_2 \tag{1}$$

are called parametric equations and t is called the parameter. The set of points (x, y) obtained as t varies over the interval I is called the graph of the parametric equations, and it is often referred as a parametric curve.

The general parametric equations for each curve may include variables other than the parameter. Once their values are fixed and the range of parameters is given, the parametric curve under consideration can be represented concretely. For example, the parametric equations

$$x(t) = a\cos t, \quad y(t) = b\sin t, \quad t \in [0, 2\pi], \quad a, b > 0 \qquad (2)$$

determines a full ellipse, centred at the origin. By specifying $a = 3$, $b = 2$ and $I = [0, \pi]$, we got the upper half ellipse with semi-major axis 3 and semi-minor axis 2. Obviously, if $a = b$ in Eq. (2), the obtained parametric curve is a circle.

Working with parametric functions is not easy for students [14], and the situation becomes even more complicated when the parameters include both fixed and changing ones. In order to facilitate understanding of the topic, we looked for a tool that students could use themselves and gain first-hand knowledge of parametric curves with it. This curve modeling tool should also be easy to use and be accessible to everyone. Another task was to find a sufficiently complex curve type that could still be modeled with simple tools. The general curve family of roulettes matched our ideas. A roulette is defined as a curve traced by a point P kept fixed with respect to a closed convex curve M as that curve rolls without slipping along a fixed curve C [18]. The point P is called the pole of the roulette. Roulettes form a general family of curves including many well-known and important curves. When M is a circle, P is on the circumference of M and C is a straight line, then the obtained roulette is the cycloid. This curve arose in connection with two famous problem in physics: the brachistochrone and the tautochrone problems [15]. If the moving circle has radius r and rolls along the x-axis and if one position of P is the origin, then the parametric equations of the cycloid are:

$$x(t) = r(t - \sin t), \quad y(t) = r(1 - \cos t), \quad t \in \mathbb{R}, \qquad (3)$$

where the parameter t is the angle of rotation of the circle ($t = 0$, when P is at the origin).

Denote by d the distance between the pole and the center of M. Obviously, in case of cycloids $d = r$. If $d > r$, then the obtained roulette is called a prolate (or extended) cycloid. The prolate cycloid contains loops, and has parametric equations

$$x(t) = rt - d\sin t, \quad y(t) = r - d\cos t, \quad t \in \mathbb{R}. \qquad (4)$$

A curtate cycloid, sometimes also called a contracted cycloid, formally has the same parametric equations of the prolate cycloid given in equation (4), but in this case $d < r$. It should be mentioned that there is some disagreement in the literature regarding the common name of the curves given by the parametric equations (4). Several authors refer these curves as trochoids, but we follow [8] and [17], where the term trochoid is used for the roulettes traced by points carried by a circle rolling on a fixed circle. There are two types of trochoids based on the circle rolling outside or inside of the fixed circle. Epitrochoid is a plane curve traced by a point on the radius or extended radius of a circle rolling on the outside of a fixed circle, while in case of hypotrochoids the rolling circle is inside the fixed one. For the parametric equations of the trochoids, assume that the center of the fixed circle is at the origin and has radius R and the meaning of r and d is the same as before. The parametric representation for the epitrochoid is

$$x(t) = (R+r)\cos t - d\cos\left(\frac{R+r}{r}t\right), \quad y(t) = (R+r)\sin t - d\sin\left(\frac{R+r}{r}t\right), \quad (5)$$

and for the hypotrochoid is

$$x(t) = (R-r)\cos t + d\cos\left(\frac{R-r}{r}t\right), \quad y(t) = (R-r)\sin t - d\sin\left(\frac{R-r}{r}t\right), \quad (6)$$

where $t \in \mathbb{R}$ denotes the angle between a line through the center of both circles and the x-axis. Similar to cycloids, we distinguish three types depending on the relation between d and r. If $d = r$, then the obtained special trochoids are called epicycloid and hypocycloid. We speak about prolate epitrochoid or hypotrochoid, if $d > r$, and in case of $d < r$ we obtain curtate epitrochoid or hypotrochoid.

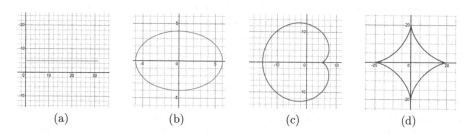

(a)   (b)   (c)   (d)

Fig. 1. Some special roulettes. (a) Cycloid with $r = 5$, $d = 0$ is a line segment. (b) Hypotrochoid with $r = 5$, $d = 1$, $R = 10$ is an ellipse. (c) Epicycloid with $r = d = R = 5$ is a cardioid. (d) Hypocycloid with $r = d = 5$, $R = 20$ is an astroid. The parameter $t \in [0, 2\pi]$ in all cases.

There are many important curves that arise as special cases of roulettes, which is one of the reasons we study this family of curves with students. These special curves can be identified both by the way the roulette is generated and by examining the parametric equations. Let's take a look at some examples.

1) In the case of cycloid, if the pole equals the centre of the moving circle, the resulting roulette is a horizontal straight line segment, since in this case 0 is substituted for d in parametric equation (4) and the coordinate y becomes constant.

2) If we form an epitrochoid, the special case $d = 0$ yields a circle with radius $R + r$. Similarly, a hypotrochoid with $d = 0$ and $R \neq r$ provides a circle with radius $R - r$.

3) A hypotrochoid with $R = 2r$ is an ellipse, because in this case equation (6) simplified to equation (2) with $a = r + d$ and $b = r - d$.

4) A cardioid is a plane curve traced by a point on the perimeter of a circle that is rolling around a fixed circle of the same radius. It means, that the cardioid is an epitrochoid obtained by choosing all three fixed parameters to be the same positive number: $r = R = d$ in equation (5).

5) Choose $r = d = R/4$ in parametric equations (6). We have

$$x(t) = 3r\cos t + r\cos 3t = 3r\cos t + r(4\cos^3 t - 3\cos t) = 4r\cos^3 t$$
$$y(t) = 3r\sin t - r\sin 3t = 3r\sin t - r(3\sin t - 4\sin^3 t) = 4r\sin^3 t, \tag{7}$$

which is the parametric equations for the astroid. Figure 1(a-d) illustrates the special curves listed in 1), 3), 4) and 5).

3   The Parametric Graph Project

3.1   Phase 1 - Drawing Roulettes

As pointed out in the previous chapter, a number of important curves belong to the general family of roulettes, in particular to cycloids and trochoids. On the other hand, when exploring the world of roulettes, you may come across curves that are perhaps not so important, but are unique and spectacular, and therefore attract the interest of students. Of course, this discovery can be done with geometric software that can interpret parametric equations, but it is much more exciting to draw these curves by hand. When designing a device that can draw roulettes, one of the most difficult problems is solving the problem of how to roll a curve along the other without slipping. This problem is solved very cleverly by a game called Spirograph, which was invented by the British engineer Denys Fisher in 1965. Spirograph sets usually consist of two types of main parts called rotors and stators. Rotors are differently sized plastic discs with toothed edges and variously placed holes in the interior. A stator is a plastic ring with gear teeth on both the inside and outside of its circumference, or a stator can be a simple tooth bar. The great idea was that Spirograph uses gears instead of normal wheels to ensure non-slip rolling. A stator is fixed in place on a sheet of paper, one of the rotors is chosen and a colored pen is placed through one of the holes. As the disc is rolled along the inside or outside of the ring or bar, a trochoid or a cycloid curve is drawn. These curves can be only curtate types, because the pen cannot be fixed on the circumference of the moving circles or outside it [3].

The Spirograph is therefore a suitable tool for drawing certain cycloids and trochoids, but unfortunately it is not usually available to students. But even if there were a sufficient number of Spirographs, it would not be easy to produce parametric equations for the curves drawn, since we would have to measure

Fig. 2. LEGO gears used for drawing roulettes.

the radius of the circle(s) that generate the curve and the distance between the pole and the centre of the rolling circle very precisely. Therefore, instead of using a Spirograph, we used the more accessible LEGO parts, namely gears and racks, to draw the roulettes in the project. Entering the data for the parametric equations is also easier in this case, as the gear radii and the pole distance d can be easily calculated using LEGO units. The pitch radius of a LEGO gear is just the half of the number of teeth, where the pitch radius represents the distance from the center of each gear such that the meshing gears touch. The rotors of our Spirograph were, of course, gears that had holes other than the central hole, because this gave us the chance to draw a variety of curves. Once one of the holes in the rotor is selected as the pole, the distance between the pole and the centre of the moving circle can be calculated using the fact that the centres of two adjacent collinear holes are 8 mm apart. Figure 2 shows the different LEGO elements used in the project. Among these parts the straight gear rack provides the fixed line when drawing cycloids, the four, attached 35 tooth curved racks form a big circle with radius 70 mm, which was the stator for plotting hypotrochoids. In addition, we had seven different sizes of gears, with 12, 20, 24, 28, 36, 40 and 60 teeth. Any of these could be the stator if drawing an epitrochoid, or could be the moving circle for cycloids or trochoids. With the exception of the two smallest gears, we can have the pole in any of the holes.

With this equipment and some coloured pens, students had the opportunity to draw and study different roulettes (Fig. 3). They have gained experience of what happens when they change gears or choose a new pole position. They noticed that in some cases the pen would return to the starting point after one or two rolls, while other curves required many more turns to return to the initial point. This problem is related to the period of the trochoid which depends on the ratio of the radii of the fixed and moving circles. If $r/R = p/q$, where p and q are relatively prime natural numbers, then the period of the trochoid is $2\pi p$

Fig. 3. Students draw different trochoids using LEGO gears.

[13]. If r/R is a rational number then we get a closed algebraic curve with finite period, otherwise the curve will never return to the initial starting point.

It soon became clear that there are a limited number of roulettes that we can produce with our simple tools. However, there were still some nice curves among the drawings, which the students liked and got them interested in the topic, so they were more enthusiastic to take the next step and study roulettes with graphical software.

3.2   Phase 2 - Desmos Graphic Calculator

A dynamic geometry software (DGS) provides the opportunity to create and manipulate geometric constructions in an interactive manner. In recent years, these programs become more advanced and popular and its use in all levels of mathematical education increased. A DGS, such as GeoGebra, can help primary school students to understand fundamental geometric concepts and support university students in their Calculus course by analyzing function graphs. Parametric curves can also be easily visualised using a DGS, and the dynamic property means that the formation of such a curve can be traced point by point. If the curve is defined as the trajectory of a moving point the process can be illustrated by moving animations. A well-constructed educational material supported by geometric software can provide a deeper understanding of parametric curves, as well as their hidden properties [5].

In our project Desmos graphing calculator was used to plot and study parametric curves. Desmos is a free application which can be downloaded to a mobile phone or a tablet so it is particularly suitable for classroom work. The program manages parametric curves in a simple and natural way. To plot a curve you should enter the parametric equations $(x(t), y(t))$ and specify an interval for the parameter t. If the formula contains additional variables you can give the values of them or change these values with a slider to see the effect of the change on the plotted curve. You can control the appearance of the graph by adding labels, changing the colour of the graph or customizing the coordinate system.

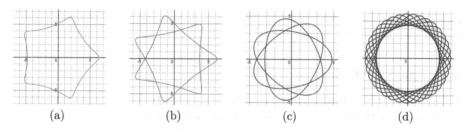

Fig. 4. Some hypotrochoids which could be drawn with the available LEGO gears. (a) $R = 7$, $r = 1.4$, $d = 0.8$, $t \in [0, 2\pi]$. (b) $R = 7$, $r = 2$, $d = \sqrt{1.6}$, $t \in [0, 4\pi]$. (c) $R = 7$, $r = 3$, $d = 0.8$, $t \in [0, 6\pi]$. (d) $R = 7$, $r = 1.8$, $d = 0.8$, $t \in [0, 18\pi]$.

The students quickly learned the basic functions of Desmos, and after entering the equations and parameters of the curves they had drawn, they realized that the software showed the same curves they have produced using the gears. Figure 4 shows some of the curves made by Desmos that have previously drawn by the students. By combining the possibilities offered by the software and their own experience of drawing, they can identify the exact parametric equations of the studied curves. For example, the hypotrochoid shown in Fig. 4(c) can be represented by the parametric equations

$$x(t) = 4\cos t + 0.8 \cos \frac{4}{3}t, \quad y(t) = 4\sin t - 0.8\sin \frac{4}{3}t, \quad t \in [0, 6\pi]. \qquad (8)$$

Desmos also made it easier to find the period of the curves by setting the interval of the parameters t to $[0, p]$, where p is the smallest number at which the start and end points of the curve coincide. Figure 5 shows an epitrochoid with different parameter ranges, and the period is the length of the smallest parameter interval of t for which a closed curve is obtained.

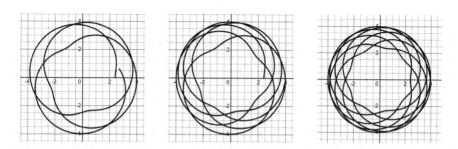

Fig. 5. Epitrochoid with parameters $r = 1.4$, $R = 1.8$, $d = 0.8$ is drawn after 3, 5 and 7 rolls. $r/R = 7/9$, the period is $2\pi \cdot 7 = 14\pi$.

With Desmos, of course, we can examine not only the curves that we produced with our modest tools. Using the software, students have almost unlimited possibilities to explore the world of roulettes and visualize countless eye-catching curves with just a few clicks.

3.3 Phase 3 - Testing

In this part of the project, students work independently. Participants were given a link to access the test through Google Classroom. Their task was to complete a 10-question online test in 30 minutes. Simple multiple-choice tests were designed to measure the level of knowledge, i.e. each question required only one correct answer out of four options to be given at the time of completion, which was written as a textual instruction on the test. Each test question applied to the following parametric curve

$$x(t) = (a + c\cos t)\cos t, \quad y(t) = (b + c\cos t)\sin t, \tag{9}$$

where $a, b, c \in \mathbb{R}$ and $t \in [0, 2\pi]$. So we have three parameters, which should be fixed and the moving parameter t. We have chosen this family of curves because with the appropriate values of parameters a, b, c we can obtain equations for several notable curves. For example circles, ellipses, cardioids as it is shown in Fig. 6.

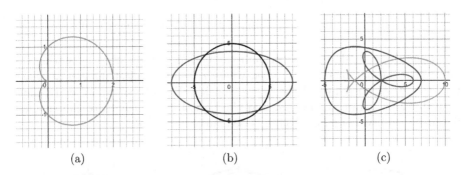

(a)   (b)   (c)

Fig. 6. Curves obtained by different choice of parameters in equation (9): (a) $a = b = c = 1$, (b) $a = 8, b = 4, c = 0$ (blue), $a = b = 5, c = 0$ (black), (c) $a = 6, b = -4, c = 1$ (green), $a = 2, b = -2, c = 4$ (purple), $a = 6, b = 1, c = 4$ (orange). (Color figure online)

The test was created using Microsoft Forms, the application used throughout the semester to create the regular weekly tests. As with the other tests, the questions in this test did not only cover the learning material of PGP, but also asked for correlations that had been learned previously. The students used their own laptops to complete the test, so they had the Desmos graphing calculator at their disposal. There were some test questions that did not require the use of Desmos, the answer could be given by the students based on the theoretical knowledge they had learned about the notable curves, knowing the exact value of the parameters a, b, c. However, some questions were easier to answer when Desmos was used in the solution. 87 students participated in the PGP, all of whom answered all the questions. The average score was 8.4. None of the students answered all the questions correctly. Figure 7 shows the total number of correct answers per questions.

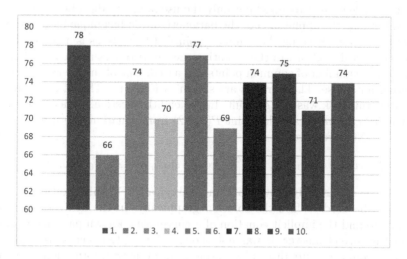

Fig. 7. Correct answers given in PGP Test. The horizontal axis shows the number of questions and the vertical axis the number of correct answers.

The first question had the most correct answers. We asked that what type of curve we get, when $a = b = c = 1$? In this case the parametric equation of curve is

$$x(t) = (1 + \cos t) \cos t, \quad y(t) = (1 + \cos t) \sin t, \quad t \in [0, 2\pi]. \quad (10)$$

The parametric equations for the $r(\varphi) = 1 + \cos \varphi$, $\varphi \in [0, 2\pi]$ cardioid was easily recognizable, so it is not surprising that so many answers were correct. The next question received the fewest good answers. Only 66 respondents knew for which value of a, b and c you get a vertical line segment of length two units for the given parametric curve. For this question, it would have been worth using Desmos. After plotting at most three curves, the correct answer could have been given. In the third question, we asked about the measure of the area of the flat surface intersected by the curve $a = b = 2$, $c = 0$. In this case, the curve is a circle with centre of origin and radius of two units. Many students recognised this famous curve and were able to calculate the area to be measured using the well-known formula. In the fourth question, we gave the implicit equation of a circle centered $P(-1, 0)$ with unit radius. We asked, for which values of a, b, c the same circle is given? This was one of the more difficult questions, since it can be solved by synthesizing the relations we have learned. The next question had the second most correct answers. In the fifth question, we wanted to know: for a fixed value of t_0, where is the point of the curve on the plane? If $t_0 = \frac{\pi}{2}$, then $\cos \frac{\pi}{2} = 0$ and $\sin \frac{\pi}{2} = 1$, i.e. the point is $P(0, b)$ and it is on the y-axis. Although many students recognized the cardioid curve in the first question, 18 students had problems finding the parameters a, b, c for the equation (9) in the sixth problem for the other cardioid $r(\varphi) = 2 - 2 \cos \varphi$, $\varphi \in [0, 2\pi]$. This proved to be the second most difficult problem, as it required not only the use of knowledge about parametric curves, but also the application of the parametrization technique for curves with polar coordinates. Finding the common points of two curves is a standard task in mathematical analysis. In the seventh question, two parametric equations are given and the number of common points was asked. One of them was a circle and the other an ellipse. Their graphs are shown in Fig. 6(b). The 74 good answers show that this task was not difficult. In the eighth question, we asked for what parameter t_0 do we obtain the point $P(2, -2)$ from equations (9) if $a = b = \sqrt{2}$ and $c = 2$? Now we have

$$(\sqrt{2} + \cos t_0) \cos t_0 = 2, \quad (\sqrt{2} + \cos t_0) \sin t_0 = -2, \quad t_0 \in [0, 2\pi]. \tag{11}$$

The solution is relatively easy to obtain algebraically. For this question, Desmos could also be used to find the solution graphically. In the next question, the task was to find the implicit equation of a curve using known parameters a, b, c. To get the correct answer, it was not enough to read the centre and radius of the circle from the figure drawn by Desmos, algebraic transformations were also needed. Despite this, 81.6 % of students answered the question correctly. In the last task, we asked a question linked to the graph in Fig. 6(c). The correct answer required the use of Desmos.

Based on good test results and student feedback, PGP is considered a success and will be repeated next year.

4   Conclusion

Parametric Graph Project was designed to discuss the topic of parametric curves by engaging students in an active learning process. In our view better results can be achieved if knowledge is taught in context by combining theory and practice (experimentation) in the right proportion. The three-phase project presented in this paper have been successful in raising students' interest related to parametric curves. The attractive figures drawn with LEGO gears in the first phase motivated the students to use of the graphical software introduced in the second phase. With Desmos, the experience of drawing by hand could be combined with the knowledge of concrete curves, including formulas, periodicity, parameter evaluation. Familiarity with the functions of the graphical software proved particularly useful in the third phase of the project in which students could test their knowledge. The results show that students have acquired a deeper knowledge of the subject, which they will hopefully remember for a longer period of time thanks to the experimental phase and the visual experience provided by Desmos.

As one of the next steps we would like to increase the variety of curves that can be drawn using gears. One way to achieve this is to use the potential of 3D printing to produce new gears in different sizes. In addition, we plan to build a programmable drawing robot which moves a gear inside or outside on a fixed gear and a pole is attached to the moving gear at any arbitrary position. This construction will make it possible to plot all three types of trochoids (not only curtate ones) completing the discussion of the topic.

References

1. Bard, Y.: Nonlinear Parameter Estimation. Academic Press, New York (1974)
2. Gura, M.: Getting started with LEGO robotics: a guide for K12 educators. International Society for Technology in Education (2011)
3. Hall, L.M.: Trochoids, Roses, and Thorns - beyond the spirograph. College Math. J. **23**(1), 20–35 (1992). https://doi.org/10.2307/2686194
4. Hartman, A., Gommer, L.: To play or not to play: on the motivational effects of games in engineering education. Euro. J. Eng. Educ. **46**(3), 1–25 (2021). https://doi.org/10.1080/03043797.2019.1690430
5. Kabaca, T., Aktumen, M.: Using GeoGebra as an expressive modeling tool: discovering the anatomy of the cycloid's parametric equation. In: Anthone, V.N. (ed.) GeoGebra, The New Language For The Third Millennium, vol. 1, pp. 63–81 (2010)
6. Kordaki, M., Gousiou, A.: Digital card games in education: a ten year systematic review. Comput. Educ. **109**, 122–161 (2017). https://doi.org/10.1016/j.compedu.2017.02.011
7. Körei, A., Szilágyi, S., Török, Z.: Integrating didactic games in higher education: benefits and challenges. Teach. Math. Comput. Sci. **19**(1), 1–15 (2021). https://doi.org/10.5485/TMCS.2021.0517
8. Lockwood, H.: A Book of Curves. Cambridge U.P, Cambridge (1967)
9. McGonigal, J.: Reality is Broken: Why Games Make us Better and How they can Change the World. Penguin Press, New York (2011)
10. Mohr, K.A.J., Mohr, E.S.: Understanding generation Z students to promote a contemporary learning environment. J. Empower. Teach. Excellence 1(1) (2017). https://doi.org/10.15142/T3M05T
11. Montesa-Andres, J.O., Garrigós-Simón, F.J., Narangajavana, Y.: A proposal for using Lego serious play in education. In: Peris-Ortiz, M., Garrigós-Simón, F.J., Pechuán, I.G. (eds.) Innovation and Teaching Technologies, pp. 99–107. Springer, Cham (2014). https://doi.org/10.1007/978-3-319-04825-3_10
12. Nerantzi, C., James, A.: LEGO® for university learning: inspiring academic practice in higher education (2019). https://doi.org/10.5281/zenodo.2813448
13. Phan-Yamada, T., Gwin, E.: Hypocycloids and Hypotrochoids. MathAMATYC Educator **6**(1), 1–3 (2014)
14. Stalvey, H.: The teaching and learning of parametric functions: a baseline study. Dissertation, Georgia State University (2014). https://doi.org/10.57709/5815413
15. Stewart, J.: Multivariable Calculus, 7th edn. Cengage Learning, Brooks/Cole (2011)
16. Watts, E.: University students who play calculus video game score higher on exams. Texas A&M Today (2019). https://today.tamu.edu/2019/02/13/university-students-who-play-calculus-video-game-score-higher-on-exams/

17. Yates, R.C.: Curves and Their Properties, Classics in Mathematics Education, vol. 4. National Council of Teachers of Mathematics (1974)
18. Zwillinger, D. (ed.): CRC Standard Mathematical Tables and Formulae, 33 Edition. Chapman and Hall/CRC, New York (2018). https://doi.org/10.1201/9781315154978

A Matching Algorithm to Assess Web Interfaces

José Paulo Leal[(⊠)] and Marco Primo

CRACS - INESC-TEC & Department of Computer Science of the Faculty of Science, University of Porto, Porto, Portugal
zp@dcc.fc.up.pt, up201800388@edu.fc.up.pt

Abstract. The work presented in this article is part of ongoing research on the automated assessment of simple web applications. The proposed algorithm compares two interfaces by mapping their elements, using properties to identify those with the same role in both interfaces. The algorithm proceeds in three stages: firstly, it selects the relevant elements from both interfaces; secondly, it refines elements' attributes, excluding some and computing new ones; finally, it matches elements based on attribute similitude. The article includes an experiment to validate the algorithm as an assessment tool. As part of this experiment, a set of experts classified multiple web interfaces. Statistical analysis found a significant correlation between classifications made by the algorithm and those made by experts. The article also discusses the exploitation of the algorithm's output to access both the layout and functionality of a web interface and produce feedback messages in an automated assessment environment, which is planned as future research.

Keywords: Automatic assessment · Web interfaces · Learning environments

1 Introduction

Web interfaces are typically built using more than one language, namely HTML, CSS, and JavaScript [4,10,13], rely on user interaction for input rather than data streams, and normally receive data as events without a predefined order. These characteristics of graphical user interfaces in general, and Web interfaces in particular, inhibit the use of black-box techniques to evaluate them.

We propose a matching algorithm that is able to map elements between two graphical interfaces with a similar layout. The proposed algorithm is flexible enough to recognize equivalent elements with different types, slightly different sizes or organized using different structures.

Element mapping is the core of the proposed algorithm. Using their properties, it is possible to identify elements from both interfaces - reference interface and tested interface - that play the same graphical role. The properties used in the matching process are either original or derived: original properties are

T. Guarda et al. (Eds.): ARTIIS 2022, CCIS 1675, pp. 115–126, 2022.
https://doi.org/10.1007/978-3-031-20319-0_9

obtained directly from the DOM API, and derived properties reflect spatial relations among elements in the interface. The output of this matching process is the cornerstone to evaluate the layout of a web application and its functionality.

A previous version of this matching algorithm [0] had a limitation: it assumed that non-leaf elements were only used for placement and did not evaluate those with graphical impact. For example, if a web interface has a container to group widgets, and this container has a different background color, it will add graphical differences to the interface. In this case, although the algorithm correctly assessed the widgets, it failed to assess the container that grouped them. The current version solves that shortcoming and produces good quality assessments. Our validation shows that the assessments produced by the algorithm correlate with 99% certainty with those of human experts.

The rest of this article is organized as follows. Section 2 presents a literature review on approaches to compare user interfaces. Section 3 details the proposed algorithm and its implementation. Section 4 validates the proposed matching algorithm by comparing it with a panel of experts. Section 5 describes how the algorithm can be used in an automatic assessment environment. Finally, Sect. 6 summarizes of the main contributions and identifies opportunities to continue this research.

2   State of the Art

Due to the growing number of students in programming classes, it is impossible to evaluate each student's exercises efficiently using manual methods [12,17]. For this reason, most schools today use automated assessment environments to support students in the learning process, particularly in programming languages [12].

Most programming language assessment systems use the so-called model black-box model [2]. In this model, the program is assessed using a set of test cases. Each test case has an input and the corresponding expected output. The assessed program is executed with the input, and the obtained output is compared with the expected one. If both outputs are equal in all test cases, the program is accepted; otherwise, it is rejected.

This assessment model has been popular for a long time [14] as it is simple to implement and programming language independent. However, it is far from being perfect. As its name suggests, it assesses the execution side effects, not the execution itself. Moreover, creating a set of tests to cover all the relevant corner cases is not straightforward.

Another shortcoming of this assessment model is that it is only applicable if the input is a data stream following a strict format. In graphic user interfaces (GUI), mouse and keyboard events deliver data directly to widgets in no particular order. For instance, the user may fill in a form's fields in any order before pressing a button to submit it.

Unsurprisingly, the GUI automatic assessment environments described in the literature inspect the GUI structure and do not use a black-box approach. Also, they are language-dependent, rely on a specific windowing toolkit, and require the identification of GUI elements to enable assessment.

English proposes JEWL [5], a simplified Java windowing toolkit based on Swing used both to create simple GUIs and to access them. It constrains widgets from the student's attempt and the teacher's reference solution to use a particular ID to compare them. Moreover, it supports only positioning using coordinates and discards the use of layout managers. Thorn and others follow a similar approach [15]. They developed a simplified GUI toolkit to support the development of JUnit tests to assess student Java programs.

The system proposed by Gray and Higgins [6] uses introspection on Java programs with a file describing the intended action to perform on the GUI. As in the system proposed by English, widgets must be identified in order to be assessed.

The previous approaches were developed for GUIs coded in a single language, namely Java, not for web applications. Nevertheless, there are a few approaches to comparing web pages, such as page internal structure or image comparison.

Štěpánek and Šimková [16] proposed algorithms to compare the internal structure of web pages. These algorithms aim at detecting plagiarized web pages and are characterized as frequency analysis, finding the same tree paths, and finding the largest subtree. Although these algorithms compare the similarity between two web pages, they are inadequate for assessing web interfaces for educational purposes. Graphically equivalent web interfaces can vary in how they are coded using HTML and CSS, and algorithms that compare the internal structure force the student to follow exactly the same structure as the reference interface.

An approach using image comparison is proposed by the software *diffee* [8]. The usage of image comparison can be an alternative way to quickly check the visual difference between two web interfaces. This strategy consists of a pixel-by-pixel comparison in each RGBA channel between the active layer and the background layer. Similar pixels become black and pixels with visual alteration will change in color by taking the absolute value of their difference: $|a - b|$ on each RGBA channel.

To the best of the authors' knowledge, no previous attempt has been made to compare web interfaces with an educational purpose. The systems described in the literature to graphically compare web pages have very different goals such as detecting phishing sites [3,11,18], and are focused on spotting small differences rather than ignoring them.

3   Web Interface Matching Algorithm

The main goal of the proposed algorithm is to map between similar elements on two web interfaces: a reference web interface provided by the exercise author, and another submitted by a student attempting to solve an exercise.

The algorithm is independent of the internal structure of both interfaces, judging their similarity based only on visual features. In addition, it is designed to help produce incremental feedback to support students in overcoming difficulties in their coding process.

The matching process is driven by attribute values of elements on both web interfaces. If a pair of elements with a visual impact, each from a different web interface, have similar attribute values, they are candidates to be matched. Moreover, if such a pair is more similar to all other possible pairs, it is confirmed as a match.

However, attributes pose different challenges when used for visual matching. On the one hand, only attributes with an impact on visualization are relevant; all others must be discarded. On the other hand, the raw values of a few attributes with a decisive impact on visualization would have unintended results. For instance, similar values of position coordinates and dimensions frequently fail to match elements with the same visual role on both web interfaces.

Based on these insights the proposed algorithm is structured in 3 stages: selection of elements to be matched, refinement of attributes of those elements, and matching of elements based on refined values. Each of these stages is detailed in the following subsections.

3.1   Element Selection

The main objective of this first stage is to produce two sets with elements from both interfaces - the elements to be matched. Each set contains graphically relevant elements, which are elements that change the layout of web interfaces.

Web interfaces are structured using HTML documents. These documents create a tree-like structure whose nodes are *elements*. However, not all elements in an HTML document are graphically relevant. For instance, a valid HTML document must have a `head` element containing general information such as document metadata and references to external files, such as style sheets and JavaScript files. But even the descendants of the HTML `body` element are not all equally relevant to the final visualization.

Consider a chessboard as the intended web interface, composed of 64 squares in an eight-by-eight grid, with alternating black and white backgrounds. There are several ways to create this layout em HTML: with a `table` element, with a `flex` container, with `grid` container, with floating `div` elements for columns, etc. These approaches can produce the same visualization with different structures, some with three intermediate levels (e.g. a table with rows and cells) and others with just 1 (e.g. a container using CSS positioning). The structural elements, i.e. those acting as containers, are instrumental for positioning black and white squares but are not themselves displayed on the web interface.

In general, the elements that most contribute to visualization are the leaves of an HTML document. These include elements such as the chessboard squares in the previous example, styled with alternating background colors. It should be noted that these elements can have different types such as `div` or `span` and still have the same appearance. Another kind of leaves on web interfaces are *widgets*, such as buttons or input fields. These usually correspond to HTML form elements but they too can be produced in different ways. For instance, a button can be created from a `button` element, a submission `input` element, or a `div` element styled with CSS.

Leave elements in the HTML documents contribute more to visualization than structural elements. Thus, all leave elements are selected for mapping. In most cases, structural (i.e. non-leave) elements contribute indirectly to visualization by changing the position and dimension of leave elements and are discarded. However, structural elements may have a direct impact on the visualization, in which case they are also selected for mapping.

This stage uses the DOM API [19] to gather all relevant predefined elements, which are the leaf elements. Relevant non-leaf elements are gathered only if certain properties have been modified, such as background color or border width.

3.2   Attribute Refinement

After the initial stage, the algorithm has two sets with HTML elements retrieved from both pages. However, the algorithm does not need all the properties of each HTML element. This stage removes most element properties, leaving only those relevant to the matching process. For instance, properties such as tag, id, and name are removed, and properties such as text, src, and style are kept.

On the other hand, the original properties directly related to positioning – x, y, width and height – are inadequate for matching. A matching based on these properties would not allow small variations in layout due to different positioning approaches.

New properties have to be added to create a satisfactory mapping. These are called *derived* properties and are based on the position of each element in the interface. Instead of position coordinates, they reflect the spatial relationships between elements. Derived properties allow the algorithm to determine how many other elements are in each quadrant of its Cartesian plane, using the upper left corner of the referent element as the origin. Using spatial relationships, the algorithm is able to map interface elements with similar, but not necessarily equal, positions and sizes.

To illustrate spatial relationships consider Fig. 1 representing a web interface with 3 non-overlapping elements, aligned horizontally, with IDs 1, 2, and 3. Using the upper left corner as referential, following the convention in windowing systems, one can define relative spatial relations with the other elements. For element 1, elements 2 and 3 are in quadrant 4, as they are mostly to the right and below the upper left corner of element 2.

This stage adds derived attributes to each element with the number of other elements (the element itself is not counted) lying in each of the 4 quadrants, using its upper left corner and referential. In the example of Fig. 1: element 1 has 2 elements in the 4th quadrant; element 1 has 1 element in the 3rd quadrant and 1 in the 4th, and element 3 has 2 elements in the 3rd quadrant. The unmentioned quadrants of each element count as 0 elements.

3.3   Element Matching

At this stage, elements belonging to both sets are matched using a similarity score based on the comparison of properties with equal values. The contribution

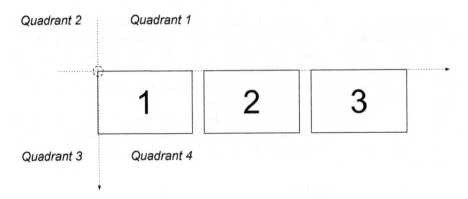

Fig. 1. Spatial relations among elements taking as reference the element 1.

of each property to the score is pondered by a weight reflecting its graphic impact. Properties with higher visual impact have higher weights.

The mapping is iteratively created by comparing elements belonging to the sets computed by the previous stage. At each iteration is selected the pair of elements with the highest score. This process is repeated with the remaining elements. That is, those already paired are ignored.

After the matching, a set with differences in properties on paired elements is computed. For each pair, an object detailing these differences is added to the set of differences. If an element cannot be matched, an object detailing this is also added to the set of differences.

The element matching stage produces two outputs: a set mapping equivalent elements, and a set of differences between matching elements. These two sets are the output of the matching algorithm. They provide a comprehensive comparison of the two web interfaces regarding their visual appearance.

4   Validation of the Matching Algorithm

An experiment was conducted to verify if the matching algorithm can be used as an assessment tool, and it discriminates errors as effectively as humans. Several web interfaces were assessed both by the matching algorithms and by a panel of experts, and the results were statistically compared.

4.1   Web Interfaces

The experiment was based on 3 web interfaces commonly found in introductory web programming courses. From these reference interfaces, variations were created by adding changes to the HTML and/or CSS codes. The amount of change varies significantly, ranging from drastically different to very similar to

the original. The interfaces chosen as starting points to create variations were
the following:

Chessboard
> The existence of 64 leaf elements (the squares) allows us to assess whether
> the algorithm is capable of handling a significant number of elements.

Curriculum vitæ
> This interface has several types of widgets and other leaf elements scattered
> on the interface. It tests how the algorithm deals with varied element types.

Dialog Box
> A challenging interface that has an element over the main layout. It tests the
> algorithm when the web interface has structural (non-leaf) elements with a
> visual role.

4.2   Web Interface Assessment

The similarity between variants and reference web interfaces was accessed by a
panel of experts. This panel was composed of 3 graduate students of the same
age - 21 years old -, 2 of which were females. All of them completed a web
technologies course in the 90% percentile. They were asked to grade each pair
of reference web interfaces and variants on a 0-to-20 scale. For each variant, its
grade was taken as the average of the grades given by the 3 experts.

The matching algorithm result was converted into a grade to compare it with
the experts' grades. The matching interface output is a list of differences and
a list of pairs of elements. The number of paired elements was divided by the
number of elements on the page and the result was multiplied by 20, to match
the range of experts' grades.

4.3   Statistical Analysis

Grades were analyzed using Spearman's rank correlation [20]. This statistical
measure, denoted as ρ, is commonly used to evaluate the relationship between
ordinal variables. It ranges between 1 and -1: if variables are in the same order
then $\rho = 1$; if they are in inverse order then $\rho = -1$; as the orders are less
correlated ρ approaches 0.

In this experiment, Spearman's rank correlation was used to compare the
orders of the experts' and algorithm's grades. The exact grades are less relevant
than their order. A variant with a higher grade is expected to be closer to the
reference solution than a variant with a lesser grade, independently of its value.

In total, 12 interfaces were evaluated both by the algorithm and the experts,
with 4 interface variants for each of the 3 reference interfaces. The ρ computed
for the 12 variants was 0.6823. The critical value for a significance of 0.01 with
$n = 12$ is 0.671. This means that the grades computed from the mappings
produced by the algorithm correlate with those of the experts' panel with a 99%
certainty. Thus, the algorithm can be used to automate the assessment of web
interfaces.

Table 1. Average grades of experts (left) and grades of the algorithm (right) for each interface variant, with Spearman's ρ

	Chessboard	Curriculum vitæ	Dialog box
Variants	18 20	15 20	19 20
	15 18	12 14	10 12
	17 18	16 16	15 16
	12 14	15 14	13 16
ρ	0.94868	0.70711	0.40000

Table 1 breaks down the results by each of the reference interfaces and their variants. For each interface, average expert grades are on the left and computed grades on the right, rounded to the nearest integer. The last row shows the ρ of each interface. These figures show a much higher correlation for the chessboard variants than the dialog box. In this case, a window (the dialog box) is positioned over the rest of the interface, making less relevant the spatial properties computed by the algorithm. This results from the procedure to compute grades from web interface differences, described in the previous subsection. In future research, we plan to adjust it to handle these cases. It should be noted that for individual interfaces the number of data points is too small ($n = 4$) to use a critical value for significance. Nevertheless, the number of data points for all variants ($n = 12$) allows us to conclude the significance of the correlation between the grades assigned by experts and computed by the algorithm.

In addition, it was observed that CSS properties related to positioning, such as margin, position, and float, have been shown to have a substantial impact on the number of mapped elements, the opposite happens with the structuring of HTML, thus ensuring the strong relationship of the mapping interfaces with based on their visual characteristics.

5   Web Interface Assessment

The proposed matching algorithm will be instrumental in building an environment to assess web interfaces. Such an environment must assess both the visual appearance and the functionality of web interfaces. It should also help students to overcome their difficulties by providing meaningful feedback. The following subsections explain how the proposed algorithm is expected to support both functional assessment and incremental feedback.

5.1   Functional Assessment

As shown in the previous section, the output of the matching algorithm can be used to assess its layout and visual properties. This subsection explains how it can also be the basis to access its functionality when the layouts of both web interfaces are similar.

If the reference and student web interfaces are too dissimilar, a bijective mapping between the elements of both interfaces may be unavailable. In this case, only the difference-set produced by the matching algorithm can be used for assessment.

Otherwise, if the two web interfaces are similar enough and a bijective mapping is available, this mapping can be the basis for functional assessment. It should be noted that the matching algorithm may produce both a bijective mapping and a nonempty difference-set.

If a bijective mapping is available, it can be used along with unit tests to assess the functionality of the interface. Firstly, unit tests are created for the reference Web interface. A typical unit test will find elements on the interface, change their properties and/or execute methods on them, and then check assertions on these elements. These unit tests can be automatically adapted to the web interface under assessment by replacing all element references. The bijective mapping is used to drive this replacement. Finally, the adapted unit tests can be applied to the interface being assessed.

After the visual and functional evaluation, many error messages may result and it is important to make the student aware of the most important ones. Presenting too many messages at once may be counterproductive. To address this issue a feedback manager is proposed.

5.2   Feedback Manager

The biggest challenge of automated assessment is to provide effective feedback that helps students overcome their difficulties [1,7]. The proposed feedback manager intends to be incremental, displaying short messages at each student attempt. These messages will be increasingly more informative and different from those previously shown to the same student, for the same exercise.

The feedback manager takes as input the result from both evaluations, functional and visual, and processes them. The generated reports are kept in memory until the exercise is solved, influencing the generation of future ones.

The feedback manager's internal process sorts visual differences from the most general to the most specific ones, giving more weight to messages reporting the lack or excess of elements than those reporting wrong element's properties. Errors related to unit tests detail those that failed or passed.

An example of an automatic assessment using the proposed features to evaluate interfaces layout and functionality is presented in Fig. 2. It illustrates successive steps of a student solving a web interface exercise until it is accepted, guided by the feedback manager.

The reference interface consists of a dialog box over an interface with a title and a navigation bar. The navigation bar buttons do not have any functionality associated with them, they only add visual features. Clicks on the buttons labeled "yes" or "no" hide the dialog box.

After the first submission, the matching algorithm produces a list of differences that is used by the feedback manager. However, the generated set of differences lists some elements from the reference interface that are not in the

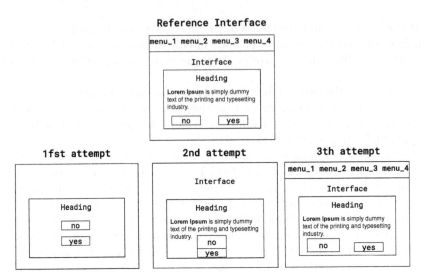

Fig. 2. Incremental assessment guided by reports from the feedback manager

tested interface, which means that the mapping algorithm was not able to create a bijective map. Then, the feedback manager builds a report message listing those with highest severity. This first feedback message replied to the student does not have much information and is not overly assertive. For instance, the message could be "Some elements are missing".

The student then adds the missing text but not the buttons. After the second submission, the feedback manager detects the missing buttons in the differences set. The feedback manager then generates a more assertive message, such as: "The button elements are still missing. There are also wrong spatial relationships among elements".

Finally, in the third submission, the algorithm manages to make the correct mapping between all the elements and marks the interface as visually correct. This guarantees that the tested interface has a layout similar to the reference interface.

Since both interfaces have a similar layout, a functional evaluation can also be performed. In this way, the unit tests are performed on the tested interface and it is checked if any errors arise from them.

Whether or not there are errors regarding the unit tests, the feedback manager delivers messages to the student detailing which unit tests failed or passed. This way the student can write features in the tested interface that approximate the functionality of both interfaces.

6 Conclusion

Automated assessment of web interfaces is particularly challenging since traditional black-box approaches are hard to use, if not impossible. The main contribution of this paper is a web interface matching algorithm that can be used as an assessment tool. A validation performed with 12 pairs of web interfaces assessed both the proposed algorithm and a panel of experts showed a correlation with 99% certainty. A secondary contribution is a plan on how to use this algorithm to enhance the functional assessment of web interfaces and the generation of incremental feedback.

The ultimate goal of this research is a learning environment targeted to web languages and technologies. Our immediate plan is to improve and extend the proposed algorithm. To improve it, we will fine-tune different features: the coordinate origin used to compute spatial relationships; property weights used in element matching; the procedure to compute grades from set differences.

We also plan to extend the algorithm to evaluate interfaces both visually and functionally, as discussed in Sect. 5. We intend to manage feedback messages through an incremental manager that facilitates student learning through intelligently structured messages.

The integration of this algorithm into an existing automatic evaluation environment aimed at web technology programming is also under consideration. A candidate environment for this integration is LearnJS - A JavaScript Learning Playground [0] [9].

Acknowledgments. This paper is based on the work done within the Automatic Assessment Of Computing Exercises project supported by the European Union's Erasmus Plus programme (agreement no. 72020-1-ES01-KA226-VET-096004)

References

1. Askew, S.: Feedback for learning. Routledge (2004)
2. Comella-Dorda, S., Wallnau, K.C., Seacord, R.C., Robert, J.E.: A survey of black-box modernization approaches for information systems. In ICSM, pp. 173–183 (2000)
3. Corona, I., et al.: DeltaPhish: detecting phishing webpages in compromised websites. In: Foley, S.N., Gollmann, D., Snekkenes, E. (eds.) ESORICS 2017. LNCS, vol. 10492, pp. 370–388. Springer, Cham (2017). https://doi.org/10.1007/978-3-319-66402-6_22
4. Duckett J.: Web design with HTML, CSS, JavaScript and jQuery set, vol. 1. Wiley IN (2014)
5. English, J.: Automated assessment of GUI programs using jewl. ACM SIGCSE Bull. **36**(3), 137–141 (2004)
6. Gray, G.R., Higgins, C.A.: An introspective approach to marking graphical user interfaces. ACM SIGCSE Bull. 38(3), 43–47 (2006)
7. Hattie, J., Timperley, H.: The power of feedback. Rev. Educ. Res. **77**(1), 81–112 (2007)

8. Kravets, U., Oliff, C.: zub4t/diffee: first release. In diffee - Instant visual diffing in the browser. Zenodo (2021)

9. Queirós, R.: Learning JavaScript in a Local Playground. In: Rodrigues, R., Janousek, J., Ferreira, L., Coheur, L., Batista, F., Oliveira, H.G., eds, 8th Symposium on Languages, Applications and Technologies (SLATE 2019), volume 74 of OpenAccess Series in Informatics (OASIcs), pp. 10:1–10:11, Dagstuhl, Germany (2019). Schloss Dagstuhl-Leibniz-Zentrum fuer Informatik

10. Robbins, J.N.: Learning web design: a beginner's guide to HTML, CSS, JavaScript, and web graphics. O'Reilly Media, Inc. (2012)

11. Roopak S.,Thomas, T.: A novel phishing page detection mechanism using html source code comparison and cosine similarity. In 2014 Fourth International Conference on Advances in Computing and Communications, pp. 167–170 (2014)

12. Saikkonen, R., Malmi, L., Korhonen, A.: Fully automatic assessment of programming exercises. SIGCSE Bull., 33(3),133–136 (2001)

13. Scott, B., Neil, T.: Designing web interfaces: principles and patterns for rich interactions. O'Reilly Media, Inc. (2009)

14. Simpson, A., Eraser, N.M.: Black box and glass box evaluation of the sundial system. In: Third European Conference on Speech Communication and Technology (1993)

15. Thornton, M., Edwards, S.H., Tan, R.P., Pérez-Quinones, M.A.: Supporting student-written tests of GUI programs. In: Proceedings of the 39th SIGCSE Technical Symposium on Computer Science Education, pp. 537–541 (2008)

16. Štěpánek, J., Šimková, M.: Comparing web pages in terms of inner structure. In: Procedia - Social and Behavioral Sciences 83, 458–462 (2013). 2nd World Conference on Educational Technology Research

17. Ullah, Z., Lajis, A., Jamjoom, M., Altalhi, A., Al-Ghamdi, A., Saleem, F.: The effect of automatic assessment on novice programming: strengths and limitations of existing systems. Comput. Appl. Eng. Educ. **26**, 02 (2018)

18. Varshney, G., Misra, M., Atrey, P.K.: A survey and classification of web phishing detection schemes. Secur. Commun. Netw. **9**(18), 6266–6284 (2016)

19. Wood, L., et al.: Document object model (DOM) level 1 specification. W3C recommendation (1998)

20. Zar, J.H.: Spearman Rank Correlation. John Wiley & Sons Ltd (2005)

Parallel Spectral Clustering with FEAST Library

Saad Mdaa, Anass Ouali Alami, Ronan Guivarch[(✉)], and Sandrine Mouysset

University of Toulouse - IRIT, Toulouse, France
`Ronan.Guivarch@toulouse-inp.fr`

Abstract. Spectral clustering is one of the most relevant unsupervised learning methods capable of classifying data without any a priori information. At the heart of this method is the computation of the dominant eigenvectors of an affinity matrix in order to work on a low-dimensional data space in which the clustering is made. We propose in this paper a study of the integration of the FEAST library to compute these eigenvectors in our parallel spectral clustering method by domain decomposition. We also show that this library allows to add a second level of parallelism in addition to the domain decomposition level.

Keywords: Kernel methods · FEAST library · Clustering · Parallel computing · Overlapping domain decomposition · Two-level parallelism

1 Introduction

Many fields from Social Science to Medicine and Biology generate a large amount of data to analyze. With the emergence of new technologies, expertise is not always available and data annotation can not be provided. As such unsupervised method are privileged [14]. In particular, spectral clustering is one of the most relevant unsupervised learning methods capable of classifying data without any a priori information on shape or locality [12]. This method consists in selecting the dominant eigenvectors of a matrix called affinity matrix, in order to define a low-dimensional data space in which the data are easily clustered. The most computationally demanding step in this algorithm remains the extraction of the dominant space from the full dense Gaussian affinity matrix. Some parallel approaches can be considered to treat large amount of data. For example, the strategies can be based on either low rank approximations of large matrices, such as Nyström methods [3,13] or subdomain decomposition [5].

In this paper, we investigate the eigensolver library called FEAST that proposes a new transformative numerical approach [9]. To take full advantage of this library, we consider a sparsification of the affinity matrix that allows a second level of parallelism on each subdomain.

The paper is organized as follows. In Sect. 2 we summarize the spectral clustering. Then we present in Sect. 3, the FEAST library, a solver for the generalized eigenvalue problem in order to perform this search of the dominant

© The Author(s), under exclusive license to Springer Nature Switzerland AG 2022
T. Guarda et al. (Eds.): ARTIIS 2022, CCIS 1675, pp. 127–138, 2022.
https://doi.org/10.1007/978-3-031-20319-0_10

eigenvectors. In Sect. 4, we include FEAST in spectral clustering by considering both full and sparsified gaussian affinity matrix. In Sect. 5, we present how we incorporate FEAST routines in our parallel spectral clustering method. As a proof of concept, we show in Sect. 6, through some experiments, the good behavior of this approach by comparison with a classical approach using LAPACK/SCALAPACK libraries. Finally, we conclude in Sect. 7.

2   Spectral Clustering

Algorithm 1 presents the different steps of spectral clustering by assuming that the number k of targeted clusters is known. First, the spectral clustering consists in building the affinity matrix based on the Gaussian affinity measure between points of the data set S. After a normalization step, the k eigenvectors associated to the k largest eigenvalues are extracted (*step 3*). So every data point x_i is plotted in a spectral embedding space of $\mathbb{R}^k$ and the clustering is made in this space by applying K-means method. Finally, thanks to an equivalence relation, the final partition of data set is defined from the clustering in the embedded space.

Algorithm 1: Spectral Clustering Algorithm

Input   :   data set $S = \{x_i\}_{i=1..n} \in \mathbb{R}^p$, number of clusters k, affinity parameter σ

1 Form the affinity matrix $A \in \mathbb{R}^{n \times n}$ defined by:

$$A_{ij} = \begin{cases} \exp\left(-\frac{\|x_i - x_j\|^2}{\sigma^2}\right) & \text{if } i \neq j, \\ 0 \text{ otherwise}, \end{cases} \tag{1}$$

2 Construct the normalized matrix: $L = D^{-1/2}AD^{-1/2}$ with $D_{i,i} = \sum_{j=1}^{n} A_{ij}$;
3 Assemble the matrix $X = [X_1 X_2 .. X_k] \in \mathbb{R}^{n \times k}$ by stacking the **eigenvectors associated with the k largest eigenvalues of L** ;
4 Form the matrix Y by normalizing each row in the $n \times k$ matrix X ;
5 Treat each row of Y as a point in $\mathbb{R}^k$, and group them in k clusters via the K-means method ;
6 Assign the original point x_i to cluster j when row i of matrix Y belongs to cluster j

---

There are several ways to compute, at *step 3*, the eigenvectors associated with the k largest eigenvalues of L. In previous works [5], we used DSYEV routine of the LAPACK library [1]. More recently, we replaced the LAPACK routines with an implementation of the SUBSPACE ITERATION METHOD [7].

We want to verify the opportunity to use the FEAST library to perform this step. We present in the next section the basic principles of this library.

3   FEAST Library

Introduced by POLIZZI [9], FEAST is a solver for the generalized eigenvalue problem $Ax = \lambda Bx$ where A and B are two square matrices of size n [10].

FEAST belongs to the family of iterative solvers based on the integration over a contour of the density matrix, which is a representation used in quantum mechanics. The FEAST algorithm decribed in Algorithm 2 requires as input:

– an interval $I_\lambda = [\lambda_{min}, \lambda_{max}]$ for the search for eigenvalues
– and M, the number of eigenvalues in this interval.

By supplying I_λ and M to FEAST, it first calculates the integral

$$U = \frac{1}{2\pi i} \oint_C (zB - A)^{-1} BY \, dz$$

where $Y \in \mathbb{C}^{n \times M}$ is made up of M random vectors and C is a curve in the complex plane enclosing the interval I_λ.

The calculation of this integral is carried out by using a numerical integration scheme (Gaussian quadrature for example), i.e. by using the approximation

$$U \approx \frac{1}{2\pi i} \sum_{i=1}^{m} w_k (z_k B - A)^{-1} BY$$

where $\{z_k\}_{k=1..m}$ are points of the curve C. For each integration node z_k, a linear system $(z_k B - A)U_k = BY$ of size n and with M right-hand sides must be solved.

The result of the integration is used in the Rayleigh-Ritz method, which results in a dense and small eigenvalue problem, whose size is of the order of the number of eigenvalues in the search interval M.

Algorithm 2: FEAST algorithm for solving the generalized eigenvalue problem $Ax = \lambda Bx$

Input   : $I_\lambda = [\lambda_{min}, \lambda_{max}]$: the search interval
            M: the number of eigenvalues in the search interval

Output: $M_0 \leq M$ eigenpairs

1 Compute $U = \frac{1}{2\pi i} \oint_C (zB - A)^{-1} BY \, dz$ where $Y \in \mathbb{C}^{n \times M}$ consists of M random vectors and C is a curve in the complex plane encompassing the interval I_λ ;
2 Compute Rayleigh quotients: $A_U = U^H A U$ and $B_U = U^H B U$;
3 Solve the generalized eigenvalue problem of size M: $A_U W = B_U W \Lambda$;
4 Compute the approximate Ritz pairs: $\Lambda, X = U.W$;
5 If convergence is not achieved, go back to the first step with $Y = X$

Regarding parallelism, the FEAST library can exploit three levels:

- **L1**: Search intervals can be processed separately without overlap;
- **L2**: The linear systems associated with the quadrature nodes in the complex contour can be solved independently;
- **L3**: Each linear system with several second members can be solved in parallel.

4 Spectral Clustering with FEAST

In this section, FEAST is included in spectral clustering by considering both full and sparsified gaussian affinity matrix.

4.1 A First Approach Considering the Dense Affinity Matrix

In the framework of spectral classification, we look for the k largest eigenvalues of the normalized affinity matrix L (*step 3* of Algorithm 1).

L is a real, dense and symmetric matrix. So according to the FEAST manual, the routine to use in this case is **dfeast_syev**. We also need to provide the search interval $I_\lambda = [\lambda_{min}, \lambda_{max}]$ and M the number of eigenvalues in this interval.

As L is a stochastic matrix, we have $\lambda_{max} = 1$. In order to determine λ_{min} and M, one can use a stochastic estimation of the eigenvalues inside the search contour by setting the flag **fpm(14) = 2** according to Algorithm 3:

Algorithm 3: Method to compute λ_{min} and M

---

1 $\lambda_{max} = 1$;
2 λ_{min} = value close to 1;
3 **loop**
4   Stochastic estimation of M on $[\lambda_{min}, \lambda_{max}]$ (by making a first call to the routine **dfeast_syev** with the option flag **fpm(14)=2**);
5   **if** $M < k$ **then**
6          $\lambda_{min} = \lambda_{min}$ - step;
7   **else**
8   **exit**;
9   **end**
10 **end**

After having determined λ_{min} and M, we make a second call to **dfeast_syev**, to compute the eigenpairs.

To test this approach on some clustering benchmark [11], we select 4 data sets available in our toolbox and we choose to solve the problem with only 1 sub-domain in order focus on the eigenvalue problem. Two data sets are respectively plotted in Fig. 1(a) and Fig. 3(a).

The benchmark results obtained using L2-level parallelism with 4 processors are summarized in Table 1.

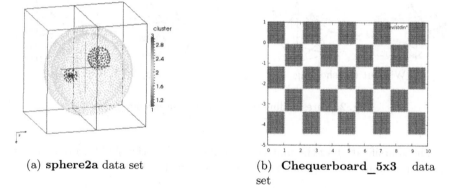

(a) **sphere2a** data set

(b) **Chequerboard_5x3** data set

Fig. 1. Examples of clustering benchmark

Table 1. FEAST execution time obtained on dense matrices with 4 processors

Data set	Size (n)	Dimension (p)	Number of clusters (k)	Time (t)
Toy	640	2	2	0.39 s
Target	650	2	4	0.75 s
Sphere2	1905	3	2	8.19 s
Sphere2a	3560	3	2	55.31 s

From these first tests, we can remark that estimating M and λ_{min} takes a long time and it is difficult to choose a good step. Moreover, The performance in terms of execution time is not satisfactory for processing large data. Further investigations should be led to identify the most computational steps in this FEAST implementation on spectral clustering. But considering a full dense affinity matrix may strongly impact the execution time. So, in the following, we consider the sparsification of the Gaussian affinity matrix.

4.2 A Second Approach with the Sparsification of the Affinity Matrix

Spectral classification is an expensive algorithm, especially for large data, as it requires computing eigenpairs of a dense matrix of size $n \times n$. To overcome this limitation and memory consumption, sparsification with a threshold can be used.

Indeed, the affinity matrix can be interpreted as a weighted adjacency graph. Thus, the thresholding will control the width of the neighbourhood, and will therefore cancel the edges that connect data points that are very far from each other as shown in Fig. 2. Thus, this reinforces the affinity between points in the same cluster and the separability between clusters [6].

(a) Without thresholding   (b) With thresholding

Fig. 2. Thresholding of the weighted adjacency graph

The sparsification of the matrix L is obtained by a threshold proportional to the Gaussian affinity parameter σ (see Algorithm 1):

$$threshold = \alpha \times \sigma.$$

The σ value (and so the threshold) can be heuristically defined to build an automatic sparsified matrix. To do so, we start by considering an uniform distribution of n points in this enclosing p-th dimensional box. This uniform distribution is reached when dividing the box in n smaller boxes all of the same size, each with a volume of order $D_{\max}^p/n$ where D_{max} is the maximum of the distance between two data point x_i and x_j, $\forall i,j \in \{1,..,n\}$. The corresponding edge size is defined by $D_{\max}/n^{\frac{1}{p}}$. The thresholding will be function of this factor which represents a reference distance for any kind of distribution of data S [8].

For sparse matrices, FEAST offers interfaces to obtain the eigenvectors associated with the largest k eigenvalues without specifying $[\lambda_{min}, \lambda_{max}]$.

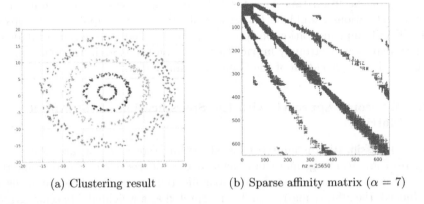

(a) Clustering result   (b) Sparse affinity matrix ($\alpha = 7$)

Fig. 3. Spectral Clustering with sparsification on the Target data set ($n = 650$ and $k = 4$)

Table 2. FEAST execution time obtained on sparse matrices with 4 processors

Data set	Size (n)	Dimension (p)	Number of clusters (k)	α	Time (t)
Target	650	2	4	7	0.5 s
Sphere2	1905	3	2	3	0.2 s
Sphere2a	3560	3	2	3	0.5 s
Cross	5120	2	5	3	10.6 s
Chequerboard2	5000	2	25	3	11.3 s

The results given in Table 2 are obtained using L2-level parallelism with 4 processors. Compared to the first approach (see Table 1), we save a lot of memory and execution time while having a correct classification. So this approach that considers sparse version of the affinity matrix, provides promising results and should be preferred.

5 Strategies of Parallelization

To parallelize the spectral clustering, we first use a domain decomposition strategy and recently implemented a new strategy to exploit more parallelism.

5.1 Domain Decomposition Principle

Our first strategy is based on domain decomposition with overlaps. Lets consider a data set $S = \{x_i\}_{i=1..n} \in \mathbb{R}^p$. This data set is included in a domain. We divide the domain in q sub-domains, thus defining q sub-sets that can have a different amount of data. By assigning a sub-domain to a processor, it applies independently the clustering algorithm on the corresponding sub-set and provides a local partition.

This grouping step is dedicated to link the local partitions from the sub-domains thanks to the overlap and the following transitive relation:
$\forall x_{i_1}, x_{i_2}, x_{i_3} \in S,$

$$\text{if} \quad x_{i_1}, x_{i_2} \in C^1 \text{ and } x_{i_2}, x_{i_3} \in C^2$$
$$\text{then} \quad C^1 \cup C^2 = P \text{ and } x_{i_1}, x_{i_2}, x_{i_3} \in P \qquad (2)$$

where C^1 and C^2 are two distinct clusters and P is a larger cluster which includes both C^1 and C^2. By applying this transitive relation (2) on the overlap, the connection between sub-sets of data is established and provides a global partition.

We can implement this algorithm using a Master-Slave paradigm as summarized in Algorithms 4 and 5.

Algorithm 4: Parallel Algorithm: Master

1: Pre-processing step
    1.1 read the global data and the parameters
    1.2 compute the uniform distance δ
    1.3 compute the overlapping bandwidth α
    1.4 split the data into q sub-sets
2: Send δ and the data sub-sets to the slaves
3: Perform the Clustering Algorithm on its sub-set
4: Receive the local partitions and the number of clusters from each slave
5: Grouping Step
    5.1 Gather the local partitions in a global partition with the transitive
    relation (2)
    5.2 Output a partition of the whole data set S and the final number
    of clusters k

Algorithm 5: Parallel Algorithm: Slave

1: Receive δ and its data sub-set from the Master
2: Perform the Clustering Algorithm on its sub-set
3: Send its local partition and its number of clusters to the Master

---

5.2   A Second Level of Parallelism

The decomposition of the domain in different sub-domains with overlaps consists of a first level of parallelism.

We can also consider that each clustering problem on each sub-domain can be solved using a parallel method. This allows us to use a large number of processors without splitting the domain into many sub-domains, which can be penalizing in some situations.

We have the possibility to use this second level of parallelism with the spectral clustering method. We can use SCALAPACK [2] and its routine PDSYEV in order to compute all the eigenvectors of the matrix L.

We have a group of leading processors that will handle the first level of parallelism. Then, for each sub-domain, there is a pool of processors, including the leading processor of the sub-domain, that perform the computation via SCALAPACK.

This organization is illustrated in the Fig. 4 for 4 sub-domains. M_1, M_2, M_3 and M_4 are the leading processors.

Or we also can exploit the different levels of parallelism in FEAST. On each sub-domain, we call FEAST using L2-level parallelism with the dedicated pool of processors. We present in the next section the comparison between LAPACK/SCALAPACK and FEAST.

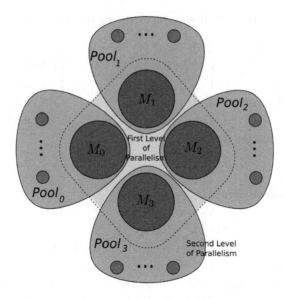

Fig. 4. Two-level Parallelism

6   Numerical Results: Proof of Concept

As proof of concept, we first performed some calculations with small data sets to compare FEAST to LAPACK/SCALAPACK. Then we give first results on larger data sets.

6.1   Clustering Benchmark

In the following, n is the size of the data, p is the dimension of the problem ($2D$ or $3D$), and **nb_sd** is the number of sub-domains. The Table 3 summarizes the time to solve the eigenvalue problem and the total time.

The number of processors in a pool is 1 or 2. With 1 processor, we use LAPACK or FEAST with no parallelization to solve a problem on a sub-domain. With 2 processors, we use SCALAPACK and FEAST with L2-level parallelism.

The following measure was used to quantify the performance of FEAST:

$$\textbf{efficiency } \% = \frac{\text{time with 1 processor}}{2 \times \text{time with 2 processors}} \times 100$$

We see that for all these problems, the results with FEAST using one processor per subdomain or two (i.e. not using, or using the second level of parallelism) are better than those with LAPACK and SCALAPACK. The times for the two problems of size n close to 10000 (time for the resolution of the problem and the total time) are better by a factor 10. We also note, that even for small problems, we benefit from the second level of parallelism, which is not the case with the

Table 3. Results on clustering benchmark

3SPHERES ($n = 4361$, $p = 3$ and **nb_sd** $= 8$)

Solver	LAPACK	SCALAPACK	FEAST		
Size of the pool	1	2	1	2	Efficiency %
Eigenvalue problem time	3.16 s	3.90 s	1.00 s	**0.81 s**	61.72%
Total time	3.35 s	4.10 s	1.11 s	**0.91 s**	60.98%

3SPHERESA ($n = 9700$, $p = 3$ et **nb_sd** $= 8$)

Solver	LAPACK	SCALAPACK	FEAST		
Size of the pool	1	2	1	2	Efficiency %
Eigenvalue problem time	34.68 s	46.45 s	3.42 s	**3.10 s**	55.16%
Total time	35.68 s	47.44 s	4.71 s	**4.39 s**	53.64%

SPHERE2B ($n = 10717$, $p = 3$ et **nb_sd** $= 8$)

Solver	LAPACK	SCALAPACK	FEAST		
Size of the pool	1	2	1	2	Efficiency %
Eigenvalue problem time	37.5 s	50.30 s	3.23 s	**2.72 s**	59.37%
Total time	38.52 s	51.27 s	3.55 s	**3.05 s**	58.19%

LAPACK/SCALAPACK implementation. We show in previous works that for the latter approach, it is only interesting to use SCALAPACK for much larger problems. The efficiency are between 50% and 60% which is promising for small problems.

6.2 Tests on Larger Data Sets

In order to test the different approaches with larger problems and in particular to observe how the speed-up behaves, we consider the **Chequerboard_5 × 3** data sets plotted in Fig. 1(b). We can change the density of the points of each dark square, in order to increase the number of points of the problem and form, for this experiment, five data sets with $\{10, 143; 42, 527; 94, 208; 197, 568; 258, 458\}$ points. We divide our domain into 16 sub-domains.

Table 4. Total execution time with LAPACK/SCALAPACK and FEAST on **Chequerboard_5 × 3_XX data sets**

Solver	Nb of points	Nb of points / subdomain	FEAST		
Data set	Pool's size				
	-	-	1	2	Efficiency %
Chequerboard_5x3_21	10,143	833	0.59 s	**0.55 s**	53.63%
Chequerboard_5x3_42	42,527	3,354	6.19 s	**4.97 s**	62.27%
Chequerboard_5x3_63	94,208	7,360	37.39 s	**25.17 s**	74.27%
Chequerboard_5x3_84	197,568	14,705	178.97 s	**124.42 s**	71.92%
Chequerboard_5x3_105	258,428	24,556	451.22 s	**330.20 s**	68.32%

With the three biggest problems, the speed-up is close to 70% which confirms the interest of using the second level of parallelism.

We have not indicated in this table the time of the LAPACK/SCALAPACK versions but they are always much slower than FEAST. For example, for the problem of size $258,428$, it takes more than two hours to get the result.

7   Conclusion

In this paper, we have shown that the use of FEAST to compute the eigenvectors in the spectral clustering method is advantageous compared to its implementation with the eigenpair computation routines of LAPACK.

This advantage remains when we consider the parallel spectral clustering with domain decomposition and allows a second level of parallelism by activating the L2-level parallelism of FEAST.

This L2-level parallelism of FEAST, when we are able to sparsify the affinity matrix, allows, with consequent problem sizes, to obtain speed-ups close to 70% compared to FEAST with no parallelism.

In the future, we plan to validate our approach on real data (images, social science, medicine and biology data) on supercomputers. Also, because we sparsify the affinity matrix, it would be interesting to compare FEAST with the routines of the ARPACK library [4] which are designed to handle sparse matrices.

References

1. Anderson, E., et al.: LAPACK Users' Guide. USA, third edn, SIAM, Philadelphia, Pennsylvania (1999)
2. Blackford, L.S., et al.: ScaLAPACK users' guide. SIAM (1997)
3. Fowlkes, C., Belongie, S., Chung, F., Malik, J.: Spectral grouping using the Nystrom method. IEEE Trans. Pattern Anal. Mach. Intell. **26**(2), 214–225 (2004)
4. Lehoucq, R.B., Sorensen, D.C., Yang, C.: ARPACK: solution of large scale eigenvalue problems by implicitly restarted Arnoldi methods. www.netlib@ornl.gov (1997)
5. Mouysset, S., Noailles, J., Ruiz, D., Guivarch, R.: On a strategy for spectral clustering with parallel computation. In: High Performance Computing for Computational Science: 9th International Conference (2010)
6. Mouysset, S., Guivarch, R.: Sparsification on Parallel Spectral Clustering. In: Daydé, M., Marques, O., Nakajima, K. (eds.) VECPAR 2012. LNCS, vol. 7851, pp. 249–260. Springer, Heidelberg (2013). https://doi.org/10.1007/978-3-642-38718-0_25
7. Mouysset, S., Guivarch, R.: ParKerC: Toolbox for parallel kernel clustering methods. In: 10th International Conference on Pattern Recognition Systems - ICPRS 2019. IET: Institution of Engineering and Technology, Tours, France (2019). https://doi.org/10.1049/cp.2019.0253
8. Mouysset, S., Noailles, J., Ruiz, D.: On an interpretation of spectral clustering via heat equation and finite elements theory. Lecture Notes in Engineering and Computer Science (2010)

 9. Polizzi, E.: Density-matrix-based algorithm for solving eigenvalue problems. Phys. Rev. B **79**(11), 115112 (2009)
10. Polizzi, E.: Density-matrix-based algorithm for solving eigenvalue problems. Phys. Rev. B **79**, 115112 (2009). https://doi.org/10.1103/PhysRevB.79.115112
11. Thrun, M.C., Ultsch, A.: Clustering benchmark datasets exploiting the fundamental clustering problems. Data Brief **30**, 105501 (2020)
12. Von Luxburg, U.: A tutorial on spectral clustering. Stat. Comput. **17**(4), 395–416 (2007)
13. Wang, S., Gittens, A., Mahoney, M.W.: Scalable kernel k-means clustering with Nyström approximation: relative-error bounds (2017)
14. Xu, D., Tian, Y.: A comprehensive survey of clustering algorithms. Annals Data Sci. **2**(2), 165–193 (2015)

A Control Problem with Passive Particles Driven by Point Vortices on the Sphere

Carlos Balsa[1]([⊠])(ID) and Sílvio Gama[2](ID)

[1] Research Centre in Digitalization and Intelligent Robotics (CeDRI), Instituto Politécnico de Bragança, 5300-253 Bragança, Portugal
balsa@ipb.pt
[2] Centro de Matemática da Universidade do Porto, Departamento de Matemática, Faculdade de Ciências, Universidade do Porto, Rua do Campo Alegre s/n, 4169-007 Porto, Portugal
smgama@fc.up.pt

Abstract. The objective of this study is to control the motion of a passive particle advected by N point vortices in a sphere. The square of the L^2 norm of control, necessary for the system to evolve from a starting point to an end point in an a priori fixed time, must be minimized. If the motion is generated by a single vortex ($N = 1$), we show that the system is controllable. The problem is also solved by a direct approach, where the control problem is transformed into a nonlinear optimization problem that is solved numerically. In the case of one ($N = 1$), two ($N = 2$), or three ($N = 3$) point vortices, the numerical results show the existence of near/quasi-optimal control.

Keywords: Vortex motion · Passive tracer · Spherical motion · Optimal control · Non-linear optimization problem

1 Introduction

Point vortices are finite-dimensional approximations to the two-dimensional vortex dynamics of incompressible ideal fluids (zero viscosity). This research topic, initiated by Helmholtz [14] and continued some years later by Kelvin [30] and Kirchhoff [17], continues to offer a wide range of work drawing on theories of dynamical systems, differential geometry, numerical analysis, control, and so on.

Point vortices [10, 25, 28] have been studied in the plane [1–4, 9], in the torus [29, 31, 32], in the sphere [12, 16, 18, 23, 26], in the hyperbolic sphere [15, 24, 27], in bounded plane regions with $C^{2,\alpha}$-boundaries [21], etc.

The study of point vortices and passive particles in a sphere is an interesting question, in particular, with issues related to understanding the evolution of atmospheric and oceanic vortices [7, 13, 16, 33].

This work is concerned with the dynamics of a passive particle advected by two-dimensional point vortex in a sphere, S^2. A passive particle is a point vortex with zero circulation. We want to drive a passive particle from a given starting point to a given destination point in a given finite time. The flow is generated by point vortices on a sphere, and we want to minimize the total amount of energy used for the motion.

© The Author(s), under exclusive license to Springer Nature Switzerland AG 2022
T. Guarda et al. (Eds.): ARTIIS 2022, CCIS 1675, pp. 139–150, 2022.
https://doi.org/10.1007/978-3-031-20319-0_11

This paper is organized as follows. In Sect. 2, we sketch the deduction of the equations that govern the dynamics of the vortices in the sphere. The formulation of the control problem is done in Sect. 3. The next section is dedicated to the numerical strategy for determining the control that drives the passive particle from its initial point to its final destination, leading to the minimization of the square of L^2 norm of the control. We considered the number of vortices from one to three. The final conclusions close this article.

2   Point Vortices on a Sphere

The two-dimensional incompressible Euler equation, written in spherical coordinates (R,θ,ϕ),

- R is the (constant) radius of the sphere, S^2;
- $\theta \in \mathbb{R} \pmod{\pi} = [0,\pi]$ is the colatitude (or polar) angle of the vortex position, i.e. the angle between the radius passing through the North Pole, here located in $(0,0,R)$ and the radius passing through the vortex, and varies from $0°$ (North Pole) to $180°$ (South Pole); and
- $\phi \in \mathbb{R} \pmod{2\pi} = [0,2\pi]$ is the longitude (or azimuthal) angle, i.e. the angle that the meridian passing through $(R,0,0)$ makes with the meridian passing by the vortex position, and varies from $0°$ to $360°$;

reads [16]:

$$\omega\,e_r = \nabla \times v, \tag{1}$$

$$v = (\nabla\psi) \times e_r, \tag{2}$$

where the differential operators act in spherical coordinates, ψ is a stream-function,

$$v \equiv (0,v_\theta,v_\phi) = \left(0, \frac{1}{R^2\sin(\theta)}\frac{\partial\psi}{\partial\phi}, -\frac{\partial\psi}{\partial\theta}\right), \tag{3}$$

is the velocity field, and

$$e_r = (\sin(\theta)\cos(\phi),\sin(\theta)\sin(\phi)\sin(\theta),\cos(\theta)),$$

is the unit vector in the radial direction. Inserting (2) into (1), we obtain

$$\nabla^2\psi = -\omega, \tag{4}$$

being

$$\nabla^2 \equiv \frac{1}{R^2\sin(\theta)}\frac{\partial}{\partial\theta}\left(\sin(\theta)\frac{\partial}{\partial\theta}\right) + \frac{1}{R^2\sin^2(\theta)}\frac{\partial^2}{\partial^2\phi},$$

the so-called Laplace-Beltrami operator on a sphere, S^2. Replacing in Eq. (4) the vorticity, $\omega(\cdot)$, by the Dirac δ function $\delta(\theta-\theta')\delta(\phi-\phi')$, the corresponding solution is the Green's function:

$$G(\theta,\phi,\theta',\phi') = -\frac{1}{4\pi R^2}\ln(1-\cos(\gamma)),$$

where γ is central angle that the points (R,θ,ϕ) and (R,θ',ϕ') form with the origin of the sphere, and it is such that

$$\cos(\gamma) = \cos(\theta)\cos(\theta') + \sin(\theta)\sin(\theta')\cos(\phi - \phi').$$

Knowing the Green's function of the Laplace-Beltrami operator on the sphere, S^2, the solution of Eq. (4) is the convolution $\psi = G * \omega$, i.e.

$$\psi(\theta,\phi) = \frac{1}{4\pi R^2} \iint \omega(\theta',\phi') \ln(1 - \cos(\gamma)) \sin(\theta')\, d\theta'\, d\phi', \tag{5}$$

and, thanks to (3), we reconstruct the velocity $\mathbf{v} = (0, v_\theta, v_\phi)$ from the stream-funtion. Assume now that the vorticity is the linear combination of N Dirac δ functions,

$$\omega(t,\theta,\phi) = \sum_{j=1}^{N} k_j \delta(\theta - \theta_j(t)) \delta(\phi - \phi_j(t)),$$

where the "singleton" $k_j \delta(\theta - \theta_j(t)) \delta(\phi - \phi_j(t))$ is interpreted as the vorticity with intensity, or circulation, $k_j \in \mathbb{R}$, at the point vortex located at $(R, \theta_j(t), \phi_i(t))$, and N is the total number of point vortices corresponding to the total circulation $\Gamma = \sum_{j=1}^{N} k_j$. Their time evolution, assuming known their positions at $t = 0$, is governed by the set of ordinary differential equations $(i = 1, 2, \ldots, N)$:

$$\dot{\theta}_i = -\frac{1}{4\pi R^2} \sum_{\substack{j=1 \\ j\neq i}}^{N} k_j \frac{\sin(\theta_j)\sin(\phi_i - \phi_j)}{1 - \cos(\gamma_{ij})}, \tag{6}$$

$$\sin(\theta_i)\dot{\phi}_i = \frac{1}{4\pi R^2} \sum_{\substack{j=1 \\ j\neq i}}^{N} k_j \frac{\sin(\theta_i)\cos(\theta_j) - \cos(\theta_i)\sin(\theta_j)\cos(\phi_i - \phi_j)}{1 - \cos(\gamma_{ij})}, \tag{7}$$

where γ_{ij}, representing the central angle between the ith and the jth vortex points, is such that
$$\cos(\gamma_{ij}) = \cos(\theta_i)\cos(\theta_j) + \sin(\theta_i)\sin(\theta_j)\cos(\phi_i - \phi_j), \tag{8}$$

or, in Bogomolov notation [7]:

$$\dot{\theta}_i = -\frac{1}{4\pi R^2} \sum_{\substack{j=1 \\ j\neq i}}^{N} k_j \frac{\alpha_{ij}}{1 - \cos(\gamma_{ij})}, \quad \sin(\theta_i)\dot{\phi}_i = \frac{1}{4\pi R^2} \sum_{\substack{j=1 \\ j\neq i}}^{N} k_j \frac{\beta_{ij}}{1 - \cos(\gamma_{ij})}, \tag{9}$$

with $\alpha_{ij} = \sin(\theta_j)\sin(\phi_i - \phi_j)$ and $\beta_{ij} = \sin(\theta_i)\cos(\theta_j) - \cos(\theta_i)\sin(\theta_j)\cos(\phi_i - \phi_j)$. Moreover, Eqs. (6)-(7) has the following Hamiltonian structure:

$$H = \frac{1}{4\pi R^2} \sum_{i=1}^{N} \sum_{j=i+1}^{N} k_i k_j \ln(1 - \cos(\gamma_{ij})),$$

and they can be rewritten as

$$\frac{d\cos(\theta_i)}{dt} = \{\cos(\theta_i), H\},$$

$$\frac{d\phi_i}{dt} = \{\phi, H\},$$

in which the Poisson bracket between two functions f and g is defined by

$$\{f, g\} = \sum_{J=1}^{N} \frac{1}{k_j} \left(\frac{\partial f}{\partial \phi_j} \frac{\partial g}{\partial \cos(\theta_j)} - \frac{\partial g}{\partial \phi_j} \frac{\partial f}{\partial \cos(\theta_j)} \right).$$

The scalar moment quantities Q, P and S defined by

$$Q = \sum_{J=1}^{N} k_j \sin(\theta_j) \cos(\phi_j),$$

$$P = \sum_{J=1}^{N} k_j \sin(\theta_j) \sin(\phi_j),$$

$$S = \sum_{J=1}^{N} k_j \sin(\theta_j),$$

are such that $\{H, Q\} = \{H, P\} = \{H, S\} = 0$, and, therefore, are invariant quantities (which are particularly useful for, among others, controlling the accuracy of numerical integration).

A passive particle is, by definition, a point vortex with circulation set to zero. Thus, the dynamics of a system with P passive particles advected by N point vortices is given by Eqs. (6)-(7) together with the equations for the passive particles

$$\dot{\theta}_p = -\frac{1}{4\pi R^2} \sum_{j=1}^{N} k_j \frac{\sin(\theta_j)\sin(\phi_p - \phi_j)}{1 - \cos(\gamma_{pj})}, \tag{10}$$

$$\dot{\phi}_p = \frac{1}{4\pi R^2} \sum_{j=1}^{N} k_j \frac{\cos(\theta_j) - \cot(\theta_p)\sin(\theta_j)\cos(\phi_p - \phi_j)}{1 - \cos(\gamma_{pj})}, \tag{11}$$

with $p = N+1, N+2, \ldots, N+P$, and the respective initial conditions.

By a reparametrization of time $(\tau := t/R^2)$ in Eqs. (6)-(7) and (10)-(11), we can henceforth fix $R = 1$.

3   The Control Problem

The control problem that we want to address here is formulated from the Eqs. (10)-(11) adding to their right hand sides the angular controls u_θ and u_ϕ, respectively, i.e.

$$\dot{\theta}_p = -\frac{1}{4\pi} \sum_{j=1}^{N} k_j \frac{\sin(\theta_j)\sin(\phi_p - \phi_j)}{1 - \cos(\gamma_{pj})} + u_\theta, \tag{12}$$

$$\dot{\phi}_p = \frac{1}{4\pi} \sum_{j=1}^{N} k_j \frac{\cos(\theta_j) - \cot(\theta_p)\sin(\theta_j)\cos(\phi_p - \phi_j)}{1 - \cos(\gamma_{pj})} + u_\phi, \tag{13}$$

The functional to be minimized is

$$f \equiv f[u_\theta(\cdot), u_\phi(\cdot)] = \int_0^T \left((u_\theta(t))^2 + (u_\phi(t))^2 \right) dt. \qquad (14)$$

The minimization of (14) corresponds to the optimal reduction of the cost of moving the particle between the initial and final points so that the particle reaches the destination at the prescribed final time T, as in [5,6,19,20].

Actually, as in [6], we shall consider an approximation of this functional by sampling the integrand at regular integrals and making an estimate based on it. This time, we used the trapezoidal rule [11], which considers a sequence of n segments to interpolate the integrand of the cost function (14), $g(t) = (u_\theta(t))^2 + (u_\phi(t))^2$, i.e.

$$f_n = \frac{\Delta t}{2} \left(g(t_0) + 2 \sum_{k=1}^{n-1} g(t_i) + g(t_n) \right), \qquad (15)$$

with $\Delta t = T/n$, and $t_i = i \Delta t$, $i = 0, 1, \cdots, n$.

We consider the admissible angular control strategy in the set

$$\mathscr{U} = \{ u = (u_\theta, u_\phi) : [0, +\infty[\longrightarrow \mathbf{U}; u \text{ measurable} \},$$

where $\mathbf{U} = [0,1]^2 \subset \mathbf{R}^2$. Rescaling the circulations, we can assume that $\|u\| \leq u_{max} = 1$.

The state space is $M =]0, \pi] \times [0, 2\pi]$. Introducing some basic notation and following [8], let $x = (\theta_p, \phi_p) \in M$, consider (12)-(13) simply as $\dot{x} = h(x, u)$, and denote the unique solution of this ODE by $x_u(\cdot, x_0)$, such that $x_u(0, x_0) = x_0$.

With $T > 0$ and $x_0 \in M$, let $\mathscr{U}_{T,x_0} \subset \mathscr{U}$ to be the set of controls $u \in \mathscr{U}$, such that the trajectory $x_u(\cdot, x_0)$ is well defined in $[0, T]$. Call $\mathscr{A}(T, x_0) = \{x_u(T, x_0) : u \in \mathscr{U}_{T,x_0}\}$ the atteignable set from x_0 in time T, and $\mathscr{A}(x_0) = \cup_{T \geq 0} \mathscr{A}(T, x_0)$ the attainable set from x_0.

The controlled system is called controllable from x_0 if $\mathscr{A}(x_0) = M$, and it is controllable, if $\mathscr{A}(x_0) = M, \forall x_0 \in M$.

4   Numerical Solution of the Control Problem

In this section, the control problem in the sphere is solved numerically by a direct approach, converting the displacement of the passive particle into a control problem.

The time available to perform the displacement is divided into a fixed number n of subintervals, where the control variables are constant. The control function $\mathbf{U}(\cdot)$ is replaced by n control variables $u_0, u_1, \cdots, u_{n-1}$ and the discretized problem is solved numerically by an optimization procedure (for details see [6]). In each subinterval, the vortex dynamics is integrated using the fourth-order numerical Runge-Kutta scheme [11].

Numerical calculations were performed in Matlab using the nonlinear programming solver fmincon, which provides some algorithms for constrained optimization, such as the interior point or the active set (see [22]).

In this work, we consider (15) with $n = 2$, i.e. $f_2 = \frac{\Delta t}{2} \left(g(t_0) + 2g(t_1) + g(t_2) \right)$.

4.1   A Particle Advected by a Single Vortex

In the one vortex ($N = 1$) and one particle ($P = 1$) problem, where the vortex is localized in the North Pole of the sphere, $V(0) = (0, 0, 1)$, and has circulation k, the dynamics of the passive particle is given by

$$\begin{cases} \dot{\theta}_p = u_\theta, \\ \dot{\phi}_p = \frac{k}{4\pi} \frac{1}{1-\cos(\theta_p)} + u_\phi, \end{cases} \tag{16}$$

with the given initial condition $P_0 = (\theta_{p0}, \phi_{p0})$. The variables u_θ and u_ϕ represent the angular controls applied on the passive particle, i.e., $u = (u_\theta, u_\phi)$.

The control (16) system can be written in the following form [8]:

$$\dot{x}(t) = F_0(x(t)) + \sum_{i=1}^{2} u_i(t) F_i(x(t)), \tag{17}$$

where $x = (\theta_p, \phi_p)$, $u = (u_1, u_2) \equiv (u_\theta, u_\phi)$, the drift $F_0(\cdot)$ is given by

$$F_0(x) = \frac{k}{4\pi} \frac{1}{1-\cos(\theta)} \frac{\partial}{\partial \phi_p},$$

and the control fields are

$$F_1 = \frac{\partial}{\partial \theta_p}, \quad F_2 = \frac{\partial}{\partial \phi_p}.$$

Proposition. The control system (17) is controllable.
Proof. The proof is similar to that given in [8].

Figure 1 shows the optimal trajectory of a passive particle whose motion is induced by a single vortex (V) with circulation $k = 2$ at the north pole, $V(0) = (0, \phi)$. The starting position of the passive particle is $P_0 = (2\pi/3, 0)$ and the target is $P_f = (2\pi/3, \pi/3)$. The time to perform the shift is $T = 10$. The number of control variables is $n = 2$ and the resulting optimal controls are $u_0 = (-0.0968, 0.1924)$ and $u_1 = (-0.1117, 0.2219)$, which are responsible for a value of the objective function equal to $f_2 = 1.1596$.

4.2   A Particle Advected by Two Vortices

In the two vortices ($N = 2$) and one particle ($P = 1$) problem, the dynamics of the vortices positions $V_1(\tau) = (\theta_1, \phi_1)$ and $V_2(\tau) = (\theta_2, \phi_2)$ are given by

$$\begin{cases} \dot{\theta}_1 = -\frac{k_2}{4\pi} \frac{\sin(\theta_2)\sin(\phi_1-\phi_2)}{1-\cos(\gamma_{12})} \\[2mm] \dot{\phi}_1 = -\frac{k_2}{4\pi} \frac{\cos(\theta_2)-\cot(\theta_1)\sin(\theta_2)\cos(\phi_1-\phi_2)}{1-\cos(\gamma_{12})} \\[2mm] \dot{\theta}_2 = -\frac{k_1}{4\pi} \frac{\sin(\theta_1)\sin(\phi_2-\phi_1)}{1-\cos(\gamma_{21})} \\[2mm] \dot{\phi}_2 = -\frac{k_1}{4\pi} \frac{\cos(\theta_1)-\cot(\theta_2)\sin(\theta_1)\cos(\phi_2-\phi_2)}{1-\cos(\gamma_{21})} \end{cases} \tag{18}$$

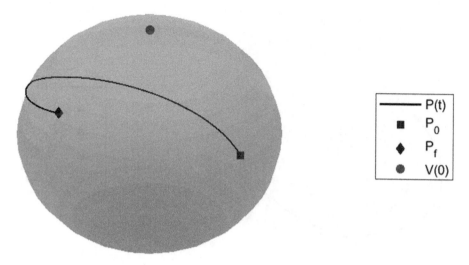

Fig. 1. Trajectory of a passive particle advected by a single vortex: $n = 2$, $P_0 = (2\pi/3, 0)$ and $P_f = (\pi/3, \pi)$.

with the given initial conditions $V_1(0) = (\theta_{10}, \phi_{10})$ and $V_2(0) = (\theta_{20}, \phi_{20})$. The value of $\cos(\gamma_{12})$ and $\cos(\gamma_{21})$ are computed in agreement with Eq. (8).

The dynamics of the passive particle induced by these two vortices and by the control is given by

$$
\begin{cases}
\dot{\theta}_p = -\frac{1}{4\pi}\left(k_1 \frac{\sin(\theta_1)\sin(\phi_p - \phi_1)}{1 - \cos(\gamma_{p1})} + k_2 \frac{\sin(\theta_2)\sin(\phi_p - \phi_2)}{1 - \cos(\gamma_{p2})}\right) + u_\theta \\[2ex]
\dot{\phi}_p = \frac{1}{4\pi}\left(k_1 \frac{\cos(\theta_1) - \cot(\theta_p)\sin(\theta_1)\cos(\phi_p - \phi_1)}{1 - \cos(\gamma_{p1})} + k_2 \frac{\cos(\theta_2) - \cot(\theta_p)\sin(\theta_2)\cos(\phi_p - \phi_2)}{1 - \cos(\gamma_{p2})}\right) + u_\phi
\end{cases}
$$
$$(19)$$

with the given initial conditions $P_0 = (\theta_{p0}, \phi_{p0})$. As in the preceding problem, $u = (u_\theta, u_\phi)$ represent the control applied on the passive particle.

Figure 2 shows the optimal trajectory of a passive particle whose motion is induced by two vortices (V_1 and V_2). The two vortices have circulation $k_1 = k_2 = 2$ and are initially located at $V_1(0) = (\pi/10, \pi/4)$ and $V_2(0) = (2\pi/3, \pi/3)$, respectively.

The initial position of the passive particle is $P_0 = (2\pi/3, 0)$ and the target position is $P_f = (2\pi/3, \pi/3)$. The time to perform the shift is $T = 10$. The number of control variables is $n = 2$ and the resulting optimal controls are $u_0 = (0, 0)$ and $u_1 = (-0.0699, 0.0274)$, which are responsible for a value of the objective function equal to $f_2 = 0.1876$.

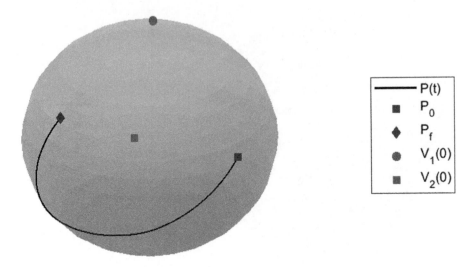

Fig. 2. Trajectory of a passive particle advected by two vortices: $n = 2$, $P_0 = (2\pi/3, 0)$ and $P_f = (\pi/3, \pi)$.

4.3   A Particle Advected by Three Vortices

In the problem of one passive particle ($P = 1$) advected by three vortices ($N = 3$), the dynamics of the vortices positions $V_1(\tau) = (\theta_1, \phi_1)$, $V_2(\tau) = (\theta_2, \phi_2)$ and $V_3(\tau) = (\theta_3, \phi_3)$ are given by Eq. (20), where the Bogomolov notation introduced in (9) is used,

$$
\begin{cases}
\dot{\theta}_1 = -\frac{1}{4\pi}\left(k_2\frac{\alpha_{12}}{1-\cos(\gamma_{12})} + k_3\frac{\alpha_{13}}{1-\cos(\gamma_{13})}\right) \\[2ex]
\dot{\phi}_1 = \frac{1}{4\pi}\left(k_2\frac{\beta_{12}}{\sin(\theta_1)(1-\cos(\gamma_{12}))} + k_3\frac{\beta_{13}}{\sin(\theta_1)(1-\cos(\gamma_{13}))}\right) \\[2ex]
\dot{\theta}_2 = -\frac{1}{4\pi}\left(k_1\frac{\alpha_{21}}{1-\cos(\gamma_{21})} + k_3\frac{\alpha_{23}}{1-\cos(\gamma_{23})}\right) \\[2ex]
\dot{\phi}_2 = \frac{1}{4\pi}\left(k_1\frac{\beta_{21}}{\sin(\theta_2)(1-\cos(\gamma_{21}))} + k_3\frac{\beta_{23}}{\sin(\theta_2)(1-\cos(\gamma_{23}))}\right) \\[2ex]
\dot{\theta}_3 = -\frac{1}{4\pi}\left(k_1\frac{\alpha_{31}}{1-\cos(\gamma_{31})} + k_2\frac{\alpha_{32}}{1-\cos(\gamma_{32})}\right) \\[2ex]
\dot{\phi}_3 = \frac{1}{4\pi}\left(k_1\frac{\beta_{31}}{\sin(\theta_3)(1-\cos(\gamma_{31}))} + k_2\frac{\beta_{32}}{\sin(\theta_3)(1-\cos(\gamma_{32}))}\right)
\end{cases}
\tag{20}
$$

with the initial conditions $V_1(0) = (\theta_{10}, \phi_{10})$, $V_2(0) = (\theta_{20}, \phi_{20})$, and $V_3(0) = (\theta_{30}, \phi_{30})$ given.

The dynamics of the passive particle induced by these two vortices and by the control is given by:

$$\begin{cases} \dot{\theta}_p = -\frac{1}{4\pi}\left(k_1\frac{\alpha_{p1}}{1-\cos(\gamma_{p1})} + k_2\frac{\alpha_{p2}}{1-\cos(\gamma_{p2})} + k_3\frac{\alpha_{p3}}{1-\cos(\gamma_{p3})}\right) + u_\theta \\[2mm] \dot{\phi}_p = \frac{1}{4\pi}\left(k_1\frac{\beta_{p1}}{\sin(\theta_p)(1-\cos(\gamma_{p1}))} + k_2\frac{\beta_{p2}}{\sin(\theta_p)(1-\cos(\gamma_{p2}))} + k_3\frac{\beta_{p3}}{\sin(\theta_p)(1-\cos(\gamma_{p3}))}\right) + u_\phi \end{cases}$$

(21)

with the given initial conditions $P_0 = (\theta_{p0}, \phi_{p0})$. As in the previous problems, the variables u_θ and u_ϕ represent the angular controls applied on the passive particle.

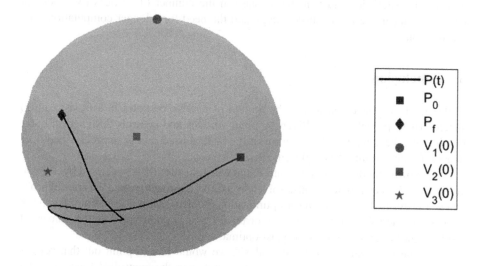

Fig. 3. Trajectory of a passive particle advected by three vortices: $n = 2$, $P_0 = (2\pi/3, 0)$ and $P_f = (\pi/3, \pi)$.

Figure 3 shows the optimal trajectory of a passive particle whose motion is induced by three vortices with circulation $k_1 = k_2 = k_3 = 2$ and which is initially located at $V_1(0) = (\pi/10, \pi/4)$, $V_2(0) = (2\pi/3, \pi/3)$, and $V_3(0) = (\pi/2, \pi)$.

The initial position of the passive particle is $P_0 = (2\pi/3, 0)$ and the target location is $P_f = (2\pi/3, \pi/3)$. The time to perform the shift is $T = 10$. The number of control variables is $n = 2$ and the resulting optimal controls are $u_0 = (-0.0254, 0.4252)$ and $u_1 = (-0.0023, -0.4456)$, which are responsible for a value of the objective function equal to $f_2 = 2.1788$.

Table 1 summarizes the results obtained in the numerical resolution of the three problems presented here. In addition, the CPU time (CPUt), in seconds, needed for the computations with the Matlab nonlinear programming solver fmincon, in a Intel Core i7 machine with 16 GB RAM, is also included.

Table 1. Summary with the results obtained for $N = 1, 2$ and 3 vortices.

N	u_0		u_1		f_2	CPUt (s)
1	−0.0968	0.1924	−0.1117	0.2219	1.1596	29
2	0.0000	0.0000	−0.0699	0.0274	0.1876	54
3	−0.0254	0.4252	−0.0023	−0.4456	2.1788	3

It can be seen in Table 1 that there is no regularity in the variation of the objective function (f_2) and CPU time (CPUt) values. This shows that each of the problems has its own characteristics and that the increase in the number of vortices (N) does not necessarily mean the use of more energy and the need for a longer computation time for its resolution.

5   Conclusion

In this work, we have considered the motion of passive particles in a (non-rotating) sphere. These particles were driven by point vortices and controls designed in order to minimize the square of the L^2 norm of the control used during the prescribed time interval for performing the displacement.

It is shown that the system is controllable when the motion is generated by a single vortex ($N = 1$). The problem is also solved by a direct approach, where the control problem is transformed into a nonlinear optimization problem that is solved numerically. In the case of one ($N = 1$), two ($N = 2$), or three ($N = 3$) point vortices, the numerical results show the existence of near/quasi-optimal control.

In connection with this type of analysis, we would like to point out that several interesting problems arise here. For example, how can the controlled trajectories be compared with the geodesics defined by the starting and ending points of the trajectories? Real applications of point vortices on a sphere consider the rotating sphere to mimic the rotation of the Earth. How does the rotation of the sphere affect the control of the passive particles? These issues will be the subject of a forthcoming work.

Acknowledgements. Carlos Balsa was partially supported by CeDRI which is financed by FCT within the Project Scope: UIDB/05757/2020.

Sílvio Gama was partially supported by (i) CMUP, member of LASI, which is financed by national funds through FCT - Fundação para a Ciência e a Tecnologia, I.P., under the project with reference UIDB/00144/2020, and (ii) project SNAP NORTE- 01–0145–FEDER–000085, co-financed by the European Regional Development Fund (ERDF) through the North Portugal Regional Operational Programme (NORTE2020) under Portugal 2020 Partnership Agreement.

References

1. Aref, H.: Motion of three vortices. Phys. Fluids **22**(3), 393–400 (1979)
2. Aref, H.: Point vortex dynamics: a classical mathematics playground. J. Math. Phys. **48**(6), 065401 (2007). https://doi.org/10.1063/1.2425103

3. Aref, H.: Relative equilibria of point vortices and the fundamental theorem of algebra. Proc. Roy. Soc. Math. Phys. Eng. Sci. **467**(2132), 2168–2184 (2011)

4. Babiano, A., Boffetta, G., Provenzale, A., Vulpiani, A.: Chaotic advection in point vortex models and two-dimensional turbulence. Phys. Fluids **6**(7), 2465–2474 (1994)

5. Balsa, C., Gama, S.: A numerical algorithm for optimal control problems with a viscous point vortex. In: Palma, L.B., Neves-Silva, R., Gomes, L. (eds). CONTROLO 2022. LNCS, vol 930. Springer, Cham (2022). https://doi.org/10.1007/978-3-031-10047-5_64

6. Balsa, C., Gama, S.M.: The control of the displacement of a passive particle in a point vortex flow. J. Comput. Methods Sci. Eng. **21**(5), 1215–1229 (2021). https://doi.org/10.3233/jcm-204710

7. Bogomolov, V.A.: Dynamics of vorticity at a sphere. Fluid Dyn. **12**, 863–870 (1977)

8. Bonnard, B., Cots, O., Wembe, B.: A Zermelo navigation problem with a vortex singularity. ESAIM: Control Optim. Calc. Var. **27**, S10 (2021)

9. Chorin, A.: Vortex methods. Tech. rep. Lawrence Berkeley Lab. CA (United States) (1993)

10. Chorin, A.J.: Vorticity and turbulence, vol. 103. Springer Science & Business Media (2013). https://doi.org/10.1007/978-1-4419-8728-0

11. Conte, S.D., De Boor, C.: Elementary numerical analysis: an algorithmic approach. SIAM (2017)

12. Crowdy, D.: Point vortex motion on the surface of a sphere with impenetrable boundaries. Phys. Fluids **18**(3), 036602 (2006)

13. Dritschel, D.G., Boatto, S.: The motion of point vortices on closed surfaces. Proc. R. Soc. A. **471**, 20140890 (2015)

14. Helmholtz, H.: Über integrale der hydrodynamischen gleichungen, welche den wirbelbewegungen entsprechen. J. für die reine und angew. Math. **55**, 25–55 (1858). http://eudml.org/doc/147720

15. Hwang, S., Kim, S.C.: Point vortices on hyperbolic sphere. J. Geom. Phys. **59**(4), 475–488 (2009). https://doi.org/10.1016/j.geomphys.2009.01.003

16. Kimura, Y., Okamoto, H.: Vortex motion on a sphere. J. Phys. Soc. Jpn. **56**(12), 4203–4206 (1987). https://doi.org/10.1143/JPSJ.56.4203

17. Kirchhoff, G.R.: Vorlesungenbër mathematische physik. Mechanik (1876)

18. Laurent-Polz, F.: Point vortices on a rotating sphere. Regul. Chaotic Dyn. **10**(1), 39–58 (2005)

19. Marques, G., Grilo, T., Gama, S., Pereira, F.L.: Optimal control of a passive particle advected by a point vortex. In: Guarda, T., Portela, F., Santos, M.F. (eds.) ARTIIS 2021. CCIS, vol. 1485, pp. 512–523. Springer, Cham (2021). https://doi.org/10.1007/978-3-030-90241-4_39

20. Marques, G., Gama, S., Pereira, F.L.: Optimal control of a passive particle advected by a Lamb-Oseen (viscous) vortex. Computation **10**(6), 87 (2022)

21. Martin, D.: Two-dimensional point vortex dynamics in bounded domains: Global existence for almost every initial data. SIAM J. Math. Anal. **54**(1), 79–113 (2022). https://doi.org/10.1137/21M1413213

22. MathWorks: Matlab Optimization Toolbox: User's Guide (R2020a). The MathWorks Inc, Natick, Massachusetts, US (2020)

23. Mokhov, I.I., Chefranov, S.G., Chefranov, A.G.: Point vortices dynamics on a rotating sphere and modeling of global atmospheric vortices interaction. Phys. Fluids **32**(10), 106605 (2020)

24. Nava-Gaxiola, C., Montaldi, J.: Point vortices on the hyperbolic plane. J. Math. Phys. **55**, 102702 (2014). https://doi.org/10.1063/1.4897210

25. Newton, P.K.: The N-vortex problem: analytical techniques, vol. 145. Springer Science & Business Media (2001). https://doi.org/10.1007/978-1-4684-9290-3

26. Newton, P.K.: The n-vortex problem on a sphere: geophysical mechanisms that break integrability. Theoret. Comput. Fluid Dyn. **24**(1), 137–149 (2010)

27. Ragazzo, C.: The motion of a vortex on a closed surface of constant negative curvature. Proc. Roy. Soc. Math. Phys. Eng. Sci. **473**, 20170447 (2017). https://doi.org/10.1098/rspa. 2017.0447
28. Saffman, P.G.: Vortex dynamics. Cambridge University Press (1995)
29. Stremler, M.A.: On relative equilibria and integrable dynamics of point vortices in periodic domains. Theoret. Comput. Fluid Dyn. **24**(1–4), 25–37 (2010). https://doi.org/10.1007/s00162-009-0156-z
30. Lord, K., Thomson, W.: On vortex motion. Trans. R. Soc. Edin **25**, 217–260 (1869)
31. Umeki, M.: Clustering analysis of periodic point vortices with the l function. J. Phys. Soc. Jpn. **76**, 043401 (2006). https://doi.org/10.1143/JPSJ.76.043401
32. Umeki, M.: Point process analysis of vortices in a periodic box. Theoret. Appl. Mech. Jpn. **56**, 259–265 (2007). https://doi.org/10.11345/nctam.56.259
33. Zermelo, E.: Hydrodynamishe untersuchungen über die wirbelbewegungen in einer kugelfläche. Math. Phys. **47**, 201 (1902)

The Dangers of Gamification

Ricardo Queirós[1]([⊠])[iD] and Mário Pinto[2][iD]

[1] CRACS - INESC TEC & ESMAD - P. PORTO, Porto, Portugal
ricardoqueiros@esmad.ipp.pt
[2] ESMAD - P. PORTO, Porto, Portugal
mariopinto@esmad.ipp.pt
http://www.ricardoqueiros.com

Abstract. In the last decade, gamification has been a widely used mechanism to influence behavioral habits in users so that they are more positively involved in learning and business processes. There are many articles or applications that materialize this adoption by showing success stories. However, few are those who mention the dangers of its use. This article shares the main precautions to be taken when creating a gamified strategy, promoting the use of gamification design and evaluation frameworks, in order to create a balanced approach that meets the profiles of its users.

Keywords: Gamification · Standardization · Design frameworks

1 Introduction

The gaming market has grown exponentially. There are several reasons for this evolution, from the growing proliferation of mobile devices, the easy availability of games on the Internet, innovations in software and, mainly, in hardware, with the advent of consoles and advanced graphics engines. A report titled "Gaming Market: Global Industry Trends, Share, Size, Growth, Opportunity and Forecast 2021-2026", state that the global gaming market reached a value of 167.9 billion USD in 2020 and is expected to reach 287 billion dollars by 2026 [18].

With this growth and consequent importance of games in the day-to-day of society, games and similar approaches began to be applied to solve problems and create better experiences in several domains. Nowadays, we can coin all these approaches with the term "game-based solutions" (GBS) which can be defined as an aggregating term for several approaches, ranging from simple playful design, to gamification, serious games, simulation and even regular games.

Many of these concepts are often confused, and when asked to use gamification, you could be referring to some game-based solution. In this sense, it is important to distinguish the different types of solutions and adapt the best solution to the problem in question. For example, for a training application in a radioactive environment, where a lot of immersion is required, or in the treatment of a phobia where gameplay is crucial, the best solutions may be a simulation

T. Guarda et al. (Eds.): ARTIIS 2022, CCIS 1675, pp. 151–162, 2022.
https://doi.org/10.1007/978-3-031-20319-0_12

application and a serious game, respectively. Games are also often confused with gamification, and the main distinction between them is in the objective. In a game, entertainment is the result the creator hopes to achieve. In gamification, there is a predefined objective, which is closely linked to the domain of the organization that conceived it and which may be related, for example, to the business processes of an organization, or to educational competences in a school course [19].

The term "gamification" emerged in 2003 by Nick Pelling, a British computer game programmer, when he made the decision to transfer his knowledge of games to other contexts. To do so, he created the first startup in the field, Conundra. However, gamification was already spreading in several organizations, with special emphasis on the sales sector, and still in a non-virtual way. For example, McDonald's created the "Employee of the Month" award to reward the employee who stood out the most and made the result public by posting the winner's photo on the store's wall. This public recognition not only boosted the employee's ego, but motivated other employees to want to win the award. With the advent of information technologies and the Internet, today, many of these concepts are applied and implemented in digital systems. A prime example is Duolingo, a language learning app that uses gamification to engage and motivate users to learn a foreign language.

Gamification has become a strong trend at the educational and business levels. The consultancy Deloitte presented in its reports that by 2025 millennials (a generation that was born between 1981 and 1996 and that grew up following the development of games) will correspond to 75% of the world's active population. However, two other reports prepared by Gallup and Deloitte show that 71% of millennials feel little or no commitment to their work and that 44% of respondents feel stressed most of the time. Being a generation raised with computers and games, it is natural that gamification helps to solve these problems. That's why organizations are gamifying their processes to meet the distinct needs of this generation's workplace and justify the importance of this technique to keep an organization motivated and competitive.

Another study (MarketsandMarkets) states that the gamification market is projected to grow from 9 billion dollars in 2020 to 30.7 billion in 2025, at an annual growth rate of 27.4%. The main factors driving the growth of the gamification market are related to the return on investment that companies obtain through the use of gamification solutions, such as the use of rewards and employee recognition of their performance, in order to increase their involvement, and profitable offers to customers and consumers.

There are several domains where gamification can be applied from sports, social networks, sustainability, e-learning, finance and shopping, productivity, etc. One of the most promising domains is health and wellness. Health and wellbeing correspond to an area where we find a significant number of successful use cases of gamification, namely, in home care, fitness and nutrition, rehabilitation and physiotherapy, emotional health and healthcare. for kids.

For example, the Mango Health app simplifies your daily health routine, making it fun, easy and rewarding. Highlights of the app include being notified to take medications according to the pre-set schedule, keeping up to date on healthy habits and the interaction with medications and their side effects, accessing the entire health history, among others. All these features are gamified through levels, points and rewards, in order to facilitate home health care. The MyFitnessPal app encourages good nutrition practices so that users have healthier eating habits and control their weight. The Physera app contains exercises created by physiotherapists to increase strength and flexibility, whether in the context of injury rehabilitation or just in the context of persistent pain. The Happify app improves your emotional well-being, mental health and helps users overcome stress through science-based activities and games. The app has more than 30 challenges (tracks) to choose from, organized by skills, and tracks the user's progress in order to monitor the progress of their skills. All challenges are based on scientific research by neuroscientists and psychologists from reputable universities such as Stanford and Harvard.

Despite the importance already demonstrated, there is the reverse side of the medal that has been little (or not at all) discussed. There are many problems that can arise when applying a gamified strategy. The next sections share some key factors to consider in this process. Section 2 presents some gamification strategies materialized in gamification design frameworks. Section 3 presents the main dangers to be taken into account when defining a gamification strategy.

2   Gamification Design Frameworks

A framework can be defined as a conceptual structure that acts as an abstract (or concrete) guide for the construction of a software product. In the field of game/gamification design there is no consensus on the use of frameworks. In fact, Crawford [7] states that game design is too complex an activity to be reducible to a formal procedure. Julius and Salo [13] conclude that the process should be treated as an agile process that does not always follow a specific design framework. Despite the existence of dozens of frameworks around the world, several researchers [8,21] claim that gamification as an academic topic is still quite young and only a few well-established models and frameworks can be useful. In order to achieve a more empirical study, a literature review was carried out, between December 8 and 15, 2021, based on works indexed in three databases, namely Google Scholar, SCOPUS and Web of Knowledge. In this research, the keywords used were gamification, design and framework. The study identified 52 articles that present or make reference to a gamification framework. From these articles, 12 frameworks were obtained. Despite the high number of frameworks identified, six frameworks were referenced in more than 75% of the total articles.

Table 1 summarizes all frameworks based on their creation date, author, context and scope.

Kevin Werbach's 6D framework (Fig. 1) models the process of designing a gamification strategy composed of six steps: 1) define project objectives; 2) outline the behavior of the target audience; 3) describe the users; 4) define activity cycles; 5) highlight the importance of fun; and 6) define the appropriate tools.

Table 1. Comparison of gamification design frameworks

Framework	Author/Date	Context	Scope
6D	Werbach & Hunter (2012)	Gamification design	Define business objectives Delineate target behavior Describe yours players Devise activity loops Don't forget the fun Deploy appropriate tools
Octalysis	Chou, Y. (2015)	Gamification design	Main units Left/right brain Black/white hat
GAME	Marczewski (2015)	Game design	Relationship Autonomy Domain Purpose
MDA	Umar, R. (2015)	Game design	Mechanics Dynamics Aesthetics
MDE	Robson, K. (2015)	Gamification design	Mechanics Dynamics Emotions
SGD	Raftopoulos, M. (2014)	Gamification design	Discover Rephrase View Create Values/Ethics Reflect/Act Understand/Do

The framework is known for the importance it gives to the study of the users of the application to be gamified and the cycles of motivational activity to be employed.

The Octalysis framework (Fig. 2) was created by Chou [6] who recognized that there are eight different types of main drives that motivate people to perform any activity. Visually, the framework has an octagonal shape where the main units (core drives) are represented in each corner. The units on the right (right brain) represent creative, artistic and social movements, while the units on the left (left brain) represent the logical and intellectual aspects. These drives favor extrinsic or intrinsic motivation. In fact, most companies aspire to design exclusively for extrinsic motivation, which is about achieving a goal or getting a reward. However, Chou states that intrinsic motivation, the use of creativity and socialization, should be the priority in the design of the gamification strategy to encourage continuous motivation and make the activity itself rewarding.

The framework also distinguishes the bottom and top sides of the octagon and Chou coined both parts as Black Hat and White Hat, respectively. The first defines negative motivations where people are being motivated to take a certain action because of fear of losing, curiosity about the next event, or the effort

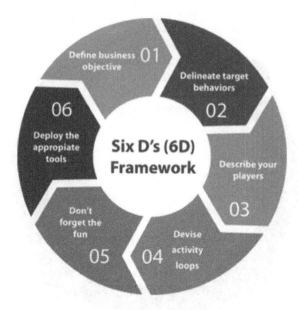

Fig. 1. 6D gamification framework.

to get things they cannot have. The latter is considered an active motivation. These positive impulses motivate individuals through creativity, make them feel powerful because of a sense of control and an impression of greater meaning. In short, to have a balance strategy, Chou points out that successful gamification requires consideration of all core units.

Marczewski in 2015 created a framework, called GAME [15] based on two phases. Firstly, planning and design, which includes collecting, through research, important information such as the types of users in the context where the gamification will be applied. Then, the best solution for goals and engagement is designed, measuring user activities and their results. It applies its own motivation framework called RAMP (Relationship, Autonomy, Mastery, Purpose).

MDA stands for Mechanics, Dynamics and Aesthetics [10] and can be defined as a framework that uses a formal approach to bridge the gap between game design and development. According to this framework, games can be divided into three elements: rules, system and fun. These elements translate directly into the respective design components, which must be defined when designing a game. The MDA framework has been modified by different authors to be suitable for various contexts. One of the changes resulted in the MDE framework, where the concept of aesthetics is replaced by emotions to describe the user experience.

Sustainable Gamification Design (SGD) is a business gamification framework developed by Marigo Raftopoulos in 2014. This work intends to value the benefits of creation, the risks of destruction, and also the concern about being ethically correct. Based on its author, this type of framework could potentially produce more responsible and sustainable results.

Fig. 2. The Octalysis gamification framework.

For a more in-depth reading on this topic, other studies [17] that gather more information about these (and more) frameworks should be consulted.

3   Dangers in the Use of Gamification

Several studies [2,9,11,12,22] were carried out in the last decade in order to identify the other side of gamification, that is, its negative side. A systematic mapping study [3] was conducted to identify the gamification negative effects in education contexts. Almost all the results presented 4 negative effects: Indifference, Loss of performance, Undesired behavior and Declining effects. In fact, loss of performance is the most cited effect and it is due mainly to the fact that learners focus more on gamified mechanics than on the assessment or some users did not understand the rules and this may have hindered their performance and, also due to demotivating effects on the inappropriate use of certain gamification elements that foster demotivation. Other negative effect is undesired behaviour when gamification causes a different effect (positive or negative) either due to bad planning or to the lack of it. Some studies reveal indifference as a common behaviour when users were not interested in the gamification that was implemented, choosing traditional methods over gamified ones.

Also some of these studies reveal the sense of undesired competition which is pointed as a big issue in the engagement process. Here the leaderboards are a common resource to promote competition, still, it can be harmful for users with low performance and low self-esteem, since they can feel forced in a competition with their peers, which can negatively affect their sense of competence and result in the reduction of their interest and engagement mostly if they are constantly positioned in the lower places of the leaderboard [4].

Based on these studies, all are unanimous in saying that those issues occurred due to the lack of proper frameworks for planning and/or deploying gamification in a organizational or learning context. Another issue that influenced on those outcomes is the absence of instructional motivational design theories to support the implementation of gamification, since they are crucial to produce well-thought gamified strategies that will have positive impacts on the users [5, 14].

In this realm, two types of motivation are typically connected to gamification topics: intrinsic and extrinsic motivation. There are several definitions of these two types of motivation that are found in the literature. Here we retrieve those of researchers Edward Deci and Richard Ryan:

- Intrinsic motivation - influences users in carrying out activities just because they want to or for their personal satisfaction;
- Extrinsic motivation - influences users in carrying out activities in order to achieve a measurable good. In terms of gamification, would be a reward given to a user (e.g. a badge).

In practice, it is simple to distinguish them: an intrinsically motivated person performs activities for pleasure, fun or as a form of growth, without need rewards. On the other hand, a extrinsic motivated person is driven solely by the measurable benefits that realization brings, such as, for example, a salary increase or a promotion, and not for wanting to do it. In this scope, there are several frameworks that model the way we are motivated, namely:

- Maslow's Hierarchy of Needs [16] - there is a sequentially in the human needs which may vary slightly depending on the context, but which, in general, defines our priorities as physiological and safety needs, then love and feeling of belonging, followed by self-esteem and, finally, self-fulfillment;
- Deci and Ryan's Theory of Self-Determination [20] - presents three needs of the human being that motivate us intrinsically: relationship (or connection), autonomy and competence. The relationship is experienced when people feel they are socially connected each other in some way. Autonomy is defined as the ability to make free and independent choices without coercion. Competence is the desire to be good at something, overcome challenges, learn and improve and eventually master the task or process;
- RAMP framework by Andrzej Marczewski [1] - the RAMP (Relatedness, Autonomy, Mastery and Purpose) is an adaptation of the theory presented previously, adding a new axis (purpose), which can be seen as the need to have a meaning for our actions, that is, we want to feel that when we do something, there is a reason and that can have a greater meaning. A good example

is Wikipedia, composed of millions of articles, all free, where whoever contributes has no other reason to do so than to provide a better understanding of topics from various domains on a global scale.

Despite being a trend these days, building a gamification strategy is often neglected or rushed, which brings a lot of inconvenience to an organization. Since time is a valuable and small variable, the tendency to apply gamification is often limited to the triad known as PBL (Points, Badges and Leaderboards). Currently, the concept is so ingrained in the market that most people confuse PBL with gamification and believe that if you put points, add some badges and provide a leaderboard, it will turn the once boring application into a engaging and fun application. If used correctly, PBL is indeed a powerful and relevant mechanism, and a good starting point for gamifying a system, but gamification is much more than using the PBL concept. Many gamification professionals are only familiar with the implementation of PBL mechanics. This does not mean that the PBL method is not important for motivating behavior and leading people to certain actions. However, the technique is reductive, taking into account all the capabilities that gamification can provide.

It is not uncommon for users to consider PBL a superficial mechanic and therefore feel discouraged from participating. If you ask any player what makes a game fun, he'll never answer that it's because of PBL. In effect, players play because there are (in)visible elements in the game design that encourage them to challenge themselves and overcome difficult obstacles. Points and badges are often a nice bonus to have, depending on the context. This is the difference between extrinsic motivation, where the user is engaged because of a goal or reward, and intrinsic motivation, where the activity itself is fun and exciting, with or without reward.

On the other hand, a gamification strategy is typically implemented without taking into account the profiles of the users who will use the gamified application. Marczewski defined a taxonomy (User Type Hexad - Fig. 3), whose main objective is to help everyone involved in the creation of gamified systems to understand the type of users that use the systems, their different types of motivations and interaction styles.

In his model, Marczewski proposes six types of users: entrepreneur, socializer, philanthropist, "free spirit", disruptor and player. Of the six types of users, four (entrepreneur, socializer, philanthropist and "free spirit") are intrinsically motivated by mastery (mastery), connection, goals (purpose) and autonomy. The remaining two (disruptor and player) are extrinsically motivated by change and rewards, respectively. For example, placing a leaderboard in an application where most users are not driven by competition or prizes can lead to frustration, distrust and abandonment of the application.

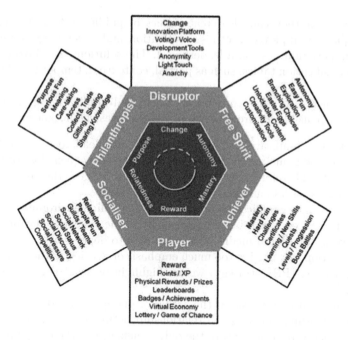

Fig. 3. User type Hexad.

Regardless of whether you want to cover all types of users, in a more balanced approach, or just the main type of users, in a more specialized approach, it is crucial to understand that a system is a living body that can scale and that its own users can change the behavior as they interact with the system. In this sense, it is convenient to have the notion that a more specialized approach may serve short-term interests, but may be limiting in the medium term.

On the other hand, a more balanced approach is more complex in its implementation, as covering all needs and interaction styles is demanding in terms of design. On the other hand, gamification must be understood as a way of encouraging a group of people and that not everyone responds in the same way to this stimulus. Therefore, gamification should not be mandatory, that is, it cannot be the only technique used.

Another risk of gamification is related to the promise of rewards that can create unrealistic expectations. While rewards are a powerful mechanism for working on extrinsic motivation, it is important that the rewards offered are sustainable. If an employee gets used to a reward, they may lose motivation if new (and better) incentives are not added. There is thus a risk of employee frustration if the reward is no longer attractive. It is therefore crucial that you make sure that sustainability is possible before adding incentives for repetitive or common tasks.

In addition to the loss of money and time, there are ethical risks in gamification practices. Leaderboards can encourage competition through socialized achievement, but they can also create issues of public pride and humiliation. For example, an employee may lose motivation and lower their self-esteem if they continually rank last on a leaderboard. The solutions may involve diversifying the classification tables, such as partial, contextual, temporal and thematic tables.

Finally, there are other consequences of a bad application of gamification that those responsible for creating gamified strategies should know:

- Distraction - gamification, if poorly applied, can lead to users getting distracted by the game and not learning, with the consequent loss of time and productivity. Therefore, it is crucial to be able to achieve the objective of the game, that is, users must know their purpose well;
- Addiction - since gamification occurs mainly in online environments, through electronic devices, it can be seen, especially in the educational context, as an incentive to use digital media, which can lead to dependence;
- Pointsification - by placing too much emphasis on scoring as the main element of gamification (PBL strategy) we are highlighting what is less essential for games;
- Exploitationware - consists of the action of manipulating/deceiving users to achieve something, making the relationship between the company and customers a one-way street, where the only beneficiary is the company itself.

4   Conclusions

This article intends to demonstrate that not "everything is rosy" in the world of gamification. Most gamified applications are built ad hoc, without any use of design frameworks and the coverage of the various types of users is almost always neglected. All these actions lead to an unbalanced gamification where success is sterile. Therefore, it is advisable to use gamification frameworks to formalize and sustain the constructive process of a gamified approach where the user is the center of attention because it is he who we want to stimulate and change his behavior towards organizational or educational goals.

In our opinion, the key to these dangers is essentially the regulation and standardization of gamification. For this, it is urgent that the responsible entities (educational and not only) begin to make efforts in this direction and in the short/medium term appear specifications that formalize the gamification processes from their dynamics, mechanics to the elements that we all interact in a gamified application. These initiatives will benefit everyone in combating the duplication, inconsistencies and lack of interoperability that plague the gamification world today.

As a future work, it is expected to create a survey to understand which gamification design frameworks are being used and to present a framework that aggregates the main valences of the most popular ones in order to find some consensus in the international community.

Acknowledgements. This paper is based on the work done within the FGPE Plus: Learning tools interoperability for gamified programming education project supported by the European Union's Erasmus Plus programme (agreement no. 2020-1-PL01-KA226-HE-095786).

References

1. Even ninja monkeys like to play: Gamification, game thinking & motivational design (2015)
2. Algashami, A., Vuillier, L., Alrobai, A., Phalp, K., Ali, R.: Gamification risks to enterprise teamwork: Taxonomy, management strategies and modalities of application. Systems **7**(1) (2019). https://doi.org/10.3390/systems7010009, https://www.mdpi.com/2079-8954/7/1/9
3. Almeida, C., Kalinowski, M., Feijó, B.: A systematic mapping of negative effects of gamification in education/learning systems. In: 2021 47th Euromicro Conference on Software Engineering and Advanced Applications (SEAA), pp. 17–24 (2021). https://doi.org/10.1109/SEAA53835.2021.00011
4. Andrade, F., Mizoguchi, R., Isotani, S.: The bright and dark sides of gamification, vol. 9684, pp. 1–1, Jun 2016. https://doi.org/10.1007/978-3-319-39583-817
5. Attali, Y., Arieli-Attali, M.: Gamification in assessment: Do points affect test performance? Comput. Educ. **83**, 57–63 (2015). https://doi.org/10.1016/j.compedu.2014.12.012
6. Chou, Y.: Actionable gamification - beyond points, badges, and leaderboards. Tech. rep, Octalysis Media, Mar 2015
7. Crawford, C.: The Art of Computer Game Design. McGraw-Hill Inc., USA (1984)
8. Hamari, J., Koivisto, J., Sarsa, H.: Does gamification work? - a literature review of empirical studies on gamification. In: 2014 47th Hawaii International Conference on System Sciences, pp. 3025–3034 (2014)
9. Hammedi, W., Leclercq, T., Poncin, I., Alkire (Ne Nasr), L.: Uncovering the dark side of gamification at work: Impacts on engagement and well-being. J. Bus. Res. **122**, 256–269 (2021). https://doi.org/10.1016/j.jbusres.2020.08.032, https://www.sciencedirect.com/science/article/pii/S0148296320305415
10. Hunicke, R., Leblanc, M., Zubek, R.: Mda: A formal approach to game design and game research. AAAI Workshop - Technical Report 1, Jan 2004
11. Hyrynsalmi, S., Smed, J., Kimppa, K.: The dark side of gamification: How we should stop worrying and study also the negative impacts of bringing game design elements to everywhere, May 2017
12. Jiang, K.: The dangers of gamification why we shouldn't build a game layer on top of the world (2011)
13. Julius, K., Salo, J.: Designing gamification. Tech. rep, Marketing (2013)
14. de Marcos, L., Domnguez, A., de Navarrete, J.S., Pags, C.: An empirical study comparing gamification and social networking on e-learning. Comput. Educ. **75**, 82–91 (2014). https://doi.org/10.1016/j.compedu.2014.01.012, https://www.sciencedirect.com/science/article/pii/S036013151400030X
15. Marczewski, A.: Game thinking. even ninja monkeys like to play: Gamification, game thinking and motivational design. Tech. rep., CreateSpace Independent Publishing Platform (2015)
16. Maslow, A.H.: A theory of human motivation. Psychol. Rev. **50**, 370–396 (1943). http://doi.apa.org/index.cfm?fuseaction=showUIDAbstract&uid=1943-03751-001

17. Mora, A., Riera, D., Gonzalez, C., Arnedo-Moreno, J.: A literature review of gamification design frameworks. In: 2015 7th International Conference on Games and Virtual Worlds for Serious Applications (VS-Games), pp. 1–8 (2015). https://doi.org/10.1109/VS-GAMES.2015.7295760
18. Mordor Intelligence: Gaming Market - Growth, Trends, Forecasts (2020–2025). https://www.researchandmarkets.com/reports/4845961/gaming-market-growth-trends-forecasts-2020 (2020), (Accessed 12 Dec 2020)
19. Queirós, R., Pinto, M.: Gamificação Aplicada às Organizações e ao Ensino. FCA - Editora de Informática, Portugal (2022)
20. Ryan, R., Deci, E.: Self-determination theory and the facilitation of intrinsic motivation, social development, and well-being. Am. Psychol. **55**, 68–78 (2000). https://doi.org/10.1037/0003-066X.55.1.68
21. Seaborn, K., Fels, D.I.: Gamification in theory and action: A survey. Int. J. Hum.-Comput. Stud. **74**, 14–31 (2015). https://doi.org/10.1016/j.ijhcs.2014.09.006, http://www.sciencedirect.com/science/article/pii/S1071581914001256
22. Toda, A., Valle, P.H., Isotani, S.: The Dark Side of Gamification: An Overview of Negative Effects of Gamification in Education Sep 2018. https://doi.org/10.1007/978-3-319-97934-2_9

Mobile Applications in Tourism: A Tale of Two Perspectives

Gorete Dinis[1,2,3(✉)] ⓘ, Maria Carlos Lopes[1,3] ⓘ, and Adelaide Proença[1,4] ⓘ

[1] Polytechnic Institute of Portalegre, Portalegre, Portugal
gdinis@ipportalegre.pt
[2] GOVCOPP - Research Unit on Governance, Competitiveness and Public Policies, Aveiro, Portugal
[3] CiTUR - Research Center for Tourism, Innovation and Development, Algarve, Portugal
[4] VALORIZA - Research Center for the Valorization of Endogenous Resources, Portalegre, Portugal

Abstract. The evolution of mobile devices has allowed the development of features, such as mobile applications (apps), which have contributed to making tourism services and destinations more accessible, significantly changing consumer habits. Currently, apps made available by mobile devices occupy a prominent place in the daily lives of individuals. Thus, the objective of this paper is, on the one hand, to understand the use and satisfaction of mobile applications in the context of tourist trips carried out by the Portuguese and, on the other hand, to know the offer of tourism-related apps available on the Google Play Store and App Store. For that, a quantitative methodology was applied, through the development and application of a survey through social media, between December 21, 2020 and January 8, 2021, and the quantification and description of travel and tourism Apps available in online stores in January 2021. In general, it can be observed that the respondents are knowledgeable and users of travel-related apps, especially in accommodation, navigation, and lodging field. The study offers a valuable contribution to the knowledge of consumer behavior in tourism and the app market.

Keywords: Tourism · Mobile applications · Apps · Technology

1 Introduction

Information and communication technologies have strongly influenced distribution and communication in the tourism sector. The deep technological transformations and their exponential adoption by consumers revolutionized the tourism market, triggering the interest of enterprises and tourism destinations and the rapid adoption of technological innovations for the distribution of products and services and communication with the consumer. Currently, it is in the digital world that tourism enterprises and destinations have started to operate, promote and commercialize a large part of the economic transactions and the provision of services in the tourism activity [1].

T. Guarda et al. (Eds.): ARTIIS 2022, CCIS 1675, pp. 163–174, 2022.
https://doi.org/10.1007/978-3-031-20319-0_13

Mobile devices have evolved rapidly, with the smartphone being the most used worldwide, exceeding in Portugal, since 2014, the use of mobile phones [2].

Applications that work explicitly on a mobile device, that is, that are installed and run on smartphones, are called "mobile apps" or, even more abbreviated, "m-apps" [3]. Therefore, m-app can be defined as "end-user software applications that are designed for a mobile device operating system and which extends the device's capabilities by enabling users to perform particular tasks." [4, p. 2].

There are apps for a variety of purposes, which can be classified into different categories, such as entertainment, commerce, education, health, interaction or social meetings, travel, among others. The apps can be obtained, free of charge or at affordable prices, mainly through the official online stores of enterprises that own the main operating systems, namely the App Store (iPhone) and Google Play (Android). The number of apps has been steadily increasing over the years, existing, in 2020, available for downloading around 3.4 million apps in Google Play while nearly 2.09 million apps are available on the Apple App Store [5].

There is a diversity of travel-related apps in the market [6], whose purpose ranges from booking accommodation and transport, through booking restaurants and cultural/sports activities, language translators, interactive and virtual reality information content, maps, itineraries, and many others [7], which makes this category of apps the seventh most popular being downloaded [8]. This process of increasing use, acceptance, and dependence of users on various tourism apps was accelerated due to the pandemic caused by Covid-19, and the need to offer touchless services by tourist attractions [9].

With a growing number of users and a wide variety of apps emerging, it is expected that in the next decade "there will be thousands of more mobile applications that will facilitate the day-to-day movement of travelers without the assistance of manpower" [10, p. 2], therefore it is essential for the tourism stakeholders to know the profile of users of travel-related apps, as well as the offer and evaluation of users of mobile applications in the market. And, to our knowledge, there are few studies that focus on tourism-related apps, mainly that approach apps from two perspectives on the demand and supply side.

Thus, the main purpose of this paper is to understand, on the one hand, the app use and satisfaction of Portuguese public in the context of a travel trip and, on the other hand, to ascertain whether the online stores provide individuals with diversity and the same opportunity to access apps.

To carry out this research, a survey was carried out that was applied to the Portuguese context, however, the methodology used can be replicated in other geo-graphic or public contexts, and a quantitative analysis of the main tourism- related apps available in online stores.

This knowledge will contribute to a deeper and more sustained reflection on consumer usage and satisfaction with apps in the context of travel, and consequently, point out paths on how to give visibility to enterprises and tourist destinations and remain competitive in the app market.

Following a brief background section presenting the most relevant approaches portrayed in scientific literature, the research methodology is outlined. Research findings are then reported and discussed. Lastly, the most pertinent conclusions are presented, along with the limitations of the study and recommendations for further research.

2 Background

Individuals may even use information technologies in their professional and social daily lives, but this does not mean that they do so in the context of tourist activities [11, 12].

Furthermore, the propensity that an individual has to use new technologies is directly related to the use of new technologies throughout their experience [13].

In turn, the technology acceptance model refers to three key assumptions to determine an individual's propensity to use a new technology: an individual's general predisposition with regard to perceived usefulness, perceived ease of use, and perceived risks [3].

Thus, regarding to perceived ease of use, a new technology is more likely to be used by individuals who have had previous experience with similar technologies [14, 15]. Regarding this first assumption, the same authors report that the probability of perceiving more perceived usefulness is also greater for individuals who have already experienced similar technology in the past.

[14–16] highlight the spillover effect in this context of using new technologies. In other words, the authors consider that workers who for professional reasons have started to adopt new technologies, denote higher levels of perceived usefulness, ease of use and reduction of perceived risks when using new technologies in the private context, including in the field of tourism.

From another perspective, individuals who work full-time use the internet more intensively and are more likely to use social networks than those who work part-time [17]. This factor was also verified by [18]. as being decisive in the use of sports applications and verified by [19]. A as being decisive in the use of applications in general.

[3] states that the age of the tourists and the foreign origin of the tourists are constraints on the use of apps by these tourists.

In the scope of the age factor, several studies were developed in order to understand the influence it has on the use of new technologies [20]. Thus, a study developed by [21] demonstrated that there is little interaction between elderly individuals and digital channels. It was also identified as a constraint for elderly tourists when carrying out a trip, the fact that important information about the trip is only available in digital format [22].

However, there are several factors that, regardless of an individual's age, do not affect their ability to use new technologies. At stake is the high level of qualifications; the fact that they are professionally active; high income and high motivation to increase their level of knowledge [23]. In the same sense, it was possible to verify the growing trend of the use of ICT by senior tourists, who benefit from new experiences [24].

For tourists in whom these conditions were verified, despite their advanced age, the use of the internet and new technologies was found to be a constant both in the preparation of their own trips and, later, during the tourism activities they carry out.

Apps, like other technologies, such as virtual reality and augmented reality, are fundamental instruments for a greater effectiveness of the tourist experience [25, 26].

The first tourism apps that appeared on the market had the function of helping with travel planning and made it possible to make hotel and transport reservations [27]. However, all the technological innovation, which boosted the functions and use of mobile devices, namely mobile phones; it intensified the use of the internet, in the sense that it increased its reach to a large part of the world's population; and triggered the speed of data and information flow, contributed to the development of a significant number of apps with the most diverse functionalities, with no slowdown in their development and production in the near future [28].

The spectrum of development and performance of apps is vast, ranging from allowing tourists to choose the route with less traffic, obtaining information on time about possible flight delays, as well as finding a place to stay in any tourism destination [29].

Since the emergence of tourism apps, tourism enterprises have recognized their importance in the sense that they have allowed the provision of services more efficiently to tourists, leading to higher levels of satisfaction, namely tourism-related apps with location services and those that allow for interactive information [30].

In this sense, also a study developed by [31] found that two enterprises in the restaurant sector had a significant increase in their turnover during the confinement period caused by Covid-19, due to the use by their customers of home food delivery apps, the that allowed them to have the food they wanted and whenever they wanted in their homes, just by using the apps and placing the desired order.

In the same context, a study developed by [32] concluded that the use of food delivery apps provides advantages for catering establishments, since they are noticeable on online sales platforms and the growth of this visibility to be a catalyst for more and more awareness. The same authors argue that tourism destinations also benefit from the use of apps by tourists, since both the catering establishments and the gastronomic culture of the destination gain notoriety in a showcase of worldwide visibility, sharpening the will of potential tourists to visit these destinations. Travelers also take advantage of new technologies, as the use of food delivery apps provides them with better value for money.

The mobile technologies add a lot of value to tourists' travel experiences as they allow them to participate and interact in a greater number of tourist activities [33].

The apps already play a significant role in tourism marketing and distribution and will play an increasingly important role in the future [34]. Furthermore, ICTs improve communication with tourists and promote more sustainable and intelligent tourist destinations, for example the most innovative apps such as augmented reality [24].

There is no doubt that applications have enormous potential for consumers [35] however, the constant emergence of new apps and the discouraging factors in the use of technology, raise challenges for mobile technology developers and distribution platforms for applications in mobile phone operating systems, justifying the need for studies in tourism sector.

From another perspective, and despite the decisive role that mobile tourism applications have in planning, preparing, carrying out and documenting travel [36] in general, and on tourist activities, in particular, other aspects and needs that can't be satisfied when using these applications to the detriment of the role played by people, such as trust, security, and other human aspects, which mobile tourism applications still cannot completely replace [35].

3   Methodology

With this study we intend to approach travel and tourism apps from two perspectives. On the one hand, it is intended to understand the use of tourism and travel apps by the

Portuguese and their satisfaction with this type of applications and, on the other hand, to know the offer of apps in the two main online stores, Google Play Store and App Store.

The appropriate procedure to understand the use of tourism and travel apps by the Portuguese and their satisfaction with this type of applications was based on a quantitative research paradigm, of a descriptive and non-experimental nature, whose objective is only to know and analyze a given phenomenon in a particular moment in time (cross-sectional study). The target population of interest in this second objective consists of individuals residing in Portugal who use tourism-related apps, aged over 15 years.

Given the size of the population and the nature of the objective of the study, it seemed appropriate to build, from scratch, a questionnaire as a data collection instrument. The survey has 14 closed questions, three of which are multiple choice. The first set of questions refers to the socio-demographic characteristics of the respondents, the second is about the characteristics of tourist trips taken and the last is about knowledge, use and satisfaction of the individuals with tourism-related apps.

This survey was developed through the Google Forms platform and distributed through social networks, namely Facebook and Instagram, between December 21, 2021 and January 8, 2022. The type of sampling used in the study is non-random – snowball. 383 surveys were collected and validated. The data is analyzed using SPSS 27.0 software. As the randomness of the sample was not guaranteed, the survey results were subject to a statistical treatment centered on univariate and bivariate analyzes (contingency tables) with a descriptive scope.

With univariate analysis, we intended to describe the profile of respondents in relation to variables such as sex, age, education, professional status, place of residence, characterize travel habits and understand the knowledge and use of tourism apps. In the bivariate analysis, different pairs of variables were crossed in order to understand whether there is any relationship between respondents who use tourism apps and which apps used with their socio-demographic characteristics and the duration of the trip; the purpose of using the apps and the gender of the responders; the apps used by the respondent's and the average length of the trips; the practice of (un)installing he tourism applications with the age of the respondents and the duration of the trip.

Bivariate tables were performed using contingency tables. The survey allowed, among other objectives, to know the opinion of the respondents about a certain type of tourism-related apps.

To complement the study, it was decided to carry out an analysis of the apps market, seeking to understand which apps are available to the user and if these vary with the service provider. To obtain data on the offer of tourism-related apps, the structured observation technique was used, and an observation grid was created with certain variables, namely the name, type of application, number of downloads, number and evaluation of users, and applied to Google Play Store and Apple App Store. The search for apps was carried out with the keyword "tourism". The data collection was carried out by the researchers in January 2021. Through the search, the various observation units were registered in the aforementioned grid. This record was the subject of a descriptive quantitative analysis with the objective of knowing, especially the offer of apps and their evaluation by users in the two main online stores, Google Play Store and App Store.

4 Findings and Discussion

From the application of the survey, 383 responses were received. In terms of characteristics of the respondents, 53% are female and 47% male. About 62% of respondents
are aged over 15 and under 29, and most reside in Alentejo, in the southern region of
Portugal (68%), and Lisbon region (14%).

Considering the academic qualifications of the respondents, 46% have completed
secondary or equivalent education, 40% have undergraduate level, 6% have the third
cycle of basic education and 5% have a master's degree. Most of the respondents are
students (46,2%), employed (39%) student worker (8%) and self-employed (5%).

When organizing the trip, 80% of the respondents stated that they prefer to use
tourism-related apps, while the remaining 20% said they preferred to use a travel agency.

In order to check if there is any group of respondents that is more likely to used
tourism-related apps, through the analysis of the contingency tables, it was found that
46% of the respondents have secondary or equivalent education, 40% have undergraduate
level, 47% are students and 67% reside in the Alentejo. These results are in line with the
conclusions drawn in the univariate analysis, focusing on the use of apps in the groups
of respondents that prevailed in the sample.

By crossing the variable with the duration of the trip, it was found that the respondents
who reported that they traveled four or more times a year were those who least expressed
a preference for the use of apps in the organization of a tourist trip, a fact that may have
been due to the smaller need for tourist information in frequent travelers.

Most of the respondents spend on their trips in average one week (56%) or less (34%),
and use tourism apps to search for information about accommodation (80%), navigation
(Global Positioning System) (50%), lodging (38%) and transport (35%). Cross tabulation
is used to understand if there is any relationship between the purpose of using the apps
and the gender of the responders. The results indicate that accommodation-related apps
are slightly more mentioned by female and, on the other hand, transport-related apps
have been mentioned most often by male (Table 1).

Table 1. Apps vs gender of the respondents

Apps purpose	Female	Male	Total
Accommodation	166	141	307
Lodging	70	76	146
Transport	59	74	133
Navigation (GPS)	94	101	195
Total	389	392	781

When asked about the knowledge and use of apps in tourism, more than half of
the respondents mentioned that they knew all the apps indicated, with the exception
of the Waze app where only 41% said they knew it. Among the apps best known by
the respondents are Google Maps (93%), Trivago (94%), Booking (89%), Uber (77%),

Uber eats (74%) and Glovo (74%). On average, respondents indicated that they used approximately 4.7 apps on trips.

A detailed analysis of the data of respondents who have already utilized tour-ism-related apps showed that 85% used Google Maps, 71% Booking.com, 54% Trivago and 53% Uber Eats. Only eight respondents reported never having used the tourism applications presented in the question. The least apps used by respondents are Momondo (21%), Airbnb (27%), Waze (28%) and Glovo (33%). This finding only corroborates with the study developed by [10] in Malaysia, in the case of Google Map, since they stated some of the most trending mobile apps examples used in that country are Grab Car, MyTaxi, GrabFood, FoodPanda, Google Map, Waze. The same applies to the study developed by [37] and applied to the Brasilian context, namely to university students, which concludes that Google Maps is the most used app, having been indicated by 88% of respondents and, on the other hand, the least mentioned are Booking.com (30%), TripAdvisor (28%), Currency Converter (22%) and Travel Translator (7%).

Relating the apps used by the respondents with their socio-demographic characteristics, it was found that the Trivago and Waze apps are more used by males, while the Momondo, Booking.com, Trivago and Glovo apps are most mentioned by females. Google Maps and Booking.com are the most used apps by respondents with different educational levels. Glovo, Uber, Uber Eats and Trivago are the most used apps by respondents with secondary education.

Regarding the Fig. 1, it is possible to observe that the higher the average duration of trips, in this case more than two weeks, the smaller the number of respondents who use the apps mentioned. The Glovo, Momomdo and Airbnb apps were not mentioned by almost any respondents who take trips with an average duration of more than three weeks, these results can be justified by the fact that this type of trips (medium/long duration) may be related to the visits to family and friends, therefore, there is no need for information or booking tourism services, namely accommodation or lodging.

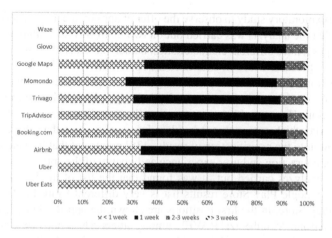

Fig. 1. Apps used by respondent's vs average length of the trips

Considering the respondents' satisfaction with the apps used on trips, 97% stated that they were "very satisfied" or "fairly satisfied", which justifies the fact that 99% of respondents said they would use tourism applications again on a future trip. However, when asked if, when the trip is over, they uninstall the tourism applications that they have used during the trip, around 53% said they uninstall some, an action that was found to be more common in the group of respondents who travel once a year, 40% do not uninstall any and 7% uninstall all apps, especially among respondents who travel two to three times a year. Through the cross tabulation between this variable and the age of the respondents, it was possible to conclude that, in the age groups from 40 to 49 and from 50 to 59 years old, even if slightly, it is where a greater number of respondents are observed to mention that they do not uninstall apps, which may suggest that these age groups are more loyal to apps and certain brands (Table 2).

Table 2. Uninstall tourism apps vs age of the respondents

Age of the respondents	None	Some	All	Total
15–19	38	87	10	135
20–29	49	50	7	106
30–39	13	15	3	31
40–49	28	27	4	59
50–59	18	17	3	38
60–69	4	8	0	12
>70	1	1	0	2
Total	151	205	27	383

From the exploratory study to observe the offer of apps on the market, it is important to point out that the analysis was carried out on two platforms that, although they have the same purpose, have different characteristics, namely in terms of presentation layout, type, categorization and selection criteria of the apps [38].

The selection criteria and the positioning of the apps in the search results for a given keyword would require a more in-depth study, which is beyond the scope of this investigation. However, [38] mentions that the App Store has more high-quality standard criteria which means that it has less low-quality apps than the Google Play Store. In relation to the prioritization of results, [38] points out that it mainly considers the relevance, interaction and user experience and quality of the app.

From the analyzes carried out, it was found that the list of the first ten apps that appear in the Google Play Store results list is very different from the App Store. In the Google Play Store, in the first positions are shown the app Booking, TripAdvisor, SkyScanner, Airbnb, Minube, iziTRAVEL, among others. These apps were downloaded by more than 1 million users, which could in some way justify why they are in the first ones, however, among the top ten apps there are also apps such as Aveiro Tourism or Visitguimaraes which only has 500 downloads. Regarding the evaluation of the apps, they were evaluated by a diverse number of users, ranging from five opinions on the Aveiro Tourism app and the two million opinions on Booking.com. Most apps were highly rated by users, with ratings above four (five is the maximum rating). With ratings of less than three, the Walkme Caminhadas de Portugal app stands out, evaluated at 1.9 in 33 opinions and the Visit Portugal Travel Guide with an evaluation of 2.5 in 386 opinions.

Regarding the analysis carried out in the App store, it was found that the apps that are available in the first 10 results differ greatly from the results of the Goggle App Store, in terms of popularity, purpose of the app and number of reviews. In the first results arise the apps walkbox, GetYourGuide, Tours&Travel, Paris Travel Guide, Tiqets - Museums & Attractions, Turijobs, DigitalPoints, among others. It should be noted that none of the apps is related to accommodation or transport, focusing mainly on attractions or tourist destination guides. Apps, in general, do not have many user reviews, however, the ratings are always higher than 4 (on a scale of 0 to 5).

5   Conclusion, Limitations and Future Research

The proliferation of apps in different areas, including tourism, and their growing adoption by consumers to search for information or book tourism services, drives the need for app developers to understand the behavior and travel habits of consumers, as well as to understand how can optimize apps so that they achieve a better positioning in online stores.

This paper aims to analyze, on the one hand, the use and satisfaction of mobile applications in the context of tourist trips carried out by the Portuguese and, on the other hand, to know the tourism-related apps available on the Google Play Store and App Store.

From the application of the survey, 383 responses were analyzed, and it can be concluded that 80% of the respondents use tourism-related apps. Some apps are more used than others, namely Google Maps, Booking.com, Trivago and Uber Eats. By crossing the variable use of apps on trips with the characteristics of the trip, it can be seen that apps are less used by frequent travelers and by those who, on average, take longer trips. The use of apps does not differ much between respondents, with their use prevailing in young students, users with secondary education and higher education. In terms of uninstalling apps after the trip, it was found that this action is more common in users under the age of 40.

From the analysis carried out on the offer of apps on the market available on the Google Play Store and App Store, it was found that these platforms have their own selection and positioning criteria in the list of results, with no similarity in the results. App Store apps are generally less popular, with lower numbers in terms of user reviews, however, the few existing reviews have a good rating by users.

This study has some limitations which are mainly due to the sampling technique used, which does not allow generalizations to the entire population, and the research carried out in online stores that needs to be repeated at other temporal moments to verify if the results were maintained in time, as well as the research carried out with other similar keywords, namely the keyword "travel" and also "tourism" in other languages.

For future research, it is suggested to use a sampling technique that allows including more users' residents in other regions of Portugal and with higher proportionality in terms of age, in addition, it would be important to deepen the study of the market for the offer of apps in online stores, in order to know better existing apps and the way they are made available to users. For future studies, it would be also important to understand the factors that influence the choice of apps and consumer loyalty.

Acknowledgements. This work was financially supported by the research unit on Governance, Competitiveness and Public Policy (UIDB/04058/2020), funded by national funds through FCT – Foundation for Science and Technology.

References

1. Haini, H.: Tourism, Internet penetration and economic growth. J. Policy Res. Tour. Leis. Events, 1–7 (2020)
2. Markteste. https://bit.ly/3NwjcRD. Accessed 30 Apr 2022
3. Beier, M., Aebli, A.: Who uses mobile apps frequently on vacation? Evidence from tourism in Switzerland. In: Inversini, A., Schegg, R. (eds.) Information and Communication Technologies in Tourism 2016, pp. 549–562. Springer, Cham (2016). https://doi.org/10.1007/978-3-319-28231-2_40
4. Pew Research Center. https://pewrsr.ch/3a2VUFD. Accessed 15 Feb 2022
5. Statista. https://bit.ly/3R3wEzl. Accessed 01 June 2022
6. Kennedy-Eden, H., Gretzel, U.: A taxonomy of mobile applications in tourism. E-Rev. Tour. Res. **10**(2), 47–50 (2012)
7. Ramos-Soler, I., Martínez-Sala, A.M., Campillo-Alhama, C.: ICT and the sustainability of world heritage sites. Analysis of senior citizens' use of tourism apps. Sustainability **11**(11), 3203 (2019). ZDNet. https://bit.ly/3uhKjt0. Accessed 10 May 2022
8. MacKay, K., Vogt, C.: Information technology in everyday and vacation context. Ann. Tour. Res. **39**(3), 1380–1401 (2012)
9. Gursoy, D., Chi, C.G.: Effects of COVID-19 pandemic on hospitality industry: review of the current situations and a research agenda. J. Hosp. Mark. Manag. **29**(5), 527–529 (2020)
10. Filho, L.M., Batista, J.O., Cacho, A.D., Soares, A.L.V.: Aplicativos Móveis e Turismo: Um Estudo Quantitativo Aplicando a Teoria do Comportamento Planejado. Rosa dos Ventos **9**(2), 179–199 (2017). Universidade de Caxias do Sul
11. Parra-López, E., Bulchand-Gidumal, J., Gutiérrez-Taño, D., Díaz-Armas, R.: Intentions to use social media in organizing and taking vacation trips. Comput. Hum. Behav. **27**(2), 640–654 (2011)
12. Vatanparast, R., Qadim, H.Z.: A cross-cultural study on mobile internet usage. Int. J. Mob. Mark. **4**(2), 14–27 (2009)
13. Kim, D.-Y., Park, J., Morrison, A.M.: A model of traveller acceptance of mobile technology. Int. J. Tour. Res. **10**(5), 393–407 (2008)
14. Oh, S., Lehto, X.Y., Park, J.: Travelers' intent to use mobile technologies as a function of effort and performance expectancy. J. Hosp. Mark. Manag. **18**(8), 761–781 (2009)
15. Venkatesh, V., Davis, F.D.: A theoretical extension of the technology acceptance model: four longitudinal field studies. Manag. Sci. **46**(2), 186–204 (2000)
16. Conroy, S., Williams, A.: Use of internet, social networking sites, and mobile technology for volunteerism, AARP report, April 2014

17. Piwek, L., Joinson, A., Morvan, J.: The use of self-monitoring solutions amongst cyclists: an online survey and empirical study. Transp. Res. Part A **77**, 126–136 (2015)
18. Lai, C.-H.: An integrated approach to untangling mediated connectedness with online and mobile media. Comput. Hum. Behav. **31**, 20–26 (2014)
19. Holt, K., Shehata, A., Strömbäck, J., Ljungberg, E.: Age and the effects of news media attention and social media use on political interest and participation: do social media function as leveller? Eur. J. Commun. **28**(1), 19–34 (2013)
20. Hwang, J., Kim, J.J., Lee, L.J.S.-H., Sahito, N.: How to form wellbeing perception and its outcomes in the context of elderly tourism: moderating role of tour guide services. Int. J. Environ. Res. Public Health **17**, 1029 (2020). https://doi.org/10.3390/ijerph17031029
21. Lopes, M.C.: Relação entre turismo e qualidade de vida no turismo sénior. Avaliação na Eurorregião. (Tese de Doutoramento). Universidade de Vigo. Vigo (2020)
22. Alén, E., Losada, N., Carlos, P.: Profiling the segments of senior tourists throughout motivation and travel characteristics. Curr. Issue Tour. **20**(14), 1454–1469 (2017). https://doi.org/10. 1080/13683500.2015.1007927
23. Neuhofer, B., Ladkin, A.: (Dis)connectivity in the travel context: setting an agenda for research. In: Schegg, R., Stangl, B. (eds.) Information and Communication Technologies in Tourism 2017, pp. 347–359. Springer, Cham (2017). https://doi.org/10.1007/978-3-319-51168-9_25
24. Zhang, H., Leung, X.Y., Bai, B., Li, Y.: Uncovering crowdsourcing in tourism apps: a grounded theory study. Tour. Manag. **87**, 104389, 39 (2021)
25. Rahimi, R., Hassan, A., Tekin, O.: Augmented reality apps for tourism destination promotion. In: Destination Management and Marketing: Breakthroughs in Research and Practice, pp. 1066–1077. IGI Global (2020)
26. Imbert-Bouchard Ribera, D., Llonch Molina, N., Martín Piñol, C., Osàcar Marzal, E.: Turismo cultural y apps. Un breve panorama de la situación actual (2013)
27. Pencarelli, T.: The digital revolution in the travel and tourism industry. Inf. Technol. Tour. **22**(3), 455–476 (2019). https://doi.org/10.1007/s40558-019-00160-3
28. Dickinson, J.E., Ghali, K., Cherrett, T., Speed, C., Davies, N., Norgate, S.: Tourism and the smartphone app: capabilities, emerging practice and scope in the travel domain. Curr. Issue Tour. **17**(1), 84–101 (2014)
29. Anacleto, R., Figueiredo, L., Almeida, A., Novais, P.: Mobile application to provide personalized sightseeing tours. J. Netw. Comput. Appl. **41**, 56–64 (2014)
30. Hall, M.C., Prayag, G., Fieger, P., Dyason, D.: Beyond panic buying: consumption displacement and COVID-19. J. Serv. Manag. (2020)
31. De Souza, J.M.M., Mondo, T.S.: A utilização de food delivery apps por turistas: ameaça ou complementaridade à oferta de alimentação em destinos turísticos?: for the use of food delivery applications by tourists: does it complement or complement the offer of food in tourist destinations?. Revista turismo estudos e práticas-rtep/uern **10**(2) (2021)
32. Minazzi, R., Mauri, A.G.: Mobile technologies effects on travel behaviours and experiences: a preliminary analysis. In: Tussyadiah, I., Inversini, A. (eds.) Information and Communication Technologies in Tourism 2015, pp. 507–521. Springer, Cham (2015). https://doi.org/10.1007/978-3-319-14343-9_37
33. Fuchs, M., Höpken, W., Zanker, M., Beer, T.: Context-based adaptation of mobile applications in tourism. Inf. Technol. Tour. **12**(2), 175–195 (2010). https://doi.org/10.3727/109830510X12887971002783
34. Tan, G.W.-H., Lee, V.H., Lin, B., Ooi, K.B.: Mobile applications in tourism: the future of the tourism industry? Ind. Manag. Data Syst. **117**(3), 560–581 (2017). https://doi.org/10.1108/IMDS-12-2015-0490

35. Rashid, R.A., Ismail, R., Ahmad, M., Abdullah, N., Zakaria, R., Mamat, R.: Mobile apps in tourism communication: the strengths and weaknesses on tourism trips. J. Phys. Conf. Ser. **1529**, 1–6 (2020)
36. Hussein, S., Ahmed, E.: Mobile application for tourism: the case of Egypt. Int. J. Cust. Relatsh. Mark. Manag. (IJCRMM) **13**(1), 1–29 (2022)
37. Usman, M.: Difference Between App Store vs Google Play Store (2017). https://citrusbits. com/difference-app-store-vs-google-play-store-2/. Accessed 15 June 2022
38. Google. https://bit.ly/3ujbnrU. Accessed 05 June 2022

Accessibility Study in Hotels in the City of Quito

Wilson Arias[1]([✉]) [iD], David Zaldumbide[2] [iD], Fausto Calderón Pineda[3] [iD],
and Marcos Cevallos[4] [iD]

[1] Heisenberg Study Centre, El Pangui, Ecuador
wilsonariasa@yahoo.com
[2] Pontificia Universidad Católica de Ecuador, Quito, Ecuador
[3] Universidad Estatal Península de Santa Elena, La Libertad, Ecuador
[4] EP Petroecuador, Quito, Ecuador

Abstract. The demand for tourist destinations with accessible and quality infrastructure has been growing steadily. The main objective of this article is to evaluate the accessibility of hotels in the city of Quito, for which a descriptive study was conducted in 106 hotels in this city, selected through a stratified sampling by hotel category. To this this purpose, indicators were defined for each hotel unit, based on Ecuadorian accessibility standards for hotels, and partial indicators were constructed based on the degree of compliance with these standards, using five measurement categories, which were aggregated to obtain an overall indicator. The results obtained indicate that the level of accessibility is very low in all the facilities in the sample evaluated, with the highest category hotels having the best levels of compliance with this requirement.

Keywords: Hotel accessibility · Torgerson model · Tourism

1 Introduction

The tourism sector is among the world's leading activities in terms of investments, financial movements and employment generated, becoming a strategic component of countries seeking to enter the era of globalization with greater elements.

Before the pandemic caused by COVID 19, tourism was considered one of the fastest growing industries worldwide. The UNWTO [1] estimated that by 2030 the number of international tourist arrivals would be around 1.8 billion; however, it has now revised those projections and estimates that by 2022 it will reach between 55% and 70% of the levels reached in 2019 [2].

In Ecuador the tourism sector had a sustained growth until 2018, where it was the third source of non-oil income (after bananas and shrimp), then there was a decrease reaching the lowest levels in 2020 [3]. To reverse this trend, the Ministry of Tourism presented a promotion plan for the entire year 2022, with goals to be met by 2025 [4].

Within the country's tourism potential, the city of Quito, with its Historic Center, has been recognized during 2013 and 2014 as a Leading Destination in South America by the Worlds Travel Awards [5], the Best in Travel 2016 guide placed it in second place among the top 10 destinations and in the same year it was part of the list published by Lonely

T. Guarda et al. (Eds.): ARTIIS 2022, CCIS 1675, pp. 175–187, 2022.
https://doi.org/10.1007/978-3-031-20319-0_14

Planet, the largest travel guide in the world [6]. Another very important recognition for the city of Quito was the inclusion by TIME magazine in the list of the 100 best places in the world in 2021 [7].

According to some trends defined for tourism, in the present decade specialization will be a determining component when it comes to differentiating destinations, products and tourist attractions. Accessible tourism is a new type of tourism that generally analyzes and meets the needs of people with disabilities in terms of leisure and recreation [8].

Accessibility benefits all types of tourists, regardless of whether or not they have any type of disability, the availability of services aimed at facilitating mobility will improve the experience of tourists and visitors in general [9]. However, despite the existence of regulations related to accessibility, there are still difficulties for full access to tourism goods and services [10].

The UNWTO (2014) estimates that 15% of the world's population suffers from some disability. These data show the potential of this group who, like other people, seek to engage in regular or health tourism activities, so if greater accessibility is implemented in tourism facilities, products and services, this group could become a key component in achieving a global policy of responsible, sustainable and profitable tourism [8].

Between 2008 and 2009, the National Federation of Ecuadorians with Physical Disabilities, began an investigation of accessible infrastructure for tourists with disabilities. In the report published in 2015, it states that both natural and cultural beauty have influenced the country to have a great national and international demand, but nevertheless the topography, coupled with inadequate infrastructure could negatively influence the access of tourists with physical disabilities or the elderly [11].

This study analyzes the accessibility of hotels in Quito to determine whether they are suitable for inclusive tourism, where barriers are not an element that limits the full participation of people in tourism activities.

The sample includes hotels of different categories, specifying global and partial accessibility indicators for each facility with compliance and non-compliance ratings.

2 Accessibility in Tourism

2.1 Accessible Tourism

Despite being one of the sectors most affected by the pandemic, the tourism sector will continue to generate jobs and also take on new challenges, one of the main ones being to offer facilities and attractions that can be accessible to all segments of society.

The World Tourism Organization determines that accessible tourism is a collaborative process so that people with special access requirements such as mobility, vision, hearing, etc. can develop under equal conditions thanks to universally designed environments [8].

The concept of accessibility has also undergone some changes over time, initially it referred only to the improvement of physical environments, nowadays it is referred to as universal or comprehensive accessibility, i.e., an environment becomes accessible if all the paths in that environment are accessible so that people with disabilities are not hindered in the development of their activities because one of those paths is not accessible enough.

2.2 Accessibility in Hotel Sector

Competitiveness within the hotel sector requires considering many aspects that allow a pleasant experience for the tourist, one of them being accessibility, taking into account that this term includes providing facilities not only to people with permanent physical disabilities, but also to senior citizens, children, pregnant women, overweight people, people with achondroplasia, mothers with babies in strollers, etc. It could be said that an accessible hotel is a quality hotel.

Regardless of the type of tourist, accessibility should focus on all the phases through which people must pass, starting with: the arrival, the tourist usually arrives in a vehicle and needs help to carry luggage; the reception, in this phase it is necessary to provide all the facilities for communication; then follows the journey to the room, where depending on the client some specific requirements will be necessary, and finally the room, which is where the person will rest and needs an environment with all possible facilities for a pleasant stay. Additionally, access to complementary services such as cafeterias and evacuation routes in case of emergency must be considered.

The specifications to be met to say that a hotel is accessible are classified in 2 levels, depending on the degree of usefulness that this measure can offer to people, being level 1 the one that is formed by essential measures that are those that will allow the client to enjoy his stay in conditions of accessibility, safety and minimum comfort, while level 2 is formed by desirable measures that to a certain extent can be omitted [12].

2.3 Ecuadorian Regulatory Framework on Accessibility

In order to eliminate physical barriers in buildings, a regulatory framework with clear objectives is necessary and the participation of the main stakeholders, such as persons with disabilities, is important.

According to Quito Metropolitan Council Ordinance No. 3457, which contains the Architecture and Urban Planning Standards, certain parameters have been established that hotel establishments must take into account for the construction or adaptation of their infrastructure. These parameters were included in the Accessibility Manual prepared by the MINTUR in 2012, which also takes into account the regulations set forth by the National Institute of Statistics and Standardization (INEN).

3 Methodology

A descriptive non-experimental cross-sectional study was carried out in hotels in the city of Quito in order to evaluate the level of accessibility in each of them.

The population studied consisted of all 1, 2, 3, 3, 4 and 5-star hotel establishments in the city, registered by the National Institute of Statistics and Census (INEC). The INEC, based on information provided by the Internal Revenue Service (SRI), the Ministry of Education and the Superintendence of Popular and Solidarity Economy, in November 2021, presented the latest version of the Directory of Companies and Establishments (DIEE), which includes 136 hotel establishments.

The sample selection was made on the basis of a stratified sampling by hotel category, guaranteeing representativeness. For this purpose, the formula was used to calculate the optimal sample size when the sample proportion is to be estimated, based on a Horvitz-Thompson estimator, with sampling error and confidence interval and normal approximation of the data.

As a result of the process, it is necessary to consider 106 hotels distributed as follows:

- One star: 8
- Two stars: 4
- Three stars: 36
- Four stars: 51
- Five stars: 7

In order to gather the necessary information, a visit was made, where an interview was conducted with the directors of each selected establishment. To determine the overall level of accessibility in each establishment, the scheme and steps described below were used (Fig. 1):

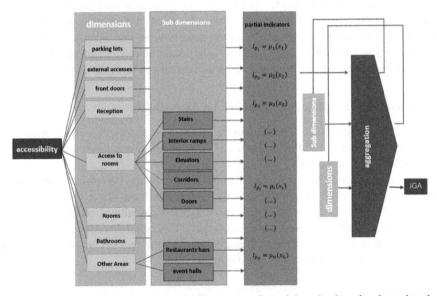

Fig. 1. Model for measuring hotel accessibility Source: Own elaboration based on interview data

Step 1: Accessibility indicators are established for each of the hotel units using the requirements established in Ecuador's accessibility manual for hotel accommodations [13].

Step 2: Partial indicators are obtained for each unit (subdimension and dimension), based on the degree of compliance with each requirement:

1. 1 is given if the requirement is met and 2 if it is not met;
2. The arithmetic mean (average) is obtained.

3. Five levels of measurement are established for each indicator: "Null", "Low", "Medium", "High" and "Very high".

Step 3: The results obtained for each unit are aggregated into a composite indicator using category aggregation based on Torgerson's multidimensional scaling model.

4 Results

Tables 1 and 2 show the degree of compliance with the indicators defined from the hotel accessibility standard for the city of Quito and the level of accessibility for each unit, respectively.

In the parking unit, five indicators were evaluated, the results indicate that only one hotel has no parking, 22.7% has one space reserved for persons with disabilities for every 25 spaces, of which only 14 of them are less than 10 m from the access door and all of them are properly marked with the international symbol of disability; a higher percentage (62.3%) comply with the minimum dimensions. From the degrees of compliance, 14.2% of the hotels have a very high level of accessibility, 26.4% high, 36.8% medium, 21.7% low and only one case does not meet any of the requirements and therefore has a zero level of accessibility.

Table 1. Results for the dependency "Parking".

Dependency		N.°	%
Parking	Has a parking lot	105	99,1
	One handicapped parking space for every 25 spaces	22	20,7
	Minimum dimensions: 3.5 m × 5 m	66	62,3
	The parking for people with disabilities is less than 10 m from the access door	14	13,2
	It is marked horizontally and vertically with the international symbol of disability	22	20,8

These results show that article 58 of the Ecuadorian Organic Law on Disabilities is not being complied with, which establishes that all construction sites must have access for people with disabilities and that at least 2% of parking spaces must be reserved for disabled people.

These results show that article 58 of the Ecuadorian Organic Law on Disabilities is not being complied with, which establishes that all construction sites must have access for people with disabilities and that at least 2% of parking spaces must be reserved for disabled people [14].

With respect to access to the hotel, a total of 20 indicators were evaluated, 14 related to exterior accesses and 6 to access doors. In the exterior accesses, the lowest percentages were found in the indicators related to the presence of tactile strips on the pavement to indicate routes for the visually impaired with 7.5% compliance, the location of tactile signs for manual perception and the circulation routes. In the access doors, the biggest problem was found in the lateral free space in addition to the door sweep.

The hotel sector should pay more attention to this indicator since the enjoyment of a service begins with access and therefore there should not be any type of obstacle and once inside, facilitate mobility with the appropriate dimensions of height, width, etc., as well as the respective signage.

Table 2. Results of dependency "Access to the hotel".

Dependency	Indicators		N.°	%
Access to the hotel	Outdoor access	Pedestrian traffic lanes with a minimum clear width of 1.6 m without obstacles	31	29,2
		Traffic lanes free of obstacles over their entire width and from the ground to a parallel plane located at a minimum height of 2.2 m.	12	11,3
		Maximum longitudinal slope of curvature of 2%.	24	22,6
		Non-slip floors with no surface irregularities	78	73,6
		Tactile strips on the pavement, parallel to buildings, to indicate routes for visually impaired persons	8	7,5
		Grips with circular or anatomical cross-sections constructed of rigid materials	44	41,5
		Handrails positioned at 0.90 cm height with good sliding, easy and safe grip	78	73,6
		Handrail with clearance from wall or other obstruction greater than or equal to 0.05 cm (0.05 in.)	82	77,4
		Minimum width of unidirectional ramps of 0.90 cm	65	61,3
		Complies with slope ranges: 6% to 8% (15 m), 8% to 10% (10 m), 10% to 12% (3 m)	21	19,8
		Rest areas with minimum free dimension of 1.2 m	26	24,5
		Illuminated visual signs, without reflections that make reading difficult, located at least 1.40 m away.	17	16,0
		Tactile signals of manual perception located at 0.8 cm and 1 m height.	9	8,5
		Dimensions of letters on embossed signs	22	20,8
	Access doors	Doors properly marked with international signs for physical, hearing and speech disabilities.	74	69,8
		Dimensions minimum width 0.90 cm and height 2.05 m	100	94,3
		Automatic doors with elliptical detection sensor on the exterior and interior.	63	59,4
		Door handles have a horizontal bar located 0.80 cm to 1.20 m from floor level.	69	65,1
		Doors with frames that contrast with the wall color	38	35,8
		They have a side clearance between 0.45 cm and 0.55 cm and a clearance depth of 1.20 m in addition to the door sweep.	26	24,5

In the reception dimension which is shown in Table 3, only one indicator obtained less than 50.0% compliance; the existence of technical aids for the visually impaired and hearing impaired.

Table 3. Results of the "Reception" unit

Dependency	Indicators	N.°	%
Reception	Flat and non-slip floor	84	79,2
	Lobby with firm seats that facilitate rest for people with disabilities and with a height of no more than 0.45 cm and a depth of no less than 0.50 cm	76	71,7
	Some section of the counter has a height of 0.70 cm free under the support surface that allows a correct approach of people with wheelchairs	64	60,4
	Routing guide strips	58	54,7
	There are technical aids for the visually impaired and hearing impaired (information in Braille or graphics)	27	25,5
	Features 300 lx illumination, so that people with low vision can identify the counter	54	50,9

The reception area is also very important because it involves communication between the receptionist and the tourist, and the physical space itself; in this study only, the physical part was evaluated, which provides the necessary amenities; however, we see that this is not met in most hotels.

The dimension of access to the rooms from Table 4, was evaluated through five sub-dimensions, the most affected in terms of accessibility are the elevators with four indicators with percentages of compliance of less than 20.0%.

Table 4. Results of the "Access to rooms" dependency.

Dependency		Indicators	N.°	%
Access to rooms	Stairs	They have a minimum width of 1 m, and riser less than 0.18 m	80	75,4
		Continuous flights with rest every ten steps	68	64,2
		Perceptible change of texture equal to the width of the harrow before starting the step	40	37,7
		Tracks with rounded edges, maximum radius of curvature 0.01 cm that does not protrude from the plane of the riser	18	17,0
		Steps of anti-slip material or adhesive anti-slip strips or emeralds on edges	38	35,8
		Continuous handrails with extensions not less than 0.30 cm at the beginning and end (one at 0.90 cm and the other at 0.70 cm height)	74	69,8

(continued)

Table 4. (*continued*)

Dependency		Indicators	N.º	%
		Stairs illuminated with minimum 100 lux	40	37,7
		Enclosed by railings or walls to prevent the cane of a visually impaired person from slipping into the void	85	80,2
	Interior ramps	Illuminated indoor access ramps	94	88,7
		They have horizontal corridors and free escape routes that are safe and easy to identify in case of emergency	67	63,2
		Ramps with handrails and curbs at edges	89	84,0
	Elevators	Minimum of 1.20 m deep and 1 m wide	101	95,3
		Opening time greater than 5 s outside call and 3 s inside call	74	69,8
		Entrance floor marked with textured pavement with a minimum area of 1.20 m × 1.20 m	23	21,7
		Boarding and disembarkation space with a minimum area of 1.5 m × 1.5 m	38	35,8
		Handrail located 0.90 cm above the ground	100	94,3
		Interior cabin with non-skid floor or carpeting or rugs subject to	21	19,8
		Opening mechanism provided with automatic sensor located at maximum 0.80 cm from the floor	18	17,0
		The button panel must be located at a maximum height of 1.20 m (4 ft)	83	78,3
		Have the outer frame in a contrasting color to the wall	42	39,6
		Interior and exterior command buttons with embossed signage, braille system, acoustic signal and contrasting colors	9	8,5
		Stops with acoustic messages	78	73,6
	Aisles	Illuminated with at least 100 lx	70	66,3
		At least 1.50 m radius to allow for full wheelchair rotation	78	73,6
		It has handrails along the aisle on one side	58	54,7
		Facilitates the movement of people with disabilities by avoiding the placement of objects that impede circulation	49	46,2

(*continued*)

Table 4. (*continued*)

Dependency		Indicators	N.°	%
		Non-slip floor	56	52,8
	Doors	They do not invade traffic areas	73	68,9
		Accessible doors (not swinging doors which represent a risk)	43	40,6
		Open to the inside of the rooms	98	92,5
		Doors with handle or lever systems, avoiding rounded plates for easy opening	47	44,3

The fact that there are hotels without elevators to access the rooms makes them practically unsuitable for people with mobility problems, this trend should be changing if we want to capture the market that demands these requirements, which is growing every day.

To determine the level of accessibility in the rooms whose results are shown in Table 5, nine indicators were taken into account, of which three of them had a degree of compliance of less than 25.0%. The worst evaluated were the location of accessible rooms on the first floor or near the elevators (17.0%), the height at which the control mechanisms are located (19.8%) and the requirements for closets (23.6%).

Table 5. Results of the "Rooms" unit

Dependency	Indicators	N.°	%
Rooms	With a rotation area of 1.5 m in diameter, with a circulation area of 0.90 cm around the bed	39	36,8
	The bed is raised from the floor 0.20 cm	94	88,7
	The bed height is 0.40 cm to facilitate transfer from the wheelchair	78	73,6
	The zone for reaching objects is not larger than 0.60 cm	46	43,4
	Control mechanisms (lighting, alarms, ventilation, etc.) are between 0.85 cm and 1.20 m high	21	19,8
	Closets with a maximum depth of 0.60 cm and hangers no more than 1.40 m high, sliding doors	25	23,6
	Televisions have unobstructed support	103	97,2
	Telephones have luminous signals	58	54,7
	Accessible rooms located on the first floor or near elevators	18	17,0

To measure accessibility in the bathrooms, 14 indicators were taken into account, related to sinks, showers, bathtubs, etc., of which four had degrees of compliance of less than 25% and eight had degrees of compliance of less than 50.0%. The results are shown in Table 6.

Table 6. Results in the "Bathrooms" unit

Dependency	Indicators	N.°	%
Bathrooms	It has frontal or oblique sinks for wheelchair approach	79	74,5
	Washbasins with a minimum height of 0.67 cm and a depth of 0.60 cm, placed at a minimum height of 0.80 cm and a maximum height between 0.90 and 0.95 cm	53	50,0
	Toilet seat height 0.45 cm (0.45 in.)	100	94,3
	The bathtub has a top rim at a maximum height of 0.45 cm	23	21,7
	The bottom surface of the bathtub is non-slip or there is a fixed mat on the floor	39	36,8
	The bottom of the bathtub and the bathroom floor are at the same level	86	81,1
	In the bathtub, there is a platform on the side or opposite the faucet to facilitate the transfer of disabled personnel	32	30,2
	The shower contains a non-fixed or folding seat with a depth of 0.40 cm	21	19,8
	The height of the shower seat is 0.45 cm	71	67,0
	The shower area does not have a curb to allow for wheelchair access	28	26,4
	There are support barriers at the sink, shower and toilet, with a diameter between 0.35 cm and 0.50 cm, with continuous travel	19	17,9
	No electrical outlets or switches near the sink, bathtub or shower	92	86,8
	Lever-operated faucets, sensor systems or other mechanisms	83	78,3
	Contrasting wall and floor colors with sanitary fixtures, accessories and grab bars	23	21,7

The rooms, as well as the bathrooms, deserve special attention since they are the place where people rest, although there are aspects that were not evaluated, such as windows, push buttons, communications systems, etc., which we consider to be the most essential, nevertheless, there are also deficiencies in the facilities analyzed, which are more noticeable in hotels that were not designed for this purpose, but were adapted to provide this service.

In the areas of bars, restaurants and event rooms, results are shown in Table 7, 6 indicators were taken into account, all above 25% compliance.

Here it is also important to emphasize that during the visits it was found that some hotels do not have these facilities, something that should not happen because this lack would force guests to move to another place if they want the restaurant service, which of course makes it less likely that a person with a disability would choose that hotel.

Table 7. Results of the "Other zones" unit

Dependency		Indicators	N.°	%
Other areas	Bars and restaurants	The layout of the furniture (tables and chairs) contemplates a circulation space of 0.90 cm and a turning space of 1.50 m	64	60,4
		The furniture area has a minimum of 10% of accessible furniture available	78	73,6
		The tables are firm, four-legged, with an inside clear height of 0.70 cm, a clear width between legs of 0.80 cm and a clear width of 0.80 cm	102	96,2
	Event rooms	There is at least one accessible route from the entrance and reception of the hotel establishment to the different areas	39	36,8
		The conference rooms have a reserved area, delimited and adapted for the use of wheelchair users, located in an open space with no slopes	54	50,9
		It has at least one computer for use by people with physical or hearing disabilities with its respective computer cabinet so that it is within reach of a person sitting in a wheelchair	78	73,6

Table 8 shows the level of accessibility of each unit, obtained from Table 1 using the steps described in the methodology. From the table we can deduce that the worst evaluated units were: access to exteriors, stairs, elevators, rooms and bathrooms, although when applying Torgerson's multidimensional model (Table 9), in general all the units had a low level of accessibility, as did the overall level of accessibility.

Table 8. Level of accessibility by unit

Units	Accessibility level									
	Very high		High		Medium		Under		Null	
	N.°	%	N.°	%	N.°	%	N.°	%	N.°	%
Parking	15	14,2	28	26,4	39	36,8	23	21,7	1	0,9
Outdoor access	4	3,8	16	15,1	32	30,2	43	40,6	11	10,4
Access doors	18	17,0	26	24,5	33	31,1	23	21,7	6	5,7
Reception	11	10,4	27	25,5	41	38,7	19	17,9	8	7,5
Stairs	4	3,8	22	22,8	36	34,0	37	34,9	7	6,6
Interior ramps	23	21,7	28	26,4	32	30,2	21	19,8	2	1,9
Elevators	3	2,8	17	16,0	23	21,7	52	49,1	11	10,4
Aisles	11	10,4	28	26,4	48	45,3	17	16,0	2	1,9
Doors	10	9,4	26	24,5	46	43,4	21	19,8	3	2,8
Rooms	3	2,8	15	14,2	29	27,4	50	47,2	9	8,5
Bathrooms	3	2,8	14	13,2	32	30,2	47	44,3	10	9,4
Bars and restaurants	18	17,0	28	26,4	31	29,2	26	24,5	3	2,8
Event rooms	9	8,5	23	21,7	37	34,9	32	30,2	5	4,7

The result obtained is an alert for the hotel sector in the city of Quito, since inclusive tourism is a growing market and they should adapt to the new trend if they want to improve occupancy levels, and at the same time become an additional attraction that seduces tourists to consider Quito as a possible destination to visit.

In many cases starting to work to be an accessible hotel is a matter of attitude, because nowadays there are tools in the cloud that allow audits on the level of accessibility, there you can provide information that will be very useful for the tourist to know in advance what will be found and at the same time help you make a decision, since according to the site techno-hotel 50% of people with disabilities do not travel for lack of information [3].

Table 9. Aggregation of indicators through Torgerson's multidimensional model.

Indicators	Very high	High	Medium	Under	Null	Average	Scale	
Parking	−1,07	−0,24	0,75	2,35	1,79	−0,656	0.90	LOW
Outdoor access	−1,78	−0,88	−0,02	1,26	−1,42	−1,330	1,57	LOW
Access doors	−0,95	−0,21	0,60	1,58	1,02	−0,585	0,82	LOW
Reception	−1,26	−0,36	0,66	1,44	0,47	−0,811	1,05	LOW
Stairs	−1,78	−0,69	0,21	1,51	−0,75	−1,233	1,47	LOW
Interior ramps	−0,78	−0,05	0,78	2,08	2,03	−0,415	0,65	LOW
Elevators	−1,91	−0,88	−0,24	1,26	−1,77	−1,395	1,63	LOW
Aisles	−1,26	−0,34	0,92	2,08	1,40	−0,799	1,04	LOW
Doors	−1,31	−0,41	0,75	1,91	0,93	−0,864	1,10	LOW
Rooms	−1,91	−0,95	−0,14	1,37	−1,63	−1,431	1,67	LOW
Bathrooms	−1,91	−0,99	−0,09	1,31	−1,68	−1,450	1,69	LOW
Bars and restaurants	−0,95	−0,17	0,60	1,91	1,39	−0,561	0,80	LOW
Event rooms	−1,31	−0,41	0,75	1,91	0,93	−0,864	1,10	LOW
Sums	−18,19	−6,60	5,53	21,96	2,70			
limits	−1,40	−0.51	0,43	2.44	0,96	0,24		

5   Conclusions

- The results of Torgerson's multidimensional scaling model show a low level of accessibility in all of the 106 hotels studied.

- The level of accessibility is proportional to the category of the hotel; those with more stars mostly comply with the regulations, although they never reach 100% of what is established in the INEN and MINTUR standards.
- The results also indicate that there is no comprehensive compliance with Ecuadorian tourism lodging regulations as well as the Organic Law of Disabilities of Ecuador.
- From the visits made, it can be deduced that many of the hotels, especially the lower category ones, were not designed to function as hotels, but rather are adapted to function as such, and this is the reason for their failure to comply to a greater extent with INEN and MINTUR requirements.
- If we consider the recognition that Quito has received as a tourist destination, it is of utmost importance that its hotel infrastructure complies with Ecuadorian regulations on this issue, although in some cases a strong investment is necessary, but in others it is a matter of will.

References

1. UNWTO: Tourism Towards 2030/Global Overview. World Tourism Organization, Madrid (2011)
2. W. T. Organization: World Tourism Organization, 6 June 2022. https://www.unwto.org/es/taxonomy/term/347#:~:text=The%20scenarios%20of%20the%20WTO,levels%20before%20the%20pandemic. Accessed 3 Apr 2022
3. INEC: Statistical Register of International Arrivals and Departures. INEC, QUITO (2022)
4. MINTUR: Ministry of Tourism of Ecuador, 9 February 2022. https://www.turismo.gob.ec/el-ministerio-de-turismo-presento-su-plan-de-promocion-para-2022/. Accessed 14 Apr 2022
5. MINTUR: Ministry of Tourism. Ministry of Tourism, 30 December 2014. https://www.turismo.gob.ec/resumen-2014-turismo-ecuatoriano-en-su-mejor-momento/. Accessed 23 Jan 2022
6. MINTUR: Semiannual bulletin. Relevant information on tourism in Ecuador. I Semester year 2015. MINTUR, Quito (2015)
7. Duggan, J.: The World's Greatest Places of 2021, 20 Julio 2021. https://time.com/collection/worlds-greatest-places-2021/. Accessed 14 Julio 2022
8. UNWTO: Panorama of International Tourism. World Tourism Organization, Madrid (2014)
9. Suriá, R., Escalona, J.: Integration, tourism and disability: are hotels accessible for people with physical disabilities. Pasos **12**(1), 209–2018 (2014)
10. Acerenza, M.: Tourism administration and planning. Trillas, Mexico (2012)
11. FENEDIF: Accessible tourism in Ecuador. National Federation of Ecuadorians with Physical Disabilities, Quito (2015)
12. Patronato, R.: Universal accessibility manual for hotels. Paradores de Turismo de España, S.A., Madrid (2007)
13. MINTUR-BRIMGEL: Universal Accessibility Manual for the Tourist Accommodation Services Sector. MINTUR -BRIMGEL International Solutions Cía. Ltda., Quito (2012)
14. Ecuador, Asamblea Nacional del: Ley Organica de Discapacidades. Registro Oficial, vol. IV, no. 796, p. 1 (2012)

A Comprehensive Study on Remote Laboratories Based on Pneumatic and Electro-Pneumatic Systems

Roger Michell Idrovo Urgilés$^{(\boxtimes)}$ [ID], Washington Daniel Torres Guin [ID],
Luis Enrique Chuquimarca Jiménez [ID], Samuel Baldomero Bustos Gaibor [ID],
and Sendey Agustín Vera González [ID]

Universidad Estatal Península de Santa Elena, Santa Elena, Ecuador
{ridrovo,wtorres,lchuquimarca,sbustos,svera}@upse.edu.ec

Abstract. This paper analyzes the different solutions of remote laboratories (RL), specifically in the area of pneumatics and electro-pneumatics. In this way, considering the design criteria of the RL, a group of articles based on the theme was selected. On the other hand, an overview of the architecture and web interface for RL based on pneumatic systems was proposed in this work according to the hardware/software used in the chosen articles. Therefore, it is possible to develop a remote laboratory under a general architecture and an user interface capable of providing an experience close to physical/face-to-face experiments.

Keywords: Remote laboratory · Pneumatic system · Industrial Internet of Things

1 Introduction

Some researchers consider that laboratory experimentation is essential in the academic field for education based on science and new technologies. Therefore, most universities use experimentation and technologies in laboratories where students apply and explore science and new technologies through the development of practical work and the improvement of their academic learning while advancing in their study plan [14].

Nowadays, an advanced technology laboratory is out of reach for most universities due to several issues, for example, high costs related to acquiring and maintaining the laboratory and investment in infrastructure [15]. However, advances in information and communication technologies (ICT) along with automation have transformed higher education, helping to solve these problems through new forms of practical activities with Augmented Reality (AR), Virtual Reality (VR), simulated and RL, creating new alternatives to learn and teach through new work environments and experiences that ease student training. RL systems are an academic experience where students interact with physical experiments through a computer with internet access. In a laboratory experience (face-to-face or distance), there are advantages and disadvantages in the pedagogical, economic, and safety area [13].

© The Author(s), under exclusive license to Springer Nature Switzerland AG 2022
T. Guarda et al. (Eds.): ARTIIS 2022, CCIS 1675, pp. 188–202, 2022.
https://doi.org/10.1007/978-3-031-20319-0_15

Table 1 shows some of the competitive edges to consider. Among the various benefits of RL (remote mode) are many access opportunities and the time needed to develop the experiments (24/7 availability). Other essential factors are the management of many students who want to perform the experiments and the students' safety due to the equipment's non-direct handling.

Table 1. Benefits of face-to-face Lab and RL.

Benefits	Face-to-face lab	Remote lab
Manage large number of students	✗	✓
Tangible feedback of the results	✓	✗
Student-instructor contact	✓	✓
Many access opportunities	✗	✓
Long access time	✗	✓
24/7 availability	✗	✓
Student safety	✗	✓
Return on investments in equipment	✗	✓

An RL allows the student to develop technical skills such as design, programming, supervision, and monitoring in experiments related to power electronics, electronics & microelectronics, pneumatic & hydraulic systems, control, automation, and SCADA systems. Several solutions have been developed for virtual or remote engineering education in recent years.

In [28] proposed a virtual laboratory for control system experiments for the education and training of Electronic Engineering students. RL Web-LABAI [11] is a Hardware-Software system that allows monitoring and controlling variables of an industrial process remotely from a Web page. This system comprises a server, a programmable logic controller (PLC), and an IP camera.

Similarly, Trentsios P. et al. work is based on an RL consisting of physical components connected to a PLC, which uses a desktop computer to run LabVIEW. This software controls and monitors all laboratory equipment and establishes remote access to an iLab server [25]. On the other hand, Viegas C. et al. analyzed the impact on student learning and motivation when using the RL named VISIR for basic and advanced courses in electricity and electronics [26]. In paper [16] a novel design and framework for an online remote digital hardware design laboratory has been presented. Students have access to a variety of System on a Chip (SoC) and Field Programmable Gate Array (FPGA) target boards in the "Hardware-as-a-Service" cloud computing model, enabling them to implement their designs online.

The rest of the document is organized as follows: Sect. 2 briefly describes the basic concepts of pneumatics and the mathematical modeling of a pneumatic system. In addition, Sect. 3 describes the comprehensive study where the architectures and user interfaces used in RL in the field of pneumatics are analyzed.

On the other hand, Sect. 4 details the results of the investigation where the hardware/software used in each RL solution is analyzed. Finally, in Sect. 5, the conclusions of the investigation are presented.

2   Pneumatic

Pneumatics is the use of compressed air to perform mechanical work. It is also used in the development of automation and control solutions. Today, pneumatic systems play an essential role in the technological field [9]. Most of the advantages of pneumatic systems are related to the low cost of components, assembly, and the use of compressed air, the latter being easy to extract from the environment. For this reason, it is practically always available in unlimited quantities.

In addition, it is ideal for absorbing shock and vibration because it can be flexibly compressed, and there is no risk of fire and explosion. Another feature highlights the insensitivity to temperature changes because it ensures proper and reliable operation in normal and extreme conditions. On the other hand, there are several disadvantages to using pneumatic systems; for example, compressed air is a relatively expensive energy medium and requires some maintenance, mainly due to dirt and condensation. Also, consistent and uniform piston speeds are not always achieved using compressed air.

2.1   Components of a Pneumatic Systems

A pneumatic system consists of the connection of different elements group. These groups form a control path for the signal flow, where we have the signal section (input) and the actuator section (output). In addition, control elements allow controlling the actuating elements according to the signal received from the processing elements [9].

A pneumatic system has the following levels: Energy supply, Input elements (sensors), Processing elements (processors), Control elements, and Power components (actuators). Table 2 shows the essential elements that belong to a pneumatic system. These elements are defined by symbols, indicating each element's function.

2.2   Mathematical Model of a Pneumatic Systems

The mathematical model of a pneumatic system involves the study of the electromagnetic, pneumatic, and mechanical subsystems present in the system, which results in a set of equations [12, 17, 23, 24]. Secondly, a traditional pneumatic system consists of a force element (pneumatic cylinder), a command device (valves),

Table 2. Basic components of a pneumatic system.

Signal Path	Type	Components	Symbol	Equipment
Command Execution	Power Component	Pneumatic cylinders, motors, visual indicators.		
Signal Output	Control Element	Directional control valve		
Signal Processing	Processing Elements	Directional control valves, non-return valves, pressure control valves, timers, sequencers.		
Signal Input	Input Elements	Push-button valves, roller lever valves, proximity switches, air barrier.		
Energy Supply	Supply Elements	Compressor, reservoir, pressure regulating valve, service unit		

connecting tubes, different sensors that detect force, position, pressure, and an external load represented by a mass connected to the piston.

The mathematical model proposed by Richer, E., and Hurmuzlu, Y. takes into consideration series of factors, including the friction present in the piston, the difference in the active areas of the piston due to the rod, the inactive volume at the ends of the piston stroke, leakage between chambers, valve dynamics, time delay and flow amplitude attenuation in valve-cylinder connecting tubes [22].

The schematic diagram of a pneumatic system, with the variables of interest specified respectively, is presented in Fig. 1. The dynamics of the piston-rod-load assembly are expressed in Eq. 1:

$$(M_L + M_p)\ddot{x} + \beta\dot{x} + F_f + F_L = P_1 A_1 - P_2 A_2 - P_a A_r \qquad (1)$$

where M_L is the external load mass, M_p is the piston and rod assembly mass, x is the piston position, β is the viscous friction coefficient, F_f is the Coulomb friction force, F_L is the external force, P_1 and P_2 are the absolute pressures in actuator's chambers, P_a is the absolute pressure, A_1 and A_2 are the piston effective areas, and A_r is the rod cross-sectional area.

The pneumatic valve is another element to consider in the mathematical modeling of a pneumatic system. Which is a critical component in the system because it should control air flows quickly and accurately. For this reason, it is known as the command element. The valve modeling presented in [22] relates two

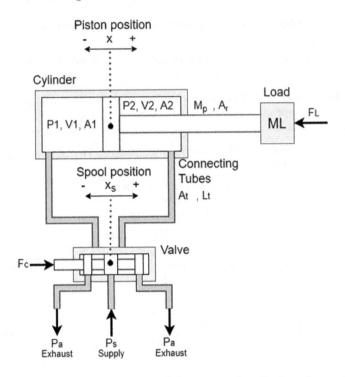

Fig. 1. Schematic representation of the pneumatic cylinder-valve system.

aspects: the dynamics of the valve spool and the mass flow through the variable orifice of the valve. Analyzing Fig. 2 and simplifying the spring and friction forces and considering the force produced by the coil as $F_c = K_{fc}i_c$, then Eq. 2 defines the motion of the valve spool.

$$M_s\ddot{x}_s + c_s\dot{x}_s + 2k_sx_s = K_{fc}i_c \tag{2}$$

where M_s is the total mass of the spool and bobbin assembly, x_s is the spool displacement, c_s is the viscous coefficient of friction, k_s is the spool spring constant, K_{fc} is the coil force coefficient and i_c is the coil current.

The cylinder chamber model is defined as a differential equation that relates the chamber pressures to the mass flow through the system and the translational velocity of the piston. In [22] a general model for a volume of gas is presented, consisting of three equations: an ideal gas law equation, the conservation of mass continuity equation, and the energy equation. In this model, the following is assumed: the gas is perfect, the pressures and temperatures inside each chamber are homogeneous, and the kinetic and potential energy terms are negligible. Equation 3 represents the time derivative of the pressure in the pneumatic cylinder chambers.

$$\dot{P} = \frac{RT}{V}(\alpha_{in}\dot{m}_{in} - \alpha_{out}\dot{m}_{out}) - \alpha\frac{P}{V}\dot{V} \tag{3}$$

Consider in Eq. 3 the following: P is the pressure, V is the control volume, T is the temperature, R is the ideal gas constant, m_{in} and m_{out} are the mass flows entering and leaving the chamber and α, α_{in} and α_{out} are a constants depending on the actual heat transfer during the process. Equations 1, 2 and 3 fully describe the pneumatic system. These equations can be solved numerically and used as a mathematical model for control design, as demonstrated in [21].

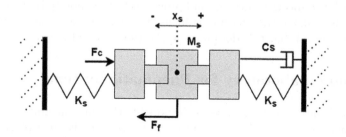

Fig. 2. Valve spool dynamic equilibrium.

2.3   Pneumatics in Industry 4.0

Due to its simplicity and accessibility, pneumatic is a favorite technology in industrial automation systems in a factory. In addition, its natural robustness allows it to withstand extreme temperatures, pressure, and environments. This technology offers a series of benefits, thanks to the characteristics of its energy source (compressed air). Among other advantages, we have security, minimum operating costs, simple implementation, and profitability, which allows many plants to have an interest in pneumatic automation [3].

Currently, modern pneumatic systems have very advanced levels of intelligence, where the use of controllers such as PLC is beginning to be considered. For this reason, industrial sectors such as the automotive and production/handling sectors have pneumatic technology as the main tool in their process lines. Likewise, pneumatic solutions are used in mining for wastewater recovery, treatment, and control processes. Similarly, these solutions allow the implementation of fluid control systems found in chemical plants [1,3,10].

As Industry 4.0 continues to change the manufacturing ecosystem significantly, the future of pneumatics remains up for debate. Still, statistics from the British Fluid Power Association indicate that sales of pneumatic equipment have risen to more than $ 1.4 billion a year in recent years [5]. This is because manufacturers such as FESTO and Camozzi have focused on innovating and adapting pneumatic solutions in Industry 4.0, thus improving the Industrial Internet of Things (IIoT) compatibility of their equipment [2]. IIoT enables a more advanced level of precision engineering, quality management, and risk assessment, where there are integrated and programmable activities, starting from the supply chain to the completion of the final product. In addition to the aforementioned, connectivity to the cloud, data analysis, and edge computing allow an essential change in the design, implementation, operation, and maintenance of devices, equipment, and the industry [4].

Some research is developing new sensor-oriented technology. These studies look at advanced electronic data collection systems using thin films. For example, these sheets could function as tags attached to a pneumatic cylinder, where they would collect and send information from sensors wirelessly to a control network. In this way, future research seeks to boost the overall effectiveness of pneumatic equipment by adapting its designs and processes to incorporate IIoT factors into its operation. Currently, attention is focused on automated systems' electronic and digital control, but this does not impede the future of pneumatics 4.0.

3   Remote Laboratory for Pneumatic Systems

New technologies and ICTs have made possible the implementation of RL for different fields of engineering. This research focuses on the area of pneumatics and electro-pneumatics, which is fundamental in the academic learning of future professionals at any university. In particular, the scientific development of RLs in this engineering field is new and has appeared in recent years. Therefore, few universities have RLs to develop pneumatic and electro-pneumatic systems experiments.

Consequently, following the RL design criteria proposed in [19], a group of articles was selected for the comprehensive study. These criteria involve the creation of an interface that allows easy configuration of new and existing equipment on the platform, the use of a server responsible for authentication, resource allocation, and user and session management, and the last criterion is based on the design of a communication policy on the client side (students, researchers or engineers). These criteria are necessary for developing an RL in any engineering field. Therefore, in this section, the hardware/software, the architecture, and the web interface used in each RL system of the selected articles were analyzed. Subsequently, a general description of the architecture and web interface of the different RL solutions studied is established.

3.1   System Architecture

One of the biggest challenges in an RL is identifying a system architecture that provides adequate access to remote hardware for hands-on development. Remote labs use two main architectures: the client/server architecture is a high-performance system, and the browser/server architecture is a more stable system [29].

However, several RL scenarios exist in various universities where the proposed architectures or hybrid architectures are used, which use different technologies, access interfaces, and administration systems. For this reason, there are no widely adopted standards for RLs that define unique sets of technologies [30].

In recent years, the University of Novi Sad, located in Serbia, has developed RLs based on pneumatic systems where they define similar communication architectures using different controllers such as CompactRIO [8], PLC [20], and Arduino YUN [7]. In general, end clients must log in to connect to the remote desktop in the on-site lab. To start the experiment, students must run a user application installed on the remote desktop. On the other hand, the remote desktop and the controller are connected using communication protocols such as TCP/IP and RS - 232. In addition, the students must have the necessary software installed and a good internet connection in these systems. Finally, a webcam is used to visualize the execution of the experiment.

On the other hand, an electro-pneumatic system, a data acquisition board (DAQ), power circuits, a web camera, and a personal computer equipped with LabVIEW® software are the components of the RL architecture developed in [27]. The DAQ board and the camera are connected to the computer's USB ports. Students can use virtual instruments (VIs) to monitor various parameters and view graphical process indicators and images of actual laboratory equipment. These VIs run on the server computer. For remote access and operation of the experiment through the web, the LabVIEW® web server was used with the Web Publishing tool.

Instead, the architecture developed in [6] consists of a central controller based on an Arduino board. The controller is in charge of exchanging information with the pneumatic scheme of the experiment, sending data to the database, and acting as a student server. The actuators and sensors are connected to the controller through analog inputs and outputs; PWM output and the I2C protocol are used. The database is installed on a server's computer to respond to the user application or controller requests. The database is based on MySQL and stores all the readings of the pneumatic system.

As can be seen, there is no general standard to define a communication architecture in an RL focused on pneumatic systems. For this reason, an overview of architectures is proposed considering the previous research works. Figure 3 shows an overview of the architecture of an RL. This architecture is made up of the following components:

1. *Client Station(CS)*: Refers to a client's personal computer with Internet access.
2. *Communication protocol*: Systems/Networks carrying out bidirectional communication between all system components.
3. *Lab Server*: System in charge of the interconnection towards the experimentation unit where the physical hardware selected during an RL experiment is located. Similarly, user administration and webcams are managed by the server. In addition, it is possible to establish a connection to services such as a database and the user interface.
4. *Experimentation unit*: Group of equipment and devices used to carry out experiments.

5. *Instrumentation unit*: Sensors/actuators used to measure the readings of the experimentation unit. Additionally, these instruments provide real-time measurements of the experiment.

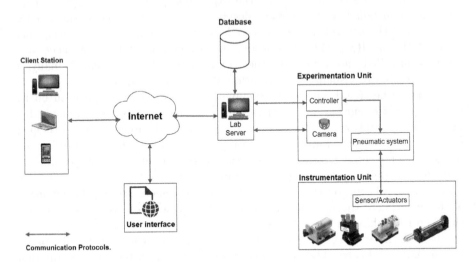

Fig. 3. Overview of the architecture of an RL.

3.2   User Interface

Students should be able to interact with various experimental practices related to pneumatic systems through a Web interface, which is considered an essential component in an RL system. Possibly different experiments require different interfaces. The user interface is intended for the end-user (students, engineers, or researchers). The web interface is a graphical representation of the experiment's state to be developed. In addition, it provides capabilities and skills that allow a unique experience in an RL.

In [8] a web interface for the RL is presented where students are provided with a list of experiments related to direct and indirect control of pneumatic actuators. In this interface, the title and a legend with indications about the experiment are in the foreground. In addition, it has an area to draw the pneumatic scheme where students must use the essential components to develop the experimental practice. Once the work is finished, the students must press a button where the simulation of the scheme will be executed, and through the camera, they will be able to visualize the operation of the actuators and the activation of the valves employing LED indicators.

On the other hand, the user interface proposed in [20] includes the work cycle control of a pneumatic circular manipulator. Students must select the operating mode of the manipulator: single cycle, single cycle with delay, and an automatic mode, as well as configure the communication parameters for data transfer to the system controller. This application was developed in LabView software and used a webcam to monitor the experiment.

The user application developed in [7] consists of four parts: the electro-pneumatic control diagram, the configuration of the valve opening percentage, the start of the experiment, and the results. Students will be able to configure the opening of the actuator through sliders. Likewise, to start the experiment and see the impact of the speed regulation, a button must be pressed, and through a webcam, the users visualize the execution of the experiment in real-time. In this interface, it will be possible to visualize the measured results through diagrams.

An automated electro-pneumatic part stamping process was developed at the Universidad Veracruzana in Mexico [27]. The user interface consists of a set of VIs (graphical indicators and animations) for the movement of the cylinder rods using LABVIEW software. On the other hand, a webcam is used to visualize the RL teams in real-time.

On the other hand, a web-based remote experiment using a pneumatic system was presented in the paper [6]. The proposed web interface is based on the XHTML language, which provides capabilities and flexibility for the control, monitoring, and data storage of a pneumatic actuator. Students will be able to connect to the interface using a web browser. The structure of the web interface consists of five parts: visual representation, database, and graphs enabling/disabling experiments, controller parameters, and Debugging messages.

Currently, there is no standard on how the areas of an RL web interface should be structured. The important thing in the design of an interface is to offer a clear and adequate general structure for the development of the experiment, easy navigation, and direct access to commonly used functionalities. Users' first impression when they log in to the interface is considered necessary. For this reason, a general structure of the web interface should have the following areas (Fig. 4):

1. *Control Panel*: Field where users can interact with commonly used actions such as start/end of the experiment, save/send, and information related to the experiment.
2. *Live monitoring*: Typically, a camera is used for this feature. Users will be able to visualize the system's operation on the laboratory workstation.
3. *Circuit Diagram*: Diagram of the experiment to be studied. It is recommended that this section be interactive so that users can see the system's current status in real-time.
4. *Graphs*: Graphs related to the readings of the variables of the pneumatic system. These variables depend on the intelligent equipment (sensors, actuators) installed in the system. The data is stored in the database.

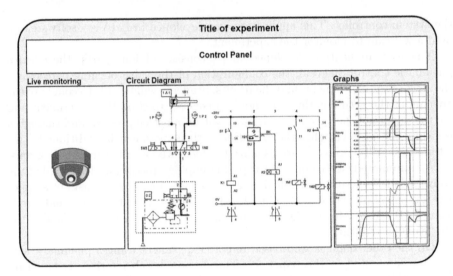

Fig. 4. Overview of an RL web interface.

4   Results

Approximately 250 implementations of RL for various applications in the field of engineering and science are distributed throughout the world's universities [29]. In addition, experimental configurations and new RL modalities focused on pneumatic and electro-pneumatic systems have been implemented in specific universities. Some of the more prominent RLs are described in the previous sections and are listed in Table 3. In this way, these laboratories are available and can share and distribute the theoretical and practical content of the experiments.

Table 3. Summary on remote pneumatics and electro-pneumatics laboratories.

Papers	University	Year	Tests in students
Bajči, B. et al. [7]	Univ. of Novi Sad	2019	Not specified
Abreu, P. et al. [6]	Univ. of Porto	2019	Future work
Reljić, V. et al. [20]	Univ. of Novi Sad	2018	Yes
Bajči, B. et al. [8]	Univ. of Novi Sad	2017	Future work
Villa-López, F.H. et al. [27]	Univ. Veracruzana	2013	Yes

Besides, a comparative analysis of the RLs' different architectures and user interfaces is carried out. In addition, Table 4 and Table 5 clearly show the differences between these RLs. For the development of the RL's [6–8,20,27], various architectures have been defined that differ in terms of hardware/software and approach to experiments in pneumatic systems and these are based on the general structure proposed in Sect. 3.1.

The RL systems developed at the University of Novi Sad [7,8,20] present a solid communication architecture compared to the other RL studied, which contains the necessary elements to establish a high-speed transmission of experimental data real-time performance. Students can access the experiments remotely using the CEyeClon network and the "CEyeClon viewer" application installed on their personal computers. This application is versatile because it can be installed on different operating systems. In addition, a dynamic firewall script is executed to increase the security level of the CEyeClon network. Regarding the user interface, students must connect to the remote desktop located in the face-to-face laboratory to access the interface and start the experiments. The distribution presented in each interface is suitable for each proposed experiment. However, the integration of measurement graphs (historical) in real-time is recommended to study the behavior of the pneumatic system. For example, in [7], there is a graph related to cylinder extraction time that allows the user to analyze the device's behavior.

Table 4. Components of each architecture of RL.

	CS	Remote access	Experimentation unit				Instrumentation unit		
			Controller	Camera	Pneumatic system		Cylinders	Valves	Sensors
[8]	✓	CEyeClon	CompactRIO	✓	✓		✓	✓	✗
[20]	✓	CEyeClon	PLC	✓	✓		✓	✗	✗
[7]	✓	CEyeClon	Arduino Yun	✓	✓		✓	✓	✓
[27]	✓	LabVIEW web server	DAQ board	✓	✓		✓	✓	✓
[6]	✓	Arduino board	Arduino board	✗	✓		✓	✓	✓

On the other hand, the architecture proposed in [27] uses the web server LabVIEW and the web publishing tool of LabVIEW software. This way, the different front panels are published in a web browser, and students can access the experiments from the Internet from anywhere. A non-critical drawback of this system is the availability of the LabVIEW Runtime on all the platforms where the students will perform the experiments. On the other hand, communications are not encrypted, and it is a complicated task to achieve. In this way, malicious users can become a big problem [18].

Instead, an architecture using low-cost components is proposed in [6] where remote access to the system is done through an Arduino board, which works as a server for clients. In addition, this board allows the control, monitoring, and data storage of the pneumatic system. Network security issues to prevent unauthorized access by outside agents are not mentioned. On the other hand, a disadvantage is the non-integration of a camera in the proposed system. Instead, the user interface is integral to the factors mentioned in Sect. 3.2. Furthermore, the authors mention a future integration of a real-time visualization system.

Table 5. Components of each user interface of RL.

	Control panel	Live monitoring	Circuit diagram	Graphs	Database	Based on
[8]	✓	✓	✓	✗	✗	JavaScript
[20]	✓	✓	✓	✗	✗	LabVIEW
[7]	✓	✓	✓	✓	✗	C#
[27]	✓	✓	✓	✗	✗	LabVIEW
[6]	✓	✗	✓	✓	✓	XHTML

5 Conclusions

Automation and ICT have transformed learning in higher education through new technologies. RLs based on pneumatic and electro-pneumatic systems are no exception. These laboratories are implemented in few universities but have enormous advantages in training engineering students by developing intelligent pneumatic solutions using a computer with Internet access. In this way, the students have been able to interact with sensors, actuators, and components belonging to a pneumatic workstation. On the other hand, from the user-side, the compatibility of the executable programs, the platform, and the operating system are problems to be considered.

The contribution of this work is based on an analysis of the architectures and user interfaces of the different RL systems related to pneumatic experiments, detailing advantages, disadvantages, hardware, software, and implemented technologies. In this way, the pros and cons of these systems were identified for future implementation in this engineering area. Additionally, RL developers will need to consider constraints, such as security, unavailability of smartphone-oriented operating systems, and mismanagement of deployed technologies. Likewise, in the design of an RL, the concepts of hardware/software of the system, digitization and data collection, data transmission and visualization, and communication networks must be learned.

References

1. Top 10 Industries Using Hydraulic & Pneumatic Seals. https://www.ozseals.com/top-10-industries-using-hydraulic-pneumatic-seals. Accessed 10 June 2022
2. Pneumatics 4.0: Penetration of Advanced Technologies through Lower Tiers (2017). https://www.frost.com/frost-perspectives/pneumatics-4-0-penetration-of-advanced-technologies-through-lower-tiers. Accessed 10 June 2022
3. Pneumatic Automation: Versatile, Attractive and Low Cost (2019). https://www.industryemea.com/market-overview/22391-pneumatic-automation-versatile,-attractive-and-low-cost. Accessed 10 June 2022
4. The Future of Pneumatics (2019). https://www.rowse.co.uk/blog/post/the-future-of-pneumatics. Accessed 10 June 2022

5. Fluid Power Industry Facts (2022). https://bfpa.co.uk/bfpa-statistics-service/industry-facts/. Accessed 10 June 2022
6. Abreu, P., Valiente, J.S., De La Torre, L., Restivo, M.T., et al.: Remote experiments with pneumatic circuit using a double rod cylinder. In: 2019 5th Experiment International Conference (exp. at 2019), pp. 410–414. IEEE (2019). https://doi.org/10.1109/EXPAT.2019.8876526
7. Bajči, B., Dudić, S., Šulc, J., Reljić, V., Šešlija, D., Milenković, I.: Demonstration: using remotely controlled one-way flow control valve for speed regulation of pneumatic cylinder. In: Auer, M.E., Langmann, R. (eds.) REV 2018. LNNS, vol. 47, pp. 144–152. Springer, Cham (2019). https://doi.org/10.1007/978-3-319-95678-7_16
8. Bajči, B., Šulc, J., Reljić, V., Šešlija, D., Dudić, S., Milenković, I.: Remote laboratory for learning basics of pneumatic control. In: Auer, M.E., Zutin, D.G. (eds.) Online Engineering & Internet of Things. LNNS, vol. 22, pp. 144–150. Springer, Cham (2018). https://doi.org/10.1007/978-3-319-64352-6_14
9. Croser, P., Ebel, F.: Pneumatik: Grundstufe. Springer, Heidelberg (2013)
10. Damrath, F., Strahilov, A., Bär, T., Vielhaber, M.: Experimental validation of a physics-based simulation approach for pneumatic components for production systems in the automotive industry. Procedia CIRP 31, 35–40 (2015). https://doi.org/10.1016/j.procir.2015.03.078
11. De La Cruz, F., Díaz-Granados, M., Zerpa, S., Giménez, D.: Web-labai: Laboratorio remoto de automatización industrial. Revista Iberoamericana de Automática e Informática Industrial RIAI 7(1), 101–106 (2010). https://doi.org/10.1016/S1697-7912(10)70013-3
12. Dihovicni, D., Medenica, M.: Mathematical modelling and simulation of pneumatic systems. In: Advances in Computer Science and Engineering, pp. 161–186 (2011). https://doi.org/10.5772/15313
13. Faulconer, E.K., Gruss, A.B.: A review to weigh the pros and cons of online, remote, and distance science laboratory experiences. Int. Rev. Res. Open Distrib. Learn. 19(2) (2018). https://doi.org/10.19173/irrodl.v19i2.3386
14. Hofstein, A., Lunetta, V.N.: The laboratory in science education: foundations for the twenty-first century. Sci. Educ. 88(1), 28–54 (2004). https://doi.org/10.1002/sce.10106
15. Lowe, D., Newcombe, P., Stumpers, B.: Evaluation of the use of remote laboratories for secondary school science education. Res. Sci. Educ. 43(3), 1197–1219 (2013). https://doi.org/10.1007/s11165-012-9304-3
16. Machidon, O.M., Machidon, A.L., Cotfas, P.A., Cotfas, D.T.: Leveraging web services and FPGA dynamic partial reconfiguration in a virtual hardware design lab. Int. J. Eng. Educ. (IJEE) (2017)
17. Obukhova, E.N., Grishchenko, V.I., Dolgov, G.A.: Formalization of dynamic model of pneumatic drive with variable structure. In: MATEC Web of Conferences, vol. 226, p. 02022. EDP Sciences (2018). https://doi.org/10.1051/matecconf/201822602022
18. Orduña, P., García-Zubia, J., Rodriguez-Gil, L., Irurzun, J., López-de Ipiña, D., Gazzola, F.: Using labview remote panel in remote laboratories: advantages and disadvantages. In: Proceedings of the 2012 IEEE Global Engineering Education Conference (EDUCON), pp. 1–7. IEEE (2012). https://doi.org/10.1109/EDUCON.2012.6201134
19. Prada, M.A., Fuertes, J.J., Alonso, S., García, S., Domínguez, M.: Challenges and solutions in remote laboratories. Application to a remote laboratory of an electro-pneumatic classification cell. Comput. Educ. 85, 180–190 (2015). https://doi.org/10.1016/j.compedu.2015.03.004

20. Reljić, V., Bajči, B., Milenković, I., Šulc, J., Šešlija, D., Dudić, S.: Development of an experimental setup for remote testing of pneumatic control. Int. J. Online Eng. **14**(1) (2018). https://doi.org/10.3991/ijoe.v14i01.7784

21. Richer, E., Hurmuzlu, Y.: A high performance pneumatic force actuator system: Part II-nonlinear controller design. J. Dyn. Sys. Meas. Control **122**(3), 426–434 (2000). https://doi.org/10.1115/1.1286366

22. Richer, E., Hurmuzlu, Y.: A high performance pneumatic force actuator system: Part I-nonlinear mathematical model. J. Dyn. Sys. Meas. Control **122**(3), 416–425 (2000). https://doi.org/10.1115/1.1286336

23. Schlüter, M.S., Perondi, E.A.: Mathematical modeling of pneumatic semi-rotary actuator with friction. J. Braz. Soc. Mech. Sci. Eng. **40**(11), 1–17 (2018). https://doi.org/10.1007/s40430-018-1434-8

24. Shilin, D., Gribkov, A., Golubev, V.: The study of the control law for carriage positioning of rodless pneumatic actuator with fuzzy regulator. EAI Endorsed Trans. Ind. Netw. Intell. Syst. **4**(11), e3–e3 (2017). https://doi.org/10.4108/eai.21-12-2017.153501

25. Trentsios, P., Wolf, M., Frerich, S.: Remote lab meets virtual reality-enabling immersive access to high tech laboratories from afar. Procedia Manuf. **43**, 25–31 (2020). https://doi.org/10.1016/j.promfg.2020.02.104

26. Viegas, C., et al.: Impact of a remote lab on teaching practices and student learning. Comput. Educ. **126**, 201–216 (2018). https://doi.org/10.1016/j.compedu.2018.07.012

27. Villa-López, F.H., García-Guzmán, J., Enríquez, J.V., Leal-Ortíz, S., Ramírez-Ramírez, A.: Electropneumatic system for industrial automation: a remote experiment within a web-based learning environment. Procedia Technol. **7**, 198–207 (2013). https://doi.org/10.1016/j.protcy.2013.04.025

28. Villar-Zafra, A., Zarza-Sánchez, S., Lázaro-Villa, J.A., Fernández-Cantí, R.M.: Multiplatform virtual laboratory for engineering education. In: 2012 9th International Conference on Remote Engineering and Virtual Instrumentation (REV), pp. 1–6. IEEE (2012). https://doi.org/10.1109/REV.2012.6293127

29. Wang, N., Lan, Q., Chen, X., Song, G., Parsaei, H.: Development of a Remote Laboratory for Engineering Education. CRC Press, Boca Raton (2020). https://doi.org/10.1016/j.compedu.2011.02.015

30. Zubía, J.G., Alves, G.R.: Using Remote Labs in Education: Two Little Ducks in Remote Experimentation, vol. 8. Universidad de Deusto (2012)

Augmented Reality in Clothing Consumer Customization in COVID-19 Pandemic: A Preliminary Study

Aylen Karina Medina-Robalino(iD), Sandra Jacqueline Solís-Sánchez(✉) (iD),
Eduardo Santiago Suárez-Abril(iD), and Nancy Margarita López-Barrionuevo(iD)

Facultad de Diseño y Arquitectura, Universidad Técnica de Ambato, 180105 Ambato, Ecuador
{aylenkmedina,sj.solis,eduardossuarez,nm.lopez}@uta.edu.ec

Abstract. Emergencies produce significant changes in people's habits and lifestyles. Further, it also impacts our clothing tastes and preferences because social interaction is reduced, and everyday activities are performed at home. Thus, this paper shows a psychographic analysis to determine the type, style, color, and other clothing characteristics users preferred across the pandemic. In addition, some considerations have been taken into account to understand the clothing characteristics users will look for in post-pandemic presential jobs. In this context, the first version of a smartphone app using augmented reality (AR) has been developed. Three-dimensional objects were designed using Blender, while the smartphone app was set up using Unity, accompanied by modules such as AR Foundation, ARCore XR Plugin, and DOTween. The application allows the overview of the selected three-dimensional garment and relevant information about its components. Statistical analysis shows a vital essential between the monthly income of the participants and their purchasing decision; likewise, between sex and upper garments usage. Experimental tests inside a retail store validate this proposal throughout a new sample of 44 people. Ultimately, they filled out a usability test (SUS) that confirmed the application acceptance with an 82.73%. Finally, they gave the corresponding feedback on their experience using the app. Consequently, relevant information that might be used in future research to understand the consumer needs in a matter of clothing emergencies or confinement is passing through has been exposed.

Keywords: Consumer customization · Clothing preferences · Augmented reality · COVID-19

1 Introduction

In the last two decades, exponential e-commerce development has been seen on all platforms [1]. Web pages have become one of the main methods for product sale and exchange. The purchase of toys, entertainment articles, jewelry and, household appliances stand out as the main ones. Also, there are some gadgets that people prefers according on how they wear it or where they live at such as clothes, furniture among other decoration products [2]. However, two-dimensional images shown in either printed magazines or online sites prevent users to have an easy purchase choice due to their lack of information or details. This is why consumers decide to better move towards the store and make a presential visit in which they can confirm the product satisfy their needs, taste and anthropometric measurements [3–5].

The human being was accustomed to perform entertainment activities, commerce and physical fitness recreation. However, technology growth has brought new ways of interaction between people. E-commerce made his appear as the variant that allows society to purchase and sale products through the net. It has been considered a disruptor that has radically changed conventional commerce, increasing convenience and diversifying benefits for sellers and customers. It even became the business model basis that some companies select. Among the different available types, B2C (business to consumer) stands out from others where attention is completely directed to the final consumer. The online store is the most habitual business model, it became the digital version of what, in the past, was a physical space. As main advantages, low initial investment, broad reach, accessibility and permanent availability for public is highlighted [6].

E-commerce has an almost unlimited growth potential due to sales never stop neither by the business hours nor seller availability. The greater the innovation of the system, the better the profitability of the business is expected to be [7]. Hence, new methodologies that nowadays are in the rise would be included in sales strategy. The extended reality (XR) systems appear bring the option of developing new scenarios, characters and computer-simulated objects [8–11]. By its definition, augmented, virtual and mixed reality are included in the above-mentioned systems [12, 13]. Augmented reality (AR) came as a new tool which is typically used in smartphones and tablets, just as describe Lucero et al. [14]. This technology allows to extend the real world's appreciation by adding virtual information that enhance user's experience. Applications have a wide variety. In fact, entertainment is the most-used field. On the other hand, this type of technology let the information to be displayed without physical contact; it means that viruses and bacteria transmission is avoided.

SARS-CoV-2 virus, since COVID-19 pandemic was officially established, has been the cause of misfortune and death throughout the world [15]. An unprecedent pandemic that started at the end of 2019 and in 2020 and 2021, it had a severe impact over population without distinction. The World Health Organization (WHO) and physicians from all over the world recommended biosafety measures to reduce the number of infections [6]. The partial or total confinement, face mask usage, hand-washing and social distancing stand out as principal measures taken. The closure of public and private establishments produced important changes in matter of economy, policy and society. The human being was required to adopt technological means to conduct activities that right before were presential. E-commerce became popular because it brought the client's ability to be assisted at any purchase; it simulates the interaction just as being physically present at the store through live chats or live videocalls to show the products to the client.

Although sensory gaps have not been completely filled, the number of online services and stores has increased. The social component in e-services is often neglected, so there is still room for improvement in the social and experiential experience. This is why nowadays we face human-machine interactions (HCI), where computer interfaces and virtual avatars could replace conventional employees, helping to generate more sociable environments. For example, PHARA [16], a mobile AR assistant that provides information about food products in grocery stores; it contributes to a better decision making. Similarly, [3] presents an AR-based application that displays the main product attributes in a physical retail store. It can even influence the change of customer consumption behavior. In [17], information on organic products is shown as a strategy to increase sustainable consumption. AR is consolidating as a marketing tool that enables business evolution. The sale of other products such as furniture and decorative accessories can also be done through virtual catalogs that include three-dimensional AR models.

As described by Ekmeil et al. [18] augmented reality environments are presented as a technological variant that have offered important benefits for marketing and e-commerce in COVID-19 context. However, there is still a lot of ground to be explored and needs to be covered. Therefore, this manuscript describes the use of AR to create an application to improve the experience of clothing consumers. Considering the need to reduce physical contact, this technology allows to obtain more information about a product without the need to interact with a store employee. To achieve the goal, the use of a mid-range smartphone whose acquisition has become widespread in recent years, is required. To validate the app, experimental and usability test are carried out with their corresponding feedback.

This document is composed by four sections including the introduction in Sect. 1. In Sect. 2 the applied methodology is described while in Sect. 3 results are presented. Section 4 address the discussion and conclusions.

2   Materials Methods

The user-centered design was the chosen methodology for this study. It began with an in-depth study of the person in order to define his or her requirements. In this case, the aim was to define the profile of the clothing consumer in an emergency context. Moreover, this study presents the development of an intuitive and easy-to-use application. Based on other existing applications, the use of video transparencies is proposed; it allows to calibrate the smartphone camera automatically. This is based on tracking markers, which avoids the person must receiving a previous preparation before using it.

2.1   Sample

The type of sample used for data gathering is non-probabilistic; usually applied in research with a more qualitative approach. As part of the ethnographic focus, samples are defined in two ways: i) in a chain ii) with voluntary participants. For the chain (also known as snowball) sample, key participants were identified, so that, they recommended other people who expand the number of people who could participate [19]. The remaining group responded affirmatively to a summon.

2.2   Participants

This study is focused on adolescents and young adults. Therefore, it was conducted with students of a university campus with a total of 254 people. Table 1 summarizes the sociodemographic variables of the participants.

Table 1. Demographic characteristics of the study population.

Variable	Range	Frequency	Percentage
Age	18–25 yo	213	83,86%
	26–30 yo	37	14,57%
	31 yo or above	4	1,57%
Sex	Female	135	53,15%
	Male	119	46,85%
Civil status	Single	243	95,67%
	Married	7	2,76%
	Divorced	1	0,39%
	De facto union	3	1,18%
Number of children	No children	233	91,74%
	One	17	6,69%
	Two	3	1,18%
	Three	1	0,39%
Family size	2–4 people	141	55,90%
	5–7 people	102	40,16%
	8–10 people	10	3,94%
Who they live with	Family	246	96,85%
	Alone	6	2,36%
	Friends	2	0,79%
Monthly income	$0$400USD	124	48,82%
	$401$1000USD	97	38,19%
	$1001$1400USD	21	8,27%
	$1401USD or above	12	4,72%

The majority are between 18 and 25 years old (83.86%), the remain people have and older age. In regards to sex, female has a higher proportion than male (53.15%). Almost the half of the families have a monthly income of less than or equal to $400 USD, followed by those earning between $401 and $1000 USD and only 11% earns further than $1000 USD.

Although married and de facto union people exists in less quantity, in this study group, as expected, the single civil status is predominant. Most of them have no kids. However, a few of them have one kid and in a less proportion have two or three children. Almost all individuals live with their family and rarely live alone or with friends. In terms of the family size, more than a half of the sample have between 2 and 4 members, followed by those with 5 to 7 people in the family and a minimum number with a family size exceeding 8 people.

2.3   Requirement Analysis

The study begins with the environment description where participants operate, i.e., their homes. The context was defined through virtuality enhanced by the confinement in terms of COVID-19 pandemic. Ethnographic method is applied to define needs in which several data collection techniques are established. In this case, a mixed model is used, the qualitative approach was obtained from surveys and observation. On the other hand, the interview was taken as a quantitative tool [19].

Semi-structured interviews are conducted to determine the socio-cultural factors that characterize the selected group. For the registry, written notes and recorded audios were taken prior the consent of the interviewed people in order to be able to use the resource. Respondents were contacted through personal references, meetings were held through Zoom digital platform because of the confinement. The preferred meeting schedule was in the afternoon or at night, after their study or job hours.

At the same time, a non-participant observation was performed with the aim to identify the clothing typology of the participants. The information registry was conducted using a record card as an instrument. It contains the screenshot of the observed individuals and a simple contextual description of the activities he or she is doing in the moment. Finally, surveys were filled out to determine demographic, psychographic and behavioral data that expose their lifestyle. This allows to identify their clothing preferences during telework and the kind of product that will be required for post-pandemic presential work.

2.4   Application Design

Technical Requirements. To guarantee the proper operation of the app, a mid to high rage smartphone is required. In general terms, the smartphone should at least include a 12 megapixels camera, an ARCore from Google compatible processor and typical sensors such as accelerometer and gyroscope. The color-quality of the clothing depends directly of the smartphone's display. For this case, we use a smartphone with 1.440x3.120px AMOLED 90 Hz display, Snapdragon 855 processor, 12 GB of RAM memory and a 48 Mpx f/1.6 OIS + EIS camera. Likewise, the AR managing requires special attention in the characteristics of the PC where it will be developed in order to avoid slowdowns or extended compilation times. It is highly recommended not using the minimum specifications for the use of Unity because later on with the installation of several packages, modules, plugins and extensions, the computer will be severe impacted on its performance. Therefore, we use a computer with an Intel Core i7 10th gen, 16 GB of RAM memory and a graphics card NVIDIA RTX 2060 4 GB.

Software. The multiplatform Unity graphics engine is used since it is compatible with the development of AR apps through installable modules. Unity facilitates the development of the application through its integrated development environment (IDE); in addition, it has a direct connection with Visual Studio for scripts creation that allow the execution of the app [1]. Version 2021.3.4f1 was used for the development of the application.

For AR development, it was required the installation of several packages such as: 1) AR Foundation. It contains the user interface that allows AR development in Unity; however, it does not include any AR feature so for its operation another package must be downloaded according to the development platform. 2) ARCore XR Plug-in. It is compatible with ARCore and allows AR development through Unity. It has several subsystems, including camera, depth, session, planes, anchors, face and image tracking, among others. 3) DOTween. It is an object-oriented animation engine compatible with C#. It can animate numeric and non-numeric values; it can even animate strings with support for rich text. Figure 1 shows the flowchart for the creation of the design interface.

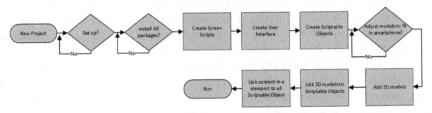

Fig. 1. General flowchart about the creation of the app.

Clothing Design. Blender software was used. It is a 3D illustration software compatible with Unity. Blender allows to transfer a 2D image to 3D by decomposing the image into a mesh of multiple geometric figures such as squares, rectangles, triangles, circles; and into three-dimensional figures, such as cylinders, cubes, etc. The clothing model was designed based on the study that characterizes the users, where black was the predominant color in men, together with navy blue and gray. In women, neutral colors predominated, with beige standing out.

Operation. When the application is launched for the first time, the permissions concerning camera, position and gyroscope are requested. On the main screen, the camera is shown in operation. On this screen, the points where clothing garment will be projected in 3D are read. After pressing the menu button, a ribbon of options is displayed with all the available 3D clothing designs (see Fig. 2). Finally, after selecting the garment, the 3D element is displayed giving the augmented reality illusion by placing the 3D model over the real view displayed through the smartphone's camera as shown in Fig. 3. The application has repositioning and rotation capabilities for the visualization of the garment. The display of 2 or more clothing garments is possible, however, it depends on the smartphone to avoid slowdowns.

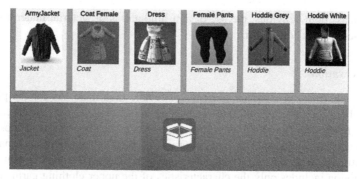

Fig. 2. Ribbon options with 3D models.

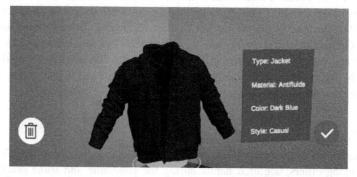

Fig. 3. App operation with three-dimensional model of a designed clothing garment

3 Experimental Results

3.1 Interviews

The prevalence of negative feelings such as stress due to isolation and concern about the need for social interaction has been identified. In the educational field, face-to-face education combined with practice is preferred; something similar occurs with work. There is also evidence of fatigue, frustration and fear of contagion of the virus and related diseases. To this is added the expectation of personal and family well-being due to inflation and the generalized economic crisis. Despite this scenario, feelings of resilience also stand out, including solidarity, honesty and valuing health and life.

Social habits have been modified, replacing for virtual meetings the face-to-face ones. Most of people prefer stay at home and just as an informant said "habits are now more virtual". New acquired habits are related to adoption of biosafety measures released from the beginning of the pandemic. The use of face mask, alcohol and antibacterial gels, hand-washing and disinfection of food, clothing, shoes and surfaces are emphasized. The most usual activities during the confinement and weekdays include telestudy and teleworking combined with watching movies and series. On weekends, other activities are carried out such as going out in open spaces, take a walk, share family moments, being online to social media and buy online grocery and some other products. With the return to classroom activities, the use of anti-fluid and anti-bacterial materials will be used, preserving the conventional style.

3.2 Observation

In this sample, there is a greater presence of female than male. As for the place and context where they are located, we are talking about their homes, specifically their bedroom, living room or study room. Among physical characteristics of these places are windows, bookcases, shelves and pictures. The predominant lighting is natural, as well as artificial, with walls in pastel colors and light shades. It should be clarified that the description includes only the characteristics of the upper clothing garments, since this is the one and only type of clothing that could be seen during virtual meetings. Active wear type clothing stands out with comfortable garments in knitted materials, with sporty characteristics. The ideal clothing for the development of these activities at home are hoodies and sports outfits. For weekends, the use of comfortable and sporty clothing is maintained. The use of semi-sheer garments has also been identified, where simplicity and very few prints predominate. In terms of color, black tones predominate, followed by white, beige and/or brown tones, as well as neutral gray tones. In much lesser incidence the clothing garments are presented in color combination.

3.3 Polls

Finally, data from polls was valuated establishing categories regarding the COVID-19 theme. Among others, acquired habits during the pandemic and some practices that became familiar are emphasized. In social context, 18.50% prefer stay at home, but, 28.74% mentioned that at least they go out twice a week. 17.72% prefer face-to-face meetings; however, the majority have adopted the virtual world or any other remote media communication. Although it has being reduced over the time, 70.87% are concern about being infected. Despite this, 87.4% still prefer making purchases physically. However, social media take center stage: Whatsapp (19.29%) and Facebook (8.66%). In regards to the clothing, 86.61% has preference for upper garments rather than lower ones. The use of jerseys (66.54%), hoods (60.63%), T-shirts (57.09%), sweaters (49.61%) and jackets (38.58%) stand out. In smaller proportion, coats (38.19%), blouses (23.63%), shirts (17.32%), tops (9.84%) and bvd (4.33%). On the other hand, lower garments just like pants are preferred: sports pants (69.29%), jeans (62.60%), pajamas (40.94%), lycra - leggings (33.46%) and tube (25.59%). Shorts (14.57%), Bermuda shorts (13%), short skirts (6.3%) and long skirts (3.15%). In terms of footwear, sports shoes (90.55%), slippers (41.73%) and formal shoes (19.69%) stand out. As for accessory items, surgical masks (55.91%) and personalized masks (36.61%), hats (31.89%), scarves (22.05%) and glasses (16.14%) are among the main ones.

From the economic point of view, 46.85% of the participants consider that prices have risen, 37% that they have remained the same, and only 16.15% that they have decreased. 57.48% prefer buying their clothes in squares and fairs, while the remaining 42.52% prefer buying their clothes in commercial establishments and supermarkets. On the other hand, participants have preferences at the time of purchasing, therefore, 24% prefer purchasing based on price, 30.31% on quality, 16.93% on aes-thetics and 6.3% on sustainability. Despite the reduction of bans, the post-pandemic consumer still maintains respect for biosafety measures. Based on this survey, it is estimated that 94.49% will continue to wear face masks, 88.98% will carry alcohol and antibacterial gel, 87.40% will continue to wash their hands frequently, and 32.677 will still change their clothes when they get home. The preferences of the material used in presses will also change to use anti-fluid (17.72%), repellent (4.33%) and antibacterial (3.15%) characteristics.

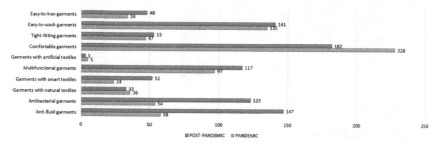

Fig. 4. Clothing preferences in pandemic and post-pandemic period.

Moreover, a statistical analysis to define if inherent conditions of the sample have an influence over the person behavior was performed. There was not any significant inference between sociodemographic factors such as age, civil status, number of children, family size or age and composed variables in the interview. However, socioeconomic level is an important variable to consider due to 79.51% of the sample belong to a high socioeconomic level. A significant inference was found between purchase behavior and the monthly income of the participants. There is also an important relation between variables such as sex and upper clothing garments usage. Crossed tables show that men prefer jeans, while women sporty pants. It is estimated that age did not influence in other variables because people's majority is concentrated in the 18–25 age range and there is not much variability.

Figure 4 shows the expected changes between a consumer in a pandemic context and after it. According to the interview data, most of the confined users prefer comfortable clothing with natural textiles. In the future, the focus will be on multifunctional clothing garments with smart textiles that include anti-fluid and anti-bacterial functions.

In order to establish the categories and carry out the analysis, it is necessary to triangulate all information sources [19]. This analysis involves studying each piece of evidence separately in its context, then, integrating it with the rest of information to form the categories and establish the findings. Triangulation involves verifying the data in at least two of the three available sources. A summary of the information obtained is shown in Fig. 5.

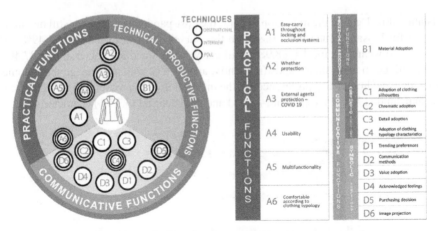

TECHNIQUES

Fig. 5. Relationship of clothing functions according to consumer preferences.

3.4 Experimental Tests.

A new sample of 44 individuals is randomly selected, who are part of the initial group that owns a mid-range smartphone. For this study, it was necessary for these people to be in a physical store which was easier with the last authority's decision about the reduction of capacity limitations on establishments. At the beginning of the test, insecurity was noted in the participants; however, it was firmly reduced when the app was socialized. Then, we helped them to install the app on their smartphones. After that, they were given 3 min to explore and get familiar with the app. In the end, they started experimental test to evaluate slowdowns, unexpected closure, or any other issue when using the app.

In the store's entry, a marker was placed to be scanned with the smartphone's camera; it shows the main biosafety measures that must be respected. Also, general rules for both store and app are displayed. During this test, users found many markers in different places inside the store that allow them to know more details about clothes. In addition, a few three-dimensional models were included to let consumers look at its structure and clarify the idea about how will it fit on their bodies, thus, the manipulation of some products were restricted in order to avoid the viruses and bacteria propagation. Figure 6 shows the experimental tests. After 15 min using the app, the experimental test is finished and now users give feedback through the usability test about this proposal.

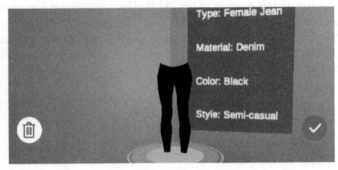

Fig. 6. Functional testing of the proposed system.

3.5   Usability Test

In order to validate the performance of this proposal, a questionnaire based on the SUS test, developed by Brooke [20], has been implemented. This instrument has been used in many other research to evaluate the performance of applications that have virtual scenarios. The evaluation is carried out on a scale of 1 to 5. Questions must be evaluated in two groups. In the first group, 1 should be subtracted from the rating obtained. This group consist of questions 1, 3, 5, 7 and 9. Conversely, in questions 2, 4, 6, 8 and 10, a base of 5 is chosen and the value obtained by the participants is subtracted from this value. At the end, a sum of all the values obtained is added up and multiplied by 2.5; the result is the score obtained in the test. This value will be in a range from 0 to 100 and the higher it is, the better the acceptance of the application. The scores are shown in Table 3.

The result of 82.73% validates that the application works correctly, positive values show that consumers will use the application to get information about products. A feeling of security is also perceived due to its interaction ease. The lower values were given because of the feedback about the function integration that maybe included in the application for next version. At the same time, there is still some inconsistencies when displaying the information due to it is yet a beta version. In addition, as an improve to the app, an information poster with indications of using the application would be added to the store's entry.

Table 3. Results summary of the SUS test.

N°	Question	Score	Result
1	I think I would like to use this system frequently	4,27	3,27
2	I find this system unnecessarily complex	1,30	3,70
3	I think the system is easy to use	4,18	3,18
4	I think you would need technical support to make use of the system	1,32	3,68
5	I find the various functions of the system quite well integrated	3,57	2,57
6	I have found too much inconsistency in this system	2,07	2,93
7	I think most people would learn to make use of the system quickly	4,07	3,07
8	I found the system quite uncomfortable to use	1,32	3,68
9	I have felt very safe using the system	4,52	3,52
10	I would need to learn a lot of things before I can manage the system	1,52	3,48
	Subtotal		33,09
	Total		82,73%

4   Discussion and Conclusions

User-centered design has a conceptual framework that, in this application, allows to identify a cognitive meaning aligned with behavioral theories and consumer motivation.

It is also related to value-perceived theory since innovation research through AR development has been arranged. Augmented reality is no longer an exclusive topic of fiction science and videogames. This technology, that is still a novel matter in some countries around the globe, will play an important role in many industries in the next years. As for this moment, most of its features are oriented to entertainment activities and tourism promotion as described in [21]. Virtual training advantage comes from a much reduced risk when performing activities (controlled environment); however, activities are carried out in an identical way to the traditional one. Although marketing has had an important growth, there's a long way to go in terms of e-commerce. Moreover, e-commerce allows services diversification by showing informative messages to the consumers as proposed in [16, 18, 22]. The mentioned research is aligned to this proposal; it shows that its use can be generalized to other industries. In other studies, the user-interaction and even more commonly the development of many products in commercial stores are emphasized [23]. This is also comparable to this research since the three-dimensional clothing models are presented so that the person can visualize them reducing the contact, but maximizing the experience.

During the pandemic time, clothing sales declined by more than 12% as shown by Shetty & Pai [6]. Thus, applications that merge technology with industry are necessary to meet the changing customer demands. The objective of a user-centered study has been met, where the system is formed based on a complete analysis of the customer's requirements. It has become evident how confinement can affect young people behaviorally and change their dressing habits and personal care. Now virtual meetings are more common just like the use of upper clothing garments. The most used, chromatic and other inherent characteristics have been also identified. Likewise, economic parameters have also been identified since the global crisis is another variable that may promote further changes in the future. This is why the success of clothing stores will depend on their adaptation to new technologies.

In the COVID-19 pandemic, e-commerce has proven to be a maintenance and growth opportunity for the textile industry [24]. However, this study results are not conclusive because of the experiment's design; the main contribution is to enhance the existent literature on the advantages the technology offers in the current marketing. AR could become the basis to improve consumers' experience, but it is required more studies and applications. It also increases the satisfaction of the customer using online shopping portals, with an extended product's view and services they receive. The need to foster new user experiences will turn online stores into serious games. When making proposals such as this one that seek to meet the needs of man, usability tests are a valuable tool that allows us to evaluate the product performance. As in [3], the acceptance of our proposal by users has been massive with 82.73% in the SUS test. It demonstrates that technology is both part of people's lives and a field to be exploited. In fact, it will allow businesses to set new satisfaction standards that do not currently exist. Even the customer can be influenced to choose a certain type of clothing as they did in [17] by displaying messages of sustainable products. These technologies settlement is already a profitable reality, thus, stores should know how to merge them as soon as possible.

One of the main limitations in the research was due to the lack of related literature. Most of the works are related to tourism or entertainment, however, recent researches that allow to determine the AR contribution into marketing nowadays has been referenced. Another limitation was the selection of a non-representative group of people because the analysis and surveys were taken from members of the university com-munity, therefore, the obtained information could be biased. Thus, it is planned to increase and diversify the amount and type of people for future research. However, this main issue would impact on the direct or indirect relation found between this proposal and the definition of the consumer behavior.

This research aims to contribute to the development of guidelines that can be used by application developers in emergency situations. Future research should aim to verify the proposed model in other areas of industry and knowledge. It could also be applied in other parts of the world and evaluate whether demographic variables have a strong influence on consumer behavior. It is also planned to develop an application that uses high-quality images only and compare with this proposal with the aim to define which one is better in terms of consumer's acceptance. Furthermore, it is intended to compare this research with online stores so that, accurate conclusions could be obtained and exposed.

Acknowledgment. This manuscript is part of the research project: "Diseño y producción de prendas emergentes para afrontar la emergencia sanitaria Covid-19 del consumidor pospandemia". It has been financed by the Investigation and Development Direction (DIDE) from Universidad Técnica de Ambato (UTA). It was approved with resolution: UTA-CONIN-2020–0324-R and keeps the code PFDAA 12. The entire researching group express their acknowledge to the Superior Education Institute UTA for the finance and support.

References

1. García-Magariño, I., Gonzalez Bedia, M., Palacios-Navarro, G.: FAMAP: A framework for developing m-health apps. En: Advances in Intelligent Systems and Computing, pp. 850–859. Springer Verlag (2018). https://doi.org/10.1007/978-3-319-77703-0_83/COVER/
2. Jílková, P., Králová, P.: Digital consumer behaviour and eCommerce trends during the COVID-19 crisis. Int. Adv. Econ. Res. **27**(1), 83–85 (2021). https://doi.org/10.1007/s11294-021-09817-4
3. Álvarez Márquez, J.O., Ziegler, J.: In-store augmented reality-enabled product comparison and recommendation. In: RecSys 2020 - 14th ACM Conf. Recomm. Syst. 20, pp. 180–189 (2020). https://doi.org/10.1145/3383313.3412266
4. Medina Robalino, A.: Indumentaria indígena: ética, política y diseño. Una mirada sobre el artefacto vestimentario de la mujer chibuleo. Cuad. del Cent. Estud. Diseño y Comun. (2020). https://doi.org/10.18682/cdc.vi120.4171
5. Medina Robalino, A.: Tesis recomendada para su publicación. Indumentaria e identidad: análisis de la vestimenta de la mujer indígena desde el Diseño. El caso del pueblo chibuleo (Tungurahua, Ecuador 1990–2016). Cuad. del Cent. Estud. Diseño y Comun. (2020). https://doi.org/10.18682/cdc.vi116.4141
6. Shetty, S., Pai, R.: Impact of Covid-19 on online shopping -a case study. EPRA Int. J. Environ. Econ. Commer. Educ. Manag. **8**, 9–15 (2021). https://doi.org/10.36713/epra7063
7. Medina Robalino, A.K.: El chumbi andino. Reflexiones en torno a la potencialidad de su estudio desde las funciones del vestido. J. Chem. Inf. Model. **8**, 167–187 (2021)

8. Varela-Aldás, J., Palacios-Navarro, G., Amariglio, R., García-Magariño, I.: Head-mounted display-based application for cognitive training. Sensors (Switzerland). **20**, 1–22 (2020). https://doi.org/10.3390/s20226552

9. Palacios-Navarro, G., Albiol-Pérez, S., García-Magariño García, I.: Effects of sensory cueing in virtual motor rehabilitation. A review. J. Biomed. Inform. **60**, 49–57 (2016). https://doi.org/10.1016/j.jbi.2016.01.006

10. Palacios-Navarro, G., Hogan, N.: Head-mounted display-based therapies for adults post-stroke: a systematic review and meta-analysis. Sensors (Switzerland). **21**, 1–24 (2021). https://doi.org/10.3390/s21041111

11. Varela-Aldás, J., Buele, J., Amariglio, R., García-Magariño, I., Palacios-Navarro, G.: The cupboard task: an immersive virtual reality-based system for everyday memory assessment. Int. J. Hum. Comput. Stud. **167**, 102885 (2022). https://doi.org/10.1016/J.IJHCS.2022.102885

12. Ortiz, J.S., Palacios-Navarro, G., Andaluz, V.H., Guevara, B.S.: Virtual reality-based framework to simulate control algorithms for robotic assistance and rehabilitation tasks through a standing wheelchair. Sensors. **21**, 5083 (2021). https://doi.org/10.3390/s21155083

13. Varela-Aldás, J., Buele, J., Lorente, P.R., García-Magariño, I., Palacios-Navarro, G.: A virtual reality-based cognitive telerehabilitation system for use in the covid-19 pandemic. Sustain. **13**, 1–24 (2021). https://doi.org/10.3390/su13042183

14. Lucero-Urresta, E., Buele, J., Córdova, P., Varela-Aldás, J.: Precision shooting training system using augmented reality. In: Gervasi, O., et al. (eds.) ICCSA 2021. LNCS, vol. 12957, pp. 283–298. Springer, Cham (2021). https://doi.org/10.1007/978-3-030-87013-3_22

15. Talahua, J.S., Buele, J., Calvopina, P., Varela-Aldas, J.: Facial recognition system for people with and without face mask in times of the covid-19 pandemic. Sustain. **13**, 6900 (2021). https://doi.org/10.3390/su13126900

16. Gutiérrez, F., Verbert, K., Htun, N.N.: Phara: An augmented reality grocery store assistant. In: MobileHCI 2018 - Beyond Mobile: The Next 20 Years - 20th International Conference on Human-Computer Interaction with Mobile Devices and Services, Conference Proceedings Adjunct, pp. 339–345. ACM, New York, NY, USA (2018). https://doi.org/10.1145/3236112.3236161

17. Jäger, A.K., Weber, A.: Increasing sustainable consumption: message framing and in-store technology. Int. J. Retail Distrib. Manag. **48**, 803–824 (2020). https://doi.org/10.1108/IJRDM-02-2019-0044

18. Ekmeil, F.A.R., Abumandil, M.S.S., Alkhawaja, M.I., Siam, I.M., Alaklouk, S.A.A.: Augmented reality and virtual reality revolutionize rusiness transformation in digital marketing tech industry analysts and visionaries during Coronavirus (COVID 19). J. Phys. Conf. Ser. **1860**, 012012 (2021). https://doi.org/10.1088/1742-6596/1860/1/012012

19. Guber, R.: La Etnografía Método, Campo y Reflexividad. Siglo XXI Editores, Buenos Aires (2019)

20. Brooke, J.: SUS: a retrospective. J. Usability Stud. **8**, 29–40 (2013)

21. Jingen Liang, L., Elliot, S.: A systematic review of augmented reality tourism research: what is now and what is next? Tour. Hosp. Res. **21**, 15–30 (2021). https://doi.org/10.1177/1467358420941913

22. Nhan, J.: Designing an Augmented Reality Experience. Mastering ARKit. 45–58 (2022). https://doi.org/10.1007/978-1-4842-7836-9_3

23. Fu'Adi, D.K., Hidayanto, A.N., Inan, D.I., Phusavat, K.: The implementation of augmented reality in e-commerce customization: a systematic literature review. In: Proceedings 2021 13th International Conference Information Communication Technology System ICTS 2021, pp. 12–17 (2021). https://doi.org/10.1109/ICTS52701.2021.9608322

24. Medina, A., Solís, S., Suárez, E.: Diseño de indumentaria y covid-19. Consideraciones de los comportamientos del consumidor en relación al artefacto vestimentario. Rev. Inclusiones. **8**, 36–57 (2021)

Identification of Mango Fruit Maturity Using Robust Industrial Devices and Open-Source Devices Applying Artificial Vision

Samuel Baldomero Bustos Gaibor⬛, Luis Enrique Chuquimarca Jiménez$^{(\boxtimes)}$ ⬛,
José Miguel Sánchez Aquino⬛, Carlos Alberto Saldaña Enderica⬛,
and David Eduardo Sánchez Espinoza⬛

Facultad de Sistemas y Telecomunicaciones, Universidad Estatal Península de Santa Elena,
Santa Elena, Ecuador
lchuquimarca@upse.edu.ec

Abstract. This article is about the communication between the programmable logic controller and the Raspberry Pi device. Due to technological advances at the Industrial level in recent years, the popularity of this interconnection has increased due to the importance of intelligent systems and the Industrial Internet of Things (IIoT). This project applied intelligent automation through a low-cost device with high efficiency, performance, precision, and monitoring in industrial processes in real-time, in order to identify mango fruit maturity according to its color. The system detects green color for unripe fruit and yellow color for ripe fruit, using computer vision techniques through an intelligent device (Raspberry Pi) and an inexpensive sensor (Pi camera module). The connection of the Siemens s7–1200 PLC with RPi3 through the Python-Snap7 library allows the transfer of information, considering the Profinet industrial communication protocol. RPi3 is used as a control node of the network through the PuTTY application to transfer data to the Siemens s7–1200 PLC, using the SSH protocol for the connection. Therefore, this work achieves real-time monitoring with low latency and high precision between the detection process and the automation of the actuators through the programmable logic controller.

Keywords: PLC · Rpi · Python-Snap7 · Artificial vision · Mango

1 Introduction

Currently, the industrial sector incorporates intelligent technologies creating a new business model and new challenges. The use of artificial vision facilitates the automation of decision processes in real-time to create a synergy between increasing product quality and reducing production time.

In addition, companies and researchers focus on the use of mid-range devices due to the cost-benefit they represent in measurement systems and the interconnection of devices focused on industrial applications [1].

T. Guarda et al. (Eds.): ARTIIS 2022, CCIS 1675, pp. 217–227, 2022.
https://doi.org/10.1007/978-3-031-20319-0_17

Industrial automation uses programmable logic controllers (PLCs) as robust control devices for industrial environments being a fundamental pillar of the third industrial revolution. But, in the fourth industrial revolution, some companies have prioritized migration towards digital transformation through the interconnection of devices, sending data to the cloud, data analysis in the cloud, predictive systems, among others [2].

Due to this, new configurations and communication protocols arise between high-end devices (PLCs) with mid-range devices such as Raspberry Pi (RPi) [3]. The PLC has communication modules such as Ethernet, serial, and USB ports [4].

Instead, the RPi has a communication protocol in common with the PLC device, which is the Profinet communication protocol through the Ethernet port of both devices [5].

Siemens s7–1200 PLC is connected with RPi3 through Profinet communication using the Snap7 library allowing the transmission/reception of data in real-time [6].

RPi is an intelligent device used as a low-cost minicomputer, running on an open operating system [7]. However, RPi3 device works as a processor of images captured by a Raspberry Pi camera to detect the yellow and green colors of the mango fruit; the processed information updates the variables of the Siemens s7–1200 via Profinet communication [8–10] as shown in Fig. 1.

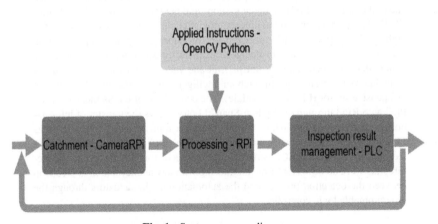

Fig. 1. System process diagram.

Real-time communication is required in image processing to control and monitor the ripeness of the mango fruit, with this system a low-cost solution, versus the techniques offered by recognized manufacturers for the application of artificial vision.

The RPi3 uses the OpenCV library based on Python, which has several functions that help process and recognize images in real-time [11].

2   Proposed System

This project allows identifying the mango's ripeness, with green color for immature and yellow for mature, using computer vision [12].

The system captures the image of the mango fruit; then, it is converted to digital format to be processed by the RPi3 device and to identify using the Python-Snap7 library [13].

In addition, the Profinet communication with the Siemens S7–1200 PLC manages the outputs to the actuators based on the result of the inspection [14].

2.1 Hardware Selection

The system comprises several processes controlled by two central devices, together with the primary sensor that is the Raspberry Pi camera applied to the detection of object movement, which allows the capture of images of the mango fruit in real-time.

The Raspberry Pi camera module connects directly to the Camera Serial Interface (CSI) standard slot of the RPi3 [15].

The RPi3 device works with Linux operating system together with its compilers and libraries [16], which allow communication with the Siemens S7–1200 PLC, which supports the automated control process [17].

2.2 Software Selection

The RPi runs on the Raspbian Stretch operating system developed on Linux. In addition, it supports the Python programming language, which contains a series of modules or special libraries for systems based on artificial vision, used in developing algorithms that work quickly and efficiently [18].

Python has the OpenCV library, commonly used in computer vision techniques to process and recognize images in real-time [19].

Python-Snap7 library is also running for communication and interaction between RPi3 and Siemens S7–1200 PLC [20].

In addition, TIA PORTAL software gives a complete range of Siemens digitalized automation devices based on control and interfaces, from digital planning to integrated engineering and easy programming [17].

2.3 Communication System

Indeed, there are various forms of communication in the industrial field, but the Profinet communication protocol is prioritized for its speed and reliability in network systems [21].

Figure 2 shows that the mentioned protocol presents a low latency and a high level of stability in the network system [22].

3 Materials and Methods

The selected devices are suitable for application in the development of the project, considering the parameters of communication, acquisition, processing, and control of the system's variables. RPi3 works like a computer, so it is possible to connect various devices to the ports such as a mouse, keyboard, monitor, Raspberry Pi camera, Siemens S7–1200 PLC, and the respective power supply of the device [23].

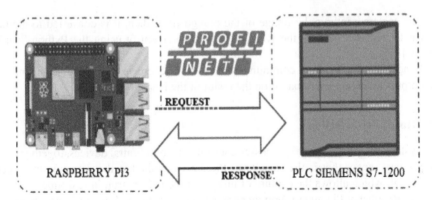

Fig. 2. Device communication via profinet protocol.

The algorithm computer vision on Python detects the ripeness of the mango fruit [24] and analyzes the green and yellow colors through OpenCV libraries [25].

The following are the functions used by the main algorithm:

- **PiCamera:** It is an exclusive function for the Raspberry pi camera module; it provides configuration settings, for example, the frame rate and image resolution [26].
- **camera.capture_continuous:** It is a function that allows the visualization in real-time of the video, which restores one frame per second. RawCapture is the format to read the frame. The configuration defines the type of image in BGR. Finally, Use_video_port determines the camera in video mode [26].
- **cv2.cvtColor:** Sets the color conversion type by defining the image name and the BGR to HSV parameter, eg cv2.COLOR_BGR2HSV [27, 28].
- **np.array:** It supports the determination of the range of colors to detect [27].
- **cv2.rectangle:** It is a function that allows to graph rectangles in the image, also, the location of the four lines of the rectangle, color, and thickness of the lines are illustrated in Fig. 3 [27].
- **cv2.circle:** It is a function to draw circles on the image. In addition, the circle parameters can be modified, such as the location, the radius, the thickness of the outline, and the padding are described in Fig. 3 [27].
- **cv2.moments:** It is a function that calculates the total moments of a detected graph [27].
- **cv2.findContours:** It determines the contour of an image through limit points, which connect, forming a precise outline. CV_RETR_EXTERNAL obtains the outer contours of the detected image, and CV_CHAIN_APPROX_SIMPLE compresses the diagonal, vertical, and horizontal parts to provide only endpoints [27].
- **cv2.convexHull:** This function allows finding the convex hull of each contour and establishes the variable that stores the count of shapes [27].
- **cv2.drawContours:** It draws contours in the image. Also, as shown in Fig. 3, it has a variable that stores the shapes, indicates the outline to remove, and its color [27].
- **cv2.putText:** It generates text on any image. Also, it coordinates to locate the text, font, font scale, RGB color, and thickness [27].

In the mango fruit detection system, Fig. 3 shows that the Raspberry pi camera module's location allows an angle variation to determine the exact one for adequate detection.

Fig. 3. Detection of green and yellow colors according to the ripening of mango fruit (Color figure online).

For communication between RPi3 and Siemens S7–1200 PLC, the main requirement is the Snap7 library.

The RPi3 device is accessed remotely through Putty, entering the IP address and port number using the Secure Shell (SSH) protocol [29].

The session is started on the RPi3 device through the Putty software, entering the username and password.

Immediately, by executing the "wget" command next to the download address, the Snap7 library package is installed, and the archive has to be uncompressed using the "tar -zxvf" command next to the file name downloaded [30]:

– wget   https://sourceforce.net/projects/snap7/files/1.4.0/snap7-full-1.4.0.tar.gz/dow nload

On the Unix OS, to get to the snap7-full-1.4.0 build folder, do it using find commands, then run "sudo make –f arm_v6_linux.mk" to build the library for the ARMV6 RPi CPU [30].

It is necessary to edit the library's location in the common.py file located at the address "/usr/local/lib/python2.7/dist-packages/snap7/". Editing the file in the WinSCP software and the external editor is selected next to the ".py" extension.

The text of the file is added the text line "lib_location = '/usr/local/lib/libsnap7.so' ", so it is created in that indicated location [30].

The correct location of the Snap7 library is verified in "usr/local/lib", using the command "ls -la" [30].

The command "sudo apt-get install Python-pip" is used to install the Python pip, which is also required for Python-Snap7 to work [30].

Python-Snap7 is a container and developer for the Snap7 library, and its installation is done with the command "sudo pip install python-snap7" [30].

The command "sudo apt-get install ipython" installs Ipython; this is an "interactive Python" [30].

Finally, in ipython, the following commands are executed:

- In [1]: import snap7  Import Snap7 Library
- In [2]: plc – snap.client.Client()  Assigning Snap7 as Client to PLC
- In [3]: plc.connect('192.168.3.147',0,1)  Entering the PLC IP address for the connection.

The RPi3 and the Siemens S7–1200 PLC communication are verified using the indicated commands.

In this project, the application of an experimental method coupled to real-time is determined, according to computer vision techniques to detect the ripeness of the mango fruit, through the algorithm compiled in the RPi3.

It modifies the variables in the programming of the Siemens S7–1200 PLC through Profinet communication, which allows controlling external devices, according to the results obtained in the detection [30].

However, consider an excellent ambient light source for a better real-time image capture through the Raspberry pi camera module.

4   Results

Figure 3 shows the implementation interface of the mango maturity detection system applying artificial vision in real-time, considering the detection of the color of the green fruit for a ripe mango or yellow for an unripe mango.

For the transport of the mangoes, a conveyor belt controlled by a device called a frequency inverter is used, which is programmed to control the motor of the conveyor belt at a constant speed, suitable for the detection process by computer vision.

By performing the green and yellow detection tests on the handle using a Raspberry Pi camera located at the positions of 0, 15, 30, 45, 60, and 85 degrees, as illustrated in Fig. 4.

In addition, the yield results in Table 1, indicating 100% accuracy in detecting mango fruit maturity.

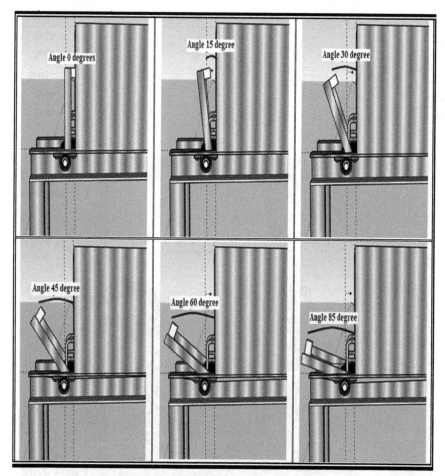

Fig. 4. Design in sketchUp of the system, with Raspberry pi camera module at 0, 15, 30, 45, 60, and 85 grades for detection according to the ripening of mango fruit.

The change of discrete state of the control variables between the RPi3 device and the Siemens S7–1200 PLC occurs every time the green or yellow color of the mango fruit is detected as illustrated in Fig. 5 and Fig. 6, with a latency of the order of milliseconds.

The Siemens S7–1200 PLC controls a series of four stepper motors, each driven by the discrete state variable of the computer vision identification system.

Table 1. Tests of the implemented system based on computer vision to detect mango maturity.

Mango detection					
Degrees of fruit capture	Number of unripe mangos	20	Number of ripe mangos	20	Precision
	Successful	No success	Successful	No success	
0	X		X		76%
15	X		X		87%
30	X		X		93%
45	X		X		100%
60	X		X		95%
85	X		X		90%

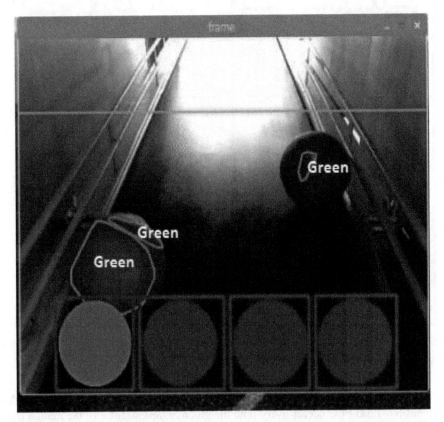

Fig. 5. Interface for the detection of unripe mangoes by computer vision (Color figure online).

Each red box, as illustrated in Fig. 5 and Fig. 6, serves as a sensor that detects a handle in a precise location to activate a motor in the same direction.

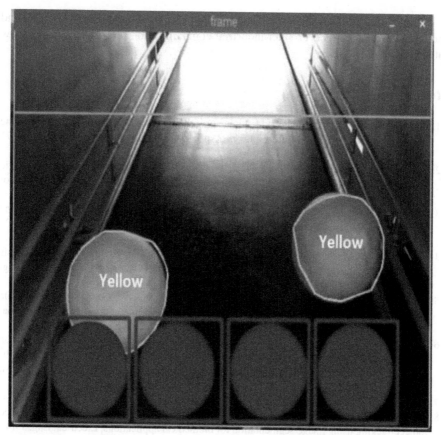

Fig. 6. Interface for the detection of ripe mangoes by computer vision (Color figure online).

In the detection interface has a specific motor for its drive.

When the fruit is not ripe, the RPi3 device communicates with the Siemens S7–1200 PLC to activate the engine in the same direction the mango is moving to divert it to another bin where there are only green mangoes.

The motor has a system of mechanical gears coupled to a paddle, which pushes the unripe mango towards the specified reservoir.

On the contrary, if the mango is ripe, it falls directly into the mature mango store without activating the mechanical system.

5 Conclusion

The implementation of the system is based on computer vision techniques for mango fruit maturity detection, using the Python programming language and the OpenCV library.

The detection of the green and yellow color of the mangoes was acquired by processing BGR-type images acquired by the Raspberry Pi camera, which was placed at different angles, providing an absolute accuracy of 100%.

The transmission/reception of information between the Siemens PLC s7–1200 and the RPi3 device using the Profinet industrial communication protocol had a very low latency in milliseconds.

References

1. Hrbček, J., Bubeníková, E.: Embedded image processing on Raspberry Pi connected to the industrial control system. Multidisciplinary Aspects of Production Engineering **2**, pp. 62–71 (2019)
2. Hatahara da Fonseca, R.H., Rocha Pinto, F.: The importance of the programmable logic controller "PLC" in the industry in the automation process. International Research Journal of Engineering and Technology (IRJET), **6**, pp. 280–284 (2019)
3. Vieira, G., Barbosa, J., Leitão, P., Sakurada, L.: Low-cost industrial controller based on the raspberry pi platform. In: IEEE International Conference on Industrial Technology (ICIT), pp. 292–297 (2020)
4. Setioko, D.A., Murti, M.A., Sumaryo, S.: Perancangan Sistem Andon Nirkabel Berbasis Internet of Things (IoT) menggunakan PLC dan Raspberry Pi. Seminar Nasional Teknologi Komputer & Sains (SAINTEKS) 1(1), 202–206 (2019)
5. Ciptaning Anindya, R.S., Haryatmi, E.: Design of 3 phase motor control system using plc with raspberry Pi based on Internet of Things (IoT) system. International Research Journal of Advanced Engineering and Science, vol. 4, pp. 278–283 (2019)
6. Alexakos, C., Anagnostopoulos, C., Fournaris, A., Kalogeras, A., Koulamas, C.: Production process adaptation to IoT triggered manufacturing resource failure events. In: 2nd IEEE International Conference on Emerging Technologies and Factory Automation (ETFA), pp. 1–8 (2017)
7. Upton, E., Halfacree, G.: Raspberry Pi user guide. John Wiley & Sons, ilustrada, p. 312 (2014)
8. Koniar, D., Hargaš, L., Loncová, Z., Simonová, A., Duchŏn, F., Beňo, P.: Visual system-based object tracking using image segmentation for biomedical applications. Electrical Eng. **99**(4), 1349–1366 (2017)
9. Bubeníková, E., Pirník, R., Holečko, P., Franeková, M.: The ways of streamlining digital image processing algorithms used for detection of lines in transport scenes video recording. IFAC-PapersOnLine **48**(4), 174–179 (2015)
10. Hruboš, M., et al.: Searching for collisions between mobile and environment. Searching for collisions between mobile robot and environment. International J. Advanced Robotic Syst. **13**(5), 1–11 (2016)
11. Fiset, J.-Y.: Human-machine interface design for process control applications. Instrumentation, Systems, and Automation Society (2009)
12. Patra, S.N., Sarkar, P.P., Nandi, C.S., Koley, C.: Pattern recognition of mango in ripening process with image processing and fuzzy logical system. FaQSaT, pp. 1–7 (2011)
13. Manage, P., Ambe, V., Gokhale, P., Patil, V., Kulkarni, R.M., Kalburgimath, P.R.: An intelligent text reader based on python. In: 3rd International Conference on Intelligent Sustainable Systems (ICISS), pp. 1–5 (2020)
14. Howse, J., Media, N.: Training detectors and recognizers in Python and OpenCV. In: IEEE International Symposium on Mixed and Augmented Reality (ISMAR), **1**, pp. 1–2, (2014)
15. Pajankar, A., Kakkar, A.: Raspberry Pi By Example, Packt Publishing Ltd. (2016)
16. Upon, E., Halfacree, G.: Meet the Raspberry Pi, John Wiley & Sons (2012)
17. Chuquimarca, L., Asencio, A., Torres, W., Bustos, S., Sánchez, J.: Development of network system for connection PLC to cloud platforms using IIoT. In: International Conference on Advances in Digital Science, pp. 433–443 (2021)

18. R.P. Foundation, «https://www.raspberrypi.org/software/operating-systems/,» Raspberry Pi Foundation, [En línea]. https://www.raspberrypi.org/software/operating-systems/. [Último acceso: Viernes Junio 2021]

19. P. S. Foundation, «Python,» Python Software Foundation, [En línea]. https://docs.python.org/3/. [Último acceso: Martes Julio 2021]

20. Bradsky, G., Kaehler, A.: Learning OpenCV: Computer Vision with the OpenCV Library, O'Reilly Media, Inc (2008)

21. Mateoiu, A.M., Korodi, A.: OPC-UA based small-scale monitoring and control solution for android devices case study for water treatment plants. In: 4th International Conference on Control, Automation and Robotics (ICCAR), pp. 190–195 (2018)

22. Forsström, S., Jennehag, U.: A performance and cost evaluation of combining OPC-UA and microsoft azure IoT hub into an industrial internet-of-things system. In: Global Internet of Things Summit (GIoTS), pp. 1–6 (2017)

23. Sivasangari, A., Deepa, D., Anandhi, T., Ponraj, A., Roobini, M.: Eyeball based cursor movement control. In: International Conference on Communication and Signal Processing (ICCSP), pp. 1116–1119 (2020)

24. Betancourt, R., Chen, S.: Python for SAS Users, Apress (2019)

25. Pajankar, A.: Raspberry Pi computer vision programming: design and implement computer vision applications with Raspberry Pi, OpenCV, and Python 3, Packt Publishing Ltd (2020)

26. Jones, D.: Picamera. Read the Docs, 2013–2014. [En línea]. https://picamera.readthedocs.io/en/release-1.10/api_camera.html. [Último acceso: Jueves Julio 2021]

27. Mordvintsev, A., Abid, K.: Opencv-Python Tutorials Documentation (2014)

28. Majare, S., Chougule, S.R.: Skin detection for face recognition based on hsv color space. Int. J. Eng. Sciences Res. Technol. 2(7), 1883–1887 (2013)

29. Wibowo, F.W., Ardiansyah, M.A.: Low cost real time monitoring system and storing image data using motion detection. Int. J. Applied Eng. Res. 11(8), 5419–5424 (2016)

30. Molenaar, G., Preeker, S.: python-snap7 Documentation (2021)

FHSS Classification System in the Spectrum Using SDR Generators for Signal Inhibitors

Washington Daniel Torres Guin[1] , Luis Miguel Amaya Fariño[1]([✉]) ,
Juan Fernando Arroyo Pizarro[1] , Vladimir Israel García Santos[2] ,
and Elsy Del Rocío Villamar Garces[3]

[1] Universidad Estatal Península de Santa Elena, La Libertad, Ecuador
luis-amayafa@outlook.com
[2] Universidad de Cantabria, Cantabria, Spain
vgarcia@upse.edu.ec
[3] Universidad Politécnica de Madrid, Madrid, Spain
e.villamar@alumnos.upm.es

Abstract. This article presents a study focused on radio interfaces defined through HackRF One instrumentation used to develop block diagrams generating interference in the dynamic access of the spectrum. The present systems are designed by implementing algorithms with logical blocks and applying a Wi-Fi network analyzer through a Radio Defined by Software. The GNU operating system processes reusable signals for Frequency Hopping Spread Spectrum (FHSS) channel hopping to jam over an 802.11 b/g/n network. Therefore, the logic block diagram is implemented in a Radio system in a GNU to intervene in the radio transceiver. Thus, the transceiver generates the classification and stop of test signals by emitting an interference signal directed towards the network with a directional antenna. The 802.11 b/g/n connectivity speed tests evaluated at the installation of any device help to achieve the efficiency of the noise produced by the logical block that interferes with the signal to measure the degradation of connectivity. The results will allow us to determine whether Wi-Fi interference is possible through the logical development of blocks, providing information on the technique used and the initial optimization instructions possible during the test environment.

Keywords: GNU · Radio · Interference · FHSS · SDR

1 Introduction

Wireless local area networks (WLAN) are more popular today due to various Wi-Fi devices' easy deployment and introduction. However, despite all its advantages, wireless communication suffers from security vulnerabilities, such as jamming attacks, analyzed by a noise signal generator system for SDR Wi-Fi 2.4 GHz equipment to measure the effects caused by noise [1].

© The Author(s), under exclusive license to Springer Nature Switzerland AG 2022
T. Guarda et al. (Eds.): ARTIIS 2022, CCIS 1675, pp. 228–240, 2022.
https://doi.org/10.1007/978-3-031-20319-0_18

The research focuses on analyzing and experimenting with the generation of noise signals in Wi-Fi networks for specific channels and frequencies, developing an interference process through an SDR communications system. However, deepening the knowledge of the detection, security, and fragility that Wi-Fi networks currently have and how noise signals affect the dynamic access to the spectrum is a critical topic handled by researchers today.

With the application of a transceiver as the final device for the analysis of the upload/download speed, through an Android application and the FHSS signal by the GNU system, it classifies the logic of the frequency block. Therefore, graphically signal inhibitors generate a loss of frequency in the dynamic application of the spectrum, which the researcher analyzes.

The following sections describe the materials and methods used and the results, discussions, and conclusions of this work.

1.1 Purpose of Technical Research

Within the 2.4 GHz ISM bands, several variables are proposed to develop interoperability between devices; each standard uses a different mechanism to avoid interference, used in WLAN wireless area networks with its IEEE 802.11 [2].

The radio technology implemented in the research uses an excellent frequency system that allows the combination of hardware and software with the correct analysis classification. Simulated SDR systems create HackRF One prototypes from Great Scott Gadgets [3].

The HackRF One can send and receiving radio signals. Compared to much more expensive hardware, its most significant limitation is that it is only half-duplex, meaning it can only send or receive and not both simultaneously. Despite this limitation, it is excellent for many analyses, such as replay attacks where we capture the transmission and then resend it. Table 1 indicates the advantages and limitations of the HackRF One device compared to others.

The RTL-SDR device has a maximum sample rate of 3.2 MS/s (mega samples per second). However, this device tends to be unstable at this speed, so sample periods are lost. The maximum frequency that does not allow loss periods is 2.56 MS/s. However, better results have been obtained with 2.8 MS/s and 3.2 MS/s [4].

The results of the investigation allow us to understand the possible attacks based on systems defined by radio, interference is a vulnerable wireless scenario with devices that emulate Rx/Tx or Tx/Rx signals, proposing a logical block diagram where the system jumps by FHSS co-channels, allowing to identify and emulate transmission and reception frequency changes.

For radio defined systems. Wireless frequencies are easy to emulate as long as the powers in dB are adequate, however there are increasingly popular Internet of Things (IoT) networks that work at low powers. These networks are not reliable due to their low connection power, which disqualifies them for use in devices such as smoke detectors, light switches, or any other intermediate element, this would be one of the scenarios not suitable for analysis. [5].

Table 1. Comparison of SDR devices.

Technical parameters	HackRF One	RTL-SDR	ETTUS B200
Frequency range	1MHz-6GHz	22MHz-2.2GHz	70MHz-6GHz
RF Band	20MHz	3.2MHz	61.44MHz
Transmission Channel	1	1	1
Receivers	1	1	1
Duplex	Half	N/A	FULL
Interface	USB 2.0	USB 2.0	USB 3.0
Chipset	MAX5864	RTL2832U	AD9364
Open Source	FULL	No	Schematic and Firmware
Transmitted power	-10dBm+	N/A	10dBm+
Price	320$	40$	902$

1.2 Development of the Proposed System

The technical specifications of the HackRF One device are by default in test mode. In wireless jamming systems, the SDR under investigation is the logical block diagram for noise generation in the GNU system. Finally, in this work, a case study is specified that shows the use of HackRF One.

The HackRF One from Great Scott Gadgets is an SDR peripheral capable of transmitting or receiving radio signals from 1 MHz to 6 GHz, designed to enable the testing and development of modern, next-generation radio technologies. This device is an open-source hardware platform that can be used as a USB peripheral or programmed for stand-alone operation [6]. Whose purpose of the device is to interact with radio frequency signals that are in the form of a radio-electric wave in space, as the main complement of the device is to recognize its parts.

Keep in mind that when starting the testing process, the 3V3, 1V8, and RF LEDs are three different power supplies inside the HackRF. Therefore, these must light up when a signal is received or transmitted. However, if the LEDs are not all on, that indicates a problem with the device. In addition, the USB LED indicates that the host computer has configured the HackRF One as a USB input device. The last two LEDs are RX and TX, which signify receive and transmit operations. One of them must be on if the HackRF One is receiving or transmitting a radio signal [7].

Figure 1 shows the corresponding interconnections of all the devices involved in the development of the investigation.

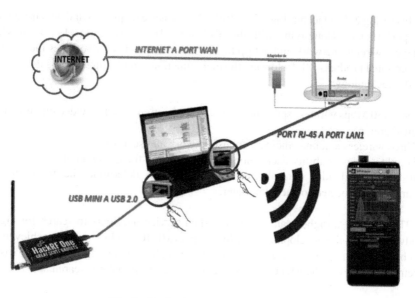

Fig. 1. Device interconnection topology.

The usual solution is to use a single frequency system with Gaussian Frequency Shift Keying (GFSK) modulation. All devices always use one narrow predefined channel. These systems are common in the sub-GHz Short Range Device (SRD) frequency band, known in Europe as 868 MHz band [5].

A diverse application for mobile devices that analyzes the status of the Wi-Fi network allows the user to test the speed of their WLAN connection. This project uses the Wi-Fi Analyzer application.

1.3 Transceiver Device

The TL-WR841N device has exceptional wireless performance, making it ideal for streaming HD video clips, VoIP, and online gaming. Complying with the IEEE 802.11n standard, the TL-WR841N can connect to a wireless network and achieve up to 15 times the speed of conventional products. Below are the main functions and features of this device:

- Ideal wireless speed of 300 Mbps for sensitive applications such as interruption of HD video clip broadcasting.
- Two antennas significantly increase wireless robustness and equality.
- Simple wireless stability encryption only by pressing the QSS button.
- IP-based bandwidth control enables managers to decide the proportion of bandwidth allocated to each computer.

Featuring MIMO technology, TL-WR940N creates exceptional and advanced wireless performance. Complying with the IEEE 802.11n standard, the TL-WR940N can engage a wireless network and get up to 15 times the speed and five times the reach of conventional products [8]. Below are the main functions and features of this device with MIMO technology:

- Ideal 450 Mbps wireless speed for sensitive applications like HD video clip broadcast interruption.
- Three wireless antennas increase robust network and security.
- Simple wireless stability encryption only by pressing the QSS button.
- IP-based bandwidth control enables managers to determine the proportion of bandwidth allocated to each computer.

The need for a higher data rate has pushed service providers to search for higher bandwidth. With the development of Multi-Input (MIMO) technology, the achievement of a higher data rate was realizable within the available bandwidth. Thus, improvising spectral efficiency by MIMO Cognitive radio has been a popular research area [9].

2 Materials

The following materials are used in the project:

- The Wi-Fi network will be configured using a router model
- An Android mobile phone as the target device (DUT) for the interference experiments.
- Only 802.11 standard b/g/n interference, with the router set to channel 1 (center frequency 2.412 GHz), high power enabled.
- The channel bandwidth was chosen to be 20 MHz or 40 MHz, depending on the scenario used.
- The hardware used for the jamming was HackRF One, an SDR equipped with an Aaronia Hyper Log 7060 directive antenna model.
- GNU Radio Companion Software Environment (GRC) is used to model the Hack RF transmission.

To represent the scenario of interference channels, it is necessary to verify the multiple unlicensed channels, for simultaneous communication in the presence of interference, it is necessary to add negative voltages to represent the noise in the transmitted signal. However, it is commonly assumed that all terminals know the channel gains and radio defined systems relate the codes of all encoders, for their respective transmission [10]. As shown in Fig. 2, the analysis scenario shows a wireless network where the DUT represents the attacked terminal.

Scenarios to consider in the measurement, each state will be represented by parameters of bandwidth and power in the channels, each scenario represents the automatic system of each non-licensed frequency change:

- Router with high broadcast power configured on channel 2 with 20 MHz bandwidth and SDR configured with 20 MHz bandwidth signal-to-noise interference.

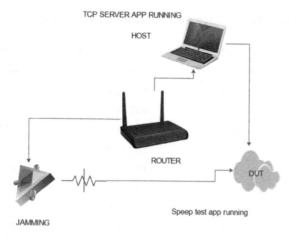

TCP SERVER APP RUNNING

HOST

ROUTER

DUT

Speep test app running

JAMMING

Fig. 2. Topology for the results of the interconnection of the devices.

- Router with high broadcast power configured on channel 2 with 40 MHz bandwidth and SDR configured with 20 MHz bandwidth signal-to-noise interference.
- Router with high broadcast power configured on channel 2 with 40 MHz bandwidth and SDR configured with 10 MHz bandwidth signal noise interference

3   Methodology

The procedure to determine the processes in interference efficiency through applications that choose Tx/Rx speeds for Wi-Fi connectivity by developing logical blocks for interference generation and end nodes for signal reception. The noise generated by each wireless radiofrequency FHSS communication channel allows analyzing the correct flow diagram for each signal inhibitor block since the frequency is interrupted by each FHSS channel.

In a highly heterogeneous wireless environment, software-defined radio (SDR) is widely considered a signal analysis solution, directly accessing the physical layer signal regardless of the underlying wireless technologies [11].

The literature has proven its effectiveness through extensive research. Range of applications such as spectrum monitoring for network operation [12], drone detection [13] for security, and activity monitoring for health [14]. Despite significant benefits, USRPs are rarely adopted in practice and rarely used by end users. This is mainly due to expensive hardware ranging from hundreds to thousands of dollars [15]. While low-cost SDRs, for example, HACK-RF-ONE variants, are available on the market.

The logical flow diagram shown in Fig. 3 explains the operation mode of the SDR system to block the signal in the spectral access dynamism at frequencies of 2.4 GHz.

By entering the router in the Local Network section, and then in the WLAN subsection, you can configure the parameters such as channel, bandwidth, model, or standard. Table 2 shows the respective configuration for this project.

Table 2. Parameters to determine the range of FHSS periods

Network Frequency	Channel	Mode or Standard	Bandwidth
2412 MHz	1	802.11 b/g/n	40 MHz
2417 MHz	2	802.11 b/g/n	20 MHz
2422 MHz	3	802.11 b/g/n	40 MHz
2427 MHz	4	802.11 b/g/n	20 MHz
2432 MHz	5	802.11 b/g/n	20 MHz
2433 MHz	6	802.11 b/g/n	40 MHz
2442 MHz	7	802.11 b/g/n	20 MHz
2447 MHz	8	802.11 b/g/n	20 MHz
2452 MHz	9	802.11 b/g/n	20 MHz
2457 MHz	10	802.11 b/g/n	20 MHz
2462 MHz	11	802.11 b/g/n	20 MHz

When configuring the parameters of Table 2 in the GNU system, the application analyzes the signal generated in radiofrequency test mode to determine the channel to use. The use of manual channels established by channel 1 for a range of 2401–2423 MHz, setting this value as a variable to relate it to the logical scheme of the GNU system.

From the first analysis of channel 1, the configurations are applied respectively in the 2437 MHz and 2462 MHz frequencies, managing to determine the specific parameters to inhibit the signal for each channel analyzed within the electromagnetic spectrum in the 2.4 GHz range.

3.1 Scope with the Investigation

HackRF One is the device in charge of the deliberate electromagnetic emission action to block or interfere in a single channel due to the device's limitations. It can only handle 20 MHz of bandwidth at best, but at 40 MB/s transfer over USB 2.0, each sample is 2 bytes, insufficient even for fundamental 2.4 GHz frequencies (802.11b/g /n/ax) since its channels have a bandwidth of 22 MHz. Therefore, it shows that 802.11n standards are vulnerable to selective interference in targeted attacks. The following channels described in Table 3 are selected in the present project.

The SNR expressed in dB is one of the essential radio parameters for analyzing the quality of a communication link. Measuring the power in a receiver is not enough and should be compared to the noise level introduced by both the channel and the receiver. High values in radio-defined networks allow more complex modulation techniques resulting in higher transmission speeds and fewer retransmissions [16]. Table 4 defines the SNR ranges associated with the communication link quality for a WLAN environment [17].

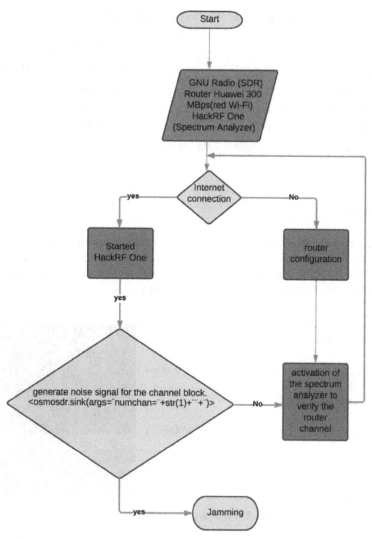

Fig. 3. Logic flow diagram of the SDR system to represent the logical process of values in the GNU radio.

Table 3. Effective transmission parameters in the 802.11 b/n/ac standards.

Channel	Initial frequency (MHz)	The frequency range in MHz
1	2412	2401–2423
6	2437	2426–2448
11	2462	2451–2473

Table 4. Permissible ranges for data transmission

Parameters	Variable dB ranges	Attention
Excellent quality, high data speeds	> 40 dB	ITU-R S.524
Exceptionally good quality, high data speeds	25–40 dB	
Very good quality, high data speeds	15–25 dB	
Acceptable quality, lower data rates	10–15 dB	
Low to no signal, usually not associated, data rate very low to nothing	0–10 dB	

4   Results

First, the frequency to attack is determined, and then the transmitted signal is amplified by copying the same received frequency to inhibit it and obtain the noise in the FM signal. Then the SDR is used to identify the correct control of dynamic openings by conducting transmission and reception tests on FM waves.

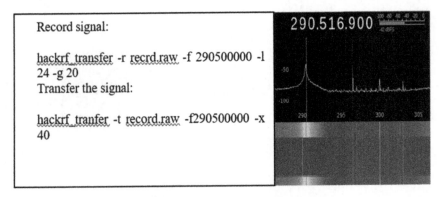

Fig. 4. Noise analysis in FM signals.

Figure 4 shows the spectral graph analyzed by the GNU system, where the signal increase of the filters is verified, evidencing the attenuation of the amplified signal. For the classification of the channels, the variables were analyzed as indicated in Table 4, where the verified channels are 1, 6 and 11, which are the ones with the best range of spectral coverage. However, channel 1 is chosen since it works at 2.462 GHz and the parameters are static, it is possible to observe its operation and behavior with the help of the Wi-Fi analyzer.

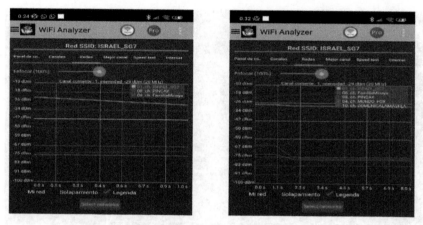

Fig. 5. Graphical analysis of the signal without noise.

The WiFi Analyzer in Fig. 5 indicates the values in dB where the powers related to Table 4 are parameterized. Therefore, to detect the jumps of each channel, the logical block diagram of the GNU system must be activated to verify the results of the analysis signal inhibitor.

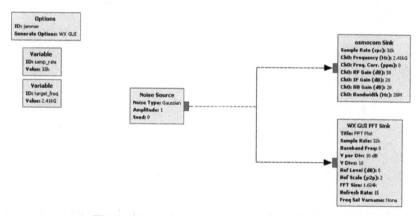

Fig. 6. Block scheme using GNU Radio software.

When generating noise with the SDR development program, the unlicensed 802.11 signals in the electromagnetic spectrum will begin to use the frequency jump technology in channels 1–6-11, as indicated in Table 3, to mitigate the noise in channel 1, as shown in Fig. 6.

Figure 7 shows how the other frequencies jump to the different channels since, internally, the GNU Radio inhibitor is blocking the signal by setting 20 MHz ranges for noise blocks at channel 1, as in Fig. 8.

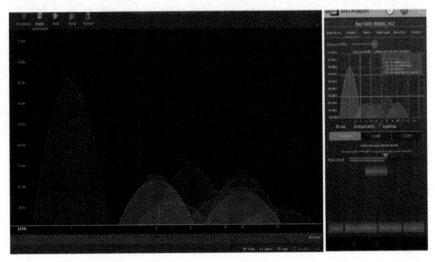

Fig. 7. FHSS graphics to mitigate noise on channel 1.

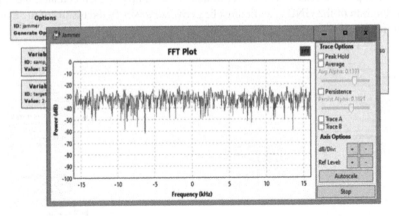

Fig. 8. GNU allows determining the noise generated in channel 1.

The graphical representation in Fig. 8 shows the logical diagram of blocks; if it is emitting a noise signal using the SRD, the signal peaks determine the measured bandwidth in kHz and dB [18].

5 Conclusions

It was possible to generate a simulated system to identify the potential changes analyzed in dB in each FHSS channel. The projection of the SMA antenna is analyzed with specific ranges from 75 MHz to 1GHz as the default range for noise block development. However, the logical blocks where the insertion of each type of noise occurs are applied directly to each channel of multiple blocks in periodic actions of 32kbps per period.

For the result, the fixed frequencies of 2.416 GHz should be considered, with spectral resolution frequencies of 1.024 GHz for each FHSS fixed channel technology, managing to centralize the adequate power for each channel hop in static frequencies of 2.4 GHz.

A noise oscillator system was generated in a numerical simulator, using variables for rigorous propagation control, which have been entered with voltages from 0V to 1V for the noise signal; furthermore, with regular periods of 10 oscillations, obtaining an inhibiting system in static ranges for each gain. Variables such as RF channel gain of 10 dB, IF Bollinger of 20 dB, and BB of 20 dB, generate additional values in the GMSK constellation plots, thus improving the Gaussian filter. Therefore, a fixed gain in dB is obtained in ranges from -25 dB to -60 dB for sampling frequencies between -15 kHz to 15 kHz, as indicated in Fig. 8.

By obtaining a logical block as a final result, it will be possible to synchronize the variables for each channel of the 2.4 GHz spectrum, changing variables in the bandwidth at 20 MHz and in the static filter channels, for example, channel 6 at 2441 MHz, respecting the properties of spectral synchronization.

References

1. Do, V.A., Rana, B., Hong, I.-P.: Identification of Wi-Fi and bluetooth signals at the same frequency using software defined radio. Journal of IKEEE **25**(2), 252–260 (2021)
2. I. S. 8.-2.-I. S. f. I. Technology, "Telecommunications and Information Exchange between Systems—Local and Metropolitan Area Networks—Specific Requirements Part 11: Wireless LAN Medium Access Control (MAC) and Physical (PHY) Specification. In: IEEE IEEE, San Francisco, CA, USA (2012)
3. Machado, J.R.: Software Defined Radio: Basic Principles and Applications. **24**(38), 7996 (2015)
4. Stewart, R.W., Barlee, K.W., Atkinson, D.S., Crockett, L.H.: Software defined radio using MATLAB & Simulink and the RTL-SDR, Strathclyde academic media (2015)
5. Jakubík, T., Jeníček, J.: SDR all-channels receiver for FHSS sensor network in Cortex-M. In: 2019 42nd International Conference on Telecommunications and Signal Processing (TSP), pp. 32–35 (2019). https://doi.org/10.1109/TSP.2019.8769064
6. Jaimes Rico, R., Salas, L.: Esquema de triangulación para detectar drones usando. **9**(1) (2021)
7. Molla, D.M., Badis, H., George, L., Berbineau, M.: Software Defined Radio Platforms for Wireless Technologies **10** (2022)
8. Schwarz, F., Schwarz, K., Fuchs, D., Creutzburg, R., Akopian, D.L: Firmware Vulnerability Analysis of Widely Used Low-Budget TP-Link Routers. **33** (2021)
9. Patil, V., Singhal, C.: Throughput improvement in hybrid MIMO cognitive radio using simultaneous narrowband and wideband system. In: 2019 11th International Conference on Communication Systems & Networks (COMSNETS), pp. 285–290 (2019). https://doi.org/10.1109/COMSNETS.2019.8711135
10. Goldsmith, A., Jafar, S.A., Maric, I., Srinivasa, S.: Breaking spectrum gridlock with cognitive radios: an information theoretic perspective. Proceedings of the IEEE **97**(5), 894–914 (2009)
11. Jeong, W., et al.: SDR receiver using commodity wifi via physical-layer signal reconstruction. In: Proceedings of the 26th Annual International Conference on Mobile Computing and Networking. Association for Computing Machinery, **32**, pp. 1–14 (2020). https://doi.org/10.1145/3372224.3419189

12. Pfammatter, D., Guistiniano, D., Lenders, V.: A software-defined sensor architecture sensor architecture for large-scale wideband spectrum monitoring. In: Proceedings of the 14th International Conference on Information Processing in Sensor Networks, pp. 71–82 (2015). https://doi.org/10.1145/2737095.2737119

13. Nguyen, P., et al.: Drone presence detection by identifying physical signatures in the drone's rf communication. In: Proceedings of the 15th Annual International Conference on Mobile Systems, Applications, and Services, pp. 211–224 (2017). https://doi.org/10.1145/3081333.3081354

14. Diraco, G., Leone, A., Sicilliano, P.: In-home hierarchical posture classification with a time-of-flight 3D sensor. Gait & Posture,Institute for Microelectronics and Microsystems, National Research Council, c/o Campus Ecotekne, Via Monteroni, Lecce, Italy 39(1), 182–187 (2014)

15. E. Research., E. Research.,. https://www.ettus.com/all-products/UN210-KIT/

16. Lara-Cueva, R., Morales, C., Fernandez, C.: Performance evaluation of WiFi technology in conformance with IEEE 802.11b/n/ac and WDS for indoor environments. 1(6) (2017)

17. Wang, M., Ma, X., Wang, Z., Guo, Y.: Analysis of Co-Channel Interference in Connected VehiclesWLAN with UAV. vol. 2022 (2022)

18. Chino, M., Miyashiro, H., Luis, A.J.: Implementation of SNR estimation algorithms, using LabVIEW Communications and GNU Radio Companion (2018)

19. Nafkha, A., Naoues, M., Cichon, K.: Experimental spectrum sensing measurements using USRP Software Radio platform and GNU-radio (2014)

Front-End Framework to Improve HCI, Evaluated Using an Eye-Tracking

Bryan Marcillo-Delgado(✉) ⓘ, Gema Giler-Velásquez ⓘ, Mónica Vaca-Cardenas ⓘ,
and Leticia Vaca-Cardenas ⓘ

Universidad Técnica de Manabí, Portoviejo 130105, Ecuador
{bmarcillo2729,leticia.vaca}@utm.edu.ec

Abstract. In the paradigm of cognitive cities, it is very important that the interfaces of web and mobile applications adapt to any type of user that interacts with them. Likewise, HCI (Human computer interaction) is an area of study that seeks to improve the user experience when interacting with a computer. Therefore, the objective of this research was to develop a front-end framework that facilitates the creation and design of interfaces aimed at improving HCI. It contains inclusive options for people with color blindness or dyslexia and considers the aspects of organization and distribution of the elements in the interfaces. For the development of the framework called UTM-Bootstrap, the eXtreme Programming (XP) software development methodology was used. Next, with the help of a visual perception device (eye-tracking), the interfaces were evaluated to measure the effectiveness of the framework parameters and elements. The evaluation was based on the metrics: Total Fixation Duration and Average Fixation Duration. This allowed to determine the effectiveness of the interfaces when interacting with different types of users. Finally, the study culminated with user interfaces that are adaptable, intuitive and easy to use, reaching an efficient user experience.

Keywords: Cognitive cities · Eye tracking · Front-end framework · HCI · Interface · User experience · UTM-bootstrap

1 Introduction

Inclusion is one of the issues that is currently impacting society; to provide with the same opportunities to all kinds of people, based on the world technological and scientific advances. The study of HCI seeks to develop systems or applications that allow any type of user to easily understand and manipulate them, and that their interaction with a system be intuitive and friendly. HCI is a very important area of research and development, which goes beyond the physical aspect. It is a multidisciplinary area that includes cognitive psychology, ergonomic applications engineering, social sciences and applied computing [1]; which objective is to improve the design of systems or applications by increasing user satisfaction and comfort when using them [2–9]. Faulkner [10] declares that the HCI provides "an understanding of how users work, and how computer systems and their interfaces need to be structured to facilitate the achievement of their tasks", as

T. Guarda et al. (Eds.): ARTIIS 2022, CCIS 1675, pp. 241–256, 2022.
https://doi.org/10.1007/978-3-031-20319-0_19

such it can be stated that HCI seeks to optimize the quality of the user experience when handling an application.

Some related studies such as, the research carried out on 2018, where the authors [11] formulated a project to define a framework for engineers and developers of mobile application that enables software quality testing focused on usability in a teaching or learning virtual environment [11]. In 2019, [12] an innovative framework was presented that classifies cognitive cities based on deep learning algorithms based on surveys for domains known as machine learning and smart cities. The framework adds the perspective of efficiency, sustainability and resilience that cities cognitive seek to solve. In 2020 the authors [13] present HCI trends and challenges in Artificial Intelligence Systems to support the urban planning process. In 2021 [14] scientifically explains how eye-tracking technologies can record what people record with their eyes and describes how user interface design can benefit the user experience to improve citizen interactions in urban computing environments.

Therefore, the objective of this research was to develop a front-end framework that facilitates the creation and design of interfaces aimed at improving HCI. For which the bootstrap framework was taken as a base and elements were added to change the color to gray scale of the objects, change the shape and size of the pointer, increase and decrease content, change typography, from dark to light option, responsive option, voice recognition and text reading, resulting in the UTM-Bootstrap Framework. For practical purposes of the study, web platforms of the Technical University of Manabí - Ecuador (UTM) were chosen. Once the interfaces were created, they were evaluated using a visual perception device, which allowed validating the efficiency of the interfaces developed with the UTM-Bootstrap framework.

For Ruiz et al. [15], the user interface development is considered an important component of the interactive system development, since the interface connects the functionality of the system with the end users. If there is no proper user interface development, the interactive systems can fail, since the User Interface (UI) development should focus on improving the HCI.

2   Background

2.1   HCI

Human-Computer interaction is made up of 3 fundamental elements: 1. The Human; since, the main objective of HCI is to improve the quality of the user experience. 2. The Computer equipment that will execute the systems, and 3. The interaction, which is any action that the user does on the interfaces. Therefore, HCI incorporates multiple disciplines in order to maximize the applications that are developed to serve the end-users [16].

2.2   Framework

A framework is considered as a base software or an incomplete and configurable generic application in which the necessary elements can be added to make a complete application.

Samaniego Larrea [17] defines a framework as "a set of tools, libraries, conventions and good practices that seek to encapsulate repetitive tasks in easily reusable generic modules".

2.3 Bootstrap

Bootstrap is a CSS framework of open code that allows web development in a simpler and more agile way. It contains design templates established in HTML and CSS and it allows to modify fonts, forms, buttons, tables, navigations, drop-down menus, among others [18].

2.4 Cognitive Cities

Cognitive cities go beyond smart cities which use data and technology to improve efficiency, sustainability, the quality of life, and the experience of working in the city [19]. In cognitive computing advances, cognitive cities expand the concept of smart cities by introducing cognition and learning [20, 21].

2.5 Eye-Tracking

Eye-Tracking is a procedure to measure the eye movements of an individual; in this way, the researcher can see what a person is looking at any given time and the order in which the eye moves from one place to another. Based on metrics, the user's eye movements are tracked. Researchers in human-computer interaction know about the processing of visual information and the possible causes that affect the usability of an interface [22].

2.6 Metrics

The metrics are objective indicators to measure the results in any strategy, in any study that is based on eye tracking. One of the key decisions is to establish the metrics to use to achieve a particular objective. In this research, the following metrics were used:

Total Fixation Duration. It is based on multiple fixations. It indicates the total time that a user looked at a given area of interest.

Average Fixation Duration. It is the average of time that a user looked at the area of interest.

2.7 Area of Interest

It is the area we want to analyze. In eye tracking devices, the linked software gives the option of selecting a certain area and displays its results based on the visual behavior of users in that area [23].

3 Methodology

For this investigation, inductive - deductive methods were used to identify the problem based on the observed needs. Additionally, the synthetic analytical method allowed to establish the requirements of the necessary components in the Front-end framework to improve the HCI in the UTM platforms [24].

3.1 Methodology of the Front-End Framework UTM-Boostrap Development

For the development of the software, the eXtreme Programming (XP) methodology was chosen, because it has a set of well-defined stages [25] that are developed one after another and fit the established need. Next, the explanation of the development of each stage is presented:

Phase 1: Project Planning Phase. The requirements were established and agreed between the researchers and the team from the UTM technology department. A series of user stories with elements to be included in the interfaces were defined. In this case, 2 platforms were chosen to redesign the interfaces: The Academic Planning and Control System (SPCA, by its acronym in Spanish) and the Pre-Professional Internship and Connection with society System (SPPPV, by its acronym in Spanish). These Systems, which were developed with the UTM Bootstrap framework are able to:

- *Change the colors of the objects to grayscale,* helping color blindness users.
- *Dark and light mode:* It gives the option to use the page in a dark or light mode.
- *Dyslexia:* Choosing the Dyslexia option will change the font for those with literacy issues.
- *Pointer change:.* It varies the size and color of the pointer.
- *Font size:.* Option to increase or decrease the font size.
- *Responsive design:.* It adapts the interfaces to all devices.
- *Voice recognition and text reading:.* Microphone to recognize the voice and convert it into text. It also has the reading option for the entered text.
- *Sidebar:.* It creates sections either on the left or right side of the interface.

Phase 2: Project Design Phase. The Bootstrap framework was chosen as a base, to which libraries were added to help meet the requirements defined in the user stories. This, in order to design interfaces that help to improve the HCI.

In the design of the framework, it was considered to create:

Responsive interfaces. That adapt to all types of devices, that are accessible, focused on graphic aspects and with different input/output capabilities, using their different interaction modalities.

Interfaces with useful designs., easy to navigate, functional and efficient; adaptable to the needs, preferences and physical capacities of the users. The main elements of UTM-Boostrap are detailed below:

Phase 3: Framework Development

It is declared constant with buttons that have the "bt-grayscale" class. When clicking on this option, it will activate it and modify the body of the html where the class is located. If the modification is made, the *"grayscale-mode"* item in the *localStorage* is modified, adding *"True"* to it. When the interface starts, it asks if the "grayscale-mode" item contains *"True"*, if so, the body is automatically modified.

It is declared constant with buttons that have the "bt-dyslexic-font" class. When clicking on this option, it will activate it and modify the body of the html where the class is located. If the modification is made, the *"dyslexic-mode"* item in the *localStorage* is modified, adding *"True"* to it. When starting the interface, it asks if the item *"dyslexic -mode"* contains *"True"*, if so, the body is automatically modified.

It is "declared const"nt with th" but"ons that have the "bt-big-cursor" class. When clicking on this option, it will be activated and will modify the body of the html where the class is located. If the modification has been made, the "cursor-mode" item in the localStorage is modified, adding "True" to it. When starting the interface, it asks if the item "cursor -mode" contains "True", if so, the body is automatically modified.

It is declared constant with the buttons that have the "switch" class. When clicking on this option, it will activate it and modify the body of the html where the class is located; in addition, the button will be modified, changing its appearance. If the modification has been made, the *"dark-mode"* item in the *localStorage* is modified, adding *"True"* to it. When starting the interface, it is asked if the item *"dark -mode"* contains *"True"*, if so, the body and the appearance of the button are automatically modified.

When clicking on a button with the "sidebarCollapse" class, the sidebar, its content, and the buttons will be displayed or removed.

When clicking on a button with the "decrease" class, it will alter those labels that contain the *"la-sm"* class by subtracting 2 points from their font size.

When clicking on a button with the "increase" class, it will alter those labels that contain the *"la-sm"* class, by adding 2 points to their font size.

When clicking on a button with "reset" class, it will alter the labels to the values that are set as default.

Phase 4: Implementation of Requirements in Interfaces

After developing the UTMBootstrap framework, the interface prototypes of the UTM platforms were developed, applying the established requirements to improve the HCI.

If you choose the gray scale mode, the interface would be as follows, see (Fig. 1):

Fig. 1. Grayscale interface [1, 26]

The dark and light option allows to change the interface as follows (Fig. 2):

Fig. 2. Interface with dark and light mode [1, 26]

The Dyslexia option modifies the text for a better appreciation (Fig. 3):

Fig. 3. Interface when applying dyslexia mode [1, 26]

The pointer option changes its shape and color for a better display (Fig. 4):

Fig. 4. Interface with different color and size of pointer [1, 26]

The interfaces created are responsive, that is, the content will be adapted to the device, whether it is a PC or a Smartphone. (See Fig. 5).

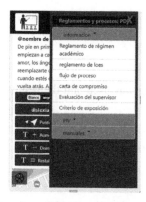

Fig. 5. Interface adapted to a Smartphone [1, 26]

Including text reading and voice recognition helps users with vision problems. (See Fig. 6).

Fig. 6. Interface with voice recognition and text reading [1, 26]

To include sidebar in the interface allows to create sections on the left or right side of the interface. It can include several buttons. (See Fig. 7).

Fig. 7. Sidebar in an interface [1, 26]

Phase 4. Tests
For this phase the eye tracking was used and the results are detailed in the following section

4 Results and Discussion

4.1 Eye-Tracking Tests

This evaluation gave information about how real users interact with the interfaces, which functions they are using, what elements are overlooked, as well as what is the focus of attention generated by the interfaces. To do this, the visual perception device called Tobbi Pro Nano [27] was used in conjunction with the Tobbi Pro Lab software. The tests carried out were essential to verify the user interface (UI) and the interaction between the user and the web interface. The interaction evaluation was carried out on 16 people.

The Following Areas of Interest (AOI) Were Analyzed:
For monitor formats (desktop computers, laptop), the captures of the interfaces were used: Main page (PC-1), Class plan (PC-2), Development of the thesis agenda (PC-3). For the Smartphone format (cell phones, Tablet) screenshots of the following interfaces were used: Main Page (Smartphone-1), Sidebar to switch between the Internship and Connection with society interfaces (Smartphone-2), Menu Options Sidebar (Smartphone -3).

In this article only the evaluation of interfaces in monitor-PC format will be addressed.

Users using eye-tracking were effectively shown interface captures with areas of interest every 5-s interval separately, but consecutively, with the test subjects. The metrics used for this analysis were: 1) Total fixation duration and 2) Average fixation duration.

4.2 Areas of Interest of the Interfaces Captures for PC Formats

The areas of interest defined for the analysis with the visual perception device in the designed interfaces are detailed below. It is important to mention that the Tobbi ProLab system attached to the equipment allowed to establish the areas of interest in order to accurately measure the interest that each user gave when interacting with the interface. (See Fig. 8, Fig. 9, Fig. 10).

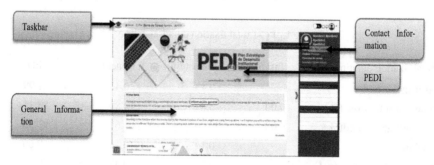

Fig. 8. Areas of interest PC-1. Source: Thesis [1, 26]

Fig. 9. Areas of interest PC-2. Source: Thesis [1, 26]

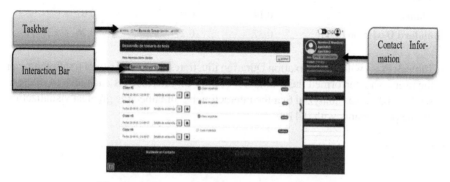

Fig. 10. Areas of interest PC-3. Source: Thesis [1, 26]

4.3 Analysis Results Based on Selected Metrics

Total Fixation Duration

- Table 1: PC-1 with Total Fixation Duration illustrates the result in total fixation time of the users who performed the evaluation of the PC1 interface for each area of interest, see Fig. 8. When analyzing these results, it is noted that the greatest interest in the fixation is found in the PEDI part (background image of the system).

Table 1. PC-1 total fixation duration metric

Total fixation duration	Taskbar	Contact info	General info	PEDI
Average		0.43	0.43	1.99
Share of total time (%)	0.00	3.89	12.80	83.31
Percentage Fixated(%)	0.00	20.00	66.67	93.33
Variance		0.14	0.10	0.60
Standard Deviation (n-1)		0.38	0.32	0.77

- Table 2: PC-2 with Total Fixation Duration illustrates the result in total fixation time of the users who performed the PC2 interface evaluation for each area of interest, see Fig. 9. Analyzing the results, the general information area of interest obtained the longest total fixation time with 0.403 s.

Table 2. PC-2 total fixation duration metric

Total fixation duration	Taskbar	Contact info	General info
Average	0.40	0.30	0.40
Share of total time (%)	16.04	35.70	48.26
Percentage Fixated(%)	20.00	60.00	60.00
Variance	0.14	0.07	0.07
Standard Deviation (n-1)	0.37	0.27	0.26

- Table 3: PC-3 with Total Fixation Duration illustrates the result in total fixation time of the users who performed the evaluation of the PC3 interface for each area of interest, see Fig. 10. It was analyzed that the interaction bar obtained the greatest visualization by the participants with 0.41 s.

Table 3. PC-3 total fixation duration metric

Total fixation duration	Interaction bar	Taskbar	Contact info
Average	0.41	0.22	0.29
Share of total time (%)	63.42	8.72	27.86
Percentage Fixated(%)	57.14	14.29	35.71
Variance	0.18	0.04	0.03
Standard Deviation (n-1)	0.42	0.20	0.18

Average Fixation Duration

- Table 4: PC-1 with Average duration of fixation illustrates the result of the average duration of fixation of the users who carried out the evaluation of the PC1 interface for each area of interest, see Fig. 8. The longest average fixation duration was obtained by the PEDI image (the system background image) with 0.28 s

Table 4. PC-1 average fixation duration metric

Average fixation duration	Taskbar	Contact info	General info	PEDI
Average		0.24	0.16	0.28
Variance		0.00	0.00	0.01
Standard Deviation (n-1)	0.00	0.06	0.06	0.11

- Table 5: PC-2 with Average fixation duration displays the result of the average fixation duration of the users who carried out the evaluation of the PC2 interface for each area of interest, see Fig. 9. The longest average duration of fixation was obtained by the general information with 0.19 s.

Table 5. PC-2 average fixation duration metric

Average fixation duration	Taskbar	Contact info	General info
Average	0.15	0.14	0.19
Variance	0.00	0.00	0.00
Standard Deviation (n-1)	0.05	0.05	0.05

- Table 6: PC-3 with Mean Fixation Duration, illustrates the result of the mean fixation duration of the users who carried out the evaluation of the PC3 interface for each area of interest, see Fig. 10. The longest average duration of fixation was obtained by the interaction bar with 0.17 s of fixation.

Table 6. PC-3 average fixation duration metric

Average fixation duration	Interaction bar	Taskbar	Contact info
Average	0.17	0.13	0.16
Variance	0.00	0.00	0.00
Standard Deviation (n-1)	0.06	0.07	0.05

4.4 Heat Maps and PC Visual Walkthroughs

They show the areas that most called the attention of users. It is presented by colors, the more intense it is, the greater the time that users put their attention on it. The resulting heat maps are presented in the different interfaces, see Fig. 11, 12, 13.

Fig. 11. Main page (PC-1)

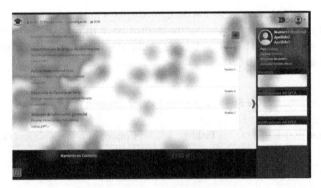

Fig. 12. Class plans (PC-2)

Fig. 13. Thesis topic development (PC-3)

4.5 Discussion of Eye-Tracking Tests for PC Formats

There are a few investigations that carry out the verification of adaptive interfaces based on metrics as it is indicated by the author [28]. The functionality of an interface is that it is adapted to the specific user to interact with the system. Based on the results, it can be affirmed that the distribution of the menus and details of the interfaces according to the fixation and the heat maps are well distributed and attract the attention of the users. The interface must be adapted [29], accordingly, in such a way that it meets certain requirements such as the needs, wishes or preferences of a user. Options that facilitate user interaction with the interfaces were developed, which are adapted to users´ abilities and cognitive limitations [30-32].

When analyzing all the results, we obtained that the Information Button, which is a tool implemented for people with disabilities, was unnoticed by the majority of participants. Therefore, it was proposed as a recommendation that, when including this button in the web page, an image should be placed in the image carousel (PEDI) which has a greater focus of attention or make it stand out with some effect to call the attention, allowing users to see the available options in case they are required.

The information button was modified, resulting in: (See Fig. 14 and Fig. 15)

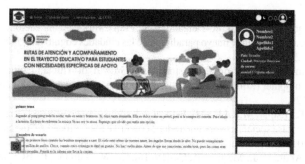

Fig. 14. Information button change in the interface

Fig. 15. Modified information button, the chosen color is friendly to the eyes of people with color blindness.

5   Conclusions

The resulting framework called UTM-Bootstrap allows the creation of interfaces aimed at improving HCI, thus allowing all types of users to manage the interfaces in an intuitive and easy way, reaching the fundamental principle of making the interface adapt to the user and not vice versa.

Carrying out the evaluation with the visual perception equipment based on the established metrics allowed to know that the help button that contained several options was not so striking. Therefore, a call to action was included and the help button color was changed so that all users can notice the available options, making their interaction with the interface friendlier.

As future work, by using the Tobii pro nano visual perception equipment from the Technical University of Manabí, it will be possible to continue interface analysis projects and human behavior studies through the various metrics that the Tobbi Pro-Lab system offers [23].

References

1. Giler-Velásquez, G.B., Marcillo-Delgado, B.S.: Framework para aplicaciones web y móviles que favorezcan la HCI en el nuevo paradigma de las ciudades cognitivas. Universidad Técnica de Manabí (2022)
2. Shneiderman, B.: Revisiting the Astonishing Growth of Human-Computer Interaction Research. Computer (Long. Beach. Calif). **50**(10), 8–11 (2017). https://doi.org/10.1109/MC.2017.3641625
3. Llantos, O.E., Estuar, M.R.J.E.: My.Eskwela: designing an enterprise learning management system to increase social network and reduce cognitive load. Procedia Computer Science **138**, 595–602 (2018). https://doi.org/10.1016/j.procs.2018.10.080
4. Cecílio, J., Andrade, J., Martins, P., Castelo-Branco, M., Furtado, P.: BCI framework based on games to teach people with cognitive and motor limitations. Procedia Computer Science **83**, 74–81 (2016). https://doi.org/10.1016/j.procs.2016.04.101
5. Mijović, P., et al.: Communicating the user state: Introducing cognition-aware computing in industrial settings. Saf. Sci. **119**, 375–384 (2019). https://doi.org/10.1016/j.ssci.2017.12.024

6. Huang, Y., White, C., Xia, H., Wang, Y.: A computational cognitive modeling approach to understand and design mobile crowdsourcing for campus safety reporting. Int. J. Hum. Comput. Stud. **102**, 27–40 (2017). https://doi.org/10.1016/j.ijhcs.2016.11.003
7. Blandford, A.: HCI for health and wellbeing: Challenges and opportunities. Int. J. Hum. Comput. Stud. **131**, 4151 (2019). https://doi.org/10.1016/j.ijhcs.2019.06.007
8. Ding, I.J., Lin, Z.Y.: A service robot design with an advanced HCI scheme for the person with disabilities. In: Proceedings of the 2017 IEEE International Conference on Information, Communication and Engineering: Information and Innovation for Modern Technology, ICICE 2017, pp. 531–534 (2018). https://doi.org/10.1109/ICICE.2017.8479297
9. Gaouar, L., Benamar, A., Le Goaer, O., Biennier, F.: HCIDL: Human-computer interface description language for multi-target, multimodal, plastic user interfaces. Futur. Comput. Informatics J.**3**(1),110130 (2018). https://doi.org/10.1016/j.fcij.2018.02.001
10. Faulkner, C.: The Essence of Human Computer Interaction20006 The Essence of Human Computer Interaction . Prentice Hall, 1998. , ISBN: ISBN 0-137-51975-3 £14.95. Kybernetes **29**(1), 144–155 (2000). https://doi.org/10.1108/k.2000.29.1.144.6
11. Mera Paz, J.A., Cano Beltrán, J.H.: Diagnóstico de pruebas de calidad en software para ambientes virtuales de aprendizaje sobre dispositivos móviles. Memorias Congr. UTP; 2018 II Congr. Int. en Intel. Ambient. Ing. Softw. y Salud Electrónica y Móvil – AmITIC 2018; 144–150. Accessed: 23 Jun 2021 (2018). https://ridda2.utp.ac.pa/handle/123456789/5177
12. Lima, S., Teran, L.: Cognitive smart cities and deep learning: A classification framework. In: 2019 6th International Conference on eDemocracy and eGovernment, ICEDEG 2019, pp. 180–187 (2019). https://doi.org/10.1109/ICEDEG.2019.8734346
13. Vaca-Cardenas, L., Avila-Pesantez, D., Vaca-Cardenas, M., Meza, J.: Trends and Challenges of HCI in the New Paradigm of Cognitive Cities (2020). https://doi.org/10.1109/ICEDEG 48599.2020.9096845
14. Vaca-Cardenas, L., Meza, J., Avila-Pesantez, D., Vaca-Cardenas, M., Vasco, J.: Enhancing user experience through an HCI research tool. Case study: Cognitive urban planning platform (PUC). In: 2021 8th International Conference eDemocracy eGovernment, ICEDEG 2021, pp. 163–171 (2021). https://doi.org/10.1109/ICEDEG52154.2021.9530960
15. Ruiz, A., Arciniegas, J.L., Giraldo, W.J.: Characterization of user interface development frameworks for interactive systems based on video content distribution. Ingeniare **26**(2), 339–353 (2018). https://doi.org/10.4067/S0718-33052018000200339
16. Mariana López Quirós: Hacia la Sociedad de la Información y el Conocimiento, 2013. COSTA RICA. Accessed: 09 Sep 2021 (2014). https://core.ac.uk/download/pdf/148340063.pdf
17. Samaniego Larrea, M.J.: Estudio Comparativo de Productividad de Frameworks PHP Orientados a objetos para Desarrollar el Sistema de Siguimiento de Incidentes de la infraestructura de Red en la ESPOCH. Escuela Superior Politécnica de Chimborazo. Accessed: 31 Mar 2021 (2015). http://dspace.espoch.edu.ec/handle/123456789/4376
18. Bootstrap: Bootstrap. https://getbootstrap.com/. Accessed 19 Sep 2021
19. Albino, V., Berardi, U., Dangelico, R.M.: Smart cities: definitions, dimensions, performance, and initiatives. J. Urban Technol. **22**(1), 3–21 (2015). https://doi.org/10.1080/10630732.2014. 942092
20. Artemis Psaltoglou: archi-DOCT: La revista electrónica de investigación doctoral en arquitectura. http://www.archidoct.net/issue11.html. Accessed 30 Mar 2021
21. Vaca-Cardenas, L., Avila-Pesantez, D., Vaca-Cardenas, M., Meza, J.: Trends and challenges of HCI in the new paradigm of cognitive cities. In: 2020 7th International Conference on eDemocracy and eGovernment, ICEDEG 2020, pp. 120–126 (2020). https://doi.org/10.1109/ ICEDEG48599.2020.9096845
22. Interaction Design: The Encyclopedia of Human-Computer Interaction, 2nd Ed. I Interaction Design Foundation (IxDF). https://www.interaction-design.org/literature/book/the-enc yclopedia-of-human-computer-interaction-2nd-ed. Accessed 08 Sep 2021

23. Neurolabcenter UCM, Eye Tracking Seguimiento ocular para investigación (2021). https://neurolabcenter.com/eye-tracking/. Accessed 11 Feb 2022
24. Giler-Velásquez, G., Marcillo-Delgado, B., Vaca-Cardenas, M., Vaca-Cardenas, L.: Software frameworks that improve HCI focused on cognitive cities. a systematic literature review. In: Guarda, T., Portela, F., Santos, M.F. (eds.) ARTIIS 2021. CCIS, vol. 1485, pp. 142–157. Springer, Cham (2021). https://doi.org/10.1007/978-3-030-90241-4_12
25. Beck, K., Hendrickson, M., Fowler, M.: Planning Extreme Programming. Accessed: 08 Sep 2021 (2001). https://books.google.com.ec/books?hl=es&lr=&id=u13hVoYVZa8C&oi=fnd&pg=PR11&dq=Beck,+K+(2001).+Planning+extreme+programming&ots=GN-5WYdU9e&sig=Y3DdOtt5sFC4AyoofEIrn0hONTk#v=onepage&q=Beck%2CK.Planningextremeprogramming&f=false
26. Briones-Villafuerte, G.T., Naula-Bone, A.A.: Prototipos De Interfaces De Usuarios Web Y Móvil Que Promuevan Una Adecuada Construcción De HCI. Universidad Técnica de Manabí (2022)
27. Eye Tracking | Tobii Pro Nano, Fusion y Spectrum | Bitbrain. https://www.bitbrain.com/es/productos-neurotecnologia/eye-tracking/tobii-pro-nano-fusion-y-spectrum. Accessed 27 Apr 2022
28. Quiroz, T., Salazar, O.M., Ovalle, D.A., Quiroz, T., Salazar, O.M., Ovalle, D.A.: Modelo de Interfaz Adaptativa basada en Perfiles de Usuario y Ontologías para Recomendación de Objetos de Aprendizaje. Inf. tecnológica 29(6), 295–306 (2018). https://doi.org/10.4067/S0718-07642018000600295
29. Figueiredo, D.G., Insfran, E., Abrahão, S., Vanderdonckt, J.: Medición De La Experiencia De Usuario Mediante Datos Encefalográficos (Eeg) Para Interfaces De Usuario
30. Pérez Pérez, M., García Morales, L., Coromina-Hernández, J.C., Álvarez-González, M.Á.: Memoria visual en la tercera edad. Regularidades para el diseño de interfaces. Scielo 41(3) (2020). Accessed: 27 Apr 2022. http://scielo.sld.cu/scielo.php?pid=S1815-59362020000300006&script=sci_arttext&tlng=en#B7
31. Kalakoski, V., Henelius, A., Oikarinen, E., Ukkonen, A., Puolamäki, K.: Cognitive ergonomics for data analysis: Experimental study of cognitive limitations in a data-based judgement task. In: ECCE 2019 - Proceedings 31st Eur. Conference Cogn. Ergon. Design Cogn., pp. 38–40 (2019). https://doi.org/10.1145/3335082.3335112
32. Kim, I.-J.: Cognitive Ergonomics and Its Role for Industry Safety Enhancements (2016). https://www.longdom.org/open-access/cognitive-ergonomics-and-its-role-for-industry-safety-enhancements-2165-7556-1000e158.pdf. Accessed 27 Apr 2022

Advanced Exploratory Data Analysis for Moroccan Shopping Places in TripAdvisor

Ibrahim Bouabdallaoui$^{(\boxtimes)}$ ⓘ, Fatima Guerouate ⓘ, Samya Bouhaddour,
Chaimae Saadi, and Mohammed Sbihi ⓘ

EST Salé, Mohammed V University in Rabat, Avenue le Prince Héritier, 11060 Salé, Morocco
bd.ibrahim@hotmail.com

Abstract. The economic impact of tourism and travel is considerable as it drives the growth of investment in infrastructure and is a source of significant foreign currency not subject to debt obligations, purchase and specific payments. Among the major expenses of tourists during their stay in Morocco are their outlays in markets and souks, since they represent a contributing element in the income of actors in the tourism sector. TripAdvisor is one of the most popular social media for travelers, it is considered as a bank of information about each country's tourism, which can be trusted and recommended. This information can be exploited for analytical purposes using data mining techniques to help decision-makers in the sphere of tourism to take measures to improve touristic shopping sites in Morocco. In this paper, we present a detailed exploratory data analysis of tourist's feelings towards Moroccan shopping places, in particular, the characteristics of each shopping place according to ratings, a discussion about types of shopping places with a detailed geographical analysis, and finally an introduction to topic discovery using N-grams and Word-Cloud.

Keywords: Data mining · Morocco tourism · Geographic information system · Topic modelling · n-grams

1 Introduction

Although artificial intelligence (AI) is still seen only as a futuristic invention for many people, its effects in the world of tourism are increasingly being felt. In particular, it made it possible to optimize exchanges as well as better organization of tourist's feelings towards tourism entities. Artificial intelligence is able to interact with clients face to face thanks to developments in speech recognition and natural language processing technologies. Machine learning algorithms analyze and interpret data to uncover patterns in datasets about tourists, business travel, and pricing strategies [1]. The AI can thus help travel agents analyze travelers' opinions, understand their preferences, estimate their budgets and get an idea of their habits in order to recommend personalized and tailor-made suggestions [2]. TripAdvisor has 340 million unique visitors and 350 million reviews. Every minute, around 280 traveler reviews are posted on the site. In addition to the conventional statistical analysis of opinion subsets, the computing power and underlying techniques of machine learning make it possible to analyze all comments related to a brand. The analysis of emotions aims to explore the data of the text to define and classify their emotional and real qualities [3]. The maturity of natural language processing and sentiment analysis allows for the adoption of precise analytical tools while avoiding data collection time. In this work, we will first present the data collection procedure, then a statistical and geographical analysis on the shopping places, then we will start a sentiment analysis, and at the end a discovery on the most frequent topics in the data.

2 Methodology

2.1 Data Collection

Data is collected from TripAdvisor website, due to its reliability and enriched content. [4]. Collected reviews contains rates and location of each Moroccan shopping place indexed in the website. Shopping places known in TripAdvisor are 91 places, grouped with their names and the average of rates and number of reviews. Reviews are grouped in each shopping place name, number of reviews varies from 1 review to more than 26000 reviews, depending the popularity of the place. Each shopping place has a presentation, photos, address and nearby places, reviews and Q&A.

For the dataset of the Shopping places, a scraping work is done at the level of the titles and the type of each market place, in fact, each type contains a sub-type incorporated within each page of the market place, however two entities are divided, and the subtype is chosen as an element of analysis for this whole part. Thus, using the Google Maps API geocoding tool, each market place is located accurately according to the data of Google Maps [5], the choice of this interface is made following the richness of geolocation data in Morocco, GPS services in Morocco depend on Google Maps to geolocate sites.

2.2 Data Preparation

After collecting data using a HTML and XML document parsing library, 2 JSON files are created: the first one contains reviews and rates, and the second one contains titles and localization of shopping places. After loading these two files, merging them into one large dataset, empty rows and undesirable data (that would generate outliers in the analysis) are deleted. The final shape of data has a size of 26244 rows and 4 major columns: "Name_of_the_shop_place", "Title_of_the_review", "Review", "Rate", "Address", "Latitude", "Longitude", "Shop_Type", "Shop_SubType". The name of shopping place may be duplicated in function of reviews number. Rate column contains 5 classes: "terrible" for 0, "bad" for 1, "regular" for 2, "good" for 3 and "excellent" for 4. Lowercasing and cleaning work are applied to reviews text (remove punctuations, links, emails, special characters and stop words). Stop words package is set to English language since we are working on English reviews. A parallelism mechanism has been applied to browse data and manipulate it easily without having memory issues and long processing time using multithreading CPU pools.

3 Results

3.1 Shopping Places

The introduced dataset has many hidden insights to be shown, from "Rate" and "Reviews" columns, these insights are presented as visualizations since it's an efficient methodology to simplify data.

Counting classes in an important stage in discovering a dataset, it's an efficient way to create compact set of features that are valuable to the analysis, the following plot shows counting of each class of the data [6]. The shopping places on TripAdvisor are 91 market places, divided into 10 types: Specialty & Gift Shops, Flea & Street Markets, Shopping Malls, Art Galleries, Antique Shops, Art Museums, Historic Sites, Lessons & workshops and Point of Interests & Landmarks. The figure below shows the number of existing markets on TripAdvisor according to their types (Fig. 1):

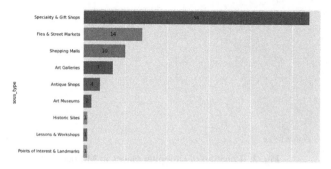

Fig. 1. Shopping places by types

"Speciality & Gift Shops" is the most popular type on TripAdvisor, tourists show more interest in this kind of market places, to give a customer experience with the products we can offer them and mark the memories during their stays in Morocco. Then, the "Flea & Street Markets" category takes second place, this ranking is due to the distribution of traditional markets across the kingdom, which attracts more tourists to visit and explore such traditional markets that are frequented by Moroccans almost [7]. "Shopping Malls" are quite numerous especially in the last decades when Morocco has adopted a vision for the creation of formal markets (e.g. malls) to promote tourism for high classes who seek entertainment and shopping in large surfaces and major brands [8]. For the other classes, they differ according to their historical and cultural characteristics (e.g. Museums, Antique shops and historic sites), these places do not have many markets due to the interest of the tourist to visit and explore places and enjoy the Moroccan historical heritage.

Geographically speaking, these shopping places are distributed in most cases in cities with a historical character (e.g. Marrakech, Fez) where they are very recognized on an international scale, and which are often publicized in Moroccan tourist posters and through social medias [9]. The figure below shows the distribution of shopping markets in the Kingdom of Morocco, according to their type (Fig. 2).

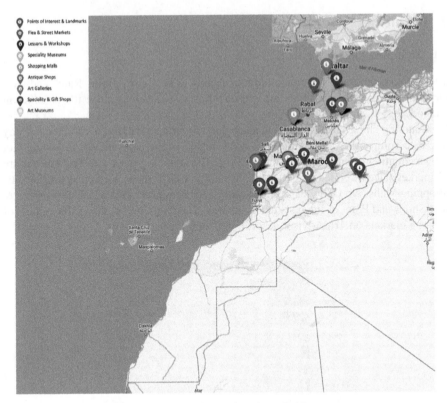

Fig. 2. Location of shopping places in Morocco

The 91 market places that have been collected are plotted in the map of Morocco, all the sites are located in the north and the middle of Morocco, which means that tourists tend to visit the most recommended cities. This map shows the concentration of markets in the most famous cities, especially for the category "Specialty and Gifts shop" which can be seen that it is distributed through the main cities of the kingdom, while for "Flea and Street Markets" are spread over cities that have a historical character (e.g. Marrakech, Fez, Agadir). Casablanca is the city that contains the large number of "Shopping malls", because it is the largest city in the kingdom and which welcomes tourists who have a high social class [10]. On the other hand, Fez, the spiritual capital of Morocco, contains a large number of art galleries, which shows that the artisanal heritage of this historic city is very present in the economy of this city, especially for the artisanal industry. The following figures are an example of the distribution of shopping places on two cities that are geographically close: that of the coastal city of Essaouira and the city of Marrakech which is located in a mountainous geography. Essaouira is a port and tourist city located on the Atlantic coast of Morocco, it is known as a city with a Jewish religious heritage and which has a significant historical character.

In the Fig. 3, art galleries are located very close to the ocean, with a strategic position that includes places at "Point of interest & Landmarks", which encourages tourists to discover tourist sites without having difficulties to move, this geographical position also

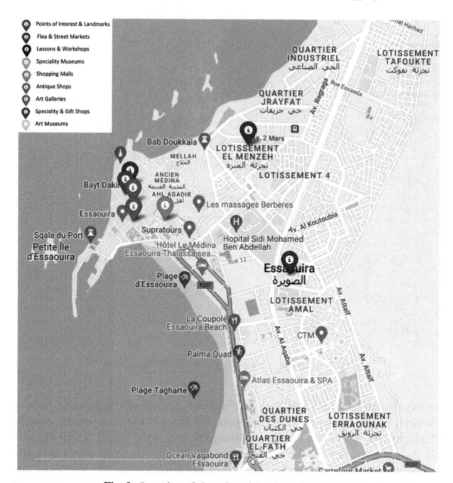

Fig. 3. Location of shopping places in Essaouira city

allows the tourist to go to the Specialty & Gifts Shops, which is practical for a tourist in terms of costs. For the other market places, they are distributed in the heart of the city where there is a Mall, a "Flea and Street Markets" and many more "Specialty & Gifts Shops". This distribution is considered fair due to the fact that this city can accommodate several profiles of tourists, who have plans to go to several sites in a homogeneous way since this city is small and welcomes thousands of tourists each year, and who give positive assessments on these sites.

Marrakech is a city located in central Morocco, at the foot of the Atlas Mountains. It is nicknamed the ocher city in reference to the red color of most of its buildings and houses. Tourist arrivals in the city of Marrakech totaled nearly 3 million visitors in 2019, all nationalities combined. The figure below shows a close up of shopping places in Marrakech (Fig. 4):

The traditional markets are located in the heart of the city, and particularly in the popular districts, with a concentration of "Speciality & Gift Shops" which can be noticed

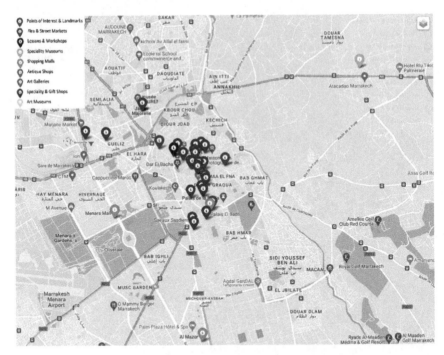

Fig. 4. Location of shopping places in Marrakech city

to be very close to each other, this gives the tourist the privilege of visiting each tourist site while enjoying the purchase of local products, and going to the places whose character of "Lessons and Workshops", and also giving the tourist the option of visiting malls while staying at the heart of the city. This concentration of locations allows the tourist not to be confused during his stay in Marrakech and gives him a desire to discover each site of the city without being far from the center of the city, despite the fact that this city is among the largest cities in the kingdom.

3.2 Sentiment Analysis

Opinion extraction is the process that determines the emotional tone conveyed by the words, used in order to obtain an interpretation of the attitudes, opinions and emotions expressed in an online comment. In the section of market places in TripAdvisor, each opinion is linked to a rate that a user should put to express his appreciation in addition to his review, which is considered as a support for what he thinks about the place. In this section, we will do an exploratory data analysis to analyze each sentiment with a constraint, to demonstrate insights. The figure below shows counting of each sentiment (Fig. 5).

The classes "excellent" and "good" have the highest numbers of reviews, which means that tourists have a good behavior through different topics related to shopping places. However, "terrible" and "bad" classes are reaching less than 1500 reviews, and as a result, negative reviews are less than positive ones.

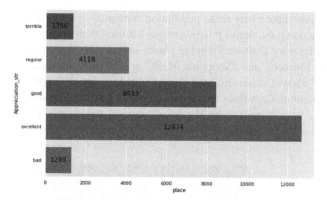

Fig. 5. Ratings of shopping places

This difference is justified by the fact that two market places contain a lot of opinions (e.g. Jamaa El Fena and Ensemble artisanal), and that the ranking of all the feelings of these two market places are present at the top of the ranking, which can bias inferences about the data. Removing these outliers is a way to solve this problem [11], especially "Jamaa El Fena" and "Ensemble artisanal" samples, to route the rest of this analysis without these two elements. However, the deletion of the reviews that concern these two market places is mandatory to perform a fair analysis between the 89 places, and leave the two markets eliminated for particular inferences given their enormous numbers of reviews [12]. The count of opinions without these two markets places is therefore displayed as follows (Fig. 6):

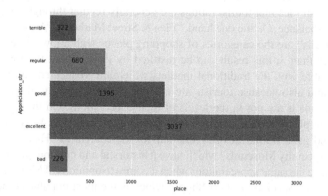

Fig. 6. Ratings of shopping places after outliers deletion

After the deletion, the count of opinions is notably decreased and the difference is slight between the classes: the "excellent" class takes the first place with 3037 positive reviews, against 332 for the "terrible" class. Basically, the number of opinions has been reduced 3 to 8 times less than that of the previous graph after the deletion of the opinions concerning the two market places in question, this insight would make a deduction: that the negative classes take a very small population compared to the positive classes, which means that tourists tend to leave positive reviews during their stays in Morocco.

For the exploratory analysis shopping places subsection, "Speciality & Gift Shops", "Flea & Street Markets" and "Shopping Malls" are the most frequent subtypes on TripAdvisor, now we will discover the average of feelings for each type, for this we will have to use the numerical values of the rating that we have collected from the site, note that the classes vary from 0 to 5. The importance of this axis is to know the major elements in the choices of tourists to visit a marketplace.

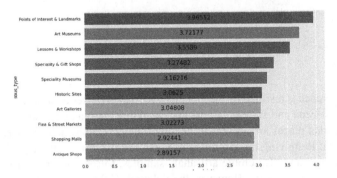

Fig. 7. Mean of ratings by shopping places types

In the figure above, the average rating varies between 3.96 and 2.77, which means that the appreciations are almost balanced between good experiences and bad ones despite the excessive distribution of "Excellent" class reviews in Fig. 7., this range would give us an idea that tourist ratings are generally regular through shopping types following this balance. On the one hand, "Flea & Street Markets", "Antique Shops" and "Shopping Malls" are the categories of shopping places with a low score, with scores that are lower than 3, this result can be justified by the fact that the tourists are not very comfortable with the traditional markets which are frequented and promoted by Moroccans, and also because tourists are not interested in going to the malls, or that the Moroccan malls are not in the levels of their expectations. On the other hand, the other shopping places have averages higher than 3 and lower than 4, which condensed the results and gave similarities in particular for the categories "Historic Sites", "Art Galleries", "Specialty Museums" which have a historical and cultural character, tourists will tend to have the same appreciations when it comes to opinions of Moroccan heritage. For the category "Specialty & Gift Shops" which is the most popular in the kingdom, we find that the appreciations are generally good, because the products offered by these stores attract the attention of tourists and can be enticing to these tourists. to recommend it. "Points of Interests & Landmarks" and "Lessons & Workshops" took first and third place respectively due to the fact that the number of places in these two categories does not exceed 1, which clearly justifies that the chances of having high or low ratings will be maximized as there is no competition. The category "Art Museum" is the most appreciated place due to its popularity in TripAdvisor.

In another context, two examples of exploration of feelings would be taken following the names of shopping places, notably for the case of the "Excellent" class and the case of the "Terrible" class which are concerned with two contradictory classes. The figure below shows the top 10 of the most appreciated/worst shopping places (Fig. 8).

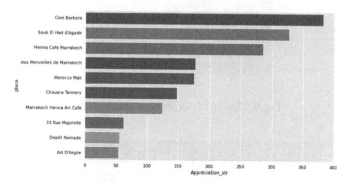

Fig. 8. Top-10 of "excellent" shopping places

For the "Excellent" class, "Coin Berbere" is the most popular place, since it is an art museum that contains Amazigh handicrafts, which represent the Berber identity of Morocco, and also "Souk El Had of Agadir" which is an appreciated place by tourists, its traditional products offered attract more and more tourists despite that it belongs to the category "Flea & Street Markets". For this ranking, we notice that there is a diversity of cities since each shopping place is located in a city (e.g. "Coin Berbere" in Fez, "Souk El Had d'Agadir" in Agadir, "Henna Cafe Marrakech" in Marrakech, "Morocco Mall" in Casablanca…), but also a diversity at the level of categories since there are "Shopping Malls" for the case of the "Morocco Mall", "Art Galleries" for the case of "Coin Berbere", "Flea & Street Markets" for the case of "Souk El Had of Agadir"…

For the rest of the rankings, the rankings are generally below 50 reviews, as there is a shortage of opinions on these shopping places, and therefore few information is available. For the case of the bad reviews in the figure below, "Souk El Had of Agadir" takes the first place, but less than 30 reviews, this is due, as we mentioned before, to the fact that tourists do not really like traditional markets [13], but it does not mean that tourists do not like the products offered, but it is likely that they cannot adapt to the climate of this kind of market place. In the "Chouara Tannery", the negative opinions can be explained by the fact that a number of tourists are not comfortable with the smells of leather during its preparation for industrialization, this tannery is traditional and represents a historical heritage of the city of Fez [14], which was a ray of Moroccan civilization. For other reviews, the more we are decreasing in the ranking, the more we have less "terrible" ideas about a shopping place, since it can tend towards positive levels, and also there is a lack of information in the market places that are not well known or doesn't reached by TripAdvisor users (Fig. 9).

We will then, at that point, project the 5 classes of sentiments on the map of Morocco, to characterize the sentiments for every city and have an overall idea of the appreciations for vacationers in every city.

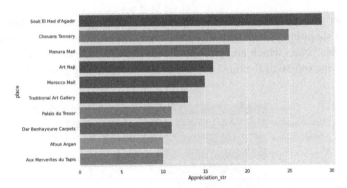

Fig. 9. Top-10 of "terrible" shopping places

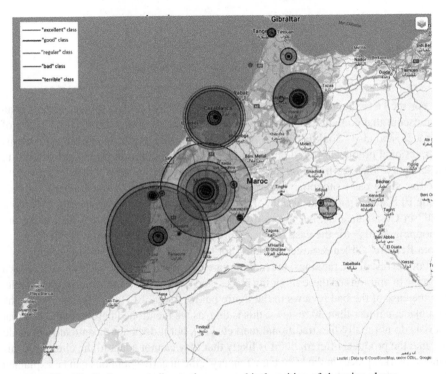

Fig. 10. Ratings according to the geographical position of shopping places

In Fig. 10, we have a general view of the appreciations of the users on each shopping place projected geographically. Marrakech is the city most appreciated by tourists of which they gave only the positive opinions on this city, on the other hand in Fez, the rating tends towards the "good" class which is generally neutral. Opinions on Agadir and Casablanca switch between the "Excellent" class and the "good" class with a minimum number of negative opinions. However, for small circles they can be persuaded in cities with the least opinion, such as the case of the city of Tangier and Chefchaouen (Fig. 11):

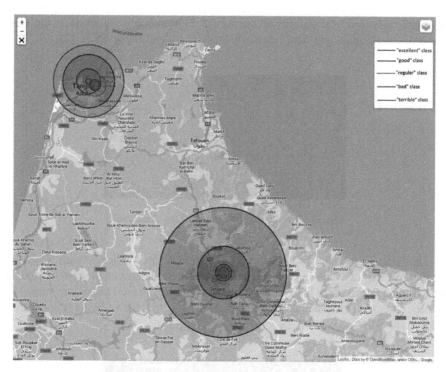

Fig. 11. Ratings in Tangier city and Chefchaouen city

As can be seen, negative opinions are the most numerous for the city of Tangier, which contains "Art Galleries" and a mall, which shows us that tourists are not really interested in these two categories in the within the city, despite the strategic position of the city which links between the Atlantic Ocean and the Mediterranean Sea, and also its rich Moroccan and Spanish cultural heritage. On the other hand, in the city of Chefchaouen, the city has very favorable or even excellent ratings with minimal negative ratings, this is due to the fact that the city is located in a mountainous and forested area which is well appreciated by tourists who love ecotourism and sustainable tourism.

3.3 Topic Discovery

Word Cloud. The keyword cloud is a visual representation of the most used keywords (tags) on a data sample. Typically, words appear in character sizes and weights that are more visible the more they are used or popular. It is a kind of semantic digest of a document in which the key concepts evoked are endowed with a unit of size allowing to highlight their importance in the current sample using this same idea of operation [15]. It is possible to prioritize this system according to an alphabetical order of popularity or even of representation in the current sample. Concretely, the more a keyword (tag) is quoted, the more it will appear in large size in the cloud represented by the word cloud. By clicking on one of these keywords, depending on whether there is a cloud of keywords organized by popularity on the sample. Figures below are results of the Word Cloud of "good" class and "bad" class which are two close classes (Fig. 12).

Fig. 12. Word Cloud of reviews of the class "bad"

The most important words in "bad" class sample are: "price", "mall", "place", "shop", "rug" …, which means that there is an intersection between these words and the analysis that we presented in previous sections: malls are the most underrated places for tourists, and tourists complains almost on prices, due to the cost-of-living in some areas in Morocco (Fig. 13).

Fig. 13. Word Cloud of reviews of the class "good"

In "good" class, relevant words are: "good", "shop", "souk", "place", "time", "see"… and these words are giving a positive attitude that a tourist has towards the popular shopping places, particularly in "Flea and Street Markets" (e.g. souk), and they enjoy shopping during their stay in Morocco.

Ngrams. An n-gram is a subsequence of n elements constructed from a given sequence. His idea was that from a given letter sequence it is possible to obtain the likelihood function of the appearance of the next letter. From a training corpus, it is easy to construct a probability distribution for the next letter with a history of size n [16]. This modelling corresponds in fact to a Markov model of order n where only the last n observations are used for the prediction of the next letter. Thus, a bigram is a Markov model of order 2. N-grams are widely used in automatic natural language processing but also in signal processing. Their use is based on the simplifying assumption that, given a sequence of k elements (k ≥ n) the probability of the appearance of an element in position *i* does not depend on only the previous *n-1* elements.

We have: $$P(w_i \mid w_1,...,w_{i-1}) = P(w_i \mid w_{i-(n-1)},...,w_{i-1})$$ (1)

With *n=3* (tri-gram): $$P(w_i \mid w_1,...,w_{i-1}) = P(w_i \mid w_{i-2}, w_{i-1})$$ (2)

Then the probability of the sequence is:

$$P(w_{1,k}) = P(w_1) * P(w_2 \mid w_1) \prod P(w_i \mid w_{i-2}, w_{i-1})$$ (3)

This model is considered as common single words that exist in reviews.

Bi-gram. A bigram is a sequence of two adjacent elements from a string of tokens, the frequency distribution of every bigram in a string is commonly used for simple statistical analysis of text.

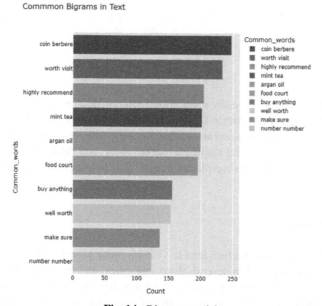

Fig. 14. Bi-gram model

In Fig. 14, many sequences are showing several topics such as gastronomy (e.g. "mint tea", "argan oil", "food court"...), places (e.g. "Coin berbère") and sentiment (e.g. "worth visit", "highly recommend"). Tourists have interests on exploring shops while expressing their reviews about food and public places.

Tri-gram. As seen in the previous section, a trigram is a sequence of 3 characters. From this point of view, trigrams are characterized by their probabilities of appearing in different corpus of texts and we do not concern ourselves with the associated sounds.

Commmon Trigrams in Text

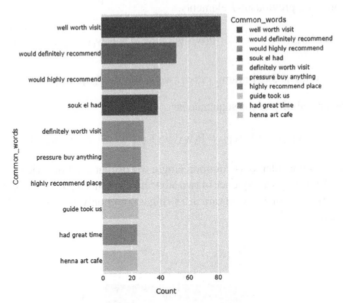

Fig. 15. Tri-gram model

In Fig. 15, the trigram gave keywords about recommendation such as "well worth visit" or "would definitely recommend", most of these keywords are varying between good and bad rating, that means tourists are tending to give their opinions in a sense where they recommend or not recommend visiting a market place, and there also more sequences that describes exactly life in shop places, squares and public places in Morocco.

4 Conclusion

This study has shown that tourists tend to visit shopping places with a traditional character which are distributed in several Moroccan cities, and in particular famous cities (e.g. Marrakech, Fez…), with a significant interest to cities with a coastal and mountainous geographical location as shown by the sentiment analysis carried out in this work. However, this analysis would bring more insights if there were many Moroccan shopping places in TripAdvisor. This work is an introduction to sentiment analysis of tourists' behaviors towards shopping places while emphasizing their reviews that could be utilized in predictive analytics.

References

1. Afsahhosseini, F., Al-mulla, Y.: Machine learning in tourism. In: 2020 The 3rd International Conference on Machine Learning and Machine Intelligence. pp. 53–57 (2020)

2. Nilashi, M., Bagherifard, K., Rahmani, M., Rafe, V.: A recommender system for tourism industry using cluster ensemble and prediction machine learning techniques. Comput. Ind. Eng. **109**, 357–368 (2017)

3. Laksono, R.A., Sungkono, K.R., Sarno, R., Wahyuni, C.S.: Sentiment analysis of restaurant customer reviews on tripadvisor using naïve bayes. In: 2019 12th International Conference on Information & Communication Technology and System (ICTS), IEEE, pp. 49–54 (2019).

4. Valdivia, A., Luz´on, M., Herrera, F.: Sentiment analysis on tripadvisor: Are there inconsistencies in user reviews? In: International Conference on Hybrid Artificial Intelligence Systems, Springer, pp. 15–25 (2017). https://doi.org/10.1007/978-3-319-59650-1_2

5. Hsu, F.-M., Lin, Y.-T., Ho, T.-K.: Design and implementation of an intelligent recommendation system for tourist attractions: the integration of ebm model, bayesian network and google maps. Expert Syst. Appl. **39**(3), 3257–3264 (2012)

6. Camizuli, E., Carranza, E.J.: Exploratory data analysis (eda). The encyclopedia of archaeological sciences, pp. 1–7 (2018)

7. Godefroit-Winkel, D., Peñaloza, L.: Women's empowerment at the Moroccan supermarket: an ethnographic account of achieved capabilities and altered social relations in an emerging retail servicescape. J. Macromark. **40**(4), 492–509 (2020)

8. Danteur, T.: Evolution of leisure patterns in morocco: from traditional spiritual pilgrims to contemporary mall wanderers. In: Mapping Leisure, Springer, pp. 235–268 (2018). https://doi.org/10.1007/978-981-10-3632-3_14

9. Karimova, G.Z.: How to transform research results into the advertising message: the example of experiential artisanal tours in morocco. Global J. Management and Business **2**(1), 45–53 (2015)

10. Mharzi Alaoui, H., Radoine, H., Chenal, J., Yakubu, H., Bajja, S.: Understanding the urban middle-class and its housing characteristics—case study of casablanca, morocco. Urban Science **6**(2), 32 (2022)

11. Pahwa, B., Taruna, S., Kasliwal, N.: Sentiment analysis-strategy for text pre-processing. Int. J. Comput. Appl **180**(34), 15–18 (2018)

12. Nikolova, M.: A variational approach to remove outliers and impulse noise. J. Mathematical Imaging Vision **20**(1), 99–120 (2004)

13. Kania, K., Kalaska, M.: Functional and spatial changes of souks in morocco's imperial cities in the context of tourism development. Miscellanea Geographica **23**(2), 92–98 (2019)

14. Merger, M.-F.: Visual and olfactory itineraries in some travel guides on morocco (1954 to 2018). LiCArC (Littérature et culture arabes contemporaines) 2020(Hors-série n° 2), pp. 101–120 (2020)

15. Cui, W., Wu, Y., Liu, S., Wei, F., Zhou, M.X., Qu, H.: Context preserving dynamic word cloud visualization. In: 2010 IEEE Pacific Visualization Symposium (PacificVis), IEEE, pp. 121–128 (2010)

16. Schonlau, M., Guenther, N.: Text mining using n-grams. Schonlau, M., Guenther, N., Sucholutsky, I.: Text mining using n-gram variables. The Stata Journal **17**(4), 866–881 (2017)

Content Richness, Perceived Price, and Perceived Ease of Use in Relation to the Satisfaction Level and Brand Equity in Streaming Platforms

Romina Dextre-Mamani, Belén Pérez-Arce, and Manuel Luis Lodeiros Zubiria[✉]

Universidad Peruana de Ciencias Aplicadas, Lima, Perú
{u201713224,u201711392,pccmmlod}@upc.edu.pe

Abstract. Streaming platforms have become popular in recent years, where consumers can view personalized content at any time on the device of their choice. Many brands in this market have been fighting to win more market share. It was seen how they improved their strategies based on several factors such as price, ease of use, content richness, or brand equity. Users tend to have high satisfaction with the streaming platform depending on what brand offers what they value the most. The objective of this study was to find the relationships that the variables content richness (CR), perceived price (PR), perceived ease of use (PEOU), brand equity (BE), and user satisfaction (US) have within this market. The study population was made up of subscribers of streaming platforms in Peru, in which the sample was 400 subscribers who used streaming platforms for more than 6 months. The methodology used was a PLS-SEM analysis using the SmartPLS 3 tool to answer the hypotheses raised in the study. All the scale items were measured by a 7-point Likert scale. The results from the investigation indicated that brand equity was significantly influenced by both content richness and perceived ease of use. Moreover, brand equity and user satisfaction have a high significance between them. This may be since users now value more the richness of content and ease of use on streaming platforms. However, the perceived price was not significantly predictive of brand equity, it could be because some streaming platforms offer more than one pricing plan and the perceptions disperse even more than with the other variables. Overall findings suggest reinforcing the relationships between CR and BE, since there have not been previous investigations.

Keywords: Streaming platforms · Multimedia · Content richness · Brand equity · User experience

1 Introduction

Streaming is the distribution of multimedia content in real-time through the internet anywhere, in which it is possible to play series, movies, music, and more [1], where streamers such a Netflix, Hulu, Disney Prime, and Amazon Prime, which control 90% of the total market, are getting massively famous around the world with 50% increase in the last years [2], since their platforms allow customers to check out their content library and find their favorite film without time or place restrictions [3] and watch personalized and recommended videos based on customer ratings and reviews [4] according to with the target needs and the provision of rich and exclusive content in an effortless way [5]. The present research will focus on the Latin-American market where a good example of this trend can be found where the platforms have developed local content in the last years to gain more engagement with the audience but also to increase their satisfaction [6].

However, it is also important to mention that all the streaming services circulate similar programming to a worldwide audience simultaneously, but only Netflix produces a notable amount of content outside the United States and has a higher available content in all nations [7]. In consequence, in the first quarter of 2020, Netflix was the leading streaming service in Latin America, with 34.32 million subscribers, and the largest local competitor - Claro Video owned by América Movil - had 3.69 million subscribers [8]. Nevertheless, some new market opportunities attract other brands into the streaming industry, that is why the current enterprises need to evolve to stay relevant to the public and adapt themselves to the digital world's trends [9].

Under these circumstances, the present work analyzes variables such as content richness, perceived price, and perceived ease of use in relation to the satisfaction level and brand equity in streaming platforms [10]. It is understood by content richness as a variety of interesting content that brings satisfaction to the consumer [11]. About ease of use, it is the consumer's perception that buying something will involve a minimum of effort [12].Perceived price is defined as the person's judgment about the product's price level [13]. Finally, brand equity is the customer's subjective and intangible assessment of the brand over and above its value [5].

On the other hand, it was mentioned that most of the research regarding streaming services tend to focus on the USA, Europe, and Asia. No research was found to analyze those services in Latin America [10]. Therefore, this research will try to analyze this market, costumers' behavior, and contribute to the theory of streaming platforms. Moreover, this research will try to analyze variables such as content richness, perceived price, perceived ease of use, satisfaction level and brand equity that have been studied several times in other sectors as vehicles, baking, e-commerce, food, but not in the streaming platforms sector [10, 14] The objective of this research will be to analyze the relationship between the variables that were mentioned.

Another investigation problem is that this paper tried to collect information about all Latin-American countries, but the sample just reflects a closer view to the Peruvian market since a big part of the people who participated in the survey came from that country.

2   Literature Review and Hypothesis

The TAM model is defined as an influential socio-technical model that points to explain user acceptance of an information system [15] and users' behaviors [16] [17] that predict the use of these technologies [18] since, in the context of user acceptance of learning system, the intrinsic motivation is derived from emotional feelings such as pleasure or unhappiness [16, 19].

Initially, the TAM model was measured with two dimensions, perceived usefulness, and perceived ease of use, and it assumes the beliefs that both determine attitude and affect the intention to use [15]. Furthermore, some studies extended the TAM model includes new dimensions as user satisfaction, task-technology fit, content richness, vividness, and digital platform self-efficacy [16], and knowledge [20].

However, the present study will investigate two dimensions of the TAM model, content richness, and perceived use, because of its current relevance in the industry but adding perceived price, brand equity, and user satisfaction related to streaming platforms [10].

Content Richness
Content richness has had different meanings through time. Above all, this variable is related to learning resources and how users enhance their knowledge across them [21]. According to other authors, content richness is a variety of interesting content that brings satisfaction to the consumer [11]. This variable implies three dimensions: Relevance, timeliness, and sufficiency [22]. Furthermore, the authors mentioned clarify that the subscribers have a better disposition to interact with content richness than with other services as banking and home shopping as a result of the accessibility, ease of use, and time to learn of it [16].

As for the results of the studies, the variable content richness is affecting media use intention is varied by availability [23]. In the same way, more authors point out that new media acceptance is based on how the media can provide a good offering of information search opportunities and the variety of technological infrastructure available to users of the various media [24]. It is explained that content richness directly affects the consumer's disposition to use the media [23]. Along with it, user-perceived video quality has an impact on perceived usefulness through content richness [25].

Perceived Ease of Use
Perceived ease of use as the degree to which a person believes that using a particular system would be without any effort that is a finite resource that a person may allocate to the various activities for which he or she is responsible [15], it's emphasized that it is one of the factors that influence the intention to subscribe [26]. Ease of use has often been termed usability in the online context [27], and for an application or service to be accepted by the community easily, it must have an easy path so that the consumer experience is enjoyable [15].

Ease of use is the consumer's perception that buying on the Internet will involve a minimum of effort and this has to do with the design of the page and various factors that can complicate the user experience [12, 19]. Besides, there are some search functions like download speed, overall design, and organization that are among the key elements that affect usability [28].

According to previous studies carried out, they have verified that ease of use is a precedent of the perception of the quality of service of streaming services [27], attitude, and intention of use of users [29], and it has a positive effect on the intention to use technology and innovation [10].

Perceived Price

According to previous studies carried out, it is worth considering that price is one of the factors that influence the decision to acquire a product [10]. Furthermore, perceived price is defined as the person's judgment about the product's price level [13]. In this context, the perceived price is right according to the offered price, the consumer probably buys the product [30].

It is often said that the price level is related to people's perception [13] and the brand's value given by the market [31]. But some authors argue that this variable has a negative relation with the intention to use technology items since if the perceived price is too high or if the search cost is expensive, the consumer will look for the item on another websites to find similar products or services with a lower price [23]. What was mentioned before may be also seen as price consciousness causing the consumer develops a tendency to only pay low prices [32].

As a result of the aspects mentioned before if the consumer thinks that a store's products are cost-effective, they will buy it there because of the benefit since, in the market, the perceived price is even more important than the real product's price [23].

Brand Equity

Brands are the best at building images that make customers identify that specialty from among others [33, 34] and brand equity is the construct used to study customer's subjective and intangible assessments of the brand over and above its value [35, 36] through the brand awareness, perceived value, brand personality, brand association, and perceived uniqueness aspects [37]. Also, conceptualizes customer-based brand equity as the differential effect of brand knowledge on consumer response to the marketing of the brand [33].

It is mentioned that positive brand equity is the degree of marketing advantage a brand would hold over an unnamed or fictitiously named competitor [34]. Negative brand equity is the degree of marketing disadvantage linked to a specific brand [34], otherwise, high brand equity implies that customers have a lot of positive and strong associations related to the brand, perceive the brand is of high quality, and are loyal to the brand [38]. The key actionable levers of brand equity are brand awareness, attitude toward the brand, and corporate ethics [36].

As for the results of the studies, there is an associative relationship among the four consumer-based brand equities, where it is envisaged that consumer's perception of quality will be associated with their brand loyalty [39]. Also, it has been studied with variables like price promotion in terms of marketing strategies, as a result, it has a significant effect on brand equity [40], and price transparency is known to result in higher brand loyalty given a positive effect between price and brand equity [35]. Therefore, the following hypothesis is developed: H1: Perceived price positively affects brand equity.

Furthermore, it is known that the brand equity has been studied with items such as content quality in terms of interactivity and vividness in the social media market where, as a result, it has been shown that those variables have a weak positive connection since they are partially linked in the short term but completely supported in the long one [41].

In addition, the brand equity was measured with other variables as the media richness in the social networking services market but with a focus on Instagram given as a result that brand equity has a partial and positive connection to media richness [42]. Consequently, while reviewing some studies, the authors present the next hypothesis: H2: Content Richness positively affects brand equity.

On the other hand, brand equity has also been evaluated with an item as perceived ease of use in the mobile market. The results demonstrated that these two variables are related to each other since, in the long term, if the perceived ease of use increases, then the brand equity will have better results too [43]. Following the previous study, the authors present the next hypothesis: H3: Perceived ease of use positively affects brand equity.

User Satisfaction

User satisfaction is considered an important factor affecting the success of learning systems [44, 45], also previous researchers have found that user satisfaction is related to the use of the e-service for extended periods affects the success of learning systems [16]. However, a conceptual difference may exist, such that attitude relates to emotion regarding the use of a system, while satisfaction concerns the evaluation of the emotion based upon the outcomes achieved by the system [46, 47].

In addition, satisfaction is the evaluative belief that customers have the choice to use and buy streaming music on a website/app that is good, that it was the right choice and that the service provided what they needed [48]. Satisfaction is an affective state that is the emotional reaction to a product or service experience [14], depends on the situation, feelings, and attitudes that a person may have so that it can affect any system [49].

It is also mentioned that if customers are satisfied with the services received through the online system, it is likely they will keep using the system [50]. Otherwise, some e-commerce research has shown that satisfaction is associated with loyalty in business-to-consumer (B2C) e-commerce in countries like Malaysia and Indonesia [51].

Some investigations demonstrated that user satisfaction is a variable that has been studied with other items such as web design, personalization, and navigation in digital sectors as well as digital services and the results have been that these variables are highly correlated with each other [14]. Additionally, a study that involves multiple brands from different sectors, it finds that brand equity has a positive effect on customer satisfaction [52] Therefore, after reviewing those and other related studies, the following hypotheses of this study are presented: H4: Brand equity positively affects customer satisfaction (Fig. 1).

3   Methodology

Data Collection and Sampling

The present study adopted an online survey approach to empirically validate the proposed conceptual framework in a non-probability sampling. The survey bears in mind that the conceptual framework consists of five constructs (content richness, perceived ease of use, price, brand equity, and user satisfaction). It is important to note that this was

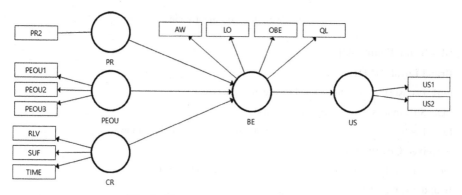

Fig. 1. The proposed conceptual framework

an online survey. There are key reasons to develop a survey in this way including the reduction of costs and time of it to be completed, the ease to reach large numbers of participants, and the possibility of providing anonymity to potential responders [53]. The study population was made up of subscribers to streaming platforms in Peru such as Netflix, Amazon Prime, Disney Plus and Spotify. An important criterion for selecting study participants was that they should have been using at least one streaming service for more than six months.

Development of Measurement Instrument

The study sample was 400 streaming users that live in Peru. The first part of the questionnaire used four fixed nominal scales to collect basic demographic information including age, gender, level of education, and use of streaming platforms. The second part employed direct measurement of the study variables. Furthermore, the sampling was further designed to exclude those with less experience in using streaming services so that the study could be controlled for any potential confounding effects that might result from the sampling.

To ensure content validity, the measurement instruments involved the adaptation of existing validated scales from prior studies. All the scale items were measured by a 7-point Likert scale with anchors ranging from 1 as "strongly disagree" to 7 as "strongly agree". The questionnaire was developed in Spanish but translated into English.

The multidimensional scale of Yoo & Donthu [38] was adapted to measure the brand equity variable depending on brand loyalty (three items), perceived quality (two items), brand awareness (five items), and overall brand equity (four items). Likewise, content richness, perceived ease of use, and user satisfaction dimensions were adapted from Lee & Lehto's scale [16] on depending on the perceived ease of use (four items), user satisfaction (three items), and content richness: relevance (three items), timeliness (three items), and sufficiency (three items). Finally, the scales of the perceived price variable were adapted from Yoo & Donthu [38] depending on three items.

Table 1. Measurement scales

BE - Brand Equity [38]
Brand Loyalty (LO)
LO1. I consider myself to be loyal to streaming services
LO2. Streaming services would be my first choice
LO3. I will not buy other brands if streaming brands are available at the store
Perceived Quality (QL)
QL1. The likely quality of streaming services is extremely high
Brand awareness (AW)
AW1. I can recognize streaming services among other competing brands
AW2. I can quickly recall the symbol or logo of streaming services
AW3. I am aware of streaming services
Overall brand equity (OBE)
OBE1. Although other streaming brands have the same features as the one I use, I would not change my current streaming platform
PEOU - Perceived ease of use [16]
PEOU1. My interaction with streaming services is clear and understandable
PEOU2. I think it easy to get streaming services to do what I want it to do
PEOU3. Using streaming services requires little mental effort
CR - Content richness [16]
Relevance (RLV)
RLV1. Streaming services have valuable content that is tailored exactly to my needs
Timeliness (Time)
TME1. Streaming services have the useful content I need
Sufficiency (SUF)
SUF1. I am satisfied with the valuable content that the streaming platform I use offers me
SUF2. Streaming services give me the content I need
US - User satisfaction [16]
US1. I am satisfied using streaming services
US2. I like to use streaming services
PR - Perceived Price [38]
PR1: The price of the streaming service is high
PR2: The price of the streaming service is low

4 Results Evaluation

Reflective Measurement Model Assessment

The evaluation of the PLS-SEM results begins with an assessment of the reflective measurement models (i.e., BE, CR, PEOU, PR, and US). From the original scales, items that did not comply with the model measures were eliminated, such as LO1. (I consider myself to be loyal to streaming services), LO3. (Will does not buy other brands if streaming brands are available at the store), AW2. (I can quickly recall the symbol or logo of streaming services), AW3. (I am aware of streaming services), SUF1. (I am satisfied with the valuable content that the streaming platform I use offers me), and PR1. (The price of the streaming service is high).

Table 1 shows the results and evaluation criteria outcomes. It was noticed that all reflective measurement models meet the relevant assessment criteria required. All the outer loadings were above 0.70, and even most parts of the indicators were above 0.90 which makes them close to 1. This indicated that all the indicators and latent variables show an efficient level of reliability too. In addition, they were all above 0.50 as it was required to prove their support for the measures' convergent validity. BE showed the lowest result with 0.580, and CR had the highest one with 0.846. These measurement models matched the relevant assessment criteria. Composite reliability had a value between 0.846 and 0.943 which indicated that they are above the minimum level of 0.70.

Also, Cronbach's alpha values were placed between 0.729 and 0.909, which is acceptable. Finally, all ρA values met the 0.70 thresholds. These results suggest that the construct measures of BE, CR, PEOU, PR and US exhibit sufficient levels of internal consistency and reliability since their results came from 0.771 to 0.912.

The PR construct is not included in the reflective into this measurement model assessment, because it had only one item. This explained why for this construct indicator data and latent variable scores resulted in 1.

The next analysis showed the degree of shared variance between the model's variables. As it was shown, the constructs' discriminant validity was established because each construct was higher than its correlation with another construct. For example, BE has a 0.761 value, and its correlation with CR, PEOU, PR, and US is lower, and placed in a range of 0.581 and 0.086. This scenario was repeated with the other constructs which indicated positive results for the model (Table 2).

All the results were clearly below the conservative threshold of 0.85 (Table 3). The results showed that this HTMT confidence intervals didn't include value 1. The results show that the HTMT confidence intervals include values between 0.022 and 0.756. They are all different from 1. It was exposed that discriminant validity has been established. The highest one was the result of PR and CR latent variables (0.814).

For the analysis of R2, its variations between 0 to 1 were considered, where higher levels indicate greater predictive precision [54] The results of the study showed the values 0.391 and 0.338 for the variables Brand Equity (BE) and User Satisfaction (US) respectively, where according to some authors, as a rough rule of thumb, the R^2 values of 0.75, 0.50, and 0.25 can be considered substantial, moderate, and weak [55, 56]. Therefore, based on our results obtained, R^2 had a weak intensity level for both cases (Table 5).

Table 2. PLS-SEM assessment results of reflective measurement models

Latent variable	Indicators	Internal consistency reliability				
		Loadings	AVE	Composite reliability	Reliability Rho A	Cronbach's alpha
		> 0.70	> 0.50	> 0.70	> 0.70	0.70–0.90
BE	AW_1	0.752	0.580	0.846	0.771	0.758
	LO_2	0.841				
	QL_3	0.726				
	OBE_4	0.721				
CR	RLV_1	0.911	0.846	0.943	0.912	0.909
	SUF_2	0.929				
	TIME_3	0.929				
PEOU	PEOU_1	0.891	0.742	0.896	0.848	0.827
	PEOU_2	0.892				
	PEOU_3	0.798				
PR	PR_1	1	1	1	1	1
US	US_1	0.919	0.784	0.879	0.772	0.729
	US_2	0.850				

Table 3. Formell Larcker Criterion

	BE	CR	PEOU	PR	US
BE	0.761				
CR	0.495	0.920			
PEOU	0.513	0.308	0.861		
PR	0.086	0.106	0.005	1.000	
US	0.581	0.672	0.456	0.019	0.885

Finally, the value of $f2$ was calculated in which as a guideline, $f2$ values of 0.02, 0.15, and 0.35, respectively, represent small, medium, and large effects of an exogenous latent variable (Cohen, 1988). According to the results, all the hypotheses represent small effects, in which BE and US obtained a value of 0.037 being the smallest effect of the group. In the same way, values were obtained for CR and BE and PEOU and BE of 0.050, and for PR and BE of 0.039 (Table 4).

Table 4. HTMT value

	BE	CR	PEOU	PR	US
BE					
CR	0.591				
PEOU	0.629	0.351			
PR	0.153	0.111	0.024		
US	0.756	0.814	0.573	0.022	

Table 5. Path coefficients of the structural model and significance testing results

	Path coefficient	95% BCa confidence interval	Significant (p < 0.05)?	$f2$ effect size
H1- PR - > BE	0.045	[-0.034–0.115]	No – 0.248	0.039
H2 -PEOU - > BE	0.400	[0.295–0.496]	Yes –0.00	0.050
H3 -CR - > BE	0.367	[0.265–0.465]	Yes –0.00	0.050
H4 -BE - > US	0.581	[0.505–0.646]	Yes –0.00	0.037

5 Conclusions

The objective of the research was to check whether the variables of content richness, perceived ease of use, price, and brand equity directly influence user satisfaction in the streaming platform market where there are brands as Netflix, Amazon Prime, HBO, and more as the main competitors.

The data described in this work concludes that the proposed conceptual framework the variables CR and PEOU influence brand equity, and there is an influence between brand equity and user satisfaction. The first hypothesis wanted to check if there was a relationship between the variables perceived price and brand equity, in which the results verified that they do not influence each other as in other investigations such as the ones made about e-commerce platforms and banking applications where the results showed those variables were highly related [16, 38]. Users value more the quality of the content and its ease of use before the perceived price. Other investigations show that there is a variable related to price (price promotion) that does affect brand equity in an online and physical store market: "The study has found a significant causal relationship between PP and all the elements of BE of the online stores. In physical stores [...] repeated or long-term use of PPs have adverse effects on some of the elements of BE" [57]. On the other hand, [4] it was demonstrated by a study that perceived price and its dimensions (price detail, and perceived value) are determinative to create a strong association with the brand, but not in the long term.

Based on this investigation, perceived price is not as functional as the other variables. This could be due to once the person is subscribed to the platform the price goes to the background, that is, the price would be relevant at the time of subscription. It may also be because some streaming platforms offer more than one pricing plan and the perceptions disperse even more than with the other variables. Brands can work efficiently into their pricing strategies; the customers give more value to the content they are receiving.

With respect to the second hypothesis, it was wanted to check if there was a relationship between content richness and brand equity. This means that users value the quality of the content offered by the different platforms, increasing the brand equity of the platform. Brand equity has been studied with items as content quality in terms of vividness in the social media market where, as a result, it has been shown that those variables have a positive connection in the long term [10, 42].

The third hypothesis affirmed the influence between perceived ease of use and brand equity in streaming platforms. It was demonstrated that these two variables are related to each other since, in the long term, if the perceived ease of use increases, the brand equity will have better results too in the mobile market [43]. The brand equity variable is very important since we relate it to user satisfaction. Also, has been shown that if the perceived ease of use and perceived usefulness are great, they can positively influence the customers' attitudes and increase mobile brand equity [58–60].

The proposed hypothesis is that brand equity positively affects user satisfaction is fulfilled in this study. According to previous studies that involve multiple brands from different sectors, it finds that brand equity has a positive effect on customer satisfaction [52, 61]. More specifically, some authors have agreed with this hypothesis after their investigations into another online market as the e-Learning brands: "We find a positive influence of consumer satisfaction on brand equity [...] customers look more into benefits and the conditional values offered by the e-Learning provider, [...] users generally take up courses from the providers which provide more value for money and have a good brand name" [62].

This indicates that brand equity improves customer satisfaction, but it's also important to see its effect on more traditional markets like the private health clinics where the author indicates that: "From a business practice standpoint, customer experience strategic management analysis recommends growing customer-based brand equity aimed at sparking emotional connections capable of supporting successful business-customer relationships." [63].

Finally, this investigation is useful for the companies and the business environment because it shows which aspects of streaming platforms a customer values the most and it is more urgent to put efforts on to gain success in this or another similar technology market. It may also help consultants to evaluate the dimensions of the streaming market, and identify the reasons behind the success of some companies such as Netflix in comparison to its competitors. This investigation may also be relevant to contrast with the results of new features some streaming brands are developing and the future improvements they will have. In addition, since the sample shows the Peruvian consumer behavior, it can be helpful for video streaming brands that decide to get into this geographic market.

Regarding the limitations of the research, it was identified that it was only focused on one country, which is recommended to expand both the geographical area and the number of study participants in South America. Thus, another geographical limitation in this study was sourced investigated focused on foreign markets, and these countries are limited to diverse cultures, customs, lifestyles, and income levels, therefore, a distinct perspective is proposed focused on a new context. Also, a recommendation for future research would be to be able to study not only streaming video platforms but also music platforms like Spotify and Apple Music, and videogames streaming platforms like Twitch to have a global vision of all the streaming markets and how the variables relevant change per each market dimension. Also, consider updates from streaming platforms such as interactive shows.

References

1. Mora Astaburuaga, A., Prado Seoane, J.A.: Estudio Comparativo de las Condiciones Generales de la Contratación de las Principales Plataformas de Reproducción en Streaming Cláusulas Potencialmente Abusivas. Revista Electrónica del Departamento de Derecho de la Universidad de La Rioja 1(15), 176–177 (2017). https://doi.org/10.18172/redur.4167
2. Zuckerman, N., Rose, J., Rosenzweig, J., Sheerin, A., TMank, T., Schmitz, L.-K.: Streaming Viewers Aren't Going Anywhere, New York: The Boston Consulting Group (2021)
3. Haridas, H., Deepak, S.: Customer perception towards networked streaming service providers with reference to amazon prime and netflix. Int. J.of Recent Technol. Eng. 9(1), 513–517 (2020). https://doi.org/10.35940/ijrte.A1911.059120
4. Kumar, J., Gupta, A., Dixit, S.: Netflix: SVoD entertainment of next gen. Emerald Emerging Markets Case Studies 10(3), 10–12 (2020). https://doi.org/10.1108/EEMCS-04-2020-0108
5. Wayne, M.: Netflix, Amazon, and branded television content in subscription. Media Cult. Soc. 40(5), 725–741 (2018). https://doi.org/10.1177/0163443717736118
6. Cornelio-Marí, E.M.: Mexican melodrama in the age of netflix: algorithms for cultural proximity. Comunicación y Sociedad 17(1), 1–27 (2020). https://doi.org/10.1177/174960202110 44444
7. Lotz, A.: In between the global and the local: mapping the geographies of Netflix as a multinational service. Int. J. Cult. Stud. 24(2), 190–200 (2020). https://doi.org/10.1177/136787792 0953166
8. Statista, V.S.: (SVoD) in Statista. Statista Inc., Hamburg (2021)
9. Schauerte, R., Feiereisen, S., Malter, A.J.: What does it take to survive in a digital world? resource-based theory and strategic change in the TV industry. J. Cult. Econ. 45(2), 263–293 (2020). https://doi.org/10.1007/s10824-020-09389-x
10. Hasan, V.A.: Analisis Faktor-Faktor Yang Mempengaruhi Willingness To Subscribe: Telaah Pada Layanan Video On Demand Netflix. Ultima Management: Jurnal Ilmu Manajemen 9(1), 22–38 (2017). https://doi.org/10.31937/manajemen.v9i1.595
11. Dimmick, J., Albarran, A.: The role of gratification opportunities in determining media preference. Mass Communication Review 21(3), 223–235 (1994)
12. Moore, G., Benbasat, I.: Development of an instrument to measure the perceptions of adopting an information technology innovation. Inf. Syst. Res. 2(3), 192–200 (1991)
13. Weniger, S.: User adoption of IPTV: a research model. In: 23rd Bled eConference eTrust: Implications for the Individual, Enterprises and Society, Slovenia (2010)
14. Al-Kasasbeh, M.M., Dasgupta, S., AL-Faouri, A.H.: Factors Affecting E-Service Satisfaction. Communications of the IBIMA 2011(1), 1–12 (2011). https://doi.org/10.5171/2011.547937
15. Davis, F.: Perceived usefulness, perceived ease of use, and user acceptance of information technology. MIS Q. 13(3), 319 (1989)
16. Lee, D., Lehto, M.: User acceptance of YouTube for procedural learning: an extension of the technology acceptance model. Comput. Educ. 61(1), 193–208 (2013). https://doi.org/10.1016/j.compedu.2012.10.001

17. Venkatesh, V., Thong, J., Xu, X.: Consumer acceptance and use of information technology: extending the unified theory of acceptance and use of technology. MIS Q. **36**(1), 157–178 (2012). https://doi.org/10.1287/isre.2.3.192

18. Surendran, P.: Technology acceptance model: a survey of literature. Int. J. Business Social Res. **2**(4), 175–178 (2012). https://doi.org/10.18533/ijbsr.v2i4.161

19. Gefen, D., Karahanna, E., Straub, D.: Trust and TAM in online shopping: an integrated model. MIS Q. **27**(1), 51–90 (2003). https://doi.org/10.2307/30036519

20. Ban, H.-K., Ellinger, A., Hadjimarcou, J., Traichal, P.: Consumer concern, knowledge, belief, and attitude toward renewable energy: an application of the reasoned action theory. Psychol. Mark. **17**(6), 449–468 (2000). https://doi.org/10.1002/(SICI)1520-6793(200006)17:6%3c449::AID-MAR2%3e3.0.CO;2-88

21. Tung, F.-C., Chang, S.-C.: Nursing students' behavioral intention to use online courses: a questionnaire survey. Int. J. Nurs. Stud. **45**(9), 1299–1309 (2008). https://doi.org/10.1016/j.ijnurstu.2007.09.011

22. Jung, Y., Perez-Mira, B., Wiley-Patton, S.: Consumer adoption of mobile TV: examining psychological flow and media content. Comput. Hum. Behav. **25**(1), 123–129 (2009). https://doi.org/10.1016/j.chb.2008.07.011

23. Lin, A., Chen, N.-C.: Cloud computing as an innovation: percepetion, attitude, and adoption. Int. J. Inf. Manage. **32**(6), 533–540 (2012). https://doi.org/10.1016/j.ijinfomgt.2012.04.001

24. Alan, R., Rubin, R.: Interface of personal and mediated communication: a research agenda. Crit. Stud. Media Commun. **2**(1), 36–53 (1985)

25. Park, S., Kang, S.-U., Zo, H.: Analysis of influencing factors on the IPTV subscription. Inf. Technol. People **29**(2), 419–443 (2016). https://doi.org/10.1108/ITP-05-2014-0100

26. Sathye, M.: Adoption of internet banking by australian consumers: an empirical investigation. Int. J. Bank Marketing **17**(1), 324–334 (1999)

27. Zeithaml, V., Parasurarnan, A., Malhotra, A.: Service quality delivery through web sites: a critical review of extant knowledge. J. Acad. Mark. Sci. **30**(4), 362–375 (2002). https://doi.org/10.1177/009207002236911

28. Swaminathan, V., Lepkowska-White, E., Rao, B.: Browsers or buyers in cyberspace? an investigation of factors influencing electronic exchange. J. Computer-Mediated Communication **5**(2), JCMC523 (1999)

29. Cebeci, U., Oguzhan, I., Hulya, T.: Understanding the intention to use netflix: an extended technology acceptance model approach. Int. Review of Manage. Marketing **9**(6), 152–157 (2019). https://doi.org/10.32479/irmm.8771

30. Chiang, C.-F., Jang, S.S.: The effects of perceived price and brand image on value and purchase intention: leisure. J. Hosp. Leis. Mark. **15**(3), 49–69 (2007). https://doi.org/10.1300/J150v15n03_04

31. Netemeyer, R., et al.: Developing and validating measures of facets of customer-based brand equity. J. Bus. Res. **57**(2), 209–224 (2004). https://doi.org/10.1016/S0148-2963(01)00303-4

32. Vazifedoost, H., Charsetad, P., Akbari, M., Kbari, J.: Studying the Effects of Negative and Positive Perceptions of Price on Price Mavenism. Research J. Applied Sciences, Eng. Technol. **5**(15), 3986–3991 (2013). https://doi.org/10.19026/rjaset.5.4465

33. Keller, K.: Conceptualizing, measuring, and managing customer-based brand equity. J. Mark. **57**(1), 1–22 (1993). https://doi.org/10.1177/002224299305700101

34. Berry, L.: Cultivating service brand equity. J. Acad. Mark. Sci. **28**(1), 128–137 (2000). https://doi.org/10.1177/0092070300281012

35. Kim, N., Kim, G., Rothenberg, L.: Is honesty the best policy? examining the role of price and production transparency in fashion marketing. Sustainability (Switzerland) **12**(17), 2–18 (2020). https://doi.org/10.3390/su12176800

36. Lemon, K., Rust, L.: Zeithaml and Valarie, "What drives customer equity? Marketing Management **1**(20–25), 10 (2001)

37. Aaker, D.A.: Managing brand equity. J. Mark. **56**(2), 125–128 (1991). https://doi.org/10.2307/1252048
38. Yoo, B., Donthu, N., Lee, S.: An examination of selected marketing mix elements and brand equity. J. Acad. Mark. Sci. **28**(2), 195–211 (2000). https://doi.org/10.1177/0092070302840022002
39. Pappu, R., Quester, P., Cooksey, R.: Consumer-based brand equity: improving the measurement – empirical evidence. J. Product Brand Manage. **14**(3), 143–154 (2005). https://doi.org/10.1108/10610420510601012
40. Chi, H.-K., Yeh, H.-R.: The Influences of advertising endorser, brand image, brand equity, price promotion, on purchase intention- the mediating effect of advertising endorser. J. Global Business Manage. **5**(1), 224–233 (2009)
41. Estrella-Ramón, A., García-de-Frutos, N., Ortega-Egea, J.M., Segovia-López, C.: How does marketers' and users' content on corporate facebook fan pages influence brand equity? Electron. Commer. Res. Appl. **36**(1), 1–25 (2019). https://doi.org/10.1016/j.elerap.2019.100867
42. Hasim, M.A., Ishak, M.F., Hamil, N.N.A., Ahmad, A.H., Suyatna, P.N.: Media richness on instagram influences towards consumer. Dinasti Int. J. Education Manage. Social Science (DIJEMSS) **1**(6), 1001–1011 (2020)
43. Sheng, M.L., Teo, T.S.: Product attributes and brand equity in the mobile domain: the mediating role of customer experience. Int. J. Inf. Manage. **32**(2), 139–146 (2012). https://doi.org/10.1016/j.ijinfomgt.2011.11.017
44. Shee, D., Wang, Y.-S.: Multi-criteria evaluation of the web-based e-learning system: a methodology based on learner satisfaction and its applications. Comput. Educ. **50**(3), 894–905 (2008). https://doi.org/10.1016/j.compedu.2006.09.005
45. Wu, J.-H., Tennyson, R., Hsia, T.-L.: A study of student satisfaction in a blended e-learning system environment. Comput. Educ. **55**(1), 155–164 (2010). https://doi.org/10.1016/j.compedu.2009.12.012
46. Liao, C., Palvia, P., Chen, J.-L.: Information technology adoption behavior life cycle: toward a technology continuance theory (TCT). Int. J. Inf. Manage. **29**(4), 309–320 (2009). https://doi.org/10.1016/j.ijinfomgt.2009.03.004
47. Oliver, R.L., Linda, G.: Effect of satisfaction and its antecedents on consumer preference and intention. J. Mark. Res. **8**(1), 88–93 (1981)
48. Cronin, J., Brady, M., Hult, T.: Assessing the effects of quality, value, and customer satisfaction on consumer behavioral intentions in service environments. J. Retail. **76**(2), 193–218 (2000). https://doi.org/10.1016/S0022-4359(00)00028-2
49. Bailey, J., Pearson, S.: Development of a tool for measuring and analyzing computer user satisfaction. Manage. Sci. **29**(5), 530–545 (1983). https://doi.org/10.1287/mnsc.29.5.530
50. Xiao, L., Dasgupta, S.: Measurement of user satisfaction with web-based information systems: an empirical study. In: Eighth Americas Conference on Information Systems, Washington (2002)
51. Khatib, S.M., Seong, L.C., Chin, W.S., Hong, K.: Factors of e-service quality among Malaysian Millennial streaming service users. Int. J. Economics Manage. **13**(1), 63–77 (2019)
52. Torres, A., Tribo, J.: Customer satisfaction and brand equity. J. Bus. Res. **64**(1), 1–8 (2011). https://doi.org/10.1016/j.jbusres.2010.12.001
53. Van, M., Jankowski, N.: Conducting online surveys. Qual Quant **40**(1), 435–456 (2006). https://doi.org/10.1007/s11135-005-8081-8
54. Sarstedt, M., Hair, J., Hopkins, L., Kuppelwieser, V.: Partial least squares structural equation modeling (PLS-SEM): an emerging tool in business research. Eur. Bus. Rev. **26**(2), 106–121 (2014). https://doi.org/10.1108/EBR-10-2013-0128

55. Henseler, J., Sinkovics, R., Ringle, C.: The use of partial least squares path modeling in international marketing. **20**(1), 277–319 (2009). https://doi.org/10.1108/S1474-7979(2009)0000020014

56. Hair, J., Ringle, C., Sarstedt, M.: PLS-SEM: indeed a silver bullet. J. Marketing Theory Practice **19**(2), 139–151 (2011). https://doi.org/10.2753/MTP1069-6679190202

57. Bhakar, S., Bhakar, S., Bhakar, S.: Impact of price promotion on brand equity model: A study of online retail store brandsImpact of price promotion on brand equity model: a study of online retail store brands. J. Content, Community Communication **10**(6), 124–142 (2020). https://doi.org/10.31620/JCCC.06.20/10

58. Ambler, T., Edell, J., Lane, K., Lemon, K.: Relating brand and customer perspectives on marketing management. J. Service Research **5**(1), 13–25 (2002). https://doi.org/10.1177/1094670502005001003

59. Homer, M.: Perceived quality and image: when all is not rosy. J. Bus. Res. **61**(1), 715–723 (2008). https://doi.org/10.1016/j.jbusres.2007.05.009

60. Konecnik, M., Gartne, W.: Customer-based brand equity for a destination. Ann. Tour. Res. **54**(2), 400–421 (2007). https://doi.org/10.1016/j.annals.2006.10.005

61. Iglesias, O., Josep, R.: How does sensory brand experience influence brand equity? Considering the roles of customer satisfaction, customer affective commitment, and employee empathy. J. Business Research **96**(1), 343–354 (2019). https://doi.org/10.1016/j.jbusres.2018.05.043

62. Ray, A., Kumar, P., Chakraborty, S., Dasguta, S.: Exploring the impact of different factors on brand equity and intention to take up online courses from e-Learning platforms. J. Retail. Consum. Serv. **59**(1), 1–12 (2021). https://doi.org/10.1016/j.jretconser.2020.102351

63. Cambra-Fierro, J.J., Fuentes-Blasco, M., Huerta-Álvarez, R., Olavarría, A.: Customer-based brand equity and customer engagement in experiential services: insights from an emerging economy. Serv. Bus. **15**(3), 467–491 (2021). https://doi.org/10.1007/s11628-021-00448-7

Data Intelligence

Augmented Virtual Reality in Data Visualization

Pedro Alves[1] and Filipe Portela[1,2(✉)] ⓘ

[1] Algoritmi Research Centre, Universidade do Minho, Guimarães, Portugal
a80539@alunos.uminho.pt, cfp@dsi.uminho.pt
[2] IOTech – Innovation on Technology, Trofa, Porto, Portugal

Abstract. As a result of data being collected daily at high speeds, it becomes extremely important for organizations to analyze it in real-time to be a decisive factor in successful decision-making. Therefore, real-time decision based on real-time generated data is seen by organizations as a decisive factor for successful decision-making. However, organizations have difficulties making a real-time analysis of this data due to its complexity, quantity, and diversity. Studying the problems inherent in processing these large amounts of data is insufficient. The way this data is visualized and presented to the end-user is crucial. Thus, this paper focuses on exploring Augmented Reality capabilities to optimize the traditional data visualization methods to support real-time decision-making. This technology offers a wide range of data visualization possibilities that can become quite attractive to the human being. A series of results inherent to this paper can be identified, namely analyzing the challenges and limitations of implementing augmented virtual reality systems for data visualization, the development of 1 augmented reality data visualization module in a real-world data science platform, based on a cross-analysis of 4 dashboards, the analysis of its impact relative to a traditional two-dimensional data visualization module through a questionnaire that serves as the first proof of concept.

Keywords: Augmented virtual reality · Big data · Data visualization · Real-time decision making

1 Introduction

The evolution of the Internet of Things has allowed huge volumes of data to be generated from devices such as sensors, and this has led to a key question "How can this information be used significantly?" [1]. Business Analytics (BA) systems involve using data science capabilities and technologies to collect, transform, analyze, and interpret data to support decision-making [2]. Those capabilities and technologies comprise data warehousing, reporting, online analytical processing, dashboarding, data visualization, predictive modelling and forecasting systems. BA systems provide value to organizations by improving business processes, supporting decision-making [2] and providing a competitive advantage [3].

As a result of data being collected daily at high speeds, it becomes extremely important for organizations to be able to analyze it in real-time to obtain crucial information for the business and consequently reach better decisions in good time [4].

T. Guarda et al. (Eds.): ARTIIS 2022, CCIS 1675, pp. 289–302, 2022.
https://doi.org/10.1007/978-3-031-20319-0_22

Organizations see real-time decision based on real-time generated data as a decisive factor for successful decision-making. However, organizations have difficulties in making a real-time analysis of this data due to its complexity, quantity, and diversity. However, it is not enough just to study the problems inherent in processing these large amounts of data in real-time. It is also very important to analyze and understand the best practices of data visualization and how data should be disposed to facilitate and simplify the decision-making processes. It is interesting to look for new concepts to optimise how data can be analyzed and visualized, and Augmented Virtual Reality (AVR) can be one of them. Augmented Virtual Reality offers a wide range of possibilities for technological solutions, which in turn can become quite attractive to the human being simply by being able to create a different reality or add information to its reality.

The main goal inherent to this paper focuses on the particular interest in Data Science and Augmented Virtual Reality, as well as its exploration, to understand to what extent it is possible to acquire new knowledge combining the area of information systems, web programming, augmented virtual reality, and data science. This paper also focuses on implementing an augmented reality data visualization module in a real-world data science platform, understanding the impact of this kind of development on the decision-making process and understanding to what extent it benefits the end-user. The experiments provided in this article are running under a research project in the area of smart cities that will use this approach to show their data.

To achieve these goals, a literature review was carried out in the Background section through the concepts of Big Data, Data Science, Visual Analytics and Augmented, Virtual and Mixed Reality to better understand the concepts and how they impact the development of this paper. Next, in the Research Methods section, it is possible to find the necessary methods that were used in this project and a description of how they were applied.

In the Case Study section, the data science platform's architecture inherent to this project was analyzed to understand how and where the implementation of the augmented reality data visualization module should be developed. In section five, the implementation of an augmented reality module for data visualization in a real-world data science platform was addressed as well as all the challenges and limitations associated with this development. Lastly, in the Discussion and Conclusion sections, a simple and concise questionnaire was conducted with the participation of the platform users to assess the impact of the augmented reality module, to discuss the achieved results and to understand how relevant these implementations are and whether they make sense in other contexts.

2   Background

This section aims to summarize the state of the art regarding the fields associated with the topics of this paper. Literature reviews are important in supporting the identification of a research topic, question or hypothesis, identifying the literature to which the research will contribute, and contextualizing the research within that literature, building an understanding of theoretical concepts and terminology, facilitating the building of a bibliography or list of the sources that have been consulted and analyzing and interpreting results. Thus, the concepts covered in this chapter are Big Data, Data Science, Visual Analytics, and Augmented, Virtual and Mixed Reality.

2.1 Big Data

Big Data's main objective is to make the information useful for the decision-making process. Data is being generated at an exponential rate, but that does not mean there are better algorithms and technologies. This confirms what Peter Norvig, Google's director of search, said: "We don't have better algorithms. We just have more data." [5]. Therefore, Big Data has become so important. Through the precepts of volume, variety, speed, veracity and value, Big Data can store many diverse pieces of information, quickly analyze them, and even check their veracity, which allows it to add value to the decision-making process, making it more effective and efficient.

Those main characteristics of Big Data are also defined as the three "V" s of Big Data: variety (refers to structured, unstructured and semi-structured data that is gathered from multiple sources), velocity (refers to the speed at which data is being created in real-time) and volume (refers to huge 'volumes' of data that are being generated daily from various sources like social media platforms, business processes, machines, networks, human interactions, etc.) [4].

There are still many organizations that have doubts about what really defines the concept of Big Data and where the limits of such a project lie. For this reason, it is advantageous to resort to frameworks such as the Big Data Project Assessment Framework (BigDAF) [6], which aims to help organizations to classify their Big Data project according to variety, velocity and volume and to understand if there is a need to invest in technologies and machines that support big data architectures, which will consequently avoid unnecessary costs [7].

2.2 Data Science

In recent years, there has been a huge explosion in the amount of data available, and since then, the problem has moved from being a lack of data to figuring out how to derive value from it [8]. Data Science emerged to make data relevant and to be able to gain knowledge [9]. According to Steele [10], the purpose of real-time analysis is to enable faster actions in the same proportion as data is received.

Data Science is the computational science of extracting knowledge from raw data, which is then communicated effectively to obtain value. Through this knowledge, specialists in the field have access to the predictive insight they need to drive change and achieve desired outcomes [11].

In summary, a sensible position can be taken that high-quality data, together with the analytical tools in a secure environment, can provide valuable benefits in the commercial sector, education, government, and many other areas [12].

2.3 Visual Analytics

The results of insight creation capability, whether they are intended to facilitate real-time decision-making or intended for the learning process, need to be provided to users in such a manner that they can be best utilized.

Visual analytics is related to data visualization, information visualization, scientific visualization, and knowledge visualization. It refers to the use of computer graphics to create a visual representation of large collections of information.

Thomas and Cook [13] define visual analytics as the science of analytical reasoning facilitated by visual interfaces to synthesize information and derive insights from massive, dynamic, ambiguous and often conflicting data, to detect the expected and discover the unexpected, to provide timely, defensible and understandable assessments and, lastly, to communicate assessments effectively so actions can be taken.

2.4 Augmented, Virtual and Mixed Reality

Although visual analytics has seen a huge stimulus in terms of its capabilities in the last thirty years, additional research is still needed to improve the decision-making process, including exploring new ways of presenting data.

Augmented Virtual Reality (AVR) is a surging area in this thematic, and due to this, it should be explored to take advantage of its benefits in data visualization [14].

Augmented Reality (AR) is a computer-based technology that combines the digital and real worlds. It works on the computer vision of real-world surfaces and objects detected by systems like object recognition, plane detection, facial recognition or movement tracking. Sutherland [15] describes AR as a technology that enhances the interaction between digital items while letting us see our real-world surroundings.

Sutherland [15] describes Virtual Reality (VR) as a technology that uses software and headset devices to replace one's view from the real world to a digitally created scene. Using full-coverage headsets completely blocks out our surroundings and shuts out the physical world, simulating actions and allowing interactive encounters with virtual scenes and components.

Mixed Reality (MR) is a combination of AR and VR. It is also specified as Hybrid Reality as it blends real-world and digital elements. While it is a technology used for mixing the physical and virtual world, the best side of MR is the realistic interaction between the users and the digital objects [16].

Concluding, AR, VR and MR are promising technologies that will soon take human-computer interaction to another level. Although there are challenges and limitations, applications for these technologies have already been found in the military, education, healthcare, industry and gaming fields.

Bellow, in Table 1, a simple representation of these technologies' main differences is presented.

Table 1. Main differences between AR, VR and MR.

	AR	VR	MR
Immerse users in an entirely virtual world		X	
Create an overlay of virtual content but can't interact with the environment	X		
Create virtual objects that can interact with the actual environment			X

2.5 Augmented Virtual Reality Challenges

From birth, people started exploring the world using visual capabilities honed over centuries. According to Olshannikova et al. [14], there are certainly important challenges and limitations related to the implementation of augmented virtual reality systems:

- Application development is the first one because, to operate with visualized objects, it is necessary to create a new interactive system for the user. However, one of the main issues regarding this direction of development is the fact that implementing effective gestural and voice interaction is not a trivial matter. To this end, there is a need to develop machine learning algorithms [14].
- Applying specific equipment and virtual interfaces is necessary for the implementation of such an interactive system. Currently, there are optical and video see-through HMDs that merge virtual objects into the real scene view. Both have issues regarding distortion and resolution of the real scene, delay, viewpoint matching and engineering and cost factors [14].
- Tracking and recognition algorithms are a down factor because of their dubious performance, which causes some challenges. The position and orientation values of virtual items are one of them since virtual objects are dynamic and must be re-adjusted [14].
- Perception and cognition can be represented as another challenge. The level of computer operation is high but still not sufficiently effective in comparison to human brain performance, even in cases of neural networks. In this sense, simplicity in information visualization must be achieved to avoid misperceptions and cognitive overload [14].
- Using these technologies can often cause a mismatch of virtual and physical objects.
- In an AR environment, virtual images integrate real-world scenarios. Consequently, there is a mismatch of virtual and physical distances that may result in incorrect focus, contrast, and brightness of virtual objects in comparison to real ones [14].
- With the current technology development level, visualized information is presented mainly on screens. Unfortunately, users can experience a lack of comfort while using these systems, caused by a low display resolution and high graininess [14].

In conclusion, the challenges of Augmented Virtual Reality are associated not only with current technology development but also with human-centric issues. It is worthwhile to note that those factors should be considered simultaneously to achieve the best outcome for the established industrial field.

3 Material and Methods

For the development of this project, two research methodologies were used, namely Case Study and Design Science Research.

The use of the Case Study is related to the fact that this research was conducted on an existing real-world data science platform, so it became necessary to study and explore its architecture, identify the problem and motivation and define the objectives of a solution prototype [17].

According to Peffers [18], the DSR approach is composed of six phases: identify the problem and motivation, define the objectives of a solution, design and development, demonstration, evaluation, and communication. However, it is possible to establish a link between problem and objectives formulation through the Case Study method and phases one and two of the DSR method. Therefore, this project was divided into two phases.

The first phase, following the Case Study method (Fig. 1), consisted in analyzing the previously mentioned data science platform to identify the problem and define the objectives and motivations that support the development of a solution.

Thus, the identified problem can be reduced to a simple question "Can data visualization be optimized using augmented reality capabilities to support real-time decision-making?" the defined objective is to develop a data visualization module using augmented reality, and the motivation inherent to this project is the acquisition of new knowledge combining the area of information systems, web programming, augmented virtual reality and data science.

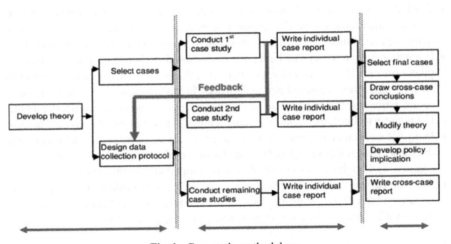

Fig. 1. Case study methodology

The second phase uses the DSR method to solve the identified problem and achieve the defined objectives through the Case Study method, enabling the development, demonstration, evaluation, and communication of a solution prototype, which consists of phases 3 to 6 of the DSR method (Fig. 2).

The Design and Development phase begins after the problem and the objectives have been identified, and this is where the actual development of the solution comes in. The Demonstration phase is about testing and validating the functionality of the prototype in some suitable context. The testing process involves the system rather than testing each component separately. In this step, users of the aforementioned platform tested the augmented reality module for data visualization, and a questionnaire was also conducted to assess the impact of the solution.

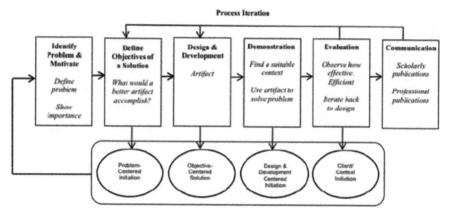

Fig. 2. Design science research methodology

The Evaluation phase involves comparing the objectives of the solution with the results observed in the demonstration phase. Depending on the nature of the problem, evaluation can take many forms. Thus, the prototype was evaluated using the fulfilment of the objectives. The communication phase refers to this document and involves communicating the problem and the importance of the artefact, its usefulness and effectiveness to researchers and other relevant target audiences.

Regarding the tools, the team explored and combined a set of programming languages and libraries to achieve the final prototype like node.js, MySQL, python, MongoDB Vue.js, AMCharts, and AR.js, A-Frame and Web XR. Section four gives a brief presentation impact of each one on the project.

4   Case Study

As this is a continuation project, it is necessary to address the data science platform inherent to this case study, which is entitled ioScience [19, 20]. The platform gave rise to the development of a patent on a method for performing offline data analysis [21]. ioScience can be described as a model, an architecture, and a web-based solution aiming to provide Data Science as a Service by retrieving information from heterogeneous data sources, processing it, and passing it through an analytical layer toward a visualization cross-platform web application. Consequently, it is important to analyze the platform's architecture to understand how and where the implementation of the augmented reality data visualization module should be developed.

As can be seen below in Fig. 3, the architecture inherent to this project is composed of 4 layers:

- Data Layer (1),
- Analysis Layer (2),
- Caching Layer (3),
- Visualization Layer (4).

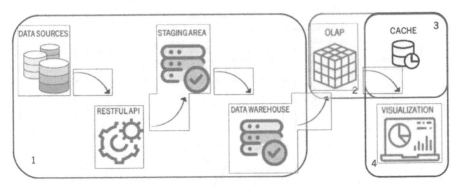

Fig. 3. Platform's architecture

In a brief analysis of Fig. 3,

- **Data Layer** includes all the necessary mechanisms to drive data from data sources to the Data Warehouse through the ETL process, which aims to improve data quality, and the Staging Area loading, which aims to refresh the data and reduce data loading time.
- **The analysis Layer** includes the necessary mechanisms for the construction of the OLAP cubes, which are multidimensional arrays of data.
- **Caching Layer** consists of a bridge between the analysis layer and the visualization layer. This intermediate layer includes mechanisms that make it possible to have a "cache database" that allows limited offline views through data.
- **The visualization Layer** includes all dashboard developments based on data stored in the caching layer. This layer involves the user's perception of the value of the work developed. Therefore, this element is considered of great importance because if the value of the solution is not well understood, it means that the whole solution is a failure. Therefore, in addition to a good dashboard development, it is necessary to develop a set of functionalities to provide interactivity and perspective on the data. Thus, the development of an augmented reality module for data visualization can be an important factor in enforcing this goal.

The novelty of this approach was included in the visualization layer. This layer offers a new way for the user to consult the data and see the dashboards. The user can explore the RVA module in three dimensions and have a real experience with an OLAP cubes analysis. For example, they can consult a cube by exploring its three dimensions. When compared with non-AR solutions, this approach also can add other features to the data visualization and create more data levels or even add dashboards to physical objects (e.g. QR Codes, books or walls).

After analyzing the platform's architecture, it was necessary to understand which technologies are being used for its development. Thus, Table 2 discusses these technologies and provides a brief explanation of their use so that it is possible to understand the environment where this implementation of augmented reality applied to data visualization was carried out.

Table 2. Technologies concerning the data science platform and the AR implementation.

Layer	Technology	Description
Data	MongoDB	Used by the platform for the registration of unstructured data
	MySQL	Based on a relational data structure. Supports the platform's data warehouse
	Python	Used to support all the ETL (Extract, Transform and Load) Processes
Analysis	NodeJs	The platform's API and all microservices are built using this technology to support part of the logical processes
Caching and visualization	VueJs	The platform's web interface is built on Vue.js since it has cross-platform support
	AmCharts	AmCharts is used in the platform to support dashboard development
	Ar.js	AR.js is a lightweight library for Augmented Reality on the Web, coming with features like Image Tracking, Location-based AR and Marker track. AR.js was used to support the implementation of augmented reality on the platform's data visualization modules
	A-Frame	A-Frame complements AR.js and WebXR. It is a web framework for building virtual reality experiences
	WebXR	WebXR provides the necessary interfaces to build augmented and virtual reality experiences as it is a tool to access AVR devices, including sensors and head-mounted displays since WebVR was deprecated in July 2020

5   Augmented Reality Module

Vision is one of the most important senses, and so it is necessary to understand how to take advantage of this potential provided by the human being. However, when it comes to analyzing and visualizing data to support decision-making, traditional dashboards provide a small amount of data compared to the capabilities of human vision, which develops about thirty-six thousand bits of information per hour [22].

Augmented Reality (AR) applied to data visualization solves this problem simply because the development of dashboards on a computer or mobile phone is limited by screen space, whereas using augmented reality provides a field of vision of approximately one hundred and fifty degrees [22]. This way, it is possible to develop dashboards with more information to take greater advantage of human vision and consequently improve decision-making.

Then, an augmented reality data visualization module was implemented on a real-world data science platform, as mentioned previously. To do this, Ar.js was chosen, which is a lightweight library for Augmented Reality on the Web, coming with features like image tracking, location-based AR and marker tracking. This library was chosen since it is the only open-source library with a strong community, despite being quite recent.

After choosing the library and performing some tests with the three types of implementations of augmented reality mentioned above, marker tracking was selected. This choice is based on the ideology of the developed web application and eliminatory factors concerning the other types of integration since the image tracking was very unstable, and the location-based is not aligned with the needs of the platform.

Next, the installation of the library and all the necessary configurations were carried out with the support of the documentation provided by Ar.Js [23]. However, several problems arose, and most of them were solved using the issues feature provided by Github, which allows developers to discuss a certain problem until they reach a solution. Nonetheless, the use of custom markers by pattern recognition has not yet been resolved by both the community and the development team of the Ar.js library to this date, only allowing the use of predefined markers.

Despite the challenges, the implementation was carried out by aggregating all the data perspectives presented on the platform's dashboards and creating objects to complement the data visualizations, such as text and images. For this purpose, A-frame was used, which is a web framework for building virtual and augmented reality experiences.

A-Frame is not just a 3D scene graph or a markup language. The core is a powerful entity-component framework that provides a declarative, extensible, and composable structure to three.js, used by Ar.js.

Finally, the module was successfully developed, taking advantage of the benefits of using augmented reality for data visualization and decision-making. It was possible to cross-analyze the data and all the business indicators defined in the platform.

The AR implementation appears after scanning the marker with the device's camera, as follows in Fig. 4. It is worth noting that, although the marker used is static, the data that feeds the presented charts are dynamic and updated in the background.

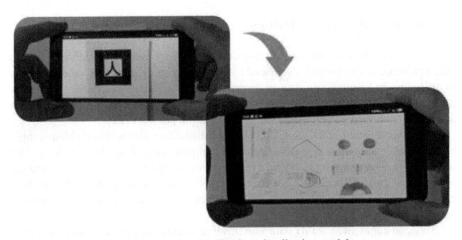

Fig. 4. Augmented reality data visualization module

It is relevant to mention that the augmented reality development shown in Fig. 4 has a background color behind its composing elements. If a background color were not applied to the image provided by the camera, the reading of the augmented reality dashboard would become less perceptible due to the contrast of colors.

6 Evaluation

As the first proof of concept, to discuss the achieved results and to understand how relevant these implementations are and whether they make sense in other contexts, a simple and concise questionnaire was conducted with the participation of the platform users to assess the impact of the augmented reality module. It should be noted that, in the first phase, participants received a brief explanation regarding the purpose and functionalities of the platform, and, in the second phase, they explored and interacted with the developed platform/solution and the same conditions of use were ensured for all participants. After using the platform, they were asked to answer the questionnaire.

Thus, all the 37 platform users who participated in the questionnaire, all aged between 20 and 30 years old, except one of the participants who presented himself as 42 years old. Of the 37 participants, 16 are female (43%), and 21 are male (57%). Each of the participants completed the questionnaire in its entirety, providing a total of 37 responses, all of which were classified as valid responses for analysis. Table 3 represents the questions that compose the questionnaire and brief analysis of the answers.

Table 3. Questionnaire responses analysis

Question	Possible response	
Is there a need to constantly try to improve the way data is visualized and analyzed to improve decision-making?	Yes	70%
	No	30%

The general opinion is that it is important to continue to improve the way data is analyzed and visualized so that decision-making can be improved. It was also concluded that the use of augmented reality in data visualization should be considered and that, according to the participants' opinion, it brings some advantages by looking across all data and all performance indicators, improving the decision-making process.

Thus, it can be assumed that traditional data analysis and data visualization is not enough and that these topics should be continuously explored and optimized. And although the augmented reality is a path that should be explored, the community should keep up the effort to reach other solutions by continuing to explore this theme, considering that there are other methods that should be properly tested within the data visualization and manipulation spectrum.

Nonetheless, augmented reality is a recent technology, still under development, and due to this fact, there is a misperception of the technology, as something new and disruptive tends to convey the image that it is something complex to implement, which, despite the challenges, is not the case with the libraries described previously in this paper.

7 Conclusion

To conclude, it is possible to make a positive overall balance of the work developed since a data visualization module using augmented reality was developed and new knowledge combining the area of information systems, web programming, augmented virtual reality, and data science was acquired.

Table 4 presents a summary of the work carried out through some metrics, quantifying what was used for the results achieved during the development of this project. So, as can be observed, this approach allowed to create four dashboards and one AR module.

Table 4. Quantification of the achieved results

Usage metrics	Count	Development metrics	Count
Programming languages	2	Queries	18
Libraries	3	KPIs	7
Frameworks	2	Dashboards	4
Databases	2	Augmented Reality Module	1

A Proof of concept was designed, and then it was evaluated by the users To show the feasibility of the solution. The evaluation process was conducted online using forms, achieved the participation of 37 users and received 70% of positive feedback.

Moreover, it is possible to respond positively to the identified problem through the Case Study method, i.e., "Yes, it is possible to optimize data visualization using augmented reality capabilities to support real-time decision making". Additionally, the questionnaire addressed in the Discussion section served as the first proof of concept and validation of the solution. In this regard, it is possible to conclude that there is a need to constantly try to improve the way data are analyzed to optimize decision-making and that traditional dashboards are not enough to analyze data and make decisions.

Thus, the implementation of augmented reality to improve this thematic is highly relevant as it is a disruptive technology that brings a series of advantages, such as ease of data analysis due to greater use of the human eye and the visual field. However, it should be noted that this technology is still in the development stage, and therefore the challenges associated with its implementation are increased.

Considering that this is a continuation project, it is necessary to make a series of in- internal improvements to increase the value of the platform; however, it is also necessary to continue the development and exploration of the augmented reality data visualization module to increase its value both at the analytical level and at the user interaction level. Nevertheless, the overall balance is positive, as the solution developed is scalable and can be easily integrated into other solutions. In the future, this approach will be applied in an actual project named ioCity, where these developments are being made.

Acknowledgements. This work has also been developed under the scope of the project NORTE-01-0247-FEDER-045397, supported by the Northern Portugal Regional Operational Programme (NORTE 2020), under the Portugal 2020 Partnership Agreement, through the European Regional Development Fund (FEDER).

References

1. Simmhan, Y., Perera, S.: Big Data Analytics Platforms for Real-Time Applications in IoT, Rao, B.P., Rao, S. (eds.). Springer India, New Delhi (2016)
2. Shanks, G., Bekmamedova, N., Willcocks, L.: Using Business Analytics for Strategic Alignment and Organisational Transformation (IJBIR), Yeoh, W., (ed.). Deakin University, Australia (2013)
3. Davenport, T., Harris, J.: The Dark Side of Customer Analytics. Harvard Business Review, US and Canada (2007)
4. Eaton, C., Deroos, D., Deutsch, T., Lapis, G., Zikopoulos, P.: Understanding Big Data: Analytics for Enterprise Class Hadoop and Streaming Data. McGraw-Hill, New York (2012)
5. Norvig, P.: Google's Zeitgeist (2011)
6. Alpoim, Â., Lopes, J., Guimarães, T.A.S., Portela, C.F., Santos, M.F.: A framework to evaluate big data fabric tools. In: Azevedo, A., Santos, M.F. (eds.) Integration Challenges for Analytics, Business Intelligence, and Data Mining, pp. 180–191. IGI Global, Hershey, PA (2021). https://doi.org/10.4018/978-1-7998-5781-5.ch009
7. Portela, F., Lima, L., Santos, M.F.: Why big data? Towards a project assessment framework. Procedia Comput. Sci. **98**, 604–609 (2016). ISSN 1877–0509. https://doi.org/10.1016/j.procs.2016.09.094
8. Loukides, M.K.: ProQuest. What Is data science? O'Reilly Media, Sebastopol (2012)
9. Cady, F.: The Data Science Handbook. John Wiley & Sons Inc., Hoboken, NJ (2017)
10. Steele, B., Chandler, J., Reddy, S.: Algorithms for Data Science. SpringerInternational Publishing, Cham (2016). https://doi.org/10.1007/978-3-319-45797-0
11. Pierson, L., Porway, J.: Data Science for Dummies, 2nd edn. John Wiley and Sons Inc., Hoboken, NJ (2017)
12. Stanton, J., Graaf, R.: Introduction to Data Science (2013)
13. Thomas, J., Cook, K.: Illuminating the Path: The Research and Development Agenda for Visual Analytics. IEEE CS Press (2005)
14. Olshannikova, E., Ometov, A., Koucheryavy, Y., Olsson, T.: Visualizing big data with augmented and virtual reality: challenges and research agenda. J. Big Data **2**, 1–27 (2015)
15. Sutherland, I., Sproull, B., Harris, D.: Logical Effort: Designing Fast CMOS Circuits. Morgan Kaufmann Publishers (1999)
16. Speicher, M., Hall, B., Nebeling, M.: What is Mixed Reality? 2 5 (2019)
17. Lubbe, S.: Development of a case study methodology in the information technology (IT) field in South Africa: a step-by-step approach. South African Journal of Information Management (2003)
18. Peffers, K., Tuunanen, T., Rothenberger, M., Chatterjee, S.: A Design Science Research Methodology for Information Systems Research (2007)
19. Fernandes, G., Portela, F., Santos, M.F.: Towards the development of a data science modular solution. In: 2019 7th International Conference on Future Internet of Things and Cloud Workshops (FiCloudW), pp. 96–103 (2019). https://doi.org/10.1109/FiCloudW.2019.00030
20. Ferreira, V., Portela, F., Santos, M.F.: A practical solution to synchronise structured and non-structured repositories. In: Rocha, Á., Adeli, H., Dzemyda, G., Moreira, F., Ramalho Correia, A.M. (eds.) WorldCIST 2021. AISC, vol. 1368, pp. 356–365. Springer, Cham (2021). https://doi.org/10.1007/978-3-030-72654-6_35

21. Portela, F., Fernandes, G.: Method to execute offline data analysis. Patent 116393 (2022)
22. Advanced Eye Care Center. https://advancedeyecarecenter.com/2016/03/31/interesting-facts-about-eyes/. Accessed 12 Jan 2022
23. Ar. Js. https://ar-js-org.github.io/AR.js-Docs/. Accessed 21 June 2021

Big Data Analytics to Measure the Performance of Higher Education Students with Online Classes

Francisco Campos[1], Teresa Guarda[1] ⓘ, Manuel Filipe Santos[1] ⓘ, and Filipe Portela[1,2(✉)] ⓘ

[1] Algoritmi Research Centre, University of Minho, 4800-058 Guimarães, Portugal
{mfs,cfp}@dsi.uminho.pt
[2] IOTECH—Innovation on Technology, 4785-588 Trofa, Portugal

Abstract. The pandemic that hit the world in 2020 created a transition period from classes to an e-learning environment. In this type of teaching, a lot of data is generated about different topics that can help improve the class's daily routine. This paper presents an online case study performed during the 1st semester of the 2020/2021 school year. Online data were analysed in order to understand the students' behaviour and the course's success regarding the TechTeach methodology. This data was collected through the ioEduc platform, used in every class, and stored information about the evaluation and day-to-day work. With this research work, it was possible to verify a strong relationship between high attendance and class participation (online activity) with excellent academic performance. In this study, 77% of the students could take a final grade above 15, most of whom attended all classes.

Keywords: Big data · Unstructured data · Data analysis · OLAP cube

1 Introduction

In today's world, the quantity of data produced and available is larger than at any point in time. This event is called "Big Data". The main importance of Big Data consists in the potential to improve efficiency using a large volume of data of several types. If Big Data is used the right way, organisations can get a better view of their business and be more successful in different areas [10]. According to Sowmya & Suneetha [11], "For modern industry, data generated by machines and devices, cloud-based solutions, business management has reached a total volume of more than 1000 Exabytes annually and is expected to increase 20-fold in the next ten years". This, by itself, should not be a problem; however, a large amount of this data is not used properly or lost along the way. To solve this problem, new tools, technologies, and techniques need to be used to transform and analyse this data so that it can help with decision-making and be accessible to users. This can also be applied to services like education.

The existence of data from thousands of students who have similar learning experiences but in very different contexts gives information that was not possible before

T. Guarda et al. (Eds.): ARTIIS 2022, CCIS 1675, pp. 303–315, 2022.
https://doi.org/10.1007/978-3-031-20319-0_23

for studying the influence of different contextual factors on learning and learners [12]. Analysing the data created from an e-learning approach allows a better description of the reality of the environment being taught and room for improvements and changes that can optimise the teaching experience.

The primary goals of this case study were to assess the viability of TechTeach in an e-learning context. Then, study the results from a real case conducted in a university environment that can help translate this methodology's success and its tools and approaches that aim to make the learning experience a lot easier for students and teachers. This article also aims to understand the main variables that can affect students' performance (in terms of class interaction) and how and which needs to be upgraded for future experiences.

The paper is divided into six sections: the Introduction, which presents the work, and the Background, providing the paper's topics and related works. Then, Sect. 3 exposes all the methods and tools used in this case study. The case study is described in Sect. 4, and the results achieved are analysed in the Discussion Section. Finally, the conclusion of the work is provided, and the future work is explained.

2 Background

2.1 Big Data

During the last few years, society has witnessed a big increase in our ability to collect data [13]. This enormous data collection has surpassed our capability to process and store this information. In that order, Big data represents this "information that can't be processed or analysed using traditional processes or tools" [14].

Big data can be defined by seven different characteristics: Velocity, Variety, Volume, Veracity, Visualization, Variability, and Value. These characteristics define the velocity at which data comes into organisations, the variety of types of data that exist, the volume of data that keeps growing, the veracity of the data that is being analysed, the visualisation of the data graphically, the way that data changes with time and finally, the value of the data to the organisation.

2.2 Data Warehouse and OLAP

A Data warehouse combines concepts and technologies that allow organisations to manage and store historical data obtained from different types of applications. [1]. Data Warehousing is an approach to integrating data from multiple different sizes, distributed databases, and other data sources [2].

According to Han [3], it can also be classified as a "subject-oriented, integrated, time-varying, non-volatile collection of data that is used primarily in organisational decision making" [3].

OLAP (On-Line Analytical Processing) is a group of data analysis techniques created for data analysis in data warehouses [4]. In OLAP, data is represented as a cube, where each cell contains measures representing facts and contextual information around, also called dimensions [5]. The OLAP needs to logically organise and process data in a multidimensional mode and illustrate and analyse data in a multidimensional way [6].

3 Materials and Methods

Although this work is not a typical Big Data project, it meets some of Big Data characteristics [15]. It addresses different types of datasets (structured and non-structured) collected in real-time, providing massive data.

3.1 TechTeach

According to Portela [8], the TechTeach paradigm is a new concept of learning and teaching in higher education that "allows the creation of a B-learning environment and uses gamification to motivate the students to participate in the class". This paradigm includes interactive classes, quizzes and surveys, and project-based learning, among others. This concept aims to show "how information systems and new technologies can contribute to reengineering processes and digital transformation" [8].

3.2 Kimball Lifecycle

The Kimball Lifecycle is a methodology used for developing Data Warehousing systems. The life cycle of the DW project is based on four principles that help to focus on the business, build an adequate information infrastructure, make deliveries in significant increments, and provide a solution that fulfils all the requirements [7]. This methodology follows the phases described below [7]:

- **Project Planning**: Phase where it's defined the goals and scope of the project, including risks and first approaches for the problem;
- **Definition of Business Requirements**: Phase that includes all the steps and processes made in order to get to know the business, meet with personnel, know about the industry and the main competitors;
- **Dimensional Modelling**: Phase where the business process is chosen, and the level of granularity of the dimensions is established, identifying the metrics and facts tables;
- **Design**: Phase where all of the previous steps come together, and the user can access the solution, accessible from the business user's desktop;

3.3 Tools

The system used for this paper was the python programming language due to many libraries available regarding data processing and visualisation techniques. It was the chosen language, mainly because of the number of libraries available that assist developers in several tasks, such as Pandas for data processing and matplotlib for data visualisation.

MySQL and MongoDB were the technologies used for data storage in terms of data warehousing and data collection.

4   Case Study

This section explains the context, challenges, and approaches used in the case study.

This article has the main objective of answering the following research questions: "Is TechTeach a viable option for education purposes?" and "Is the student grade directly related to the different variables of a course?".

The main goal of this article is to develop a group of dashboards that make it possible to consult the information about the data that was processed and that can answer the research questions.

4.1   Context

The data used in this project was collected from a real case from the 5th of October in 2020 to the 29th of January in 2021. It was from the subject "Web Programming" taught by Professor Filipe Portela.

According to Portela [9], This course had the value of 10 ECTS (European Credit Transfer and Accumulation System), and 168 students were registered in it, from where 90% of them were active participants (attended more than 50% of the classes). These classes were divided into three different formats: Theoretical (T), Theoretical practice (TP), and laboratory practices (LP), and used different learning approaches and techniques for each one of them. Since this was with online classes only, the researcher used different platforms for the e-learning process and to collect data from it: ioEduc, ioChat, Zoom, and Kahoot! And HackerRank. Google Analytics was also used to collect data as well as the students' responses to surveys made during the course. The evaluation for this course was divided into two different types: A project in teams that were made during theoretical practice and laboratory practice classes, and continuous evaluation methods to evaluate professors, students, and the course. It included weekly quizzes, a card system, and three individual mini-tests during the year to evaluate different types of knowledge.

The data for this project includes the evaluation process as well as the day-to-day records, class by class. Some of this data is structured in tables within a database (relational) called "webitclo_ioeduc". This database has 57 tables and contains almost all the data. However, not all of these tables were used, only the ones that are the most relevant for this project and for this theme. The selected tables made a total of 11 different tables (19% of the total tables).

Besides these tables, another part of the data about the quizzes that were made in each class (records of each question and answer) is stored in json files in a MongoDB database (non-relational database). It has three different collections where it was used only the file "ioquiz_answers" containing the data from the answers for each quiz.

In order to achieve the proposed goals, the definition of a set of business requirements was distinctly discussed with the different parts that interacted in the project and compared with similar work to understand the focal points and the biggest needs during the whole process. Relative to the project plan, it was developed and implemented following the proposed methodologies and considering the time-space scheduled for its development.

4.2 Software Architecture

At this stage, the main objective is to develop a simple framework that allows the integration of various technologies from different sources and with different functionalities.

Figure 1 represents the architecture of this prototype. It starts by collecting the data from the "ioEduc" platform. This data was stored in MySQL and MongoDB databases. Once the data is collected, it starts the process of extracting, transforming and loading (ETL) to different dimensions and facts tables that make the data ready and available for analysing and applying machine learning algorithms. Every step of the way was made using the Visual Studio Code characteristics that made it the best solution for it and the Python coding language. Once this process is completed, the results are represented in a simple manner for every user to understand. The visualisation section was also made using Visual Studio Code with python libraries like Seaborn and Matplotlib.

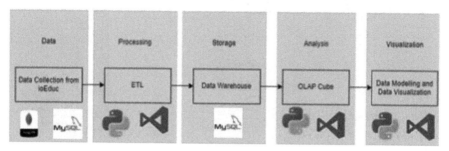

Fig. 1. Software architecture

4.3 Multidimensional Model

After establishing the software architecture, a data warehouse creation was needed, where it was possible to organise the data in the best way possible to accomplish the analytical and predictive goals. Firstly, a group of business requirements was set that guaranteed every area of the targeted data was included. Once this phase was set, it was defined that five different dimensions were needed for this project:

- Time – Dimension that allows controlling every record temporally;
- Course – Where all the data about classes will be stored;
- Assessment – Where every assessment will be stored;
- Student – Where student personal data will be stored;
- Moment – Where information about evaluation moments is stored;
- Once the dimensions that would be a part of the data warehouse were decided, it was also defined that this model would have two facts tables:
- Attendancefacts – Table that receives the students' and classes' primary keys and stores every attendance-related fact, like logins, presences, number of benefits, and penalties;

- Evaluationfacts – Table that receives the student, moment and assessment primary keys and that will store every evaluation-related fact, the grade in each evaluation moment, every assessment made to the students, or if it applied to the rescue system;

Figure 2 represents the multidimensional model that resulted from this process.

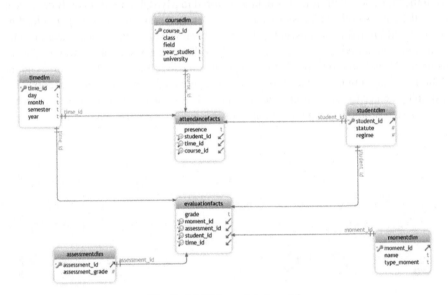

Fig. 2. Multidimensional model

4.4 Data Preparation

In order to get the best information possible, a group of processes was made for the correction and creation of attributes that suited the goals of this project.

Starting with the unstructured data, in order to get the quizzes that got the most answers given, a projection was made to filter the title of the quizzes on each record, as well as their time. Following it by filtering to the dates that are being analysed.

In terms of structured data, it was needed the carry out a treatment to inconsistencies that were encountered in the tables. These inconsistencies were missing data and uncoded data. The user_id was turned into a hexadecimal number, and the students with missing evaluation moment data were filtered out of the system.

4.5 OLAP Layer

The data processing and development of the data warehouse have provided the possibility for creating a visualisation environment, with the aim of helping the understanding and analysis of the data by the prototype user. This environment is based on the data that comes from the facts tables, dimensions and metrics that are contained in the OLAP cube. Then, to meet the different needs, a group of indicators was designed to facilitate the development of the viewing environment and to answer the main questions. The indicators created were:

- Total number of goals - Sum of benefits given to a student;
- Total number of penalties - Sum of penalties given to a student;
- Redeem - Indication if the student applied to the rescue system or not;
- Total assessment grade - Sum of all the grades given to the student by his group during the evaluation moments;
- Total Logins - Sum of all logins made by a student;
- Total Presences - Sum of all presences in classes by a student;
- Total number of quizzes answered - Number of total quizzes answered by the student;
- Final grade - Final grade by student, calculated using a formula: 25% x grade_MTs + 15% x grade_quizzes + 60% x grade_project

4.6 Numbers

This section reflects the main results in terms of analysis, with a numerical description of the several variables studied.

Statute

Firstly, it a study was made on how a total of 166 students were divided in terms of the statute. The analysis represents, as expected, a vast majority of full-time students (E), which means students that have to study as their sole occupation, with 149 (92%) as their statute. It was also possible to know that two students had a physical disability statute (EPD), while 1 was the class delegate (DLG) and the other a Student Association Member (EDAEE). On the other hand, 13 (7%) students were student-workers (TE), a statute given to students studying and working simultaneously. Figure 3 represents the statute distribution.

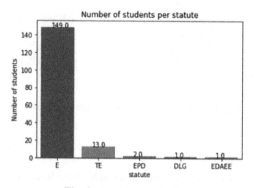

Fig. 3. Statute distribution

Card and Rescue System

After studying the distribution of students in the different statutes, it was possible to analyse the impact of the card system in class.

- **Card System** - The card system is where the teacher gives the students white (positive) or yellow (negative) cards. When the limit number of positive or negative cards was achieved, consequences would happen. In this case, two positive cards would give a blue card that translates into an extra point in the group project. On the other hand, three negative cards (or penalties) result in a red card that translates to the student having a grade of 0 in the group project. In this case, six students received one positive card, and five received the full two positive cards, resulting in a blue card. In terms of penalties, seven students received a single warning, and one student had two warnings. Finally, three students received the limit of 3 warnings which resulted in a red card and consequent failure in the group project. Figure 4 represents the distribution in terms of penalties during the year.
- **Rescue System** - The rescue system was a tool available to failed students (grade = − 1) on the MT2 moment who thought they deserved more. The professor analysed the situation, and, in the case of acceptance, they allowed them to continue with a penalty of fifteen per cent (15%) in the final MT grade. After analysis, it was concluded that 11 students (6%) used this option, and three of them still ended up with a negative grade in MT2, failing the course. On the other hand, eight students were able to go through by using this system. Additionally, from the students that were able to be saved, they were able to bounce back and achieve at least a grade of 16, corroborating the success of this system.

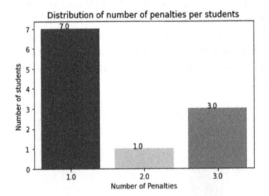

Fig. 4. Penalties distribution in the card system

Attendance and Logins

In a more generalist analysis, it is important to understand how the number of presences in classes and logins on the platform changed during the semester.

- **Presences** - For this, the total presences in classes per week was calculated. It includes Theoretical (T), Theoretical practice (TP) and laboratory practices (LP) classes. The results made it possible to see that the first few weeks (3,4, and 5) were when the students most attended classes, with over 420 attendances registered in all of them, when the average number of attendances per week is 350. The first two weeks had also a low number of presences both TP and LP classes started later. After this, a drop happened during the semester, going up again in the second to last week, which can be explained by the final grades period. The final weeks (from 14 to 16) were occupied with exams which means that no classes were given in that period. Concluding, there is a big percentage of students that attended more than 50% of the classes, with the maximum number of attendances recorded being 36 (100% of the classes) while the minimum was 12, meaning that every student attended at least, one-third of the classes.

- **Logins** – In the same analysis, the distribution of logins in the platform was studied per week. The number of logins follows the same path as the number of presences with a big number of records (over 3000 when the average number of logins per week is 2371) in weeks 3,4, and 5 with a decrease in number after that. The weeks with a smaller number of logins follow the same pattern and explanation as the presences graphic (start of classes and exam period). In contrast, the weeks with the highest number of logins are the ones where the evaluation moments were scheduled.

After mixing both variables, it was possible to see that they are directly related. Students with a high number in one variable also have a high number in the second one, as represented in Fig. 5.

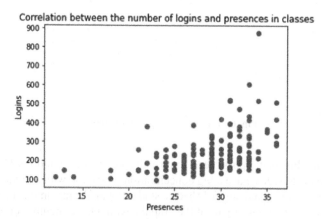

Fig. 5. Relation presences/logins

Grades

Following to the next topic, it is important to understand how each of these variables affects the final grade of students, which is the most important aspect of this project.

- **Relation between logins and grades** - good grades are usually related to a high number of logins. Still, they especially show that bad grades (or failed students) are related to a low number of platform interactions, meaning a lack of interest or motivation in the course.

- **Relation between presences and grades** – Both variables are related, with the highest grade having the biggest attendance rate, and it is also noticeably the big number of high grades with a grade over 16. Failed students also had a good attendance rate which means that this factor is not really related to the failing aspect but more about the excellence in terms of grades.

In order to resume the results, it was made a study splitting the grades into four different groups:

- A for the students with grades in the top 25%
- B for students with grades between the top 25% to 50%
- C for students with grades between the top 50% and 75%
- D for the students with the worst 25% grades

With this division, it was possible to investigate the relation between these four groups and the number of presences in classes of each group.

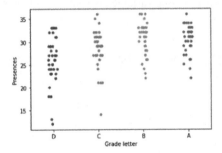

Fig. 6. Presences per group of students

By analysing Fig. 6, it is possible to confirm the previous assumptions. Groups A and B, with the highest grades, have a big concentration on the top with a higher number of presences. On the other hand, group D had no students with the maximum attendance and several students in the inferior part of the graphic, with a lower number of attendances, compared to the average.

Evaluation Moments
Then, it was time to understand how students were holding each phase. The three different moments were:

- **Quizzes**: Quiz made in the final of every class. The final grade for this component is calculated with the average of the grade in each quiz and in how many of them the student has participated in. It weighs 15% of the final grade. Through the results, it was possible to see that 68 (44%) had completed 100% of the quizzes (11) and most of the students (79%) had at least nine quizzes completed. Checking each quiz individually, it was possible to conclude that every quiz had at least 114 students

(75%) participating in it, while the best performing quiz (T2 – HTML) had a total of 149 students (97%). 52% of the students achieved at least a grade of 15 as the final quiz grade.

- **MTs**: Three mini tests during the year to test students in sine areas. MT2 needs to be positive, or the student not go through to the rest of the course or can apply to the rescues system, as explained earlier. It weighs 25% of the final grade. Only two students failed during this component, while 91 students (53%) had a grade over 15. This evaluation component can be understood as successful and the rescue system since it saved eight students from failing the class and allowed them to pass the course.
- **Group Project**: Project made during the year, divided into groups with evaluation in checkpoints and final presentation. It weighs 60% of the final grade. Only three students, the same that got three penalties during the year, consequently had a grade of 0 in the group project. Most of the students had a very good grade (>15), with 5 of them getting the biggest grade possible, 20. The results show that the checkpoints created to help students during the project were a big help, and they ensured that almost no group was left alone in terms of work management.

Finally, applying the formula to get the final grade, only three students failed the course (the same that got the three penalties), while the rest was able to complete it, with 77% of them with a grade over 15. This distribution is represented in Fig. 7.

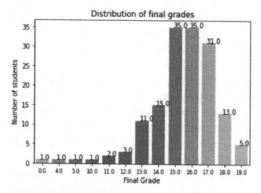

Fig. 7. Distribution of final grades

5 Discussion

Considering the whole theme of this article and from a critical perspective, the dashboards developed allowed the professors to reach the following conclusions:

- Attendance in classes and participation in the platform is directly related to better grades;
- 77% of students were capable of getting a grade over 15;

- The attendance in classes is bigger at the beginning of the semester and at the end, during the evaluation period
- The card system created an impact on the final grade. Three students received three penalties and a red card consequently, failing the course, while five students got two benefits and a blue card, which allowed them to get an extra point in the project;
- The rescue system had a total of 11 students applying and saved 73% of them (8), allowing them to finish the course;
- Every student attended at least 1 class in 3;
- Every quiz made during the semester had at least a 75% participation rate, and 44% of the students participated in every quiz, of a total number of 11.

With these numbers, it is possible to confirm the success in terms of classes, with high values in attendance and logins, which confirms a good motivation from the students and the appliance of the right mindset in terms of effort. The relation between grades and these high values confirms good teaching by the professors and understanding from the students in the tools used during the year (classes and ioEduc) since the students were able to reach good grades when these were used correctly.

6 Conclusions

To answer the questions, which served as a motivational basis for the development of the project, "Is TechTeach a viable option for education purposes" and "Is the student grade directly related to the different variables of a course?", a case study was developed on the evaluations and evaluative method. It was applied to the discipline of Web programming in the Integrated Master's course in Information Systems Engineering and Management regarding the academic year 2020/2021.

After analysing the results, it is possible to say that TechTeach achieved a level of success in terms of education purposes with a high number of grades of over 15 (77%) and high attendance and participation in the different activities by the students. It was also proven that the student grade is directly related to their behaviour in classes, with both attendance and participation directly correlated to better results in terms of grades.

Concluding this article, it is possible to say that the goals set for this project were accomplished successfully. However, this project's future consists of web mining techniques that can help to create models using data mining algorithms to complement this project with predictive analytics, bringing new intel for the researchers in the area. The goal is also to extend past the Web Programming course for other areas of work and schools in order to improve the education sector as a whole.

Acknowledgements. This work has been supported by FCT – Fundação para a Ciência e Tecnologia within the R&D Units Project Scope: UIDB/00319/2020. The data used was collected from the ioEduc platform and anonymised and provided by IOTECH.

References

1. Santoso, L.W.: Data warehouse with big data technology for higher education. Procedia Comput. Sci. **124**, 93–99 (2017)

2. Theodoratos, D., Sellis, T.: Data warehouse configuration. In: VLDB, vol. 97, pp. 126–135 (1997)
3. Chaudhuri, S., Dayal, U.: An overview of data warehousing and OLAP technology. ACM SIGMOD Rec. **26**(1), 65–74 (1997)
4. Han, J.: OLAP mining: an integration of OLAP with data mining. In: Proceedings of the 7th IFIP, vol. 2(6), pp. 1–9 (1997)
5. Etcheverry, L., Vaisman, A.A.: QB4OLAP: a new vocabulary for OLAP cubes on the semantic web. In: Proceedings of the Third International Conference on Consuming Linked Data, vol. 905, pp. 27–38 (2012). CEUR-WS.org
6. Zhao, H.L.: Application of OLAP to the analysis of the curriculum chosen by students. In: 2008 2nd International Conference on Anti-counterfeiting, Security and Identification, pp. 97–100. IEEE (2008)
7. Delgado, A., Rosas, F., Carbajal, C.: System of business intelligence in a health organisation using the kimball methodology. In: 2019 IEEE CHILEAN Conference on Electrical, Electronics Engineering, Information and Communication Technologies (CHILECON), pp. 1–5. IEEE (2019)
8. Portela, F.: Techteach—an innovative method to increase the students engagement at classrooms. Information (Switzerland) **11**(10), 1–32 (2020). https://doi.org/10.3390/info11100483
9. Portela, F.: Towards an engaging and gamified online learning environment-a real casestudy. Information **13**(2), 27–28 (2022). https://doi.org/10.3390/info13020080
10. Alsghaier, H., Akour, M., Shehabat, I., Aldiabat, S.: The importance of big data analytics in business: a case study. Am. J. Softw. Eng. Appl. **6**(4), 111–115 (2017)
11. Sowmya, R., Suneetha, K.R.: Data mining with big data. In: 2017 11th International Conference on Intelligent Systems and Control (ISCO), pp. 246–250. IEEE (2017)
12. Baker, R.S.J.D.: Data mining for education. Int. Encycl. Educ. **7**(3), 112–118 (2010)
13. Fan, W., Bifet, A.: Mining big data: current status and forecast to the future. ACM SIGKDD Explor. Newsl. **14**(2), 1–5 (2013)
14. Zikopoulos, P.C., Eaton, C., Deroos, D., Seutsch, T., Lapis, G.: Understanding Big Data: Analytics for Enterprise Class Hadoop and Streaming Data. Mc Graw-Hil (2012)
15. Portela, F., Lima, L., Santos, M.F.: Why big data? Towards a project assessment framework. Procedia Computer Science - WoTBD 2016 - The Second International Symposium on Web of Things and Big Data **98**, 604–609. Elsevier (2016). ISSN: 1877–0509. https://doi.org/10.1016/j.procs.2016.09.094

COVID-19 Fake News Detection Using Joint Doc2Vec and Text Features with PCA

Hector Mejia[1,2] , Carlos Chipantiza[1,2(✉)] , Jose Llumiquinga[1] ,
Isidro R. Amaro[1] , and Rigoberto Fonseca-Delgado[1]

[1] Yachay Tech, School of Mathematical and Computational Sciences,
San Miguel de Urcuqui, 100119 Imbabura, Ecuador
{hector.mejia,carlos.chipantiza,jose.llumiquinga,iamaro,
rfonseca}@yachaytech.edu.ec
[2] Factored AI, Palo Alto, CA, USA

Abstract. With the current pandemic, it is imperative to stay up to date with the news and many sources contribute to this purpose. However, there is also misinformation and fake news that spreads within society. In this work, a machine learning approach to detect fake news related to COVID-19 is developed. Specifically, Doc2Vec language model is used to transform text documents into vector representations, and handcrafted features like document length, the proportion of personal pronouns, and punctuation are included as complementary features as well. Then, Principal Component Analysis (PCA) is performed on the original feature vectors to reduce dimensionality. Both, the original and reduced data are fed to various machine learning models and finally compared in terms of accuracy, precision, recall, and execution time. The results indicate that the reduced set of features had minimal accuracy impact. However, the execution times are greatly reduced in most cases, specifically at testing time, indicating that dimensionality reduction can be useful on projects already in production that would need model inference on large volumes of documents to detect fake news.

Keywords: Fake news · Principal Component Analysis · Text classification

1 Introduction

As a result of the COVID-19 pandemic, multiple news articles started to emerge from multiple sources, and with it, misinformation, speculation, and fake news were disseminated as well. Since the internet plays a very important role in the propagation of information, news with false information can influence people either in their perception of the facts, generate social or economic problems, and manipulate public opinion, and change political outcomes [11]. With this current problem, people around the world have been influenced many times by

T. Guarda et al. (Eds.): ARTIIS 2022, CCIS 1675, pp. 316–330, 2022.
https://doi.org/10.1007/978-3-031-20319-0_24

the dissemination of information about the origin, spread, and treatment of this disease, as they have been left in a situation of helplessness or uncertainty about their future. Therefore, it is important to detect fake news content.

The most accurate way of detecting fake news is manual detection but it is a very slow process, making it unfeasible to tag large amounts of news. Nowadays with the widespread popularity of scientific computing and artificial intelligence, an scalable model for automatic detection of fake news using machine learning and feature engineering can be made just if the data that has been previously identified by a rigorous classification analysis is used. However, the text classification task needs vector representations from the textual documents, as well as discriminatory features, and with increasing vector dimensionality, training and inference times become slow and unpractical for real-time processing.

We proposed a method to identify COVID-19-related fake news utilizing feature extraction, normalization, dimensionality reduction, and classification. This study uses data that was previously labeled and verified by experts. For the feature extraction component, a language model called Doc2Vec is employed to create vector representations from text documents. Moreover, a set of hand-crafted features, derived from the lengths of the documents and punctuation, is concatenated to the previous document vectors to aid in the classification. These resulting feature vectors are normalized by subtracting the mean vector to each instance and dividing by the standard deviation.

Furthermore, Principal Component Analysis is employed to reduce the dimensionality of the features, while minimizing performance reduction. The purpose of adding this procedure is to reduce inference time when using classification models in production environments.

Then, a set of the most common machine learning algorithms are trained and tested on the original features, as well as the reduced components on two separate experiments to classify truthful and fake news. Specifically, the models employed are: Stochastic Gradient Descent optimized linear model, Support Vector Classifier, Random Forest, AdaBoost, and K-Nearest Neighbors.

Finally, training and testing performance metrics, as well as time, are compared between the models that were developed using the original features and the models built with the reduced principal components.

2 Previous Work

The pandemic of COVID-19 presented multiple opportunities in research across many areas, and sciences related to digital information are no exception. Many works explored the task of fake news detection related to this current world problem using machine learning approaches.

Some authors developed frameworks that employed traditional feature engineering and machine learning models. For instance, the work of Felber [7] utilized linguistic features like n-grams, emotional tone, and punctuation and machine learning models like support vector machines (SVM), linear regression (LR), random forest (RF), naive Bayes (NB) and multi-layer perceptron to classify fake and truthful reviews. This work achieved accuracies ranging 90.79% to 95.70% with a dataset of 10700 news related to COVID-19 for the Constraint@AAAI2021 challenge [18].

Morover, Shushkevich and Cardiff [23] proposed the use of an ensemble model consisting of bidirectional long short-term memory, support vector machine, logistic regression, Naive Bayes, and a combination of logistic regression and Naive Bayes. For the feature engineering phase, they used term frequency-inverse document frequency (TF-IDF) to transform text to vector representation and consequently feed the model for training and testing. This work achieved an F1-score of 0.94 using the same dataset of the Constraint@AAAI2021 challenge.

Other authors harnessed the state of the art in natural language processing (NLP), using transformers in their frameworks. Transformers are deep learning-based language models that are pretrained on large corpora of text and then fine-tuned for the desired task, like text classification.

The work of Bang et al. [4] explored two methodologies for fake news detection. The first is fine-tuning ALBERT-base [12], BERT-base, BERT-large [6], RoBERTa-base, and RoBERTa-large [15] with different loss functions, and the second is data cleansing using an influence score, inspired by the work of Kobayashi et al. [10]. Finally, these two approaches achieved weighted F1-scores of 98.13% using the dataset for the Constraint@AAAI2021 challenge and 38.18% weighted-F1 on the Tweets-19 dataset [2].

Furthermore, Vijjali et al. [24] proposed a two-stage transformer model to detect fake news related to COVID-19. The first stage retrieves the most relevant facts concerning user claims about particular COVID-19 news, while the second verify the level of truth in those claims by computing the textual entailment between the claim and the facts retrieved from a manually curated dataset. This dataset is based on a publicly available information source consisting of more than 5000 COVID-19 false claims and verified explanations. As for the results, this work achieved 85.5% accuracy on the aforementioned dataset using BERT+ALBERT as the transformer models for the two-stage detector.

All the mentioned methods have in common a first step that receives the text and returns a feature vector. The training time required by these methods depends on the size of the vector. Several studies have shown the efficacy of using PCA to reduce the dimensionality of the problem [19]. In the work of Akkoyunlu et al. [1], with the intention of understanding eating habits in order to build a context-aware recommender system that provides personalized dietary recommendations, they propose a *Doc2Vec*-based method for representing food consumptions in order to identify eating behavior clusters. Furthermore, comparing their method to the state of the art methods used in the nutrition community, especially with the CPA method, which is applied for deriving eating behaviours. The dataset used is The INCA2 which consists of individual 7-day food records collected during 2006–2007 from 2,624 adult French consumers over several months in order to take into account seasonality. They used an unsupervised setting and applied Doc2Vec directly to users to challenge state-of-the-art methods in food-based approaches to see how the NLP method performed on this task. The results obtained are as follows: a) The *Doc2Vec* method produces fewer clusters on users, and the clustering results are quite different; b) the method cannot be used to inspect eating behaviors as easily as state-of-the-art methods; c) additional analysis is required to understand why clustering results are so disparate; and d) this method is adequate if the goal is to extract consumer clusters. In this work, we propose to use PCA to reduce the size of the feature vector, while maintaining the commitment to performance.

3   Materials and Methods

In this section, the employed dataset, as well as the steps taken to develop the fake news classification model are described in detail.

3.1   Dataset Description

The dataset used in this work is called COVID19-FNIR and was downloaded from the IEEE DatePort. It contains two sets of text news, collected between February 2020 and June 2020, that are related to the COVID-19 global pandemic, one set corresponding to verified truthful news, and the other is a compilation of fake news. This data was gathered from sources in multiple regions: India, the United States of America and various countries of Europe. This data does not contain special characters neither non-vital information [21]. Two papers have worked with this dataset. The first one [5] proposes an automatic detection system using different Machine Learning techniques to check the reliability of medical news related to the COVID-19 pandemic. The system works in several stages of classification, from classifying the scope of the news, selecting documents similar to the COVID-FNIR dataset, to performing a Stance Classification. The work achieves a system capable of finding documents identical to a query, but the stance classification is not so reliable to automatically classify fake news. The second paper [3] examines the performance of some traditional machine learning techniques for fake news detection on COVID-19 and English. In this paper, it is determined that Support Vector Machine and Naive Bayes models outperform other strategies.

The dataset contains a total of 7588 examples. As shown in the Fig. 1, the dataset has balanced classes, 3794 samples for trustworthy news and 3793 for false news.

3.2   Data Processing

To develop a model to detect COVID-19 related fake news, textual data has to be preprocessed. In this work, three stages of data processing that will allow us to perform training of various machine learning models are defined. These stages are dataset consolidation, feature extraction, and feature normalization.

The original dataset consisted of two files. One file contained all verified truthful news collected from many sources, while the other contained fake news

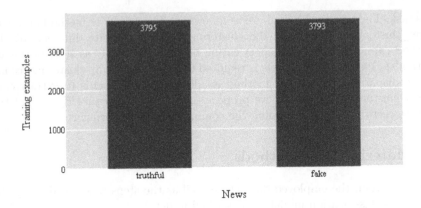

Fig. 1. Distribution of classes.

that was manually labeled by the author of the dataset. Furthermore, these files were loaded and concatenated. In addition, an integer label was assigned to each example: 1 to denote "fake news" and 0 to denote "truthful news".

After the dataset is consolidated and tagged a feature extraction is performed on the textual information. Since machine learning models can only use numerical data to learn patterns, a transformation has to be carried on the text corpus to vector representations.

Doc2Vec is a neural network designed by Mikolov and Le [13], with the purpose to map text to a number considering the meaning of the words. It is trained for language modeling, i.e., predicting words given previous words that are used as context. *Doc2Vec* is based on *Word2Vec* developed by Mikolov *et al.* [16].

3.3   Word2Vec

Given a sequence of training words $w_1, w_2, w_3, ..., w_T$, where T is the total number of words in the vocabulary plus the number of paragraphs, the objective is to maximize the average log probability:

$$\frac{1}{T} \sum_{t=k}^{T-k} log p\left(w_t|w_{t-k}, ..., w_{t+k}\right),$$

where k is the maximum distance of the words. In this framework, every word is mapped to a unique vector, represented by a column in a matrix W. The column is indexed by the position of the word in the vocabulary. Moreover, these vectors are averaged or concatenated and used as features for the prediction of the next word. This prediction is done by adding a softmax classification layer. Therefore:

$$p\left(w_t|w_{t-k}, ..., w_{t+k}\right) = \frac{e^{y_{w_t}}}{\sum_i e^{y_i}}.$$

Then each y_i is computed as:

$$y = b + Uh\left(w_{t-k}, ..., w_{t+k}; W\right),\tag{1}$$

where U, b are the softmax parameters and h is the concatenation or average of each words vectors extracted from W (see Fig. 2) [13].

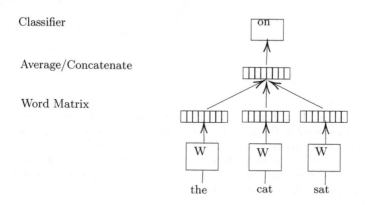

Classifier

Average/Concatenate

Word Matrix

Fig. 2. A framework for learning word vectors. Context of three words ("the," "cat," and "sat") is used to predict the fourth word ("on"). The input words are mapped to columns of the matrix W to predict the output word. Source [13].

3.4 Doc2Vec

Doc2Vec's primary goal is to generate numerical representations of documents. Documents do not have logical (grammatical) structure, whereas words do. Another vector (Paragraph ID) must be added to the *Word2Vec* model to solve this problem. The only difference between *Word2Vec* and *Doc2Vec* is this. *Doc2Vec* is available in two ways:

Paragraph Vector: A Distributed Memory Model. Every paragraph is mapped to a unique vector, represented by a column in matrix D, in our Paragraph Vector framework (see Fig. 3), and every word is also mapped to a unique vector, represented by a column in matrix W. To predict the next word in a context, the paragraph vector and word vectors are averaged or concatenated. More formally, the only difference between this model and the word vector framework is in (1), where h is built from W and D. The paragraph token can be compared to another word. It functions as a memory, recalling what is missing from the current context - or the paragraph's topic. The name given for this model is the Distributed Memory Model of Paragraph Vectors (PV-DM) [13].

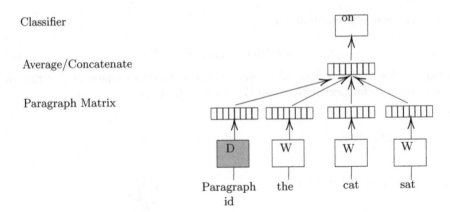

Fig. 3. A framework for learning paragraph vector. This framework is similar to the framework presented in Fig. 2 1; the only change is the additional paragraph token that is mapped to a vector via matrix D. In this model, the concatenation or average of this vector with a context of three words is used to predict the fourth word. The paragraph vector represents the missing information from the current context and can act as a memory of the topic of the paragraph. Source [13].

Paragraph Vector Without Word Ordering: Distributed Bag of Words.
The above method considers the concatenation of the paragraph vector with the word vectors to predict the next word in a text window. Another approach would be to ignore the context words in the input and force the model to predict words from the paragraph at random in the output. In practice, this means that for each iteration of stochastic gradient descent, we sample a text window, then sample a random word from the text window, and form a classification task given the Paragraph Vector. This technique is shown in Fig. 4. The name of this version is the Distributed Bag of Words version of Paragraph Vector (PV-DBOW) [13].

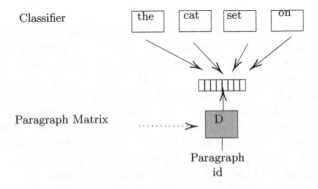

Fig. 4. Distributed Bag of Words version of paragraph vectors. In this version, the paragraph vector is trained to predict the words in a small window. Source [13].

Once the language model is trained, the softmax layer was removed and retain only the embeddings of each document.

In addition to the document vectors, manual features were computed from the text, inspired by the work of Li *et al.* [14]. The features are defined as follows:

Length of a Document (L). For a document d, L is defined as the total number of words that compose d.

Ratio of Exclamation Sentences (RES). For a document d, composed of s sentences, where each sentence is delimited by a period ".", then RES is defined as the number of sentences within d that contain at least a single exclamation symbol "!".

Ratio of First Personal Pronouns (PP1). For a document d, composed of the total number of words t and f being the total number of words inside d that correspond to the first personal pronouns included in the list (i, me, we, us, myself, ourselves, my, our, mine, ours). Then:

$$PP1 = \frac{f}{t}.$$

Percentage of Capital Letters (PC). For a document d, composed of the total number of characters t, including white-spaces and non alpha-numeric symbols and u, the total number of characters in uppercase. Then:

$$PC = \frac{u}{t}.$$

After the features are computed, feature normalization is performed since the resulting document embeddings present different scales across its dimensions. This is done by simply subtracting the mean u and dividing by the standard deviation s:

$$z = \frac{x - u}{s}.$$

These feature vectors have numbers in each dimension, in a range from 0 to 1. Furthermore, using the training data, we generate a correlation matrix of features, as depicted in Fig. 5. The determinant of the correlation matrix is 0.134; then, there is a significant correlation between the variables, and therefore PCA is useful to reduce the dimensionality of the problem.

The aforementioned procedure was implemented using python 3.8 with the help of scikit-learn and gensim libraries for feature extraction and matplotlib for plotting. The implementation details can be seen in Algorithm 1.

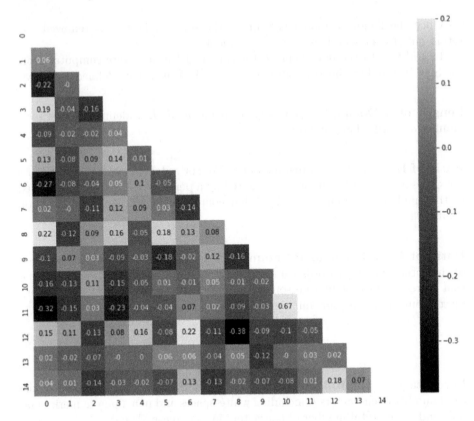

Fig. 5. Correlation matrix from the computed features.

3.5   Principal Component Analysis

One of the main objectives when analyzing high-dimensional data is to obtain a representation in a reduced space that demonstrates the main patterns of similarity between individuals. This problem can be addressed by using multivariate techniques such as the Principal Component Analysis (PCA) [9,20].

In other words, principal component analysis reduces a large number of multivariate variables into a relatively small number of linear combinations of these that can be used to account for much of the variability in the data. The central idea of PCA is to reduce the dimensionality of a data set with minimal information loss [20].

According [20], there are several parameters to consider when deciding how many components to deal with; one of them is that at least 80% of the total variance must be considered. In our case, we can operate with ten components (82%).

Algorithm 1: Feature extraction

Data: Truthful news directory d_T, Fake news directory d_F
Result: Scaled train and test features datasets S_{train}, S_{test}, train and test
        principal components PC_{train}, PC_{test}
$D_T, L_T \leftarrow load\_data\_and\_labels(d_T)$;
$D_F, L_F \leftarrow load\_data\_and\_labels(d_F)$;
$D \leftarrow D_T \cup DF$;
$L \leftarrow L_T \cup LF$;
$D_{train}, L_{train}, D_{test}, L_{test} \leftarrow train\_test\_split(D, L, test\_size = 20\%)$;
$M_E \leftarrow train\_Doc2Vec\_LM(D_{train})$;
$E_{train}, E_{test} \leftarrow encode\_documents(D_{train}, D_{test}, M_E)$;
$f_{1train}, f_{1test} \leftarrow get\_documents\_length(D_{train}, D_{test})$;
$f_{2train}, f_{2test} \leftarrow get\_exclamation\_ratio(D_{train}, D_{test})$;
$f_{3train}, f_{3test} \leftarrow get\_caps\_percentage(D_{train}, D_{test})$;
$f_{4train}, f_{4test} \leftarrow get\_1stpersonalpronoun\_ratio(D_{train}, D_{test})$;
$f_{train} \leftarrow concatenate(f_{1train}, f_{2train}, f_{3train}, f_{4train})$;
$f_{test} \leftarrow concatenate(f_{1test}, f_{2test}, f_{3test}, f_{4test})$;
$F_{train} \leftarrow concatenate(f_{train}, E_{train})$;
$F_{test} \leftarrow concatenate(f_{test}, E_{test})$;
$M_S \leftarrow fit\_standard\_scaler(F_{train})$;
$S_{train}, S_{test} \leftarrow scale\_features(F_{train}, F_{test}, M_S)$;
$M_{PC} = fit\_PCA(S_{train})$;
$PC_{train}, PC_{test} = get\_principal\_components(S_{train}, S_{test}, M_{PC}, min_variance = 80\%)$;

3.6 Machine Learning Training and Testing

At this stage, K-fold cross validation is used to estimate the skill of five different supervised machine learning algorithms. The algorithms are tested for fake news classification in two different settings. The first setting uses the original set of features, while the second uses the ten first principal components. The procedure was implemented using python 3.8 with the help of Scikit-learn to train various machine learning models and to implement a 10-fold cross validation. The machine learning algorithms are briefly described below:

SGD Classifier: Stochastic Gradient Descent (SGD) Classifier is a classification algorithm that works with regularized linear models and gradient descent learning (SGD), hence the reason for its name. In this algorithm the error gradient is estimated each sample at a time and the model is updated over time with a learning rate [17].
Support Vector Machine Classifier (SVM): Builds a model that finds the best separation between classes and assigns new examples to one or the other category. It does this by separating the classes into two spaces by means of a separation hyperplane that is defined as a vector between the two classes [8].
Random Forest Classifier: Uses the fundamentals of decision trees, except that the Random forest uses many decision trees that it builds at training

time and makes predictions by averaging the predictions of each component tree. It generally has a much higher prediction accuracy than a single decision tree and works well with predetermined parameters [17].

AdaBoost Classifier: This algorithm is part of boosting algorithms. Boosting is an approach that relies on creating an accurate prediction rule by combining many relatively weak and inaccurate rules, also the boosting algorithm can track the model that failed in accurate prediction. AdaBoost stands for Adaptive Boosting and uses 1-level decision trees as weak rules that are sequentially added to the ensemble, the importance of the tree in the final classification is calculated, then the weights are updated so that the next decision tree takes into account the errors made by the previous decision tree [22].

K Neighbors Classifier: Implements the nearest neighbor algorithm where the input is the number of k nearest training examples in the feature space. This algorithm searches the observations closest to the observations it is trying to predict and classifies a point based on the surrounding points [17].

K-Fold Cross Validation: This method is used to evaluate the performance of machine learning models in classification tasks on unseen data [25]. This method divides a data set into k groups. Once the data set is divided into k folds, the model is trained using $k-1$ folds and the missing fold for validation. Then, the results of the validations are used to calculate a performance metric. Finally, the calculated metrics are averaged to know the model's performance in a generalized way.

Various metrics are computed by each fold to assess performance. These metrics are precision, recall, $F1$-score, and accuracy.

Precision is the ability of the classifier not to label as positive an observation that is negative and is given by:

$$\text{Precision} = \frac{tp}{tp + fp},$$

where tp are the True positives and fp are the False Positives.

Recall is the ability of the classifier to find the positive samples and is defined by:

$$\text{Recall} = \frac{tp}{tp + fn},$$

where tp are the True positives and fn are the False Negatives.

The f1-score is a weighted harmonic measure of precision and recall, where at 1 it reaches its best value and at 0 it reaches its worst value. It is given by:

$$F_1 = 2\frac{\text{Precision} * \text{Recall}}{\text{Precision} + \text{Recall}}.$$

Finally, the accuracy measures the ratio of correct predictions against all the instances of a test set and it is formulated as:

$$Acc = \frac{tp + tn}{tp + tn + fp + fn}.$$

4   Results and Discussion

Table 1 shows the average run times of the ten folds. In general, it can be seen that the run times of the models are shorter after having performed the PCA analysis, except for the Random Forest Classifier. It can be seen that the models in general have a high percentage of improvement. It would be an important topic for future work to treat the Random Forest model in more detail, under the influence of PCA analysis, to examine why the execution time increased after dimensionality reduction.

Table 1. 10-fold cross validation time.

Machine Learning Method	TIme Before PCA (s)	Time After PCA (s)	Improvement (%)
SGDClassifier	0.0770	0.0277	64.03
Support Vector Machines	2.137	1.3	39.17
Random Forest Classifier	1.9837	1.932	2.61
AdaBoost Classifier	1.7847	1.448	18.87
KNeighbors Classifier	0.1008	0.0855	15.18

Tables 2 and 3 show the precision, recall, and F1-score for the two classes of the COVID-19 news dataset, i.e. the labels 0 for truthful and 1 for fake news. Comparing these two tables containing performance metrics before and after PCA shows that, in general, the dimensionality reduction produced by PCA has a minimal influence over performance. It can be observed that the precision, recall, and F1-score metrics after PCA indicate that most of the information needed to correctly predict news about COVID-19 is still present.

Table 2. Performance Parameters before PCA.

	Precision		Recall		F1-score	
Machine Learning Method	0	1	0	1	0	1
SGDClassifier	0.8042	0.855	0.8674	0.8333	0.8213	0.8305
Support Vector Machine	0.889	0.87	0.8723	0.8865	0.8804	0.8778
Random Forest Classifier	0.9030	0.8863	0.888	0.9013	0.8953	0.8936
AdaBoost Classifier	0.8750	0.8723	0.8731	0.8742	0.8738	0.8730
KNeighbors Classifier	0.8771	0.8744	0.8749	0.8763	0.8759	0.8752

In terms of accuracy, the models using the full dimensionality of the features have a higher number of correctly classified elements than the models using the features after a PCA, as shown in Fig. 6, but the difference is still very minimal, which means that using the same models, but with a lower computational cost can still rely on the reduced features for classification tasks.

Table 3. Performance Parameters after PCA.

	Precision		Recall		F1-score	
Machine Learning Method	0	1	0	1	0	1
SGDClassifier	0.8513	0.8123	0.8190	0.8448	0.8345	0.8278
Support Vector Machine	0.8950	0.8686	0.8719	0.8922	0.8832	0.8801
Random Forest Classifier	0.8801	0.8576	0.861	0.8767	0.8703	0.867
AdaBoost Classifier	0.8372	0.8360	0.8358	0.837	0.8362	0.8361
KNeighbors Classifier	0.8917	0.8418	0.8491	0.8858	0.8698	0.8632

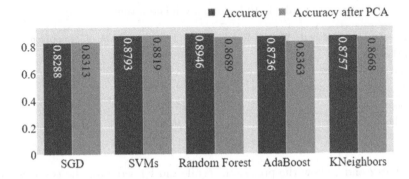

Fig. 6. Performance based on accuracy

5 Conclusion

To detect fake news related to COVID-19, using the COVID19-FNIR Dataset, the effectiveness of the Principal Component Analysis (PCA) procedure was analyzed against several Machine Learning models, widely known in the field for classification tasks, both before and after applying dimensionality reduction. When compared to the performance evaluation using the original set of features, in terms of accuracy, the PCA analysis only resulted in a reduction of 4%, maintaining high performance for every machine learning model. Furthermore, the experiments also show that machine learning methods together with Principal Component Analysis are more efficient in terms of COVID-19-related news classification than only using the original features; since the training and evaluation times of the models were greatly reduced while maintaining high-performance metrics. This reduction in time would be greater, when the training corpus becomes much larger, or when is used in production environments for inference. In addition, the Doc2Vec model with PCA for dimensionality reduction allows keeping a large amount of feature information, maintaining good accuracy, and reducing training and test execution time for classification tasks. This is useful since detecting false news in near-real-time helps to mitigate many social problems, problems that have to do with the spread of false information about COVID-19. Finally, this work contributes to the research about fake news and helps to identify fake news related to COVID-19, for future work an attempt will be made to explore other dimensionality reduction techniques that allow better performance, in combination with machine learning methods.

References

1. Akkoyunlu, S., Manfredotti, C., Cornuéjols, A., Darcel, N., Delaere, F.: Exploring eating behaviours modelling for user clustering. In: HealthRecSys@ RecSys 2018 colocated with ACM Recsys 2018 (ACM Conference Series on Recommender Systems), pp. 46–51 (2018)
2. Alam, F., et al.: Fighting the covid-19 infodemic in social media: a holistic perspective and a call to arms. In: Proceeding of the Fifteenth International AAAI Conference on Web and Social Media (ICWSM 2021) (2021)
3. Almatarneh, S., Gamallo, P., ALshargabi, B., Al-Khassawneh, Y., Alzubi, R.: Comparing traditional machine learning methods for covid-19 fake news. In: 2021 22nd International Arab Conference on Information Technology (ACIT), pp. 1–4 (2021). https://doi.org/10.1109/ACIT53391.2021.9677453
4. Bang, Y., Ishii, E., Cahyawijaya, S., Ji, Z., Fung, P.: Model generalization on COVID-19 fake news detection. In: Chakraborty, T., Shu, K., Bernard, H.R., Liu, H., Akhtar, M.S. (eds.) CONSTRAINT 2021. CCIS, vol. 1402, pp. 128–140. Springer, Cham (2021). https://doi.org/10.1007/978-3-030-73696-5_13
5. De Magistris, G., Russo, S., Roma, P., Starczewski, J.T., Napoli, C.: An explainable fake news detector based on named entity recognition and stance classification applied to covid-19. Information 13(3) (2022). https://doi.org/10.3390/info13030137, https://www.mdpi.com/2078-2489/13/3/137
6. Devlin, J., Chang, M.W., Lee, K., Toutanova, K.: BERT: pre-training of deep bidirectional transformers for language understanding. In: Proceedings of the 2019 Conference of the North American Chapter of the Association for Computational Linguistics: Human Language Technologies, Volume 1 (Long and Short Papers). pp. 4171–4186. Association for Computational Linguistics, Minneapolis, Minnesota, June 2019. https://doi.org/10.18653/v1/N19-1423, https://aclanthology.org/N19-1423
7. Felber, T.: Constraint 2021: machine learning models for COVID-19 fake news detection shared task, January 2021. CoRR, abs/2101.03717
8. Fletcher, T.: Support vector machines explained, January 2009. https://www.cs.ucl.ac.uk/staff//T.Fletcher/
9. Jolliffe, I.T.: Principal Component Analysis for Special Types of Data. In: Principal Component Analysis, pp. 338–372. Springer, New York (2002). https://doi.org/10.1007/0-387-22440-8_13
10. Kobayashi, S., Yokoi, S., Suzuki, J., Inui, K.: Efficient estimation of influence of a training instance. In: Proceedings of SustaiNLP: Workshop on Simple and Efficient Natural Language Processing, Stroudsburg, PA, USA, pp. 41–47. Association for Computational Linguistics (2020). https://doi.org/10.18653/v1/2020.sustainlp-1.6, https://www.aclweb.org/anthology/2020.sustainlp-1.6
11. Koirala, A.: Covid-19 fake news classification with deep learning, October 2020. https://doi.org/10.13140/RG.2.2.26509.56805
12. Lan, Z., Chen, M., Goodman, S., Gimpel, K., Sharma, P., Soricut, R.: Albert: a lite Bert for self-supervised learning of language representations. In: International Conference on Learning Representations (2020). https://openreview.net/forum?id=H1eA7AEtvS

13. Le, Q., Mikolov, T.: Distributed representations of sentences and documents. In: International Conference on Machine Learning, pp. 1188–1196. PMLR (2014)
14. Li, F.H., Huang, M., Yang, Y., Zhu, X.: Learning to identify review spam. In: Twenty-Second International Joint Conference on Artificial Intelligence (2011)
15. Liu, Y., et al.: RoBERTa: A Robustly Optimized BERT Pretraining Approach, July 2019. https://arxiv.org/abs/1907.11692
16. Mikolov, T., Chen, K., Corrado, G., Dean, J.: Efficient estimation of word representations in vector space. arXiv preprint arXiv:1301.3781 (2013)
17. Paper, D.: Hands-on Scikit-Learn for Machine Learning Applications: Data Science Fundamentals with Python. Apress (2019). https://books.google.com.ec/books?id=kqy-DwAAQBAJ
18. Patwa, P., et al.: Fighting an Infodemic: COVID-19 fake news dataset. In: Chakraborty, T., Shu, K., Bernard, H.R., Liu, H., Akhtar, M.S. (eds.) CONSTRAINT 2021. CCIS, vol. 1402, pp. 21–29. Springer, Cham (2021). https://doi.org/10.1007/978-3-030-73696-5_3
19. Peluffo-Ordóñez, D.H., Rodríguez-Sotelo, J.L., Castellanos-Domínguez, G.: Estudio comparativo de métodos de selección de características de inferencia supervisada y no supervisada. TecnoLógicas pp. 149–166 (2009)
20. Rencher, A.C.: Methods of Multivariate Analysis (2002). https://doi.org/10.1002/0471271357
21. Saenz, J.A., Kalathur Gopal, S.R., Shukla, D.: Covid-19 fake news infodemic research dataset (covid19-fnir dataset) (2021). https://doi.org/10.21227/b5bt-5244, https://dx.doi.org/10.21227/b5bt-5244
22. Schapire, R.E.: Explaining AdaBoost. In: Schölkopf, B., Luo, Z., Vovk, V. (eds.) Empirical Inference, pp. 37–52. Springer, Heidelberg (2013). https://doi.org/10.1007/978-3-642-41136-6_5
23. Shushkevich, E., Cardiff, J.: TUDublin team at Constraint@AAAI2021 - COVID19 Fake News Detection, January 2021. https://arxiv.org/abs/2101.05701
24. Vijjali, R., Potluri, P., Kumar, S., Teki, S.: Two stage transformer model for COVID-19 fake news detection and fact checking, November 2020. https://arxiv.org/abs/2011.13253
25. Wong, T.T., Yeh, P.Y.: Reliable accuracy estimates from k-fold cross validation. IEEE Trans. Knowl. Data Eng. **32**(8), 1586–1594 (2020). https://doi.org/10.1109/TKDE.2019.2912815

Eye Tracking and Visual Attention in a Retail Context: Can Point-of-Sale Stickers Guide Customers?

Hanne Sørum[1]([⊠]) and Jannicke Johansen[2]

[1] Kristiania University College, Kirkegata 24–26, 0153 Oslo, Norway
`hanne.sorum@kristiania.no`
[2] Kristiania University College, Urtegata 9, 0187 Oslo, Norway

Abstract. Knowing how users navigate in a physical store is vital to facilitate the best experiences along their purchasing journey. A grocery store houses a variety of products, placed in different in-store locations. It is not always easy to spot products, due to location, labels, placement, and the store's physical premises. The present study examines the use of eye tracking glasses to investigate visual attention among consumers. We focus on the effect of using stickers on the floor that symbolize product categories and present the following research question: To what extent do customers pay visual attention to point-of-sale stickers on the floor in a buying situation? The findings show that customers notice such stickers to a small or no degree and that stickers (with color and a product symbol) attract attention to a low extent. The idea of how the floor can be used to guide consumers turns out not to have the effect that was first assumed. It appears this concept needs to be better established in physical stores before such stickers can be a useful and helpful way to facilitate efficient grocery shopping. Moreover, we conclude that eye tracking glasses as a method has worked in regard to the study context and what we intended to investigate. Additionally, the contribution is relevant for both academics and the retail industry itself, to gain a better understanding of user experiences in physical stores.

Keywords: Eye tracking glasses · Visual attention · User experiences · Grocery store · Retail design · Point-of-sale

1 Introduction

Imagine that you go into a physical store to shop one or more specific products. You know exactly what to buy but are not sure where in the store the item(s) is/are located. It is therefore essential how your eyes move to get an overview of the selection that is available. You must move around in the search for the right product. If, on the other hand, you had visited an online store, you could have easily searched for products – and if they were not found within a reasonable time, competitors are just a click away. In both contexts, user experiences are significant. What has piqued our curiosity and led to the current study is how the floor in a store can be used to guide customers to the right

T. Guarda et al. (Eds.): ARTIIS 2022, CCIS 1675, pp. 331–344, 2022.
https://doi.org/10.1007/978-3-031-20319-0_25

product in an efficient way. User experiences in a physical store can be studied in many ways; the use of mobile eye tracking glasses is one approach. When test subjects wear such glasses, the movements of their eyes (pupils) can be tracked, stored, and analyzed, which is not possible with any other method or technology. One explanation is that "Eye tracking delivers unique insights into shopper behavior and gives a clear indication of what factors influence purchase choices by revealing visual attention and subconscious actions. This information allows you to make the most informed decisions on how you engage consumers and nurture their journey with your brand" [1]. This ability to generate unique insights shows us how the use of eye tracking technology can be brought into the retail industry to understand consumers' behavior, attendance, and glances in a shopping context, enabling their visual attention to be measured.

Consumers' visual attention is required for purchases, and visual stimuli are generally the most important in relation to cognitive processing in retail environments [2]. As Soomro et al. observe, "getting consumers' attention and consideration is something very important for the store managers to increase their buying. Store managers should use visual merchandising strategies to communicate with the customers and making them visit their stores" [3, p. 35]. This insight testifies to the importance of creating good user experiences in physical stores, ensuring attention is focused on different places in the store location and specific products, to stimulate purchases and communicate with customers in a way that creates profitability for the store itself.

To delve into the area of interest, the present paper explores the following research question: *To what extent do customers pay visual attention to point-of-sale stickers on the floor in a buying situation?* The question is related to how to use the floor in a store to guide customers so they can find products more easily. The contribution of this paper should therefore be of interest to both research communities (in various disciplines using eye tracking) and the retail industry itself (to gain a better understanding of user experiences in physical stores).

2   Related Work

Norwegian trading patterns have been investigated by the Norwegian Consumer Council to map out how often Norwegian households make food purchases [4]. In their grocery survey they found that eight out of ten Norwegian households purchase from a grocery store every day or several times per week. Moreover, 7% of the respondents visit the grocery store every day, and 74% make food purchases several times per week. Persons aged between 18 and 29 visit the grocery store more frequently than elderly people. In the same survey, only 23% of the respondents in the oldest age group (60 +) visited the grocery store only once a week. A very small proportion of the same group (1%) visited the grocery shop less than once a week.

People spend a great deal of time looking for products when they are in a store; in grocery stores, more than 80% of consumers' in-store time is spent finding products [5]. Hence, there is great potential for making grocery shopping more efficient for customers by labeling shelves or other places in the locations that attract customers' visual attention. [4] have carried out surveys of shop experiences that can be used for analysis and research of Norwegian consumer behavior. In this regard, the survey carried out by Statistics

Norway shows that four out of ten respondents think it is important that the store is clear, clean, and tidy. Among elderly (60 +) respondents, half emphasized and appreciated a clear, clean, and tidy store. Another key finding from the research is that the respondents want the store to have all the items they need. In total, 35% of the respondents considered this important, and this is particularly important for those who shop only once a week or less often. A further important insight was that 16% of the respondents need a store that has an extra-wide range of goods. Elderly (60 +) respondents considered this to be more important than those who are younger. A study by [6] investigated the impact of store attributes (atmosphere, promotion, convenience, facilities, merchandise, staff interaction, and services) on food and grocery shopping behavior in India. The findings show that store attributes influence store choice decisions and that age matters.

Moreover, [7] investigated the effect of making a shopping list before undertaking online grocery purchases to see how this affected purchasing behavior among consumers. Those who made a shopping list before shopping bought significantly fewer items than those who did not, indicating that if you make a shopping list, you shop less. [8] compared how people shop in an online context versus buying groceries in stores, drawing on data from 137 household customers in the United States. Findings show that the participants shopped differently in the two contexts: When shopping online, 44% more was spent per transaction and the participants bought more. Online shopping was associated with reduced expenditure per transaction on sweets, cold or frozen desserts, and cereal-based desserts. Moreover, online shopping of grocery purchases was associated with lower spending on unhealthy products.

Customer experiences in physical stores and how to facilitate an efficient customer journey in the search for products are phenomena of particular interest. Grocery stores offer many and various products in different in-store locations. It is not always easy to find them, especially for consumers visiting the store for the first time. Given the importance of marking the placement of products and to investigate the use of stickers on the floor, the present study explored the use of eye tracking through glasses. There is considerable interest in using eye tracking as a method in the retail industry to better understand, among other things, the behavior of consumers in a store and which factors are significant in relation to purchasing decisions. Moreover, there is a need to understand which elements attract visual attention, as well as how customers select products from a large and varied range [9]. The tool eye tracking is growing in popularity within various research disciplines and is more accessible than ever before [10].

Within the field of user experiences in physical stores, the use of eye tracking glasses can create value to facilitate a good customer experience and uncover what the shopper perceives from poster material in a store [5]. Several research studies have used eye-tracking technology in a retail context to measure visual attention [11]. Moreover, to make it easier for customers to shop in physical stores, retailers have developed various types of apps that can be used during the shopping trip, such as editable shopping lists, scanning bar codes, and voice-based systems [12]. These solutions allow customers to largely personalize their shopping trip through various types of technologies and lead to increased productivity. When shopping in a store, many elements can attract customers' visual attention, among them other people who are in the store at the same time, employees working there, product placement, and labeling. Visual attention can also be drawn by poster material; therefore, it is interesting to investigate how much of this is noticed by customers, both consciously and unconsciously.

According to [5], the placing of posters in stores is crucial in how or whether they are perceived by customers. One study shows that fewer than 20% who observed poster material noticed posters hanging from the ceiling, whereas 70% observed those placed at eye level, and approximately 60% observed those placed on the floor. This is key knowledge regarding the placement of posters in the store to attract visual attention. A study by [3] investigated how visual merchandising elements, namely window display, store layout, colors and lighting, and interior design, influence consumers' attention in a retail store. The findings show that color, lighting, interior design and window display have a positive impact on consumer attention. On the other hand, store layout does not have a significant positive impact on consumer attention. From these findings, we learn what store managers should focus on with regard to elements of visual merchandising when promoting goods and in the effort to gain a competitive advantage over their competitors.

Moreover, a study by [11] shows that, among other things, signage in stores is significant in relation to customers' visual attention during decision-making and increases the attention they direct to products. Thus, signage is important to consumers and can help guide them through the shopping journey. Furthermore, [13] reports on a study with a mixed methods design, combining mobile eye-tracking analysis (fixations) and pre- and post-tracking questions, which investigated visual attention among consumers within a retail context. The results indicate that both internal and external motivations (such as lighting, sight lines, signage, and product presentation) played a role in the observed consumer behavior.

3   Background and Case Description

3.1   Choice of Case – Wheat Flour

Bread and other baked goods are important in the Norwegian food tradition and diet, and in 2020 the grain consumption per capita was 79.8 kg [14]. On average, Norwegians eat around 75 kg of bread per year. In this context, 1 kg of wheat flour was chosen as the case study product in the research project, as everyone who lives in Norway knows about the product. The task for the respondents in the research project was to buy 1 kg of wheat flour in a grocery store. The current Norwegian government aims to increase the degree of self-sufficiency in Norwegian agricultural food production to 50%. Minister of Agriculture and Food Sandra Borch points out that food grain is one of the key products in Norwegian agriculture [15]. In this context, preliminary figures from the Norwegian Directorate of Agriculture show that about 63% of the wheat that went to flour production in 2021 was Norwegian [16].

The government and other actors in the value chain have, therefore, because of this low Norwegian share, gathered around the "food grain initiative," whose goal is that 90% of food grain will be Norwegian by 2030 [16]. The global Covid-19 pandemic and uncertainty surrounding the war in Ukraine have contributed to the need to become more self-sufficient in the years to come and, in this context, food grains play a key role in meeting this political goal. The Covid-19 pandemic has also caused Norwegians to eat more bread, as most meals are prepared and eaten within the four walls of their homes. Division Director Linda Granlund of the Norwegian Directorate of Health [18] also points out that this is interesting in relation to The Norwegian Directorate of Health's report on the Norwegian diet from 2020 [17], as it is the first time that total consumption in Norway can be measured without cross-border trade and Norwegians traveling abroad. In this context, it turns out that the proportion who want to reduce bread (i.e., wheat flour and other grain products) has been stable since the survey started in 2009.

3.2 Study Context

The research team collaborated with a large grocery store chain in Norway. The present project has received internal funding from Kristiania University College, but has not received any support beyond this. In addition, there has been a collaboration with a grocery store that made its store location available for data collection. The location for data collection was Oslo (the capital of Norway), and the data were collected in one of their physical stores. As a stimulus, we placed a sticker (self-designed) on the floor, representing the product (graphical element) which was available on the shelf next to the sticker (Fig. 1).

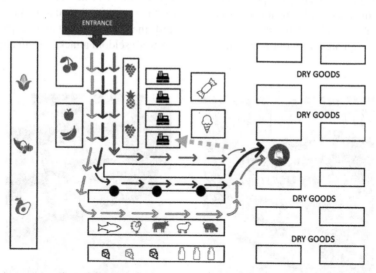

Fig. 1. A representation of the grocery store floor, showing the placement of the sticker. (Colour figure online)

The sticker that was designed by the research team (authors of the present paper) got a red color, because red is a color that may create attention. The research team, that are also into the field of design, used pictograms as graphic design elements in the actual design of the sticker. The idea was to create a more universal approach to wheat flour as a product. The combination of using the color red and pictograms may create visual attributes in the shop space. The initial thought and idea were that this design would create a good visual attention and guide the customers through their journey in the store.

We collected eye tracking data by using mobile glasses. The respondents were asked to buy a specific product, and the idea was that the sticker on the floor should lead them effectively to the product. After the test was completed, we followed up with qualitative interviews with each of the respondents. The data collection took place on two Sundays (December 2021 and February 2022), and the store was closed, so there were no other customers in it. As a gesture of thanks, the participants received a gift card of NOK 100 (which can be used in over 5500 stores in Norway).

3.3 Floor and Graphical Symbols in Retail Spaces

In the research project, the floor in the retail space of the grocery shop was crucial. As [18] observes, the floor has three main functions. It directs us from one place to another; it delimits a space from its surroundings; and it supports us by providing a firm footing. The floor also functions as an architectural commonality that defines the exterior space that is beneath us. It balances the forces of inside and outside with those of the walls and roof. The plan for the research was to investigate how the floor could be used as both a way of finding and an information area. The research team's hypothesis was that using stickers as stimuli on the floor would cause the floor in the grocery store to function as an arena to guide consumers to product categories. The stimulus (the sticker) was glued in front of the shelf with wheat flour. According to [5], a customer's usual field of view is straight ahead and 15% to 30% downwards towards the floor. The fact that people rarely look up originates from our reptilian brain, as we were seldom attacked from above [5] (Fig. 2).

Fig. 2. How the sticker looks on the floor (the design).

The graphical symbol used in the study was a pictogram of wheat flour, of 1 m in diameter. In the Oxford Learners' Dictionaries, a pictogram is defined as a pictorial symbol for a word or phrase, a kind of visual communication that was used as early as before 3000 BC in both Egypt and Mesopotamia. In recent years, emojis have become a new way of using pictograms and sending instant messages between people [19]. The pictogram in the study was designed in red and white. The motif consisted of a bag of grain and some sheaves of wheat against a red background. The idea around the motif and selected product was to use a common product to which most Norwegians can relate. The color red was, as earlier mentioned, selected to trigger attention and motivate respondents to take action at the moment of purchase.

The question might be asked why a graphical symbol of wheat flour was on the floor instead of text. First, a graphical symbol, pictogram, or sign takes up less space than written text, and it is easier to see and identify from a distance than pure text, as was shown by the research project "Signal ahead" by Jacobs, Johnston, and Cole in 1975 [20]. Their investigation showed that graphical symbols are 50% easier to read than text at longer distances. Second, graphical symbols work in multilingual environments, as shown by researchers Cairney and Sless [20], as well as for people who cannot read. Third, graphical symbols and signs have better visibility for viewers of all ages [20]. By drawing on the related literature and using the wheat flour pictogram as stimulus on the floor, our hypothesis was that the floor in the grocery store could function as a wayfinding area to guide consumers to product categories. The choice of using a pictogram versus text was therefore based on the research mentioned above.

4   Method

4.1   Data Collection

For data collection in the present study, we used tracking glasses from Tobii (Tobii Glasses 2) and software from iMotions (iMotions 9.1). The software was installed on a Microsoft surface (Surface Pro 7 128 GB i5) with Windows 10. There were no challenges or problems associated with the data collection process using this equipment. The equipment was carefully tested in advance, and the software on the computer was updated to the latest version available. Respondents were given the task of finding a specific product in the store (a packet of wheat flour). They put on the eye tracking glasses and, after the glasses were calibrated, they were taken to the entrance of the store. They were asked to imagine that they were on a regular shopping trip and that they should search for the product as they normally do. The respondents were told which product to find (buy), and after they had found it, they went to the checkout. The research team observed the respondents as they walked around the store and was placed at the end (near the entrance/exit). We strove not to influence participants in any way.

After the eye tracking test was completed, the respondents were asked questions related to shopping habits, the degree to which they liked to cook, and whether they had noticed the sticker placed on the floor (close to the wheat flour). The interviews took place in the store, and written notes were taken. The purpose of the interviews was to gain background information about the respondents, as well as to understand whether they had seen the sticker on the floor and the extent to which it had any effect on their ability to locate the product. The participants willingly shared their thoughts and expressed how they experienced their participation in this project (experiences they had during the test and what they noticed with their eyes).

As a separate empirical component, the data from the qualitative interviews gave us a deeper understanding of user experiences in a grocery store. To ensure that the analyses were carried out in an appropriate manner, without subjective interpretation, both researchers participated. There was an opportunity to have fruitful discussions about how the data should be understood and communicated in a satisfactory way.

4.2 Participants

The present study draws on data from 31 participants of various age groups and genders. Before the participants put on their glasses and the data collection started, they were carefully informed about their rights and the content of the consent form. Participation in the study was completely voluntary, and they could withdraw at any time without providing any explanation. In Table 1, we give an overview of the respondents included in the analysis.

Table 1. Overview of respondents.

Gender	n	%
Female	15	48.39%
Male	16	51.61%
Age	**n**	**%**
< 20	3	9.68%
21–30	16	51.61%
31–40	6	19.35%
41–50	1	3.23%
51–60	2	6.45%
> 60	3	9.68%

Table 1 shows an equal distribution by gender in this study and that approximately half of the participants are aged between 21 and 30. During the qualitative post-test interviews, questions were asked that could be linked to the respondents' preferences regarding the grocery trade. On the question related to the extent to which they like to cook, 36% answered that they are very fond of cooking, 29% like it to some extent, 13% are neutral, 19% are not very fond of cooking, and 3% are not fond of cooking at all. When it comes to habits in a grocery store, 39% answered that they are targeted, while 29% like to look at the selection (without rushing). Thirty-two percent of the respondents do both, depending on the situation and the time they have available.

To the question of which criteria must be met to ensure a good user experience in a physical grocery store, the answers varied, but certain common denominators recurred: it should be easy to find products, the store should be tidy, and there should be clear marking of where items are located, a good selection (assortment), and pleasant and helpful service.

4.3 Data Analysis

Software from iMotions (version 9.1) was used to perform analyses of the eye tracking data. To examine the effects of the sticker on the floor (close to the wheat flour), we defined an area of interest (AOI) – AOIs refer to regions of display – where the sticker was clearly visible to the respondents. Since the first-person view video (POW) is a constantly moving medium, unlike an image, it was a time-consuming task to highlight AOI throughout the video sequence in which each of the respondents was exposed to the sticker. The area of the AOI had to be moved every second, as the test persons moved around in the space. This marking had to be done manually for each individual respondent.

During the analysis, the focus was on the following activities: (1) Movements and flow in the space from the respondents entered the store and until they found the product; (2) Extent to which they focused their gaze on the sticker on the floor; and (3) Extent to which they remembered seeing the sticker on the floor compared to whether they looked at the sticker. Overall, this gave us an understanding of whether the sticker had a function and was helpful in a shopping situation.

Regarding the analysis, both actual numbers and data offered by the software were reviewed. Note that in this study, we have not performed any separate (additional) static analysis, other than the numbers (values) reported by the software. It could have been appropriate if many of the respondents noticed the sticker on the floor and if we had more than one AOI. More precisely, since there were so few respondents who gave attention to the sticker on the floor (see Sect. 5.1), we discussed that it was not appropriate. In addition, a qualitative analysis was undertaken for each respondent which emphasized where, on an individual level, they fixed their gaze during the test process.

Furthermore, manual analyses were performed to gain an overall overview of the data in which the respondents were studied as one group (not on an individual level). When working with eye tracking data collected using glasses, it is necessary to work with each respondent individually.

5 Findings

5.1 Attention to the Sticker on the Floor

The present paper draws on data collected by eye tracking glasses, along with qualitative interview data from participants in the eye tracking test. As the sticker on the floor (symbolizing wheat flour) is investigated in this study, this was the AOI when analyzing the video recorded. In addition to data recorded by the eye-tracking glasses, we draw on outcomes from the interviews. The respondent count reveals that only three respondents gazed at the AOI during the test (respondent ration is about 10%). The findings show that AOI duration (the average duration of how long the AOI was active on this stimuli) was 3.8712 s. Regarding time spent looking at the AOI (sticker on the floor), the results show this was 0.7395 s on average. Moreover, the hit time since the AOI's start time until gaze entered for the first time the AOI, the analysis shows 1.6069 s on average. Overall, the findings from the eye-tracking test show that the respondents paid extremely little visual attention to the sticker on the floor, and many of them gave it no visual attention at all. Consequently, the sticker had little or no effect in the search for the product they were to find (a packet of wheat flour).

5.2 Post-test Interviews

Moving on to the analysis of the results from the post-test interviews with the respondents, the findings reveal that 28 out of 31 could not remember seeing the sticker on the floor, even after they were shown a picture of it. This means that only three people remembered seeing the sticker on the floor. Furthermore, our analysis shows that the respondents who focused their eyes on the sticker were those who remembered it during the post-test interview. Of those respondents who could remember the sticker (n = 3), two of three remembered it only after they were shown a picture of the design. In the post-test interview, the respondents expressed that if they had been told by the grocery shop to use the floor as a guide for indoor navigation and wayfinding, they would probably have looked at it more often. They also pointed out that the floor in today's grocery stores is seldom used as a wayfinding arena for navigation, marketing, or communication.

5.3 Navigation and Visual Attention in the Store

Based on qualitative analysis of the eye tracking data, the illustration below (Fig. 3) shows our findings related to how the participants navigated in the store and the elements to which they paid visual attention. An explanation is given of each of the pictures (picture 1–3). The conclusion from the qualitative analysis of the eye tracking data is that a retail space should not be too open but have a certain spaciousness and long lines of sight. Another insight is that goods should not be placed behind obstacles in the room, such as columns, as they will not easily be noticed by customers.

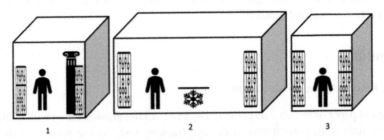

Fig. 3. Navigation and visual attention in the retail space.

The first image in Fig. 3 shows how obstacles in the retail space such as columns make it difficult to navigate in the store. The eye tracking data from the respondents show that their visual attention was reduced due to the obstacles. Furthermore, the eye tracking data showed that there was a dead spot behind the column in the space in which they moved. None of the respondents was aware of items or goods one meter or more behind the column. The second image illustrates the qualitative analysis of the eye tracking data; this shows that in open spaces in the store, the respondents were looking further beyond themselves, which gave them a bigger overview of the retail space. However, they did not look at goods, but at the retail space itself. The last image (number 3) illustrates how the respondents in narrow spaces tended to focus on and look at the goods, probably because they were closer to them.

6 Discussion

Our research question, *To what extent do customers pay visual attention to point-of-sale stickers on the floor in a buying situation?* was prompted by the fact that floors in stores are used to a low extent (or not at all) to inform customers about market products. Many stores have a large floor space available, and there is potential to use it for various purposes. We know that eight of ten Norwegian households purchase goods from a grocery store every day or several times a week [4], proving that grocery stores are frequently and regularly visited by most people. As the Norwegian population consumes a great deal of wheat flour, we used a graphical symbol of wheat flour on the floor sticker instead of pure text. Symbols are easier to see from a distance than text. In addition, graphical symbols have better visibility for viewers, regardless of age [20], and need less space than text. In the search for specific products in a grocery store, customers are used to looking for product categories using, among other things, posters or shelf dividers.

What we have tested in this study is, in many ways, innovative because it has not, to the best of our knowledge, been examined by any previous research studies. Eye tracking is a method that, to a large extent, is of interest for use within the retail industry to understand the behavior of consumers when navigating in a store [9]. This technology has also enjoyed an increasing degree of popularity among researchers [10] as well as practitioners. No other method can measure precisely where the eyes (pupils) focus at any time through a customer journey in a store. The combination of the idea and the use of eye tracking gave us a unique insight into consumers' attention when they are shopping in a grocery store. The use of the glasses and post-test interviews with participants led to unambiguous findings. Our analysis revealed that the respondents noticed the sticker on the floor to a very low or no extent. Although in-store signage may have an impact on customers' visual attention during decision-making processes, as well as increasing attention to products [11], our study shows that a sticker on the floor had no effect, in terms of visual attention, and customers did not remember seeing it. Most of the respondents were relatively young. A study by the Norwegian Consumer Council [4] shows that persons aged between 18 and 29 visit the grocery store more frequently compared to elderly people. Thus, the question arises in our study of whether we would have gained different data if we had only focused on customers aged 60 +. The collected and analyzed data show that age has no significant impact on how customers navigate in a store, although a study of Norwegian trading patterns [4] revealed that the 23% of respondents in the oldest age group (60 +) visited the grocery store only once a week. This finding has piqued our curiosity in relation to how a shop could be designed for an older target group. Although our findings do not give any clear evidence of differences across age groups regarding visual attention in physical stores, we need to investigate further to achieve an accurate answer. In the present study, we point out that we do not make any separate analysis at the intersection of gender, age or other variables. This is because of a little variation in the findings and very few respondents noticed the sticker.

Furthermore, we found from our qualitative data that the respondents did not use the floor as a way finder in the store. However, they told us in the post-test interviews that they were open to using the floor as a path guiding indoor navigation and wayfinding. Their feedback on this possible outcome – of using the floor as a communication and navigation area – was dependent on the grocery store's desire to teach them to use the floor in a new way. We therefore see potential in the future of using the floor as a way finder or marketplace for marketing products in grocery stores. These findings are interesting in themselves and can also be used as a starting point for discussion. Is it a good idea to use the floor to guide customers to the right product in a fast and efficient way, and why do very few customers notice what is on the floor? According to [5], people rarely look up. Most people look straight ahead, and 15% to 30% look down towards the floor. This is vital knowledge regarding placing items in stores with the intention to attract customers' visual attention.

A floor has different functions, according to [18]. When the floor is experienced as something safe, it is something you do not regard as special, as long as you have firm footing. In contrast, if the floor is unstable or directly dangerous, you will immediately become preoccupied with looking down and checking where you step. As the floor in stores is normally safe to walk on, customers pay little visual attention to it and spend more time navigating the retail space and looking at goods, shelves, and walls. We nevertheless highlight another function of the floor, according to [18], which is to direct us from one place to another. This function can create an opportunity and make customers more aware of the floor. Furthermore, the floor as an area for navigation can also become a place of communication to spread information about goods and offers. In this regard, stickers on the floor may be used as a new form of point-of-sale material. As the floor is a large part of the physical retail space, it has the potential to be used as a marketing and information area in the store.

Our study found that this may be possible if customers are told by the store to look at the floor as a navigation and information area. In our view, the retail industry could therefore carry out more research on how this may be possible. To enhance user experiences and make it easy to shop, various mobile apps can also guide the customers during the shopping journey in physical stores [12]. Such apps can replace signs or other attributes that contribute to enlightenment. In this regard, we present the idea of creating a mobile app that uses the floor as a guiding area in a grocery shop. As most customers who use the store weekly are young people, aged 21 to 30 [4], we see a golden opportunity and a connection between using new technology such as a mobile app for the use of the floor in a physical retail space.

In our study, we have seen that the sticker on the floor drew little or no attention from the respondents. On the other hand, we have seen that space management can have an impact on how customers see and move in the store. What has captured our interest is the possible outcome if the sticker were placed elsewhere in the retail space. An idea could be to place the sticker in the open spaces where the customers gain a more extensive overview of the retail space. In relation to this, we would argue that a sticker on the floor can have a greater effect. At the same time, we wonder if the lack of visual attention paid to the sticker is due to the huge number of competing elements in the store, possibly creating a visual overload for the respondents. This may be the reason the respondents did not notice the sticker on the floor.

Grounded in the idea of using the floor as a guide to products, the results were somewhat surprising and interesting. In our research we noticed that our hypothesis of using color and pictograms as visual attention on the floor had little or no effect. This was not necessarily that it was something wrong with the actual design of the sticker, but the fact that the customers did not notice the floor in the store.

More research is therefore needed to be able to give concrete and precise advice on where to place stickers on the floor. Although we can see from our study that the retail space must not be too open and should not have visual obstacles, a certain spaciousness in the store is important to gain customers' visual attention. Additionally, further research should be done on the effect of color and visual attributes in space to accurately state a clear finding. In this regard, an idea is to include several AOI's (beyond one as in this study). For example, conduct a study with multiple stickers (AOI's) on the floor and compare the degree to which each of these receive visual attention, as well as the effect of different shapes, symbols, colors, sizes and so on.

7   Conclusion

We conclude that eye tracking as a method has worked in regard to the study context and what we intended to investigate. The objection to using point-of-sale stickers on the floor is that they did not have a large impact on respondents' visual attention, and if they are to work, customers must be trained to use the floor as a navigation, information, or marketing channel. Stickers on the floor gain little or no attention from the users (buyers), but space management can have an impact on how customers see and move in the store. Consequently, we see the potential to use the floor, currently an unused retail space, but it will be important to carry out more research on what it is used for and where in the store it can be used. Furthermore, one should examine whether it should be used in closed space or open space in the shop and whether in relation to marketing of goods or purely for purposes of information and navigation in stores.

References

1. Tobiipro. https://www.tobiipro.com/applications/marketing-user-research/shopper-research/
2. Huddleston, P.T., Behe, B.K., Driesener, C., Minahand, S.: Inside-outside: using eye-tracking to investigate search-choice processes in the retail environment. J. Retail. Consum. Serv. **43**, 85–93 (2018)
3. Soomro, Y.A., Kaimkhani, S.A., Iqbal, J.: Effect of visual merchandising elements of retail store on consumer attention. J. Bus. Strat. **11**(1), 21–40 (2017)
4. Forbrukerrådet. https://www.forbrukerradet.no/wp-content/uploads/2015/09/Dagligvareun dersøkelsen.pdf
5. Hillesland, J.: Shopping. Link Analytix, Oslo (2019)
6. Suja, R., Nair, S.M., Riad, S.: Impact of store-attributes on food and grocery shopping behavior: insights from an emerging market context. EuroMed J. Bus. **16**(3), 324–343 (2021)
7. Davydenko, M., Peetz, J.: Shopping less with shopping lists: planning individual expenses ahead of time affects purchasing behavior when online grocery shopping. J. Consum. Behav. **19**(1), 240–251 (2020). https://doi.org/10.1002/cb.1812

8. Zatz, L.Y., et al.: Comparing online and in-store grocery purchases. J. Nutr. Educ. Behav. **53**(6), 471–479 (2021). https://doi.org/10.1016/j.jneb.2021.03.001

9. IntoTheMinds. https://www.intotheminds.com/blog/en/eye-tracking-retail-sector/

10. Holmqvist, K., Nyström, M., Andersson, R., Dewhurst, R., Jarodzka, H., van de Weijer, J.: Eye Tracking: A Comprehensive Guide to Methods and Measures. Oxford University Press, Oxford (2011)

11. Otterbring, T., Wästlunda, E., Gustafsson, A.: Eye-tracking customers' visual attention in the wild: dynamic gaze behavior moderates the effect of store familiarity on navigational fluency. J. Retail. Consum. Serv. **28**, 165–170 (2016)

12. Niemeier, S., Zocchi, A., Catena, M.: Reshaping Retail: Why Technology is Transforming the Industry and How to Win in the New Consumer Driven World. John Wiley & Sons (2013)

13. Harwood, T., Jones, M.: Mobile eye-tracking in retail research. In: Horsley, M., Eliot, M., Knight, B.A., Reilly, R. (eds.) Current Trends in Eye Tracking Research, pp. 183–199. Springer, Cham (2014). https://doi.org/10.1007/978-3-319-02868-2_14

14. Helsedirektoratet. https://www.helsedirektoratet.no/rapporter/utviklingen-i-norsk-kosthold/ Utviklingen%20i%20norsk%20kosthold%202020%20-%20Kortversjon.pdf/_/attachment/ inline/0d856999-7cec-49ac-a580-db2664506be3:265cbe603d4cf786d5fbf2272c6c34a36 e4cb540/Utviklingen%20i%20norsk%20kosthold%202020%20-%20Kortversjon.pdf

15. Regjeringen. https://www.regjeringen.no/no/aktuelt/mer-norsk-mathvete/id2900203/

16. Landbruksdirektoratet. https://www.landbruksdirektoratet.no/nb/nyhetsrom/nyhetsarkiv/nor skprodusert-mathvete-oker

17. Landbruk24. https://landbruk24.no/dette-spiste-vi-i-2020/

18. Thiis-Evensen, T.: Archetypes in Architecture. Universitetsforlaget, Oslo (1987)

19. Oxford Learners Dictionaries. https://www.oxfordlearnersdictionaries.com/definition/eng lish/pictograph

20. Black, A., Luna, P., Lund, O., Walker, S.: Information Design, Research and Practice. A Gower Book, Routledge, London (2017)

Error Classification Using Automatic Measures Based on n-grams and Edit Distance

L'ubomír Benko(✉) ⓘ, Lucia Benkovaⓘ, Dasa Munkovaⓘ, Michal Munkⓘ, and Danylo Shulzenko

Constantine the Philosopher University in Nitra, 949 01 Nitra, Slovakia
lbenko@ukf.sk

Abstract. Machine translation (MT) evaluation plays an important task in the translation industry. The main issue in evaluating the MT quality is an unclear definition of translation quality. Several methods and techniques for measuring MT quality have been designed. Our study aims at interconnecting manual error classification with automatic metrics of MT evaluation. We attempt to determine the degrees of association between automatic MT metrics and error classes from English into inflectional Slovak. We created a corpus, which consists of English journalistic texts, taken from the British online newspaper The Guardian and their human and machine translations. The MT outputs, produced by Google translate, were manually annotated by three professionals using a categorical framework for error analysis and evaluated using reference proximity through the metrics of automated MT evaluation. The results showed that not all examined automatic metrics based on n-grams or edit distance should be implemented into a model for determining the MT quality. When determining the quality of machine translation in respect to syntactic-semantic correlativeness, it is sufficient to consider only the Recall, BLEU-4 or F-measure, ROUGE-L and NIST (based on n-grams) and the metric CharacTER, which is based on edit distance.

Keywords: Machine translation · Automatic metrics · Error classification

1 Introduction

Machine translation (MT) is one of the most popular natural language processing applications. It is the automatic translation of text from one natural language into another natural language. The quality of the translation, its accuracy or, on the other hand, its error rate, plays a key role in interpersonal communication. Evaluating the MT quality is essential for improving MT systems, as it presents a strong indicator of the correlation between an MT output and its corresponding human translation [1:2]. The biggest issue in evaluating MT quality is an unclear definition of translation quality together with its criteria and measures for translation quality. There are no explicit criteria for "good translation" [1:2]. For this reason, several methods and techniques for measuring translation quality have been designed. In general, they can be divided into a manual approach to MT quality assessment and an automatic approach to MT quality assessment [2]. Both

T. Guarda et al. (Eds.): ARTIIS 2022, CCIS 1675, pp. 345–356, 2022.
https://doi.org/10.1007/978-3-031-20319-0_26

approaches have their advantages, but also their disadvantages. The manual evaluation assesses the translation more likely as a whole, i.e. it assesses cohesiveness and coherence of the translation, but this evaluation is very subjective and time-consuming [3]. The standard criteria used within manual evaluation are fluency (grammatical correctness), adequacy (preservation of the meaning) or usability. In addition to standard criteria of MT quality, human evaluators also use task oriented methods for quality evaluation such as post-editing or error analysis, and/or error classification. Error classification (i.e. identification and classification of errors occurring in a machine translated text) is not only a time-consuming, but also a resource intensive task. It provides a distribution of errors over the defined error classes, but it suffers from low consistency of human evaluators [4].

On the other hand, automatic evaluation brings speed, objectivity, and reusability to the measurement. The objective of automatic MT evaluation is to calculate the numerical score (between 0–1), which represents the quality of MT output and/or the performance of the MT system. This evaluation is less reliable compared to manual evaluation, as the evaluation lies in a lexical comparison of two strings - MT output with reference/human translation - in a target language. Within automatic MT evaluation, there are two main approaches for evaluating quality (MT output) automatically - reference proximity and performance-based techniques [5]. In this study we focus on reference proximity techniques, which are based on statistical principles (lexical similarities) or linguistic features [6]. They compare translation to the human reference in that way, that the closer MT output is to the reference the better the quality is considered to be. Distance between MT output and reference translation is calculated automatically (e.g. WER, TER or CharacTER) or their overlap (e.g. BLEU, F-measure, METEOR or NIST).

Our study aims at interconnecting manual error classification with automatic metrics of MT evaluation. Through error analysis, we point out the degree of association between automatic MT metrics and error classes from English into inflectional Slovak.

The structure of the paper is as follows. The second section introduces automatic MT metrics based on reference proximity. The third section focuses on the methodology of experiment with assumptions, methods, and dataset. The fourth section describes the results of the experiment. Subsequently, the last two sections discuss the obtained results and draw conclusions.

2   Automatic MT Metrics Based on Reference Proximity

Automatic MT metrics provide quantified scores of overall translation quality. They do not require high human effort and they can be used quite easily to compare the performance of two or more MT systems. Therefore, they are not only popular, but also in great demand. Based on their results, MT systems are subsequently developed or optimized.

In this study, we focus on automatic MT metrics that compare MT output with reference based on exact lexical matches between MT words, and/or phrases and reference.

Lexical similarity is a measure of the degree to which the word or phrase of MT output is similar to the corresponding word or phrase in reference. A lexical similarity of 1 means a total overlap between MT output and reference, whereas 0 means there is no match. *Precision* and *recall* belong to the basic MT metrics [7], where precision is the proportion of words in MT output/hypothesis (Y) that are present in the reference (X), and recall is the proportion of words in reference (X) that are present in the hypothesis (Y). F-measure is a harmonic mean of precision and recall:

$$P = precision(Y|X) = \frac{|X \cap Y|}{|Y|}, \tag{1}$$

$$R = recall(Y|X) = \frac{|X \cap Y|}{|X|}, \tag{2}$$

$$F1 = \frac{2PR}{P+R}. \tag{3}$$

Bilingual Evaluation Understudy (BLEU) is a standard automatic measure, which is a precision-oriented metric. *BLEU-n* [8] is a geometric mean of n-gram precisions with a *brevity penalty* (BP), i.e. penalty to prevent very short sentences:

$$BLEU(n) = exp \sum_{n=1}^{N} w_n \log p_n \times BP \tag{4}$$

where w_n is weights for different p_n,

$$BP = \begin{cases} 1, \text{ if } h > r \\ e^{1-\frac{r}{h}}, \text{ if } h \leq r \end{cases} \tag{5}$$

where r is a reference of a hypothesis h.

The *BLEU* represents two features of translation quality- *adequacy* and *fluency* by calculating words or lexical *precisions* [9]. The *BLEU* score has several variations, depending on the number of words in the reference used to compute the brevity penalty. The IBM version of *BLEU* uses the average value of the length of the reference. The *NIST* version of *BLEU* uses the shortest references to compute the brevity penalty. To not get confused, there exists the *NIST* metric which is not equal to the *NIST* version of *BLEU*, using the arithmetic mean of the n-grams counts instead of the geometric mean, which is used in the ordinary *BLEU-n* metric.

Measure for Evaluation of Translation with Explicit Ordering (METEOR) is a recall-oriented measure. It calculates not only *precision* (like *BLEU*), but also *recall*. Both are combined with a preference to *recall* when calculating the harmonic mean. It is based on a combination of unigram-precision and unigram-recall, and on direct capture of how well-ordered the matched words/phrases in MT outputs are in respect to the reference [10]:

$$METEOR = \frac{10PR}{R+9P}(1 - BP), \tag{6}$$

where the unigram-recall and unigram precision are given by P and R, and

$$BP = 0.5 \left(\frac{\#chunks}{\#unigrams\_matched} \right), \tag{7}$$

L'. Benko et al.

where chunk (a group of matched unigrams between MT output and reference) is a minimum number of words required to match unigrams in the MT output with corresponding references [11].

NIST [12] is a metric based on *BLEU*. It was designed to improve *BLEU* by rewarding the translation of infrequently used words, i.e. it uses heavier weights for rarer words [11]. The *BLEU* metric calculates n-gram precision with equal weight to each one, but the *NIST* metric calculates how much information is preserved in a particular n-gram.

Character n-gram F-measure (ChrF) is a language- and tokenization-independent metric, which correlates well with human judgments on the system- and segment-level [13]:

$$chrF\beta = (1 + \beta^2)(\frac{chrP \cdot chrR}{\beta^2 chrP + chrR}), \tag{8}$$

where the character n-gram *precision* and *recall* are given by *chrP* (percentage of n-grams in the hypothesis) and *chrR* (percentage of n-grams in the reference). β is a parameter which assigns β times more important to recall than to precision. For instance, if $\beta = 1$, both (precision and recall) have the same weight and if $\beta = 2$, recall is two times more important than precision and vice versa, if $\beta = \frac{1}{2}$, precision is two times more important than recall [4, 14].

Recall-Oriented Understudy for Gisting Evaluation (ROUGE) counts the number of overlapping units such as n-gram, word sequences, and word pairs between the computer-generated summary to be evaluated and the ideal summaries created by humans [15]. It includes several automatic evaluation measures that determine the similarity between summaries. In this study, we used *ROUGE-N* and *ROUGE-L*. *ROUGE-N* is an n-gram recall between a hypothesis summary and a set of reference summaries. *ROUGE-L* is the longest common subsequence F-measure and counts only in sequence co-occurrences.

The second approach to measure the lexical similarity of two words, and/or phrases is to calculate the minimum edit distance to transform an MT output/hypothesis into a reference (to transform one string into another) through edit operations. Sets of string operations depend on the type of edit distance. One of the simplest sets of edit operations is defined by Levenshtein [16:107-111]:

- Insertion of a character. If $a = uv$, then insert the character x produces uxv. This can also be denoted $\varepsilon \rightarrow x$, using ε to denote the empty string.
- Deletion of a character x changes uxv to $uv(x \rightarrow \varepsilon)$.
- Substitution of a character x for a character $y \neq x$ changes uxv to $uyv(x \rightarrow y)$.

Word Error Rate (WER) counts the Levenshtein distance between the hypothesis and reference, without allowing the words reordering [17]:

$$WER(h, r) = \frac{min\#(I+D+S)}{|r|}), \tag{9}$$

where r is a reference of a hypothesis h, I- insertion, D - deletion, and S - substitution.

The minimum number of edit operations (insertions, substitutions, and deletions of the words necessary to transform the hypothesis/MT output into the reference) is divided by the number of words in the reference [7].

Translation Edit Rate (TER) is defined as the minimum number of edit operations required to change a hypothesis/machine translation to an exact match with the reference [18]:

$$TER\,(h, r) = \frac{min\#(I + D + S + shift)}{|r|}),\qquad(10)$$

where r is a reference of a hypothesis/machine translation h, I - insertion, D - deletion, S - substitution and shift (number of changes in word order).

CharacTER [19] is an edit distance metric, which is based on character-level and calculates the character-level edit distance while performing the shift edit on word level. Like *TER*, *CharacTER* also calculates the minimum number of character edit operations required to change a hypothesis to the exact match of the reference, divided by the length of the hypothesis:

$$CharacTER\,(h, r) = \frac{min\#(shift + I + D + S)}{|h|}\qquad(11)$$

where r is a reference of a hypothesis h, I- insertion, D - deletion, S - substitution and shift (number of changes in word order).

3 Experiment

Our objective is to investigate the relationship between automatic MT metrics and a distribution of errors over the defined error classes. We attempt to determine which of the examined metrics (based on lexical similarity and edit distance) associate the best with individual error classes of a categorical framework for error analysis [20:100]. The examined texts (1903 sentences/3271 segments) were of the journalistic style, taken from the British online newspaper The Guardian. In 2021, the texts were translated by the freely available Neural Google Translate (NGT) engine and subsequently manually annotated by three professionals. The annotation was performed according to the categorical framework for error analysis for translation into Slovak [20:100]. The framework consists of five error classes (categories):

1. Predication,
2. Modal and communication sentence framework,
3. Syntactic-semantic correlativeness,
4. Compound/complex sentences,
5. Lexical semantics.

In this study, we focus only on one particular category - Syntactic-semantic correlativeness - characterizing inflectional languages like Slovak. This category corresponds to the category of *language,* and/or *fluency,* both belonging to the core of harmonized DQF-MQM Error typology [21].

The category of Syntactic-semantic correlativeness is more deeply divided into subcategories: Nominal morphosyntax, Pronominal morphosyntax, Numeral morphosyntax, Verbal morphosyntax, Word order, Other morphosyntactic phenomena, and Others.

3.1 Assumption

Given that the metrics of automatic evaluation are constantly developing, we have been encouraged to examine which of the MT metrics (based on lexical similarity or edit distance) used so far are appropriate and/or best capture the errors that occurred in machine translation into the inflectional language. Besides free word order, inflectional languages are also characterized by inflection and declension. Both linguistic features are particularly captured in the category of Syntactic-semantic correlativeness.

We assume that:

Automatic MT metrics based on lexical similarity (precision, recall, F-measure, ChrF, NIST, ROUGE, METEOR, and BLEU) associate better with the occurrence of errors in a given category than automatic MT metrics based on edit distance (CharacTER, WER, and TER).

To prove our assumption, we used Goodman and Kruskal's gamma. Gamma represents the degree of association between two variables, i.e. the probability of whether two variables are in the same or opposite order.

3.2 Dataset

The dataset consists of machine-translated journalistic texts from English (STs) to Slovak (NMTs). The readability and lexico-grammatical features of our corpus are as follows (Table 1):

Table 1. Dataset composition

Feature type	Feature name	NMTs_SK	STs_EN
Readability	Average sentence length	17.12034	19.26274
	Average word length	5.696361	4.996122
	#short sentences ($n < 10$)	469	395
	#long sentences ($n \geq 10$)	1434	1508
Lexico-grammatical	Frequency of proper nouns	1501	3078
	Frequency of nouns	10070	8627
	Frequency of adjectives	3324	2968
	Frequency of adverbs	933	1667
	Frequency of verbs	5198	6473
	Frequency of pronominals	2371	2124
	Frequency of particles	592	149
	Frequency of foreign words	841	0
	Frequency of interjections	3	3
	Frequency of numerals	617	777
	Frequency of prepositions & conjunctions	6028	6697
	Frequency of interpunction	5958	3547

3.3 Methods

For the metrics as *BLEU*, *NIST*, *METEOR*, and *ChrF* Python Natural Language Toolkit (NLTK) library was used.

```
from nltk.translate.bleu_score import sentence_bleu, sen-
tence_nist, meteor_score, chrf_score
bleu_scores_1.append(sentence_bleu([ref], hyp,
weights=(1,0,0,0)))
bleu_scores_2.append(sentence_bleu([ref], hyp,
weights=(0,1,0,0)))
bleu_scores_3.append(sentence_bleu([ref], hyp,
weights=(0,0,1,0)))
bleu_scores_4.append(sentence_bleu([ref], hyp,
weights=(0,0,0,1)))
nist_scores.append(sentence_nist([ref], hyp, n=1))
meteor_scores.append(meteor_score([ref], hyp))
chrf_scores.append(chrf_score.sentence_chrf(ref, hyp))
```

For *ROUGE*, *TER*, and *WER* open-source libraries were used.

```
import jiwer
import pyter
from rouge_metric import PyRouge
wer_scores.append(jiwer.wer (ref, hyp))
rogue_scores.append(rouge.evaluate_tokenized([hyp], [ref]))
ter_scores.append(pyter.ter(hyp,ref))
```

Precision, recall, F-measure were implemented separately from the others. The *CharacTER* was implemented as an edit distance function.

4 Results

After manual error classification, we identified 1851 errors in the category of syntactic-semantic correlativeness, of which 394 errors were identified in nominal morphosyntax, 88 errors in pronominal morphosyntax, 4 errors in numeral morphosyntax, 276 errors in verbal morphosyntax, 453 errors in word order, 617 errors in other morphosyntactic phenomena, and 19 errors in the subcategory others.

Based on a Cochran Q test ($N = 3271$, $Q = 1371.86$, $df = 6$, $p < 0.001$) we showed that there are statistically significant differences between the individual subcategories. These results were also proved by *Kendall's Coeff. of concordance* (0.07), where were identified a small agreement, and/or almost no agreement between the examined subcategories.

Based on the results of multiple comparisons, we showed statistically significant differences between Other morphosyntactic phenomena/Word order/Pronominal morphosyntax and other subcategories and, conversely, there were no statistically significant differences between Numeral morphosyntax and Others, or between Nominal morphosyntax and Word order (Table 2).

Table 2. Multiple comparisons: Homogenous groups, $p < 0.05$

	Incidence	1	2	3	4	5
Numeral morphosyntax	0.12%	****				
Others	0.58%	****				
Pronominal morphosyntax	2.69%			****		
Verbal morphosyntax	8.44%				****	
Nominal morphosyntax	12.05%		****			
Word order	13.85%		****			
Other morphosyntactic phenomena	18.86%					****

Using Goodman and Kruskal's gamma, we determined the rank associations between the individual subcategories and the automatic MT metrics based on lexical similarity or edit distance (Tables 3 and 4).

Table 3. Nominal morphosyntax - rank association

Error category & automatic metrics	Valid N	*Gamma*	Z	p-value
Nominal morphosyntax & BLEU-4	3271	**0.08****	2.9868	**0.0028**
Nominal morphosyntax & NIST	3271	**0.05***	2.0931	**0.0363**
Nominal morphosyntax & BLEU-3	3271	0.05	1.9018	0.0572
Nominal morphosyntax & BLEU-2	3271	0.04	1.7635	0.0778
Nominal morphosyntax & precision	3271	0.04	1.5416	0.1232
Nominal morphosyntax & ChrF	3271	0.04	1.4759	0.1400
Nominal morphosyntax & F-measure	3271	0.04	1.4083	0.1591
Nominal morphosyntax & METEOR	3271	0.03	1.2716	0.2035
Nominal morphosyntax & recall	3271	0.03	1.1908	0.2337
Nominal morphosyntax & BLEU-1	3271	0.03	1.1790	0.2384
Nominal morphosyntax & WER	3271	−0.03	−1.1804	0.2379
Nominal morphosyntax & TER	3271	−0.03	−1.2338	0.2173
Nominal morphosyntax & ROUGE1	3271	−0.04	−1.7095	0.0874

(continued)

Table 3. (*continued*)

Error category & automatic metrics	Valid N	Gamma	Z	p-value
Nominal morphosyntax & ROUGE2	3271	−0.04	−1.7095	0.0874
Nominal morphosyntax & ROUGE-L	3271	**−0.07****	−2.8404	**0.0045**
Nominal morphosyntax & CharacTER	3271	**−0.09*****	−3.6744	**0.0002**

Note: 0.00 to 0.10 (0.00 to −0.10) – trivial positive (negative) measure of association; 0.10–0.30 (−0.10 to −0.30) – low positive (negative) measure of association; 0.30–0.50 (−0.30 to −0.50) – moderate positive (negative) measure of association; 0.50–0.70 (−0.50 to −0.70) – high positive (negative) measure of association; 0.70–1.00 (−0.70 to −1.00) – very high positive (negative) measure of association; *** $p < 0.001$, ** $p < 0.01$, * $p < 0.05$

The subcategory Nominal morphosyntax (Table 3) is partially identified by the metrics *BLEU-4* and *NIST*, where a trivial, but statistically significant degree of positive association was achieved (*Gamma* $< 0.1, p < 0.01/0.05$), similarly, in the case of the metrics *ROUGE-L* and *CharacTER*, there were achieved statistically significant, but trivial degrees of a negative association (*Gamma* $< −0.1, p < 0.01/0.001$).

The automatic metrics *BLEU-4* and *NIST*, both based on precision, associated best with MT errors in the subcategory of nominal morphosyntax. On the other hand, in terms of edit distance, the metric *CharacTER* associated best with this subcategory.

In the case of the subcategories of pronominal morphosyntax and other morphosyntactic phenomena, there were achieved only trivial, statistically insignificant degrees of association between automatic MT metrics and the given subcategories (*Gamma* $\approx$ 0.00).

In the case of the subcategory of numeral morphosyntax, the degree of association oscillates between a low (0.10–0.30 and/or −0.10––0.30) and a very high (0.70–1.00 and/or −0.70––1.00) either positive or negative degrees of association (Table 4).

Table 4. Numeral morphosyntax - rank association

Error category & automatic metrics	Valid N	Gamma	Z	p-value
Numeral morphosyntax & CharacTER	3271	0.32	1.3681	0.1713
Numeral morphosyntax & TER	3271	0.30	1.2536	0.2100
Numeral morphosyntax & WER	3271	0.30	1.2519	0.2106
Numeral morphosyntax & ROUGE-L	3271	0.30	1.2566	0.2089
Numeral morphosyntax & ROUGE1	3271	0.22	0.9428	0.3458
Numeral morphosyntax & ROUGE2	3271	0.22	0.9428	0.3458
Numeral morphosyntax & BLEU-3	3271	−0.26	−1.0836	0.2786
Numeral morphosyntax & ChrF	3271	−0.40	−1.7115	0.0870
Numeral morphosyntax & BLEU-2	3271	**−0.49***	−2.0522	**0.0401**

(*continued*)

Table 4. (*continued*)

Error category & automatic metrics	Valid *N*	*Gamma*	*Z*	*p*-value
Numeral morphosyntax & METEOR	3271	**−0.57***	−2.4312	**0.0151**
Numeral morphosyntax & BLEU-4	3271	**−0.62***	−2.2520	**0.0243**
Numeral morphosyntax & NIST	3271	**−0.63****	−2.6330	**0.0085**
Numeral morphosyntax & BLEU-1	3271	**−0.65****	−2.7494	**0.0060**
Numeral morphosyntax & precision	3271	**−0.70****	−2.9358	**0.0033**
Numeral morphosyntax & F-measure	3271	**−0.74****	−3.1129	**0.0019**
Numeral morphosyntax & recall	3271	**−0.77****	−3.2238	**0.0013**

Note: 0.00–0.10 (0.00 to −0.10) – trivial positive (negative) measure of association; 0.10–0.30 (−0.10 to −0.30) – low positive (negative) measure of association; 0.30–0.50 (−0.30 to −0.50) – moderate positive (negative) measure of association; 0.50–0.70 (−0.50 to −0.70) – high positive (negative) measure of association; 0.70–1.00 (−0.70 to −1.00) – very high positive (negative) measure of association; *** $p < 0.001$, ** $p < 0.01$, * $p < 0.05$

In the case of verbal morphosyntax, we achieved similar results as for the subcategory of nominal morphosyntax, i.e. only for *ROUGE-L, ROUGE1, ROUGE2*, and *CharacTER* were achieved a statistically significant, but trivial degrees of negative association (*Gamma* > −0.1, $p < 0.01$).

We obtained slightly better results for the subcategories Word order and Others, but still with a low positive, and/or negative degree of association. Only for metrics *Recall, Precision, F-measure, BLEU-3*, and *BLEU-4* (*Gamma* ≥ −0.1, $p < 0.001/0.01/0.05$) were achieved a statistically significant negative degree of association, in the case of the category of Word order. For the category Others, only the *ChrF* metric has achieved a low, but statistically significant positive degree of association (*Gamma* = 0.23, $p = 0.0345$).

5   Discussion

Metrics like *Precision, Recall, F-measure, BLEU-n, NIST, METEOR, WER, TER*, and *ROUGE* are more reliable and have a higher association with linguistic errors within these subcategories: word order, nominal morphosyntax, and numeral morphosyntax. Although they have high associations, the *CharacTER* metric (based on edit distance) has the highest statistical significance among them in nominal morphosyntax. The *ChrF* metric compared to other metrics, which are based on n-grams, showed a poor performance and is not suitable for this linguistic subcategory (error class).

In the case of numeral morphosyntax, the metrics based on n-gram outperform the metrics based on edit distance in all aspects, i.e. in terms of a degree of association with linguistic category, they achieved a higher level of statistical significance ($p < 0.01$). Linguistic categories like verbal morphosyntax, other morphosyntactic phenomena, pronominal morphosyntax, and others do not show the clear associations to automatic metrics (based on n-grams or edit distance) due to approximately the same low degree of association and a low level of statistical significance ($p < 0.05$).

6 Conclusions

The results of our study showed that not all automatic metrics based on n-grams or edit distance should be implemented into a model for determining the MT quality of journalistic texts translated from English into inflectional Slovak. When determining the quality of machine translation in respect to syntactic-semantic correlativeness, it is sufficient to consider only *Recall, BLEU-4* or the *F-measure, ROUGE-L* and *NIST* (based on n-grams) and the metric *CharacTER*, which is based on edit distance. The results can be also applicable to other inflectional languages.

The results of our study also showed certain pitfalls and limitations that open up space for further research. The first question that arises here is whether automatic MT metrics based on statistical principles (lexical similarity) are suitable for determining the quality of machine translation into the inflectional Slovak language? Or rather to accept into the model automatic MT metrics based on linguistic features? On the other hand, whether the categorical framework used for error analysis is suitable (for translation of journalistic texts from English into Slovak), as the strong associations between automatic MT metrics and the error category under study were not proved.

We consider the size of the corpus to be the main limitation of our study along with the limitation to only one style and genre. In future work, we want to focus on the expansion of our corpus in terms of size and style.

Acknowledgements. This work was supported by the Slovak Research and Development Agency under contract No. APVV-18-0473 and Scientific Grant Agency of the Ministry of Education of the Slovak Republic (ME SR) and of Slovak Academy of Sciences (SAS) under the contract No. VEGA-1/0821/21.

References

1. Chow, J.: Lost in translation: fidelity-focused machine translation evaluation (2019). https://www.imperial.ac.uk/media/imperial-college/faculty-of-engineering/computing/public/1819-ug-projects/ChowJ-Lost-in-translation-fidelity-focused-machine-translation-evaluation.pdf
2. Castilho, S., Doherty, S., Gaspari, F., Moorkens, J.: Approaches to human and machine translation quality assessment. In: Moorkens, J., Castilho, S., Gaspari, F., Doherty, S. (eds.) Translation Quality Assessment. MTTA, vol. 1, pp. 9–38. Springer, Cham (2018). https://doi.org/10.1007/978-3-319-91241-7_2
3. Sepesy Maučec, M., Donaj, G.: Machine translation and the evaluation of its quality. In: Recent Trends in Computational Intelligence. IntechOpen (2020). https://doi.org/10.5772/intechopen.89063
4. Popović, M.: Error classification and analysis for machine translation quality assessment. In: Moorkens, J., Castilho, S., Gaspari, F., Doherty, S. (eds.) Machine Translation: Technologies and Applications. Springer, Cham (2018). https://doi.org/10.1007/978-3-319-91241-7_7
5. Babych, B.: Automated MT evaluation metrics and their limitations. In: evista Tradumàtica: Tecnologies De La Traducció, 12 (2014). https://doi.org/10.5565/rev/tradumatica.70
6. Munk, M., Munková, D., Benko, Ľ: Identification of relevant and redundant automatic metrics for MT evaluation. In: Sombattheera, C., Stolzenburg, F., Lin, F., Nayak, A. (eds.) MIWAI 2016. LNCS (LNAI), vol. 10053, pp. 141–152. Springer, Cham (2016). https://doi.org/10.1007/978-3-319-49397-8_12

7. Munk, M., Munkova, D.: Detecting errors in machine translation using residuals and metrics of automatic evaluation. J. Intell. Fuzzy Syst. **34**, 3211–3223 (2018). https://doi.org/10.3233/JIFS-169504

8. Papineni, K., Roukos, S., Ward, T., Zhu, W.: BLEU: a method for automatic evaluation of machine translation. In: Proceedings of the 40th Annual Meeting of the Association for Computational Linguistics, pp. 311–318, Philadelphia (2002)

9. Munk, M., Munkova, D., Benko, L.: Towards the use of entropy as a measure for the reliability of automatic MT evaluation metrics. J. Intell. Fuzzy Syst. **34**, 3225–3233 (2018). https://doi.org/10.3233/JIFS-169505

10. Banerjee, S., Lavie, A.: METEOR: an automatic metric for MT evaluation with improved correlation with human judgments. In: Proceedings of the ACL Workshop on Intrinsic and Extrinsic Evaluation Measures for MT and/or Summarization (ACL-05), pp. 65–72. Michigan (2005)

11. Wołk, K., Koržinek, D.: Comparison and Adaptation of Automatic Evaluation Metrics for Quality Assessment of Re-Speaking (2016)

12. Doddington, G.: Automatic evaluation of machine translation quality using n-gram co-occurrence statistics, pp. 138–145 (2002)

13. Popović, M.: chrF: character n-gram F-score for automatic MT evaluation. In: Proceedings of the Tenth Workshop on Statistical Machine Translation. pp. 392–395. Association for Computational Linguistics, Stroudsburg, PA, USA (2015). https://doi.org/10.18653/v1/W15-3049

14. Popović, M.: chrF deconstructed: beta parameters and n-gram weights. In: Proceedings of the First Conference on Machine Translation: Volume 2, Shared Task Papers, pp. 499–504. Association for Computational Linguistics, Stroudsburg, PA, USA (2016). https://doi.org/10.18653/v1/W16-2341

15. Lin, C.-Y.: ROUGE: a package for automatic evaluation of summaries. In: Text Summarization Branches Out. pp. 74–81. Association for Computational Linguistics, Barcelona, Spain (2004)

16. Jurafsky, D., Martin, J.: Speech and Language Processing (2020)

17. Nießen, S., Och, F.J., Leusch, G., Ney, H.: An evaluation tool for machine translation: Fast evaluation for MT research. In: Proceedings of the 2nd International Conference on Language Resources and Evaluation (LREC-2000), pp. 39–45 (2000)

18. Snover, M., Dorr, B., Schwartz, R., Micciulla, L., Makhoul, J.: A study of translation edit rate with targeted human annotation. In: Proceedings of Association for Machine Translation in the Americas, pp. 223–231 (2006)

19. Wang, W., Peter, J.-T., Rosendahl, H., Ney, H.: CharacTer: translation edit rate on character level. In: Proceedings of the First Conference on Machine Translation: Volume 2, Shared Task Papers. pp. 505–510. Association for Computational Linguistics, Stroudsburg, PA, USA (2016). https://doi.org/10.18653/v1/W16-2342

20. Vaňko, J.: Kategoriálny rámec pre analýzu chýb strojového prekladu. In: Munkova, D. and Vaňko, J. (eds.) Mýliť sa je ľudské (ale aj strojové), pp. 83–100. UKF v Nitre, Nitra (2017)

21. Lommel, A.: Metrics for translation quality assessment: a case for standardising error typologies. In: Moorkens, J., Castilho, S., Gaspari, F., Doherty, S. (eds.) Translation Quality Assessment. MTTA, vol. 1, pp. 109–127. Springer, Cham (2018). https://doi.org/10.1007/978-3-319-91241-7_6

Understanding and Predicting Process Performance Variations of a Balanced Manufacturing Line at Bosch

Ângela F. Brochado[1]([✉])[iD], Eugénio M. Rocha[2,3][iD], and Carina Pimentel[1,4][iD]

[1] Department of Economics, Management, Industrial Engineering and Tourism,
University of Aveiro (UA), Aveiro, Portugal
`filipabrochado@ua.pt`
[2] Department of Mathematics, UA, Aveiro, Portugal
[3] Center for Research Development in Mathematics and Applications,
UA, Aveiro, Portugal
[4] Systems for Decision Support Research Group (GOVCOPP),
UA, Aveiro, Portugal

Abstract. Industry 4.0 takes advantage of data-driven approaches to improve manufacturing processes. Root cause analysis (RCA) techniques are naturally required to support the identification of reasons for (in)efficiency processes. However, RCA methods tend to be sensitive to data perturbations and outliers, compromising the confidence of the results and demanding the implementation of robust RCA approaches. Here, methods of graph theory (queue directed graphs), operational research (multi-directional efficiency analysis), machine learning (extreme gradient boosting), and game theory (Shapley analysis) are merged together, in order to obtain a robust approach that is able to benchmark the workers acting on a discrete manufacturing process, determine the relevance level of process variables regarding a worker belonging to the (in)efficient group, and predict the worker performance variation into its next working session. A use case at Bosch ThermoTechnology is analysed to show the methodology's applicability.

Keywords: Discrete manufacturing processes · Benchmarking · Machine learning · Root cause analysis

1 Introduction and Previous Work

RCA can be defined as a set of methodologies for identifying the (fundamental) causes/factors of a problem, based on the analysis of deviations from a standard reference, in order to prevent its future occurrence, reduce overall process variability, and/or optimize costs. For RCA, three main types of approaches can be found in the literature: quantitative, qualitative and mixed. The most addressed and also the most used by companies' continuous improvement teams (namely in the manufacturing industry) are the mixed approaches. They comprise tools brought by the Six Sigma area, such as the 5 Why's, Fault-tree Analysis, Ishikawa Diagram (also known as Fishbone Diagram), Pareto Chart, 8Ds,

T. Guarda et al. (Eds.): ARTIIS 2022, CCIS 1675, pp. 357–371, 2022.
https://doi.org/10.1007/978-3-031-20319-0_27

Failure Mode and Effects Analysis (some recent studies are [1,2]). However, after more than 10 years of the *Industry 4.0 Era*, where companies have systems capable of extracting data from their manufacturing processes, most continuous improvement activities, namely RCA, continue to be developed through conventional methods, such as manual data analysis, or the utilization of basic business analytic tools [3]. These conventional methods conducted by process experts are time-consuming and provide results with high variability [4]. However, the reason why it keeps happening is quite simple to explain. Many companies dealing with big data still lack human resources with the expertise of applying data-driven methodologies with some level of machine learning to automate (and therefore, speed up) their RCA processes.

Moreover, one of the aims of any production manager is to increase the productivity of their production processes. For such, understanding the reasons for deviations in (current) performance is fundamental to devise effective countermeasures for continuous improvement. Manufacturing production lines (MPL) that are balanced, meaning that, globally, the duration of the jobs are designed to minimize bottleneck workstations and maximize operators' work time usage, are particular challenging since, by construction, the deviations are smoother and difficult to grasp.

In this work, we consider the problem of applying an effective and scientific valid data-driven approach to answer the following research questions:

(Q1) Is it possible to identify significant performance variations in a balanced MPL by evaluating process KPIs, metrics and/or variables associated with workers' consecutive work sessions?

(Q2) How can we determine the causes (variables) that led to high/low performance deviations?

(Q3) Is it possible to predict future performance variation based on current calculated process metrics?

In what follows, we introduce some relevant works found in the literature within the scope of automatic approaches for RCA in manufacturing lines. An automatic approach is defined as a sequence of algorithms/methods that follow a set of implicit/explicit rules, measuring relevance, and which are capable of extracting in-depth information from real-data without human intervention, giving variable relevance scores with respect to a process of study.

In fact, there are still few studies that address automatic RCA in manufacturing production problems and the majority focuses on quality problems. In [5], it was developed an approach for constructing digital cause-and-effect diagrams with quality data, where the K-means algorithm is implemented to cluster the problems and causes, and then a classification model based on a random forest is employed to classify cause text into the main cause categories. Similarly, [6] also follow the idea of constructing an automated version of a well-known lean manufacturing tool, the Value Stream Map (VSM), for multi-varieties and small-batch production, with timely on-site waste identification and automated RCA. In addition, [7] developed a two-stage automatic root cause analysis (ARCA) for the phenomenon of overlap in manufacturing. The authors propose a first stage of Problematic Moment Identification (PMI), where relevant data is selected for the analysis by using a Exponentially Weighted Moving Averages control chart. Then factor ranking algorithms were developed and used to avoid hiding highly correlated factors and enabling information on equally probable root causes. The factor ranking algorithms are Co-Occurrences (CO), Chi-Square (CS) and Random Forest (RF). Lastly, [8] presents a big data-driven RCA system including three modules of (1) Problem Identification (to describe multiple and different types of quality problems using data mining methods), Root Cause Identification (using K-Nearest Neighbor (KNN) and Neural Network (NN) classifiers to automatically predict root causes), and Permanent Corrective Action. The authors validated the approach by using data from an automobile factory.

2 Methodology and Mathematical Model

For the problem addressed in this work, it was necessary to implement a more adjusted methodology capable of encompassing not only quality variables but also variables related to the own workers, some of them calculated in a very particular way, with the support of a formal abstract structure, as will be explored in Sect. 3. Additionally, up to the author's knowledge, none of the found RCA methodologies in the literature adopts a robust approach. Robustness is fundamental to get more reliable estimates for unspecified parameters in the presence of outliers or data perturbations, for more trustworthy root cause identification and model predictions.

In particular, the approach in this work generally follows the methodology introduced recently in [9], applied to a Ceramic Industry manufacturing, which has quite different characteristics in comparison with the ones of the manufacturing process of our use case at Bosch. The methodology is schematically described in Fig. 1.

The approach intends to deter-

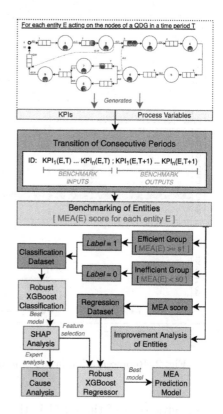

Fig. 1. A data-driven methodology for RCA.

mine the causes, i.e., the variables associated to workers, machines or processes of an MPL that most contribute to an entity being considered efficient or inefficient, according to the KPI values of consecutive work sessions and also predicting future performance variation scores. As displayed in the figure, the approach fuses an operational research method (multi-directional efficiency analysis), a machine learning method (extreme gradient boosting), and a game theory method (Shapley analysis), in order to obtain a robust approach for RCA. Each step of the methodology has been applied to the problem introduced in the next section, and the main results are displayed in Sect. 4.

First, an MPL is chosen and the notion of "entity" is defined (in this problem) as a worker, who operates on the MPL during a certain work shift. Each worker applies a set of actions to a set of workstations in the MPL. The layout and flows in the MPL can be modelled according to a formal abstract mathematical structure, called *Queue Directed Graph* (QDG) (see the bottom block of Fig. 2 and [11]). This mathematical structure consists of nodes (in the case of an MPL nodes are workstations) that act on tokens (i.e., parts or products), which in turn may have to wait in queues if nodes are busy processing previous tokens.

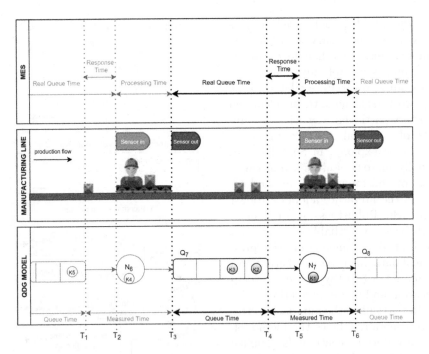

Fig. 2. Representation layers of a MPL segment - retrieved from [11].

The advantage of the QDG is that it is capable of representing any type of MPL with a discrete production environment, so this work can be easily extended to other use cases of discrete manufacturing. Additionally, the QDG is based on *minimal information* (MI), which is meant as the most elementary information from production line operations, enough to autonomously generate the abstract manufacturing layout and calculate metric variables, for example the so-called *AMPM* (the Average Measured Period of time a workstation is occupied processing a part), and the *AQPM* (the Average Queue Period of time a part spends at the queue of a workstation), see [11] for further details about MI and the mathematical formulas of those metrics.

Commonly, the notion of workstations' *Processing Time* is associated with time readings obtained by hardware devices on the workstations, which are further sent to the manufacturing execution system (see first block "MES" of Fig. 2). This metric comprises the amount of time between the beginning of the first operation in a workstation and the moment the product leaves because all tasks, in that workstation, were completed. An QDG gives a similar metric, the so-called *Measured Time*, described in the same figure. It comprises the amount of time between the moment a part/product leaves the queue of a workstation and the moment the product leaves the workstation after all tasks have been performed. So, by setting the difference between the *Measured Time* and the *Processing Time*, it is possible to compute the amount of time a worker spent to "respond" to a part in a queue, the so-called *Part Response Time*. Then, the **Response Time** directly associated with MPL workers is defined as the average of Part Response Times in a time period (usually a shift), see [12].

Hence, taking into account the impact that workers' variability have on the performance of an MPL, it seems clear to study some of the variables that may cause such variability. In this work, these variables are designated as *worker-related variables*: the **Wage**, the **Experience Time** (the amount of training hours invested by the company and benefited by the worker), the **Response Time**, and the **Delay Time**. The latest is a penalization value that measures the lapse between the planned shift start time and the time a worker effectively started working, by using a Gaussian function, defined by

$$\mathrm{DT}(t) = G_\sigma\left(t_b\right) - G_\sigma(t) \quad \text{where} \quad G_\sigma(t) = \frac{1}{\sigma\sqrt{2\pi}} \exp\left(-\frac{1}{2}\frac{(t - t_b)^2}{\sigma^2}\right),$$

for a given standard deviation σ that accounts for the penalization curve spread. The reason for such penalization is the fact that earlier starting workers (artificially) increase the next workstation queue and later starting workers create a gap in the working flow, so both perturb the theoretical balancing of the line, see [26] for data-driven simulations showing this phenomena.

Hence, both *Response Time* and *Delay Time* vary along with workers and different work sessions, while the *Experience Time* and *Wage* may differ between workers, however, both values are fixed per work session (except when events such as pay raises, job promotions and/or job training, where there's an update).

Finally, global quality metrics are also added to the previous ones and introduced to answer all research questions, namely the percentage of *Reworks* and **Quality**. This work, as continuation of previous work based on an optimization problem with a maximization function, uses the complementary values of the AMPM, AQPM and Reworks, defined here as **cAMPM, cAQPM** and **cRework** (see [12] to assess the mathematical formulas). A complement of a variable is given as the maximum possible value of the variable minus their current value.

Further details regarding the data sets used in this work shall be discussed in the section that follows.

3   Data Characterization and Correlation

A chosen MPL of Bosch Thermotechnology (Bosch TT), the business unit facility of residential hot water located in Aveiro, Portugal, is analysed through the proposed approach. At this MPL, usually 2 to 3 daily work shifts operate with a specific number of workers (shift 1 has 14 workers, shift 2 has 8 workers, shift 3 has 14 workers). The MPL is composed by 18 workstations where each worker is assigned to either 1 or 2 of them, depending on the shift, workers' experience with certain machines/processes, and even workers' availability (although not very often). In this study, the 5 chosen data sets contain information related to shift 1 on different time instances, so we will be dealing with 14 entities and 5 time periods. The *Response Time, Delay Time, cRework, cAMPM and cAQPM* are first calculated and then added as new columns to each data set, which already contain information regarding the *Experience Time, Wage* and *Quality* for each entity and time period. Although, each data set represents a specific time period, for confidentiality purposes the actual date is not provided here. Tables 1 and 2 show the statistical characterization of the data sets. In the same way, the wage and experience values change by a offset to preserve anonymity. Notice that the results obtained by the proposed methodology are not affected, since the methods are variable translation invariant.

Table 1. Data sets characterization (part 1 of 2) - mean and standard deviation of the worker-related variables.

| Data set | Worker-related variables | | | |
	Response time	*Delay time*	*Wage*	*Experience time*
d01	1.16 ± 0.99	0.26 ± 0.14		
d02	0.59 ± 0.45	0.17 ± 0.13		
d03	0.59 ± 0.53	0.21 ± 0.14	666.21 ± 46.32	1060.71 ± 586.66
d04	0.96 ± 0.88	0.19 ± 0.15		
d05	1.06 ± 0.96	0.18 ± 0.13		
Units	seconds	per unit	euros	hours

Table 2. Data sets characterization (part 2 of 2) - mean of the shift metrics plus mean and standard deviation of the production variables.

| Data set | Shift metrics | | Production metrics | |
	cRework	*Quality*	*cAMPM*	*cAQPM*
d01	0.726	94.07	7.10 ± 3.70	28.13 ± 10.53
d02	1.260	97.98	7.28 ± 3.44	11.05 ± 05.80
d03	0.782	97.78	7.26 ± 3.50	12.02 ± 06.20
d04	0.813	72.59	6.64 ± 2.87	15.91 ± 07.05
d05	0.416	81.48	6.17 ± 3.21	14.35 ± 07.66
Units	percentage	percentage	seconds	seconds

Figure 3 represents the Person's correlation heatmap of the variables and KPIs, where the values can be (briefly) interpreted as measuring the strength of the linear relationship between variables (similar results where obtained by Spearman's correlation). Looking at the figure, both *Wage* and *Experience Time* have a reasonable negative correlation with the *cAMPM*. This fact is interesting, as it tells us that workers with high wages and high experience time have a lower complementary value of *AMPM* (remember that *AMPM* is the Average Measured Period of time a workstation is occupied processing a product, so the lower the complementary value, the higher is the measured time on the workstation). Such may seem against common sense, but the reason relies on the fact that, for production efficiency, the most experienced workers are allocated to the most complex workstations, with higher processing times and problematic jobs. Hence, to eliminate this bias, the *cAMPM* variable has been removed from the model, and it will not be used from this point further in the analysis.

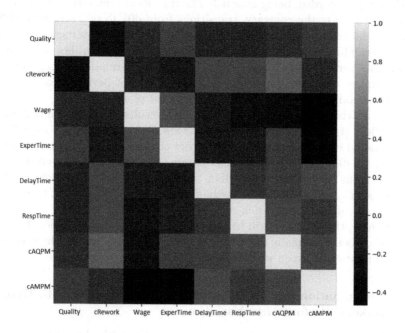

Fig. 3. Variables' correlation matrix/heatmap.

4   Main Results

4.1   Benchmark of Performance Variation Between Consecutive Work Sessions

Proposed by [13] as a derivative of the well-known data envelopment analysis (DEA) methodology, multi-directional efficiency analysis (MEA) is a nonparametric approach that has been widely used nowadays (some applications

are [12,14,15]). This refined approach aims to provide further insights about the
potential improvement for each factor involved in the model, to make a more efficient and cost-based plan to either maximize efficiency or minimize inefficiencies.
For advantages of using MEA over DEA, see [16–18].

The benchmark done here (in the output orientation version) over the tuples
(*worker*, *day*) can be briefly interpreted as the best ranked tuples being the
ones who are capable of maximizing the KPIs of the next work session, when
compared with their KPIs of the current work session, if somehow it was possible
to normalize and compare all input variables between workers.

The MEA algorithm was applied to analyze the variation of performance of
14 workers from shift 1 on 5 work sessions (the data sets). Both shift metrics
presented in Table 2 were selected as inputs (the values at t) and outputs for
the MEA model (the values at $t+1$) to compute the efficiency scores. From the
results, the average MEA score of the 14 workers in the transition from d03 to d04
was the lowest recorded, being near 0.4. The transition from d04 to d05 obtained
a score of 0.92. On the contrary, transitions from d01 to d02 and from d02 to
d03 were the transitions with the best performance improvements, attaining
a 1.0 score. This represents a first level of RCA, as it identifies a significant
performance variation in the data. With the above information, experts are now
able to explore these situations identified as significant performance variations
and derive good practices for future improvement plans.

Based on this first outcome, benchmarked results were split into 2 groups
and labelled: (i) the so-called *Efficient Group* (G_+) was labelled as "1", and
it is composed of workers with a MEA score equal to or bigger than a defined
threshold $s \in]0,1[$; (ii) the *Inefficient Group* (G_-) which was labelled as "0",
and it contains all entities with MEA scores below the s threshold. For our
problem, s was chosen to be the median of the obtained scores. These groups
define the so-called *Classification data set*.

From here, the next step will be to determine the factors/variables that most
influence or better explain the MEA scores, measuring the production line's
ability to improve between work sessions.

4.2   Determination and Analysis of Variables' Relevance to Explain Workers' Performance Variation

Researchers and industrial engineers have built up wealthy literature on classification and regression models and their applications to real-life industrial cases
(the literature is quite extensive). In RCA, one of the recent approaches fits
a machine learning model and uses feature importance (FI) to get the fac-
tors/causes relevance. However, FI is an explainable characteristic of the particular fitted model, which may not represent the problem correctly when the
model used is prone to sensibility through data perturbations.

A critical issue in the classical FI approach in machine learning is that it
is generally not stable to small perturbations of the features' data because the
used model is not robust to perturbations. The *robustness problem* has been
studied thoroughly during the last decades, with a fast-paced development of

robust approaches in some contexts (e.g., see [19–21]). Sometimes, robust models attain worse performances than not robust ones, but by construction they are far more reliable for FI. For the above reasons, the work from [22] combining a robust machine learning model with eXtreme Gradient Boosting (XGBoost) has been studied and employed in the methodology. XGBoost has been greatly recognized in the well-known Kaggle competitions due to its great performance and fast response to classification/regression predictive modelling problems, for structured or tabular data sets (some recent examples of its effectiveness are [23,24]). In our case, after hyper-parameters optimization, the best model can be selected as a good representation of a function mapping features into the Efficient/Inefficient Groups classes. Because we focus on getting variable relevance, over-fitting is a desired situation and it was promoted, because it means that the machine learning model best characterizes the relation between inputs (features) and the output (label).

For explaining the model results, allowing a sort of RCA, we use the so-called SHapleyAdditive exPlanation (SHAP). This method is a game-theoretic approach proposed in [25], which aims to analyse complex models when there is a set of features that work as inputs and which produce a set of outputs (or predictions). The goal is to explain the predictions by computing the contribution of each feature, in the form of a value denominated the **Shapley value**. The SHAP value provides insight into how to fairly distribute the prediction among the features. Therefore, it gives a powerful measure of the importance of each individual feature in a model. The larger the SHAP value, the bigger the importance of such feature to the model explanation.

Following the steps of the proposed methodology of Fig. 1, a grid hyper-parameter optimization of the (robust) XGBoost classifier was performed, and the best model metrics are described in the Table 3. Notice that this is a binary classification problem which is slightly imbalanced (27.8% vs 72.2%). These metrics are considered good enough to assume the relevance of the SHAP analysis.

Table 3. Results metrics of the XGBoost.

	Precision	Recall	F1-score	Support
G_-	1.00	0.93	0.97	15
G_+	0.98	1.00	0.99	41
macro avg	0.99	0.97	0.98	56
weighted avg	0.98	0.98	0.98	56

At the beginning of the methodology, we address SHAP analysis when applied on a robust machine learning method as a RCA approach for the difference between the Efficient Group (G_+) and the Inefficient Group (G_-) of workers. Figure 4 shows the SHAP performance variance relevance plot. All seven variables are sorted in descending order based on their relevance to attain the specific classification class by the model. The red colour represents a high value of the variable for a specific observation, while blue represents a low value of the variable.

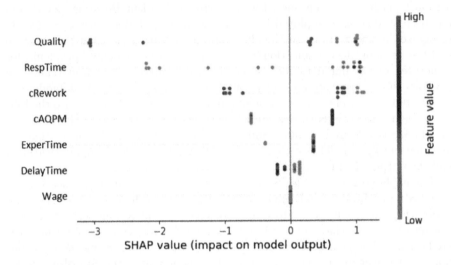

Fig. 4. Variables relevance plot computed with XGBoost+SHAP.

A global analysis of the SHAP results shows that variables *Wage*, *DelayTime*, and *Experience Time* are the less relevant, whereas *Quality* and *cRework* are the most relevant. So, looking at the top relevant variables *Quality* and *cRework*, it can be said that lower values of both metrics are determinant for obtaining the respective classification. The same thing can be mentioned about lower complementary values of *Reworks*: if there is a big number of reworks in a current work session, it is determinant to define the classification class. For higher *Quality* values, the interpretation is not as obvious, so in this situation, Fig. 5(left) can help clarify what is the most prominent impact on the model - a negative impact, however it can be slightly positive for some cases, as seen in Fig. 4.

On the other hand, higher values of *Response Time* are also associated with better determinant where, again, it is not clear about lower values. Figure 5(left) indicates a (global) positive model impact through this variable.

For this work, the partial dependence plot was also computed with SHAP. However, because the outcome did not provide any significant conclusion, it was decided not to include it at the analysis.

4.3 Prediction of the Performance Variation Benchmark

By the end of our RCA approach, the regression data set with the MEA scores, plus the outcomes provided by the SHAP analysis, were used to train the robust XGBoost algorithm, and a regression model was obtained. This model is able to predict the entities' performance (MEA score) for the next work

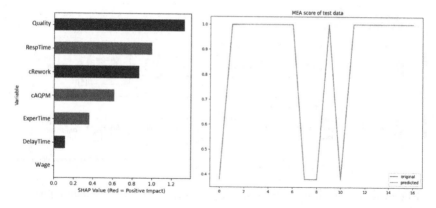

Fig. 5. (left) Variables relevance plot computed with SHAP; (right) MEA score prediction results of workers' performance for the next work session.

session based on some variables from the current work session, in particular, $(Quality, RespTime, cRework)$ were used.

These features were selected, based on the results of an algorithm created to detect which feature (or, in this case, which set of features) could better predict the value of the MEA score. Figure 5(right) compares the MEA performance results of the test data set with the predicted outcomes of the XGBoost robust regression model. The registered RMSE metric is 0.00376, indicating that the model has a quite good fit. Just by looking at the result in Fig. 5(right), the same conclusion of good fit can be taken. Thus, with this magnitude of error, managers may truly rely on the prediction model results to accurately predict future benchmark performance variations. This is quite useful for situations when the algorithm detects significant drops, so managers can try to identify the reasons or root causes for such events.

5   Conclusion and Future Work

In this work, several data sets from a use case problem of a discrete manufacturing process at Bosch TT were analysed and it was possible to:

1. Identify significant performance variations of 14 workers, operating on a balanced MPL, between the transition of consecutive work periods;
2. Determine the causes/factors, i.e., the variables that led to high/low performance variations;
3. Build a prediction model capable of detecting future performance variations scores in the MPL based on the values of the current variables produced by the 14 line workers on the (current) shift.

With these results, experts are now able to explore specific events identified as significant performance variations, derive good practices for improvement plans, or even identify, in time, the causes/variables that will lead to future variation.

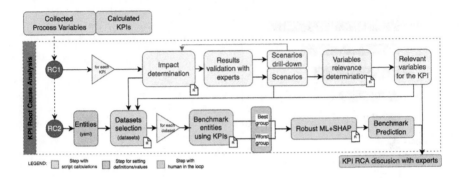

Fig. 6. KPI root cause analysis approaches for the DMAIC's *Analyse* phase.

The followed methodology fuses techniques from operational research (MEA), machine learning (XGBoost) and game theory (SHAP). The attained XGBoost regression model registered a quite good RMSE metric. One of the limitations described in [9] is that although the model is robust by construction, its applicability depends on the set of process variables chosen. Because these variables become the model features, they may induce low values of the machine learning evaluation metrics for the classification model, the foundation for the SHAP analysis. In this work, this problem was overcome, by drawing, analysing and eliminating redundant variables detected with the correlation matrix. Another concern mentioned in [9] is that the methodology approach does not deal (automatically) with the existence of unbalanced classes.

After further real-data validations, this work is planned to be deployed to production testing as a set of micro-services, communicating with Kafka brokers connected to the manufacturing execution system.

Regarding future work, one of the main goals of the research team is the design and development of a data-driven platform to support continuous improvement activities in companies. Although in a prototype phase, this platform will follow the structure of an extensive protocol (a well-defined set of rules and steps), in order to deliver a unified continuous improvement tool for all areas of operation of a company, from the top management to the operational level. The DMAIC (Define-Measure-Analyse-Improve-Control) strategy, well-known as a data-driven improvement approach to help reduce process variation, and deriving from the Six Sigma area, will be used as the protocol foundation.

The methodology applied to the problem addressed in this paper (see Fig. 1) will pertain to the *Analyse* phase of the DMAIC, and it represents one of two possible approaches developed by one of the authors for RCA of key performance indicators (KPIs) (see Fig. 6, RC2 path). The RC1 approach was tested and applied to another use case presented by Bosch TT, which can be found in the following work [27].

Subsequently, it is intended to introduce in the *Improve* stage of the DMAIC, the PDCA cycle (Plan-Do-Check-Act), a widely known approach for continuous improvement and problem-solving [28]. Thus, the Improve phase can integrate multiple PDCA cycles, as many as necessary, to effectively produce an improvement, which must be measured based on a quantifiable metric.

Acknowledgements. The present study was developed in the scope of the Project Augmented Humanity (PAH) [POCI-01-0247-FEDER-046103], in which the first author has a PhD grant, financed by Portugal 2020, under the Competitiveness and Internationalization Operational Program, the Lisbon Regional Operational Program, and by the European Regional Development Fund. The second author was partially supported by the Center for Research and Development in Mathematics and Applications (CIDMA), through the Portuguese Foundation for Science and Technology, reference UIDB/04106/2020.

Data Availability Statement. All data sets used in the present study are confidential information of Bosch company manufacturing systems, so they are not publicly available.

References

1. Rathi, R., Reddy, M.C.G., Narayana, A.L., Narayana, U.L., Rahman, M.S.: Investigation and implementation of 8D methodology in a manufacturing system. Materials Today: Proceedings **50**, 743–50 (2022). https://doi.org/10.1016/J.MATPR.2021.05.273
2. Zhai, G.F., Liu, X.H., Deng, J., Sulistiyowati, W., Adamy, M.R., Jakaria, R.B.: Product quality control based on lean manufacturing and root cause analysis methods. J. Phys: Conf. Ser. **1402**(2), 022038 (2019). https://doi.org/10.1088/1742-6596/1402/2/022038
3. Peças, P., Encarnação, J., Gambôa, M., Sampayo, M., Jorge, D.: PDCA 4.0: a new conceptual approach for continuous improvement in the Industry 4.0 paradigm. Appl. Sci. **11** (16), 7671 (2021). DOI: https://doi.org/10.3390/APP11167671
4. Kim, B., Jeong, Y.-S., Tong, S.H., Jeong, M.K.: A generalised uncertain decision tree for defect classification of multiple wafer maps. Int. J. Prod. Res. **58**(9), 2805–2821 (2020)
5. Xu, Z., Dang, Y.: Automated digital cause-and-effect diagrams to assist causal analysis in problem-solving: a data-driven approach. Int. J. Prod. Res. **58**(17), 5359–5379 (2020)
6. Wang, H., He,Q., Zhang, Z., Peng, T., Tang, R.Z.: Framework of automated value stream mapping for lean production under the Industry 4.0 paradigm. J. Zhejiang Univ.-SCIENCE A (Appl. Phys. Eng.) **22**(5), 382–95 (2021). https://doi.org/10.1631/JZUS.A2000480
7. e Oliveira, E., Miguéis, V.L., Borges, J.L.: On the influence of overlap in automatic root cause analysis in manufacturing. Int. J. Prod. Res. (2021). https://doi.org/10.1080/00207543.2021.1992680
8. Ma, Q., Li, H., Thorstenson, A.: A big data-driven root cause analysis system: application of machine learning in quality problem solving. Comput. Ind. Eng. **160**(October), 107580 (2021). https://doi.org/10.1016/J.CIE.2021.107580

9. Rocha, E.M., Brochado, A.F., Rato, B., Meneses, J.: Benchmarking and prediction of entities performance on manufacturing processes through MEA, robust XGBoost and SHAP analysis. In: IEEE 27th International Conference on Emerging Technologies and Factory Automation, 1–8 (2022). https://doi.org/10.1109/ETFA52439.2022.9921593

10. Lopes, M.J., Rocha, E.M., Georgieva, P., Ferreira, N.: General model for metrics calculation and behavior prediction in the manufacturing industry: an automated machine learning approach. In: Handbook of Research on Applied Data Science and Artificial Intelligence in Business and Industry, (January), 263–290 (2021). https://doi.org/10.4018/978-1-7998-6985-6.CH012

11. Brochado, A.F., Rocha, E.M., Almeida, D., de Sousa, A., Moura, A.: A data-driven model with minimal information for bottleneck detection - application at Bosch thermotechnology. Int. J. Manage. Sci. Eng. Manage. (2022). https://doi.org/10.1080/17509653.2022.2116121

12. Rocha, E.M., Brochado, Â.F., Moura, A.: Workers benchmarking using multi-directional efficiency analysis in a manufacturing production system. Procedia Comput. Sci. **200**, 1451–1460 (2022). https://doi.org/10.1016/J.PROCS.2022.01.346

13. Bogetoft, P., Hougaard, J.L.: Efficiency Evaluations Based on Potential (Non-Proportional) Improvements. J. Prod. Anal. **12**(3), 233–47 (1999)

14. Manevska-Tasevska, G., Hansson, H., Asmild, M., Surry, Y.: Exploring the Regional Efficiency of the Swedish Agricultural Sector during the CAP Reforms - Multi-Directional Efficiency Analysis Approach. Land Use Policy **100**, 104897 (2021)

15. Lei, X., Zhang, X., Dai, Q., Li, L.: Dynamic evaluation on the energy and environmental performance of China's transportation sector: a ZSG-MEA window analysis. Environ. Sci. Pollut. Res. **28**(9), 11454–68 (2021)

16. Asmild, M., Matthews, K.: Multi-directional efficiency analysis of efficiency patterns in Chinese banks 1997–2008. Eur. J. Oper. Res. **219**(2), 434–41 (2012)

17. Dyson, R.G., Allen, R., Camanho, A.S., Podinovski, V.V., Sarrico, C.S., Shale, E.A.: Pitfalls and protocols in DEA. Eur. J. Oper. Res. **132**(2), 245–59 (2001)

18. Hahn, G.J., Brandenburg, M., Becker, J.: Valuing supply chain performance within and across manufacturing industries: a DEA-based approach. Int. J. Prod. Econ. 108203 (2021)

19. Wang, Q., Wang, Z., Zhang, L., Liu, P., Zhang, Z.: A novel consistency evaluation method for series-connected battery systems based on real-world operation data. IEEE Trans. Transp. Electrif. **7**(2), 437–51 (2021)

20. Qian, J., Wong, W.K., Zhang, H., Xie, J., Yang, J.: Joint optimal transport with convex regularization for robust image classification. In IEEE Trans. Cybern. **52**(3), 1553–64 (2022)

21. Liu, W., Mao, X., Zhang, X.: Fast and robust sparsity learning over networks: a decentralized surrogate median regression approach. IEEE Transa. Sig. Process. **70**, 797–809 (2022)

22. Chen, H., Zhang, H., Boning, D., Hsieh, C.J.: Robust decision trees against adversarial examples. In: Proceedings of 36th International Conference on Machine Learning, ICML 2019 2019-June (February), 1911–1926 (2019)

23. Dairu, X., Shilong, Z.: Machine learning model for sales forecasting by using XGBoost. In: IEEE International Conference on Consumer Electronics and Computer Engineering, ICCECE 2021, pp. 480–483 (2021)

24. Gautam, V., Kaur, P.: Malware classification based on various machine learning techniques. In: Proceedings of 2nd International Conference on Artificial Intelligence: Advances and Applications, pp. 141–151 (2022)
25. Shapley, L.: A Value for N-Person Games. In: Contributions to the Theory of Games II, pp. 307–317. Princeton University Press (1953)
26. Rocha, E.M., Lopes, M.J.: Bottleneck prediction and data-driven discrete-event simulation for a balanced manufacturing line. Procedia Comput. Sci. **200**(January), 1145–1154 (2022). https://doi.org/10.1016/J.PROCS.2022.01.314
27. Lopes, M.J., Rocha, E.M.: Impact analysis of KPI scenarios, automated best practices identification, and deviations on manufacturing processes. In: IEEE 27th International Conference on Emerging Technologies and Factory Automation, 1–6 (2022). https://doi.org/10.1109/ETFA52439.2022.9921462
28. Brochado, Â.F., Rocha, E.M., Pimentel, C.: PDCA protocol to ensure a data-driven approach for problem-solving. In: Proceedings of the 12th Annual International Conference on Industrial Engineering and Operations Management, Istanbul, Turkey (2022)

A Comparative Analysis on the Summarization of Legal Texts Using Transformer Models

Daniel Núñez-Robinson, Jose Talavera-Montalto, and Willy Ugarte[✉] [iD]

Universidad Peruana de Ciencias Aplicadas, Lima, Peru
{201622489,201516424}@upc.edu.pe, willy.ugarte@upc.pe

Abstract. Transformer models have evolved natural language processing tasks in machine learning and set a new standard for the state of the art. Thanks to the self-attention component, these models have achieved significant improvements in text generation tasks (such as extractive and abstractive text summarization). However, research works involving text summarization and the legal domain are still in their infancy, and as such, benchmarks and a comparative analysis of these state of the art models is important for the future of text summarization of this highly specialized task. In order to contribute to these research works, the researchers propose a comparative analysis of different, fine-tuned Transformer models and datasets in order to provide a better understanding of the task at hand and the challenges ahead. The results show that Transformer models have improved upon the text summarization task, however, consistent and generalized learning is a challenge that still exists when training the models with large text dimensions. Finally, after analyzing the correlation between objective results and human opinion, the team concludes that the Recall-Oriented Understudy for Gisting Evaluation (ROUGE) [13] metrics used in the current state of the art are limited and do not reflect the precise quality of a generated summary.

Keywords: Abstractive text summarization · Benchmark · Deep learning · Natural language processing · Transformers

1 Introduction

Currently, the problem of the Peruvian Justice System is the excessive delay in procedures carried out on a daily basis. This problematic is backed by the analysis of the accessibility barriers done by [4], with the most important barriers being the economic and institutional ones.

The economic component of barrier consists mainly on general poverty, which is about 20.4% of the current population. This statistic is then correlated with a lack of education and financial resources to seek legal counsel. The institutional component of the barrier describes obstacles which involve the general population. This includes the procedural burden issue (obligations which require

© The Author(s), under exclusive license to Springer Nature Switzerland AG 2022
T. Guarda et al. (Eds.): ARTIIS 2022, CCIS 1675, pp. 372–386, 2022.
https://doi.org/10.1007/978-3-031-20319-0_28

manual reading work, case-studying and other activities), geographical barriers and poor legal education. According to the research done, it was shown that the procedural burden issue is the most important factor in the delays of judicial processes because of the number of lawsuits filed for a lawyer and the amount of cases a judge has to study and hear, which both imply a large amount of manual reading work.

In the past years, transformer architectures have been a hot topic, with around 5 to 10 relevant works done per year, each one of them surpassing the metric scores of the previous ones in different text generation tasks, such as text summarization, which involves the shortening of textual documents through a learning process involving neural networks. This task can be extractive, where models learn to weigh and select the most important sentences in a text, or they can be abstractive, where models learn to understand the given text and provide a summary with their own words. Most of these solutions have been benchmarked with a text summarization dataset called CNN/Daily Mail[1].

This dataset has been the main ground work for the selection process carried out by the team, as it helped with them find which models are currently the best and let them investigate the possibility of execution. To solve the problem, the team has decided to develop proof of concept benchmarks for the summarization of legal files based on the fine-tuning of different state-of-the-art Transformer models that generate legal abstractive summaries. The team chose a wide range of models worked within the past 5 years (since 2017), when Bidirectional Encoder Representations from Transformers (BERT) [5] was introduced.

These state-of-the-art models have been manually fine-tuned by observing and comparing their performances. To be able to obtain a measured result, the team searched for the fundamental metric for this task. The team found that most of the works use the ROUGE metric as their main metric for evaluation. According to [9], the ROUGE metric is the best metric for text summarization tasks, as this automatically measures the quality of a summary generated using statistical measures in n-dimensions. This metric has 5 variants, but the most important ones are ROUGE-1, ROUGE-2 and ROUGE-L, which are present in all of the papers investigated. The higher the value (which ranges from 0 to 100), the better the score.

The BART [11] architecture is generally considered as the best architecture thanks to its adaptability to fine tuning. With some modifications, for example [12], the model presents a considerable increase in ROUGE metrics. For example in BART, the Rouge metrics for the CNN/DailyMail dataset are, $R1 = 44.16$, $R2 = 21.28$ and $RL = 40.90$ and in comparison, in BART + R-Drop [12], the metrics for the same experiment improve to $R1 = 44.51$, $R2 = 21.58$ and $RL = 41.24$; although the difference is not significant, it is shown that fine-tuned versions of BART provide better results. The research done on the Transformer architecture has been, as one can see, plentiful. However, research done specifically on the legal domain is rather scarce.

The contributions of the team can be summarized as follows:

---

[1] https://paperswithcode.com/dataset/cnn-daily-mail-1

1. We have an updated benchmark for legal datasets BillSum and GovReport with state-of-the-art results,
2. We have fine-tuned each model to reach the best possible results and
3. We have demonstrated the current state of Transformer models along with any challenges identified within the legal domain.

In Sect. 2, the background, the most important concepts and definitions will be explained. In Sect. 3, the contribution of the scientific articles will be explained in depth. In Sect. 4, the process to land this research will be shown as well as which scientific articles were the most impacting. In Sect. 5, the experiments conducted to prove the feasibility of the approach will be presented in three steps. This will begin with the methodology, followed by the results and finally a comparative analysis. Finally, Sect. 6, will conclude the research and focus on future works.

2   Background

2.1   Abstractive Summarization Models

Abstractive Summarization [14] is a task in natural language processing whose objective is to generate a summary from a given a text. Unlike extractive summarization, important sentences/phrases from the source input are not copied, but understood, which also allows this task to come up with new sentences/phrases which are relevant or paraphrasing. This type of summarizing was employed using a attentive sequence-to-sequence model, composed by an encoder and decoder; it has also been developed using reinforcement learning, and has shown improvements in the area.

Previously, Long Short-Term Memory (LSTM) models, which are evolved Recurrent Neural Networks (RNN) were the predominant model for this task. These models were mainly used in text summarization tasks, as RNNs use the LSTM module to provide context for the words the model receives and subsequently generate outputs. Also, Generative Adversarial Networks (GAN), which consists on the merging of a pretrained generative and discriminatory model were used in this task.

But, in 2017, with the development of the attention mechanism [18], the transformer architecture became the dominant approach in the natural language understanding processes. For the researchers work, the selection of Transformer models to be used was carefully selected by studying different publications from colleagues in the computer science department and by testing different state of the art models with a generic dataset (CNN/Daily Mail).

2.2   Transformer Architecture

Transformer models are new state of the art deep learning neural networks which were first introduced in BERT [18]. Its self-attention module introduced a new standard for text generation tasks which were improved over the years through models such as the BART [11] and T5 [15] models. The BART model innovates by allowing the model to corrupt and attempt to restore text sequences as part of its learning process, while T5 was trained for many different text generation tasks, ranging from translation and classification to text summarizing, which makes it an excellent model in general for each of these tasks (Fig. 1).

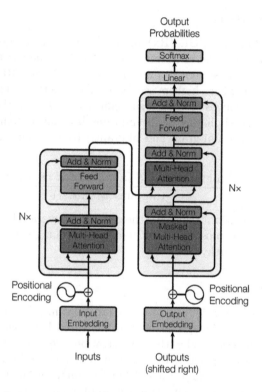

Fig. 1. The Transformer Model Architecture [18]

The core of transformer language model is composed of a variable number of encoder and decoder layers and the self-attention mechanism. Transformer architecture is unique within the encoder-decoder architecture, as it also contains the self-attention head. These heads assign a value of importance to each input of a sentence so, afterwards, it will be used in the reconstruction of the text. All transformer architectures involve this self-attention mechanism as well as an encoder layer, embedding layer, soft-max layer and decoder layer. The embedding layer involves receiving a word from the source text and maps it in a vector representation which is sent to the encoder. The encoder is a bidirectional LSTM layer, whose input is the vector representation obtained previously.

With this input, a hidden state will be produced at the output in a forward and reverse order. These hidden states are actually the merge of the hidden state vectors of both directions of the bidirectional LSTM. After the attention mechanism focuses the relevant words, the decoder, composed of a unidirectional LSTM, will predict the next word in the summary based on its hidden state to fulfill its task. To finalize the transformer architecture, the soft-max layer is the last layer of the decoder, which generates the probability distribution of the next word over a group of candidate words.

2.3   Evaluation Metric

As mentioned before, ROUGE (Rx) metrics are the most important way to evaluate a computer generated summary compared to one written by a human. According to [8], the most common metrics are R1, R2 and RL, and the scores range from 0 to 100, where highers scores represent better summaries. The RL metric measures the longest common subsequence present in the text, while R1 and R2 compare the similarity of the n-grams in a given computer generated summary (in this case, uni-gram and bi-grams) to a human one using the following formula:

$$Rx = \frac{\sum(\text{n-grams } found \; in \; model \; and \; reference)}{\sum(\text{n-grams } in \; model)} \tag{1}$$

These metrics are meant to show if the computer generated summary achieves its goal of selecting the most pertinent information in a given text, thus making the summary a trustworthy one.

2.4   Legal Datasets

The legal datasets chosen for the research are Billsum [10] and GovReport [7]. These datasets contain the specialized and advanced language required for the analysis of these models under the investigation premises. The first dataset, BillSum, consists of law projects of USA congress and California State and was created by Anastassia Kornilova and Vlad Eidelman in 2019. This consists of more than 21,000 records which are made up of a summary, a text and a title. The dataset is already split up in train and test sets using the Hugging Face[2] library. The training part contains 18,949 records and the testing 3,269. The second dataset, GovReport, consists of long document summaries based on reports written by research agencies such as the congressional research service and the US government accountability office. This dataset was created by Huang in 2021 and, like the previous dataset, it contains information regarding the title, summary and report.

3   Contribution

3.1   Benchmark of Legal Transformer Summarization Models

The team carried out an exhaustive analysis of different Transformer models and manually tuned model and training parameters in order to achieve considerable

---

[2] https://huggingface.co/.

improvements to the ROUGE metrics. The maximum length of summaries were fixed to a cap of 500 and 2,000 characters in order to evaluate the models' performances with longer summaries. The selection process for these models was executed through a careful read through the current state of the art, followed by an analysis of each of the models[3]. The models were selected according to their availability in documentation and code, overall ROUGE metrics and GPU requirements. The metrics shown for the models are comparable to other models evaluated using the same dataset.

The following models were selected:

- BART [11]
- T5 [15]
- LED [1]
- DISTILBART [17]
- PEGASUS [19]

The legal datasets used for training were the following:

- Billsum [10]
- GovReport [7]

In order to use these datasets, they were imported from the datasets library, split into train and test sets, preprocessed, labelled and tokenized to be used in the training process. Afterwards, the same library was used to load the ROUGE metrics and use them for the evaluation processes before and after training. Tables 1a and 1b represent the evaluations of the selected models before training and fine-tuning.

Before the training process was started, the models needed to be investigated further to understand which were the hyper-parameters with the biggest influence in the metrics. Using the Hugging Face library, the team was able to execute all models successfully and evaluate which hyper-parameters were the most important through the documentation. Also, there were some hyper-parameters which needed to be constant numbers due to the teams GPU restriction and processing power.

After the training process was completed, the models were evaluated and sampled in order to take notes of the models' ROUGE metrics before and after training. This and any noteworthy observations during the training processes were later integrated into a new legal Transformer benchmark which includes the study of the two legal datasets. This new benchmark seeks to analyze the current state of Transformer models in the legal domain and to explore the challenges at hand for this specific task.

After the development of the benchmark, further work was required. Even though the ROUGE metrics have been a good indicator to compare between the models in an objective manner, sometimes the best metrics fail to offer the best summary quality. Because of this, the team has an obligation to question and validate this metric as the sole and only summarizing indicator.

---

[3] Spreadsheet with the benchmark - https://bit.ly/3HxYuPT.

4   Target Approaches of the Study

In [8], the authors completed a thorough analysis of the current state of text summarization tasks. Along with this, several machine learning models were tested and evaluated in order to determine any challenges that lay ahead in this task. This paper is important because it lays the ground work for many of the experiments done with models other than Transformers and this work will be useful when comparing the team's results after training modern Transformer models on the same tasks. The team will use this paper as ground work for the experiments done.

In [11], the authors present the Transformer model called BART. This work is interesting because it proposes a unique training process which seeks to add noise to a given text and asks the model to denoise it so that it may learn the intricacies of said text. This model has been reported to be adaptive to fine tuning and, thanks to the unique denoising training, has also proved to offer state of the art results in metrics, making the BART model the baseline for modern Transformer models. The team will use this architecture and models evolving from it to fine tune and experiment on them by manually exploring the hyper-parameters of these models.

In [6], the authors present a study of the current state of automatic text summarization as a whole. The authors analyse different techniques and metrics within this environment and shows what is the current state of the art. The most important contribution for this paper is the definition of the ROUGE metrics and

Table 1. Pre-training Model Evaluation for both datasets.

	Rouge Metric Scores				Rouge Metric Scores		
Model	ROUGE1	ROUGE2	ROUGEL	Model	ROUGE1	ROUGE2	ROUGEL
BART				BART			
Large	32.69	16.86	24.46	Large	24.17	**10.97**	16.96
Small	**35.88**	**18.38**	**26.50**	Small	20.27	9.33	14.50
DISTILBART				DISTILBART			
Large	18.70	4.43	13.74	Large	13.67	3.06	9.30
Small	15.12	3.11	11.05	Small	22.74	4.96	16.40
LED				LED			
	13.12	4.05	9.64		22.7	7.97	15.57
PEGASUS				PEGASUS			
Large	29.38	16.56	23.64	Large	25.19	6.71	18.24
Small	15.10	7.14	12.86	Small	12.07	2.88	8.84
T5				T5			
Large	29.46	12.16	21.39	Large	27.18	8.22	18.58
Small	30.05	13.40	23.25	Small	**27.26**	8.24	**18.61**

(a) Pre-Training Model Evaluation for Billsum

(b) Pre-Training Model Evaluation for GovReport

the workflow of automatic text summarization, as there will need to be a pre-processing, processing and finally a post-processing phase. Finally, it summarizes various datasets which have been used for this task. For this investigation, the paper was used to set the metrics for the generated summaries' evaluation, and also to question if ROUGE metrics should be the only metrics used, as stated by [8].

In [1], the authors propose an improvement to the limitations of long document summarization by developing the Longformer model. This transformer architecture has an attention mechanism that scales linearly with the length of the sequence, therefore making it possible to process documents of thousands of tokens or more. This attention mechanism is replaced with a local attention which then persuades the global attention. This paper has been used to evaluate the generation of longer summaries in the experimental phase of this research by setting different lengths for each model.

After investigating the best models and evaluating the team's computational resources (assisted by Google Colaboratory Pro and a local anaconda environment), the selected models were T5, BART, DISTILBART, LED and PEGASUS. This was mainly due to the literature review and the limited computational resources.

5   Experiments

5.1   Experimental Protocol

For the training process, the team used the following hardware during the beginning training phases executed with Python 3.7 in Google Colaboratory Pro Plus with the following specs: (i) 24 GB RAM, (ii) T4/P100 GPU 16 GB.

This allowed the team to train the models with the highest computational resources available. As for software used, development was done through the cloud service of Google Colaboratory, so no other software was used. Through Python, the Pytorch library was the main tool used for model training, accompanied by the datasets and metrics libraries for evaluation and training data. The team used the Hugging Face library function called Seq2SeqTrainer. This function enabled the allocation of a model, tokenizer, testing and training data (split from the dataset used) as well as the definition of the training arguments to be executed. This function also allows for metric evaluations before and after the training process. Additionally, the hyper-parameters were fine-tuned manually per training iteration, as any automatic hyper-parameter exploration exceeded the computational resources available.

Table 2. Legal Summarization Benchmark for both datasets.

	Rouge Metric Scores					Rouge Metric Scores			
Model	ROUGE1	ROUGE2	ROUGEL	Survey Score	Model	ROUGE1	ROUGE2	ROUGEL	Survey Score
BART					BART				
Large	20.76	13.53	17.74	**66.64**	Large	32.20	9.00	21.00	25.57
Small	58.80	41.30	51.30	66.07	Small	39.89	18.45	29.29	58.29
DISTILBART					DISTILBART				
Large	**59.24**	**42.04**	**51.86**	64.29	Large	39.76	18.40	29.04	53.00
Small	19.69	12.58	16.64	58.93	Small	14.96	6.33	10.85	58.36
LED					LED				
	20.23	12.56	16.97	55.36		27.8	10.39	17.59	**58.93**
T5					T5				
Large	42.64	28.38	36.68	24.43	Large	23.05	10.01	16.98	45.86
Small	57.93	40.44	50.70	64.29	Small	**57.93**	**40.44**	**50.70**	-

[a] Survey scores standardized to fit ROUGE scores   [a] Survey scores standardized to fit ROUGE scores

(a) Legal Summarization Benchmark for Billsum   (b) Legal Summarization Benchmark for GovReport

The code is publicly available at GitHub (https://github.com/TheBigBam/Summarizator) and Zenodo (https://zenodo.org/record/6859402).

The datasets are available at: Billsum (https://paperswithcode.com/dataset/billsum) and GovReport (https://paperswithcode.com/dataset/govreport).

5.2   Results

Once the training of the fine-tuned models was completed (through manually tweaking model and training parameters), all of the models were evaluated in order to calculate their ROUGE metric scores.

These scores were then compiled into a new legal benchmark for the Billsum and Govreport datasets. Each model was trained with a specific max length in mind, which is why there are S and L variants for most of the models used.

Due to computational resources, some larger models were unable to be trained with the entirety of the data or with reduced parameters like epochs and batch sizes. These models were LED, PEGASUS and DISTILBART. Other models like BART and T5 had their batch sizes reduced for the training process of the GovReport dataset.

After acquiring all of the objective data, it was important for the team to validate the results through human interaction, since ROUGE metrics compare directly to human developed summaries.

Through this line of thinking, the team decided to distribute various surveys involving many models' sample summaries and the human target summary. Through a series of questions, respondents participated in ranking the samples in order from best to worst in terms of readability and the understanding of the main ideas of the texts (target summaries were presented beforehand). https://es.surveymonkey.com/r/57VFBMG.

Table 3. Individual survey scores

Model	BillSum S_1	BillSum S_2	GovReport S_1	GovReport S_2
BART				
Large	**71.43**	61.89	29.71	21.43
Small	69.00	63.14	58.29	**58.29**
DISTILBART				
Large	65.43	63.14	**63.14**	53.57
Small	54.71	63.14	48.86	57.14
LED				
	56.00	54.71	60.71	57.14
T5				
Large	23.86	25.00	39.29	52.43
Small	59.57	**69.00**	-	-

It is important to note that all models were labelled, so there were no hints as to which model's sample was being read. After receiving all 12 survey results, these were compiled into the benchmark after a standardization of the scores so that they could fit the ROUGE metric score range. The benchmark for each dataset is presented in Tables 2a and 2b, along with Table 3, which shows the survey scores for the participating models:

SECTION 1. ENVIRONMENTAL INFRASTRUCTURE.

(a) Summary before training.

Amends the Water Resources Development Act of 1992 to authorize the Secretary of the Interior to make grants to: (1) Jackson County, Mississippi, for the elimination or control of combined sewer overflows for Jackson County; and (2) State, local, and tribal governments for the cleanup and control of such

(b) Summary after training.

Fig. 2. Summary Example - BARTS-Billsum

In Figs. 2a and 2b, the improvements in the quality of summaries generated by models are shown. These models are able to capture important information of the target text samples but are not able to fully capture the main idea of the texts due to their length. Currently, these models should not be used as a solution, but rather as an experimental tool for these tasks.

To further analyze the results of these tables, parallel coordinates plots were developed (Figs. 3a, 3b, 4a, 4b and 5) to identify trends and relations between metric scores and subjective scores from the respondents surveyed. With all the data processed and visualized, key information has been determined and discussed.

5.3   Discussion

After a careful analysis of the results, there are two key topics to discuss. The first topic to analyze is the metrics after the fine-tuning of the Transformer models. As one can observe from the new benchmarks (see Tables 2a and 2b), the top 3 models for the Billsum dataset were DISTILBART L, BART S and T5S, while the top 3 for GovReport were BARTS, DISTILBART L and BARTL. This shows that older Transformer models excel at capturing and understanding important parts of a given texts at a shorter length (around 350–450 characters and), whilst more recent and refined Transformer models (based on the BART training process) have reached a new level of understanding for long sequences of text (ranges from 1300–1800 characters for LED, PEGASUS and DISTILBART models, whilst older models with large generated summaries did not exceed 600 coherent characters).

This shows that Transformer models in general are capable of capturing and understanding key ideas from legal texts with varying lengths, and that newer Transformer models have achieved a limit of about 1500 characters in length for summary generation related to this topic.

The second topic to discuss is the survey scores. The main idea of these surveys was to find a correlation between metrics and human opinion for the best models. To begin, the best models for this category are presented. On one hand, for Billsum, the top 3 models in the survey were BART L, BART S and DISTILBART L tied with T5S. On the other hand, the top 3 models for GovReport were DISTILBART L, LED and BART S.

Through an analysis of the different Figs. 3a and 3b, one can observe that, from Billsum's point of view, high ROUGE scoring models generally result in a better opinion on the surveys, while average scores may result in negative opinions. More importantly, though, one can observe that, in Fig. 3a, low ROUGE scoring models have achieved positive results in the surveys, with one of them (BARTL) surpassing the top 3 models based on ROUGE scores.

From GovReport's point of view, however, further discussion is required. As opposed to Billsum, which had the better scoring models generally at the top of the survey opinions, Figs. 4a and 4b show that this dataset only kept one of these higher scoring models (BART S), and it was in third place (by deci-

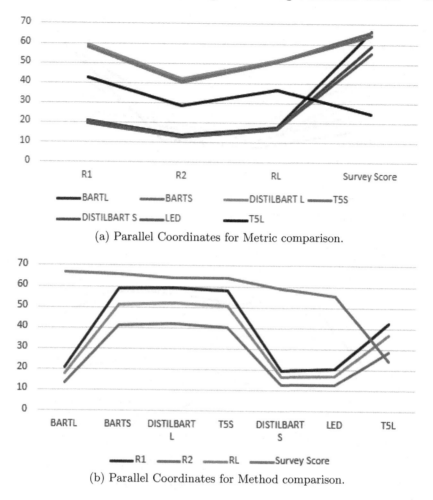

(a) Parallel Coordinates for Metric comparison.

(b) Parallel Coordinates for Method comparison.

Fig. 3. Parallel coordinates for Billsum.

mal points), surpassed by DISTILBART S and LED, two of the worst ROUGE scoring models. One way to interpret this is.

Contained in a dataset by dataset basis, Fig. 5 shows that the abstraction of texts (specifically legal texts) becomes harder the longer the text sequences become through the difference between the results of one sample to another (as shown by the large deviations in GovReports survey scores for models like DISTILBART L and T5L) and because GovReport has larger target summaries, the performance of the models is shown to depend on specific seeds or text samples analyzed.

This means that future Transformer models need to work on achieving better, more generalized learning that allows them to consistently generate abstractive summaries. Another way to interpret this, however, is that there are faults with

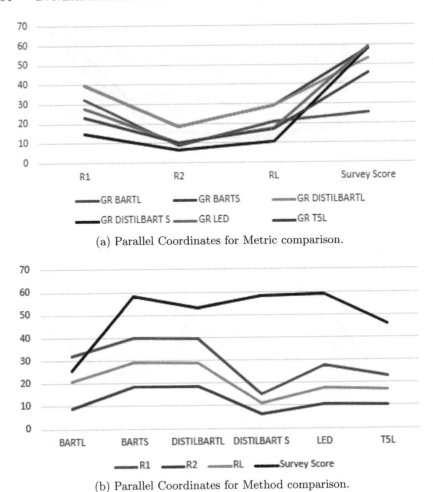

(a) Parallel Coordinates for Metric comparison.

(b) Parallel Coordinates for Method comparison.

Fig. 4. Parallel Coordinates for GovReport.

the current metrics used in the state of the art. Highly specialized texts contained in the legal domain have now shown a discordance between objective and subjective assessments which can be observed on both of the datasets investigated (as shown when comparing the top 3 models for each case in Figs. 3a and 4a), which means that ROUGE scores are not representing the quality of a generated summary with the precision needed when contrasted with the general opinion of the respondents.

It is important to consider that, in the future, new metrics should be developed that improve the evaluation of from specialized domains (like the legal domain) and attempt to maintain a similar relation between the objective metrics and human opinion.

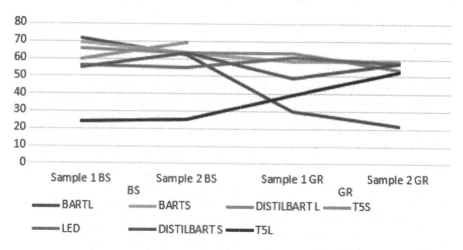

Fig. 5. Individual survey scores.

6   Conclusion

To conclude this paper, the team has reached two main takeaways. The first one is that the Transformer architecture has shown great progress in recent years. Older Transformer models have achieved a good understanding of important topics in the legal texts when generating short texts, whilst newer Transformer models have achieved the same goal with a larger text threshold (around 1500 coherent characters), with most of these models achieving high ROUGE scores. This shows promise for future Transformer models as they get closer to target lengths of legal summaries (around 3000–3500 characters).

The second takeaway is that some challenges have been identified in the current state of the art and Transformer models. The architecture needs work on consistency when understanding datasets with larger dimensions, as the results are varied and depend on seeds or given samples. This challenge has also shown that the ROUGE metrics have presented inconsistencies when evaluating texts, as models with low ROUGE metric scores were preferred during the evaluation of the samples in the surveys. The researchers recommend that work is put on a new, more precise metric that reflects the quality of the specialized texts summarized.

Regarding future works, we plan on developing a solution focused on the summarization of longer texts [16] through segmentation techniques so that the texts are summarized in lengths that models can understand similarly than videos [3]. Adding to this, we plans on acquiring more computational resources so that it may be able to finish the training phases with more demanding models and training parameters, which would be an improvement to the current work. Finally, we also plans on identifying the key aspects of legal texts so that this may aid on the development of a new metric for specialized texts [2].

References

1. Beltagy, I., Peters, M.E., Cohan, A.: Longformer: The long-document transformer. CoRR abs/2004.05150 (2020)
2. Burga-Gutierrez, E., Vasquez-Chauca, B., Ugarte, W.: Comparative analysis of question answering models for HRI tasks with NAO in spanish. In: SIMBig (2020)
3. Chancolla-Neira, S.W., Salinas-Lozano, C.E., Ugarte, W.: Static summarization using pearson's coefficient and transfer learning for anomaly detection for surveillance videos. In: SIMBig (2020)
4. Chavez-Chavez, E., Zuta-Vidal, E.I.: El Acceso a La Justicia de Los Sectores Pobres a Propósito de Los Consultorios Jurídicos Gratuitos Pucp y la Recoleta de Prosode. Master's thesis, Pontifica Universidad Católica del Perú (2015)
5. Devlin, J., Chang, M., Lee, K., Toutanova, K.: BERT: pre-training of deep bidirectional transformers for language understanding. In: NAACL-HLT (2019)
6. El-Kassas, W.S., Salama, C.R., Rafea, A.A., Mohamed, H.K.: Automatic text summarization: a comprehensive survey. Expert Syst. Appl. 165 (2021)
7. Huang, L., Cao, S., Parulian, N.N., Ji, H., Wang, L.: Efficient attentions for long document summarization. In: NAACL-HLT (2021)
8. Jain, D., Borah, M.D., Biswas, A.: Summarization of legal documents: where are we now and the way forward. Comput. Sci. Rev. **40**, 100388 (2021)
9. Kanapala, A., Pal, S., Pamula, R.: Text summarization from legal documents: a survey. Artif. Intell. Rev. **51**(3), 371–402 (2019)
10. Kornilova, A., Eidelman, V.: Billsum: A corpus for automatic summarization of US legislation. CoRR abs/1910.00523 (2019)
11. Lewis, M., et al.: BART: denoising sequence-to-sequence pre-training for natural language generation, translation, and comprehension. In: ACL (2020)
12. Liang, X., et al.: R-drop: Regularized dropout for neural networks. In: NeurIPS (2021)
13. Lin, C.Y.: Rouge: a package for automatic evaluation of summaries. In: Proceedings of the ACL Workshop: Text Summarization Braches Out 2004 (2004)
14. Liu, L., Lu, Y., Yang, M., Qu, Q., Zhu, J., Li, H.: Generative adversarial network for abstractive text summarization. In: AAAI (2018)
15. Raffel, C., et al.: Exploring the limits of transfer learning with a unified text-to-text transformer. J. Mach. Learn. Res. **21**, 1–67 (2020)
16. de Rivero, M., Tirado, C., Ugarte, W.: Formalstyler: GPT based model for formal style transfer based on formality and meaning preservation. In: KDIR (2021)
17. Shleifer, S., Rush, A.M.: Pre-trained summarization distillation. CoRR abs/2010.13002 (2020)
18. Vaswani, A., et al.: Attention is all you need. In: NIPS (2017)
19. Zhang, J., Zhao, Y., Saleh, M., Liu, P.J.: PEGASUS: pre-training with extracted gap-sentences for abstractive summarization. In: ICML (2020)

Determination of the Factors Influencing Proper Face Recognition in Faces Protected by Face Masks, an Analysis of Their Algorithms and the Factors Affecting Recognition Success

Shendry Balmore Rosero Vásquez[✉] [ID]

Universidad Estatal Península de Santa Elena, Santa Elena, Ecuador
srosero@upse.edu.ec

Abstract. One of the many collateral effects that the entire planet has suffered with the appearance of covid-19 and the declaration of this as a pandemic, has been evidenced in the treatment of facial recognition algorithms and the variety of applications, both commercial and for exclusive use in research for this same purpose. For the time being, there are already reports of effectiveness with respect to the analysis of these algorithms and that are paving the way to understand the degree of affectation that the use of face masks can have on facial recognition processes. In this context, it is important to determine how it is possible that throughout these almost two years of confinement and use of face shields and masks, the human being, regardless of his age, has been able to maintain its advantage over artificial intelligence systems when recognizing the face of a relative, friend or simply an acquaintance; that is why, the present study aims to evaluate some face recognition systems in order to determine the main problems faced by these algorithms when recognizing a face protected with a mask.

Keywords: Artificial intelligence · Data augmentation · Deep learning · Eigenfaces · Face mask · Face recognition

1 Introduction

Long before the COVID-19 pandemic and in general, face recognition (RF) systems focused on finding a set of descriptive patterns within the human face to compare with a given database and because of this comparison, the aforementioned face recognition systems were able to recognize to whom a human face belonged. Of course, this ability has been overshadowed to some extent by the need for people to wear a mask as a means of protection and thus avoid infection with Sarscov2, which causes COVID-19.

According to the World Health Organization (WHO), the use of a facemask as of this writing is one of the most effective protections against infectious and airborne diseases, such as COVID-19.

It is in this sense that since its appearance, infected countries have applied a strict regulation of face masks and their use both in enclosed spaces and in public spaces has

T. Guarda et al. (Eds.): ARTIIS 2022, CCIS 1675, pp. 387–400, 2022.
https://doi.org/10.1007/978-3-031-20319-0_29

become mandatory. Of course, although the use of a mask is a protection, the position and type of mask must be taken into account to increase its effectiveness. COVID-19.

This context, the pandemic has made it difficult for conventional facial recognition technology to effectively identify people and has affected the way in which security controls have been applied over the past two years and even in the systematic advance of crime, at least from the daily evidence in the national news. Therefore, it is worth asking whether a means of protection such as the face mask should be set aside in favor of having a secure method of facial recognition or simply the algorithms that use it should be structured in order to adapt to this new reality.

Parallel to this, it is important to note that although most people have decided to protect themselves by wearing masks, this has not prevented other people from identifying them under certain basic criteria of human nature, which apparently the current facial recognition systems are obviously not considering.

This research based on the analysis of object recognition algorithms, pattern recognition and face recognition as well as the study of platforms such as YOLO, TensorFlow, Keras to name the most recognized, aims to highlight the main problems that prevent a human face can be identified as most people can do once they recognize certain basic patterns in the face of acquaintances.

The second section of this paper discusses the main RF and object identification techniques and how mask detection, mask type classification, mask position classification and identity recognition using Convolutional Neural Networks (CNN), AlexNet, VGG16, and Facial Recognition Pipeline with FaceNet (with special emphasis on the latter for recognition testing) are deep learning algorithms used to classify features in each scenario.

This analysis is structured by five components including training platform, server, support frameworks, hardware and user interface. Comprehensive unit tests use cases and results analysis are used to evaluate and monitor recognition performance and issues.

The third section contains the current discussion and results while the fourth section contains the conclusion and the fifth section contains the results.

2   Facial Recognition Techniques and How They Work

One of the most reiterative questions about artificial intelligence systems and specifically those of computer vision are focused on determining how it is possible that a computer without reasoning capacity can recognize a face and perhaps what causes more controversy is that this lack of reasoning is compensated by the large volume of information which currently makes it the ideal tool for machine learning algorithms (automated/machine learning), So much so that facial recognition techniques date back to 1960[1]; however, due to advances in technology and equipment, it is only in the first decade of the 2000s that it has been possible to develop applications that not only identify a face from among multiple objects, but there are now applications capable of recognizing who that face belongs to (Fig. 1).

---

[1] Scientist and mathematician Woodrow Wilson Bledsoe designed a system of measurements to classify and categorize faces.

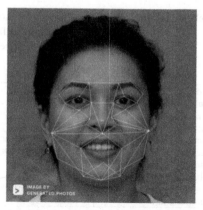

Fig. 1. The figure shows a cheerful Asian adult female with medium brown hair and brown eyes, generated by artificial intelligence systems, downloaded from https://generated.photos/.

2.1 Definition

By simplification, facial recognition can be understood as a way of recognizing a human face through technology, by using biometric data to map individually defined facial features contained in video or images.

From a more technical point of view, it is a matter of storing the characteristics of a parameterized face in a database that serves as a reference for later comparisons of a particular face, the comparisons and parameterizations will depend on the technique to be used; currently you can find from traditional face recognition models based on mathematical models of varying utility to complex algorithms based on artificial neural networks and deep learning networks [1], each technique maintains a similarity in form (parameter-comparison) but differ in terms of implementation and effectiveness, in an academic environment is complex to try to decide which technique is the best.

2.2 Analysis of Facial Recognition Techniques

Face recognition is a problem of subclassification of visual pattern recognition techniques, you could easily (not literally) develop a face recognition application based on object recognition. Perhaps this seems reasonable to you since humans recognize visual patterns all the time, through visual information provided mainly by eyes. This information is recognized by the brain and interpreted as appropriate. In the case of a computer, both an image and a video are recognized as a numerical array of pixels that is defined as a bitmap, each computer must find by mathematical calculations, which concept parameterizes a certain part of the data to be stored. It is the development and technology used in the parameterization of stored data that has allowed us to have efficient facial recognition algorithms, a development [2] that can be seen in Fig. 2 of summary.

Facial recognition development stage	Related technologies	Characterization of the different stages of face recognition development.
Early stages	• Principal component analysis • Linear discriminant analysis	In the initial stages, Face Recognition is considered as a general pattern recognition problem and the main streams are based on the geometric structure of the face.
Characteristics and stage of classifiers	• Support vector machines • Adaptative boosting (adaboost- statistical classification)	This is the effervescent stage of face recognition in which applications for this purpose are appearing.
Deep Learning Stage	• Neural networks • Deep learning	At this stage, researchers pay special attention to real-time recognition and its complications.

Fig. 2. Stages in the development of face recognition techniques taken from "a review of phase recognition technology" by LIXIANG LI et al.

As can be seen in the previous image, face recognition uses computer-generated filters to transform images of faces into numerical expressions. Nowadays, these filters, which are based on the aforementioned techniques, are currently limited to the use of deep "learning" and artificial neural networks as an alternative that has achieved results with percentages higher than 90% effectiveness [3].

2.3 Eigenfaces

Although the use of eigenfaces might not be considered as a state-of-the-art technique, at least there is no dispute that it is the most recognized technique by data analysts and computer scientists, so the reader can verify that most computer vision libraries include it as a technique in the face recognition functions they offer.

The Eigenfaces algorithm was presented by Sirovich and Kirby in 1987 through the paper "Low-dimensional procedure for the characterization of human faces" [4], as a complement to this article we can also analyze the studies performed by Turk and

Fig. 3. Set of images with faces belonging to CALTECH (California Institute of Technology).

Pentland in their research presented at the 1991 CVPR (Computer Vision and Pattern Recognition Conference of 1991), "Facial recognition using Eigenfaces" formalizing the previous studies of eigenfaces [5].

The eigenfaces technique consists of having and entering a set of N faces (figure, currently it is debated how many faces per class (person) and how many classes should be handled, however, for didactic reasons it is agreed that a set of images of faces that allow to appreciate the different facets of the same face would be enough, while the number of classes will depend on the type of identification to be performed.

Each face inside a computer will be represented as a matrix of $K \times K$ dimensions, eigenfaces takes this arrangement to form a single numerical vector from an image (Fig. 4 and Fig. 5).

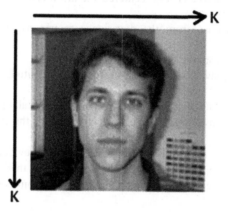

Fig. 4. Image sizing based on its size and the way a computer could define it.

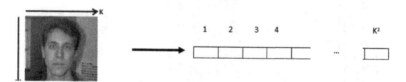

Fig. 5. Feature vector not yet processed

The set of images will subsequently form a $Z \times K$ matrix, where K is the number of matrix elements and Z the number of images to be used (Fig. 6).

From what has been presented up to this point, the reader may realize the need for the images to be standardized in terms of size, something that is generally not read anywhere but which becomes very necessary when working in practice. From the resulting matrix and from this moment on, one could play with clustering techniques that are considered basic for obtaining patterns; however, the PCA or principal component analysis (principal component analysis) is a fundamental technique to be used for eigenfaces, whose implementation detail is beyond the scope of this study, however a brief summary of the technique is shown below:

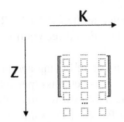

Fig. 6. Resulting data set matrix.

- Calculation of the average of each column in the matrix (average pixel intensity).
- Calculation of data center according to the mean (mandatory component of the PCA).
- Once the original matrix is now centered on the mean values, the covariance is calculated.
- Decompose eigenvalues from the covariance matrix to obtain eigenvalues and eigenvectors.
- Arrange the results from the largest to the smallest.
- Take the top N eigenvectors with the eigenvalue magnitude corresponding to the largest.
- Transform the input data by projecting it (i.e., taking the scalar product) into the space created by the N eigenvectors; these eigenvectors will be the eigenfaces.

A brief result can be seen in Fig. 7, in which it can be evidenced that each row in the NxK^2 matrix has a representation of eigenfaces and that this can be reshaped into a bitmap resulting from the image averaging and the most prominent patterns.

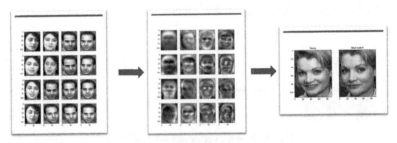

Fig. 7. Simplified processing of the result of an eigenfaces process.

Face identification will then consist of taking the vector of a new face and comparing it with the eigenfaces:

$$Query\ Face = 36\%\ of\ Eigenface\ \#1+$$
$$-8\%\ of\ Eigenface\ \#2+\ldots+21\%\ of\ Eigenface\ N \qquad (1)$$

Sirovich and Kyrbi then propose to identify a face by taking the Euclidean distance between the projected eigenface representations; this is, in essence, a *k-NN* classifier, the smaller the distance, the greater the similarity between images (faces), see Fig. 7c and Fig. 8.

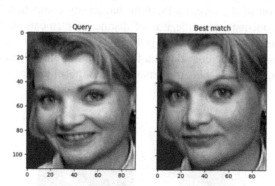

Fig. 8. Comparison result using eigenfaces.

2.4 Deep Learning

To understand how a deep learning algorithm works when recognizing a face, a set of previous steps must be analyzed, such as face detection (identifying the face object among other objects), face alignment, feature extraction, face recognition and verification, among the most important.

Face Detection

Initially it is mandatory that the system to be developed can identify a face in an image or video, i.e. to separate this object and distinguish it from other objects of similar characteristics, even for humans this is not such an easy task when appropriate distractors appear on the scene as shown in Fig. 3 (Fig. 9).

Fig. 9. Block A shows images of objects that could easily be considered faces under parameterization, without losing that perspective, block B shows faces of real people.

Face Alignment

As in other pattern recognition techniques, image preprocessing becomes mandatory, because the position of the face, its location, luminosity components, among others, would prevent an adequate identification of distinctive elements such as eyes, nose, mouth and their respective "geometric" positions. Not to mention the fact that a face far away from what could be considered a focal point or point of interest, would look different despite belonging to the same person, an example of this technique can be seen in Fig. 10.

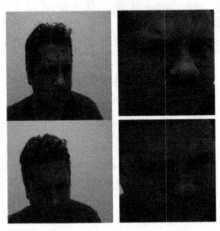

Fig. 10. Comparison of images, the left side shows the face of a person without any preprocessing, while the right side shows the same face already aligned.

Feature Extraction and Measurement

At this stage, the aim is to measure and extract as many features as possible from a face identified as a face object and aligned so that the face recognition algorithms can compare these features stored in structural arrays according to the algorithm and techniques used with a database of faces stored under the same considerations. It is at this stage that deep learning techniques differ from traditional techniques due to the debate on what features should be stored, leaving the DL algorithm to decide through the training of its network the optimal method of collection, usually deep convolutional neural networks whose work is adequate in image processing excels in preparing a dataset of images and to distinguish the specific parameters that would allow to differentiate one face from another.

A Convolutional Neural Network (CNN) works by obtaining an image, assigning it some weight based on the different objects in the image and then distinguishing them from each other [6]. A CNN requires little preprocessing data compared to other deep learning algorithms. Its main capability is that it applies primitive methods to train its classifiers, which makes it good enough to learn the features of the target object, like how the human brain uses object feature abstraction to define a given object. The workflow of a CNN consists of (see Fig. 11):

- Obtain an input image
- Generate a convolution layer called kernel
- Generate a grouping layer
- Classify features
- Generate architecture

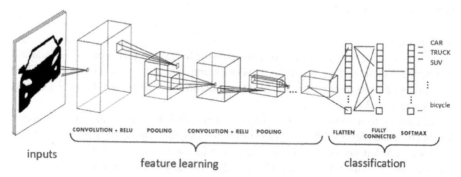

Fig. 11. Simplified process of a convolutional neural network.

Considering that an image is a matrix of pixels; in fact three matrices if we talk about RGB images (red, green and blue), and that the dimensions of that matrix are a function of how they were captured (consider the megapixel capabilities of cell phones), it is not difficult to imagine the amount of information that can be contained in a dataset of 30 classes with at least 30 images per class and 3 matrices per image; The role of a convolutional network is to reduce the images to a structure that is easy to process and without losing the main characteristics of the images as shown in Fig. 12, which

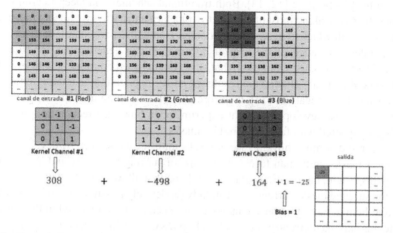

Fig. 12. Convolutional process of dimensional reduction of the original image. (Color figure online)

shows how the dimensional reduction process is structured, where later one of the main problems of facial recognition can be observed when identifying a face using masks.

Facial Recognition
Near the end a deep learning algorithm will compare the measurements of each face with faces stored in a database, using the unique measurements of each face. The result will be whichever face in your database most closely matches the measurements of the face under evaluation.

Verification
Finally, the deep learning algorithms will match the face with other faces in the database, if it matches then the face is said to be verified and if not, it remains unverified. These measurements will then be translated into an algorithmic form and thus a 2-D image will be created [7–10].

According to its objective, the comparison can also be divided into two categories. Verification and identity. The integration of these templates into a given face recognition software makes it possible to detect and recognize faces, even when their expressions vary (smiles, frowns, blinks, etc.). Usually, the accuracy of the software is not affected by the appearance of a beard. However, prematurely it can be stated that the effectiveness rates of face recognition systems with the use of masks tend to reach at most 10% at best when a person wears a mask and is subjected to an RF system. Based on the latter context, it is safe to say that training a network with images containing faces with face masks could easily harmonize with face recognition systems.

3   Materials and Methods

Most of the problems that researchers may encounter when developing face recognition codes [11] are found in the amount of information that is currently used when training a system for this purpose [12, 13]. Both traditional schemes and Deep Learning based schemes, focus on taking most of the features of a face and try to save all that information in databases with which to make a future comparison with a particular face to recognize, this generates that much of the helpful information can generate the opposite effect (beard, glasses, scars, use of masks); that is, a system based on training with or without beard could drastically change the results of an RF application generating either false positives and false negatives [14], therefore and without being the ultimate goal of this research, we have developed a slight experiment on how face recognition algorithms have been impacted with faces covered by masks.

In order to determine how the use of masks impacts, we worked by developing code that places masks on human faces; at the time of starting this study and at the time of writing this article, there were no datasets at hand that allow working with faces hidden under the surgical mask, currently it is already moderately possible to find blocks of data related to human faces that have characteristics such as those required in this research, despite this and that currently sites such as http://www.surfing.ai/face-recognition-data/ could provide datasets with such characteristics, it was preferred to recreate situations of mask use based on [11, 13, 15, 16]. A working pipeline was developed based on generic codes found on the Internet [12] and [17] as well as a line of work based on:

Dataset Generation
The following steps were followed:

- Choice of the Data Augmentation (DA) method [17] that allows the aggregation of training data allowing the generalization of a model.
- Selection of benchmarks.
- Process triangulation.
- Matching search.

Already in practice:

- Clone and build repositories.
- Download and import SDK (mask phase).
- Generate reference point estimators using the "face_alignment" library.
- Draw the point triangulation.
- Search for matches (Fig. 13).
- Result.

The execution of this type of code can be verified with Figs. 13 and 14.

Fig. 13. Data augmentation process to place masks in the dataset.

Fig. 14. Final result of data augmentation.

Testing Process

In the testing processes and based on [5, 12, 18] for traditional and optimized eigenfaces methods, and [19, 20] as well as [21, 22] for Deep Learning based methods, test codes were developed to try to determine the main problems of recognizing a face based on face images with masks, counting at least 10 different estimations (tests on python code).

Under this context it should be explained that the masks were added artificially; despite finding detractors of this technique due to the limitations that may arise from the results of synthetically adding the masks, the author of this study believes that it is a good starting point to understand how increasing raw data with little nuance variability by the technique employed affects the performance of a face recognition system.

The experiments were conducted on a 40-class basis and with 10 photographs per class giving a total of 400 photographs of faces with a simple random selection of "out-of-sample" photographs over an existing class (Fig. 15).

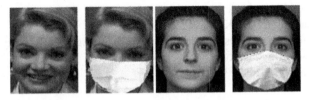

Fig. 15. Masked data set augmented for experimental purposes.

4   Discussion and Results

Similar works that were the basis of this study can be found in [23] as well as case studies based on the applications of device manufacturers that incorporate RF such as [24] that show the concern that the obligation to rid the planet of Covid is facing a scenario in which impersonation [25] will be regular news in 2022, with this answer and from what was evaluated in this study it was determined that:

- The variation in the percentage of face concealment by the mask reaching a range of less than 50% of the face provided the possibility that with the algorithms evaluated, at least 30% of the experiments performed were successful.
- Based on the previous point and considering a higher range of concealment, that is, an area greater than 50%, the effectiveness of the evaluated algorithms dropped to less than 10% of successful cases, the latter being subject to discussion since the results were not conclusive due to the randomness of the cases of successful recognition.
- Similar to the first point, the false positive rate remained between 65% and 70% of cases, so impersonation scenarios may not be a potential security risk at the time of writing.
- The effectiveness and success rates obtained were a result of the way traditionally used methods approach image processing, both for classical methods and those based on Deep Learning [1, 26], in which component reduction and feature parameterization

are affected by the "continuity matrices" (values without nuances or specific texture variation in an image) of an image that are under a mask.

- Given the way the experimental dataset was constructed, the study did not include the differentiation by type of mask to be used, which is understood to have an influence on RF systems [27, 28].
- As a complement to this study, tests were carried out in commercial and security applications, which failed categorically in recognizing a face with a mask.

5 Conclusion

From the present investigation and the data analyzed, it can be concluded that:

- As of this writing, most applications that rely on traditional techniques as well as deep learning have at least 30% effectiveness despite the fact that they were developed to work without the information hiding that masks represent.
- The success rate of facial recognition on masked faces can go up considerably if the wearer clears at least 40% of the face for recognition purposes.
- It is perhaps the conclusion of the previous point that leads us to think that the use of masks would not represent a security or identity theft problem as long as the purposes of their use are specifically adjusted to protection and health situations.
- Given the ease with which images can currently be manipulated by means of data augmentation, it is indisputable that there will soon be applications based on face training with and without masks.

References

1. Mohammad, S.M.: Facial recognition technology. SSRN Electron. J. (June) (2020)
2. Li, L., Mu, X., Li, S., Peng, H.: A review of face recognition technology. IEEE Access **8**, 139110–139120 (2020)
3. Al-Yazidi, S.A., Berri, J., Hassan, M.M.: Novel hybrid model for organizations' reputation in online social networks. J. King Saud Univ. Comput. Inf. Sci. (2022)
4. Sirovich, L., Kirby, M.: Low-dimensional procedure for the characterization of human faces. **4**(3) (1987)
5. Turk, M., Pentland, A.: Face recognition using eigenfaces. p. 6 (1991)
6. Yang, J., Hua, G.: Deep learning for video face recognition. Adv. Comput. Vis. Pattern Recogn. 209–232 (2021)
7. Yi, D., Lei, Z., Liao, S., Li, S.Z.: Learning Face Representation from Scratch, November 2014
8. Wen, Y., Zhang, K., Li, Z., Qiao, Y.: A discriminative feature learning approach for deep face recognition. In: Leibe, B., Matas, J., Sebe, N., Welling, M. (eds.) ECCV 2016. LNCS, vol. 9911, pp. 499–515. Springer, Cham (2016). https://doi.org/10.1007/978-3-319-46478-7_31
9. Abudarham, N., Shkiller, L., Yovel, G.: Critical features for face recognition. Cognition **182**, 73–83 (2019)
10. Calder, A.J., Keane, J., Young, A.W., Dean, M.: Configural information in facial expression perception. J. Exp. Psychol. Hum. Percept. Perform. **26**(2), 527–551 (2000)

11. Ding, F., Peng, P., Huang, Y., Geng, M., Tian, Y.: Masked face recognition with latent part detection. In: MM 2020 - Proc. 28th ACM International Conference on Multimedia, pp. 2281–2289, October 2020

12. Frank, C., Nöth, E.: Optimizing eigenfaces by face masks for facial expression recognition. In: Petkov, N., Westenberg, M.A. (eds.) CAIP 2003. LNCS, vol. 2756, pp. 646–654. Springer, Heidelberg (2003). https://doi.org/10.1007/978-3-540-45179-2_79

13. Brouton, L.: Cómo funciona el reconocimiento facial con máscaras facials. Blog y asesoría sobre investigación (2022). https://broutonlab.com/blog/how-facial-recognition-works-with-face-masks. Accessed 13 May 2022

14. Castelluccia, C., Le Métayer Inria, D., Le Métayer, D.: Impact Analysis of Facial Recognition (2020)

15. Jayaweera, M., Perera, H., Gunawardana, B., Manatunge, J.: Transmission of COVID-19 virus by droplets and aerosols: a critical review on the unresolved dichotomy. Environ. Res. **188** (2020)

16. Saib, Y.M., Pudaruth, S.: Is face recognition with masks possible? Int. J. Adv. Comput. Sci. Appl. **12**(7), 43–50 (2021)

17. Deng, J., Guo, J., Xue, N., Zafeiriou, S.: ArcFace: additive angular margin loss for deep face recognition. In: Proceedings of IEEE Conference on Computer Vision and Pattern Recognition, vol. 2019-June, pp. 4685–4694 (2019)

18. Ejaz, M.S., Islam, M.R., Sifatullah, M., Sarker, A.: Implementation of principal component analysis on masked and non-masked face recognition. In: 1st International Conference on Advances in Science, Engineering and Robotics Technology 2019, ICASERT 2019, May 2019

19. Song, Z., Nguyen, K., Nguyen, T., Cho, C., Gao, J.: Spartan face mask detection and facial recognition system. Healthcare **10**(1) (2022)

20. Vijitkunsawat, W., Chantngarm, P.: Study of the Performance of machine learning algorithms for face mask detection. In: CIT 2020 - 5th International Conference on Information Technology, pp. 39–43, October 2020

21. Alzu'bi, A., Albalas, F., Al-Hadhrami, T., Younis, L.B., Bashayreh, A.: Masked face recognition using deep learning: a review. Electron **10**(21) (2021)

22. Patel, V.S., Nie, Z., Le, T.-N., Nguyen, T.V.: Masked face analysis via multi-task deep learning. J. Imaging **7**(10) (2021)

23. Reconocimiento facial en tiempos de pandemia - Mobbeel. https://www.mobbeel.com/blog/reconocimiento-facial-en-tiempos-de-pandemia/. Accessed 10 June 2022

24. Cómo usar el reconocimiento facial con mascarilla: cuando los algoritmos se adaptan a la nueva normalidad. https://www.xataka.com/privacidad/como-usar-reconocimiento-facial-mascarilla-cuando-algoritmos-se-adaptan-a-nueva-normalidad. Accessed 10 June 2022

25. ¿Es posibleel robo de identidad a través del reconocimiento facial ? - Revista Transformación Digital. https://www.revistatransformaciondigital.com/2021/02/13/es-posible-el-robo-de-identidad-a-traves-del-reconocimiento-facial/. Accessed 10 June 2022

26. Bruce, V., Young, A.: Understanding face recognition. Br. J. Psychol. **77**(3), 305–327 (1986)

27. Carbon, C.C., Wearing face masks strongly confuses counterparts in reading emotions. Front. Psychol. **11** (2020)

28. Fitousi, D., Rotschild, N., Pnini, C., Azizi, O.: Understanding the impact of face masks on the processing of facial identity, emotion, age, and gender. Front. Psychol. **12**, 4668 (2021)

Evaluation Metrics in Explainable Artificial Intelligence (XAI)

Loredana Coroama$^{(\boxtimes)}$ and Adrian Groza

Computer Science Department, Technical University of Cluj-Napoca, St. Memorandumului 28, 400114 Cluj-Napoca, Romania
loredana.coroama@campus.utcluj.ro , adrian.groza@cs.utcluj.ro

Abstract. Although AI is spread across all domains and many authors stated that providing explanations is crucial, another question comes into play: How accurate are those explanations? This paper aims to summarize a state-of-the-art review in XAI evaluation metrics, to present a categorization of evaluation methods and show a mapping between existing tools and theoretically defined metrics by underlining the challenges and future development. The contribution of this paper is to help researchers to identify and apply evaluation metrics when developing an XAI system and also to identify opportunities for proposing other evaluation metrics for XAI.

Keywords: Explainable artificial intelligence · Interpretability · Explanation methods · Explanation quality · Explanation metrics

1 Introduction

Artificial intelligence has experienced a significant growth in the last decade, especially in critical decision-making systems (e.g. medicine or justice related applications), recommendation systems or different processes such as credit lending or employment. An issue arises when the system rely upon black box models such as Deep Neural Networks rather than a simple statistical model because increasing the model complexity comes with the trade-off of decreasing the interpretability, therefore, quantifying and explaining the effectiveness of XAI to the people that system interacts with becomes a challenge.

There is also an increasing demand for a responsible and accountable AI that are achieved by providing explainability. Explainable AI systems aim to detect unwanted biases such as gender or social discrimination ensuring fairness, safety, privacy through algorithmic transparency. The main issue is that most algorithms collect and analyze user data affecting decision making. Each individual should have a right to an explanation according to GDPR commission. One negative recent example was in political elections where personal information of people has been collected and used against their will. Their feed was flooded with spam during political elections to influence their decision. The strategy of politicized social bots is outlined by Samuel C. Woolley in his study [36].

T. Guarda et al. (Eds.): ARTIIS 2022, CCIS 1675, pp. 401–413, 2022.
https://doi.org/10.1007/978-3-031-20319-0_30

Another great advantage of providing explanations is gaining user trust. A system that provides explanations is perceived more human-like by users because it is part of human nature to assign causal attribution of events. Figure 1 shows the architecture of XAI process where for each decision generated by an intelligent system, explanations are provided to the user increasing trust and confidence. It is very important to assess the quality of explanations as many evaluation metrics are addressed in the literature.

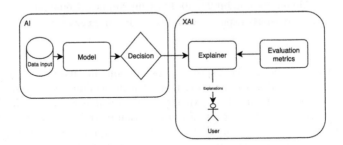

Fig. 1. XAI process

XAI is applied in various industrial applications. In recommendation systems, recommended posts and news are explained to establish trust between users and content providers. In sales, prediction are made to upsell and the most relevant features are perturbed in order to influence the result. In human resources, it might be needed to discriminate between many candidates for a certain role. In medicine, one example is the Predict tool developed by David Spiegelhalter [31] that shows how different treatments for breast cancer might improve survival rates after surgery. In credit lending, counterfactual explanations are mandatory. Other uses are in explaining energy consumption or critical systems such as object detection.

The paper is organised as follows. Classification of XAI metrics, methods and existing studies are presented in Sect. 2, existing XAI evaluation metrics are discussed in Sect. 3, while implementations are describes in Sect. 4 and conclusions are drawn in Sect. 5.

2   XAI Classifications

Regarding the state of the XAI research, existing studies are split in three main categories. Some papers review existing XAI methods or propose new techniques for explainability [18, 20, 33]. Second category is focused on the notions of explainability [6, 11, 34], while the third one tends to evaluate all these approaches proposing new evaluation metrics [15, 17, 23, 28, 38].

G. Vilone et al. [34] classify existing XAI methods based on five criteria. The first one is related to the stage in which explanations are generated. Explanations can be generated during training or a post-model (agnostic or specific) can

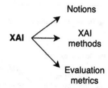

Fig. 2. Current state of XAI research

be built which is less computationally expensive. The second one deals with the type of explanations which can be global or local. The third one splits the methods based on the problem type (classification and regression). Also, input data is important because not all the methods work for all data types such as text, images or tabular data. Finally, one more criteria is related to the output format. Explanations can be numerical, textual, visual, mixed or rules-based. They also performed a classification of evaluation metrics. According to the authors, there are human-centred and objective metrics. Human-centred metrics involve users feedback. Users can be randomly selected or domain experts. Also, depending on the questions addressed to people, there are qualitative metrics which aim to achieve deeper insights and quantitative metrics for statistical analysis. On the other hand, objective metrics such as explanation completeness, rules cardinality or perturbation metrics are defined based on formal definitions. Explanation completeness captures the highest number of features that determine the prediction while perturbation metrics refers to the sensitivity to input perturbation by altering the input and comparing the outputs and to model parameter randomization by comparing with same models but with different parameters (Fig. 2).

F. Doshi-Velez et al. [11] divided XAI evaluation in tree categories: user-based evaluation, application-based evaluation and functionality-based evaluation. They also considered first two types as a part of human-centred evaluation and split it in subjective and objectives metrics. Moreover, we claim that functionality-based evaluation which assesses the quality of explanations using formal definitions of explainability could be divided in method-specific metrics and agnostic metrics.

Other evaluation approach is related to features perturbation. Perturbing relevant features should lead to a change in prediction, therefore higher the change, better the method. Secondly, example-based explanations seems to be another type of evaluation that is better designed for humans [8,18]. Another category of explanations depends on data, P. Hase et al. [14] performed experiments by generating forward and counterfactual explanations. On the other side, [9] shows that visual explanations are not always of use. Another way of evaluating explanations is from a developer point of view [7].

Taking into consideration related work discussed in Sect. 3, we categorize existing XAI evaluation metrics as it is shown in Fig. 3. We consider the metrics that rely on human feedback as subjective. The feedback can be provided by randomly selected persons or by domain experts such as doctors in medicine or judges in justice. They are subjective as each user might consider that a

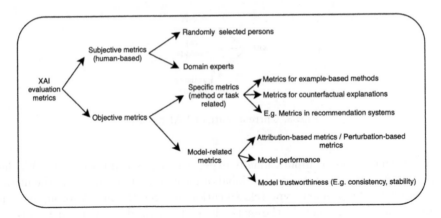

Fig. 3. XAI evaluation metrics

particular method or application is more appropriate for them relying also on different aspects including user experience or application design which does not necessarily assess the explanation quality. On the other hand, objectivity could be achieved through formal definitions. Many explanations methods have been developed in the past years, some metrics were developed only for specific methods or tasks, while others are focused on the model behaviour. Example-based methods provide explanations by generating the most similar instances for the sample being explained, therefore aspects such as non-representativeness or diversity stand as valid options for quantifying the effectiveness of explanations. Counterfactual explanations are used when knowing the outcome is not enough and explanations are required to determine what should be changed for obtaining another result. These could be evaluated with metrics such as diversity of changes and their feasibility. Other specific metrics could be related to a certain task such as generating explanations in recommendation systems. The last category covers model-related metrics. Attribution-based metrics are computed taking into consideration feature importance. Examples of such metrics are sensitivity or the monotony. Some methods build another oversimplificated version of the initial model (post-model) in order to generate explanations which is efficient because avoids model retraining and reduces the computational cost. In this case, evaluating the quality of explanations comes down to the post-model evaluation with metrics such as size, complexity or accuracy. Performance aspects refer to metrics such as computational cost which can be highly expensive or even stopping the execution of the algorithm for very large datasets. Model trustworthiness is another aspect that comes into play. Metrics such as consistency or stability increase confidence when quantifying the quality of explanations.

Numerous metrics underlying the quality of explanations were proposed in the literature as summarised in Table 1.

Table 1. Existing metrics

XAI metric	Type	Observations	Implementation
D	Objective	The performance difference between the model and the logic presented as an explanation	No
R	Objective	The number of rules in the explanation, the fewer, the better	No
F	Objective	The number of features used to construct the explanation, less features, clearer the explanation	No
S	Objective	The stability of the explanations	Yes
Simplicity	Objective	The ability to choose only the necessary and sufficient features for explaining the prediction	No
Sensitivity	Objective	Measure the degree to which the explanation is affected by insignificant perturbations from the test point	Yes
Completeness	Objective	Captures the highest number of features that determine the prediction	No
Soundness	Objective	How truthful each element in an explanation is	No
Stability of explanation	Objective	Test the consistency of explanation methods consisting in many repeated experiments; Close inputs with similar predictions yields similar explanations	Yes
Robustness	Objective	Similar inputs should result in similar explanations, measure the sensitivity to noise	Yes
Computational cost	Objective	How expensive is to generate explanations	Yes
Post-model evaluation metrics	Objective	Model size (number of rules, length of rules or depth of trees), model complexity, interaction strength, etc.	Yes
Monotonicity	Objective	It is measured by adding each feature in order of increasing importance and observing an increase in the model performance; Features attributions should be monotonic, otherwise the correct importance of the features is not provided	Yes
Perturbation-based metrics	Objective	The capacity of underlying the variations after perturbing the inputs	Yes
Non-representativeness	Objective	Measure of the fidelity of the explanation; used in example-based methods	No
Diversity	Objective	Used in example-based methods	No
Explanation correctness	Objective	Assessed through sensitivity and fidelity	Yes
Explanation confidence	Objective	High confidence predictions	Yes
Fidelity (MuFidelity, Deletion and Insertion)	Objective	Explanations describe correctly the model behaviour; Ensure there is a correlation between a random subset of pixels and their attribution score	Yes
Representativity (Generalizability)	Objective	How much seeing one explanation informs you about the others; the more representative an explanation is, the more it persists when we remove a point	Yes
Consistency	Objective	The consistency score of the explanations, it informs about the confidence of the explanations, how much two models explanations will not contradict each other; The explainer should capture the same relevant components under various transformation to the input	Yes
Faithfulness	Objective	Computes which feature has the most impact on the model output when individually changed; Removing each important feature should result in decreasing the model performance	Yes
ROAR	Objective	Retrains the model with the most relevant features removed	Yes
GT-Shapley	Objective	Determine which technique compute most accurately the approximations to the Shapley values	Yes
Infidelity	Objective	Included in XAI-Bench tool [21]	Yes
Metrics for counterfactual explanations (diversity, feasibility, validity, sparsity)	Objective	Diversity implies a wide range of suggested changes and feasibility the possibility to adopt those changes; Validity measures the uniqueness and the sparsity refers to the number of features that are different	Yes
Transparency	Subjective	Describe how the system takes a certain decision; Used in recommendation systems (not only)	No
Scrutability (similar with actionability or correctability)	N/A	Ability to correct the system if its assumptions are wrong; Used in recommendation systems	No
Trust	Subjective	Measured through user questionnaires or metrics such as products sold in recommendation systems	No
Effectiveness	Subjective	Used in recommendation systems to discard unwanted options	No
Persuasiveness	Subjective	Used in recommendation systems to convince the user to take an action (e.g. buy a product) after receiving the explanations	No
Efficiency	Subjective	Used in recommendation systems/conversational systems and can be measured by counting the explanations needed	No
Satisfaction	Subjective	Usefulness and ease of use; used in recommendation systems	No
Comprehensibility	Subjective	How much effort is required for humans to understand the explanations	No
Justifiability	Subjective	Assess if the model is in line with domain knowledge	No
Explanation goodness, User curiosity or attention engagement, User understanding, User performance, System controllability or interaction, Explanation usefulness	Subjective	Used in psychology	No
Interactivity, interestingness, informativeness, human-AI task performance	Subjective	User experience	No

3   Discussion and Related Work

If an XAI agent (system or application) works in tandem with a specialist then a maximum accuracy can be achieved. Avi Rosenfeld considers state-of-the-art imaging techniques in radiology in order to identify diseases [28]. Radiologists have a successful rate of 97% in finding the disease, while the agent has achieved 99.5% accuracy. As this area is very sensitive and the decisions are crucial, it would be ideal to have meaningful explanations for those misclassified samples; in this manner, doctors with knowledge expertise will identify the mistakes. In presented paper, four metrics are suggested in order to evaluate generated explanations: i) D, the performance difference between the model and the logic presented as an explanation; ii) R, the number of rules in the explanation; iii) F, the number of features used to construct the explanation; iv) S, the stability of the explanations. The author claims that these objective metrics are critical raising the issue that existing studies using methods such as post-models are a oversimplication of the initial models logic and they didn't evaluate legal, ethical or safety concerns. Also, an advantage of the metrics developed is that they are not dependant of the task being performed or the XAI algorithm.

Black-box algorithms such as neural networks achieve a higher accuracy than white box algorithms, but are less transparent. D measures if choosing black box algorithms is really necessary. It quantifies the change in performance (δ) between the black box model (P_b) and the transparent model (P_t). The decision is made comparing $P_b - \delta$ and P_t. R focuses on the size of the explanations, the fewer, the better: $\lambda * L$, where $L = [size(m) - c]$, m is number of rules and c a penalization. This metric is more suitable for transparent methods. F focuses on the number of features used to create the explanation, less features, clearer the explanation. This metric is quantified similarly with the previous one except that represents the number of inputted features instead of outputted rules. S is the stability of the explanations which quantifies the ability to handle small noise perturbations: $\lambda * (1 - similarity)$. Some metrics for quantifying similarity are Jaccard and Tanimoto.

There are three ways to generate explanations: directly using a transparent algorithm, through feature selection or by creating a post-model. The last option aims to describe the inner working of a black-box algorithm that is not inherently understood. This is achieved by approximating model's logic via white-box algorithms or by highlighting superpixels or using model perturbations. Also, some authors consider a difference between explainability and interpretability claiming that explainability focuses on the ability of humans to understand model logic and interpretability clarifies the system's internal logic. On the other side, in many papers these terms are used synonymously.

In recommendation systems, N. Tintarev et al. [33] claim that metrics such as user satisfaction, serendipity, diversity and trust are as important as accuracy metrics such as precision and recall. To asses explanation quality, they have proposed the following metrics: transparency, scrutability, trust, effectiveness, persuasiveness, efficiency and satisfaction. These metrics were analysed in many recommendation systems. Transparency should explain how a system works and why it recommended a certain decision. There is no work on evaluating transparency. Scrutability allows users to correct the system if its assumptions were wrong. It is also known as user control. It was proved that some recommendations are made based on the user profile, therefore changing his attributes would result in generating different recommendations. Trust is linked with transparency and accuracy, but sometimes explanations can compensate faulty recommendations. Moreover, Bj Fogg et al. [12] demonstrated that the design of the system might affect the users credibility. Trust has been measured through user questionnaires or user loyalty by counting metrics such as the number of logins or products sold. Persuasiveness is a technique to convince the user to buy or try and it can be measured after the users receive explanations. Effectiveness help users to discard unwanted options by generating good explanations. Efficiency is mostly used in conversational systems and measures how quickly a task can be performed. An evaluation metric could be the number of explanations needed. Satisfaction is related to usefulness and ease of use and can be evaluated using user-based metrics.

G. Vilone et al. [34] have presented many notions related to the explanation quality. Actionability and correctability describe the capacity to transfer knowledge to the users allowing them to explain necessary corrections. Causality [16] refers to the relationship between input and output. Completeness defines the extent to which a system is described by explanations. Comprehensibility [5] quantifies how much effort is required for humans to understand the explanations. Faithfulness represents the capacity to select truly relevant features. Justifiability assess if the model is in line with domain knowledge. Robustness means that similar inputs should result in similar explanations, David et al. [1] quantifies this metric and claim that current XAI methods do not perform well. Scrutability allows inpecting a training process that fails. Simplicity is the ability to choose only the necessary and sufficient features for explaining the prediction. Sensitivity reflects the capacity of underlying the variations after perturbing the inputs. Stability measures the consistency. Soundness analyses how truthful each element in an explanation is. Todd Kulesza et al. [19] claim that completeness is more important than soundness. Many other notions and metrics such as transparency, effectiveness, efficiency, interactivity, interestingness, informativeness, persuasiveness, satisfaction and security are discussed, but there are no formal definitions or implementations developed.

Other domains in which XAI research takes advantages are cognitive science and psychology. 7 cognitives metrics were introduced by J. H. Hsiao et al. in their study [17]: explanation goodness, user satisfaction, user curiosity/attention engagement, user trust/reliance, user understanding, user performance/productivity and system controllability/interaction. They claim that existing evaluation methods are inherited from cognitive processes. There are 3 processes in cognitive science and psychology: measuring and comparing the system's behavior under different conditions (e.g. perturbation-based methods), building predictive models to simulate the behaviour (XAI post-models) and explaining the behaviour by analysing features through factor analysis (XAI methods based on feature importance). Presented metrics can be measured using subjective methods as they require user interaction.

S. Mohseni et al. [23] classified evaluation methods based on targeted users such as AI novices, domain experts and AI experts. Primary interpretability measures refers to user's mental model, explanation usefulness and satisfaction, user trust and reliance and the human-AI task performance. Last type covers the computational measures such as explanation correctness which is strong related to model consistency, explainer fidelity and model trustworthiness and do not rely on human-subject studies.

Stability of explanation, robustness of referee classifier and computational cost are discussed when quantifying the informativeness of explanation methods for time series classification [27]. T. Nguyen et al. studied the saliency maps method for explanations which highlight the most important parts when making a prediction. They define an explanation as being truly informative if it points out the part of time series that are most relevant for the prediction. The stability of explanation test the consistency of explanation methods consisting in many repeated experiments. Robustness measures how sensitive to noise are presented methods. The computational costs measures how expensive is to generate explanations.

J. Zhou et al. [38] define explainability as a combination of interpretability (explanations understandable by humans) and fidelity (explanations describe correctly the model behaviour). They claim that general computation metrics for XAI methods evaluation is unlikely to be possible due to many factors such as the subjectivity of explanations, the context, the models, the users dependency and the type of explanations required. They also divided objective evaluation metrics in tree types: model-based explanations, attribution-based explanations and example-based explanations. Model-based explanations use the model itself or create new models to explain ML. Evaluating the quality of explanations means evaluating that model. Examples of such metrics are model size (number of rules, length of rules or depth of trees), interaction strength or model complexity. Attribution-based explanations are based on feature importance or feature ranking. Examples of metrics are monotonicity or sensitivity. Example-based explanations select most similar instances from the dataset. Examples of metrics are non-representativeness and diversity [26].

A. B. Arrieta et al. [6] suggest as future improvement the development of certain evaluation metrics: the goodness, usefulness and satisfaction of explanations, the improvement of the mental model of the audience induced by model explanations and the impact of explanations on the performance of the model and on the trust and reliance of the audience. Goodness checklist, explanation satisfaction scale, elicitation methods for mental models, computational measures for explainer fidelity, explanation trustworthiness and model reliability are described in [15,24].

The reasoning of Bayesian Networks has been applied in different applications. BayLime [37] is an extension of LIME, a well-known XAI technique that it was proved to be unstable do to the lack of consistency when generating different explanations for same instances. BayLime takes advantage of prior knowledge and Bayesian reasoning to improve the consistency and the robustness to kernel settings. The need for explaining bayesian networks for legal evidence was also addressed [35]. C. Lacave et al. [20] review the explanation methods for Bayesian networks. They defined some properties that each explanation should satisfy. There are three aspects that should be taken into consideration: the content (what to explain), communication (how the system interacts with the user), adaptation (to whom the explanation is addressed). The content covers the focus, purpose, level and causality of explanations. First property is the focus of explanation and defines 3 basic issues that should be explained by any expert system: the knowledge base (explaining the model), the reasoning (explaining obtained results and the reasoning process or hypothetical reasoning) and the evidence (which unobserved variables justify the available evidence). The purpose refers either to the description of the model or other aspects or the comprehension which explain how each finding affects the results. The level of explanation in Bayesian networks consists in micro-level explanations by generating detailed explanations for a particular node or macro-level explanations which analyses the main lines in the network. Causality is one of the most important features because humans tend to interpret events in terms of cause-effects relations. The communication represents the way in which it is offered to the users and covers the user-system interaction, display of explanations (text, numbers or graphs) and expressions of probability (numerical, quantitative or linguistic such as "very likely"). The adaptation consists in the ability to address each user's needs depending on the knowledge he has and covers the user's knowledge about the domain and reasoning method and the level of detail. There are various tools for explaining Bayesian Networks (Hugin [3], Analytica, Ideal [32], David [30], Diaval [10], Elvira[1] Medicus [29], B2 [22], Banter [13]), but no metrics developed to assess their correctability. This can be a starting point for future research.

4   Implementations

Predict Tool[2] [31] helps doctors and patients to decide which treatment to take after breast cancer surgery. The tool explains its decisions and provides graphics, text and tables with how that treatment affected other women after surgery. Similar tools could be developed for other types of cancer.

There are different ways to explain a decision. Different users require different explanations for different purposes and with different objectives. A doctor wants to know why a certain treatment is recommended (trust), the government wants to prove that there is no discrimination (compliance, safety) and a developer is concerned about how is the system performing or how it can be improved (quality, debug). In all the cases, the explanations quality is crucial. IBM AIX360 [4] developed a similar application[3] with 3 types of users: developer (ensure the

---

[1] Elvira tool available online: https://leo.ugr.es/elvira/.

[2] PredictTool available online: https://breast.predict.nhs.uk/tool.

[3] IBM AIX360 available online: http://aix360.mybluemix.net/data.

model works appropriately), loan officer (needs to assess the model's prediction and make the final judgement), bank customer (wants to understand the reason for the application result). They also implemented 2 metrics in order to evaluate the explanations methods: faithfulness and monotony. Faithfulness measures the correlation between the model attributes and the model performance. Removing each important feature should result in decreasing the model performance. On the other hand, monotony is measured by adding each feature in order of increasing importance and observing an increase in the model performance.

Main drawbacks when developing new metrics are: computational cost, inability to be extended to non-image domains or simply focusing only one desirable attribute of a good explainer.

XAI-Bench tool [21] uses synthetic datasets to evaluate the faithfulness, monotonicity, ROAR, GT-Shapley and infidelity of five XAI techniques. Faithfulness computes which feature has the most impact on the model output when individually changed, while monotonicity computes the effect of the features added sequentially. Remove-and-retrain (ROAR) consists in retraining the model with the most relevant features removed, while GT-Shapley metric determine which technique compute most accurately the approximations to the Shapley values. Infidelity computes the difference between the change in function value and the dot product of the change in feature value with the feature importance vector, considering that each feature is replaced with a noisy baseline conditional expectation.

DiCE [25] is a tool that generates and evaluates counterfactuals explanations. In some cases such as credit lending, knowing the outcome is not enough, the applicant might want to know what to do to obtain a better outcome in the future. The metrics developed are diversity and feasibility. Diversity implies a wide range of suggested changes and feasibility the possibility to adopt those changes (proximity to the original input). Other constraints are validity (unique examples which correspond to a different outcome than the original input) and sparsity (the number of features that are different).

Implementations for correctness, consistency and confidence[4] are developed in the literature. For example, consistency refers to the fact that the explainer should capture the same relevant components under various transformation to the input. Correctness is the same thing with sensitivity and fidelity and represents the ability of the explainer to determine the most relevant features. Confidence is concerned with whether the generated explanation and the masked input result in high confidence predictions. This metrics are computationally inexpensive because do not require model retraining.

Xplique[5] is a tool dedicted to explainability for neural networks based on Tensorflow. It contains a module that allows testing the current evaluation metrics. Fidelity is addressed through 3 metrics: MuFidelity, Deletion and Insertion. The deletion metric measures the drop in the probability of a class as the input is gradually perturbed. The insertion metric captures the importance of the pixels

---

[4] Available online: https://github.com/amarogayo/xai-metrics.

[5] Available online: https://github.com/deel-ai/xplique.

in terms of their ability to synthesize an image and is measured by the rise in the probability of the class of interest as pixels are added according to the generated importance map. MuFidelity ensure there is a correlation between a random subset of pixels and their attribution score. Stability ensure that close inputs with similar predictions yields similar explanations. Representativity (or Generalizability) gives you an overview of the generalization of your explanations: how much seeing one explanation informs you about the others. Consistency is the consistency score of the explanations, it informs about the confidence of the explanations, how much two models explanations will not contradict each other. Explicitness, faithfulness, stability are also presented in [2].

5 Conclusions and Future Improvements

The integration and evaluation of XAI methods have become very important as the AI is more and more widespread in almost all domains. In the last years, artificial intelligence has been used in unethical purposes such as computational propaganda, fake news spreading and different campaign to manipulate public opinion. Two well-known events are the war in Ukraine and COVID-19 in China. Some datasets are provided by the university of Oxford[6] which can be used for future research.

This paper summarizes existing evaluation methods and metrics in the literature underlining two issues. A big part of the research limits itself to theoretical definitions that have not been implemented or adopted in real applications. Then it seems that general evaluation metrics for XAI methods are unlikely to be implemented due to many factors such as the task being performed, the internal logic of the XAI method or the type of the explanations. However, some metrics could be generally applicable (e.g. each method should be consistent and return same explanations at different runs for the same sample). This issue should drive future research in this direction.

Moreover, many metrics come with a trade-off. It is desired to achieve all these features at their maximum capacity, but in reality it might be impossible (e.g. an increase in transparency comes with the decrease in efficiency and so on). The evaluation metrics should be mapped to the system goal and what the explanation is trying to achieve.

References

1. Alvarez-Melis, D., Jaakkola, T.S.: On the robustness of interpretability methods. CoRR abs/1806.08049 (2018). arxiv.org/abs/1806.08049
2. Alvarez-Melis, D., Jaakkola, T.S.: Towards robust interpretability with self-explaining neural networks. CoRR abs/1806.07538 (2018). arxiv.org/abs/1806.07538
3. Andersen, S., Olesen, K., Jensen, F., Jensen, F.: HUGIN - a shell for building Bayesian belief universes for expert systems. IJCAI **2**, 1080–1085 (1989)

---

[6] https://demtech.oii.ox.ac.uk/research/data-sets/.

4. Arya, V., et al.: One explanation does not fit all: a toolkit and taxonomy of AI explainability techniques (2019). arxiv.org/abs/1909.03012

5. Askira-Gelman, I.: Knowledge discovery: comprehensibility of the results. In: 2014 47th Hawaii International Conference on System Sciences, vol. 5, p. 247. IEEE Computer Society, Los Alamitos, January 1998. https://doi.org/10.1109/HICSS.1998.648319. https://doi.ieeecomputersociety.org/10.1109/HICSS.1998.648319

6. Barredo Arrieta, A., et al.: Explainable artificial intelligence (XAI): concepts, taxonomies, opportunities and challenges toward responsible AI. Inf. Fusion **58**, 82–115 (2020). https://doi.org/10.1016/j.inffus.2019.12.012. https://www.sciencedirect.com/science/article/pii/S1566253519308103

7. Bhatt, U., et al.: Explainable machine learning in deployment. CoRR abs/1909.06342 (2019). arxiv.org/abs/1909.06342

8. Borowski, J., et al.: Exemplary natural images explain CNN activations better than feature visualizations. CoRR abs/2010.12606 (2020). arxiv.org/abs/2010.12606

9. Chu, E., Roy, D., Andreas, J.: Are visual explanations useful? A case study in model-in-the-loop prediction. CoRR abs/2007.12248 (2020). arxiv.org/abs/2007.12248

10. Díez, F., Mira, J., Iturralde, E., Zubillaga, S.: Diaval, a bayesian expert system for echocardiography. Artif. Intell. Med. **10**, 59–73 (1997). https://doi.org/10.1016/S0933-3657(97)00384-9

11. Doshi-Velez, F., Kim, B.: Towards a rigorous science of interpretable machine learning (2017)

12. Fogg, B., et al.: Web credibility research: a method for online experiments and early study results. In: CHI 20001 Extended Abstracts on Human Factors in Computing Systems, pp. 295–296 (2001)

13. Haddawy, P., Jacobson, J., Kahn, C.E.: BANTER: a Bayesian network tutoring shell. Artif. Intell. Med. **10**(2), 177–200 (1997). https://doi.org/10.1016/S0933-3657(96)00374-0. https://www.sciencedirect.com/science/article/pii/S0933365796003740

14. Hase, P., Bansal, M.: Evaluating explainable AI: which algorithmic explanations help users predict model behavior? CoRR abs/2005.01831 (2020). arxiv.org/abs/2005.01831

15. Hoffman, R.R., Mueller, S.T., Klein, G., Litman, J.: Metrics for explainable AI: challenges and prospects (2019)

16. Holzinger, A., Langs, G., Denk, H., Zatloukal, K., Müller, H.: Causability and explainability of artificial intelligence in medicine. Wiley Interdisc. Rev. Data Mining Knowl. Disc. **9**, e1312 (2019)

17. Hsiao, J.H., Ngai, H.H.T., Qiu, L., Yang, Y., Cao, C.C.: Roadmap of designing cognitive metrics for explainable artificial intelligence (XAI). CoRR abs/2108.01737 (2021). arxiv.org/abs/2108.01737

18. Jeyakumar, J.V., Noor, J., Cheng, Y.H., Garcia, L., Srivastava, M.: How can i explain this to you? An empirical study of deep neural network explanation methods. In: 34th Conference on Neural Information Processing Systems (2020)

19. Kulesza, T., Stumpf, S., Burnett, M., Yang, S., Kwan, I., Wong, W.K.: Too much, too little, or just right? Ways explanations impact end users' mental models. In: 2013 IEEE Symposium on Visual Languages and Human Centric Computing, pp. 3–10 (2013). https://doi.org/10.1109/VLHCC.2013.6645235

20. Lacave, C., Dez, F.: A review of explanation methods for Bayesian networks. Knowl. Eng. Rev. **17** (2001). https://doi.org/10.1017/S026988890200019X

21. Liu, Y., Khandagale, S., White, C., Neiswanger, W.: Synthetic benchmarks for scientific research in explainable machine learning. In: Advances in Neural Information Processing Systems Datasets Track (2021)
22. Mcroy, S., Liu-perez, A., Haller, S.: B2: A tutoring shell for Bayesian networks that supports natural language interaction, February 1996
23. Mohseni, S., Zarei, N., Ragan, E.D.: A survey of evaluation methods and measures for interpretable machine learning. CoRR abs/1811.11839 (2018). arxiv.org/abs/1811.11839
24. Mohseni, S., Zarei, N., Ragan, E.D.: A multidisciplinary survey and framework for design and evaluation of explainable AI systems (2020)
25. Mothilal, R.K., Sharma, A., Tan, C.: Explaining machine learning classifiers through diverse counterfactual explanations. In: Proceedings of the 2020 Conference on Fairness, Accountability, and Transparency, pp. 607–617 (2020)
26. Nguyen, A., Martínez, M.R.: On quantitative aspects of model interpretability. CoRR abs/2007.07584 (2020). arxiv.org/abs/2007.07584
27. Nguyen, T.T., Le Nguyen, T., Ifrim, G.: A model-agnostic approach to quantifying the informativeness of explanation methods for time series classification. In: Lemaire, V., Malinowski, S., Bagnall, A., Guyet, T., Tavenard, R., Ifrim, G. (eds.) AALTD 2020. LNCS (LNAI), vol. 12588, pp. 77–94. Springer, Cham (2020). https://doi.org/10.1007/978-3-030-65742-0_6
28. Rosenfeld, A.: Better metrics for evaluating explainable artificial intelligence: blue sky ideas track, May 2021
29. Schröder, O., Möbus, C., Thole, H.J.: Knowledge from linguistic models in complex, probabilistic domains, January 1996
30. Shachter, R.D.: DAVID: influence diagram processing system for the Macintosh. CoRR abs/1304.3108 (2013). arxiv.org/abs/1304.3108
31. Spiegelhalter, D.: Making algorithms trustworthy: what can statistical science contribute to transparency, explanation and validation? In: NeurIPS (2018)
32. Srinivas, S., Breese, J.S.: IDEAL: a software package for analysis of influence diagrams. CoRR abs/1304.1107 (2013). arxiv.org/abs/1304.1107
33. Tintarev, N., Masthoff, J.: A survey of explanations in recommender systems, pp. 801–810, May 2007. https://doi.org/10.1109/ICDEW.2007.4401070
34. Vilone, G., Longo, L.: Explainable artificial intelligence: a systematic review, May 2020
35. Vlek, C.S., Prakken, H., Renooij, S., Verheij, B.: A method for explaining Bayesian networks for legal evidence with scenarios. Artif. Intell. Law **24**(3), 285–324 (2016)
36. Woolley, S.C.: Automating power: social bot interference in global politics. First Monday **21**(4) (2016). https://doi.org/10.5210/fm.v21i4.6161. https://journals.uic.edu/ojs/index.php/fm/article/view/6161
37. Zhao, X., Huang, X., Robu, V., Flynn, D.: BayLime: Bayesian local interpretable model-agnostic explanations. CoRR abs/2012.03058 (2020). arxiv.org/abs/2012.03058
38. Zhou, J., Gandomi, A.H., Chen, F., Holzinger, A.: Evaluating the quality of machine learning explanations: a survey on methods and metrics. Electronics **10**(5), 593 (2021)

Real-Time Condition-Based Maintenance of Friction Welding Tools by Generalized Fault Trees

Pedro Nunes[1,2]([✉]) [iD], Eugénio M. Rocha[3,4] [iD], Jorge Neves[5],
and José Santos[1,2] [iD]

[1] Centre for Mechanical Technology and Automation, Aveiro, Portugal
pnunes@ua.pt
[2] Department of Mechanical Engineering, University of Aveiro, Aveiro, Portugal
[3] Center for Research and Development in Mathematics and Applications,
Aveiro, Portugal
[4] Department of Mathematics, University of Aveiro, Aveiro, Portugal
[5] Business Digitalization Office (TT/BDO-M-PO),
Bosch Termotecnologia, S.A., Aveiro, Portugal

Abstract. In manufacturing processes, root cause analysis of tools' failures is crucial to determine the system reliability and to derive cost minimizing strategies. Condition-based maintenance (CBM) is one of the relevant policies to reduce costs of tools usage subjected to degradation processes. In a previous work, the authors introduced a new statistical methodology entitled Generalized Fault Tree (GFT) analysis that demonstrated good results for reliability analysis and root cause analysis. In this work, we propose a new dynamic CBM methodology, through real-time failure forecasting of the replacement instant of friction welding tools at a Bosch TermoTechnology facility, based on the dynamic update of the GFT root probability. The GFT structure is described by data-driven basic events (BEs), obtained from an embedded accelerometer, and the tree that best describes the tools' failures is obtained through a new training process that employs a pruning technique to reduce computational complexity. The results show that we can reduce at least 12% of the costs per welding cycle by applying the GFT approach and CBM, when compared with the current policy of preventive maintenance in (optimized) constant cycles replacement periods.

Keywords: Generalized Fault Tree · Condition-based maintenance · Data-driven · Friction welding · Industry 4.0

1 Introduction

Root cause analysis, together with reliability analysis, increases the availability and safety of systems [12]. The first concept consists of determining the main causes or events that lead to a given failure or problem, while the second one is

© The Author(s), under exclusive license to Springer Nature Switzerland AG 2022
T. Guarda et al. (Eds.): ARTIIS 2022, CCIS 1675, pp. 414–428, 2022.
https://doi.org/10.1007/978-3-031-20319-0_31

closely related to the determination of the failure probability of a given component. A well-known and exploited technique to handle these tasks is the Fault Tree Analysis (FTA) [27]. A fault tree (FT) is a directed acyclic graph that represents the failure path or chain of events that originated a problem. It consists of a tree model approach, where the root represents the failure or top event (TE), leaves are the basic events (BEs), and intermediate nodes are gates. The BEs are the causes that lead to the TE, while the gates are operators that represent the way BEs interact to generate the TE. For example, an OR gate triggers when at least one of its BEs occurred, while an AND gate is activated when all its BEs occurred.

FTA became more popular with the development of dynamic gates that describe the temporal dependency of some parts, such as spares. These gates allow the reliability assessment of large and complex systems [6,23], by using different techniques, such as simulation methods [3,7,31], model checkers [5,30], state-space models [11,13,15], algebraic approaches [8,22], among others [1]. For this reason, this technique is being used in several real use cases. For example, [28] employed FTA to assess the reliability of a power transformer, [9] evaluated the reliability of a diesel generator system, and [24] performed a risk assessment of fires on rooftops with photovoltaic systems. Even very well-known entities, such as NASA, employed FTA in aeronautic applications [29].

In [26], was discussed the limitations of some variations of FTA, namely the fact that existing approaches assume that BEs follow an exponential (or Weibull) distribution, which in general can be a rough approximation of the real distribution. Moreover, reliability analysis with FTA strongly depends on expert knowledge to define the tree-shaped structure that describes a given failure or problem. The recent work proposes a data-driven methodology, the so-called Generalized Fault Tree (GFT) analysis, that proved to be effective in more realistic scenarios, either to automatically determine the root cause of mechanical failures in a stamping press based on data driven-events, or for determining its reliability.

The term CBM came up with the development of the Internet of Things (IoT) and the increasing necessity to monitor the condition of industrial assets by means of sensors and embedded devices [17]. Its key point is the fact that maintenance actions are taken based on the actual degradation state of industrial equipment. It may represent important savings in comparison with other maintenance policies, such as the corrective (CM) or preventive maintenance (PM). In the CM scenario, actions are made only when there is a fail and the equipment is unable to perform without any intervention, which may cause huge losses since healthy parts may be damaged in consequence of other part's failure. In the PM scenario, actions are programmed, usually in equally spaced intervals. Adopting this strategy may lead to replacing a part when the failure is too far from occurring, or, when the failure already occurred. To improve PM, predictive maintenance policy was developed and has attracted much of nowadays's attention, by applying techniques such as machine learning beside others. Our approach stands on this topic by applying statistical based techniques.

In fact, following the advances in the CBM field, data-driven techniques have been proposed to address the health condition of industrial assets. For example, [14] and [32] used sensor-based degradation models to predict the remaining useful life (RUL) of equipments and validated their approaches on data from a simulation model. The authors in [20] and [10] exploited the Wiener process model (WPM). While [20] employed this model together with particle filtering (PF) to estimate the RUL of turbofan engines, the authors in [10] employed the WPM to estimate the degradation of automotive components that are subjected to hard failures (lead-acid batteries). Theoretically, considering hard failures increases the complexity of the problem due to its unpredictability. However, authors simplify the problem by approximating the hazard rate by a Weibull distribution.

The rolling bearings are one of the most studied components in the literature that uses a data-driven approach to assess the health condition of industrial equipments. The authors in [19] exploited a PF to estimate the RUL of rolling bearings, while [21] addressed a similar use case by applying a self organized map (SOM) [16]. The fact that there are a plethora of experiments and equations describing the failures of some components, such as the Paris-Erdogan model [25], which describes the propagation of micro fatigue cracks, favors the health condition assessment of some mechanical components, such as the rolling bearings, however these models could hardly be generalized for other use cases.

Machine learning techniques, such as XGBoost, random forests (RF), support vector regression (SVR), artificial neural networks (ANN), among others, have been used to estimate the health condition of equipments. For example, [2] tested several ML algorithms in components of a production factory, while [4] proposed an innovative approach where ML algorithms are used together with anomaly detection and segmentation techniques to predict mechanical failures in stamping presses.

Despite the number of solutions proposed to assess the health condition of industrial assets, none of the mentioned solutions has the capacity to be effective in all industrial scenarios. ML learning models are good at finding patterns and non-linear relations in data, but they are less efficient to globally capture the failure behavior of industrial equipment in the presence of high imbalanced datasets [18], where failures represent a very small percentage of the data, which is very common in industry industrial scenarios, since, usually industrial assets have a normal behavior most of the time. To address high amounts of data, ML classification models exploit aggregation techniques, and use data from a few time-windows. In scenarios where there is a degradation process of tools, it is interesting to address all the data since the beginning of the component's life cycle, to accurately determine its reliability or health condition.

Statistical methods, such as the FTA, have the capability to capture a plethora of behaviors with minimal loss of information by means of distributions. In our previous work [26], we addressed and solved the main issues of traditional FTA with the so-called GFT approach, where events may follow an arbitrary compact support distribution and the building of the tree-shaped structure does not rely on expert knowledge, since a training method can find the structure that best fits the TE distribution automatically. Traditionally, FTA is employed for reliability analysis or risk assessment. In this work, besides considering a new use case, and a larger dataset, we propose a new methodology to perform a dynamic CBM based on the dynamic update of the GFT's root. For this, we explore a friction welding use case at Bosch TermoTechnology, where the tools' replacement is optimized based on a failure probability, that is calculated by a GFT and accounts with the number of working cycles, and with data-driven BEs obtained from an accelerometer.

The remaining of this document is organized as follows; Sect. 2 presents the friction welding use case at Bosch TermoTechnology. Section 3 and its subsections describe the GFT approach for root cause analysis, reliability analysis and health condition assessment. Section 4 highlights the main results, and Sect. 5 presents the conclusions and final remarks.

2   Friction Welding Use Case

The use case addressed in this paper is the optimization of tool's replacement in a friction welding process at Bosch TermoTechnology. It is a solid-state welding in which heat is generated by the mechanical friction between a rotating tool and the workpieces to fuse the materials, as depicted by Fig. 1. In addition, the tool has a lateral displacement in the direction of the X-axis to displace the materials.

As expected, this process causes degradation of the welding tools that have to be regularly replaced. At the moment, the maintenance policy for replacing these tools is the PM at the end of an assigned number of welding cycles (780 cycles). This value is considered the best constant replacing value for the problem. However, as verified by the production engineers, the great majority of tools have a catastrophic failure before the assigned period, which requires the tool to be replaced before the assigned number of welding cycles. In these situations, the workpieces are considered scrap, so there is an additional cost to the enterprise.

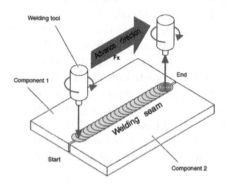

Fig. 1. Schematic of the friction welding process.

The process is monitored in real-time by embedded sensors, thus important variables such as the force in the X-axis and Z-axis are collected by a programmable logic controller (PLC), with a period of 14.5 ms. Then, the data are standardized from a specific proprietary format, sent to the *Nexeed* Manufacturing Execution System (MES), and also sent to a representational state transfer application programming interface (REST API), as depicted by Fig. 2. The REST API, when receiving a request, generates a Kafka message [33] that is forwarded to the Kafka Cluster, where processing will take place. Since the main goal is to optimize the replacement of welding tools, in order to decrease the operational cost of the process, we exploit the collected data to build a GFT from data-driven events. Then, we propose the change from a PM policy to a CBM policy, where the health condition of tools is given by a failure probability calculated by the GFT, which accounts for the data-driven events that already occurred and the number of performed welding cycles.

3   GFT Approach

The GFT approach encompasses several steps to perform the CBM. One part of the process is the training phase and the other is the real-time health condition assessment, as depicted by Fig. 3. The first phase of both processes consists in pre-processing the data, which encompasses the following steps:

- The data are enriched with the derivatives of the force in the X-axis and Z-axis;
- The (continuous) data are discretized in classes based on cutting parameters calculated from its distributions (see below);
- The data for the same welding cycle are aggregated, and its mean, standard deviation, maximum and minimum are extracted as new variables.

The next step in the training phase consists in the calculation of the BEs and TE distributions. These distributions together with the discretization thresholds and the number of leaves are the configuration settings that will be used to generate the best GFT model, and to dynamically update the GFT root probability in real-time. The GFT training intends to generate the tree-shaped structure that best fits the TE distribution, by automatically exploring a list of operators and the set of BEs. A given criterion is defined to allow a minimization problem by a given metric (e.g., the root-mean-square error (RMSE) between the TE distribution and the GFT root distribution). Then, the failure probability that minimizes the cost with tools' replacements for a training dataset is obtained, and then, the best GFT structure is employed with real-time data to assess the failure probability of the current tool. A replacement is suggested when the failure probability is higher than the obtained threshold probability. The next Subsections describe in more detail the mentioned steps.

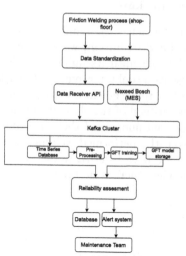

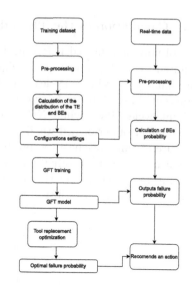

Fig. 2. Data pipeline of the friction welding process.

Fig. 3. Overview of the GFT approach for CBM.

3.1 Definition of Basic Events (BEs)

The BEs are generated by discretizing the continuous data collected in the classes: outlier low (OL), low (L), normal (N), high (H) and outlier high (OH), as depicted by Fig. 4. Each class represents a different BE and generates new variables V, where the definition of each class is made according to threshold values. The values $L_1(V)$ to $L_4(V)$ are calculated by Eqs. (1)–(4), where $Q_0(V)$ and $Q_4(V)$ represent the minimum and maximum values of the considered variable V; $Q_1(V)$, $Q_2(V)$ and $Q_3(V)$ are the standard quartiles; $a_1 = a_2 = 1.5$ and $b_1 = b_2 = 0.5$ are configuration parameters.

$$L_1(V) = max\{Q_0(V), Q_1(V) - a_1\left(Q_3(V) - Q_1(V)\right)\}, \tag{1}$$

$$L_2(V) = b_1\,Q_1(V) + (1 - b_1)\,Q_2(V), \tag{2}$$

$$L_3(V) = b_2\,Q_2(V) + (1 - b_2)\,Q_3(V), \tag{3}$$

$$L_4(V) = min\{Q_4(V), Q_3(V) + a_2\left(Q_3(V) - Q_1(V)\right)\}. \tag{4}$$

Then, the continuous values v of the variable V are categorized using the rules: V_**OL** if $v < L_1(V)$, V_**L** if $L_1(V) \leq v < L_2(V)$, V_**N** if $L_2(V) \leq v \leq L_3(V)$, V_**H** if $L_3(V) < v \leq L_4(V)$, and V_**OH** if $v > L_4(V)$. The BEs distributions are generated from this categorization, as explained in the next subsection.

3.2 Calculation of the TE and BEs Distributions

A tool may be replaced before its failure when it reaches the number of cycles required for a PM intervention. Thus, for the TE distribution, we account for the number of welding cycles performed by the tool until its failure, which is represented in red in Fig. 5a, where "OK" represents a tool replacement after 780 welding cycles (PM), while "NOK" represents a tool replacement due to a failure. The number of performed welding cycles is used instead of the elapsed time as a measure of time, because the production is not continuous and there are times in which there is no production. For this reason, the performed welding cycles describe more accurately the degradation process over time than the elapsed time, eliminating biases introduced by periods when there is no production.

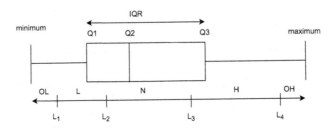

Fig. 4. Discretization of continuous data into new BEs.

Analogously, the BEs distributions are calculated considering the number of welding cycles performed between the last tool replacement and the occurrence of the BE, which is depicted by Fig. 5b. The distributions of TE and BEs, as well as the limits L_1 to L_4 are calculated in the training phase and are passed in the configuration settings to be applied in real-time data.

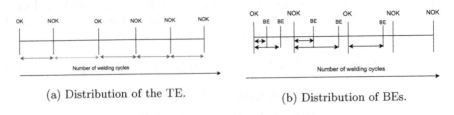

(a) Distribution of the TE.   (b) Distribution of BEs.

Fig. 5. Calculation of distributions.

3.3 Training a GFT

Training a GFT consists in finding the tree-shaped structure that best fits the cumulative density function (CDF) of the TE, using the operators and the CDF of the BEs. Since there are BEs that may not be important to characterize the TE, we define a maximum number of BEs to use in the training phase, limiting the number of leaves in the tree. A full search requires a lot of computational effort, because the number of possible trees explodes with the number of leaves and with the size of the BEs' set. For this reason, we apply an algorithm with a pruning technique, represented by Algorithm 1.

To understand the training algorithm described by the pseudocode, it is important to note that here we only use binary operators that take the CDF of 2 input BEs and outputs a new CDF according to the Eqs. 5 and 6. The function *calculateProb* calculates a CDF according to the given inputs. In the beginning of the process, a dictionary of dictionaries (Python data structure) exists to save the CDF of each tree $Tree$, which is initialized with the CDF of each BE. Then, all the combinations with two BEs are performed and all the trees with 2 BEs are calculated. After that, evaluation is made by using the root-mean-square error (RMSE) between the CDF of each tree and the CDF of TE, as indicated by Eq. 7.

To reduce computational time, calculation of more complex trees is made from the less complex ones. For example, a tree with 4 BEs can be calculated with a gate that has a tree with 3 BEs and a single BE as inputs, or 2 trees with 2 BEs each. These trees are saved in the data structure $Tree$ to speed up the calculation process. This is performed until the trees with a number of BEs less or equal to N are calculated. The pruning strategy consists in calculating, for a tree with K BEs, only the trees that contain all the BEs of the tree with $K - 1$ BEs that has the lowest RMSE. For example, when calculating the trees with 4 BEs, only the ones that contain all the BEs of the tree with 3 BEs with the best RMSE score will be calculated. This technique avoids the explosion of possible trees and reduces the computational time of the process, compared with an exhaustive search made in [26].

$$AND(F_X, F_Y) = F_X \, F_Y, \tag{5}$$

$$OR(F_X, F_Y) = F_X + F_Y - F_X \, F_Y, \tag{6}$$

$$RMSE_{X,Y} = \sqrt{\frac{1}{N} \sum_{j=1}^{N} .(x_j - y_j)^2} \tag{7}$$

3.4   CBM with a GFT

Having the best GFT structure from the training step for a given metric, a root cause analysis can be performed from the path or chain of events that best describes the occurrence of the TE, giving the variables that most influence the failure. The reliability analysis is made by estimating the failure probability of the tool for a given number of performed cycles. Moreover, a qualitative analysis can be made by determining the minimal cut sets (MCS), which are sets with the minimum number of BEs whose occurrence ensures that the TE occurs [7].

The fact that the BEs of the GFT are data-driven generated, a better estimation of the failure probability with the GFT in real-time can be established, when compared with the CDF of the TE. This happens, because for a given number

---

Algorithm 1. Training a GFT with a pruning strategy

     INPUT: $\mathfrak{D}(BE_i), i \in \{1, 2, 3, ..., n\}$ as the CDFs of BEs, n is the number of BEs, $\mathfrak{D}(TE)$ is the CDF of TE, O is the set of operators, and N the maximum number of BEs to use in the leaves.

     OUTPUT: GFT structure, GFT

 1: $Tree[1][BE_i] = \mathfrak{D}(BE_i)$
 2: Compute all the combinations, $combs$ of 2 from all the BEs
 3: **for** $\forall\, operator \in O$ **do**
 4:     **for** $\forall\, comb \in combs$ **do**
 5:         $cdf = calculateProb(comb, operator)$
 6:         $Tree[2][comb + operator] = cdf$
 7:     **end for**
 8: **end for**
 9: **for** $i \in \{3, 4, ..., N\}$ **do**
10:     $RMSE(\mathfrak{D}(TE), \mathfrak{D}(T_t)), \forall\, T_t \in Tree[i-1].items()$
11:     Find the tree with best $RMSE$ and create a list $BestBEs$ of their BEs
12:     **for** $j \in \{1, 2, ..., floor(i/2)\}$ **do**
13:         **for** $key1, value1 \in Tree[i-j].items()$ **do**
14:             **for** $key2, value2 \in Tree[j].items()$ **do**
15:                 **if** $BestBEs \in BEs(key1) | BEs(key2)$ **then**
16:                     $cdf = calculateProb(value1, value2, operator)$ $\forall\, operator \in O\}$
17:                     $Tree[i][(key1, key2) + operator] = cdf$
18:                 **end if**
19:             **end for**
20:         **end for**
21:     **end for**
22: **end for**
23: Output the tree with best $RMSE$ from $Tree$

---

of performed working cycles the probability of each BE can be estimated from the CDF calculated in the training step, and updated according to the occurrence of this BE in real-time. For example, consider a BE, BE_i. The probability of BE_i, after t working cycles, $P_{BE_i}(t)$, is given by its CDF calculated in the training phase. However, if BE_i already occurred in the current tool data, we update this probability to the maximum value, "1", allowing to estimate the failure probability of the welding tools based on the actual condition captured from the data-driven BEs using the GFT fitted model.

    The proposed CBM policy intends to optimize the replacement of the friction welding tools, in order to minimize the costs due to failures (i.e., NOKs). For this purpose, we need to find the failure probability that optimizes the cost per welding tool given by Eq. 8, where N_{NOKs} is the number of NOKs in a training dataset, N_{OKs} is the number of tools that were replaced by PM (i.e., after 780 welding cycles), and C_{ok} and C_{scrap} are respectively the cost of replacing a tool, and the cost of the scrapped workpieces when a failure occurs.

$$Cost = \frac{N_{OKs}\, C_{ok} + N_{NOKs}\, (C_{ok} + C_{scrap})}{N_{cycles}}. \tag{8}$$

Although a lower failure probability p is more effective to avoid failures, the number of cycles performed by the tool is also going to be lower. To determine the optimal probability threshold, an iterative process is implemented where the cost per welding cycle is calculated for p varying from 0.5000 to 1.0000 in intervals of 0.0125. The p value with the lower cost is then set as the probability threshold for generating a recommendation to change tools.

4   Results

In the friction welding use case, the maximum number of BEs used in training was set to 6, since it allows relatively complex structures in a timely manner. The best approximation obtained through the process described by the Algorithm 1 is depicted by Fig. 6a, and the skeleton of the best tree-shaped structure is represented in Fig. 6b.

From the skeleton of the GFT, the following three MCS are obtained:

- $C_1 = C \cup \{\text{Fx\_max\_OL}\}$,
- $C_2 = C \cup \{\text{Fx\_mean\_OH}, \text{Fz\_1dev\_mean\_OL}\}$,
- $C_3 = C \cup \{\text{Fx\_mean\_OH}, \text{Fx\_mean\_OL}\}$,

where $C = \{\text{Fz\_1dev\_std\_OH}, \text{Fx\_1dev\_min\_OL}\}$.

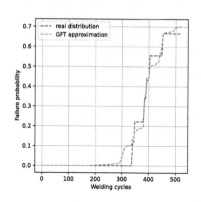

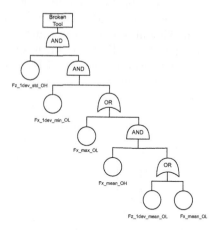

(a) CDF of the number of cycles between NOKs.

(b) Skeleton of the GFT obtained.

Fig. 6. Root cause and reliability analysis.

The description of the BEs used in the GFT structure is presented in Table 1. Note that from the 80 initial BEs, the ones that describe the path or chain of events that originate a failure are outliers. This fact was somehow expected, since when a failure occurs there are considerable changes in the force in the X-axis and Z-axis, compared to the normal behavior, which was corroborated by the engineers and technicians from Bosch TermoTechnology. The fact that the BEs related to the derivatives in the force of X-axis and Z-axis, namely Fz_1dev_std_OH and Fx_1dev_min_OL are present in all MCS demonstrate that these are the variables with more importance for the tools' failure, which actually makes sense, since a tool's break causes an abrupt change in the contact force (Z-axis) and advance force (X-axis).

Table 1. Basic Events used in the GFT

BE	Description
Fz_1dev_std_OH	The standard deviation of the first derivative of force in Z-axis is a high outlier
Fx_1dev_min_OL	The minimum of the first derivative of force in X-axis is a low outlier
Fx_max_OL	The maximum of force in X-axis is a low outlier
Fx_mean_OH	The mean of force in X-axis is a high outlier
Fz_1dev_mean_OL	The mean of the first derivative of force in Z axis is a low outlier
Fx_mean_OL	The mean of force in X-axis is a low outlier

To test the real impact of the proposed CBM approach, the optimal threshold probability was determined, as described in the previous Section, and the costs per welding cycle were compared with the actual PM policy adopted by Bosch TermoTechnology, that consists in the tool replacement after 780 welding cycles. The graph in Fig. 7 shows the obtained results. It can be noted that there is a cost reduction for a failure probability between 0.92 and 0.99. The training dataset contains tools that were replaced due to a failure and due to reaching the maximum number of working cycles for PM. For this reason, the maximum value for the CDF of the TE is smaller than 1 (about 0.80, as can be seen in Fig. 6a). However, since the BEs' probabilities are dynamically updated to "1" when they occur, the dynamic root probability of the GFT can assume values up to 1.

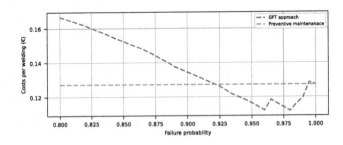

Fig. 7. Costs per welding cycle regarding the threshold probability.

The fact that the failure probability calculated by the GFT takes into account the BEs that already occurred and updates their probability in real-time, allows the health condition assessment based on the actual condition of equipments, which results in the decrease of the cost per welding cycle in 12.05%. Note that the cost C_{scrap} of the scrapped workpieces is about 68.62% of the tool replacement cost C_{ok}. In other industrial use cases, the cost associated with a failure may be much higher than the cost to replace a tool. In these cases, the cost reduction would be even more considerable, which opens good perspectives for the GFT approach to be applied in other industrial scenarios.

5   Conclusions

In this work, we propose a new methodology to perform the CMB of industrial assets subjected to degradation processes, based on the dynamic update of the root of a GFT. The proposed methodology demonstrated to be effective to perform different tasks in the exploited use case, a friction welding process at Bosch TermoTechnology. The fact that the tree-shaped structure that fits the TE distribution is automatically generated in the training phase allows a root cause analysis, since the path or chain of events that leads to the TE, and the BEs that are the causes of the TE are determined. The reliability analysis was performed either quantitatively, calculating the failure probably (and hazard function if needed) from the CDF of the TE, and qualitatively, obtaining the causes from the MCS obtained from the skeleton of the GFT. However, the most important feature of the GFT approach (highlighted in this work) is the fact the probability of the TE can be updated based on the data-driven BEs that have already occurred in real-time. Such makes possible to assess the health condition of the friction welding tools in real-time with a model that considers both, the number of performed working cycles of the tool and its actual health condition.

In comparison with other techniques, such as ML, the proposed approach has some characteristics that make it more suitable to address the health assessment of components that suffer from a degradation process. It considers all the BEs that have occurred since the last tool's replacement for each tool, instead of the data that occurred in a given number of time-windows before, which means that more information is used by the model to decide the replacement in real-time. It can also address huge amounts of data, and capture the behavior of a component during a considerable period of time in a lightweight manner through the distribution representation of the BEs.

Regarding the traditional FTA, the GFT approach enables knowledge to be generated directly from data and allows CBM policies, since the failure probability takes into account the actual state of industrial assets. Furthermore, as discussed in previous work [26], BEs may follow an arbitrary compact support distribution, which is more realistic than approximating distributions to the exponential/Weibull distribution. The pruning technique employed in the GFT training is another advance to the previous work, and allows a good fitting of the TE distribution with a huge decrease in the computational complexity. We notice that the values a_1 and a_2 can behave as extra hyperparameters.

The exploitation of the GFT approach in the use case presented in this work demonstrated that the costs related to the replacement of tools can be reduced 12.05%, in comparison with the actual PM policy of the enterprise. The cost of a failure (NOK), in this use case, is only 68.62% higher than the tool replacement cost. Usually this difference is bigger, since a failure may damage other healthy parts or have more serious consequences than only scrapped workpieces. This fact opens interesting perspectives to apply this approach in other industrial scenarios and reduce considerably the enterprises' costs with maintenance. Nevertheless, there are several other points that can be improved, namely the exploitation of anomaly detection techniques or time series Fourier decomposition techniques to enrich the dataset with other BEs that may describe with more accuracy the TE, as well as the exploitation of dynamic gates in the CBM context that were not used in this use case, since the aims proposed for it were attained.

Acknowledgments. The present study was partially developed in the scope of the Project Augmented Humanity (PAH) [POCI-01-0247- FEDER-046103], financed by Portugal 2020, under the Competitiveness and Internationalization Operational Program, the Lisbon Regional Operational Program, and by the European Regional Development Fund. The first author has a PhD grant supported FCT - Fundação para a Ciência e a Tecnologia, I.P. for the PhD grants ref. 2020.06926.BD. The second author was partially supported by the Center for Research and Development in Mathematics and Applications (CIDMA), through the Portuguese Foundation for Science and Technology, reference UIDB/04106/2020. The first and fourth authors would like to acknowledge the University of Aveiro, FCT/MCTES for the financial support of TEMA research unit (FCT Ref. UIDB/00481/2020 & UIDP/00481/2020) and CENTRO01-0145-FEDER-022083 - Regional Operational Program of the Center (Centro2020), within the scope of the Portugal 2020 Partnership Agreement, through the European Regional Development Fund. The third author was supported by Bosch Termotecnologia, SA.

Data Availability Statement. The data sets used in this work are confidential information of Bosch company manufacturing system, so they are not publicly available.

References

1. Aslansefat, K., Latif-Shabgahi, G.R.: A hierarchical approach for dynamic fault trees solution through semi-Markov process. IEEE Trans. Reliab. **69**(3), 986–1003 (2020). https://doi.org/10.1109/TR.2019.2923893
2. Ayvaz, S., Alpay, K.: Predictive maintenance system for production lines in manufacturing: a machine learning approach using IoT data in real-time. Expert Syst. Appl. **173**, 114598 (2021). https://doi.org/10.1016/j.eswa.2021.114598
3. Chiacchio, F., Iacono, A., Compagno, L., D'Urso, D.: A general framework for dependability modelling coupling discrete-event and time-driven simulation. Reliab. Eng. Syst. Saf. **199**, 106904 (2020). https://doi.org/10.1016/j.ress.2020.106904
4. Coelho, D., Costa, D., Rocha, E.M., Almeida, D., Santos, J.P.: Predictive maintenance on sensorized stamping presses by time series segmentation, anomaly detection, and classification algorithms. Procedia Comput. Sci. **200**, 1184–1193 (2022). https://doi.org/10.1016/j.procs.2022.01.318
5. Dehnert, C., Junges, S., Katoen, J.P., Volk, M.: The probabilistic model checker storm (extended abstract), October 2016

6. Dugan, J., Bavuso, S., Boyd, M.: Dynamic fault-tree models for fault-tolerant computer systems. IEEE Trans. Reliab. **41**(3), 363–377 (1992). https://doi.org/10.1109/24.159800

7. Durga Rao, K., Gopika, V., Sanyasi Rao, V.V., Kushwaha, H.S., Verma, A.K., Srividya, A.: Dynamic fault tree analysis using Monte Carlo simulation in probabilistic safety assessment. Reliab. Eng. Syst. Saf. **94**(4), 872–883 (2009). https://doi.org/10.1016/j.ress.2008.09.007

8. Elderhalli, Y., Hasan, O., Tahar, S.: A methodology for the formal verification of dynamic fault trees using HOL theorem proving. IEEE Access **7**, 136176–136192 (2019). https://doi.org/10.1109/ACCESS.2019.2942829

9. Guo, D., Yang, M., Wu, H., Ge, D., Cao, X.: Dynamic reliability evaluation of diesel generator system of one Chinese 1000MWe NPP considering temporal failure effects. Front. Energy Res. **9**, 816 (2021). https://doi.org/10.3389/fenrg.2021.793577

10. Hu, J., Chen, P.: Predictive maintenance of systems subject to hard failure based on proportional hazards model. Reliab. Eng. Syst. Saf. **196**, 106707 (2020). https://doi.org/10.1016/J.RESS.2019.106707

11. Jiang, G.J., Li, Z.Y., Qiao, G., Chen, H.X., Li, H.B., Sun, H.H.: Reliability analysis of dynamic fault tree based on binary decision diagrams for explosive vehicle. Math. Probl. Eng. **2021**, 1–13 (2021). https://doi.org/10.1155/2021/5559475

12. Kabir, S.: An overview of fault tree analysis and its application in model based dependability analysis. Expert Syst. Appl. **77**, 114–135 (2017). https://doi.org/10.1016/j.eswa.2017.01.058

13. Kabir, S., Walker, M., Papadopoulos, Y.: Dynamic system safety analysis in HiP-HOPS with Petri Nets and Bayesian Networks. Saf. Sci. **105**, 55–70 (2018). https://doi.org/10.1016/j.ssci.2018.02.001

14. Kaiser, K.A., Gebraeel, N.Z.: Sensor-based degradation models. IEEE Trans. Syst. Man Cybern. **39**(4), 840–849 (2009)

15. Khakzad, N., Khan, F., Amyotte, P.: Risk-based design of process systems using discrete-time Bayesian networks. Reliab. Eng. Syst. Saf. **109**, 5–17 (2013). https://doi.org/10.1016/j.ress.2012.07.009

16. Kohonen, T.: The self-organizing map. Proc. IEEE **78**(9), 1464–1480 (1990). https://doi.org/10.1109/5.58325

17. Lee, J., Kao, H.A., Yang, S.: Service innovation and smart analytics for Industry 4.0 and big data environment. Procedia CIRP **16**, 3–8 (2014). https://doi.org/10.1016/j.procir.2014.02.001

18. Leevy, J.L., Khoshgoftaar, T.M., Bauder, R.A., Seliya, N.: Investigating the relationship between time and predictive model maintenance. J. Big Data **7**(1), 1–19 (2020). https://doi.org/10.1186/s40537-020-00312-x

19. Lei, Y., Li, N., Gontarz, S., Lin, J., Radkowski, S., Dybala, J.: A model-based method for remaining useful life prediction of machinery. IEEE Trans. Reliab. **65**(3), 1314–1326 (2016). https://doi.org/10.1109/TR.2016.2570568

20. Li, N., Lei, Y., Yan, T., Li, N., Han, T.: A wiener-process-model-based method for remaining useful life prediction considering unit-to-unit variability. IEEE Trans. Industr. Electron. **66**(3), 2092–2101 (2019). https://doi.org/10.1109/TIE.2018.2838078

21. Liao, L., Jin, W., Pavel, R.: Prognosability regularization for prognostics and health assessment. IEEE Trans. Industr. Electron. **63**(11), 7076–7083 (2016)

22. Merle, G., Roussel, J.M., Lesage, J.J., Bobbio, A.: Probabilistic algebraic analysis of fault trees with priority dynamic gates and repeated events. IEEE Trans. Reliab. **59**(1), 250–261 (2010). https://doi.org/10.1109/TR.2009.2035793

428   P. Nunes et al.

23. Merle, G., et al.: Function to cite this version: HAL Id: hal-00566334 Dynamic Fault Tree Analysis Based on the Structure Function (2011)
24. Mohd Nizam Ong, N.A.F., Sadiq, M.A., Md Said, M.S., Jomaas, G., Mohd Tohir, M.Z., Kristensen, J.S.: Fault tree analysis of fires on rooftops with photovoltaic systems. J. Build. Eng. **46**(2021), 103752 (2022). https://doi.org/10.1016/j.jobe.2021.103752
25. Paris, P., Erdogan, F.: A critical analysis of crack propagation laws. J. Basic Eng. **85**(4), 528–533 (1963). https://doi.org/10.1115/1.3656900
26. Rocha, E.M., Nunes, P., Santos, J.: Reliability analysis of sensorized stamping presses by generalized fault trees. In: Proceedings of the International Conference on Industrial Engineering and Operations Management Istanbul, Turkey, 7–10 March 2022 (2022)
27. Ruijters, E., Stoelinga, M.: Fault tree analysis: a survey of the state-of-the-art in modeling, analysis and tools, February 2015. https://doi.org/10.1016/j.cosrev.2015.03.001
28. Sihite, J.F., Kohda, T.: Assessing the reliability of power transformer by quantitative fault tree analysis. Adv. Mater. Res. **694**(697), 901–906 (2013). https://doi.org/10.4028/www.scientific.net/AMR.694-697.901
29. Stamatelatos, M., et al.: Fault tree handbook with aerospace applications. Technical report (2002)
30. Sullivan, K., Dugan, J., Coppit, D.: The Galileo fault tree analysis tool. In: Digest of Papers. Twenty-Ninth Annual International Symposium on Fault-Tolerant Computing (Cat. No. 99CB36352), pp. 232–235, December. IEEE Computer Society (2003). https://doi.org/10.1109/FTCS.1999.781056
31. Xu, Z., Guo, D., Wang, J., Li, X., Ge, D.: A numerical simulation method for a repairable dynamic fault tree. Eksploatacja i Niezawodnosc **23**(1), 34–41 (2021). https://doi.org/10.17531/EIN.2021.1.4
32. You, M.Y., Liu, F., Wang, W., Meng, G.: Statistically planned and individually improved predictive maintenance management for continuously monitored degrading systems. IEEE Trans. Reliab. **59**(4), 744–753 (2010). https://doi.org/10.1109/TR.2010.2085572
33. Zelenin, A., Kropp, A.: Apache Kafka. In: Apache Kafka, pp. I-XVII. Carl Hanser Verlag GmbH & Co. KG, München, November 2021. https://doi.org/10.3139/9783446470460.fm

Minimizing False-Rejection Rates in Gas Leak Testing Using an Ensemble Multiclass Classifier for Unbalanced Data

Diogo Costa[1]([⊠]) [ID], Eugénio M. Rocha[2,3] [ID], and Pedro Ramalho[4]

[1] Department of Mechanical Engineering, University of Aveiro, Aveiro, Portugal
d.costa@ua.pt
[2] Center for Research and Development in Mathematics and Applications, Aveiro, Portugal
[3] Department of Mathematics, University of Aveiro, Aveiro, Portugal
[4] Manufacturing for Digitalization (AvP/MFD), Bosch Termotecnologia, S.A., Aveiro, Portugal

Abstract. Leak testing is a fundamental stage in the manufacturing process of leak-tight products providing a non-destructive quality measurement. However, leak tests are often influenced by environmental and external factors that increase the risk of test inaccuracy. These phenomena are difficult to properly account for through mathematical models, as they are particular to each individual testing setup, nonetheless, they signify great expense to manufacturers due to substantial bottlenecking. In this paper, we introduce a real-world use-case at Bosch Thermotechnology facilities where over 23.98% of testing instances result in false-rejections. We then propose a data-driven, equipment agnostic, procedure for leak testing fault classification. We first identify seven relevant classes for fault diagnosis, and, due to the highly unbalanced nature of these classes (minority class represents only 0.27% of all data), we apply a novel unbalanced multiclass classification pipeline based on an ensemble of heterogeneous classifiers. Through this method, we are able to obtain $F_1\text{-}macro$ of 90%, representing a performance improvement of over 120% in comparison with conventional Auto-ML approaches.

Keywords: Leak testing · Machine learning · Multiclass classification · Ensemble classifier · Unbalanced data

This study was developed in the scope of Project Augmented Humanity (PAH) [POCI-01-0247-FEDER-046103], financed by Portugal 2020, under the Competitiveness and Internationalization Operational Program, the Lisbon Regional Operational Program, and by the European Regional Development Fund. The first author has a PhD grant supported by PAH. The second author was partially supported by the Center for Research and Development in Mathematics and Applications (CIDMA), through the Portuguese Foundation for Science and Technology, reference UIDB/04106/2020. The third author was supported by Bosch Termotecnologia.

T. Guarda et al. (Eds.): ARTIIS 2022, CCIS 1675, pp. 429–443, 2022.
https://doi.org/10.1007/978-3-031-20319-0_32

1   Introduction

Leak testing is the identification and quantification of leaks and is a common industrial procedure, providing a non-destructive quality measurement for components requiring leak-tight behavior. A leak, defined as an excessive material flow above specified limits, is caused by factors such as open flow paths, pinholes, broken or tampered seals or from material porosity [6]. Leak detection is mandatory in the production of containers for pressurized fluids (e.g., boilers or tanks), and improper testing may lead to manufacturing bottle-necking at later stages of the productive cycle. One of the most widespread leak detection methods, for its low cost, simplicity, and sensitivity, is the differential pressure method [20], where a flow meter measures a pressure drop with a differential sensor across the extremities of a calibrated flow tube. However, this method has been known to be deeply impacted by varying environmental conditions such as temperature or ambient humidity, as well as showing a high dependence on operator skill [7], creating an elevated number of false-negative tests. Each failed test represents additional cost during manufacturing and introduces a bottleneck, particularly when the number of false negatives is highly prevalent, as failed parts are often retested.

Conventionally, these issues were tackled through model-driven approaches where mathematical and physical models are created to deal with the uncertainty factors that lead to inaccurate leak results [6,7,20]. Furthermore, higher-end leak testing equipment provides automated calibration systems to compensate for current atmospheric conditions, applying corrections to readings according to the real temperature of flowing fluid through the system [2]. Nonetheless, these methods, including ones provided by manufacturers, fail to consider each test-jig's unique set-up, and characteristics of external elements such as seal jig restrictions or tube lengths and diameters, which can result in unsatisfactory calibrations. Alternatively, data-driven methods can be speedily tailored for specific use-cases, doing away with complex physical or mathematical models, relying instead on large levels of quality historical data enriched by expert knowledge. This allows for the determination of normal and abnormal working conditions [3], after which we can apply statistics-based, Artificial Intelligence (AI) and Machine Learning (ML) algorithms and techniques [26] for future event prediction. Despite these benefits, data-driven methodologies bring forth new sets of challenges to tackle. For instance, in spite being sufficiently common to create disruptions in manufacturing, the proportion of false-rejection tests to correctly evaluated tests is heavily skewed. This leads to data unbalancing, where the number of instances between each classification class differ greatly. Common in real-world data [15], unbalanced datasets are challenging for data-driven techniques such as ML, as the number of samples in minority classes may not be sufficient as to make classifiers correctly identify decision boundaries.

Literature review shows several efforts regarding improving performance of binary classifiers in unbalanced datasets, both from algorithm-level methods and data-level methods [10]. For instance, [12] studied the application of different oversampling techniques in imbalanced data and found that Adaptive Synthetic

(ADASYN), Safe-Level Synthetic Minority Oversampling Technique (SSMOTE) and Synthetic Minority Oversampling Technique (SMOTE) methods yielded the best results. Similarly, [21] improved AUC score in the classification of industrial machine failures using SMOTE-based oversampling techniques. More complex approaches for dealing with data unbalance rely on models created through the combination of several heterogeneous and homogeneous ML algorithms, forming ensemble models. In [25] an ensemble method of various resampling strategies combined with extreme gradient boosting classifiers is used, and in [24] an ensemble of weak learners is applied to a classification problem for fault classification of power transformers. Authors of [10] reduced data unbalance through a bagging algorithm in combination with Support Vector Machines (SVM) classifiers, and further proposed a new weighted cross-entropy loss function to reduce effect of noisy data in model performance. A new approach to ADASYN resampling together with stacking algorithm meta-learning is proposed in [17], where the SVM and Random Forest (RF) stack employed ADASYN for data resampling, using Logistic Regression (LR) as an aggregation algorithm that weighed each classifier's contribution to results based on their performance. The same authors further refined their approach to allow for use in multiclass classification [15], however the issue of class imbalance in multiclass problems is comparably understudied regarding binary classifications, as the additional number of class instances further increases complexity in identifying decision boundaries.

The multiclass paradigm is frequently observed in data-driven fault identification, diagnosis, and classification applications, with faults being commonly classified into pre-defined categories derived from expert knowledge and data mining for subsequent fault categorization [23]. For example, [22] used a multiclass classification task for fault diagnosis in gears, and similarly [8] constructed a multiclass fault detection and classification system based in SVM for induction motors. In [1] SVM was also used for fault classification for centrifugal pumps, where discriminant features were computed to aid classifiers in correctly determining respective classes. In [16] it is proposed a big-data platform for integration of expert knowledge and data-mining techniques for Root Cause Analysis (RCA), or problem cause determination [13], of real-world manufacturing processes, based on multiclass classification through ML techniques. Ensemble models are also usually considered when tackling the multiclass problem, for instance, [19] developed a cost-sensitive heterogeneous ensemble approach for multiclass.

To the best of authors' knowledge, there remains a gap in applications of data-driven methods for improved performance of leak testing procedures. In this paper we introduce a real-world use case of a leak testing procedure at the production line of boiler water heaters at the Bosch Thermotechnology facilities. Testing uncertainty leads to an elevated false-rejection rate, where over 23.98% of test instances incorrectly fail with unknown cause. As it is a mandatory stage at later productive steps this deeply influences efficiency levels of the assembly line. Currently the risk of false positives, where faulty parts obtain a passing result in testing, is minimized through tighter testing standards and testing margins, yet this solution contributes to an even more demanding and time-consuming process.

Novelty introduced in this paper is two-fold: 1) we cover the current literature gap by proposing a data-driven method applied to leak testing for multiclass classification of test result instances, enabling both the identification, as well as, in case of unsuccessful tests, the determination of the failure root cause, while assuring it stays equipment, set-up, and operator agnostic; 2) to deal with multiclass unbalanced datasets, we propose a ML pipeline centered around an ensemble algorithm for sequential problem reduction and improved predictive performance. The final solution is validated using real-world data and is finally implemented at Bosch Thermotechnology facilities.

This paper is organized as follows: Section 1 contextualizes problem and motivation; Sect. 2 introduces current testing procedure and industrial data flow; Sect. 3 details implementation of the proposed ensemble classifier and feature extraction; Sect. 4 discusses obtained results using real-world data; and concluding remarks are provided in Sect. 5.

2   Industrial Data Pipeline

2.1   Testing Procedure

Testing is carried out by a PLC (Programmable Logic Controller) that controls an ATEQ D520 flow meter, used to determine leakage flow rates by measuring a pressure drop across a calibrated flow tube. When a fluid moves through a calibrated flow tube in laminar flow, a drop in pressure occurs with a value proportional to flow [2], as determined by

$$\Delta P = \frac{8\mu L Q}{\pi R^4} \tag{1}$$

where ΔP is the pressure drop across the calibrated flow tube; μ is the fluid viscosity; L is the length of calibrated flow tube; Q is the flow; and R is the radius of the calibrated flow tube. Each measurement cycle is comprised by four phases, namely:

- **Coupling:** initial set-up in which the coupling between test parts and test jig is sealed. A specified air pressure is set on the leakage meter and testing part. This pressure must be within an interval, defined as the pressure tolerances.
- **Fill:** test part is pressurized until compensation flow is obtained.
- **Stabilization:** pre-determined wait time for a stable flow value to be established.
- **Test:** differential pressure sensor measures the pressure variation across the calibrated flow tube, determining air flow induced by leaks on the testing part. The measured air flow must be between a given interval (flow tolerance) in order to be recognized as a good part.

The duration of each of the cycle's phases are preset as testing parameters with the fill stage taking 35 s; stabilization 30 s; and testing 10 s.

Complementing test pressure and flow records measured by the ATEQ D520, a set of PLC-controlled additional external sensors were installed on the machine as shown in Fig. 1. Elements marked T1 through T5 are temperature sensors; element P1 is a atmospheric pressure sensor; and element H1 is a humidity sensor. Sensors T5, P1, and H1 capture environmental conditions, whilst remaining elements operate within the testing circuit. Four samples are recorded for elements T1 through T4 at different testing moments: once at the start of ATEQ test (beginning of fill step); 15 s after the beginning of the fill; 50 s after beginning of the fill (approximately half time of stabilization); and at the end of ATEQ testing.

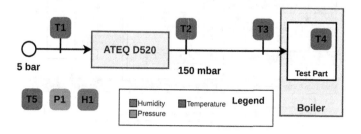

Fig. 1. Simplified schematic of the jig assembly of the testing procedure.

The ATEQ D520 features a mechanism for automatic compensation of atmospheric conditions by performing a measurement cycle on a known master part. At the beginning of each shift (at a maximum of three shifts per day) a master part is connected to a calibrated leak device so that a well known leak flow is induced. The master is tested twice, once per each of two calibrated leak devices named "OK Leak" and "NOK Leak", each having well-defined theoretical leak rate values of 5.9 cc/min and 8.7 cc/min, respectively. The equipment is locked from normal operation until an initial master part calibration is successfully achieved for each calibrated leak device. The same sensor data points are generated for both master parts and regular production parts. Upon each testing cycle completion, results returned by ATEQ D520 include: pressure within test part; final leak rate (computed through (1)); total test duration in seconds; and an error code in case of failed test, being omitted in a successful run. Results are stored along with sensor data collected during each phase. In total, combining external sensors, ATEQ D520 variables, and default operational parameters, twenty-seven features are originally associated to each individual test.

2.2   Integration with Smart Manufacturing Platform

The test assembly is integrated within a smart manufacturing platform, with Fig. 2 illustrating information flow. Data is gathered at the test-jig which interfaces an edge device responsible for basic data pre-processing and for re-routing data both to the existing Manufacturing Execution System (MES) and the predictive platform's Data Receiver API. The Annotation Generation microservice is responsible for annotating historical data with additional metadata (e.g., expert-knowledge) and for labelling data for supervised learning tasks that will occur at the ML-Models Training module. To account for possible variations in procedural conditions, or to account for model degradation, re-training is also possible at this stage. Predictions are stored and injected into alert systems and dashboards, alerting maintenance personnel in real-time of the predicted status of each tested component.

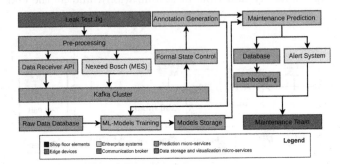

Fig. 2. Diagram of smart manufacturing platform. In blue, the developed or enhanced micro-services for this project. (Color figure online)

2.3   Data Preparation

Data is retrieved from databases unlabeled, requiring dataset pre-processing prior to model application. Preliminary data analysis together with expert knowledge allowed for the identification of seven relevant classes that will serve as targets for the proposed machine learning classification pipeline. Table 1 illustrates each class label together with a brief description. Determined classes closely follow events that can be differentiated when performing data analysis making it possible to have a more concise idea of what caused a failed test. Thus, we can provide some interpretability to the machine learning models later employed, contributing to the solution's relevancy for organizational operations by aiding in preliminary fault diagnosis analysis. This follows a *factors into root cause* approach, were specific conditions are linked to pre-determined factors, thus increasing the importance of predictive performance, seeing as now classification becomes the primary objective [13].

To provide useful data for the supervised classification algorithms a dataset labelling pipeline was created, and steps are shown in Fig. 3. The initial stage for labelling the dataset requires the generation of sequences that describe the historical test results associated with each unique part identifier, and as such, with each individual part. The label reflects the interim state between part classifications: consider the case when a part is first classified as a "fail" and subsequently is retested being now considered as "pass"; the generated sequence would be comprised of a single F-NOK (false-NOK), which would also correspond to the label of the initial test. The rationale for more complex sequences is

Table 1. Taxonomy of employed class labels.

Label	Description
OK	Successful test with results within valid specification
T-NOK	True-NOK - Valid test results, but part not up to specification. Subsequent test will return a T-NOK classification
F-NOK	False-NOK - Valid test results, but part not up to specification according to current test. Yet, subsequent testing will classify the part as OK
MF-NOK	Machine-False-NOK - Valid test results and within specification, however the equipment still failed to classify results as valid
M-NOK	Machine-NOK - Test failed due to the leak test machine's inability to establish adequate testing conditions
H-NOK	Human-NOK - No fault error occurred and result values were within specification, yet several more tests were conducted
D-NOK	Data-NOK - Rejected from further use due to invalid data (e.g., errors in data storage, transmission, format, or missing values)

analogous, e.g., "fail-fail-fail-pass" would reproduce the labels "T-NOK - T-NOK - F-NOK" where the first two labels are represented with a true-NOK as each subsequent test also produced a failure. Tests that have a result within allowable specifications are classified as "OK"; however, if the number of fails in any given part sequence is none ($n = 0$), but the number of passing results is greater than one ($m \geq 1$), that translates into a passing part being tested multiple times which can be attributed only to operator judgement and are thus classified as H-NOK (human-NOK).

A machine-NOK (M-NOK) is set whenever an element within a test sequence did not comply with appropriate conditions to produce a test result. This can be attributed to equipment failures, e.g., the equipment is unable to ensure constant pressurization to the test part, or a leak exists due to poor coupling of the test part to the test jig. Alternatively, a machine-false-NOK (MF-NOK) is used for tests that show valid results that fall within specification, but the testing equipment still rejected the parts. Note that, those instances labeled T-NOK or F-NOK are associated with tests that were performed under valid conditions, but the test results themselves were unsatisfactory, i.e., the determined leak rates were above the maximum stipulated value. The D-NOK label is associated to occurrences where any other label cannot be reliably applied due to missing or invalid data, caused by bandwidth issues, system bugs, or unreliable transmissions.

The provided dataset contains records from leak tests spanning across a five-month time period, representing a total of 49.649 separate testing instances. The histograms in Fig. 4, depict class distribution of the seven previously identified classes, after label generation process. From Fig. 4a it is determined that the second most significant class (D-NOK) accounts for just 19.86% of the size of

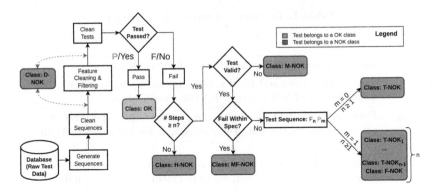

Fig. 3. Diagram of required steps to perform dataset labelling using as basis the raw test data.

the most represented class (OK), which itself totals 80.66% of data. Disparity between the most well represented and the least represented classes is even more blatant, with the minority class (H-NOK) accounting only for 0.33% of the majority class, and for only 0.27% of the total dataset size.

3 Proposed Solution

3.1 Feature Extraction

Each test instance originally contained the twenty-seven previously specified features, and was later enriched by associating a test to the last valid master part calibration test. Effectively, this tripled the number of features per test instance to a total of eighty-one. However, most show little to no variance between each other. For instance, sensors T1 through T4 will collect four different temperature readings during a test cycle, which typically lasts only about a minute, and therefore no substantial variation will take place. Hence, for each sensor all measurements taken during a single test cycle are grouped and only the average value is used. Furthermore, enriching each test's feature set with last known master part calibration results will increase redundancy between features, as multiple tests fall within the same master part calibration group. Consequently, these features were replaced using the following transformation

$$F_i^T = \epsilon\left(\bar{F}_i - \bar{M}_{OK_i}\right) - (1 - \epsilon)\left(\bar{F}_i - \bar{M}_{NOK_i}\right) \tag{2}$$

where $\bar{F}_i$ is the average value of each one of the grouped features, i; $\bar{M}_{OK_i}$ is the average grouped value of the master part calibrated for "OK Leak"; $\bar{M}_{NOK_i}$ is the average grouped value of the master part calibrated for "NOK Leak"; and ϵ is a calibration factor, which will later by tuned as an hyperparameter.

Even after data transformation, and due to the process' naturally stable behavior, it is still further required to increase the variability within data points to aid classifiers into determining appropriate decision boundaries between

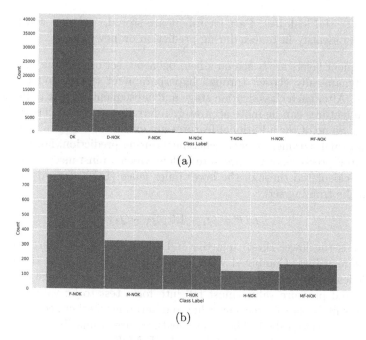

Fig. 4. Histogram depicting class distribution for: (a) all seven classes; (b) class distribution excepting the two most populous classes (OK and D-NOK).

classes. Logarithmic transformations are classically used to reduce variability in data; however, it is found that under certain conditions it may increase skewness [5]; as such, a log-transform of each existing feature was computed.

3.2 Ensemble Algorithm for Unbalanced Classification

The ensemble algorithm is comprised by six classifiers (one per layer in the classifier stack) where each learner is working in a binary classification problem following a one-versus-all paradigm. Through problem subdivision it becomes easier for each individual learner to capture a decision boundary between its target label and remaining data as the effective working dataset is being reduced, and thus decreasing overall class imbalance. Being a supervised learning algorithm, the proposed ensemble requires a training or fitting stage prior to producing predictions. Stages taken by the two initial layers during training are summarized as follows:

- The first layer runs a rule-based algorithm to check for data validity, fundamentally acting as a data filter. Invalid or improperly formatted instances are automatically labeled D-NOK, and the corresponding unique part identifier is stored, for use during the prediction stage.
- In the second layer, a deterministic algorithm checks for H-NOK instances by determining that no unique part identifier was subjected to more than

one successful leak test. Part identifiers are stored, and thus can be used to correctly identify instances during prediction on new data.

Subsequent layers are based on a heterogeneous set of machine learning algorithms, dynamically chosen through hyperparameter tuning and k-fold cross-validation. After each classification stage and subsequent dataset reduction, new statistical features can be more accurately inferred as removed classes no longer skew data. Some of the additional features are extracted from training data and used as internal parameters of the classifiers during prediction. For instance, the outlier cutoff pressure, or the pressure bellow which an instance is considered an outlier, is calculated through the lower inner fence (LIF) of good test pressure values in the training set.

$$LIF = Q_1 - 1.5\,(Q_3 - Q_1) \tag{3}$$

where $Q1$ is the lower (first) quartile and $Q3$ is the upper (third) quartile of the pressure values. Combined with other parameters, such as the maximum allowable leak rate value, we can now compute an acceptable range within which leak rate and pressure values must fall into for a test to be valid. The outlier cutoff pressure is also of excellent value to determine whether acceptable testing conditions are established. These new features are primarily used during the identification of classes OK, M-NOK, and MF-NOK.

Each layer contributes to the final prediction by determining if a given instance belongs to its own target class, with the final classifier being the only that classifies between two definitive classes. Consequently, target class at each stage should be the one most easily differentiable, typically, but not necessarily, coinciding with the current majority class, and hence, also allowing for the most significant reduction in working data for the remaining classifications. If the first five classifiers have adequate performance, we have in fact reduced the dataset into closely containing only the final two most difficult classes.

In the validation use-case, target classes were chosen based on an increasing classification difficulty determined through feature overlapping. The final step distinguished classes F-NOK and T-NOK, where, despite removing most of all classes from the work data, remains a significant imbalance between classes, as shown in Fig. 4b. Moreover, there must be a certain care taken, as misclassifying a F-NOK as a T-NOK is more costly in terms of manufacturing process, however the inverse would be much more hazardous as it could lead to incorrectly classifying faulty parts as being leak-tight. It is, therefore, justifiable that the final classifier is the most complex and requires the most robust training out of the ensemble.

4   Results and Discussion

4.1   Performance Metrics

Due to the imbalanced nature of the dataset, using accuracy alone is insufficient to correctly describe model behavior, as properly classifying the majority class would be sufficient to provide strong results [10]. As such, the final model is evaluated according to a more complete set of metrics commonly employed to evaluate imbalanced datasets [10,12,15,17,19,21,25], including Accuracy (Acc), Precision (P), Recall (R), geometric mean ($GMean$), and F_β value. For F_β, parameter β weighs the relative importance of P versus R, and for all considered testing $\beta = 1$, and therefore we computed the F_1 score. Macro variants of metrics, e.g. F_1-*macro*, are computed through the unweighted mean of all corresponding scores of each class, and represent a much more pessimistic final score than the weighted mean, as each class classification is treated equally towards the final score, regardless of support value.

4.2   Implementation of Results

Table 2 shows results obtained using a convectional Auto-ML approach (TPOT [9], version 0.11.7). All classifiers are available from the scikit-learn Python library, version 1.0.2 [14], with the exception of XGBoost (XGB) [4], and were trained to optimize the F_1-*macro* score. The inadequacy of using the accuracy metric alone in unbalanced datasets is clear, as the number of misclassified classes is large, as seen by the low F_1-*macro* scores that never surpassed 40.5%, however, accuracy is high, achieving 92.4% for XGB. These results serve as a baseline for the proposed solution, further revealing the necessity for its implementation.

Table 2. Results of several classifiers optimized through an Auto-ML platform.

Classifier	Acc	F_1-macro	Classifier	Acc	F_1-macro
SGD	0.768	0.196	KNeighbors	0.921	0.392
GaussianNB	0.775	0.343	Decision Tree	0.923	0.396
Logistic Regression	0.810	0.128	Extra Trees	0.923	0.400
MLP	0.908	0.237	Gradient Boosting	0.923	0.405
BernoulliNB	0.912	0.239	Random Forest	0.924	0.405
LinearSVC	0.912	0.239	XGB	0.924	0.392

The train-validation-test proportion for the ensemble model was: 60% of data allocated for model training; 10% for validation and hyperparameter optimization; and 30% set aside for final model evaluation. The proposed ensemble algorithm's hyperparameters were tuned through a randomized search across a large search space; with 250 iterations per classifier candidate for hyperparameter tuning; performing stratified k-fold with three splits at each stage for candidate evaluation. Eight candidate classifiers were evaluated: Decision Trees (DT), RF, LR, Gradient Boosted Trees (GBT), Gaussian Naïve Bayes (GNB), Adaboost, SVC, and Stochastic Gradient Descent (SGD). All classifiers are available using scikit-learn. The randomized search was set to optimize the final F_1-*macro* score.

Completed algorithm training, layers three-to-five used RF classifiers with 100 estimators. To deal with class unbalance, layers four and five used "balanced" class weighting to compensate for class size differences. As expected, the final classifier required the most complex solution, and the minority class of the final classifier was over-sampled with SMOTE using the 10 closest neighbors to construct synthetic samples. The number of features to use was reduced through recursive feature elimination with cross-validation ($n\_splits = 2$), using Linear-SVC as base estimator. Final estimator was SVC with a linear kernel, one-versus-one ("ovo") decision function, balanced class weights, and $C = 0.177$. Parameter ϵ of (2) was set as $\epsilon = 0.5$. Results for the proposed classifier ensemble on the holdout test set are seen in Table 3, and Fig. 5 illustrates corresponding confusion matrices.

Table 3. Results of ensemble classifier on test set left aside for model evaluation.

Acc	P-macro	R-macro	F_1-macro	GMean
0.994	0.904	0.912	0.905	0.901

The F_1-*macro* score saw an improvement of 123.46% using the proposed ensemble classifier in comparison with best performing conventional approach, whilst also seeing an improvement in total accuracy. Four classes were all correctly identified, and class H-NOK, which is the minority class of the dataset, saw only one misclassification. As expected, distinguishing F-NOK from T-NOK proved to be most difficult, however, care was taken as to not invert the balance of these classifications, as there is a security cost with increasing the number of incorrectly identified F-NOK, Fig. 5b. With such high results, the question for the risk of the model suffering from over-fitting emerges, however, due to the relatively static nature of the process and of the master part's behavior, the training and testing dataset can be considered highly representative of the use-case. Likewise, the deploy system will supervise the algorithm's predictive

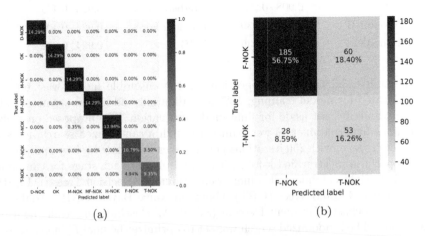

Fig. 5. Confusion matrix of: (a) obtained results, with percentage of classifications of each class (assuming each class as equal weighted); (b) only F-NOK and T-NOK classes, including absolute values of total classifications instances in each class.

performance by monitoring any variation of the metrics discussed in Subsect. 4.1, as depicted in Fig. 2, and re-training with fresh data is contemplated within the smart manufacturing platform. Furthermore, data-drift is also monitored, analyzing changing data distributions and the variability of relationships between input and output variables [11].

5   Conclusions

In this paper, we introduce a real-world use case at the Bosch Thermotechnology facilities, where unsatisfactory leak testing performance led to substantial bottlenecks at their water heater production lines. Conducted literature review reveals a lack of related work regarding data-driven methodologies for leak testing. As such, a data-driven methodology is proposed, agnostic to equipment, test setup, or operator, and using an unbalanced data pipeline centered around an heterogeneous ensemble algorithm capable of reducing a complex multiclass classification problem into simpler, more distinctly differentiable instances, and therefore increasing predictive performance.

Nonetheless, there remains possible improvements to be explored in future work. For instance, it is possible to enrich the ensemble with added layers of regression models for a deeper study of the overall length of failed test sequences that finalize with a successful test. This would also contribute to increasing the explainability of the model as the final classifier, despite performing adequately, lacks true explainability of physical phenomena, creating an opportunity for added application of techniques such as SHAP (SHapley Additive exPlanations) further explaining the output of machine learning models [18].

However, we can conclude that the obtained result of 90.5% for $F_1\text{-}macro$ allows this tool to operate reliably and provide added organizational value as it stands, delivering maintenance personnel with direct and actionable information for the continuous improvement of their leak testing procedures.

Data Availability Statement. Datasets used to obtain results are confidential information of Bosch company manufacturing system, and as such, not publicly available.

References

1. Ahmad, Z., Rai, A., Maliuk, A.S., Kim, J.M.: Discriminant feature extraction for centrifugal pump fault diagnosis. IEEE Access **8**, 165512–165528 (2020). https://doi.org/10.1109/ACCESS.2020.3022770
2. ATEQ: ATEQ D520 user manual - version 1.32 (2009). https://atequsa.com/wp-content/uploads/2014/07/PREMIER-D-USER-MANUAL-ENGLISH.pdf
3. Bousdekis, A., Lepenioti, K., Apostolou, D., Mentzas, G.: A review of data-driven decision-making methods for industry 4.0 maintenance applications. Electronics **10**(7) (2021). https://doi.org/10.3390/electronics10070828

4. Chen, T., Guestrin, C.: XGBoost: a scalable tree boosting system. In: Proceedings of the 22nd ACM SIGKDD International Conference on Knowledge Discovery and Data Mining, KDD 2016, pp. 785–794. ACM, New York (2016). https://doi.org/10.1145/2939672.2939785

5. Feng, C., et al.: Log-transformation and its implications for data analysis. Shanghai Arch. Psychiat. **26**, 105–109 (2014). https://doi.org/10.3969/j.issn.1002-0829.2014.02.009

6. Garcia, A., Ferrando, J.L., Arbelaiz, A., Oregui, X., Bilbao, A., Etxegoien, Z.: Soft computing analysis of pressure decay leak test detection. In: Herrero, Á., Cambra, C., Urda, D., Sedano, J., Quintián, H., Corchado, E. (eds.) SOCO 2020. AISC, vol. 1268, pp. 299–308. Springer, Cham (2021). https://doi.org/10.1007/978-3-030-57802-2_29

7. Guntur, H., Cai, M., Kawashima, K., Kagawa, T.: Analysis of temperature effect on differential pressure method for air leak detection. In: SICE 2004 Annual Conference, vol. 1, pp. 159–162 (2004)

8. Jyothi, R., Holla, T., Rao, K.U., Jayapal, R.: Machine learning based multi class fault diagnosis tool for voltage source inverter driven induction motor. Int. J. Power Electron. Drive Syst. **12**, 1205–1215 (2021). https://doi.org/10.11591/ijpeds.v12.i2.pp1205-1215

9. Le, T.T., Fu, W., Moore, J.H.: Scaling tree-based automated machine learning to biomedical big data with a feature set selector. Bioinformatics **36**(1), 250–256 (2020)

10. Liu, H., Liu, Z., Jia, W., Zhang, D., Tan, J.: A novel imbalanced data classification method based on weakly supervised learning for fault diagnosis. IEEE Trans. Ind. Inform. **18**, 1583–1593 (2022). https://doi.org/10.1109/TII.2021.3084132

11. Lu, J., Liu, A., Dong, F., Gu, F., Gama, J., Zhang, G.: Learning under concept drift: a review. IEEE Trans. Knowl. Data Eng. **31**(12), 2346–2363 (2019). https://doi.org/10.1109/TKDE.2018.2876857

12. Malhotra, R., Lata, K.: Improving software maintainability predictions using data oversampling and hybridized techniques. In: 2020 IEEE Congress on Evolutionary Computation (CEC), pp. 1–7 (2020). https://doi.org/10.1109/CEC48606.2020.9185809

13. e Oliveira, E., Miguéis, V.L., Borges, J.L.: Automatic root cause analysis in manufacturing: an overview & conceptualization. J. Intell. Manuf. (2022). https://doi.org/10.1007/s10845-022-01914-3

14. Pedregosa, F., et al.: Scikit-learn: machine learning in Python. J. Mach. Learn. Res. **12**, 2825–2830 (2011)

15. Pristyanto, Y., Nugraha, A.F., Dahlan, A., Wirasakti, L.A., Ahmad Zein, A., Pratama, I.: Multiclass imbalanced handling using ADASYN oversampling and stacking algorithm. In: 2022 16th International Conference on Ubiquitous Information Management and Communication (IMCOM), pp. 1–5 (2022). https://doi.org/10.1109/IMCOM53663.2022.9721632

16. Pristyanto, Y., Nugraha, A.F., Dahlan, A., Wirasakti, L.A., Zein, A.A., Pratama, I.: A big data-driven root cause analysis system: application of machine learning in quality problem solving. Comput. Ind. Eng. **160** (2021). https://doi.org/10.1016/j.cie.2021.107580, start by analysing this paper

17. Pristyanto, Y., Nugraha, A.F., Pratama, I., Dahlan, A., Wirasakti, L.A.: Dual approach to handling imbalanced class in datasets using oversampling and ensemble learning techniques. In: 2021 15th International Conference on Ubiquitous Information Management and Communication (IMCOM), pp. 1–7 (2021). https://doi.org/10.1109/IMCOM51814.2021.9377420

18. Ribeiro, M.T., Singh, S., Guestrin, C.: "Why should i trust you?": explaining the predictions of any classifier. In: Proceedings of the 22nd ACM SIGKDD International Conference on Knowledge Discovery and Data Mining, KDD 2016, pp. 1135–1144. Association for Computing Machinery, New York (2016). https://doi.org/10.1145/2939672.2939778

19. Rojarath, A., Songpan, W.: Cost-sensitive probability for weighted voting in an ensemble model for multi-class classification problems. Appl. Intell. **51**, 4908–4932 (2021). https://doi.org/10.1007/s10489-020-02106-3/Published

20. Shi, Y., Tong, X., Cai, M.: Temperature effect compensation for fast differential pressure decay testing. Meas. Sci. Technol. **25** (2014). https://doi.org/10.1088/0957-0233/25/6/065003

21. Sridhar, S., Sanagavarapu, S.: Handling data imbalance in predictive maintenance for machines using smote-based oversampling. In: 2021 13th International Conference on Computational Intelligence and Communication Networks (CICN), pp. 44–49 (2021). https://doi.org/10.1109/CICN51697.2021.9574668

22. Tang, Z., Liu, X., Wei, D., Luo, H., Jiang, P., Bo, L.: Enhanced multiclass support vector data description model for fault diagnosis of gears. Measurement **194**, 110974 (2022). https://doi.org/10.1016/j.measurement.2022.110974

23. Webert, H., Döß, T., Kaupp, L., Simons, S.: Fault handling in industry 4.0: definition, process and applications. Sensors **22**(6) (2022). https://doi.org/10.3390/s22062205

24. Xu, C., Li, X., Wang, Z., Zhao, B., Xie, J.: Improved BLS based transformer fault diagnosis considering imbalanced samples. Energy Rep. **8**, 1446–1453 (2022). https://doi.org/10.1016/j.egyr.2022.02.223

25. Yang, Y., Xiao, P., Cheng, Y., Liu, W., Huang, Z.: Ensemble strategy for hard classifying samples in class-imbalanced data set. In: 2018 IEEE International Conference on Big Data and Smart Computing (BigComp), pp. 170–175 (2018). https://doi.org/10.1109/BigComp.2018.00033

26. Zonta, T., da Costa, C.A., da Rosa Righi, R., de Lima, M.J., da Trindade, E.S., Li, G.P.: Predictive maintenance in the industry 4.0: a systematic literature review. Comput. Ind. Eng. **150**, 106889 (2020). https://doi.org/10.1016/j.cie.2020.106889

Pattern Mining and Classification Techniques for Agriculture and Crop Simulation

Javier Rozas-Acurio, Sergio Zavaleta-Salazar, and Willy Ugarte$^{(\boxtimes)}$

Universidad Peruana de Ciencias Aplicadas, Lima, Peru
{u201711814,u201515982}@upc.edu.pe, willy.ugarte@upc.edu.pe

Abstract. Research shows that data analysis and artificial intelligence applied to agriculture in Peru can help manage crop production and mitigate monetary losses. This work presents SmartAgro, a system based on pattern mining and classification techniques that takes information from multiple sources related to the agricultural process to extract knowledge and produce recommendations about the crop growth process. The problem we seek to mitigate with our system is the economic losses generated in Peruvian agriculture caused by poor crop planning. Our results show a high accuracy in regards to type of crop recommendation, and a knowledge base useful for agricultural planning.

Keywords: Agriculture · Classification · Crop simulation · Pattern mining

1 Introduction

The agricultural sector in Peru is one of the pillars of economic growth, but because of poor crop management and poor planning in the face of climate change, it never reaches its potential. In Peru there are multiple sources of relevant information such as crop intentions, weather conditions, prices of food products in real time, amount of production by region, and many others, provided by public institutions and ministries. However, many farmers are unaware of this information, and have little to no knowledge of the technological tools that could allow them to improve their crop planning.

The vast majority of farmers apply tradition-based decision making without any prior knowledge of the demand or crops that can generate better profits. Therefore, it is important that they have knowledge about the best way to plan the crop and what food products should be grown in a given area and period of time[1]. The dispersion of land represents a limit to the efficiency of agricultural production in Peru, around 85% of farmers own crops smaller than 10 ha. In

---

[1] Crop Guidance Framework (in spanish) - Peruvian Ministry of Agrarian Development and Irrigation (2020) - https://cdn.www.gob.pe/uploads/document/file/1113474/Anexo_-_Marco_Orientador_de_Cultivos.pdf.

T. Guarda et al. (Eds.): ARTIIS 2022, CCIS 1675, pp. 444–458, 2022.
https://doi.org/10.1007/978-3-031-20319-0_33

this sense, it is of great importance to implement protocols to give easy access to agricultural technology in the country in small areas of land and increase production efficiency[2].

According to the multi-year strategic plan of the Ministry of Agrarian Development, there is limited progress in research and technological development in agriculture. This includes low technical assistance and insufficient capacity for innovation in farming techniques, which results in low adoption of new technologies. Within the economically active population, agriculture employs 26% of the national population and 65% of the rural population.

In contrast to its capacity to generate employment, it is one of the sectors with the lowest productivity due to the low educational level of the labor force(See footnote 1). This situation causes the country to have a low level of competitiveness with other agricultural countries, which is reflected in the productivity of agricultural units, with low yields in crops and breeding, below the average recorded in agricultural countries.

Some techniques and systems to evaluate agriculture attributes and generate recommendations have been proposed and studied in different parts of the world. For example, soil fertility classification [13], association rules for problem solving in farms [3]; these proposed solutions work well for a specific type of data sources and are focused on only one set of recommendations.

There are also integrated Internet of Things (IoT) systems [1,12], which have excellent results, but require a lot of setup and tend to be expensive. The system proposed from our part, in contrast, is aimed at utilizing multiple sources of publicly available data, integrated to build an extensive database [10], and a more general set of recommendations without the need of installing expensive monitoring systems and sensors on each farm(See footnote 2).

To make this system accessible for most Peruvian agricultural workers, we have designed a method that implements algorithms of pattern mining and classification techniques, to generate recommendations based on crop intentions, weather attributes, and supply of products. All of these would be oriented to a region selected by the user.

Our main contributions are as follows:

- We develop an implementation of Pattern Mining algorithms for association rule mining of crop intentions.
- We develop an implementation of K-Nearest Neighbors (KNN), Support Vector Machines (SVM) and Random Forests (RF) algorithms for simulation of crop production and recommendation based on weather and supply factors.
- We present an analysis of our results and generation of crop recommendations.

In Sect. 2, we explain some of the current solutions implemented in the literature. In Sect. 3, we elaborate on some of the definitions of the research and technologies related to smart farming and knowledge discovery, the design of the

---

[2] Problems in Peruvian Agriculture (in spanish) - Peruvian Ministry of Agrarian Development and Irrigation (2015) - https://www.midagri.gob.pe/portal/22-sector-agrario/vision-general/190-problemas-en-la-agricultura-peruana.

architecture of the solution, and some terms from the agriculture and computer science sector and then we explain the main contribution of the project.

Then, the experiments and their outcomes will be detailed in Sect. 4. Finally, in Sect. 5, the main findings will be discussed.

2   Related Works

In Godara [3], the authors propose a knowledge discovery model that makes use of survey information collected by the government of India from multiple workers in different branches of the agricultural sector. This type of data specifies and categorizes the challenges that farmers face in relation to the agricultural process, like yield of specific crops, availability of resources, and others. They implement a pattern mining algorithm to find association rules that can be interpreted to specify some unseen relationship between these challenges and the relationship between regions in which they are present. In our work we also make use of pattern mining to discover knowledge about the relationship between agricultural products and regions. Unlike this, we focus specifically on crop intentions in a time period because this type of information can give a better insight into the planning process and provide options for agriculture campaigns based on this knowledge.

In Cambra [1], the authors propose a smart farming system to control fertilization and irrigation on crops. This system is implemented using an association rule mining platform with weather and crop data sensors, and a web application. This would generate recommendations and automate commands for water distribution and fertilization with the goal of better crop management and reducing waste. We aim to develop a similar solution that can be accessed from the web and generate recommendations for crop management from association rules. The difference is our work is not aimed at generating recommendations for automation solutions, instead we generate recommendations and knowledge for planning solutions.

In Gumuscu [4] the authors propose using classification algorithms with weather attributes to estimate wheat planting dates for better yield. They implemented three classification algorithms: KNN, SVM and Decision Trees (DT), to compare performances and select the best results. The data used was meteorological measurements from multiple years, and the attributes selected were Maximum Temperature (°C), Relative Humidity (%), Average Temperature (°C), Minimum Temperature (°C), and Accumulated Precipitation (mm). In our work we used the same type of meteorological measurements with some variations and two of the algorithms mentioned and one similar to DT, but we aggregated the production volume and price of each product, to create a prediction model, not for planting date, but for type of product. We decided on this because the problem we were trying to tackle was monetary losses and this would orient the crop planning towards that goal.

In Rajeswari [13] the authors proposed a classification model that used decision trees to classify the type of soil in different fertility categories, that then equates to the type of product recommended for that soil. The attributes of the data were the soil proteins from lab testing. We proposed a similar method of recommendation for types of products, but instead of lab testing for the soil nutrients we integrated meteorological data with production data to create a different type of dataset that could do the same type of product recommendation with the ones available for Peru. This is because the system is aimed to be used at a big scale, and relying on that type of soil measurement would take too long and be too expensive.

In Rupnik [14] the authors propose a decision support system for agricultural processes based on data analysis and predictive models. This system is implemented using a Random Forest algorithm and a web service open to the public for generation of recommendations based on the data provided by the user. Their system is oriented at pest population dynamics and is evaluated in terms of crop price variation affected by the quality of the product, and crop spraying costs. In comparison with our project, we are also building a service open for the public via the web and utilize data from different sources to give recommendations. The difference is in the type of recommendation we provide, and, as mentioned before, in the type of data we collect to generate recommendations and knowledge.

3 Agriculture and Crop Simulation

The generation of recommendations for crop management present challenges for data integration and knowledge discovery. Some of these problems include the measurements of farm attributes and data collection, the generation of rules for crop selection, the classification of floor by fertility level, the simulation of crop for optimal production planning, and others.

3.1 Preliminary Concepts

In the following paragraphs, some of the important concepts and approaches taken to tackle these issues are presented.

Precision Agriculture. Pierre Robert is considered as the founder of precision agriculture due to his promotion of this idea and the organization of the first crop workshop in 1990 [8].

The International Society for Precision Agriculture (ISPA) defines it as "a management strategy that considers temporal and spatial variability to improve the sustainability of agricultural production"[3].

This involves the use of modern technology to increase the quality and volume of agricultural products. Among the most prominent resources supporting this objective are the use of the internet of things (IoT), big data, artificial intelligence and system automation.

These technologies contribute to large-scale crop monitoring and optimization of information analysis to improve production and reduce costs [11].

---

[3] Precision Ag Definition - International Society of Precision Agriculture (2021) - https://www.ispag.org/about/definition.

Crop Data Management. Data has become a vital component of modern agriculture, assisting producers with management and planning, and when this crop data is managed efficiently the knowledge they provide can be translated into economic growth.

The foundations for sustainable agriculture are laid by data-driven agriculture, mixed with automation technologies that use artificial intelligence approaches to enhance efficiency while reducing resource waste and contamination.

The cycle for this type of advanced agriculture can be detailed, and divided in five main sectors, that are crop, platform, data, decision, and actuation; and what type of technology intervenes in the interaction between these five sectors [15].

IoT Platforms Large-scale smart farming models make use of integrated technologies with specialized sensing sensors and knowledge discovery techniques.

The configuration of smart farms requires the installation of this technology in large spaces, where it is complicated and costly to make network connections across the entire area where the technology is needed.

One approach is the use of edge computing, a distributed information technology architecture in which client data is processed as close as possible to the original source [12]. Sensor-based monitoring and data collection involves the constant and massive transmission of data.

When predictive models are applied, certain attributes can be identified as dependent on others after an analysis of the data.

There are ways for prediction models to supplement data collected by environmental sensors with high accuracy that can be used to reduce the storage, operation time and installation cost of these sensors [7].

Pattern Mining. In data mining, it refers to identifying rules that describe a behavior within a database.

For example, the analysis of a transactions type database can identify situations in which a selection behavior is repeated according to the items found.

It is also possible to discover sequential patterns to anticipate an unforeseen scenario[4].

Association Rule Mining. There are multiple types of data that can be used to obtain knowledge about a particular aspect of the agricultural process.

These types of algorithms can help provide hidden insights regarding the information that is analyzed.

Some popular algorithms are Apriori, FP-Growth, and Eclat. For the Apriori algorithm, which is well known and widely used for finding association rules, a dataset of transactions is necessary, a shopping registry would be a common example of a dataset used for basket analysis.

---

[4] Data Mining - Encyclopedia Britannica, inc. (2019) - https://www.britannica.com/technology/data-mining.

It starts by calculating product frequencies and identifying the most frequent products bought. Products are referred to as items, and sets of products are called itemsets.

Each item or group of items in an itemset has a frequency value and a confidence value associated with it. Each itemset is composed of an antecedent and a consequent, which is an item or group of items that make up the itemset.

In Fig. 1 we can observe the work flow of the Apriori algorithm.

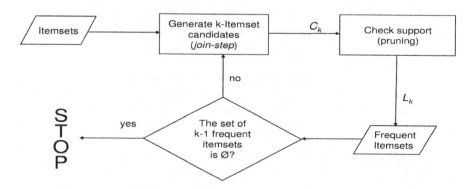

Fig. 1. Apriori algorithm process [19]

Unlike Apriori, which makes multiple scans through the data to check the support, the FP-Growth algorithm only needs to scan it twice.

The way it works is that it creates a tree structure (FP-tree) to store the information of transactions in nodes from this tree. That's why it is often faster than Apriori and considered an improvement.

The Eclat algorithm also tries to improve on the Apriori algorithm by using the intersection of the original single item sets to produce the second set of itemsets, rather than scanning the data again.

This method further improves the time that would be needed to generate association rules.

Crop Yield Prediction. Predicting suitable crop products and circumstances is an essential part of farming, and machine learning algorithms have played an important role in that task in recent years.

Manual prediction has largely failed due to climatic changes and environmental factors affecting crops, and feature selection and classification have become critical machine learning techniques [16].

Classification Algorithms. A classification algorithm is a type of supervised machine learning algorithm, where the user acts as a guide, providing a series of data instances with a previously defined class for each instance, which the algorithm must learn to select as a conclusion according to the data input presented.

In the training stage it evaluates the input attributes of a data instance to select an output class. The training of the classification algorithm is performed to identify the weights that provide the best and most accurate separation of the data classes.

It is also possible to train and use multiple classifiers, and then make a classification decision based on the results of all classifiers [9]. Three popular classification algorithms are KNN, SVM, and RF. The KNN algorithm belongs to the category of supervised learning and is used for classification and regression.

This algorithm takes the nearest data points within a plane to predict the class or continuous value of new data points. The SVM algorithm finds the optimum decision line for dividing a data space into classes and assigning a new data point to the correct category.

In the n-dimensional space, there might be several decision lines to split classes, however the best decision boundary that helps classify the data points must be found. The RF algorithm is based on the concept of ensemble learning, which is a technique for solving difficult problems and improving model performance by combining many classifiers.

It's a classifier that averages the results of multiple decision trees on distinct subsets of a dataset to improve the dataset's prediction accuracy. Rather than depending on a single decision tree, it considers the forecasts of each tree and predicts the ultimate result based on the majority votes of the predictions.

3.2   Method

For the development of the SmartAgro system to generate crop recommendations we proposed an association rule generation module that provides insights about the crop planning at a national scale.

Followed by a simulation module that implements a classification algorithm applied to a database that comprehends crop planning by region data, weather attributes data (temperature, humidity, and precipitations), and production data (average product price, and produce volume).

Pattern Mining. In this section, we first describe the data pre-processing, the algorithms that were implemented, and the pattern mining process.

Before selecting a set of algorithms, we did a benchmark based on literature, where we took different algorithms from three articles [2,5,20] to evaluate the execution time and memory use, and rank the most effective in terms of these metrics.

In the end we selected the top three, that were Apriori, FP-Growth, and Eclat.

For the extraction of frequent items and item sets, the pattern mining models are implemented, supported by the fim python library.

A public source of crop intentions (obtained from https://www.datosabiertos.gob.pe/dataset/midagri-informacion-estadisticas-intenci%C3%B3n-de-siembras), described in Table 1 is used as a dataset.

Table 1. Crop intention dataset description

Column	Description
Department	Name of a department in Peru
Province	Name of a province of in Peru
District	Name of a district in Peru
Product	Name of an agricultural product
Total	Total of hectares designated for a crop in a region

The data preparation process starts by selecting the relevant columns of the planting intention dataset, which are the product to be grown and the department where it is grown.

Then, this data is reduced to obtain only the unique crop pairs per department, and from this information it is possible to proceed with the execution of the algorithms to find the association rules.

The algorithms implemented are Apriori, as explained and illustrated in Fig. 1, FP-growth and Eclat. For these algorithms, given a set of transactional data, the first step is to calculate the frequencies of the elements in the dataset and identify the frequent elements.

Then, we follow with the execution of the selected algorithms to obtain the association rules. In addition to obtaining the relationships between crops by region, the data can be further analyzed from these results to determine the percentage of land allocated to each product in each region of Peru.

Machine Learning. For this section, we started by selecting a set of machine learning algorithms, for which we did a benchmark based on literature, as we did for the previous section.

We took different algorithms from two articles [6, 21] to evaluate the accuracy and rank the most effective in terms of this metric.

In the end we selected the top three, that were KNN, SVM, and RF. We implemented these classification models in a python environment.

The scikit-learn library was used for their implementation, since it provides simple and efficient tools for predictive data analysis. For the preparation of the prediction dataset, three data sources were integrated.

The first is the supply and price source (obtained from http://sistemas. midagri.gob.pe/sisap/portal2/mayorista/#), from which the average price and the average production volume of the products are obtained.

Then follows the source of climatic reports by region (obtained from https://www.datosabiertos.gob.pe/dataset/datos-hidrometeorol%C3%B3gicos-de-libre-acceso), from which the temperature, relative humidity, and precipitation accumulation of the available regions are taken.

These two data sources are then integrated to the third source, which is the crop intention, where the type of product is integrated referencing the supply source, and the regions with the source of climatic reports, to create a data table which can be described in Table 2.

This integrated dataset contains sufficient information to make a prediction, where the result is the recommendation of the type of crop.

Table 2. Classification dataset description

Column	Description
Department	Name of a department in Peru
Province	Name of a province of in Peru
District	Name of a district in Peru
Price	Average price of product
Volume	Volume of produce in tons inside a time frame
Temperature	Average of measured daily temperature in centigrade
Humidity	Average of measured humidity relative to air
Precipitation	Millimeters of rain inside a time frame

To visualize our results we implemented a web application in python, using the Flask framework.

Our system shows the results from the pattern mining process in the form of tables and some colored maps where regional information was displayed.

Then, in another view, the user could input some data to generate a product recommendation and analyze some information related to the crop.

4   Experiments

In this section, we will go over the experiments that our project has gone through, as well as what is required to repeat those experiments and a discussion of the outcomes acquired as a result of this procedure.

4.1   Experimental Protocol

To recreate the process of building, training and testing the models implemented in our project, we begin to describe what was needed to accomplish this task.

Development Environment. The environment used as our main platform, and where all our models were trained, was Google Colab, which provided us a total RAM of 12 GB and 100 GB storage.

For the development of our web application, we also used two personal computers with 16 GB RAM and 2TB storage, and a 3.4 Ghz Ryzen 5 Processor.

Our system was implemented in python 3, using the Anaconda distribution and the Flask framework, and the main libraries were scikit-learn and fim.

Dataset. We had three main datasets that were obtained using open data from Peruvian government ministries.

The first dataset (available at https://www.datosabiertos.gob.pe/dataset/midagri-informacion-estadisticas-intenci%C3%B3n-de-siembras) was a national survey of crop intentions from august 2020 to july 2021, published on the national open data platform.

The second dataset (available at https://www.datosabiertos.gob.pe/dataset/datos-hidrometeorol%C3%B3gicos-de-libre-acceso) was built from weather reports from multiple weather stations across the country of Peru. A web scraper was implemented to collect and organize the data, which can be accessed from the national open data platform.

Then our third dataset (available at http://sistemas.midagri.gob.pe/sisap/portal2/mayorista/#) was built from the national supply and pricing system.

Models Training. All our models were trained in Google Colab. For the machine learning models we used the SVM, KNN and RF classification algorithms from the scikit-learn library, as well as the preprocessing and optimization methods. We used Stratified Cross-validation with k folds, where k is equal to 10. Additionally, the results that each algorithm obtained based on accuracy, precision, recall and f1 metrics are used to evaluate performance. For pattern mining models, we used the PyFim library. What is sought is that the training time be as short as possible. To do this, we initially compared the three algorithms that presented the lowest times according to benchmarking results. The comparison was made in 10 different epochs and the algorithm that gave the best average time in the 10 epochs was chosen, in this case it was the Eclat algorithm. In the implementation of Eclat, a closed element set mining was used with 10% for min_freq and 2 for min_size.

Testing Environment. We evaluate the performance of each model individually. For the machine learning models we use the accuracy, precision, recall and F1 metrics, where accuracy is the main metric to be maximized. In these models, what is sought is that the results of the simulation are as close as possible to reality, which is precisely why we seek to maximize accuracy. For the pattern mining models, we chose two metrics to evaluate its performance, these are model execution time, and confidence percentage of the association rules. The execution time is measured in seconds and what is sought is that it be as short as possible. As mentioned previously, the project is deployed in the form of a web application, for this reason it is important that waiting times are not very high. Regarding the confidence of the association rules, only the rules that present a confidence greater than 80% are accepted, to guarantee that the results are reliable.

Source Code. Our code and datasets are publicly available at https://github.com/JavierRozas/SmartAgro-Notebooks. Our models and validation have been uploaded at the same repository.

4.2   Results

In order to guarantee the quality of the information provided to decision makers
in the agricultural sector, a quantitative validation was carried out to evaluate
the efficiency of the models according to certain selected metrics.

To validate the pattern mining models, comparisons were made between some
of our implementations and other similar algorithms in Google Colab. These were
FP-Growth, Eclat, RElim and SaM. Figure 2 shows the comparative results of
execution time in seconds for 10 runs.

As explained in Sect. 4.1, the metrics that have been chosen to evaluate the
results are time, accuracy, precision, recovery and F1 for the machine learning
model, and execution time and confidence for the pattern mining model. It is
sought that the web application has reduced loading times and guarantee the
quality of the results, in that sense, according to the research that was carried
out in the state of the art, the metrics described above are the ones that best
lend themselves to this task.

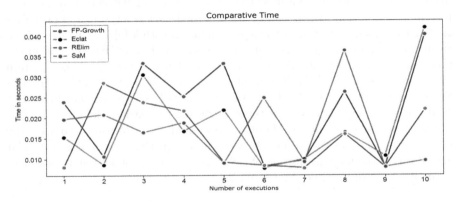

Fig. 2. Comparison of execution times of pattern mining algorithms in 10 runs

After comparing the results, we found that the algorithm with the best execution times was Eclat. Table 3 shows the average execution time registered for
each algorithm.

Table 3. Pattern mining algorithms average run time

Algorithm	Time (S)
Eclat	**0.012402**
RElim	0.012443
SaM	0.012491
FP-Growth	0.013606

With respect to the association rules obtained, histograms were prepared on
the itemsets generated to see the number of items per itemset and the confidence.

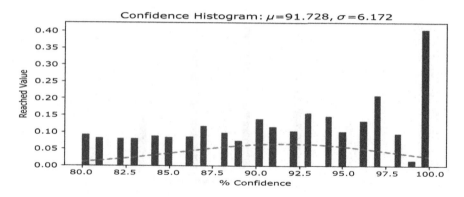

Fig. 3. Confidence histogram for pattern mining results

Figure 3 shows the histogram for the confidence of association rules and shows that the mean confidence is 91.7%.

In Fig. 4 we can see the itemset frequency histogram where one can clearly see how the frequency that each itemset of products is repeated and distributed with.

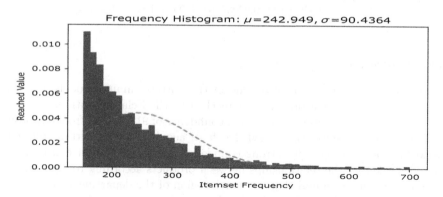

Fig. 4. Histogram for itemset frequency

In Fig. 5 we show a histogram of the number of items per itemset, where we can see the number of products that have been identified for the regions explored. Most of them have around 5 types of crops planned for a region.

To perform the validation of our machine learning models, the previously mentioned metrics, accuracy, precision, recall and f1, were used for the SVM, KNN, and RF algorithms. The results obtained can be verified in Table 4.

These models were able to generate a recommendation of a type of crop, taking weather and supply values as inputs for the classification.

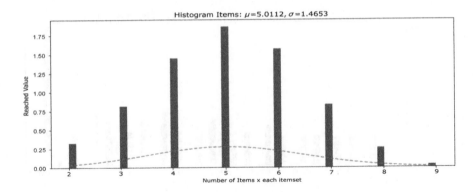

Fig. 5. Histogram for number of items per itemset

Table 4. Classification models evaluation results

Method	Evaluation metrics			
	Accuracy	Precision	Recall	F1
SVM	0.99755058	0.99768217	0.99755058	0.99755493
KNN	0.94739084	0.95128870	0.94739084	0.94736654
RF	0.99936102	0.99938204	0.99936102	0.99935455

4.3   Discussion

As it was presented in our evaluation of the pattern mining models, the best result in terms of execution time was reached by the Eclat algorithm.

The association rules have a median confidence of 91.7%, and from our observation of these results, the knowledge base acquired shows certain relations between types of crops with strong confidence and support, that can be interpreted to identify the relationships between products according to each region.

For example, we found that the north region of the department of Loreto is focusing with a 97% confidence on the plantation of cassava and beans, and as a consequent, yellow corn. From this knowledge we could recommend a campaign for these products in the north district of San Juan Bautista, where we see a high potential for production but no current planning for these types of crops.

Our results also show a high accuracy for the classification model, which allows the system to provide accurate crop recommendations for the end user. As an example, our system recommended Native Potatoes for a region with low temperature, and medium humidity and accumulation of precipitation, for a high production volume and competitive price, which is congruent with the common climate and projected supply for cultivating this type of crop.

It is observed that the highest accuracy value obtained was 99.9% and the lowest result was 94.7%, which if we compare with similar implementations of these models, like the results of Gumuscu [4], using the same algorithms and type of weather measurements, the highest accuracy reached was 92.5%.

From this we can assert that our model, using similar parameters and with the addition of product supply measurements, has a high accuracy for crop prediction and planning.

5   Conclusions

We conclude that by taking into account the regional characteristics according to crop type groupings, and in parallel, the crop associations generated by the pattern mining model, this knowledge could prove useful for promoting targeted crop campaigns by type of crop and by region in the different agricultural districts of Peru.

It was also concluded that the results obtained by our crop recommendation system, based on the machine learning models, present very encouraging results, reaching a high prediction accuracy. We can use this system to enhance what is developed in the pattern mining model and thus improve the results of the project.

In future works, it could be considered to perform an analysis on the results to measure the influence of each column on the results, as well as to add more evaluation metrics in our pattern mining validation [17, 18] to guarantee statistical independence in the association rules.

References

1. Cambra Baseca, C., Sendra, S., Lloret, J., Tomas, J.: A smart decision system for digital farming. Agronomy **9** (2019)
2. Gashaw, Y., Liu, F.: Performance evaluation of frequent pattern mining algorithms using web log data for web usage mining. In: CISP-BMEI (2017)
3. Godara, S., Toshniwal, D.: Sequential pattern mining combined multi-criteria decision-making for farmers' queries characterization. Comput. Electron. Agric. **173** (2020)
4. Gümüşçü, A., Tenekeci, M.E., Bilgili, A.V.: Estimation of wheat planting date using machine learning algorithms based on available climate data. Sustain. Comput. Informatics Syst. **28** (2020)
5. Kuang, Z., Zhou, H., Zhou, D., Zhou, J., Yang, K.: A non-group parallel frequent pattern mining algorithm based on conditional patterns. Frontiers Inf. Technol. Electron. Eng. **20** (2019)
6. Liu, Y., Bi, J., Fan, Z.: Multi-class sentiment classification: The experimental comparisons of feature selection and machine learning algorithms. Expert Syst. Appl. **80**, 323–339 (2017)
7. Mancipe-Castro, L., Gutiérrez-Carvajal, R.: Prediction of environment variables in precision agriculture using a sparse model as data fusion strategy. Inf. Process. Agric. **9**, 17—183 (2022)
8. Mulla, D., Khosla, R.: Historical Evolution and Recent Advances in Precision Farming, pp. 1–36. CRC Press, Boca Raton (2015)
9. Netoff, T.I.: Chapter 14 - the ability to predict seizure onset. In: Iaizzo, P.A. (ed.) Engineering in Medicine. Academic Pres, San Diegos (2019)

10. Ngo, V.M., Kechadi, M.T.: Electronic farming records - a framework for normalising agronomic knowledge discovery. Comput. Electron. Agric. **184**,106074 (2021)
11. Pivoto, D.: Smart farming: concepts, applications, adoption and diffusion in southern Brazil. Ph.D. thesis, Universidade Federal do Rio Grande do Sul, Porto Alegre, Brazil (2018)
12. Pérez-Pons, M.E., Plaza-Hernández, M., Alonso, R.S., Parra-Domínguez, J., Prieto, J.: Increasing profitability and monitoring environmental performance: a case study in the agri-food industry through an edge-IoT platform. Sustainability (Switzerland) **13** (2021)
13. Rajeswari, S., Suthendran, K.: C5.0: advanced decision tree (ADT) classification model for agricultural data analysis on cloud. Comput. Electron. Agric. **156** (2019)
14. Rupnik, R., Kukar, M., Vracar, P., Kosir, D., Pevec, D., Bosnic, Z.: Agrodss: a decision support system for agriculture and farming. Comput. Electron. Agric. **161**, 260–271 (2019)
15. Saiz-Rubio, V., Rovira-Más, F.: From smart farming towards agriculture 5.0: a review on crop data management. Agronomy **10** (2020)
16. Suruliandi, A., Ganesan, M., Raja, s.: Crop prediction based on soil and environmental characteristics using feature selection techniques. Math. Comput. Model. Dyn. Syst. **27** (2021)
17. Ugarte, W., Boizumault, P., Loudni, S., Crémilleux, B., Lepailleur, A.: Mining (soft-) skypatterns using constraint programming. In: EGC (best of volume) (2013)
18. Ugarte, W., Boizumault, P., Loudni, S., Crémilleux, B., Lepailleur, A.: Soft constraints for pattern mining. J. Intell. Inf. Syst. **44**(2) (2015)
19. Vannozzi, G., Della Croce, U., Starita, A., Benvenuti, F., Cappozzo, A.: Knowledge discovery in databases of biomechanical variables: application to the sit to stand motor task. J. Neuroeng. Rehabil **1** (2004)
20. Yun, U., Lee, G., Lee, K.: Efficient representative pattern mining based on weight and maximality conditions. Expert Syst. J. Knowl. Eng. **33** (2016)
21. Zhang, C., Liu, C., Zhang, X., Almpanidis, G.: An up-to-date comparison of state-of-the-art classification algorithms. Expert Syst. Appl. **82** (2017)

Peruvian Sign Language Recognition Using Recurrent Neural Networks

Geraldine Fiorella Barrientos-Villalta, Piero Quiroz, and Willy Ugarte(✉)

Universidad Peruana de Ciencias Aplicadas, Lima, Peru
{u201711590,u201710398}@upc.edu.pe, willy.ugarte@upc.pe

Abstract. Deaf people generally face difficulties in their daily lives when they try to communicate with hearing people, this is due to the lack of sign language knowledge in the country. Deaf people have to go on their everyday lives in company of a interpreter to be able to communicate, even wanting to go to buy bread every morning becomes a challenge for them and being treated in health centers also becomes a challenge, a challenge which should not exist since they have the fundamental right to health. For that reason this paper attempts to present a system for dynamic sign recognition for Peruvian Sign Language and our main goal is to detect which model and processing technique is the most appropriate to solve this problem. So that this system can be used in deaf people everyday life and help them communicate. There have been many projects around the world trying to address this situation. However, each Sign Language is unique in its own way and, therefore, a global and complete solution is not possible. There have also been similar projects in Peru, but all of them share the same flaw of only recognizing static signs. Since sign language is not just the static signs like the alphabet, a solution which addresses also words that can be used in sentences is needed. For this a dynamic recognition is needed, and this is the system that will be presented in this paper.

Keywords: Deep learning · Recurrent neural networks · Sign language

1 Introduction

Deaf people generally face difficulties in their daily lives when they try to communicate with hearing people, because of the lack of Sign Language knowledge in society. This situation is usually ignored, because the number of deaf people is underestimated. There are more than 232,000 deaf people in Peru[1] and approximately 70 million deaf people in the whole world [5].

---

[1] Resultados definitivos de los censos nacionales Perú (2017) - https://www.inei.gob.pe.

T. Guarda et al. (Eds.): ARTIIS 2022, CCIS 1675, pp. 459–473, 2022.
https://doi.org/10.1007/978-3-031-20319-0_34

Last year[2] , during the presidential campaign, there was a debate between all the candidates, which was crucial for the Peruvian population because it allowed them to decide their vote. During this important event, one issue that caught the attention of the hearing population was the absence of a sign language interpreter. This incident alone shows the lack of inclusion of deaf people in our country.

There have been many works around the world trying to address this situation. However, each Sign Language is unique in its own way and, therefore, a global and complete solution is not possible. There have also been similar works in Peru, like the mobile application Kinesika[3] or the work of [4]. The former allows a deaf user to use a keyboard of static signs and translate it to text, but it can't translate videos. The latter can translate videos but it only recognizes static signs. In Peruvian Sign Language, an static sign represents a letter, while a dynamic sign represents a whole word. Deaf people need words to express themselves, as hearing people do.

To overcome this issue, a sign language model is proposed, which pre-process videos and extracts landmarks as series for later using them in a Long short-term memory (LSTM) Neural Network. A Long short-term memory network is used, since it is well-suited to classifying, processing and making predictions based on series data.

The presented work is limited by the dataset, since there is little to no research in this area in Peru finding a dataset for the work was not possible. In addition to that, since Peru is not a country in which there is a lot of support towards disabled communities, finding information around Peruvian Sign Language and interpreters that could help to develop the dataset was difficult.

Our contribution are as follows:

- The construction of a A Peruvian Sign Language Dataset that contains the main words used in a Medical Environment, which is expected to be used by other professionals in the future to create works that can help to create a better place for deaf people in Peru.
- An experimental analysis on which are the best subset of words and pre-processing techniques to get better accuracy in the classification model.
- The development of a mobile application so the users can send Peruvian Sign Language videos for translation.

In Sect. 2, similar solutions currently implemented in the literature will be explained. In Sect. 3, the definitions of the technologies related to recurrent neural networks, the appropriate components selected for the design of the architecture of the solution, and some terms from the forestry sector and then the contribution of the work will be explained. Then, the experiments and their

---

[2] ¿Cuánto más se debe esperar?: Ausencia de interpretación de la lengua de señas en espacios primarios de nuestro país - https://www.enfoquederecho.com/2021/04/18/cuanto-mas-se-debe-esperar-ausencia-de-interpretacion-de-la-lengua-de-senas-en-espacios-primarios-de-nuestro-pais.

[3] Kinesika: app que elimina barreras de comunicación (2020) - https://noticias.upc.edu.pe/2020/09/27/kinesika-app-elimina-barreras-comunicacion/.

outcomes will be detailed in Sect. 4. Finally, in Sect. 5, the main findings will be discussed.

2   Related Work

For defining the problem, different approaches to Sign Language have been made in both the context as a social problem and the needs of the deaf community and in a technical context in the Sign Language Recognition in the last years.

In [9], the authors revolve around the peruvian deaf community and their needs in education; also in [11], since it is a deep survey and extensive study on different Sign Language Recognition Systems that use artificial intelligence.

There are also various techniques to tackle this problem, most of them are based on Recurrent Neural Networks [6–8,10,14–16] and measure the effectiveness of types of RNNs is checked and video processing techniques. This solutions are hybrid models and focus on traditional sequential models to deal with video such as LSTM.

3   Sign Language Recognition with RNN

3.1   Preliminary Concepts

In the following sections, the main definitions involved in our work and our main hypotheses are provided.

Sign Language. A language is a system that allows us to communicate with other people and express our thoughts and feelings. This is the most important aspect of our lives, because it allows us to form emotional and cultural ties and to interact with other individuals. Sign language is a natural complete language and should always be considered as that, because of the following reasons [13]:

- It is the result of a human capacity
- It is rational
- It is arbitrary
- It is in constant evolution

Artificial Intelligence

Machine Learning. It's an area of Artificial Intelligence focused on using data and algorithms to replicate the way we humans learn, improving precision gradually. The learning is focused on identifying patterns and using them to predict future behavior [2].

Deep Learning. It's an area of Artificial It's a group of machine learning techniques which exploit non-lineal information to extract, transform and analyse complex relationships between data. They try to model high-level abstractions using multiple layers of processing with complex structures or non-lineal transformations [2].

Neural Network. It's a group of algorithms that try to understand existing relationships in a dataset by imitating the human brain. They recognize numeric patterns, contained in vectors which are interpreted by machine perception, labelling or brute data grouping [2].

Training. It's the process of teaching a deep neural network to perform a desired task by feeding it data, resulting in a trained deep learning mode[4].

Inference. It's the process of using a trained deep neural network to make predictions against previously unseen data (see Footnote 4).

Types of Neural Networks

Convolutional Neural Networks (CNN). The most common types of neural networks used in computer vision to recognize objects and patters in images. One of their defining traits is the use of filters within convolutional layers, which transform the input before being passed to the next layer. They are suited for interpreting visual data and data that does not come in a sequence [3].

Recurrent Neural Networks (RNN). These networks are designed to interpret sequential information, such as videos (which are essentially a sequence of individual images). They take an input and reuse the activations of previous nodes or later nodes in the sequence to influence the output [3].

Recurrent Neural Network Arquitectures

Long Short-Term Memory (LSTM). It's a type of RNN capable of learning long term sequences and it's explicitly designed to avoid long term dependency problems. At each time. The popularity of LSTM is due to the Getting mechanism involved with each LSTM cell. It takes input from three different states like the current input state, the short term memory from the previous cell and lastly the long term memory. Figure 1a illustrates LSTM architecture.

Gated Recurrent Units (GRU). The workflow of the Gated Recurring Unit is the same as a regular RNN, but the difference is in the two gate operating mechanisms associated with each unit called update gate and reset gate. The update gate is responsible for determining the amount of previous information that needs to pass along the next state. The reset gate is used from the model to decide how much of the past information is needed to neglect. Figure 1b illustrates GRU Architecture.

---

[4] The Difference Between Deep Learning Training and Inference - https://community.intel.com/t5/Blogs/Tech-Innovation/Artificial-Intelligence-AI/The-Difference-Between-Deep-Learning-Training-and-Inference/post/1335634/.

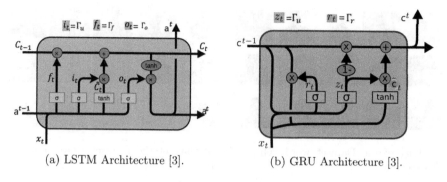

(a) LSTM Architecture [3].   (b) GRU Architecture [3].

Fig. 1. Part of the dataset for two words.

3.2   Method

The main contribution of the work can be summed up in 3 important points: the creation of the dataset for Peruvian Sign Language, the experimental analysis on subsets of words and how they behave in the classification model and the development of the first application that classifies Peruvian Sign Language in the country.

Dataset. In Peru there is not a lot of research or help toward the Deaf community. Resources are very limited and just the action of trying to find a recent an proper dictionary of Peruvian Sign Language is hard. Finding videos or compilations of people doing Peruvian Sign Language is even more hard considering the current pandemic.

Building the Dataset. Given that, working towards creating a more inclusive space for Deaf people becomes difficult and requires a lot of help from experts which are not easy to find.

We believe it is important to have a database with videos of words of Peruvian Sign Language for people to be able to learn from it and also be encouraged to work on further works.

Having a dataset like this available will allow future professionals to use it too for other application with the some objectives as out work. A dataset of 17 words was created, with words which are the most used in a Health context given by California Department of Social Services Office of Deaf Access (2020).

Our dataset contains 439 videos with 8 different people between ages of 14 to 60, men and women. Figure 2a and 2b depict some video examples for two words.

Dataset Processing. Given that this work is from a field in which there is little to no research in Peru it is hard to know the best words that go with each other.

(a) Part of the Dataset word "Gracias" (b) Part of the Dataset word "Pastilla"
(Thank you)   (Pill)

Fig. 2. Part of the dataset for two words.

In video processing, classification becomes harder, because in a video there are many factors that can change the results. These factors include light, quality of camera, angles and environment.

Classification becomes even more hard in sign language recognition due to words not having a fixed time of execution.

In some words, when there is a 1 min video a person can go and make just 1 word of sign or can go and make 30, there is no fixed timing for how many words can a person spell in a minute.

A constant prediction is necessary and then filtering, which makes processing a problem. Apart from that, the coordinates of points representing a persons face, body and hands in a dynamic series of events the description for words that might be completely different in humans eyes can become similar for the computer for the sensitive of the same.

This is explains why, although we have a dataset of 17 words, it is concluded that the best choice is to work with a group of words that work good together and lets our model have better accuracy results.

Mobile Application. A mobile application was developed in Flutter to provide users an interface so they can translate Peruvian Sign Language videos to text using our trained model. Figure 3 illustrates the main functionality of the mobile application.

To prove the concept of the work carried out, an application was proposed which will be using the classification model. With this the users will be able to get a text translation from videos of people doing Peruvian Sign Language.

Fig. 3. Mobile application

Figure 4 shows the flowchart for the use of the proposed application in which the user can enter the platform, then upload a video to the application through the camera or gallery for it to be translated. This video is send to a web service which will give the classification to the application, when this process is finished, the user can see the text translation.

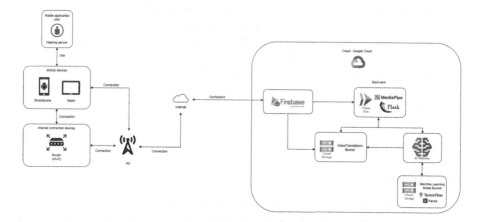

Fig. 4. Architecture diagram

The solution has been developed using the backend web service Flask, which is hosted using Google Cloud services. Flutter was used for the frontend development of the mobile application, in addition to TensorFlow for the operation of the LSTM which works inside the web service. Parts of the architecture are explained bellow:

- *Mobile Application User* Users are hearing people who want to translate Peruvian Sign Language videos to text.
- Mobile Devices In order to access the mobile application, users need a mobile device with the Android operating system.
- *Internet Connection Devices* In order to access the mobile application, users need a mobile device with internet connection.
- *Google Cloud* Cloud services provider.
- *Firebase Authentication* Firebase service that provides authentication functionalities.
- *Google Cloud Storage - Video/Translations Bucket* Storage Web Service used to store videos sent by users and their corresponding translations.
- *Google Cloud Run* Container service used to deploy a Flask web server.
- *MediaPipe* Library used for face, pose and hand recognition in the processing of videos.
- *Flask* Asynchronous web framework used to develop the API consumed by the mobile application.
- *AI Platform* Service that manages cloud resources for machine learning models.
- *Google Cloud Storage - Machine Learning Model Bucket* Storage Web Service used to store our trained model.

Our proposal is to make a Peruvian Sign Language system with machine learning. Image processing algorithms were used, Google Mediapipe which offers a ML solution for extracting key-points of images and a Long-Short Term Memory neuronal network (LSTM). Our proposal relies also in a comparison between 2 image processing techniques, wiener and median.

Furthermore, a mobile solution for the public to use and translate videos of sign language to text was developed.

Figure 5 illustrates the flow of the proposed application, the user must enter the platform, upload a video, then process it to finally display the text result. As an additional feature, the user can translate text to audio.

4   Experiments

4.1   Dataset

Due to the current lack of works in the Peruvian Sign Language area, it was necessary to create a dataset for the project. Thus, a stage had to be carried out where resources external to the organization of the work could support the recording of videos. For this, the following resources were used, some of them collected videos of not only themselves but also friends and family in order to have a more diverse dataset.

Table 1 describes each person who participated in the dataset's construction.

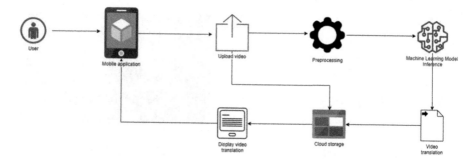

Fig. 5. Proposed application.

Table 1. Dataset subjects

	Gender	Age
1	Male	14
2	Male	16
3	Male	20
4	Male	21
5	Male	21
6	Male	22
7	Male	24
8	Female	65

493 videos were collected. The format of the videos varies, there are videos in MOV, MP4 and AVI format. However, that is not an impediment for the model since it accepts any format. The name of the videos also varies, there is no format, but this is not relevant to the model. Some evidence of the dataset, images of the collection and videos are presented below:

4.2 Preprocessing

Of every video, 30 frames per second were extracted, resulting 30 images per second. For every of these images, key-points, coordinates of the pose, hands and skeleton of the person in the video were extracted, since that was used as series for our LSTM model. Before extracting the key-points a image preprocessing is performed prior to the key-point extraction in order to obtain more samples and better accuracy when processing the training and validation of the algorithms.

Wiener Filter. The Wiener filtering executes an optimal tradeoff between inverse filtering and noise smoothing. It removes the additive noise and inverts the blurring simultaneously. Figure 6a illustrates Wiener Filter.

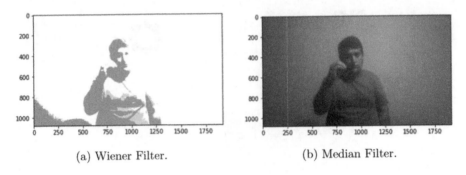

(a) Wiener Filter.   (b) Median Filter.

Fig. 6. Filters in an images from our dataset.

Median Filter. Median filters are widely used as smoothers for image processing, as well as in signal processing and time series processing. A major advantage of the median filter over linear filters is that the median filter can eliminate the effect of input noise values with extremely large magnitudes. Figure 6b illustrates Median Filter.

Mediapipe Google. Mediapipe Pose, Face and Hand are used to extract the landmarks from the person in the image. These are the coordinates in space that are later concatenated in arrays as series and used in the LSTM model. Figure 7 illustrates landmarks.

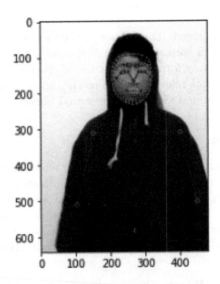

Fig. 7. Landmarks from image with Mediapipe.

4.3 Classification Model

For the model, an LSTM network is used which will have as input arrays of the coordinates in sequence of the video, that is to say that a single video will be represented as a list of lists of coordinates which will be evaluated sequentially when working with a network of this type. The AUC metric will be used for performance. Figure 8 shows more details of the model.

Model: "sequential"

Layer (type)	Output Shape	Param #
lstm (LSTM)	(None, 30, 64)	82688
lstm_1 (LSTM)	(None, 30, 128)	98816
lstm_2 (LSTM)	(None, 64)	49408
dense (Dense)	(None, 64)	4160
dense_1 (Dense)	(None, 32)	2080
dense_2 (Dense)	(None, 7)	231

Total params: 237,383
Trainable params: 237,383
Non-trainable params: 0

Fig. 8. LSTM model summary.

For the training process, the Python programming language is used.

In order to optimize the time in the analysis and experimentation, TensorFlow together with Keras were used. This framework allows us to use the LSTM network, which we will use for the training process. When we started the configuration, Keras functions were applied with 11 epochs.

With these, experiments have been carried out in different groups to see which group has the best performance.

This is because in the area of dynamic sign recognition when working with videos, which has many factors to take into account in the classification, performance is usually low in related jobs.

For pre-processing prior the training part, there were 4 scenarios to compare:

- No Filter
- Wiener Filter
- Median Filter
- Wiener + Median Filter

This for being able to see under which circumstances it is easier for the system to recognise the keypoints properly with mediapipe and then use this as input for our LSTM network.

Table 2 shows the results of the experimentation in terms of accuraccy and loss.

Table 2. Experimental results

classes	no filter		median		wiener		wiener+median	
	Loss	Accuracy	Loss	Accuracy	Loss	Accuracy	Loss	Accuracy
all	1.61	.25	1.59	.26	1.56	.28	1.54	.27
S1	1.67	.27	1.53	.28	1.45	.31	1.47	.32
S2	1.67	.27	1.53	.28	1.45	.31	1.47	.33
S3	1.70	.37	1.68	.39	1.56	.39	1.52	.38
S4	1.71	.30	1.69	.32	1.52	.33	1.53	.34
S5	1.79	.38	1.73	.38	1.66	.40	1.71	.41
S6	1.36	.44	1.62	.41	1.25	.45	1.16	.47
S7	1.54	.41	1.49	.43	1.44	.43	1.46	.43
S8	1.45	.43	1.25	.46	1.20	.46	1.18	.48
S9	.57	.68	.47	.71	.45	.71	.42	.72
S10	1.00	.47	1.13	.44	.94	.48	.93	.48
S11	.66	.69	.52	.69	.64	.70	.63	.72
S12	.94	.55	.93	.55	.89	.57	.92	.56

The subsets were made in groups of 3, 5 and 7 to test which ones got the best results in terms of accuracy, the details of the sets are shown below, initials referring to previous table:

- S1: Alergia, Ayuda, Baño, Bien, Dolor, Donde, Gracias
- S2: Baño, Bien, Dolor, Donde, Gracias, Hora, Mi
- S3: Mi, Necesito, Nombre, Pastilla, Pecho, Que, Resfriado
- S4: Nombre, Pastilla, Pecho, Que, Resfriado, Sentir, Tomar
- S5: Alergia, Ayuda, Baño, Bien, Dolor
- S6: Dolor, Donde, Gracias, Hora, Mi
- S7: Necesito, Nombre, Pastilla, Pecho, Que
- S8: Pecho, Que, Resfriado, Sentir, Tomar
- S9: Alergia, Ayuda, Baño
- S10: Dolor, Donde, Gracias
- S11: Necesito, Nombre, Pastilla
- S12: Resfriado, Sentir, Tomar

Table 3 shows the average performance of the groups (G7: Sets of size 7, G5: Sets of size 5, G3: Sets of size 3).

Table 3. Average performance per group

AVG ACC	No-filter	median	Wiener	Wiener+median
G7	.3351	.3507	.3910	.3903
G5	.4129	.4195	.4361	.4450
G3	.5970	.6008	.6141	.6167

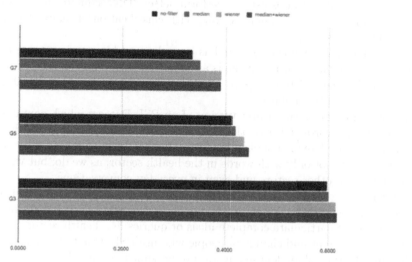

Fig. 9. Average accuracy comparison between sets

Figure 9 shows the average accuracy comparison between sets.
Table 4 shows the best performing technique for each of the groupings.

Table 4. Best technique per grouping

BEST ACC	Set	Technique	Accuracy
G7	S1	Wiener	.5235
G5	S8	Wiener + Median	.4718
G3	S9	Wiener + Median	.7148

As we can see, the larger the number of classes the accuracy is greatly reduced. We also see that the best result is achieved by using both filters (Wiener + Median) in the processing of the images. In groupings, the best performance number with a high number of classes achieved was for "Alergia, Ayuda, Baño, Bien, Dolor, Donde, Gracias" with Wiener. For the entire dataset, a performance of 28.4% has been achieved by having 17 classes in a dataset of 939 one-second videos with 6 different people using Wiener. In addition, the wiener filter in all scenarios presented better results than the other filters.

5   Conclusions

From previous works, it was found that wiener is the best pre-processing method which gives a better accuracy no matter which aggroupation is being used. In addition to that, smaller groups usually perform better. This is due to the size of the dataset, and also because when working with classification of many classes the margin of error is bigger.

Peruvian Sign Language Dataset: As has been discussed in previous parts of the document, Peruvian Sign Language is an area that is not very developed at present. There is a lack of resources to be able to learn from it and to be able to carry out works in this regard.

This work aimed to create a first version of an PSL Dataset which contains 939 videos with 17 words. Clearly, the PSL is a fairly extensive topic and has a vocabulary as complete as a spoken language. In this sense, it is necessary to extend this dataset, not only with words in the health sector, as we do; but with words to be used in other sectors and even in everyday conversations.

This work tries to work with 17 words focused on the health sector which could help make sentences quite simple and generic. However, 17 words are not enough to be able to articulate complete ideas or queries in a health sector that can really have a weight and change in people who use PSL. Due to the dataset limitation and the type of model used, it was not possible to cover a large number of words.

In the world of Machine Learning, the more classes you have in a prediction model, you need to take into account different factors and greater computational capacity [1,12], which was not available for this work. Likewise, when working with dynamic and not static signs, the prediction is even more complicated since the classification of videos and series is a more advanced topic than that of images with static signs (such as the alphabet).

Serve as a forum and community for PSL speakers: Our work has a social purpose, which is to help deaf people who use PSL to have easier interactions with speakers in their daily lives. For this reason, this application could also serve as a point of communication between people who want to learn or learn about PSL.

As you know, in Peru there is no community and no incentive for Peruvians to learn or interact with people who speak PSL. Therefore, if this application could not only serve as a translator, but also have a module for forums, events, and chats that promote inclusion in the PSL community, this would create a safe and happy space for deaf people.

References

1. Alfaro-Paredes, Edwin, Alfaro-Carrasco, Leonardo, Ugarte, Willy: Query by Humming for song identification using voice isolation. In: Fujita, Hamido, Selamat, Ali, Lin, Jerry Chun-Wei., Ali, Moonis (eds.) IEA/AIE 2021. LNCS (LNAI), vol. 12799, pp. 323–334. Springer, Cham (2021). https://doi.org/10.1007/978-3-030-79463-7_27
2. Alpaydin, E.: Introduction to Machine Learning, 2nd edn. MIT Press, Adaptive Computation and Machine Learning series (2009)
3. Bendarkar, D.S., Somase, P.A., Rebari, P.K., Paturkar, R.R., Khan, A.M.: Web based recognition and translation of American sign language with CNN and RNN. Int. J. Online Biomed. Eng. **17**(1) (2021)
4. Berrú-Novoa, B., González-Valenzuela, R., Shiguihara-Juárez, P.: Peruvian sign language recognition using low resolution cameras. In: INTERCON (2018)
5. Chong, T.W., Lee, B.: American sign language recognition using leap motion controller with machine learning approach. Sensors **18**(10) (2018)
6. Cui, R., Liu, H., Zhang, C.: A deep neural framework for continuous sign language recognition by iterative training. IEEE Trans. Multim. 21(7) (2019)
7. Elhagry, A., Gla, R.: Egyptian sign language recognition using CNN and LSTM. CoRR abs/2107.13647 (2021)
8. Farooq, U., Rahim, M.S.M., Sabir, N., Hussain, A., Abid, A.: Advances in machine translation for sign language: approaches, limitations, and challenges. Neural Comput. Appl. **33**(21) (2021)
9. Goico, S.A.: The impact of "inclusive" education on the language of deaf youth in Iquitos, Peru. Sign Lang. StudD. !9(3), 348–374 (2019)
10. Ibrahim, N.B., Selim, M.M., Zayed, H.H.: An automatic Arabic sign language recognition system (ARSLRS). J. King Saud Univ. Comput. Inf. Sci. **30**(4) (2018)
11. Rastgoo, R., Kiani, K., Escalera, S.: Sign language recognition: a deep survey. Expert Syst. Appl. **164** (2021)
12. Rodriguez-Meza, B., Vargas-Lopez-Lavalle, R., Ugarte, W.: Recurrent neural networks for deception detection in videos. In: ICAT (2021)
13. Schein, J., Mark, M.: Speaking the Language of Sign: The Art and Science of Signing. Doubleday, Garden City (1984)
14. Sherstinsky, A.: Fundamentals of recurrent neural network (RNN) and long short-term memory (LSTM) network. CoRR abs/1808.03314 (2018)
15. Ullah, A., Ahmad, J., Muhammad, K., Sajjad, M., Baik, S.W.: Action recognition in video sequences using deep bi-directional LSTM with CNN features. IEEE Access **6**, 1155–1166 (2018)
16. Yao, R., Lin, G., Xia, S., Zhao, J., Zhou, Y.: Video object segmentation and tracking: a survey. ACM Trans. Intell. Syst. Technol. **11**(4) (2020)

Opinion Clustering About Mobility Decisions
A Practical Case Study

Francisca Barros[1] , Carlos Fernandes[1], and Filipe Portela[1,2](✉)

[1] IOTECH—Innovation on Technology, 4785-588 Trofa, Portugal
{franciscabarros,carlosfernandes}@iotech.pt
[2] Algoritmi Research Centre, University of Minho, 4800-058 Guimarães, Portugal
cfp@dsi.uminho.pt

Abstract. This study aims to show the profile of people about the factors that influence decision-making about public and individual transport. First, a survey was carried out to determine several critical factors, and then an online form was created with these criteria. After obtaining the answers, a study was performed with the k-Modes technique to get the profiles. Several statistical analyses for a better understanding of the data were defined. Three different models were built. After a study developed by clustering, it was concluded that there are five groups of people. Those that consider that all variables are essential or not necessary (extremes). Those that consider that all variables have medium importance. The weighted ones present a more excellent dispersion of values and are selective for priority level five. And then, there is the group with the most answers around the medium/low values. The final degree of importance was obtained by the general average of responses and the correlation average. Nine variables were identified, which respect the defined range of values, mean response greater than 3,431 and indicate correlation more significant than 0,228, for degree five of importance.

Keywords: Clustering · Mobility · Decision

1 Introduction

Nowadays, there is a massive amount of data available. Without study and data analysis, it is challenging to interpret the data and take out essential conclusions that help the decision. The data science trend has been growing in the past years, and consequently, the tools and techniques [1]. In Porto city, 25% of transport was responsible for greenhouse gas emissions. In Lisbon, 60% use induvial vehicles and only 16% use public transport [2]. This article was born with the necessity of interpreting the correct data and the possibility for the population to access goods and services that improve their quality of life. There are many advantages and disadvantages to the chosen method of transport. Individual vehicles negatively impact the environment (pollution) and mobility (traffic congestion and a parking seat). However, public transport limited the passengers regarding timetables, flexibility, and comfort [2]. This topic is related to smart cities and the research and development project ioCity[1], which proposes through the analysis of a set

---

[1] ioCity (https://iocity.research.iotech.pt/).

T. Guarda et al. (Eds.): ARTIIS 2022, CCIS 1675, pp. 474–487, 2022.
https://doi.org/10.1007/978-3-031-20319-0_35

of data (sensors, occupancy rate, traffic, parking, among others) to help the customers to have a more informed and real-time decision regarding car parks and public transport.

Consequently, this article aims to understand which factors influence the decision between particular or public transport and create a profile of people to describe travellers clearly. The data were obtained through an online form containing the previously identified and defined critical factors through reading several articles. With data science, using the clustering technique, it was possible to clean and transform all data into a consistent form and take out essential conclusions to classify the people into different groups. For this, the clustering technique with K-Modes was used.

This article is divided into eight sections. The Sect. 1, the Introduction, presents the basis for this work. The Sect. 2 talks about the background of the article, the most critical aspects and workflow. The Sect. 3 describes the material and methods used. The next is a developed study like data understanding, preparation, and evaluation. The analysis results are presented in the six sections, and then the discussion of these outcomes. The last is a conclusion and launched the basis for further work.

2 Background

This section described the most relevant elements to the project, like car parking, public transport, and clustering. Various studies were analyzed, and information was taken from the most pertinent topics about each theme.

2.1 Parking and Public Transport

In urban mobility, the existing traffic is due to the extensive use of personal vehicles and low use of public transport, as well as the great difficulty for drivers to find a parking lot [3]. Citizens justify the use of individual transport to the detriment of collective vehicles for the low quality of public transport [2]. Comfort, privacy, and flexibility are advantages that lead citizens to adopt private cars. However, there are associated disadvantages: high energy consumption, accidents, congestion, and increased pollution [2]. Car parks are also a disadvantage, "parking affects the ease of reaching destinations and therefore affects general accessibility" [4]. There are parking supply problems and car park management problems [4]. Thus, variables that influence drivers' decision-making in choosing car parks will be described.

Accessibility is one of the most important outcomes of the public transport system. However, improving sustainability and quality of urban life is also a great result of using this means of transport. The increase in population has caused a rise in the demand for mobility. If the transport infrastructure cannot meet the needs, it will cause an increase in waiting times and congestion in public transport and on the streets [5]. Several perspectives can be considered depending on the position from which we approach the problem. It is possible to think and act as users, vehicle drivers, operators, authorities, pedestrians, traders, etc. [3]. Service quality is subjective, depending on the relationship between expectations and the service performed. For public transport to grow in its use, it is necessary to understand the various aspects that significantly impact users' satisfaction [6]. The sustainability of transportation, the environmental conditions of an area, public health, and residents' economic condition can all be increased by shifting from private vehicles to public transport, walking and cycling [5]. In this way, the many factors influencing the decision were defined.

2.2 Clustering

The cluster analysis aims to split the data into different groups. In each group, the observations are similar, identifying a set of similar patterns in a data group. There are various algorithms to perform clustering [7]. Considering the sample and the amount of data, one of the most efficient clustering techniques is K-means. However, it only works for numerical data since one of the measures used for clustering is the mean. The K-Modes method extends this technique used to group categorical variables. Through differences between the data points, modes are created. The smaller the differences, the more similar the data set will be [8].

The first step is to clean the data and get a set of K's in several divisions, and the data will have according to the distance of each data point to the centroid. A centroid is a prototype for the cluster [9]. The elbow plot method was selected to determine the optimal number of clusters from the data. Calculating the sum of differences between clusters (cost), the ideal value of K was set. To do this, the data were iterated, and clusters for different numbers of k were generated starting at one and ending at nine. Then, a graph was generated that plots the cost of each value of k. The Elbow method presents the ideal value of K at the point where the value does not significantly decrease with the addition of the value of K. The next step was to generate the final clustering object and get the cluster labels for all the records. Consequently, it is essential to summarize all clusters' features and determine each cluster's profiles [7].

2.3 Related Works

A similar study was developed to identify the impact of taxi mobility. Taxi trajectories reflect human mobility; in this way, group taxi drivers are essential to group the taxis with the same characteristics and take out various information to understand the mobility. Taxis run along the same streets. However, each earns extra daily profits. With the k-means clustering, drivers were grouped into three levels of profitability according to their driving duration and distance travelled income. Combining the results of each clustering group with the cruise stops, it was concluded that there is a significant relationship between human mobility patterns and the profitability of taxi drivers. Drivers who obtain greater profitability are due to their knowledge of the busiest streets and the best times to pass on each street [10].

3 Material and Methods

This section describes the tools, methodology used, and a clear and brief description of the research procedures. Several factors were defined to identify the impact of each one on decision-making. A general search was carried out based on pre-defined key-words: "Parking Management", "Public Transport Accessibility", and "Requirements of a decision support for Mobility" to identify and select the most important papers to read. The research strategy was based on manual processes, where the relevant information for the topic was found through visiting specific sites. As well as through auxiliary platforms such as Google Scholar, Science Direct, Google, Web of Science, Scopus and the University of Minho repository, various articles are available. Also, the list of references for a given theme makes it possible to find references to articles relevant to the project's development. Then, the selection was made by name, publication data and abstract. Considering the background of the report, the data that did not add quality or relevant information was excluded.

Figure 1 presents the workflow of the study flow. The study started on March 14 2022, and finished on April 10 2022. After reading all articles, the criteria were defined, and a form was published on a social network and sent an email to universities in the country. Through the responses to the form, the data for the study were obtained. Statistical analyses and clustering technique was performed to understand which factors impact the decision-making.

Fig. 1. Workflow

3.1 Crisp-DM

The CRISP-DM (cross-industry process for data mining) methodology is a standard inter-industry process. This project helps with the clustering analysis. It describes an approach data mining experts use to attack problems, offering a model to guide data mining projects. According to the previously mentioned methodology, this project is divided into six stages: Business Understanding, where the main objective is to determine the goals for the project. Data understanding, where it matters to collect the data and describe it. Date preparation: Select the data and analyze it in the previous step. Modelling: where appropriate modelling techniques are selected for different scenarios and tests. Finally, evaluation where the impacts of the results of the models generated from the previous step are analyzed and checked if they are all in coherence [13].

3.2 Tools

To identify the degree of importance that each decision criterion has, a survey was developed in google forms so that all citizens can select the factors they prioritize in decision making. This study is for all the people who use Individual or public transport and have an opinion to give. For each aspect, it is supposed to vote between 1 and 5. This survey used google forms, an open platform from Google that allows users to create forms and quizzes and share them with the team and other people [11]. The goal is to collect data for developing the project. The form was carried out in March 2022 and published on social networks so that any citizen can have an active voice in this participatory process. This way, it is possible to quickly and efficiently obtain relevant information regarding the most important criteria.

The Past program was used to effectively evaluate the results obtained, a software program for analyzing statistical data called PAleontological STatistics [12]. With PAST, several statistics were explored like minimum, maximum, mean, standard deviation, variance, etc. With this software, an analysis was also performed to determine each question's correlation level through the correlation coefficient non-parametric Kendall's tau. The results are between -1 and 1. If the result is closer to 1, there is a level of agreement and, therefore, a minor variation [12].

4   Study

According to the study developed to identify the factors, the defining criteria are categorized: availability, accessibility, information, time, comfort, security, and environmental impact. The total responses obtained in the form are the basis of the study. However, the results may not be valid for different populations.

4.1   Business Understanding, Data Understanding and Preparation

The main goal of this study is to understand how and what factors influence citizens in choosing between using public or individual transport. The idea is to profile the citizens and see how people behave in decision-making. Categorize them according to their characteristics.

In this case, data understanding and practice were elementary because the data resulted from the form. Table 1 shows the data that citizens voted in the form. After selecting and reading the articles, these factors were defined by category and group. In other words, criteria had been defined for public and individual transport. For each group, the criteria definition was governed by the categories mentioned in Sect. 4.

Table 1. All data and definitions

Num	Data	Definition
1	Average distance between the geographic location of the passenger and the transport	Refers to the average distance the passenger must travel to the nearest stop
2	Total vehicle capacity	The capacity of the total number of passengers that the transport admits
3	Capacity percentage	Transport occupancy percentage
4	Percentage of passenger flow	The inbound and outbound flow of passengers
5	Number of transfers between means of transport	Several changes must be made to reach the destination
6	Number of intermediate stops (long-distance trips)	The transport will make several stops to the destination desired by the passenger

(continued)

Table 1. (*continued*)

Num	Data	Definition
7	Ticket cost	The average cost the passenger has at the time of purchase of the ticket
8	Charge cost	The average cost that the passenger has in the acquisition of extra loads
9	Versatility percentage	Percentage of Transport suitable for passengers with physical difficulties, children, and seniors
10	Total number of different types of transport	Entire existing public transport
11	Percentage of transport frequency	Percentages of the average amount that public transport transports passengers
12	Percentage of information made available	Percentage of information made available for users to have access to travel data
13	Time from the passenger's geographic location to the stop	Refers to the average time a passenger takes to arrive at the finish
14	Travel time (duration)	The average time it takes transport to travel the line
15	Waiting time	The average waiting time between the arrival and departure of the transport
16	Transfer time	The average time it takes a passenger to pass from one line to another is the time between leaving one transport and entering another
17	Total travel time	The average time is taken between the trip's origin and its destination
18	Punctuality rate	Percentage of public transport that are punctual on their itineraries
19	Percentage of electronic devices	Percentage of public transport that in real-time through electronic devices have information about schedules, delays, ticket purchases, etc.
20	Percentage of physical comfort	Percentage relative to the comfort of public transport, such as the transport's ambient temperature, humidity, cleanliness, noise level, availability of walking/sitting places, etc.
21	Percentage of stop conditions	If the stop has waiting for conditions such as coverage in case of bad weather, night lighting, benches, etc.

(*continued*)

Table 1. (*continued*)

Num	Data	Definition
22	Technological percentage	Transport that has charging sockets, wi-fi, among others
23	Accident percentage	Percentage of annual public transport accidents
24	Percentage of malfunctions	Percentage of annual public transport breakdowns
25	Theft percentages	Percentage of annual public transport robberies
26	Percentages of conditions	Percentage of the quality of the road where public transport runs
27	Hybrid vehicle percentages	Annual percentage of hybrid public transport
28	Percentages of gasoline and diesel vehicles	Annual percentage of gasoline and diesel-type public transport
29	Pollution percentages	Percentage of pollution from public transport: gases, noise level, energy consumption, etc.
30	Fuel cost	The average cost that the driver presents annually
31	Average distance between vehicle parking and desired location	Total of the average length the driver needs to make between where he leaves the car and the desired position
32	Availability rate of car parks	Percentage of availability that the car park has for personal vehicles
33	Percentage of public parks	Percentage of public parks that do not incur costs for car owners
34	Average park price	Cost of expenses in terms of parking in the park
35	Total travel time	The average time is from entering the park to finding a parking space
36	Parking search time	The average time the driver spends looking for a parking space for his vehicle
37	Punctuality Percentage	The average percentage of traffic in the parking process
38	Accident percentage	Percentage of annual individual vehicle accidents
39	Percentage of malfunctions	Percentage of annual individual vehicle breakdowns

(*continued*)

Table 1. (*continued*)

Num	Data	Definition
40	Theft percentage	Percentage of annual individual vehicle thefts
41	Percentage of pollution	Percentage of pollution of individual vehicles: gases, noise level, energy consumption, etc.
42	Percentage of physical comfort	Percentage of comfort about the park's ambient temperature, humidity, cleanliness, noise level, availability, etc.
43	Percentage of car park condition	Whether the car park has soil conditions (earth or cement), building conditions (open-air or enclosed parking) and lighting (dark or bright)
44	Technological percentage	Fee for car parks with real-time surveillance cameras of the car is parked
45	Percentage of payments with electronic systems	Percentage of car parks with an electronic payment system (credit, debit, mbway, among others)
46	Car wash parks	Parks have the possibility of washing the interior and exterior of the vehicle
47	Parks with charging for electric cars	Parks that have charging zones for hybrid and electric cars
48	Security check percentage	The percentage of parks with a security system allows for the prevention of robberies and robberies
49	Geographic location	Percentage of parks that are centrally located and close to business buildings and close to public transport

The data is survey results, and for each question, it is only possible to answer between 1 and 5, according to the Likert scale, except for the age, location, and preference between individual and public transport. This way, the data for these three variables were changed to a numeral scale with the panda's library. The name of all variables changed too for a simple name to simplify the data and clarify to which question each criterion corresponds. After the first release of the form, a new question was introduced. This question is "What type of transport do you prefer? Individual or public?". Consequently, this question has a lot of null values, and it was necessary to create a function so that all null values go to 0. The number chosen to represent the null values was selected at random.

4.2   Modelling and Evaluation

The first step of this stage was to select modelling techniques, and for this case, the K-modes method was used. This method was chosen because the variables are categorical (Sect. 2.2). Scenarios are subsets of the total data. The data obtained has two different areas (private and public transport). Thus, three scenarios were created to interpret the results and investigate significant differences (Table 2). Scenario A was studied with the total data set. Scenario B only with data relating to individual transport. And scenario C with the variables referring to public transport. Consequently, the model was built with the panda's library and assessed and interpreted the results.

Table 2. Scenario

Scenario	Variables	Technique
A	All	K-modes
B	Individual Transport Variables	K-modes
C	Public Transport Variables	K-modes

Evaluation is the part where it is necessary to look at the results and see which factors meet the business success criteria, which ones should be approved for the project, and the importance grade.

5   Results

It is essential to refer that these results are based on this specific sample and obtaining other results for other populations is possible. Two hundred eleven respondents actively

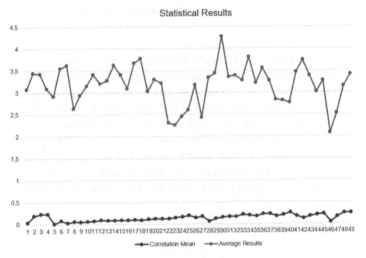

Fig. 2. Statistical results

participated in the form, and as expected, the minimum possible answer is one, and the maximum is 5. Most of the sample is between 18 and 24 years of age (63% of the total sample). As for geographic location, most of the answers are from the population of the North, occupying 61% of the entire model. Regarding the preference between public or individual transport, it must be considered that the question was only asked after the questionnaire was launched, with a sample of 76 people (36% of the total sample). However, it was found that 71% prefer individual transport.

Figure 2 presents a figure with the criteria associated with the average results and the correlation mean based correlation coefficient non-parametric Kendall's tau. For example, the criterion capacity percentage (number 3 in the figure) has an average response of 3.431 and an average correlation of 0.228.

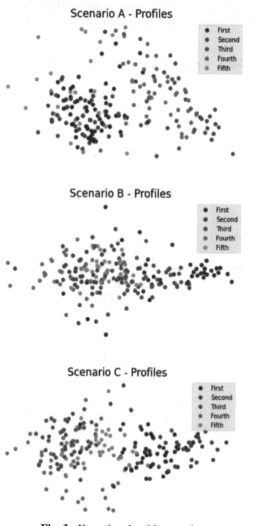

Fig. 3. K-modes algorithm results

484   F. Barros et al.

Subsequently, the K-Modes Clustering algorithm identified five profiles for three different scenarios. The Elbow method takes the ideal value of K at the point where the value does not significantly decrease with the addition of K (Sect. 2.2). These scenarios were defined in Sect. 4.2.

Figure 3 shows the differences between each system and cluster visually. All scenarios have five colours, meaning they have five different groups identified, and every colour represents a cluster.

The building model obtained the following results for each scenario (Table 3, Table 4 and Table 5). These results, for each cluster, indicate a certain amount of degree of importance. For scenario A, cluster 1 has 37 questions with an essential degree of 3. When the result is NaN, there is no question with an associated degree of importance. For scenario B, cluster 5 has a value NaN for the important degree of 2. To cluster 5, in scenario B, only the fuel cost variable has an essential degree of 5, and the percentage of physical comfort has a degree of 4. The rest of the variables all have a degree of 3.

Table 3. Results of scenario A with K-modes algorithm

Importance	Cluster 1	Cluster 2	Cluster 3	Cluster 4	Cluster 5
0	2	2	2	2	2
1	6	15	2	2	29
2	4	10	NaN	1	3
3	37	14	4	5	3
4	2	9	NaN	37	1
5	1	2	44	5	14

Table 4. Results of scenario B with K-modes algorithm

Importance	Cluster 1	Cluster 2	Cluster 3	Cluster 4	Cluster 5
0	2	2	2	2	2
1	3	3	1	11	1
2	NaN	5	1	2	NaN
3	NaN	11	1	4	18
4	NaN	2	16	1	1
5	18	NaN	2	3	1

Table 5. Results of scenario C with K-modes algorithm

Importance	Cluster 1	Cluster 2	Cluster 3	Cluster 4	Cluster 5
0	2	2	2	2	2
1	1	1	9	18	2
2	4	1	4	NaN	3
3	4	1	13	1	22
4	17	2	4	1	3
5	4	25	NaN	10	NaN

6 Discussion

The average of the correlations obtained for each question was calculated, and, in turn, the degree of importance of each criterion associated with the question was determined. The importance of degree 5 was defined by the requirements that present a mean more significant than three and a correlation level greater than 0.19. As expected, the answers diverged a lot, and therefore, the level of correlation is low. However, it should be noted that the questions percentage of capacity, passenger flow, rate of public car parks, parking search time, percentage of punctuality, percentage of technology, percentage of payments with electronic systems, allocation of security control and geographic location are those that respect the defined range.

Analyzing the cluster results, it is perceived that for the three scenarios studied, the variable age, location, and preference are constant in each cluster, with no value changes. This phenomenon is because the distribution of results is asymmetric. Both age and location represent more than half of the total percentage of the sample, 63% and 61%, respectively. Likewise, for the preference variable, it presents 135/211 answers without value. In conclusion, the impact these represent on the cluster is more potent and, therefore, more significant, assuming the most relevant characteristics in the analysis.

After analyzing the groups found by the K-Modes Clustering algorithm, it was possible to identify profiles of the importance each respondent gives to each variable. Since, for the northern region and ages between 18–24 years, five profiles were determined for each scenario. In scenario A, despite the classification of several profiles, in all identified clusters, the fuel cost has an importance level of 5. In scenario B, the variables: average park price and fuel cost, present in all clusters, except for the fifth, are of high importance (clusters 1, 3 and 4 take values of 5, and in cluster 2, they bring values of 4). In cluster 5, the fuel cost is the only variable with an essential degree of 5. In this way, their impact and importance on different groups are demonstrated. For scenario C, the variables: total capacity, percentage of occupancy and number of transfers between means of transport occupy a high degree of importance in clusters 2, 4 and 5. The number of transfers between means of transportation in cluster 1 also ranks five in importance.

These results are crucial to understanding which factors citizens prioritize. Variables that reach a higher value of importance are the ones that will be considered in the future stages of the study, as these are the critical variables that influence decision-making.

7 Conclusion

This work demonstrates, in this specific example, which variables citizens prioritize in the decision-making between public transport and private car. For another sample of data, the results may be different. The dispersion of existing values proves that people are sure which criteria they consider most important and those they prioritize in decision making. It was identified 5 clusters for three scenarios performed. It is essential to mention that there are extreme and median clusters in all scenarios available. For example, people who prioritize every variable in making a decision and other people who consider non-variable important. However, some believe that all variables have a median degree of importance. Other citizens are more critical and only vote 5 (highest significance level) for the variables central to them in decision making. They are more selective. It is a group that selects various levels of importance for different variables. Digital transformation of the cities must follow the population's priorities to add value to the town. They promote social well-being and sustainable, social, and economic development strategies. Similar studies were also reviewed, and the concept of parks and public transport was explored.

The tools and methodologies were previously studied so that the most appropriate for the study could be selected. For scenario A, the cost of fuel stands out. Average Park price and fuel cost are highlighted in scenario B. In scenario C, total capacity, occupancy percentage and number of transfers between modes of transport occupy a high degree of importance.

This study is a starting point for data collection and, consequently, to respond to the need to optimize and build intelligent models that meet the demands of the population and the city. The next step is building an OLAP (online analytical processing) and predictive models.

Acknowledgements. This work has also been developed under the scope of the project NORTE-01-0247-FEDER-045397, supported by the Northern Portugal Regional Operational Programme (NORTE 2020), under the Portugal 2020 Partnership Agreement, through the European Regional Development Fund (FEDER).

References

1. Amadebai, E.: The importance of data analysis in research—analytics for decisions 2022. https://www.analyticsfordecisions.com/importance-of-data-analysis-in-research/. Accessed 13 July 2022
2. Lima, F.: INE, Mobilidade e funcionalidade do territórionas Áreas Metropolitanas do Porto e de Lisboa 2017. Instituto Nacional de Estatística, Lisboa, 2018 (2018). https://www.ine.pt/xportal/xmain?xpid=INE&xpgid=ine_publicacoes&PUBLICACOESpub_boui=349495406&PUBLICACOESmodo=2&xlang=pt. Accessed 13 July 2022
3. Costa, A.: Manual de Planeamento das Acessibilidades e da GestãoViária (2008)
4. Litman, T.A.: Parking Management, vol. 32 (2021)
5. Saif, et al.: View of public transport accessibility: a literature review (2018). https://pp.bme.hu/tr/article/view/12072/8027. Accessed 30 March 2022

6. de Sousa, J.N.L.: Especificação de requisitos para o desenvolvimento de um sistema de apoio à decisão para gestão de transportespúblicos intermodais (2020)
7. Patil, V.: Clustering and profiling customers using k-means. Analytics Vidhya (2021). https://medium.com/analytics-vidhya/clustering-and-profiling-customers-using-k-means-9afa42 77427. Accessed 1 Apr 2022
8. Aprilliant, A.: The k-modes as clustering algorithm for categorical data type. Geek Culture (2021). https://medium.com/geekculture/the-k-modes-as-clustering-algorithm-for-categorical-data-type-bcde8f95efd7. Accessed 19 Apr 2022
9. Alves, G.: Unsupervised learning with K-means. Neuronio (2018). https://medium.com/neu ronio/unsupervised-learning-with-k-means-3eaa0666eebf. Accessed 1 Apr 2022
10. Naji, H.A.H., Wu, C., Zhang, H.: Understanding the impact of human mobility patterns on taxi drivers' profitability using clustering techniques: a case study in Wuhan. China Inf. **8**, 67 (2017). https://doi.org/10.3390/info8020067
11. Educ. Google Forms—Online Tools for Teaching & Learning (n.d.). https://blogs.umass.edu/onlinetools/assessment-centered-tools/google-forms/. Accessed 5 Apr 2022
12. Hammer, Ø., Harper, D.A.T., Ryan, P.D.: PAST - PAlaeontological Statistics, vol. 31 (2001)
13. Rodrigues, I.: CRISP-DM methodology leader in data mining and big data. Medium (2020). https://towardsdatascience.com/crisp-dm-methodology-leader-in-data-mining-and-big-data-467efd3d3781. Accessed 1 Apr 2022

An Exploratory Study on Hindcasting with Analogue Ensembles of Principal Components

Carlos Balsa[1]([✉]) [iD], Murilo M. Breve[1] [iD], Carlos V. Rodrigues[2] [iD],
Luís S. Costa[3] [iD], and José Rufino[1] [iD]

[1] Research Centre in Digitalization and Intelligent Robotics (CeDRI),
Instituto Politécnico de Bragança, Bragança, Portugal
{balsa,murilo.breve,rufino}@ipb.pt
[2] Vestas Wind Systems A/S, Design Centre Porto, Porto, Portugal
calvr@vestas.com
[3] Mountain Research Center (CIMO), Instituto Politécnico de Bragança,
Bragança, Portugal
lcosta@ipb.pt

Abstract. The aim of this study is the reconstruction of meteorological data that are missing in a given station by means of the data from neighbouring stations. To achieve this, the Analogue Ensemble (AnEn) method was applied to the Principal Components (PCs) of the time series dataset, computed via Principal Component Analysis. This combination allows exploring the possibility of reducing the number of meteorological variables used in the reconstruction. The proposed technique is greatly influenced by the choice of the number of PCs used in the data reconstruction. The number of favorable PC varies according to the predicted variable and weather station. This choice is directly linked to the variables correlation. The application of AnEn using PCs leads to improvements of 8% to 21% in the RMSE of wind speed.

Keywords: Hindcasting · Analogue ensembles · Principal Component Analysis · Time series

1 Introduction

Classical weather *hindcasting* is the recreation of past weather conditions by applying a forecast model on a past starting point (reanalysis). This is done to validate the forecast model if comparable past observations are available. It may also be used to derive absent past data (non-recorded past observations) from the forecast model (reconstruction).

Hindcasting is also a field of research aiming to improve methods in other fields of meteorology such as *downscaling* or *forecasting*. Meteorological data reconstruction techniques are essentially based on the Analogue Ensembles (AnEn) method [8,9]. Hindcasting with the AnEn method allows to reconstruct

T. Guarda et al. (Eds.): ARTIIS 2022, CCIS 1675, pp. 488–499, 2022.
https://doi.org/10.1007/978-3-031-20319-0_36

data of a meteorological variable i) based on data of other variable(s) at the same location, or ii) based on data of the same or other variable(s), from one or several nearby locations.

AnEn benefits from large training datasets. However, the amount of data that must be processed to determine the analogues sometimes makes the computational cost prohibitive [12]. Therefore, there is a great interest in improving the computational efficiency of the AnEn method. Concerning recent works that present solutions to improve the computational performance of the AnEn method, we highlight the development of the Parallel Analogue Ensemble (PAnEn) library [7] and of the cluster-based AnEn method [3].

This work exploits the reduction of the dimension of the number of meteorological variables by the application of Principal Components Analysis (PCA). PCA is widely used in multivariate statistics to reduce the dataset size, retaining only the most relevant information. In the context of forecasting, PCA has already been applied together with post processing techniques like Neural Networks (NN) and the AnEn method, to forecast wind power and solar radiation [5].

In this study, the PCA technique is used in the context of hindcasting. A total of five variables, recorded at a meteorological station, are reconstructed from the same variables recorded at two different neighbour stations.

We begin in Sect. 2 by presenting the dataset used in the study. In Sect. 3 the correlations between the different meteorological variables and stations are studied. Section 4 introduces the PCA technique and Sect. 5 revises the AnEn method. Section 6 is dedicated to the application of the AnEn method to the principal components, for the reconstruction of meteorological variables of a single station. Some final considerations are presented in Sect. 7.

2 Meteorological Dataset

The data used in this work was obtained from meteorological stations belonging to the Polytechnic Institute of Bragança (IPB). The oldest records started in 1999. The stations are located in the northeast region of Portugal, near the villages of Edroso (*latitude* : 41.912778; *longitude* : −7.152833), Soutelo (*latitude* : 41.92116; *longitude* : −6.808528) and Valongo (*latitude* : 41.923056; *longitude* : −6.950833), which are very close to the border line with Spain (see Fig. 1).

The meteorological variables available in this dataset, measured at each station, are: high relative humidity (HRH) [%]; air temperature ($ATMP$) [°C]; wind speed ($WSPD$) [m/s] averaged over a 30 min period; peak gust speed (GST) [m/s] during the same 30 min period; wind direction ($WDIR$) [°] from the North in a clockwise direction.

All three stations have data available from 2000 to 2007, with a sampling frequency of 30 min. However, one often finds time windows where there is no record, and also different time series intervals. To overcome these problems, an interpolation (nearest-neighbour or linear) was performed on the data, in order to standardize the data intervals to every 30 min. This interpolation process is limited to 4 missing values, since larger intervals could distort the data in an

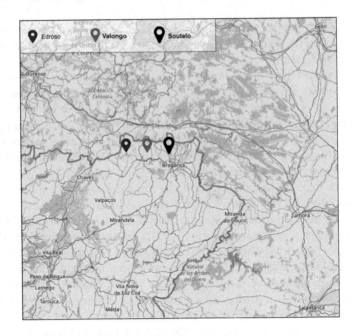

Fig. 1. Geolocation of the meteorological stations.

excessive manner. The filling of wider gaps in time series could be done through other techniques, namely based on Takens' theorem, which seeks to reconstitute the underlying dynamics of the time series (see [10], for instance). But these alternatives are yet to be exploited in future work.

Despite the interpolation process, a considerable amount of values not available (NA) persisted. Table 1 displays the number of missing values, the minimum and maximum values for each variable, and the percentage of data availability. The Valongo station has most data, while Soutelo is the sparsest.

In this work, the meteorological stations of Soutelo and Edroso are used as predictor stations, while Valongo is the predicted station. The data was separated into two datasets. The first has data for a training period, from the beginning of 2000 to the end of 2006. The second contains data from the year of 2007, for a prediction (reconstruction) period.

3   Data Correlation

Let the original multivariable historical dataset be represented by the matrix $H_0 \in \mathbb{R}^{m \times n}$, where m is the number of records of n meteorological variables ($n = 5$ in this work):

$$H_0 = \begin{bmatrix} h_0^1 \, h_0^2 \cdots h_0^n \end{bmatrix} \tag{1}$$

Each column of H_0 includes the historical dataset of one of the n variables.

Table 1. Meteorological datasets characterization.

Station	Variable	Min	Max	#NA	Availability (%)
Soutelo	WSPD	0	17	63915	47.93
	GST	0	30.3	49114	59.98
	WDIR	0,00	337.5	66628	45.71
	ATMP	−10.3	33.6	63915	47.93
	HRH	10.0	100	65353	46.75
Edroso	WSPD	0	113.5	27330	77.73
	GST	0	114.0	27330	77.73
	WDIR	0	337.5	56898	77.73
	ATMP	−32.10	33.2	28411	76.85
	HRH	9	100	28410	76.86
Valongo	WSPD	0	10.3	18279	85.11
	GST	0	19.2	18279	85.11
	WDIR	0	337.5	20253	83.50
	ATMP	−9.60	40.1	18307	85.08
	HRH	−11.0	100	18307	85.08

The matrix of the means of the observations for each variable is given by

$$\bar{H}_0 = \begin{bmatrix} \bar{h}_0^1 \, \bar{h}_0^2 \cdots \bar{h}_0^n \end{bmatrix} \tag{2}$$

where $\bar{h}_0^i \in \mathbb{R}^{m \times 1}$, for $i = 1, \ldots, n$, is a constant vector with value $\bar{h}_0^i$. Including the standard deviation s_i of each variable $i = 1, \ldots, n$, in a diagonal matrix $S \in \mathbb{R}^{n \times n}$ and subtracting the means and dividing by the standard deviation of each observation leads to the matrix of the scaled meteorological variables:

$$H = S^{-1}\left(H_0 - \bar{H}_0\right) = \begin{bmatrix} \dfrac{h_0^1 - \bar{h}_0^1}{s_1} \, \dfrac{h_0^2 - \bar{h}_0^2}{s_2} \cdots \dfrac{h_0^n - \bar{h}_0^n}{s_n} \end{bmatrix} = [h_1 \, h_2 \cdots h_n] \tag{3}$$

The matrix H is then used to obtain the correlation matrix, given by

$$C = \frac{1}{m} H^T H \tag{4}$$

where each (i, j)-entry of the matrix C is the correlation between the meteorological variables h_0^i and h_0^j.

Figure 2 shows the correlation between the five variables, for each station. It can be observed that $WSPD$ and GST were the most correlated variables. HRH and $ATMP$ showed inverse correlation almost equally in all stations. At Valongo station, $WSPD$ and GST presented a low correlation with $WDIR$ and $ATMP$; also, HRH was somewhat inversely correlated with $WSPD$ and GST.

Similarly, Fig. 3 presents the correlations between stations, for all the five variables. The three stations showed high correlation in the $ATMP$ and HRH.

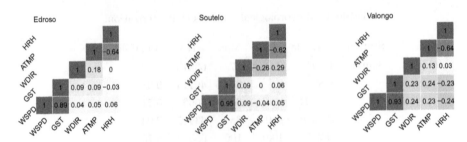

Fig. 2. Correlation between variables.

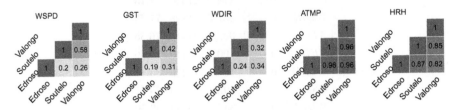

Fig. 3. Correlation between stations.

Between Valongo and Soutelo, $WSPD$ and GST showed a moderate correlation and a slightly lesser correlation from Edroso and Valongo. It is worth noting that all the variables presented some degree of correlation.

4   Principal Components Analysis of the Dataset

The main goal of PCA is to define a few number of new variables that replace all the original ones without loss of information. The number of new variables must be as small as possible in order to facilitate computational processing. This is achieved by the thin singular value decomposition of the data matrix H.

Assuming that $H \in \mathbb{R}^{m \times n}$ is the scaled data matrix, previously introduced in Eq. (4), the singular value decomposition of H is given by

$$H = U \Sigma V^T \tag{5}$$

where $U \in \mathbb{R}^{m \times n}$, $\Sigma \in \mathbb{R}^{n \times n}$ and $V \in \mathbb{R}^{m \times n}$ (see [6]). The diagonal matrix Σ contains the singular values σ_i of H, for $i = 1, \ldots, n$, where $\sigma_1 > \sigma_2 > \ldots > \sigma_n$. The right singular vectors v_i are called the *principal components directions* of H.

The vector

$$z_1 = H v_1 \tag{6}$$

has the largest sample variance, given by σ_1^2/m, amongst all normalized linear combinations of the columns of H. Vector z_1 represents the first new variable and is called the first principal component (PC_1). The second principal component (PC_2) is $z_2 = H v_2$ because v_2 corresponds to the second largest variance (σ_2^2/m), and the remaining principal components are defined similarly. The new variables are linear combinations of the columns of H, i.e., they are linear combinations of the normalized variables $h_1, h_2, \ldots, h_n$:

$$z_i = v_{1i}h_1 + v_{2i}h_2 + \ldots + v_{ni}h_n \quad \text{for} \quad i = 1, 2, \ldots, n \tag{7}$$

where the coefficients v_{ji}, $j = 1, 2, \ldots, n$ (named *loadings*) are the entries of the vector v_i. The magnitude of a coefficient is related to the relative importance of the corresponding variable to the given principal component.

The substitution criterion of the original variables by a few of the new variables must take into account the influence of the new variable on the variance of the original data. This influence is directly related to singular values. Usually, the first few principal components, corresponding to the largest singular values, account for a large proportion of the total variance, so they are all that is needed for future analyses [11].

A decomposition into principal components (*PCs*) of the five original meteorological variables was performed. Tables 2 and 3 show the loadings (entries of the vectors v_i) of each *PC* in the case of the stations of Soutelo and Edroso. The Valongo station did not participate in this analysis because it was used only as the predicted station. Additionally, it is also included the proportion between the variance of each *PC* and the sum of the variances over all the *PCs*.

Table 2. Variable loadings in each PC and variance proportion of each PC.

Station	Variable	PC_1	PC_2	PC_3	PC_4	PC_5
Soutelo	*WSPD*	0.616	−0.341	0.058	−0.067	0.704
	GST	0.611	−0.352	0.047	0.034	−0.706
	WDIR	0.267	0.338	−0.901	−0.037	0.001
	ATMP	−0.278	−0.574	−0.326	0.694	0.058
	HRH	0.313	0.561	0.274	0.714	0.043
	Variance Proportion	**0.404**	**0.350**	**0.161**	**0.075**	**0.010**
Edroso	*WSPD*	−0.668	0.221	−0.089	−0.061	−0.701
	GST	−0.684	0.166	−0.057	0.120	0.699
	WDIR	−0.137	−0.144	0.962	0.178	−0.053
	ATMP	−0.218	−0.670	0.002	−0.707	0.058
	HRH	0.132	0.675	0.251	−0.671	0.114
	Variance Proportion	**0.385**	**0.330**	**0.199**	**0.067**	**0.020**

Table 2 presents the coefficients that multiply each variable into the principal components. It shows that for both stations, PC_1 mainly contains the effects of the variables *WSPD*, *GST*, and accounted for 40.4% of all the variance. These are wind-related variables, and therefore more correlated, in according with Fig. 2. The 2nd PC mainly reflects the effect of the *ATMP* and *HRH*, the second highest correlation between variables. Note also that the 3nd PC is essentially dominated by the $WDIR$. Regarding the variance proportion, the 2nd and 3rd PC represent 35.0% and 16.1% of the total variance, respectively.

It should be mentioned that for Soutelo, PC_1, PC_2 and PC_3 accounted for 91.5% of all variances and, for Edroso, the three PCs accounted for 91.4%. This shows that in addition to presenting the same PC decomposition pattern, both stations also showed almost the same proportion of variance in the first three components.

Table 3. Variable loadings in each PC and variance proportion of each PC, without the $WDIR$ variable.

Station	Variable	PC_1	PC_2	PC_3	PC_4
Soutelo	$WSPD$	0.677	−0.201	0.060	−0.705
	GST	0.674	−0.213	−0.034	0.706
	$ATMP$	−0.195	−0.681	−0.703	−0.053
	HRH	0.219	0.671	−0.706	−0.042
	Variance proportion	**0.496**	**0.400**	**0.092**	**0.012**
Edroso	$WSPD$	−0.562	0.439	−0.069	−0.698
	GST	−0.582	0.391	0.023	0.712
	$ATMP$	−0.401	−0.591	−0.699	0.020
	HRH	0.429	0.551	−0.711	0.072
	Variance proportion	**0.568**	**0.331**	**0.088**	**0.013**

Table 3, similarly to Table 2, shows the contribution of each variable in each principal component, but without $WDIR$ in the analysis. It can be observed that, for Edroso, the variable loadings are more evenly distributed for PC_1 and PC_2. However, at both stations, the same pattern observed with $WDIR$ repeats in the first two components. That is, the predominance of wind-related variables in PC_1 and temperature-related ($ATMP$ and HRH) in PC_2.

As expected, since there are only 4 variables in the analysis, the first three components represent 98.8% and 98.7% of the proportion of variance, respectively for Soutelo and Edroso. This shows that by decreasing the number of variables in the analysis, it is possible to keep more information in the first principal components and, at the same time, have less information overall.

5   AnEn Method

The AnEn method can be used for reconstruction of missing or incomplete data from a weather station. The data is reconstructed according to a database of predictor stations close to the one with missing data.

The AnEn method also allows using more than one predictor station (or variable). In this case, the data from the predictor stations (or variables) can be used either dependently or independently (i.e., with the analogues selected in different predictor series having to overlap in time, or not – see [1] and [2]).

In Fig. 4 the AnEn method uses a time series with two stations, one with historical data (predictor station) and another with observed data (predicted station). The historical data is complete, while the observed data is missing in the prediction period. In this study, the available historical data ranges from 2000 to the end of 2006 and the reconstruction period is 2007.

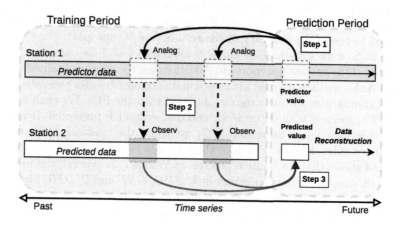

Fig. 4. Hindcasting with the Analogue Ensembles method.

Firstly (step 1), a certain number of analogues are selected in the historical dataset, due to being the past observations most similar to a predictor at instant t. Both the predictor and the analogues are vectors of $2k + 1$ elements, where each element is the value of a meteorological variable at successive $2k+1$ instants of the same time window, and $k > 0$ is an integer that represents the width of each half-window (into the past, and into the future) around the central instant of the time window. In this study $k = 1$, which is equivalent to saying that each time window corresponds to one hour (records are made every 30 min).

Note that comparing vectors, instead of single values, accounts for the evolutionary trend of the meteorological variable around the central instant of the time window, allowing for the selection of analogues to take into consideration weather patterns instead of single isolated values.

In step 2, the analogues map onto observations in the training period (years from 2000 to 2006) of the predicted station. This mapping is done only for the central instant of the analogue time window, meaning that for each analogue vector a single observational value is selected in the observation dataset.

Finally, in step 3, the observations selected in the training period are used to predict (hindcast) the missing value, through its average, weighted or not. When this value is actually available as real observational data (as it happens in this work), it then becomes possible to assess the prediction/reconstruction error.

In this study the AnEn method is applied to the PCs instead of the original variables. This means the historical dataset variables are replaced by the PCs.

6   Hindcasting with AnEn Method on PCs

In this section the AnEn method is applied to a hindcasting problem with the dataset presented in Sect. 2. Several experiments were conducted with the aim of evaluating the effects of using principal components instead of the original historical variables. The Bias error (BIAS) and the root mean square error (RMSE) were used to assess the accuracy of the results (see [4] apropos).

The tests were divided into three combinations of PCs, according to the magnitude of the variance proportion. Additionally, the results obtained with the classical AnEn method applied to the original variables are also presented, allowing for a comparison with the results obtained with the PCs. For each combination of PCs, one test with dependency and one without is presented. It is important to note that when using only PC_1, or using the classical AnEn method, there cannot exist dependency, since there is only one time-series (see [3]).

Table 4 shows that for Soutelo predicting Valongo, in general, the use of two or three PCs results in smaller errors in $WSPD$, GST and $WDIR$. Meanwhile, AnEn was superior in comparison to all PC combination in the HRH and $ATMP$ variables, with the exception of the BIAS measure in the HRH.

Table 4. Valongo variables predicted by Soutelo PCs and by the classical AnEn.

Soutelo predicting Valongo								
Variable	Dependency	1 PC		2 PC		3 PC		AnEn	
		BIAS	RMSE	BIAS	RMSE	BIAS	RMSE	BIAS	RMSE
WSPD	Yes	−0.131	0.763	−0.052	**0.647**	−0.079	0.654	−0.079	0.708
	No	—		−**0.040**	0.725	−0.057	0.761	—	
GST	Yes	−0.285	1.781	−0.089	**1.499**	−0.154	1.517	−0.240	1.643
	No	—		−**0.062**	1.724	−0.092	1.822	—	
WDIR	Yes	1.248	1.749	1.230	1.743	1.256	1.781	1.275	1.835
	No	—		1.230	1.731	**1.226**	**1.726**	—	
ATMP	Yes	−1.177	8.546	0.481	4.325	−0.955	4.217	**−0.077**	**2.306**
	No	—		−0.424	6.173	−1.411	6.604	—	
HRH	Yes	−4.182	19.885	−8.755	18.696	−5.139	15.741	−5.05	**13.888**
	No	—		−6.163	16.742	−**4.046**	16.279	—	

In turn, Table 5 shows the results of Valongo variables predicted by Edroso PCs. It can also be observed that, for most variables, the smallest errors are obtained with two or three PCs. The AnEn method achieves good results in the case of the RMSE measure in the $ATMP$ and HRH variables.

Table 5. Valongo variables predicted by Edroso PCs and by the classical AnEn.

Edroso predicting Valongo									
Variable	Dependency	1 PC		2 PC		3 PC		AnEn	
		BIAS	RMSE	BIAS	RMSE	BIAS	RMSE	BIAS	RMSE
WSPD	Yes	−0.061	0.702	−0.044	**0.684**	−0.047	0.706	**−0.042**	0.857
	No	—		−0.043	0.741	**−0.042**	0.757	—	
GST	Yes	−0.075	1.636	−0.043	**1.600**	−0.052	1.652	−0.049	1.879
	No	—		**−0.035**	1.767	−0.031	1.814	—	
WDIR	Yes	0.632	1.755	0.633	1.755	**0.606**	**1.698**	0.619	1.786
	No	—		0.631	1.746	0.635	1.754	—	
ATMP	Yes	−0.512	8.149	0.351	4.125	0.228	4.025	−0.188	**2.777**
	No	—		0.066	5.891	**−0.014**	6.835	—	
HRH	Yes	**−0.903**	18.882	−3.049	18.042	−3.018	17.528	−8.150	**16.617**
	No	—		−2.281	16.499	−2.191	16.758	—	

Table 6. Valongo variables predicted by Soutelo PCs and by the original AnEn method without the $WDIR$ variable.

Soutelo predicting Valongo									
Variable	Dependency	1 PC		2 PC		3 PC		AnEn	
		BIAS	RMSE	BIAS	RMSE	BIAS	RMSE	BIAS	RMSE
WSPD	Yes	−0.063	0.724	**−0.030**	0.651	−0.018	**0.645**	−0.079	0.708
	No	—		−0.043	0.721	−0.041	0.759	—	
GST	Yes	0.108	1.681	0.040	1.500	**−0.006**	1.469	−0.240	1.643
	No	—		−0.062	1.715	−0.052	1.817	—	
ATMP	Yes	−1.538	8.832	−0.532	4.150	−0.173	**2.097**	**0.077**	2.306
	No	—		−1.049	6.024	−1.141	6.188	—	
HRH	Yes	**3.118**	19.911	−5.612	16.373	−4.947	13.965	5.018	**13.888**
	No	—		−4.504	15.451	−3.591	15.238	—	

Tables 6 and 7 concern to the same type of experiments presented in Tables 4 and 5, but now without the wind direction ($WDIR$) variable. Thus, in these tests the $WDIR$ variable was not used to obtain the PCs.

In Table 6, relative to Valongo predicted by Soutelo, the best scores of RMSE are generally obtained with three PCs, with the exception of the HRH variable, where the smallest RMSE is obtained with the AnEn method.

In the case of Valongo predicted by Edroso (Table 7), the lowest errors obtained were more equally distributed among the different combinations of components. But PC_3 still remained superior in two ($ATMP$ and HRH) of the four variables analyzed.

Without $WDIR$ in the analysis, the method was able to predict the $ATMP$ and HRH variables more successfully at both stations. For example, in comparison to the analysis with all the 5 variables, $ATMP$ had an RMSE decrease

Table 7. Valongo variables predicted by Edroso PCs and by the original AnEn method without the $WDIR$ variable.

Edroso predicting Valongo

Variable	Dependency	1 PC		2 PC		3 PC		AnEn	
		BIAS	RMSE	BIAS	RMSE	BIAS	RMSE	BIAS	RMSE
WSPD	Yes	**−0.035**	0.813	−0.063	**0.792**	−0.079	0.814	−0.042	0.857
	No	—		−0.036	0.828	−0.042	0.836	—	
GST	Yes	−0.058	1.957	−0.124	1.884	−0.163	1.944	**−0.049**	**1.879**
	No	—		−0.068	1.999	−0.076	2.024	—	
ATMP	Yes	0.055	6.056	0.430	3.990	−0.299	**2.683**	−0.188	2.777
	No	—		0.444	5.479	**0.003**	5.549	—	
HRH	Yes	**−3.163**	15.361	−4.258	15.762	−5.708	**15.012**	−8.150	16.617
	No	—		−4.192	15.052	−4.607	15.253	—	

of 50.27% at Soutelo, which allowed the 3 PC combination to outperform the classic method (AnEN).

The predictions of the wind-related variables were weakened by the absence of wind direction at Edroso, since the $WSPD$ and GST errors increased. This was not observed at the Soutelo station, indicating that only at Edroso the $WDIR$ was important towards predicting the wind-related variables.

7   Conclusion

This study explores the possibility of applying the AnEn method to principal components instead of original variables. The results show that this technique is effective in reconstructing wind-dependent variables, allowing to reduce the number of original variables to be processed in the historical dataset. Such reduction happens because the variables are correlated with each other. Consequently, the five original variables can be replaced by only two or three principal components.

With the $WDIR$ in the analysis, the effectiveness of the reconstruction is not as good in the non-wind dependent variables, such as relative humidity and temperature. The presence of wind direction can slightly improve the prediction of wind-related variables at Edroso, but at the cost of significantly worsening the $ATMP$ and HRH reconstruction at both stations. Therefore, the non-presence of $WDIR$ promoted more balanced predictions among the variables, enabling the combination of 3 PC to have lower errors in 6 out of 8 RMSE measures.

This study was very conditioned by the dataset used, where there are many missing records. On the other hand, most of the variables, with the exception of the wind-dependent variables, are not correlated with each other and, therefore, it is difficult to reduce their dimension.

In the future, we plan to apply the same methodology to better-quality datasets, already used in previous research. Such will also allow to better assess the virtues of this new approach, in comparison to others already investigated.

Acknowledgement. This work has been supported by FCT - Fundação para a Ciência e Tecnologia within the Project Scope: UIDB/05757/2020.

References

1. Balsa, C., Rodrigues, C.V., Lopes, I., Rufino, J.: Using analog ensembles with alternative metrics for hindcasting with multistations. ParadigmPlus **1**(2), 1–17 (2020). https://journals.itiud.org/index.php/paradigmplus/article/view/11

2. Balsa, C., Rodrigues, C.V., Araújo, L., Rufino, J.: Hindcasting with cluster-based analogues. In: Guarda, T., Portela, F., Santos, M.F. (eds.) ARTIIS 2021. CCIS, vol. 1485, pp. 346–360. Springer, Cham (2021). https://doi.org/10.1007/978-3-030-90241-4_27

3. Balsa, C., Rodrigues, C.V., Araújo, L., Rufino, J.: Cluster-based analogue ensembles for hindcasting with multistations. Computation **10**(6), 91 (2022). https://doi.org/10.3390/computation10060091

4. Chai, T., Draxler, R.R.: Root mean square error (RMSE) or mean absolute error (MAE)? – arguments against avoiding RMSE in the literature. Geosci. Model Dev. **7**(3), 1247–1250 (2014). https://doi.org/10.5194/gmd-7-1247-2014

5. Davò, F., Alessandrini, S., Sperati, S., Monache, L.D., Airoldi, D., Vespucci, M.T.: Post-processing techniques and principal component analysis for regional wind power and solar irradiance forecasting. Solar Energy **134**, 327–338 (2016). https://doi.org/10.1016/j.solener.2016.04.049

6. Eldén, L.: Matrix Methods in Data Mining and Pattern Recognition. SIAM, Philadelphia (2007)

7. Hu, W., Vento, D., Su, S.: Parallel analog ensemble - the power of weather analogs. In: Proceedings of the 2020 Improving Scientific Software Conference, pp. 1–14. NCAR, May 2020. https://doi.org/10.5065/P2JJ-9878

8. Monache, L.D., Eckel, F.A., Rife, D.L., Nagarajan, B., Searight, K.: Probabilistic weather prediction with an analog ensemble. Mon. Weather Rev. **141**(10), 3498–3516 (2013). https://doi.org/10.1175/mwr-d-12-00281.1

9. Monache, L.D., Nipen, T., Liu, Y., Roux, G., Stull, R.: Kalman filter and analog schemes to postprocess numerical weather predictions. Mon. Weather Rev. **139**(11), 3554–3570 (2011). https://doi.org/10.1175/2011mwr3653.1

10. Paparella, F.: Filling gaps in chaotic time series. Phys. Lett. A **346**(1–3), 47–53 (2005). https://doi.org/10.1016/j.physleta.2005.07.076

11. Spence, L., Insel, A., Friedberg, S.: Elementary Linear Algebra: A Matrix Approach. Pearson Education Limited, London (July 2013)

12. Vannitsem, S., et al.: Statistical postprocessing for weather forecasts: Review, challenges, and avenues in a big data world. Bull. Am. Meteorol. Soc. **102**(3), E681–E699 (2021). https://doi.org/10.1175/bams-d-19-0308.1

Classification of Food Types in a Box with Gas Sensors Using a Machine Learning Method. Case Study of Intelligent Electronic Nose

Alicia Montoro-Lendínez[1], Nuno Pombo[2], Bruno Silva[2],
Macarena Espinilla-Estévez[1], and Javier Medina-Quero[1(✉)]

[1] Department of Computer Science, University of Jaén, Jaén, Spain
{amlendin,mestevez,jmquero}@ujaen.es
[2] Department of Informatics, University of Beira Interior, Covilhã, Portugal
{ngpombo,bsilva}@di.ubi.pt

Abstract. The Active and Assisted Living (AAL) paradigm has helped the expansion of the use of sensors, which is increasingly common in research work related to activity monitoring. However, one of the major disadvantages found in using sensors inside the home or other types of environment to monitor activities is the non-acceptance by users of having sensors around them because they may see their privacy compromised. Therefore, nowadays it is important to search for non-invasive and low-cost sensors that provide the user with the security and accessibility to feel comfortable with them. In this work a case study has been carried out with the design and construction of a Metal Oxide Semiconductors (MOS) sensor array with which it is intended to monitor the type of food used in the kitchen by means of the K-Nearest Neighbours (K-NN) machine learning method. Specifically, the case study presented seeks to differentiate between bananas, lemons, chorizo and prawns in a first approach as an intelligent electronic nose. Gas sensors have been used to take advantage of their non-invasive character for the user, although the disadvantage of not being widely explored in the scientific literature has been found. The results obtained in the case study presented in this paper to classify these four foods have been promising to advance in this research topic.

Keywords: Gas sensors · Metal oxide semiconductors sensors · Classification of food · k-nearest neighbors · Intelligent electronic nose

Funding for this research is provided by EU Horizon 2020 Pharaon Project 'Pilots for Healthy and Active Ageing', Grant agreement no. 857188. This contribution has been supported by the Spanish Institute of Health ISCIII by means of the project DTS21-00047 and by the Spanish Government under the project RTI2018-098979-A-I00 MCIN/AEI/10.13039/501100011033/, FEDER "Una manera de hacer Europa".

T. Guarda et al. (Eds.): ARTIIS 2022, CCIS 1675, pp. 500–510, 2022.
https://doi.org/10.1007/978-3-031-20319-0_37

1   Introduction

Nowadays, there are paradigms such as Active and Assisted Living (AAL) which looks for the improvement of life's quality of elderly and disabled people with the aim of a more friendly integration into society. In order to achieve this, a variety of technologies are used in the daily life of these people [15].

Due to this trend of using technology to improve human life, paradigms, such as the Internet of Things (IoT) paradigm, have been extending to areas such as home life or life support [6]. IoT in one of its definitions is constituted as a connection of a network of physical objects or devices where these smart objects have the ability to self-manage, share information, data, resources, react and act against situations and changes in the environment [10].

One of these smart objects are sensors, whose use has spread throughout the world and in different applications. Sensors are used to measure different magnitudes and can be of many different types: audio, vision, presence, temperature, etc. There is a wide variety of sensing technologies, some cheaper than others, some with greater accuracy and sensitivity and with different sizes and shapes.

However, it is not all advantages, and the use of some of these sensors in home applications has a major limitation. This major limitation is the lack of privacy, which leads to a discomfort on the part of users to use these devices in their homes.

Therefore this proposal is based on the use of gas sensors to identify different 4 types of food (lemon, banana, prawns and chorizo). Benefiting from a great characteristic of gas sensors, their non-invasiveness. In the process of generating the first tests for a future prototype capable of monitoring human activity in the kitchen.

This work is structured as follows. Section 2 presents a review of the literature related to different gas detection technologies and current applications using gas sensors. Section 3 presents the materials and methods carried out. Then, Sect. 4 continues with the case study. Finally, Sect. 5 gives the conclusions and future lines of work.

2   Related Works

This section, on the one hand, reviews the different existing gas sensing technologies and, on the other hand, the current IoT devices or applications based on gas sensing.

2.1   Gas Sensing Technologies

The differences between the various gas sensing technologies reside in the various methods of gas detection. While some sensor use physical variables such as the speed of propagation of light and sound, others sensors use the reaction of the target gas with the sensing element.

The following is a description of the most popular gas sensors that will be used in our proposal.

- *Electrochemical*
  This type of sensor consists of a membrane which separates the ambient gases from the electrolyte solution and uses chemical reactions to detect the target gas. Speed of the reaction is proportional to the concentration of the target gas present [13].
- *Metal Oxide Semiconductors (MOS)*
  This type is generally applied to detect target gases through redox reactions between the target gases and the oxide surface. The process has two stages. A first stage where the redox reaction takes place and results in an electronic variation of the oxide surface and, a second stage where the previous electronic variation results in a variation of the electrical resistance of the sensor [19].
- *Catalytic*
  In this type of sensor, there is a variation of the internal resistance and an increase in temperature when there is contact between the catalytic element and the combustible gases in the environment, which is how the detection takes place [8].
- *Polymers*
  These types of gas sensors are more sensitive to inorganic gases, such as ammonia and some volatile organic compounds (VOCs). For this reason, in general, they are most commonly used to detect solvent vapours in gas phase, such as aromatic compounds, alcohols or halogenated compounds and a wide range of VOCs but some studies apply them to the detection of inorganic gases such as CO_2 and H_2O. Their mode of detection is the same as MOS, in this case the polymer layers change upon exposure to the target gas [7].
- *Carbon Nanotubes*
  This type of sensor with electrical properties is very sensitive to small quantities of gases at ambient temperature without the need for heating and without the need for a pre-concentration phase. Examples of such gases are alcohol, ammonia (NH_3), carbon dioxide (CO_2) and nitrogen oxide (NO_x) [9].
- *Acoustics*
  This type of sensor uses the different speeds of sound propagation depending on the gases present in the environment to detect them. This can be through signal attenuation, sound velocity, acoustic impedance or a mix of some of them. [14].
- *Optic*
  This type of sensor is similar in behaviour to acoustic sensors in that it uses waves. But it type of sensor makes use of the different wavelength absorption properties of gases to detect them [4].

2.2   Applicactions Based on Gas Sensing

Gas sensing is very diverse and can be applied to different areas. For instance, in the food sector, Chen et al. [3] design an electronic nose (E-Nose) in combination with a camera to classify the ripening time of bananas into 4 stages: unripe, half ripe, fully ripe and overripe.

Also in the same sector, Ramón Aparicio et al. [1] have developed a work where they detect the rancid defect of virgin olive oil with an E-Nose. To select the sensors which compose the E-Nose, they use a training set from admixtures of virgin olive oil from Portuguese origin with different percentages (0–100%) of a rancid standard oil. Other authors such as Chen, Jun et al. [2] have presented a paper where their aim was to detect and predict the freshness of beef, pork and lamb and classify it into three states: fresh, sub-fresh and putrid. The results were quite good and encouraging with accuracies of 89.5%, 84.2% and 94.7% for pork, beef and lamb, respectively.

In other sectors such as the animal sector, there are some scientific works like the one by Manzoli, Alexandra et al. [11] which present the use of an E-Nose for monitoring volatile compounds as an indicator of the fertile period of bovine females with the aim of providing an improvement in genetics and in the control of genetic or acquired diseases. In addition, Cramp, A. P. et al. [5] have developed an E-Nose to detect cutaneous myiasis in sheep. This disease is debilitating, painful and potentially lethal for sheep and early detection, which is currently difficult, will allow sheep to be treated in time without it spreading through the flock.

In the health sector, there is some work such as the work by Westenbrink, E. et al. [18] where they present the development and application of an E-Nose to detect colorectal cancer (CRC). They used 92 urine samples from CRC patients, irritable bowel syndrome (IBS) patients and controls to detect through the E-Nose. Also, Yu, Kai et al. [20] present an E-Nose dedicated to home healthcare. This E-Nose is able to detect benign lung diseases, such as pneumonia and pneumoconiosis and is able to perform with high accuracy a classification between healthy control or lung cancer patients.

So this literature review shows that the use of this type of E-Nose composed of gas sensors have a wide variety of applications but all of them with good results and with the advantages of being non-invasive. At the same time there are a wide range of gas sensing technologies, some cheaper than others, some more suitable for certain conditions. Taking into account all this, our proposal, based on the collection and subsequent analysis of data derived from the recognition of food in the kitchen, will be carried out thanks to the design of an array of MOS type sensors, whose main advantage is its low cost.

3   Materials and Methods

This section presents the materials used in the proposal and includes the selection of the gas sensors and the architecture of components.

3.1   Gas Sensor Selection to the E-Nose

This subsection details the selection of gas sensors used to the sensor array or E-Nose to monitor the type of food used in the kitchen by means of machine learning methods.

This E-Nose is composed with MOS sensors. However, in the wide range of gas sensor devices, Figaro sensors have been selected because they have provided a prominent performance in scientific and technical field [3,12,16,17].

In this contribution, the selection of devices, which have been integrated to configure E-Nose, are shown in the Table 1.

Table 1. Sensors type used in the sensor array.

Sensor type	Main applications
2600	Hydrogen, Hydrocarbons
2602	Ammonia, Hydrogen Sulfide (high sensitivity to VOC and odorous gases
2610	Alcohols, Butane, Liquid Petroleum Gas, Propane
2611	Natural Gas, Methane
2620	VOC, Alcohols, Organic Solvents Steam

3.2 Architecture of the Intelligent E-Nose

The architecture of the proposed intelligent E-Nose is presented in this section. The general architecture is shown in Fig. 1 which integrates a smart board with the array of gas sensors.

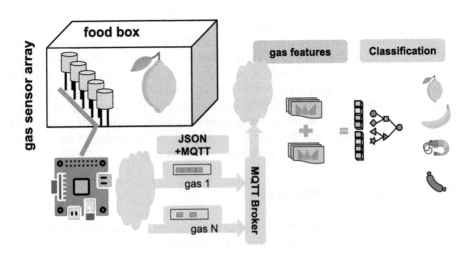

Fig. 1. Arquitecture of components

The components of the architecture are described as follows:

- **Raspberry Pi 4 Model B.** This is the development board used to collect the data from the sensor array to send it to the database and display it. In short, it is the one responsible for data flow control.
- **MCP3008 chip.** This integrated chip is an analogue to digital converter with 8 channels and 10 bits resolution. Thanks to this integrated chip the Raspberry Pi is able to read the values of the sensor array as it provides it with an analogue/digital converter pin that it does not have by default.
- **Figaro sensors.** These sensors make up the array in charge of detecting the different gases. They have all been described in Table 1.
- **Nipron HPCSA Desktop PC Power Supply.** The sensor array requires an external power supply for proper operation due to the fact that the voltage pins of the Raspberry Pi are not enough.

In Fig. 2 is illustrated the schematic diagram of connections of the proposed intelligent E-Nose.

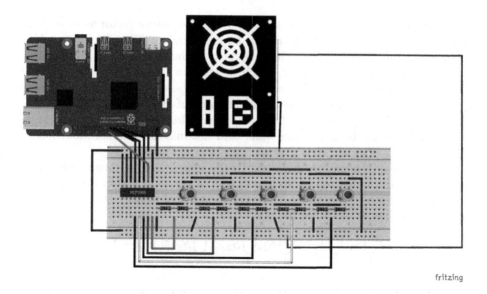

Fig. 2. Schematic diagram of connections.

Furthemore, a controller in Python has been developed for measuring the gas sensors in real-time and distributing under MQTT using JSON format to provide value and timestamp for each sensor which is defined in a given topic. The controller runs within the Raspberry Pi under an edge computing paradigm, providing: persistence, publication in real-time under MQTT and dashboard with the visualization from previous information under ssh. The Raspberry Pi also includes computational capabilities to develop machine learning in streaming for future work proposal.

3.3 Features and Classification with Machine Learning Methods from Gas Sensor Streams

In this section, the machine learning methods for processing the gas sensor streams collected by the E-Nose is presented in order to classify the nearest food box are described.

To do so, a sensor s collects data in real time in the form of a pair $\overline{s_i} = \{s_i, t_i\}$, where s_i represents a given measurement and t_i the timestamp. Thus, the data stream of the sensor source s is defined by $\overline{S_s} = \{\overline{s_0}, \ldots, \overline{s_i}\}$ and a given value in a timestamp t_i by $S_s(t_i) = s_i$.

The opening and closing of the food determine a window size of a time interval $W_w = [W_w^-, W_w^+]$ which enable segmenting the samples of a the sensor streams $\overline{S_s}$, which aggregates the values $\overline{s_i}$ by means of a :

$$\bigcup S_s \cap W_w = \bigcup_{s_i}^{\overline{s_i}} s_i, t_i \in [W_w^-, W_w^+] \tag{1}$$

Next, several aggregation functions $\bigcup$ define the feature vector for describing the sensor stream S_s. In this work, we have determine: $Tbasal)$ $\bigcup = t_0$ which determines the basal value of the food box at the beginning of the opening $s_i, t_i = W_w^-$, $Tmax)$ $\bigcup = max$ which determines the maximal value of the food box between the opening and closing $max(s_i)t_i \in [W_w^-, W_w^+]$, , $Tmin)$ $\bigcup = min$ which determines the minimal value of the food box between the opening and closing $min(s_i)t_i \in [W_w^-, W_w^+]$. and $Tinc)$ $\bigcup = \Delta$, which represents the higher interval between basal value and maximal or minimal $max(max - t_0(S_s \cap W_w), t_0 - min(S_s \cap W_w))$.

So, all sensor streams are described by the aggregation functions configuring a feature vector which represents the signals of the food within the box. This feature vector is served as input of classification model which relates to the label which defines the food within the box.

$$(\bigcup_1 S_1, \bigcup_2 S_1 \ldots \bigcup_1 S_2, \bigcup_2 S_2 \ldots \bigcup_N S_s) \cap W_w \rightarrow Y_y \tag{2}$$

4 Case Study to Classify 4 Types of Food

In this section, the case study developed in real time in a real environment are presented to classify 4 types of food.

The feature extraction following the proposal presented in Sect. 3.3 is shown in Table 2.

The experimental setup were defined by a case study which includes 5 scenes developed in a kitchen where 4 food items (banana, lemon, chorizo and prawns) where evaluated in the box. Figure 3 shows images of the box where two types of food are introduced. To carry out each scene, an user introduces one of the foods into the intelligent E-Nose where the array of sensors is located and then cover it. The food will remain in the covered box for 5 min. Then the lid will be

Table 2. Feature vector for scene 1 of sensors 2600 and 2602

	2600			
Label	Tbasal	Tmax	Tmin	Tinc
Lemon	720	764	720	44
Banana	712	756	712	44
Chorizo	717	732	717	15
Prawns	716	716	692	-24
	2602			
Label	Tbasal	Tmax	Tmin	Tinc
Lemon	495	834	495	339
Banana	520	718	520	198
Chorizo	500	550	500	50
Prawns	488	576	488	88

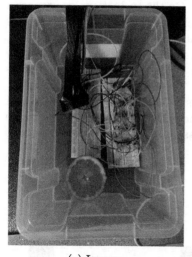

(a) Lemon.

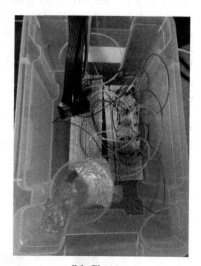

(b) Chorizo.

Fig. 3. Photographs of the box where two types of food are introduced.

opened and the food will be taken out. The box will remain open and without food for another 5 min as if it were being cleaned.

Before using this sensor array, the gas sensors were pre-heated for seven days as recommended by the manufacturer. On the day of the test, a simple 30 min pre-heat was performed to check that the measurements collected by the sensor array were stabilised to the environment in which they were being taken.

To obtain the results of the measurements collected from the array of sensors, first a preprocessing was performed to have all the measurements collected within a range of 0–1, where 0 is the minimum value and 1 is the maximum value.

Table 3. Results of scene 1, scene 2, scene 3, scene 4 and scene 5.

Scene 1		Scene 2		Scene 3		Scene 4		Scene 5	
Precision	1	*Precision*	0.625	*Precision*	1	*Precision*	1	*Precision*	1
Recall	1	*Recall*	0.75	*Recall*	1	*Recall*	1	*Recall*	1
f1_score	1	*f1_score*	0.6666	*f1_score*	1	*f1_score*	1	*f1_score*	1

For classification purposes, the model of Nearest Neighbours (K-NN) is proposed. It enables a light computing capabilities for learning and evaluation of the data which is compatible with smart and IoT boards. The K-NN integration was developed using the scikit-learn Python library. On the evaluation, we propose a rigorous method based on cross validation: developing the learning from 4 scenes and leaving the other unseen and unknown data of the other scene for testing. In order to evaluate the entire dataset, the learning and testing of scenes are combined under cross-validation approach. In Table 3, we describe the results obtained in the case scene.

And in addition the confusion matrixes are shown in Fig. 4. As can be seen in the results table, which is illustrated in Fig. 3, and in the confusion matrices for the 5 scenes, which is illustrated in Fig. 4, the results obtained were generally good.

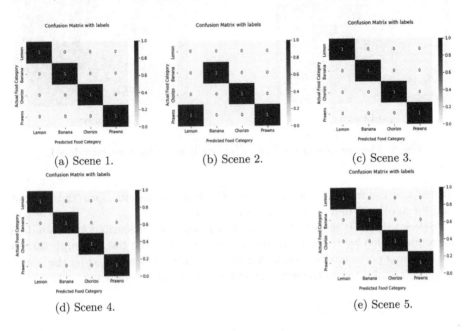

(a) Scene 1.　　　　(b) Scene 2.　　　　(c) Scene 3.

(d) Scene 4.　　　　　　　　(e) Scene 5.

Fig. 4. Confusion matrixes.

In scenes 1, 3, 4 and 5 the foods being sampled were predicted with complete accuracy. However, in scene 2 all foods were correct except for the lemon which was confused with the spraw, so the accuracy is 62.5°%, the recall is 75% and the f1_score is 66.66%.

5   Conclusions

In conclusion, in this work we have carried out the construction of an array of gas sensors. To do so, Figaro gas sensors have been used for their great advantage of non-invasiveness so that users feel more comfortable and feel that they are not intruding on their privacy.

In this case, this sensor array has been used for a case study in the kitchen. This case study was to identify four foods (banana, lemon, prawns and chorizo) in five different scenes developed by a user.

The results obtained from the measurements collected by the gas sensor array have been very encouraging as only one food in one of the scenes was not accurate. Although this first case study has its limitations, the good results obtained promise a very interesting future line of work.

In addition, some of the improvements that could easily be included would be the following: introducing more gas sensors in the array, which would allow a wider range of foods to be detected, and carrying out a case study involving more types of food and providing new results.

References

1. Aparicio, R., Rocha, S.M., Delgadillo, I., Morales, M.T.: Detection of rancid defect in virgin olive oil by the electronic nose. J. Agric. Food Chem. **48**(3), 853–860 (2000). https://doi.org/10.1021/JF9814087
2. Chen, J., Gu, J., Zhang, R., Mao, Y., Tian, S.: Freshness evaluation of three kinds of meats based on the electronic nose. Sensors **19**(3), 605 (2019). https://doi.org/10.3390/S19030605
3. Chen, L.Y., Wu, C.C., Chou, T.I., Chiu, S.W., Tang, K.T.: Development of a dual mos electronic nose/camera system for improving fruit ripeness classification. Sensors **18**(10), 3256 (2018). https://doi.org/10.3390/S18103256
4. Chen, R., Formenti, F., McPeak, H., Obeid, A.N., Hahn, C.E.W., Farmery, A.D.: Optimizing design for polymer fiber optic oxygen sensors. IEEE Sens. J. **14**(10), 3358–3364 (2014). https://doi.org/10.1109/JSEN.2014.2330359
5. Cramp, A., Sohn, J., James, P.J.: Detection of cutaneous myiasis in sheep using an 'electronic nose'. Vet. Parasitol. **166**(3–4), 293–298 (2009). https://doi.org/10.1016/j.vetpar.2009.08.025
6. Dudhe, P., Kadam, N., Hushangabade, R., Deshmukh, M.: Internet of things (iot): an overview and its applications. In: 2017 International Conference on Energy, Communication, Data Analytics and Soft Computing (ICECDS), pp. 2650–2653. IEEE (2017). https://doi.org/10.1109/ICECDS.2017.8389935
7. Emadi, T.A., Shafai, C., Freund, M.S., Thomson, D.J., Jayas, D.S., White, N.D.G.: Development of a polymer-based gas sensor - humidity and coinf2/inf sensitivity. In: 2009 2nd Microsystems and Nanoelectronics Research Conference. pp. 112–115 (2009). https://doi.org/10.1109/MNRC15848.2009.5338948

8. Grossel, S.S.: Hazardous gas monitoring: a guide for semiconductor and other hazardous occupancies (2000)-logan t. white, noyes publications/william andrew publishing, 13 eaton avenue, norwich, ny 13815, 206 pages, $85.00. Journal of Loss Prevention in the Process Industries 3(15), 249–250 (2002)

9. Liu, X., Cheng, S., Liu, H., Hu, S., Zhang, D., Ning, H.: A survey on gas sensing technology. Sensors **12**(7), 9635–9665 (2012). https://doi.org/10.3390/s120709635

10. Madakam, S., Lake, V., Lake, V., Lake, V., et al.: Internet of things (IoT): a literature review. J. Comput. Commun. **3**(05), 164 (2015). https://doi.org/10.4236/jcc.2015.35021

11. Manzoli, A., et al.: Volatile compounds monitoring as indicative of female cattle fertile period using electronic nose. Sens. Actuators B: Chem. **282**, 609–616 (2019). https://doi.org/10.1016/j.snb.2018.11.109

12. Qiao, J., Su, G., Liu, C., Zou, Y., Chang, Z., Yu, H., Wang, L., Guo, R.: Study on the application of electronic nose technology in the detection for the artificial ripening of crab apples. Horticulturae **8**(5), 386 (2022). https://doi.org/10.3390/horticulturae8050386

13. Ruiz Simões, F., Xavier, M.: Electrochemical Sensors, pp. 155–178 (2017). https://doi.org/10.1016/B978-0-323-49780-0.00006-5

14. Shengyin, Y., Minglei, S.: An acoustic method on sulfur hexafluoride concentration detection. In: 2014 IEEE Workshop on Electronics, Computer and Applications, pp. 485–488 (2014). https://doi.org/10.1109/IWECA.2014.6845663

15. Siegel, C., Dorner, T.E.: Information technologies for active and assisted living-influences to the quality of life of an ageing society. Int. J. Med. Informatics **100**, 32–45 (2017). https://doi.org/10.1016/j.ijmedinf.2017.01.012

16. Srinivasan, P., Robinson, J., Geevaretnam, J., Rayappan, J.B.B.: Development of electronic nose (shrimp-nose) for the determination of perishable quality and shelf-life of cultured pacific white shrimp (litopenaeus vannamei). Sens. Actuators, B Chem. **317**, 128192 (2020). https://doi.org/10.1016/j.snb.2020.128192

17. Voss, H.G.J., Mendes Júnior, J.J.A., Farinelli, M.E., Stevan, S.L.: A prototype to detect the alcohol content of beers based on an electronic nose. Sensors **19**(11), 2646 (2019). https://doi.org/10.3390/s19112646

18. Westenbrink, E., Arasaradnam, R.P., O'Connell, N., Bailey, C., Nwokolo, C., Bardhan, K.D., Covington, J.A.: Development and application of a new electronic nose instrument for the detection of colorectal cancer. Biosens. Bioelectron. **67**, 733–738 (2015). https://doi.org/10.1016/j.bios.2014.10.044

19. Yamazoe, N., Shimanoe, K.: Theory of power laws for semiconductor gas sensors. Sens. Actuators, B Chem. **128**(2), 566–573 (2008). https://doi.org/10.1016/j.snb.2007.07.036

20. Yu, K., Wang, Y., Yu, J., Wang, P.: A portable electronic nose intended for home healthcare based on a mixed sensor array and multiple desorption methods. Sens. Lett. **9**(2), 876–883 (2011). https://doi.org/10.1166/sl.2011.1635

A Micro-interaction Tool for Online Text Analysis

Rita Pessoa Correia[1], Bruno M. C. Silva[1]($\boxtimes$), Pedro Jerónimo[2], and Nuno Garcia[1]

[1] Instituto de Telecomunicações, Department of Informatics, University of Beira Interior, Covilhã, Portugal
rita.pessoa.correia@ubi.pt, bruno.silva@it.ubi.pt, ngarcia@di.ubi.pt
[2] LABCOM, University of Beira Interior, Covilhã, Portugal
pj@ubi.pt

Abstract. With the constant increase of new technologies and mobile device usage for content consumption, also more misinformation, fake news, and questionable content have been published in many ways and forms all over the Internet. This is undoubtedly a current problem because the public's knowledge and the respective opinions on several global matters are being easily persuaded and distorted. The circulation of fake news and malicious content is not new, but its visibility and impact increased with the emergence of social networks and online social media. There is so much misinformation spread around, that people no longer know what to believe. The line between journalism and other content has blurred, making it important for all writers, regardless of their platform, to check their facts. Unlike the conventional verification process, which requires checking information before it is published, fact-checking is dedicated to post-hoc checking, or in other words, verifying statements and alleged facts after they have been published. Many techniques and mechanisms have been studied for fake news detection and fact-checking, most of them using the synergy between Machine Learning (ML) and Artificial Intelligence (AI) algorithms with Human sensibility, sense, and emotion. Hence, this paper presents a micro-interaction tool for online text analysis focused on malicious content reporting. The system conceptual design and architecture are also presented in detail and finally, the implementation and preliminary validation of the proposed tool are described including primary system evaluation results.

Keywords: Fake news · Fact-checking · Mobile devices · Content producers · Chrome extensions

1 Introduction

The introduction of mobile devices in the early 90s allowed people to remain connected anywhere and anytime. Over time, it has become a personal mobile device that integrates

This work is funded by FCT/MCTES through national funds and when applicable co-funded EU funds under the project UIDB/EEA/50008/2020.

both communication and multimedia functionality [1]. Multimedia can be defined as media that enables content and information processing through audio, video, graphics, text, and animation in an interactive way. The mobile device, as a multimedia tool, has four main characteristics: it is portable, constantly connected, personal, and has a small screen [2]. Unlike other media, mobile news encourages users to immerse themselves in diversified manners of news consumption. Unique characteristics of mobile devices, including mobility, hyperlinks, and downloading, allow mobile users to quickly access and dispense with various content [3]. The mobile device is becoming an additional news medium to other news media, enhancing people's ability to acquire news about current events in the world, independent of time and space [1]. The migration of audiences toward digital news advanced to a new level in 2011 and early 2012, the era of mobile and multi-digital devices.

According to [4], much of the desktop news experience is built around search - people looking for what they need or want to know now. On the other hand, the way people interact with news on mobile devices is quite different than news behavior on desktop/laptop computers. Data from Localytics [5], a client-based mobile analytics firm, indicates that people spend far more time with news apps on the smartphone and tablet, visit more pages at a sitting, and return more frequently than they do on conventional computers [4]. Furthermore, as mobile news-delivery services have become diversified, users can select online news channels on mobile devices based on their specific preferences. For example, mobile users can easily access news content anywhere and anytime by visiting mobile news websites and/or logging into their social media accounts [6]. As so, moving toward mobile holds some promising options for news producers, including increasing the amount of overall news being consumed [4]. Nevertheless, despite mobile devices can increase access to news, it doesn't necessarily increase attention to news or even access to the truthful ones [7].

False and distorted news have been a part of human communication since at least Roman times. However, the arrival of the Internet in the late 20th century, followed by social media in the 21st century, drastically multiplied the dangers of misinformation, disinformation, propaganda, and hoaxes. Both questionable and fraudulent content now go viral through peer-to-peer distribution. In these circumstances, where trust becomes polarized around what "news" aligns with their views, many news consumers feel entitled to choose or create their own "facts". Combined, these actions present an unprecedented threat level that can drown out journalism, as well as contaminate it with the implication that there is nothing to distinguish it from false and fraudulent information more broadly [8]. Mobile devices allow users to remain connected to the World in a ubiquitous way, creating new contexts of media use. Considering the structural changes in the journalistic market, media organizations are trying to lead this digital transition, (re)gaining the attention of the public [9]. This digital evolution can bring either many advantages or open the door to rushed journalism, such as the publication of fake news and malicious content, which can have critical effects on both individuals and society. For this reason, it's becoming important to fact-check the sources of information.

Misinformation is incorrect or misleading information, which can lead to the distortion of people's opinions on several matters and unintended consequences. According to Wessel et al. (2016) [10], the cumulative effect of misinformed users on social media has a very negative impact. Thus, fact-checking claims with reliable information from credible sources is perhaps the best way to fight the spread of misinformation. By double-checking a claim, you can verify whether it's true. However, it's important to use verifiable and reputable sources to fact-check that information, otherwise, you risk perpetuating the cycle [11]. In order to help to fight this global issue, we can use the interaction from Internet users (within reputation rules) with the content producers/journalists, so those users can interact with Web content, validating, commenting, or expressing emotions about it to decrease the percentage of false, malicious or questionable content. With this strategy, online content producers can get dynamic interaction and feedback from the public about the published content, so they can fact-check it and have a greater degree of truthfulness.

This paper presents a micro-interaction tool for online text analysis. The main goal of this solution is for fake or malicious content reporting through a web browser extension. The paper starts by presenting the most significant research work on the fake news detection field and discusses the main issues in this field. Then, it presents the conceptual design of the proposed tool, which is a chrome extension that allows users to interact at a microlevel with the online text, whereas this information is then reported through an online platform for the journalists and content producers to evaluate and properly fact-check it. Finally, implementation and evaluation details are presented elaborating on future works.

The remainder of this paper is organized as follows. Section 2 presents the conceptual design of the proposed tool, covering the use-cases, the activity diagram, the database, the systems architecture, and the used technologies. Section 3 presents the implementation and evaluation details, and finally, the paper is concluded in Sect. 4.

2 Conceptual Design and System Architecture

In this chapter, it will be presented the conceptual design of the system and the mechanisms used in the domain of software engineering, mainly the use-case and activity diagrams, the relational DB model, the system architecture, and the technologies that were used to develop and implement both the Chrome extension tool and the platform for the content producers to receive the data.

2.1 System Use Cases

In this section, the use-case diagrams considered during the extension and platform development will be presented. As we can see in Fig. 1, the regular extension user, which is the system actor, after registering and correctly authenticating into his account, can highlight content/text excerpts on several online websites that he considers to be either fake or questionable.

The content is then stored in a DB, along with the user name, email, and URL of the respective page. That information can then be then visualized in a user-friendly platform for the content producers, which in this case are the system actors, so they can analyze it, fact-check the information and proceed most adequately (as shown in Fig. 2).

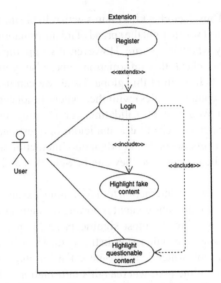

Fig. 1. Use-case diagram for the micro-interaction tool.

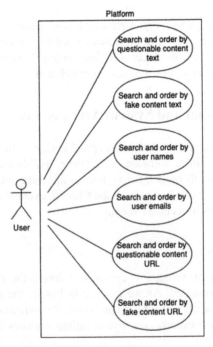

Fig. 2. Use-case diagram for the platform.

2.2 Activity Diagram

Figure 3, presents the activity diagram of the micro-Interaction tool functions. As we can see, the first page that the user reaches after installing the extension is the login page. If no account has been created so far, the user must access the registration page. If the registration process is done successfully, the user returns to the login page where he can authenticate, otherwise, he remains on the same page. If the login credentials are correct, the user can finally view the main page of the extension, otherwise, he remains on the login page. In order for the user to classify some content as fake or questionable, he must first do that text selection on the browser and then click on the respective extension button. If a button is pressed without a previous selection, an alert appears and the user remains on the main page, otherwise, the selection becomes red, if the user considers it to be fake, or yellow if he considers it to be questionable.

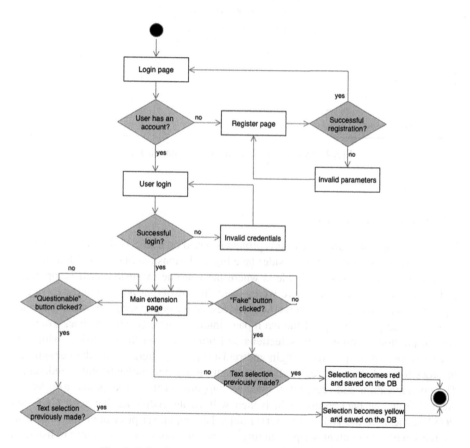

Fig. 3. Micro-interaction tool functions activity diagram.

2.3 Database

The schema represented in Fig. 4, describes the implemented Entity Relational Diagram of the database (DB). As we can see, we have three tables: "Fake", "Questionable" and "User". The "Fake" one stores all the information that the users consider to be false as well as the user's unique identifier and the respective page URL. The "Questionable" table is the same as the previous one but related to the content that the users consider to be questionable. The "User" table stores all the names, emails, and encrypted passwords of the users registered in the extension.

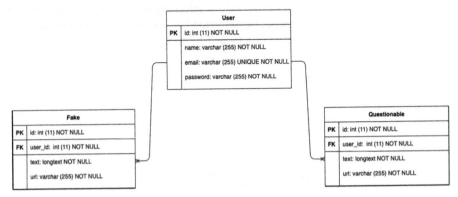

Fig. 4. System database entity relational diagram.

2.4 Systems Architecture

The system's architecture style of this project is based on a RESTful API [12, 13]. Here we can distinguish three different sides (see Fig. 5) Extension, Server, and Journal.

The micro-interaction tool side is where the Chrome extension itself is, operates, and interacts with the users. Here we can see three different popup interfaces (login, register, and main page) that interact with the respective popup scripts to make the pages dynamic. The popup script of the main page interacts directly with the background to get the previously stored user selections and print them on the extension, while the other two popup scripts (from login and register pages) interact with the background in order to send the user registration information and the authentication credentials. The authentication and registration process happens on the server.js due to a *fetch()* method from the background, which then will create endpoints that send *GET* and *POST* requests to the DB on the Server side. The popup script of the main page also interacts with the content script, sending the action codes from the buttons listeners (fake and questionable buttons). The content script will act from there as it accesses and injects code on the browser page. If the action received from the popup script of the main page comes by clicking the fake button, the selection previously made by the user on the browser becomes red, otherwise, it becomes yellow. After that, the content script sends that selection to the background script which will communicate with the server.js through a *XMLHttpRequest* object in order to store that selected content on the DB, as well as the respective user name, email, and page URL. This happens through endpoints that send *GET* and *POST* requests from the server.js to the Database on the Server side. Then, after the DB stores all the data, an endpoint from the Journal side to the DB is created, through a GET request. This last side will contain a website that will display all the relevant information for the journalist to factcheck and handle the appropriate content. When possible, resources should be cacheable on the client or server side. Server responses also need to contain information about whether caching is allowed for the delivered resource. The goal is to improve performance on the client side, while increasing scalability on the server side.

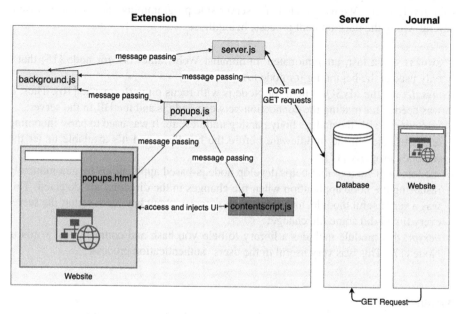

Fig. 5. System's architecture.

2.5 Used Technologies

In order to develop and correctly implement the system represented in the previous section, it was necessary several back-end and front-end technologies such as HTML, Cascading Style Sheets (CSS), Bootstrap, PHP, JavaScript, jQuery, Node.js and its dependencies and packages, and MAMP. Implementation details are going to be presented in the next section.

3 Implementation and Results

This chapter intends to explain in detail every step of the development of both the extension and platform. After all the implementation process is explained, it will be analyzed the obtained results.

3.1 Browser Extension: A Tool for Fact-Checking and Reporting

In this section, it will be approached the steps that were followed through the extension development, including the dependencies needed, all the adjacent files created, as well as some elucidative screenshots of the tool's functioning.

The initial goal of this extension was for it to work in a specific regional Journal, however, it was extended for all websites in order to perform the deepest content analysis in the future.

Server-Side Dependencies

There are some dependencies and modules that were needed to install through the extension development. We used node.js for server side programming and we had to install several within the development process, being those:

- *express*: it's a fast, unopinionated, minimalist Web framework for node [15] that I only used at the beginning for node test purposes;
- *mysql2*: it's the MySQL client for Node.js with focus on performance [16]. Thus, it was needed for making the connection between node.js and the DB in the server;
- *body-parser*: it's the node.js body parsing middleware. It was used to parse incoming request bodies in the middleware before the handlers, and it's available under the req.body property [17];
- *-nodemon*: it's a tool that helps develop node.js-based applications by automatically restarting the node application when file changes in the directory are detected. This was a very useful module, as I didn't need to worry about having to restart the server every time I did some file change;
- *bcrypt*: this module includes a library to help you hash and compare passwords in Node [17]. This was very useful in the users' authentication process.

Manifest

The Manifest is the most important file in an extension, as it stores all the information, proprieties, rules, and permissions about the extension itself. It is first described the manifest version and the extension name on Chrome, in this case, "iColabCheck". After that is the extension version and description for the user to see in the extension installation process. I also defined some icons sizes to be shown depending on the device that the extension is operating. After, we have the author's name and the background script file that it should point to with the persistent value as "true". Then, it is all the permissions that the extension has, as well as the scripts that the background file should have direct access to such as the content script.

Popup:

The popup is the UI of the extension. It should be minimalist, userfriendly, and efficient. In this case, we can distinguish three different popups: the login page, the register page and the main page. The first page that the user sees after installing the extension is the login page, where he has to insert his email and password. If the user doesn't have an account, he should click on the option "Register" below on that page, which will redirect him to the register interface, where he has to insert some parameters like his name, email, and password or return to the login page. If some registration field is left blank, it should become red and not proceed until the user fills it. Also, if the user inserts some already existing email, it should appear an error message and the user must register again. As we can see, there are two different password fields (password and confirm password). The user must insert the same password on both fields, or the registration process won't proceed, showing an error message. After the user is logged in, it will appear the main extension page (Fig. 6), which has two buttons: one for the fake content and another one for the questionable one. For the correct usage of those buttons, the user must firstly select with the mouse or computer track-pad some content that he considers to be fake or questionable and then open the extension and click on the respective button. After this action, the selected content will become highlighted in red or yellow on the chosen website, depending on if the user selected it as being fake or questionable, respectively. That selected content will also appear in the extension main popup, as we can see with an example in Fig. 6. When the content is selected by the user and one of the buttons is pressed, that content is stored on the DB along with the user name, email, and page URL, so it can be presented to the content producers on the platform, as we will see in further sections.

iColabCheck

Please check the content that you consider to be fake or questionable, by first selecting it on the website and then clicking on the respective extension button.

Fake content:

Lorem Ipsum is simply dummy text of the printing and typesetting industry. Lorem Ipsum has been the industry's standard dummy text ever since the 1500s, when an unknown printer took a galley of type and scrambled it to make a type specimen book. It has survived not only five centuries, but also the leap into electronic typesetting, remaining essentially unchanged.

Questionable content:

There are many variations of passages of Lorem Ipsum available, but the majority have suffered alteration in some form, by injected humour, or randomised words which don't look even slightly believable. If you are going to use a passage of Lorem Ipsum, you need to be sure there isn't anything embarrassing hidden in the middle of text.

Fig. 6. Extension main page.

Popup Script

The popup script interacts directly with the popup.html file. It has the functions of what to do when a button is clicked and what to output to the extension popup. In this case, beyond the popup.html, this file also interacts directly with the content script and the background script. The first one contains the highlight functions and the second one interacts mainly with the server to get or store data.

Content Script

The content script interacts directly with the Web page and it contains the browser highlight functions that result from clicking the popup buttons. Beyond those functions, it also contains a function that counts the number of the same words in the console, for future purposes. It contains a listener for when the user presses the fake or questionable buttons. If the request action from the popup script is the "executeCode" one, it means that the user clicked on the fake content button. As result, the content script will get that text selection from the window.getSelection() JavaScript function as a String. Then, if the selection is valid, the extension will send a request to the background script with the message "setTextFake" and the respective text selection and wait for a re-sponse. After that, the text selection is stored in an array and the selected text from the

In Fig. 7, is the result on the extension from clicking the fake and questionable buttons, on an example selection. As we can see, both of the selected text excerpts are printed on the respective box area on the extension. At the same time, the selections became highlighted in the browser page in red and yellow, being those, content that the user considers to be fake and questionable, respectively.

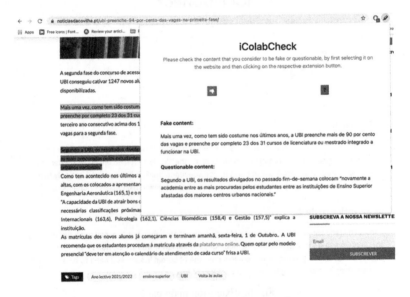

Fig. 7. Selection results on the extension.

Background Script

The background script is basically something that runs in the background and listens for triggers while the user interacts with the Chrome browser. As so, it has a listener so it can make actions according to the message received. In this case, we have a *switch-case* statement inside the listener, which will define which condition will be executed according to the request message received. It has conditions for user login and register, as well as to send the text selection to the server, in order for them to be stored in the DB.

Server

The server interacts directly with the DB and with the background script. In this file, we firstly define the dependencies and make the mysql connection to the DB through the npm mysql2 module. After that, we began to implement the routing process. Routing refers to how an application's endpoints (URIs) respond to client requests. You can define routing using methods of the Express app object that correspond to HTTP methods; for example, app.get() to handle GET requests and app.post() to handle POST requests. These routing methods specify a callback function called when the application receives a request to the specified route (endpoint) and HTTP method [18]. When it comes to adding content that the user considers being fake to the respective DB table, we need to get the text itself, the user email and ID, and the page URL. All of these parameters, except for the user id, are sent to the server through the background script. After that, it was implemented a function (*get_info(c)*) that makes a query to the DB so we can get the ID of the user that selected the content, returning that value. When that function is called we can finally execute the query that will add the "fake" content to DB, as we already have all the necessary parameters. The process of adding the content that the user considers being "questionable" to the respective DB table is similar.

3.2 Web Platform for Content Producers

This section will approach the steps and the main components that constitute the platform for the content producers on the Journal side. The server that is under the platform is MAMP localhost, It is running on Apache port 8888 and the PHP version is 7.4.12. As we can see in Fig. 8, on the platform main page we have a navtab so we can distinguish the fake content stats from the questionable ones. Inside each tab, and with the help of

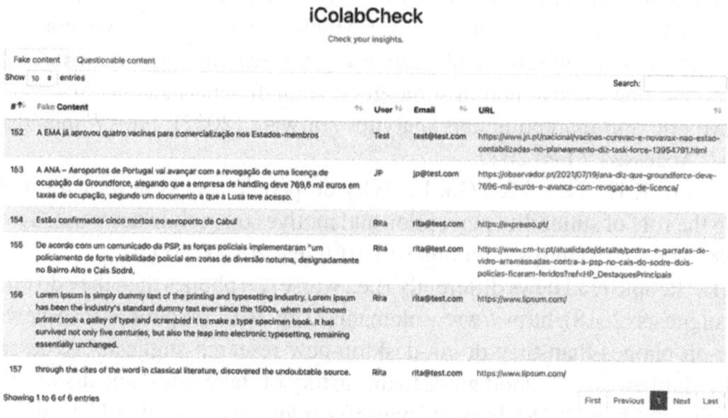

Fig. 8. Platform page.

Bootstrap, we created a table so the content producer can see the organized content and the respective information such as the user who highlight it, his email, and the page URL. It is also possible to arrange those parameters ascending or descending, show a certain number of entrances at once, search for keywords and see the first, previous, next, and last table pages. The table in the questionable content tab works similarly. The content in each tab is being retrieved from the same DB that interacts with the extension.

4 Conclusions

In this paper, we present a micro-interaction tool for online text analysis focused on malicious content reporting. The system conceptual design and architecture are presented in detail, showing all the software engineering process that was conducted. The tool implementation is also described in detail, including the used main technologies and frameworks for its development. Moreover a preliminary validation of the micro-interaction tool including a primary system evaluation was performed. The feasibility of the system was shown and for this purpose, some relevant screens of the respective visual results were presented.

References

1. Tewari, N., Datt, G.: A study on the systematic review of security vulnerabilities of popular web browsers. In: 2021 International Conference on Technological Advancements and Innovations (ICTAI), pp. 314–318 (2021). https://doi.org/10.1109/ICTAI53825.2021.9673463
2. Sundet, V.: The dream of mobile media. In: Storsul, T., Stuedahlz, D. (eds.) Ambivalence Towards Convergence. Digitalization and Media Change, pp. 87–113. Nordicom (2007))
3. Kiousis, S., Dimitrova, D.: Differential impact of Web site content: exploring the influence of source (public relations versus news), modality, and participation on college students' perceptions. Public Relat. Rev. **32**(06), 177–179 (2006). https://doi.org/10.1016/j.pubrev.2006.02.013
4. Tewari, T., Datt, D.: A study on the systematic review of security vulnerabilities of popular web browsers. In: 2021 International Conference on Technological Advancements and Innovations (ICTAI), pp. 314–318. https://doi.org/10.1109/ICTAI53825.2021.9673463
5. Mitchell, A., Rosenstiel, T., Christian, L.: Mobile devices and news consumption: some good signs for journalism (2012). https://www.pewresearch.org/journalism/2012/03/18/mobile-devices-and-news-consumption-some-good-signs-for-journalism/. Accessed 7 Feb 2022
6. Upland. Mobile app marketing and analytics software (2022). https://uplandsoftware.com/localytics/. Accessed 7 Feb 2022
7. Shim, H., You, K.H., Lee, J.K., Go, E.: Why do people access news with mobile devices? Exploring the role of suitability perception and motives on mobile news use. Telemat. Inform. **32**(1), 108–117 (2015). https://doi.org/10.1016/j.tele.2014.05.002
8. Owen, L.H.: People read news differently (i.e., worse) on phones than they do on desktop, new research suggests (2018). https://www.niemanlab.org/2018/04/people-read-news-differently-i-e-worse-on-phones-than-they-do-on-desktop-new-research-suggests/. Accessed 7 Feb 2022
9. Posetti, J., Matthews, A.: A short guide to the history of 'fake news' and disinformation: a New ICFJ learning module (2018). https://www.icfj.org/news/short-guide-history-fake-news-and-disinformation-new-icfj-learning-module. Accessed 7 Feb 2022

10. Wolf, C., Schnauber, A.: News Consumption in the Mobile Era. Digit. Journal. **3**(5), 759–776 (2015). https://doi.org/10.1080/21670811.2014.942497

11. Wessel, M., Thies, F., Benlian, A.: The emergence and effects of fake social information: evidence from crowdfunding. Decis. Support Syst. **90**(2016), 75–85 (2016). https://doi.org/10.1016/j.dss.2016.06.021

12. Ohio University: Fake News, Misinformation, Fact-Checking I Ohio University MPA I Ohio University (2021). https://onlinemasters.ohio.edu/masters-public-administration/guide-to-misinformation-and-fact-checking/. Accessed 7 Feb 2022

13. Sardinha, A.: Modelo entidade-associação (EA) (2021) https://fenix.tecnico.ulisboa.pt/downloadFile/3779579572812/mod02-1-Modelo-EA.pdf. Accessed 7 Feb 2022

14. Red Hat.s What is a rest API? May 2020. https://www.redhat.com/en/topics/api/what-is-a-rest-api. Accessed 10 Mar 2021

15. Gillis, A.S.: What is rest API (restful Api)? September 2020. https://searchapparchitecture.techtarget.com/definition/RESTful-API. Accessed 10 Mar 2021

16. IBM Cloud Education: What is a rest API?IIBM. April 2021. https://www.ibm.com/cloud/learn/rest-apis. Accessed 10 Mar 2021

17. NPMJS: Express (2022). https://www.npmjs.com/package/express. Accessed 19 Aug 2021

18. NPMJS: mysql2 (2022). https://www.npmjs.com/package/mysql2. Accessed 19 Aug 2021

19. NPMJS: bodyparser (2022). https://www.npmjs.com/package/body-parser. Accessed 19 Aug 2021

20. Cory LaViska. Hashing passwords with node.js and bcrypt. February 2017. https://www.abeautifulsite.net/posts/hashing-passwords-with-nodejs-and-bcrypt. Accessed 19 Aug 2021

21. Express. Express routing (2022). https://expressjs.com/en/guide/routing.html. Accessed 19 Aug 2021

Use of Classification Techniques for the Analysis of Data Related to COVID-19 in México

Ivan Rael Núñez-Harper$^{(\boxtimes)}$, Bogart Yail Marquez , and Arnulfo Alanis

Instituto Nacional de México, Tijuana, Baja California, México
{ivan.nunez,bogart,alanis}@tectijuana.edu.mx

Abstract. SARS-CoV-2 has bought many challenges to the world, socially, economically, and healthy habits. Even to those that have not experienced the sickness itself, and even though it has changed the lifestyle of the people across the world nation wise the effects of COVID-19 need to be analyzed and understood, analyzing a large amount of data is a process by itself, in this document details the analysis of the data collected from México by the Secretary of Health, the data was analyzed by implementing statistics, and classification methods known as K-Means, C&R Tree and TwoStep Cluster, using processed and unprocessed data. With the main emphasis on K-means. The study has the purpose of detecting what makes the highest impact on a person, to get sick, and succumb to the effects of the disease. In the study, it was found that in México the age of risk is at its highest at the age of 57, and the ones at the highest risk of mortality are those with hypertension and obesity, with those that present both at the age of 57 having a 19.37% of death.

Keywords: *SARS-CoV-2* · COVID-19 · K-Means · C&R Tree · Clustering · Data classification · TwoStep Cluster

1 Introduction

Coronaviruses (CoV), are not an unknown disease though before the current novel Coronavirus (nCoV) known as COVID-19 it was never identified in humans, a disease caused by the SARS-CoV-2 virus. causing mild to very serious illnesses to anyone that contracts the disease, requiring medical attention, or even death. Anyone with declining health issues presents themselves at the highest risk possible, though anyone of any range of age range is threatened by the disease as such, the priority in informing people, on how to prevent the transmission of the virus and viruses work in general [1], has been the high priority as through the disease was originated in bats in the Rhinolophus genus [2], it has adapted to humans cells, and humans as such the best way to preventing virus transmission is to keep informed, to keep you and those around you safe.

This study utilizes the open data collected by the Secretary of Health of the México government, to classify present conclusions extracted from the data, analyze it and process the information to observe the effects of COVID-19 in the country of México and analyze who were the most affected, and what were the observed effects of the virus

T. Guarda et al. (Eds.): ARTIIS 2022, CCIS 1675, pp. 524–534, 2022.
https://doi.org/10.1007/978-3-031-20319-0_39

in the general population according to attempt to classify the risk in contracting the virus and the possible effects of the illness according to the data of the confirmed cases studied for COVID-19. The data is being processed and analyzed using 3 classification techniques, K-Means, Two-Step Cluster, The Classification and Regression Tree (C&R Tree).

2 Objectives

In the investigation, the main objectives are to find the effects of COVID-19 in the people of México varying on their personal data, to find how common is contracting COVID-19. The likeliness of contracting COVID-19 according to the data recollected. To classify what is more likely to make someone prone to COVID-19's effects, namely how severely affected by the sickness itself, the effect results being the body recovering on its own, diagnosed with pneumonia, intubated, requiring intensive care, or death. Along with the effects of contracting the virus, as such some cases, studies present that SARS-CoV-2 can be contracted, without the user presenting the illness finding.

In specific, the research is looking to implement the different classification techniques previously mentioned to correlate the data of a person's age, smoking, if the person was pregnant, and pre-existing afflictions. The preexisting affliction being analyzed are; asthma, diabetes, hypertension, cardiovascular disease, obesity, pneumonia, COPD, immunosuppression, and renal insufficiency. Another objective is to analyze the relation of the cases of the people that had contracted SARS-CoV-2 previously, and the effect of the Virus on them.

3 Justification

The impact of COVID-19 is not a small one this can be observed, in the educational system this can be observed by the three impact phases it went through. The immediate impact was the initial phase in which information was very limited, and responses had to be made upon an issue. After the immediate impact, decisions on how to deal with the pandemic have varied, some opening programs to facilitate resources and services for virtual platforms, where the jobs of those that were set on lockdown, though not everyone got access to these resources, and through other solutions were set, they were reactive on what the local government allowed for it to function. In México, there has been an increase in household income loss and an increase in hunger, presented at the early stages of the pandemic, such the information, and how people have been on hold for the reactive information on how to deal with the pandemic, has affected them in varied and unexpected ways [3], where the article wants to focus, on the real data of impacted people according to the data recollected by the Secretary of Health of México, to interpret and analyze how the impact of COVID- 19 affected the country itself.

4 State of the Art

The prevention measures are taken to becoming ill of COVID-19, with the increasing spread growing exponentially from late 2020 towards 2021, by October 24, 2020, having killed 2.7% of the 42.549.383 cumulative cases of the patients that got ill of COVID-19, and 168,040871 by May 27 of 2021 [3], the threat COVID-19 brought, was not of the disease itself. Still, the response, implementing a lockdown, increased the mental health challenges, limited basic needs, and reduced the general income. People became more sedentary and engaged in other unhealthy behaviors. All of them are part of the life changes surrounding COVID-19 [4]. México documented a 6.7% increase in hunger and a 30% loss in household income between May and July of 2020 [3], a household survey in Latin America and the Caribbean shows how the income was affected across the countries, with the study revealing that 58% that owned a small family business closed their business, and 45% reported that a member of their household lost their job [5].

The analysis of the data produced on health responses crises is something that is not unheard of, Machine Learning has been attempted to integrate into hospitals and other health institutions, one example is are those of chest pain issues in an emergency department, those heart pains can be simple muscle pain to life-threatening issues, as such distinguishing the source of issues is very important, one was conducted at Chi Mei Medical Center, where a real-time prediction model was integrated, the method was trained using data from three hospitals, the data being from between the years 2009 and 2018 [6].

The implemented methods for data classification implemented in this research can be separated in two groups, first C&R Tree is a tree-based classification and prediction that functions by dividing the datasets into subgroups of two, and subsequently those groups get divided in two until the method is satisfied by the classification of data, the disadvantage of such a method is that it can only target a single field meaning it can only predict, or function to classify into a single output at a time. Meanwhile the other classification method group being clustering models, such as K-Means and Two-Step Cluster don't target a field, instead, they try to predict the outcome by uncovering the given pattern grouping the method according to how similar are to each other, mainly used to corroborate or to make groups according to patterns [7–9].

4.1 K-means

K-means works by making clusters of perfect circles, where at the start has a non-optimal clustering, and through various iterations of relocating the center point of the circles, through recalculating its members, until a set of iterations, or given criteria is me [10]. K-means is mathematically expressed as (1). Where (2) is a data set in a d dimensional Euclidean space (3) are the cluster centers (4) where Z_{jk} Z_{jk} is a binary variable that indicates if the data point X_i X_i belongs to the k-th, (5) with the updating equation resulting in (6,7) [11]. With the end result in grouping the data into distinct groups based on their characteristics (see Fig. 1).

$$X = \{X_1, \dots, X_n\} \tag{1}$$

$$J(z, A) = \sum_{i=1}^{n} \sum_{k=1}^{c} z_{ik} \|x_i - a_k\|^2 \tag{2}$$

$$A = \{a_1, \ldots, a_n\} \tag{3}$$

$$Z = \left[Z_{jk} \right]_{nxc} \tag{4}$$

$$k = 1, \ldots, c \tag{5}$$

$$a_k = \frac{\sum_{i=1}^{n} z_{ik} x_{ij}}{\sum_{i=1}^{n} z_{ik}} \text{ and} \tag{6}$$

$$z_{ik} = \begin{cases} 1 & \text{if } \|x_i - a_k\|^2 = \min_{1 \leq k \leq c} \|x_i - a_k\|^2 \\ 0, & \text{otherwise.} \end{cases} \tag{7}$$

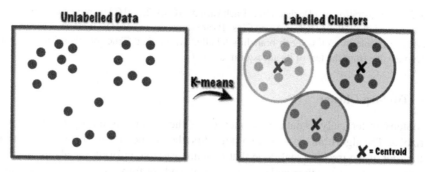

Fig. 1. K-means grouping of data [12]

4.2 C& R Tree

Decision tree models and test data items, to classify them into an structure similar to that of a tree, the top node is called root node. And other internal ones represent the test and inputs, and depending on the outcome it branches into certain node, until it reaches a leaf, or a node without a child that determines the corresponding outcome, and what components does it have in common creating a classification of samples [13], an Illustration of this is depicted in Fig. 2.

C&R Tree is a tree-based classification splitting into segments by examining the input fields by the best split based on impurity defining two subgroups, and subsequently they split, until a stopping criterion is meet. The splits are binary, they can only form two sub groups [7]. These trees can be adjusted based on a cost-complexity, enabling smaller trees with better cross validation when classifying data and one wants to avoid leaving an estimate on its own branch or classification.

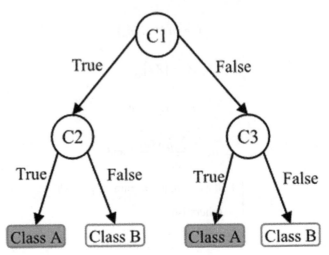

Fig. 2. An illustration of a Decision tree. Each variable (C1, C2, and C3) is represented by a circle and the decision outcomes (Class A and Class B) are shown by rectangles. In order to successfully classify a sample to a class, each branch is labelled with either 'True' or 'False' based on the outcome value from the test of its ancestor node [13]

4.3 TwoStep Cluster

TwoStep Cluster analyses data by the measure of the distance assuming the independent variables. The algorithm works in two steps, first the tree begins by placing the first case at the root of the tree in a leaf node that contains variable information about that case. Each successive case is then added to an existing node or forms a new node, based upon its similarity to existing nodes and using the distance measure as the similarity criterion. A node that contains multiple cases contains a summary of variable information about those cases. Thus, the CF tree provides a capsule summary of the data file. Then The leaf nodes of the CF tree are then grouped using an agglomerative clustering algorithm. The agglomerative clustering can be used to produce a range of solutions and determine which is better [8].

5 Proposition

Using the collected data referring to cases of COVID-19 in México as of the date of 2022–05-21, we will pick the relevant data to the situation of the patient defined by its health history and conditions, such data is composed of 15, 950, 212 as of date [14–17] cases registered in the country, such cases include, people affected by COVID-19, infected with SARS-CoV-2 virus, and negative results, using it to study the historical state of the data analyzed by the aforementioned classification methods, along with the processing of its statistical data, both done in two ways, data with minimum processing, and preprocessed data where the data is optimized before going into the classification methods.

6 Methodological Framework

To analyze the data first it was recollected, the general statistics presented in Table 1, that shows the results of the studies made on the people, and Table 2 that shows the statistics of the values themselves, with most of the cases resulting in the negative, and the second, most common result being testing positive for the virus, but not the disease. Out of the implemented variables, in both cases, where the classification methods were run for the processed and non-processed data, both had a variable added that sets if the patient is deceased or not according to the data of defunction date (FECHA_DEF), which marks the date the patient deceased. The input values that were implemented from the data tables of collected data referring to cases of COVID-19 in México are; estate (ENTIDAD_UM), sex (SEXO), intubated (INTUBADO), pneumonia (NEUMO-NIA), age (EDAD), pregnancy (EMBARAZO), diabetes (DIABETES), COPD (EPOC), asthma (ASMA), immunosuppression (INMUSUPR), hypertension (HIPERTENSION), cardiovascular disease (CARDIOVASCULAR), obesity (OBESIDAD), chronic kidney disease (RENAL_CRONICA), smokes (TABAQUISMO), defunction (DEF), indigenous heritage (INDIGENA), and ICU (UCI), the target value was defined for the value final classification (CLASIFICACION_FINAL). The definition of the values is on Table 3 [14].

Table 1. Results of cases of study of SARS-COV-2 in México

Parameters	No. cases	Percent
CASE OF COVID-19 CONFIRMED BY EPIDEMIOLOGICAL CLINICAL ASSOCIATION	339,068	2.1
CASE OF COVID-19 CONFIRMED BY JUDGMENT COMMITTEE	15,524	2.2
SARS-COV-2 CASE CONFIRMED	5,404,005	33.9
INVALID BY LABORATORY	11,644	0.1
NOT PERFORMED BY LABORATORY	90,669	0.6
SUSPICIOUS CASE	600,445	3.8
NEGATIVE TO SARS-COV-2	9,488,857	59.5

The data was then processed with the afford mentioned classification methodologies, where the unprocessed data, though gave the largest number of results, presented most of the data tightly correlated. Two steps set up a cluster with 60% Male, 40% presented pregnancy, 58.8% pneumonia, 20.1% obesity, 10.4% chronic renal disease, 8.4% immunosuppression, 32.1% diabetes, 54.8% hypertension, 9.1% COPD, 21.6% intubated, 17.1% ICU, intubated, 37.1% deceased, and a 56 average of age. Which the group highlights the biggest percentage in all groups and almost 100% of all the ICU patients, and 100% of the deceased patients. K-Means show similar results where it's easier to observe the opposite, the groups with the least age average and least percentages of diseases and health factors, presented the largest percentage of people not affected by the disease. C&R Tree did present a tight relationship between pneumonia with the disease, with most of the patients that went through the tests, presenting cases of COVID-19 and showcases of pneumonia.

Table 2. Number of cases and Mean of age and values of patients of cases of study of SARS-COV-2 in México

Parameters	No. cases	Mean
EDAD	N/A	38.522
NEUMONIA	761,272	0.048
EMBARAZO	162,081	0.019
INDIGENA	129,192	0.009
DIABETES	1,236,894	0.078
EPOC	109,709	0.007
ASMA	324,515	0.020
INMUSUPR	95,505	0.006
HIPERTENSION	1,688,152	0.106
CARDIOVASCULAR	161,031	0.010
OBESIDAD	1,395,469	0.088
RENAL_CRONICA	155,543	0.010
TABAQUISMO	1010665	0.064
UCI	81,576	0.067
INTUBADO	115,384	0.095
DEF	419,624	0.026

Table 3. Data input definition in the case study of SARS-COV-2 in México.

Parameters	Definition
EDAD	Age of the patient registered
ENTIDAD_UM	Identifies the state the patient registered the data
NEUMONIA	Identifies if the patient has pneumonia
EMBARAZO	Identifies if the patient is pregnant
INDIGENA	Identifies if the patient is self denominates as n indigenous person
DIABETES	Identifies if the patient has a diabetes diagnosis
EPOC	Identifies if the patient has chronic obstructive pulmonary disease(COPD)

(*continued*)

Table 3. (*continued*)

Parameters	Definition
ASMA	Identifies if the patient has an asthma diagnosis
INMUSUPR	Identifies if the patient has immunosuppression
HIPERTENSION	Identifies if the patient has hypertension
CARDIOVASCULAR	Identifies if the patient has a diagnosis of cardiovascular disease
OBESIDAD	Identifies if the patient has a diagnosis of obesity
RENAL_CRONICA	Identifies if the patient has a diagnosis of chronic renal failure
TABAQUISMO	Identifies if the patient has a habit of smoking tobacco
UCI	Identifies if the patient required an intensive care unit(ICU)
INTUBADO	Identifies if the patient was intubated
DEF	Identifies if the patient died
SEXO	Identifies the sex of the person
CLASIFICACION_FINAL	Identifies if the patient is a case of COVID-19

The processed data where the values were set to 0, 1 and other cases are set as undefined, reduced the amount of data processed by a large amount as most of the data didn't fulfill having enough registry data about the patients for the clustering methodologies, even so. Patterns were easier to observe; TwoStep presented the risk factors in order of importance of obesity, as the highest followed by (see Fig. 3), being intubated, obesity,

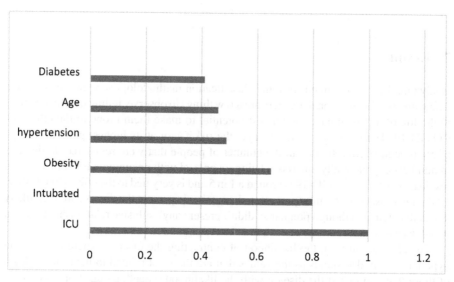

Fig. 3. SPSS importance predictor using TwoStep Cluster

hypertension, age, diabetes, and smoking, the clusters showing how the risk factors, though being intubated and requiring an ICU presenter the major clustering factors. K-Means identifying most of the causes as important highlighting obesity, cardiovascular diseases, hypertension, COPD, diabetes, age, and pneumonia, as with the non-processed data, detecting the fewer people that presented the least risk factors to be in the same group like the ones that didn't present any of the effects of COVID, C&R Tree presented that pneumonia as the factor with the highest importance (see Fig. 4).

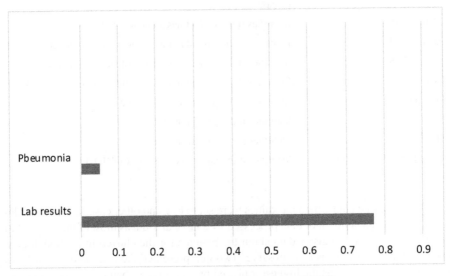

Fig. 4. SPSS importance predictor using C&R Tree

7   Results

Analyzing the data obtained from the classification methodologies, with the statistical data with the classification data, there are a few things to observe, telling us which factors in the life of a person have the highest potential to make them prone to the effects of COVID-19, The main one being the age, the risk factor at its highest point at the age of 56, though starting that point the number of people that were registered diminished in numbers exponentially, the risk o being diagnosed with pneumonia for someone that resulted positive in COVID-19 is around a 1 in 5 and is very tied to the effects of COVID-19 though most don't seem to present it, those who do present the disease are very likely to be intubated, and though pregnancy didn't present any exclusive relationship between it and deceases.

The closest values in the likelihood of contracting the disease, where obesity and hypertension, it also stands as the values that are the most related to the ratio of death of those that contracted the disease with the likelihood o death rising if one presented with both cases, 52.38% of the deceased where either prognosticated with obesity or

Hypertension. The value also closely related to being intubated, and not only the effects of the disease but suffering from any of those ailments also increases how likely the patient to contract the disease, as such patients over the age of 56 that present both cases of obesity and hypertension 19.37% chance of death according to the statistics

8 Conclusions

Though it's hard with the data collected to determine effect or causation, as its mainly classification data of the patient, when the user was diagnosticated with COVID-19, the value of the data, does not only serve to reinforce the need for a healthy life to improve the likeliness of being affected by the virus of SARS-Cov-2 but also tell us how important is to deal with the symptoms, as the study shows that the risks of being affected by the virus are not small, as almost half of the studied population did present the virus.

Though is suggested that the data itself should be more rigorously filled with less, unclear data that is not predictable should be agreed on how to be dealt with, and in most cases should be dealt with both, pre-processed and processed as in this case of study, where the processed data showed a big amount of data loss, passing from the millions to the thousands, Also repeated usage of the algorithm is important as sometimes a value is obstructing a result, wherein the case of the C&R Tree pneumonia appeared so tightly related to the case of study that obfuscated the data and attempting the method again excluding it provided information that was not apparent at first. The classification shouldn't be the end, after finding tendencies through multiple iterations, working statistics of that data, or the findings themselves is imperative in corroborating the results, and really observing how the data is actually interacting with each other.

References

1. United Nations : Coronavirus | United Nations. United Nations (2020). https://www.un.org/en/coronavirus
2. Bülent, Ç.A.K.A.L.: Origin of SARS-CoV-2. Turkiye Klinikleri Journal of Medical Ethics-Law and History 28(3), 499–507 (2020). https://doi.org/10.5336/mdethic.2020-76286
3. Reimers, F.M. (ed.): Primary and Secondary Education During Covid-19: Disruptions to Educational Opportunity During a Pandemic. Springer International Publishing, Cham (2022). https://doi.org/10.1007/978-3-030-81500-4
4. Matovu, J.K.B., Kabwama, S.N., Ssekamatte, T., Ssenkusu, J., Wanyenze, R.K.: COVID-19 Awareness, Adoption of COVID-19 Preventive Measures, and Effects of COVID-19 Lockdown Among Adolescent Boys and Young Men in Kampala, Uganda. J. Community Health 46(4), 842–853 (2021). https://doi.org/10.1007/s10900-021-00961-w
5. Bottan, N., Hoffmann, B., Vera-Cossio, D.: The unequal impact of the coronavirus pandemic: Evidence from seventeen developing countries. PLoS ONE, 15, e0239797 (2020). https://doi.org/10.1371/journal.pone.0239797
6. Zhang, P.: Real-time AI prediction for major adverse cardiac events in emergency department patients with chest pain. Scandinavian J. Trauma, Resuscitation Emerg. Med., 28(1), 93 (2020) https://doi.org/10.1186/s13049-020-00786-x
7. IBM Corporation: C&R Tree node - IBM Documentation (2022). https://www.ibm.com/docs/en/cloud-paks/cp-data/4.0?topic=modeling-cr-tree-node

534   I. R. Núñez-Harper et al.

8. TwoStep Cluster Analysis - IBM Documentation. (n.d.). July 18 (2022). https://www.ibm.com/docs/en/spss-statistics/23.0.0?topic=option-twostep-cluster-analysis%0Ahttps://www.ibm.com/docs/en/spss-statistics/24.0.0?topic=option-twostep-cluster-analysis%0Ahttps://www.ibm.com/docs/en/spss-statistics/27.0.0?topic=features-twostep-clu
9. IBM Corporation: K-Means node - IBM Documentation (2022). https://www.ibm.com/docs/en/cloud-paks/cp-data/4.0?topic=modeling-k-means-nodes
10. Mannor, S., et al.: K-Means Clustering. Encyclopedia of Machine Learning, pp. 563–564 (2011). https://doi.org/10.1007/978-0-387-30164-8_425
11. Sinaga, K.P., Yang, M.S.: Unsupervised K-means clustering algorithm. *IEEE*. Access **8**, 80716–80727 (2020). https://doi.org/10.1109/ACCESS.2020.2988796
12. Jeffares, A.: K-means: A Complete Introduction. K-means is an unsupervised clustering… | by Alan Jeffares | Towards Data Science. Towards Data Science (2019). https://towardsdatascience.com/k-means-a-complete-introduction-1702af9cd8c
13. Uddin, S., Khan, A., Hossain, M.E., Moni, M.A.: Comparing different supervised machine learning algorithms for disease prediction. BMC Med. Inform. Decis. Mak. **19**(1), 1–16 (2019). https://doi.org/10.1186/s12911-019-1004-8
14. Secretaría de Salud.: Datos Abiertos - Dirección General de Epidemiología | Secretaría de Salud | Gobierno | gob.mx. Gob. (2020). https://www.gob.mx/salud/documentos/datos-abiertos-152127
15. Secretaría de salud.: COVID-19 Tablero México - CONACYT - CentroGeo - GeoInt - DataLab. Coronavirus (2020). https://datos.covid-19.conacyt.mx/%0Ahttps://datos.covid-19.conacyt.mx/%0Ahttps://datos.covid-19.conacyt.mx/#DOView%0Ahttps://datos.covid-19.conacyt.mx/#COMNac%0Ahttps://coronavirus.gob.mx/datos/#DownZCSV
16. Gobierno de México.: Datos Abiertos de México - Información referente a casos COVID-19 en México. Secretaría de Salud. (2021). https://datos.gob.mx/busca/dataset/informacion-referente-a-casos-covid-19-en-mexico
17. Secretaria de Salud.: Secretaría de Salud | Gobierno | gob.mx. ¿Qué Hacemos? (2020). https://www.gob.mx/salud%0Ahttps://www.gob.mx/salud/que-hacemos

Artificial Neural Networks Applied to Natural Language Processing in Academic Texts

Bogart Yail Marquez$^{(\boxtimes)}$ ⓘ, Arnulfo Alanis ⓘ, Jose Sergio Magdaleno-Palencia ⓘ, and Angeles Quezada ⓘ

Departamento de Sistemas y Computación, Mestría en Tecnologías de la Información y Comunicación, Instituto Tecnológico de Tijuana, Av. Castillo de Chapultepec 562, Tomas Aquino, 22414 Tijuana, B.C. México, Germany
bogart@tectijuana.edu.mx

Abstract. In the last decade, Artificial Intelligence (AI) has become lead on the field of information generation and processing tasks through the emergence of Machine Learning (ML), as well as the data specialist mentions Machine Learning is a master of pattern recognition, and is capable of transform a data sample into a computer program capable of drawing inferences from new data sets for which it has not been previously trained, based on artificial neural networks (ANN) processing in academic texts, which are used to identify patterns and classify different types of information, currently treated as Deep Learning (DL) which is a subset of Machine Learning, this algorithm tries to imitate the human brain by continuously analyzing data with a given logical structure, which has led to its applicability to different fields such as robotics, voice processing, artificial vision, natural language processing (NLP), with the intention to provide computer systems with the ability to learn. Natural language processing has traditionally been a complex and non-trivial task in algorithm design. Making use of AI, new thresholds are being reached in the state of the art of different problems and with constant advances in the models in use, they are being reached faster and faster.

Keywords: Artificial neural networks · Natural language processing · Academic texts · Machine learning · Deep learning

1 Introduction

1.1 Problem Statement

As can be seen, the implementation of AI has considerable potential to be able to automate tasks with degrees of abstraction. In our case, in the DL branches, making use of a language branch such as NLP, we can provide systems with the ability to process the textual structures that shape our language [1], and thus be able to give a response that contains the logic of an output message to an input message, of course the state of the art of this type of algorithm is constantly evolving and throughout this investigation we will see which ones may be adequate to be able to process text structures [2].

T. Guarda et al. (Eds.): ARTIIS 2022, CCIS 1675, pp. 535–545, 2022.
https://doi.org/10.1007/978-3-031-20319-0_40

There is currently a clear understanding problem about the vast amount of information that exists, as users in the web environment, we are exposed to enormous amounts of data in the different information media that we use [3], on internet there are books, articles, texts of all kinds, if you want to learn basic programming, there are texts, to learn medicine concepts, there are texts, learn recipes, learn chemistry, processors, cars, etc., for everything there is information being a considerable point that not everything is precisely clear for each viewer, so we have this vast amount of information on the internet with different structures and that does not usually have a clear type of user other than a person with an interest in the subject.

The problem that is addressed lies in the difficulties that exist in today's information overload, of having accessible information but not with diversity of formats such as forms or tutorials in which one as a student or a user, can understand a topic of interest in the best way. Currently, the NLP has been improved considerably with tools such as GPT-3, a chatbot capable of generating coherent responses and texts by analyzing the inputs given by us or even being able to generate conversations with consistency with itself, all due to computational power [4] that has led to great advances in artificial intelligence, in this case oriented to deep learning.

It is proposed to create a simplified way of learning based on online tutors that work by NLP and use the best algorithms oriented to this field in order to be able to innovate with them different ways to use it and be able to promote a new way of learning, through tutors that are not necessarily a person, are always available to other users, and most importantly, they adapt and understand what is the best way to make the user learn and to know the academic and learning objectives that are persuading.

Currently there are various investigations on Artificial Intelligence, Machine Learning, Deep Learning, among other topics related to Natural Language Processing that take the state of the art to new horizons [5, 6]. This research will focus on studying different algorithms, models and methodologies used for the creation and training of Neural Networks Applied to Natural Language Processing so that they can later be applied to our text restructuring system [7, 8], in order to be able to compare the characteristics that make the use more or less convenient between the different types that exist, also considering the complexity of its implementation, the computational cost that they require, the training time that must be implemented, the ease of its scalability, and its constant or low use that exists among the scientific community that studies the area, to be able to contemplate that there is enough study, to entail adaptations between the different ideas that surround the implementation of the same problem since a low documentation would implicitly bring more time in testing and develop algorithms that do not guarantee that may be optimal for the present work.

The purpose is to be able to create a tool that can be helpful to the average student, in this case the objective is to focus on a system that can be capable of summarizing the main ideas of texts, thereby being able to help students who are starting a topic and they need a basic solid knowledge to be able to continue with a firm understanding about topic, exemplifying, to understand from basic mathematical concepts, to know biology of basic principles, all making use of the existing information from a simpler and more user-friendly approach.

2 State of the Art

2.1 Background

Noam Chomsky published his book [9], Syntactic Structures published in 1957, in which some of the already known linguistic concepts were revolutionized, in this it was concluded that for a computer to understand a language, the structure would have to be changed. Chomsky created a style of grammar which was called "Phase Structure Grammar", which consisted of methodically translating sentences from natural language into a format that computers could understand. In 1964, ELIZA, a comment and response process, was created to imitate a psychiatrist using reflection techniques with his patients. In that same year, the US National Research Council (NRC) created the Automatic Language Processing Advisory Committee, or ALPAC. This committee was tasked with evaluating the progress of natural language processing research [10, 11].

In 1966, the NRC and ALPAC were the ones to start the first AI and NLP strike, by stopping funding for research on natural language processing and machine translation, after twelve years of research, machine translations were still more expensive than manual human translations, and no computers yet came close to being able to hold a basic conversation. The next record was made 14 years later, in 1980, for Natural Language Processing and Artificial Intelligence research to recover from unfulfilled expectations created by extreme enthusiasts [12]. In a way, the AI disruption had ushered in a new phase of new ideas, with earlier machine translation concepts abandoned and new ideas fueling new research, including expert systems [13].

In the year of 1990, statistical models for the analysis of natural language processes gained a lot of popularity and this led to an incredible increase. Purely statistical NLP methods had become remarkably valuable in keeping up with the tremendous flow of text online. In 1997, LSTM recurrent neural network (RNN) models were introduced and found their strong point in 2007 for speech and text processing. Currently, neural network models are at the forefront of research and development in understanding the NLP of text and speech generation.

In 2001, Yoshio Bengio and his team proposed the first neural "language" model, using a feedforward neural network [14]. The feed-forward neural network describes an artificial neural network that does not use connections to form a loop. In this type of network, data moves in only one direction, from input nodes, through hidden nodes, and then to output nodes. The feedforward neural network has no cycles or loops and is quite different from recurrent neural networks. Currently as such there are constant progress within the field of ML, according to Oguzhan Tas [15] artificial neural networks (ANN) are one of the most popular and powerful classes of machine learning algorithms.

According to Oguzhan Tas [15], if the extractive digest method is used, it can be divided into different phases, the first being pre-processing and the second processing. In the pre-processing phase, there is a wide variety of techniques, such as tagging, stopword filtering, and stemming.

As shown in Fig. 1, several blocks are made from the source document, each block performs a task dependent on continuous relationships:

Part of Speech Labeling. Part of speech labeling is the process of grouping or specifying the words of the text according to the category of speech such as nouns, verbs,

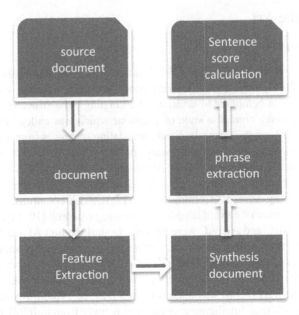

Fig. 1. How part of speech tagging works, Modified from Part of speech tagging: a systematic review of deep learning and machine learning approaches [16].

adverbs, adjectives, etc., the voice labeling process can be carried out by many algorithms such as the model hidden Markov and Viterbi.

Word Filtering. The "stopwords" are words that are filtered before or after processing the text, examples of stopwords and filtered from the plain text without: a, one/an, in, by, etc.

Stemming. Unfolding is the process of reducing inflected or sometimes derived words to their root, for example, eliminating verbs in the past and present continuous, using the singular instead of the plural, etc. There are many NLP tools that use stemming algorithms to do the stemming.

Title Similarity. A phrase scores well if it has the maximum number of similar words in the title. The similarity of the title can be calculated by the number of words of the phrase that appears in the title and the total number of the words of the title.

We will define title similarity as:

$$f_1 = S \cap T / t \tag{1}$$

where:

- $S = $ *Set of words in the sentence*
- $T = $ Set of words of the title

- $S \cap T =$ *Similar words in the phrase and the title of the Document*

Phrase Position. In this function, a sentence is evaluated by its position in the text, if it is the first five sentences of the paragraph, the position of the sentence in the text gives the information of the sentences we consider the first five sentences of the paragraph.

The score for this characteristic is calculated by:

$$f_2 = 5/5 \, for \, 1st, \, 4/5 \, for \, 2nd, \, 3/5 \, for \, 3rd, \, 2/5 \, for \, 4th, \, 1/5 \, for \, 5th, \, or \, 0/5 \, for \, other \, phrases \tag{2}$$

Term Weight/Term Frequency. The total weight of the term is calculated by calculating *tf* and *idf* for the document. In this case, *idf* refers to the inverse document frequency, which simply indicates whether the term is common or rare across all documents. The score of the important punctuation of word i can be calculated by traditional methods.

Phrase Length. This function is suitable for removing sentences that are too short, such as dates or authors' names. Short sentences are not expected to belong in the abstract.

Topic Word. This feature is related to domain-specific words that appear frequently in a document and are likely to be related to the topic. The score for this feature is calculated as the ratio of the number of topic words that appear in the sentence to the maximum summary of topic words in the sentence.

Proper Names. In general, the phrase that includes proper names is essential and is the one that is most likely to be contained in the abstract of the document. The score for this feature is calculated as the ratio of the number of proper nouns that appear in the sentence to the length of the sentence that contains the maximum number of proper nouns.

Similarity Between Sentences. The cosine similarity formula gives the similarity between S and each of the phrases. The weight of the term *wi* and *wj* of the term t with respect to the term n of the sentence *Si* and *Sj* are represented as vectors.

2.2 Tools for the Implementation of NLP

To implement analysis on the data, it is recommended that the texts go through a pre-processing usually called text normalization, in which the following is implemented:

1. Tokenization: This is the process by which we will divide tokens, whether letters, words, or sentences. In general, tokenization by words is the most common.
2. Lemmatization: In it, each of the words/tokens of a phrase or a text string is converted to its fundamental root, that is, if you have a word or a verb, what you do is convert it into the original word of which that conjugation was derived.
3. Segmentation: Phrases or sentences (the same topic) are identified in it.

In addition to the, the elimination or omission of punctuations as well as the so-called "stopwords" (such as a, one/an, in, by, etc.) are usually considered by means of regular expressions to avoid redundancy of insignificant words. NLP contains without adding AI a wide range of applications and functions, as such NLP tools can be considered as the algorithm world 2 vec (Source), which in short is an algorithm that giving input a corpus(a text normalized) outputs a vector representation of each word (in order to establish the neighboring words, that is, they enter into that context), in their case they used the word 2 vec variant called "Continue bag of words" (CBOW). Which can be used to limit context words below the threshold called "window size".

3   Methods for Extracting Information

The need for clear and concise texts is not new, there are studies where the different ways of obtaining information in the texts are proposed, which are divided into two: the extractive and the abstractive. The extractive way consists of generating summaries by making a copy of fragments of the original text, that is, extracting information (words and phrases) from the text to be summarized. On the other hand, abstractive methods generate words and phrases from scratch, which are very likely not to be found in the text, as we normally do.

According to Javier Alonso [17], extractive methods are considered to be simpler because they guarantee a minimum linguistic coherence, one possibility of obtaining them is by doing a statistical study of the most common words and those that are most repeated in a text, that is, the ones that are most often used and copy the phrases in which these are usually found, this because if it is repeated the most there is what is most talked about in the text. On the other hand, abstractive methods require more study and understanding of language, commonly use paraphrasing to form shorter sentences, and are capable of stringing sentences together.

Blue. "Bilingual Evaluation Understudy" or by its acronym BLEU is a metric that in the field of natural language generation provides a score that will serve to measure the quality of responses given by our model, interpreting that in our case, a text restructuring it is given based on a text entry that will give the restructuring as an output/answer. This score that BLEU awards is given by the coincidence it has with respect to another reference, which is supposed to be correct, considering a section of candidate answers or answers.

3.1   Market Positioning

When launching a product to the market, it is not enough to think about the patent of the name and to have an error-free version that has passed the corresponding quality tests. According to research by The Software Alliance (BSA) foundation, software generated $1.4 billion in the United States [18]. In 2016 there was an increase of 70 billion compared to the previous year, it is estimated that all this is thanks to the strategic plans that are implemented for its launch. Software companies today are leveraging content marketing, paid ads, and non-traditional strategies to drive and build awareness of the product or service and reach a larger audience.

In this case, the same strategy is applied so that future potential clients can be known and reached, the internet today is a tool that can open many doors for you if you know how to handle it in the correct way and as already mentioned above many companies make use of it to make themselves known and attract more potential customers, advertising on social networks is the most viable option to give us publicity since it is in this where many users spend hours of the day browsing and investigating things, this being the most viable way that many companies that provide services or products make themselves known.

4 Research Methodology

How is the quality of learning related to tools that are responsible for restructuring texts and how much impact can it have on mexican education?

The analysis and data collection, the information that is being analyzed is qualitative data since these are presented verbally or in our case in graphs. it is based on the interpretation of such information. The most common way of collecting information is through open interviews and through information where researchers generally analyze the patterns in the observations throughout the data collection phase, this being the case, it was decided to conduct surveys to carry out the collection of information, making a form with questions to reach the users who decided to study through the group of tijuana's technological institute and answered by students of the same institution Fig. 2.

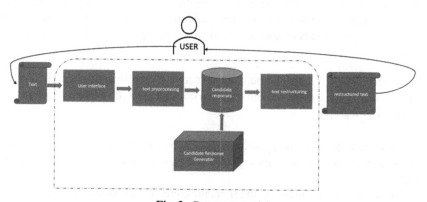

Fig. 2. Boost me model

Model Development. Given the nature and purpose of our project, it was fundamental and useful restructuring the text for the user, since it would not be of much use to generate a version of the given text as input that is visual, structural and, in short, more complex than the original which would be a result opposite to that required, with this we consider that the generation of valid text structures will have to go through a quality threshold to be able to reach what would be our response recovery module to be able to compare them with texts with similar structures and like these as an example of a success story, they were restructured with the minimum objective of having coherence, change of font and meaning of the text.

During the experimentation phase, problems were found related to the lack of candidate answers that were available to be able to compare with the text entries, which showed that validating one by one manually was not the most efficient way to achieve a large volume of candidate responses and thus a better restructuring of texts, a way to partially solve this problem was to manually validate which responses could be considered as candidate responses to pass them to our response recovery module.

With the studies and surveys carried out, the following information can be interpreted: The learning style that predominates in the study population is the visual style, that is, it seems easier for them to study with documentation, series, videos, documentaries, with a percentage of 49%, almost half of our studied sample, while therefore, it can be seen that the auditory learning style is only found in 21.6%, 23.5% is kinesthetic and only 5.9% do not have a notion of what is the correct way to study to achieve a greater understanding of the topics. These values are positive for us since our tool has much more potential to have a greater impact on people with visual learning styles. To study how the study population would react when comparing a normal text and a modified one, we propose two different texts:

Normal Text: "A semantic network or network representation scheme is a way of representing linguistic knowledge in which concepts and their interrelationships are represented by a graph. In case there are no cycles, these networks can be visualized as trees. Semantic networks are used, among other things, to represent conceptual and mental maps. In a semantic graph or network, the semantic elements between which the semantic relationship that the network represents is admitted, will be joined by a line, arrow or link or edge. Certain kinds of non-symmetric relationships require directed graphs that use arrows."

Restructured Text: A semantic network or network representation scheme is a way of representing linguistic knowledge in which concepts and their interrelationships are represented by a graph.

- In a case where there are no cycles, semantic networks can be visualized as trees.
- Semantic networks are used, among other things, to represent conceptual and mental maps.
- In a graph or semantic network, the semantic elements are represented by nodes.

Participants were asked how understandable Text 1 was, and Fig. 3 shows the results. And these were the results when asked how understandable the Text 2 was Fig. 4.

This leaves us with an average comprehensibility of Text 1 of 1.76 and Text 2 of 4.20 within the user's consideration based on a score of 0 to 5 of degree of comprehensibility Table 1.

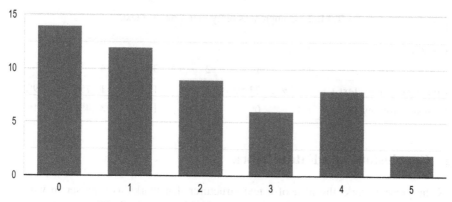

Fig. 3. Comprehensibility of information in the Text 1.

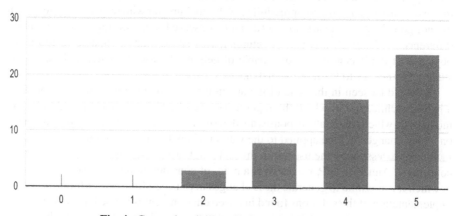

Fig. 4. Comprehensibility of information in the Text 2.

Table 1. Waste of study and tools to increase comprehension in texts.

Questions	Maybe	Yes	No
Would you study a subject of your interest that you have left behind if it were easier to study?	19.6%	68.6%	11.8%
Would you use a tool that explains your texts (of your study topics) in a more understandable and structured way for you?	23.5%	68.6%	7.8%

Table 2. Comprehensibility in informative texts.

Question	Rating					
	0	1	2	3	4	5
Comprehensibility Text 1	27.5%	23.5%	17.6%	11.8%	15.7%	3.9%
Comprehensibility Text 2	0%	0%	5.9%	15.7%	31.4%	47.1%

5   Conclusions and Future Work

IN the present work, the idea of a text structurer that works as a parser in which a candidate text input was presented to structure it, this to make educational, informative, and explanatory texts more understandable. For this case the prospective users that used this text restructured find a compressibility of 40.66% greater with respect to the texts that did not go through the restructuring (it can be observed in the average compressibility difference of Table 2), this text structurer leaves shows that is capable to fulfill the objective of implementing a tool capable of helping the user to better understand the study texts they try to learn or understand.

As could be seen in the state of the art, in the implementation of ml, we opted for a hybrid architecture in which the input texts given by the user pass through different modules on which candidate responses are determined as input to the generative modules, on which changes will be applied to the way in which the text is structured, in order to facilitate processing by the user, with this, although we do not enter into very complex concepts of Ann with NIP, we arrive at a point of consideration of simple architectures in which it is possible to generate these changes in a successful way. for future work the implementation of the solutions found in a web environment is needed, the construction and determination of a model that increases the compressibility of texts, and the power to make this something scalable towards new ways of being able to help the user from DI with NIP.

During the experimentation phase it can be found that our manual validation process is counterproductive with the objective of automating the tasks, this is a part for improvement into the model. The generative model and the response recovery model have a filter that automatically contemplates with a high level of reliability what is a correct structure from a text, this can be achieved with different combinations, such as text generator models that would pass to the restructuring model to have a source of combinations of texts and different structures so that it feeds on a wide variety of texts, of course this is achieved by bringing other issues to consider, however it seems to be an optimal way to reach a level of automation and autonomy that increases the success of the model.

Adaptation of the system for other learning styles when talking about text restructuring, it is understandable that the learning style that best suits this is the visual one, this being one of the points that we want to extend so that it covers other types of styles, for example, the auditory style, that option will be inserted so an audio can be played that reads the new generated text, this being a new way in which people who find it difficult to retain information through reading can also achieve a better retention of information from the inserted text.

References

1. Sancho Escrivá, J.V,: Utilidad de las nuevas tecnologías en la mejora de la comunicación médico-paciente en el área de salud mental: aportaciones de la inteligencia artificial y el procesamiento del lenguaje natural. Universitat Jaume I (2021)
2. Beltrán, N.C.B., Mojica, E.C.R.: Procesamiento del lenguaje natural (PLN)-GPT-3.: applicación en la Ingeniería de Software. Tecnol. Investig. y Acad. 8(1), 39–49 (2020)
3. Masip, P., Aran-Ramspott, S., Ruiz-Caballero, C., Suau, J., Almenar, E., Puertas-Graell, D.: Onsumo informativo y cobertura mediática durante el confinamiento por el Covid-19: sobreinformación, sesgo ideológico y sensacionalismo. El Prof. la Inf. 29(3) (2020)
4. OpenAI.: No Title (2022)
5. Ho, T.K., Luo, Y.-F., Guido, R.C.: Explainability of Methods for Critical Information Extraction From Clinical Documents: A survey of representative works. IEEE Signal Process. Mag. 39(4), 96–106 (2022)
6. Márquez, B.Y., Magdaleno-Palencia, J.S., Alanís-Garza, A., Romero-Alvarado, K., Gutiérrez, R., Ibarra, M.: Biomechanical Analysis of Human Gait with Inertial Sensors Using Neural Networks. In: Chen, Y.-W., Zimmermann, A., Howlett, R.J., Jain, L.C. (eds.) Innovation in Medicine and Healthcare Systems, and Multimedia. SIST, vol. 145, pp. 213–221. Springer, Singapore (2019). https://doi.org/10.1007/978-981-13-8566-7_21
7. Zhou, M., Duan, N., Liu, S., Shum, H.Y.: Progress in neural NLP. Model. Learn. Reason. Eng. 6(3), 275–290." 2020
8. Hinton, G., et al.: Deep neural networks for acoustic modeling in speech recognition: The shared views of four research groups. IEEE Signal Process. Mag. 29(6), 82–97 (2012)
9. Chomsky, N.: Syntactic structures, 2nd edn. Berlin & New York: Mouton de Gruyter (2002)
10. Khyani, D., BS, S.: An Interpretation of Lemmatization and Stemming in Natural Language Processing. Shanghai Ligong Daxue Xuebao/J. Univ. Shanghai Sci. Technol. 22 350–357 (2021)
11. Josh, V.: Application Research on Latent Semantic Analysis forInformation Retrieval (2019)
12. Waltz, D.L.: Semantic Structures (RLE Linguistics B: Grammar). In: Advances in Natural Language Processing. Routledge (2014)
13. Khurana, D., Koli, A., Khatter, K., Singh, S.: Natural language processing: State of the art, current trends and challenges. Multimed. Tools Appl. 3 1–32 (2022)
14. Sarzhan, N.: Transformers and their applications in natural language processing.
15. Tas, O., Kiyani, F.: A survey automatic text summarization. Press. Procedia 5(1), 205–213 (2007)
16. Chiche, A., Yitagesu, B.: Part of speech tagging: a systematic review of deep learning and machine learning approaches. Journal of Big Data 9(1), 1–25 (2022). https://doi.org/10.1186/s40537-022-00561-y
17. Alonso Hernández, Á.J.: Deep learning aplicado al resumen de texto (2017)
18. Cadence C.N.C. et al.: Competition and Consumer Protection in the 21st Century Hearings, Project Number P181201 BSAI The Software Alliance Comments on Topic 2: Competition and Consumer Protection Issues in Communication, Information, and Media Technology Networks

Relationship of the Socioeconomic Conditions with the Emotional Well-Being of the Students of the Tecnológico Nacional de México Campus Tijuana: An Analysis Using Data Mining

Irving Diaz-Hernandez[✉] , Bogart Yail Marquez , Maribel Guerrero-Luis , and Raúl Barutch Pimienta Gallardo

Departamento de Sistemas y Computación, Mestría en Tecnologías de la Información y Comunicación, Instituto Tecnológico de Tijuana, Av. Castillo de Chapultepec 562, Tomas Aquino, 22414 Tijuana, B.C., México
{irving.diaz,bogart,maribel.guerrero,
raul.pimienta}@tectijuana.edu.mx

Abstract. The present work seeks to analyze the relationship that exists between aspects of the social and family environment with the emotional well-being of the students of the Tecnológico Nacional de México campus Instituto Tecnológico de Tijuana. During the period 2013–2019, a descriptive level field investigation is carried out. A non-probabilistic sampling of intentional type is carried out, where a questionnaire-type instrument was applied to a population of 768 students of the tutoring program to obtain the necessary information and focus the object of study on the satisfaction that the student presents about the chosen career. Decision trees are elaborated through data mining and the results show that the importance that the family gives it and the fact that the costs of studying are assumed by the parents tend to be related to greater student satisfaction with their studies, while having a sexually active life is an important aspect, since the evidence shows that these students would feel less insecure, but on the other hand, they would show greater dissatisfaction with the chosen career.

Keywords: University students · Emotional well-being · Socioeconomic status · Data mining

1 Introduction

The present investigation will consist of knowing the main relationship between the socio-economic conditions of the students with their emotional well-being by analyzing the answers from a questionnaire carried out in a special course that is taught throughout their academic life. This is to recognize the impact they can have on the student's satisfaction with her career choice.

The journey through university life has become a great step in one's career, in the process the individual acquires the knowledge and skills necessary to carry out their profession for future growth. However, university life and the environment of its institutions

T. Guarda et al. (Eds.): ARTIIS 2022, CCIS 1675, pp. 546–557, 2022.
https://doi.org/10.1007/978-3-031-20319-0_41

have been consistently described as highly stressful places [1]. In general, university students begin this new stage full of uncertainty and with a small degree of stress that can accumulate in the classroom, where the greater demand and academic activity translates into more work [2]. In the process, the individual's desire to manage college life most successfully (which may to some extent require better professional training), is an additional element of stress. Greater strength for students [3]. Likewise, other differences can contribute negatively to the development of university life; The first is the social factor, followed by the economic, cultural, and finally psychological level that each student has to face at university [4].

Psychological well-being is a concept that is difficult to define conceptually, due to the inherent complexity of the term, the diversity in its use, and the scope of the research devoted to its study. The term is multi-deterministic and involves both objective and subjective factors [5]. However, their study is of great scientific interest, since it can determine why some students feel dissatisfied with the choice of their university career, while others do not [6].

The objective of the present study was to determine the predictors related to the general well-being of adolescent students of the National Technological Institute of Mexico using a data collection tool collected for 6 years.

Several studies have shown that the frequent use of forms of emotional regulation leads to different results at the emotional, cognitive and social levels [7]. Emotionally, those who tended to be repressive experienced negative emotions, including depressive symptoms and a lack of positive emotions. At a cognitive level, students who use suppression regularly suffer from memory loss. Socially, repression reduces support and contact with others. In contrast, at the emotional level, those who used cognitive reappraisal tended to experience more positive emotions, fewer negative emotions, and fewer depressive symptoms. At the cognitive level, reappraisal was positively associated with improved memory. At the social level, reappraisal increases positive relationships with others [8–11]. Among the other variables studied, emotional inhibition was reported to be associated with lower optimism, lower life satisfaction, and lower self-esteem and self-esteem. While cognitive reappraisal is associated with higher levels of optimism, self-esteem, personal growth, life purpose, and life satisfaction [12]. These data reinforce the idea that reassessment is more practical and desirable than elimination. However, as mentioned above, context is important in determining the most appropriate or generally beneficial strategies [13].

It has been shown that the development of skills related to emotional intelligence has a positive impact on social, academic, and professional aspects [14, 15]. Emotionally intelligent students show higher self-esteem, emotional and personal regulation, happiness and satisfaction, quality of network interactions, social support, and little willingness to express themselves. They also showed lower levels of physical symptoms, anxiety, and depression. This increases their academic performance by adequately coping with stressful school situations, with less drug use [16].

2 State of Art

In a study by Ryff in 1989 [17], significant differences in age, gender, and educational level were found between various aspects of psychological well-being. When it comes to sex, women have a more positive relationship than men [18]. Other studies (eg, [19, 20]) also confirm gender differences in psychological well-being. The most common interpretations in the literature on the subject affirm that women tend to be more defensive and in tune with others than men, while the latter tend to give more importance to self-promotion, denunciation, and pursuit of personal goals and objectives. Zubieta, Fernández, and Sosa (2012) [21] evaluated 947 people from different Argentine cities and found significant differences by sex in aspects of self-acceptance and self-control (high value compared to men), positive relationships, and personal growth (higher value in women). This is not a case of environmental mastery and life purpose, where there is no difference. In summary, the authors point out that their findings confirm the tendency of women toward social, social, and social values to show more, while men emphasize self-acceptance and independence as the source of their well-being. In another study [22], similar evidence has often been explained by the social contexts in which social skills, such as social, emotional, and interpersonal skills, are formed. Society emphasizes qualities such as self-discipline, goal orientation, self-determination, etc.

Colombia is one of the Latin American countries most affected by dropout, a survey was conducted to contribute to a decision to reduce the dropout rate of students in university programs, due to their use. Discovery of the knowledge database (KDD) and implementation in the design of predictive mathematical models, including the four factors proposed by the Colombian Ministry of Education related to the socio-economic aspects of each student, whether social, personal, academic, or institutional, allowing to visualize the individual dropout rates of students in the Various Academy programs [23].

3 Methodology

3.1 Data Recollection

The present investigation seeks to understand the impact that it´s generated when the socioeconomic characteristics affect the emotional stability of the institute students, finding out the main factors that influence that even the students do not feel satisfied with the career they chose when entering the institution. A request was made to the administration of the institution to be able to use a database that comes with a total of 768 records, the questionnaire was applied over for almost 6 years, the first record being added on March 12, 2013, and the last one on January 9, 2019. Table 1 shows the questions answered by students from different careers at the University.

Table 1. Questions that comes in the data base.

Questions
Semester
Sex
Date of Birth
Age
Marital status
Number of children
Current partner: Yes or No
You live with
Total number of siblings
Work: Yes or No
People who work in your house
Dad
Mother
Brothers
Partner
How many rooms are there in the house where you live? (including kitchen-bathroom-etc.)
What services does the house have?
Water
Sewer system
Light
TV
Cable or satellite TV
Internet
Telephone
Do you have a private space at home to study and/or do your school work?
Indicate the means with which you support yourself to study at home
Computer equipment
Desk
Printing machine
table and/or dresser
Internet
Comfortable chair
Bookcase
Specialized books and dictionaries
Adequate light and ventilation
How important is your studies in your family?
In your family you like to spend free time together: Yes or No
There are difficulties or problematic situations: Yes or No
They communicate easily and with respect: Yes or No
They help each other: Yes or No
Expenses with which his father supports
Tuition

(*continued*)

Table 1. (*continued*)

Questions
Materials
Clothing
Foods
Living place
Others
Expenses with which his mother supports
Tuition
Materials
Clothing
Foods
living place
Others
Do you have any chronic illness or serious health situation?
How many hours do you sleep per day?
Have you consumed alcohol in the last year?
If your answer is yes, how often do you consume?
Have you used any drugs?
How often have you been consuming?
How many meals do you eat a day?
Do you have any problem with food?
Do you have an active sex life?
Do you use contraceptive methods?
How often do you usually feel depressed?
How often do you usually feel pressured?
How often do you usually feel fearful?
How often do you usually feel angry?
How often do you usually feel annoyed?
How often do you usually feel insecure?
Are you satisfied with the career you chose to study?

How these data were collected was through a course called *"Tutorias"*, which is an accompaniment that is carried out for students from the time they enter the first semester until they finish, there are 3 types of *"Tutorias"*, the first is the entrance tutorials *"Tutoria de Ingreso"*, which help the newly admitted student to know the TecNM system, the structure of the personnel, social, cognitive and personal skills. The second is an accompanying tutorial *"Tutoria de Acompañamiento"*, which consists of monitoring students through their academic progress, and personal and group counseling. And the last one is a graduation tutorial *"Tutoria de Egreso"*, which advises the student in the course of social service, professional residence, and entry into the world of work. Because of these three programs, it is necessary to know the socio-economic and emotional aspects of the students (Fig. 1).

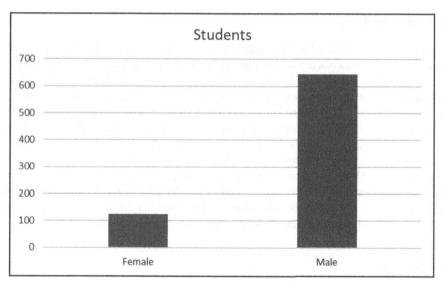

Fig. 1. Number of those surveyed according to sex.

It should be noted that of the 768 records, 124 are female student responses, which represents 16.3% of the total records, and 644 are male student responses, representing 83.7%.

It is of great importance to clarify that the database was cleaned, eliminating some fields whose response was open and there was no way to characterize these responses, the questions that are being presented in Table 1 were dichotomous responses and scale Likert since it is ideal to measure the reactions, attitudes, and behaviors of a person.

3.2 The Steps that Any Data Mining Process Includes

- The data mining process begins with the selection of variables to be processed, those that are a function of the variables to be calculated or predicted, the objective variables guide the choice of the objectives of the analysis and the independent variables determine how process will take place.
- Subsequently, the characteristics of the data set are analyzed, which will go through trend analysis, pattern detection, recognition of atypical values, and values with null information will be discarded. This previous cleaning will guide the processing of the data and will allow them to be classified and grouped according to the chosen predictive model, after which knowledge models will be built.
- It concludes with the validation of the knowledge models for which they are compared and interpreted and the one that best satisfies the objective is selected. If the model does not meet expectations, the process is carried out again, but changing the variables until obtaining a model that satisfies the needs and the proposed mining objective [24].

3.3 Decision Trees

Data mining is understood as the process of discovering interesting knowledge, such as significant patterns, associations, changes, anomalies, and structures from large amounts of data stored in a database, data warehouse, or other information storage media [26]. The application of data mining algorithms requires previous processes to prepare the data uniformly. This first step is also known as ETL (Extract, Transform, and Load) [27]. An integral process of applying mining techniques, also known as the database knowledge discovery process [28], makes data mining one of its steps. In this framework, what is the decision tree algorithm can be used, this algorithm is classified as learning based on similarity [25], the decision tree is one of the simplest and most popular algorithms, easy to implement and in turn easy to implement. The most powerful algorithms. This algorithm iteratively generates a decision tree by observing the criteria for the highest profit rate [26], that is, it selects the best attributes to classify the data.

4 Results

The analysis carried out shows that satisfaction with the choice of career is predicted by the insecurity felt by the student. The results indicate that 94.5% of the students surveyed are satisfied with their chosen careers. The fact of feeling insecure very frequently results in a variable that better predicts student satisfaction by showing a higher chi-square statistic (4.919) than any other option of said question. The following branch shows that 94.3% of the students who are supported by their mother, with the payment of tuition, are satisfied with the career they chose. In a concrete way and based on the questions raised, the tree indicates that the satisfaction of the career chosen by the student is influenced by the frequency with which he feels insecure and by the fact that the student is supported by the mother in the process. tuition payment (See Fig. 2).

Regarding the insecurity felt by the student, feeling fearful is the main predictor of it. The chi-square statistic of 62,530 allows us to argue that, of the people surveyed, 66.3% of those who answered that they rarely felt fearful also answered that they rarely felt insecure. In the same way, the level of fear is related to a low level of depression, concluding that having an active sexual life is linked to students feeling less insecure, since 85.3 percent of the people who show little insecurity declared who lead an active sexual life (See Fig. 3).

If the results shown in Figures 2 and 3 are taken into consideration, it can be argued that there is a relationship between the satisfaction provided by the choice of career with the fact of feeling more insecure, while having an active sexual life generates a perception of greater security, so that people who have sex on a regular basis would be more likely to show some dissatisfaction with the chosen career.

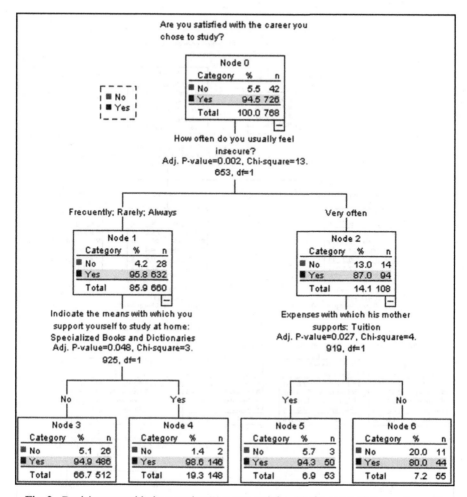

Fig. 2. Decision tree with the question "Are you satisfy with the career that you choose?".

On the other hand, if we approach the analysis from the student's environment and take as a reference the importance given to studies in their family environment, we have that the degree of family help and cooperation that exists adequately predicts the importance that is given to studies.

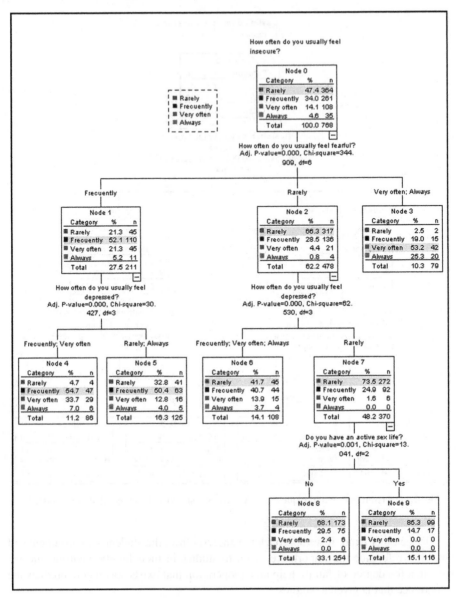

Fig. 3. Decision tree with the question "How often do you usually feel insecure?".

The data shows that 78.5% (See Fig. 4) of those surveyed consider that studies are very important for the family and that 89.7% of those who declare that there is mutual help in their families, showed a high level of importance in studies by their families. . While 95% indicated a high level of importance of studies in the family since their father pays the tuition.

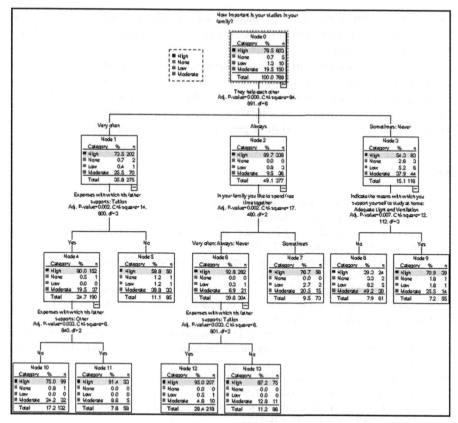

Fig. 4. Decision tree starting with the question "How important is your studies in your family?".

5   Conclusions

The descriptive analysis carried out contributes to a certain extent to the discussion about the importance of the family and social environment in the emotional well-being of the students of the Technological Institute of Tijuana.

Fundamentally, it was found that satisfaction with the choice of career, as an approximate measure of the student's well-being, is predicted by the level of insecurity felt by the student. In general, it is found that 94.5% of the students are satisfied with the chosen career and that the insecurity felt by the student better predicts said satisfaction. Likewise, the participation of the mother results in an aspect that contributes to reducing the effect of feeling insecure, since 94.3% of the students who are supported by their mother, with the payment of tuition, are satisfied with the career they chose.

If we focus more closely on the insecurity felt by the student, feeling fearful is the main predictor of it. There is a relationship between a low level of insecurity with a low level of fear felt by the student, while the low level of fear is related to a low level of depression, and this in turn with an active sexual life. This gives us elements to conclude that a low level of insecurity is linked to having an active sexual life. The data also showed that the importance given to studies in their family environment as well as the degree of family help and cooperation that exists are linked to the fact that the father is the one who assumes the cost of enrollment.

In conclusion, we can affirm that aspects such as the importance that the family gives it and the fact that the costs of studying are assumed by the parents tend to be related to greater student satisfaction with their studies, while having a sexually active life is an aspect important, since the evidence shows that these students would feel less insecure, but on the other hand, they would show greater dissatisfaction with the chosen career.

References

1. Mundo, A.: Estrés académico y burnout en los estudiantes de psicología (Tesis maestría). Universidad Rafael Urdaneta, Maracaibo (2014)
2. Barraza, A.: Estrés académico y burnout estudiantil. Análisis de su relación en alumnos de licenciatura. Psicogente **12**(22), 272–283 (2009)
3. Vélez, A., Roa, C.: Factores asociados al rendimiento académico en estudiantes de medicina. Educación Médica **8**(2), 74–82 (2005)
4. Caballero, C., Abello, R., Palacio, J.: Relación del burnout y el rendimiento académico con la satisfacción frente a los estudios en estudiantes universitarios. Avances en Psicología Latinoamericana **25**(2), 98–111 (2007)
5. García-Viniegras, V., González Benítez, I.: La categoría bienestar psicológico: Su relación con otras categorías sociales. Revista cubana de medicina general integral **16**(6), 586–592 (2000)
6. Strack, F., Argyle, M., Schwartz, N. (eds.): Subjective Well-Being: An Interdisciplinary Perspective. Pergamon Press, Oxford (1991)
7. Gross, J.: Emotion regulation: taking stock and moving forward. Emotion **13**(3), 359–365 (2013). https://doi.org/10.1037/a0032135
8. Garrido-Rojas, L.: Apego, emoción y regulación emocional. Implicancias para la salud. Revista Latinoamericana de Psicología **38**(3), 493–507 (2006)
9. Gross, J., John, O.: Individual differences in two emotion regulation processes: implications for affect, relationship, and well-being. J. Pers. Social Psychol. **85**, 348–362 (2003)
10. Nezlek, J., Kuppens, P.: Regulating positive and negative emotions in daily life. J. Pers. **76**, 561–580 (2008). https://doi.org/10.1111/j.1467-6494.2008.00496.x
11. Richards, J., Gross, J.: Emotion regulation and memory: the cognitive cost of keeping one's cool. J. Pers. Soc. Psychol. **79**, 410–424 (2000). https://doi.org/10.1037/0022-3514.79.3.410
12. Gross, J., Thompson, R.: Emotion regulation: conceptual foundations. In: Gross, J.J. (ed.) Handbook of Emotion Regulation, pp. 3–24. GuilfordPress, New York (2007)
13. Gross, J.: Emotion regulation: current status and future prospects. Psychol. Inquiry **26**, 1–26 (2015). https://doi.org/10.1080/1047840X.2014.940781
14. Palomera, R., Fernández-Berrocal, P., Brackett, M.: La inteligencia emocional como una competencia básica en la formación inicial de los docentes: algunas evidencias. Revista Electrónica de Investigación Psicoeducativa **6**(15), 437–454 (2008)
15. Bueno García, C., Teruel Melero, M.P., Valero Salas, A.: La inteligencia emocional en alumnos de Magisterio. La percepción y comprensión de los sentimientos y las emociones. Revista Interuniversitaria de Formación del Profesorado **19**(3), 169–194 (2005)
16. Extremera, N., Fernandez-Berrocal, P.: El papel de la inteligencia emocional en el alumnado: Evidencias Empíricas. Revista Electrónica de Investigación Educativa **6**(2), 1–17 (2004)

17. Barra, E.: Bienestar psicológico y orientación de rol sexual en estudiantes universitarios. Terapia psicológica **28**(1), 119–125 (2010). https://doi.org/10.4067/S0718-48082010000100011

18. Ryff, C., Keyes, C.: The structure of psychological well-being revisited. J. Pers. Social Psychol. **69**(4), 719–727 (1995). https://doi.org/10.1037/0022-3514.69.4.719

19. Delfino, G., Zubieta, E.: Valores y política. Análisis del perfil axiológico de los estudiantes universitarios de la ciudad de Buenos Aires (República Argentina). Interdisciplinaria **29**(1), 93–114 (2009)

20. Zubieta, E., Mele, S., Casullo, M.: Estructura de valores y religiosidad en población adulta urbana argentina. Psicodiagnosticar **16**, 53–60 (2006)

21. Zubieta, E., Fernández, O., Sosa, F.: Bienestar, valores y variables asociadas. Boletín de Psicología **106**, 7–27 (2012)

22. Zubieta, E., Muratori, M., Mele, S.: Bienestar, clima emocional, percepción de problemas sociales y confianza. Anuario de Investigación de la Facultad de Psicología de la Universidad de Buenos Aires **19**(1), 97–106 (2012)

23. Argote, I., Jimenez, R.: Detección de patrones de deserción en los programas de pregrado de la Universidad Mariana de San Juan de Pasto, Aplicando el proceso de descubrimiento de conocimiento sobre base de datos (KDD) Y su implementación. In: IV Conferencia latinoamericana sobre abandono en la educacion superior, pp. 1–7 (2014)

24. Corporacion ICEMD TV. Mineria de Datos. Obtenido de (2017). https://www.icemd.com/digital-knowledge/articulos/mineria-datos-proceso-areas-sepuede-aplica/

25. Han, J., Kamber, M.: Data Mining: Concepts and Techniques. The Morgan Kaufmann Publishers, Burlington (2006).ISBN: 1558609016

26. Britos, P., Hossian, A.: Minería de Datos. Nueva Librería, Argentina (2005). ISBN: 9871104308

27. Kimball, R.: The Data Warehouse Toolkit: The Complete Guide to Dimensional Modeling. Wiley Computer Publishing, Hoboken (2002). ISBN: 780471200246

28. Cabena, P., Hadjinian, P.: Discovering Data Mining, From Concept to Implementation. Prentice Hall, Upper Saddle River (1988).ISBN: 9780137439805

Classification of Defects in Injected Parts Through: Moments of Image and Multilayer Perceptron

Blanca Ruiz[✉], Rosario Baltazar, Miguel Casillas, Raul Santiago, and Francisco Mosiño

Instituto Tecnológico de León, León, Mexico
{m14241007,rosario.baltazar}@leon.tecnm.mx
https://leon.tecnm.mx/

Abstract. Quality control at industry is an important factor to find the desired specifications of the manufactured products, this is often achieved manually with the support of the work staff. It implies that some defects are not detected by workers due to fatigue. This article describes a technological proposal, applied to the quality control of injected parts, using vision machine to give support to quality control. In this article we achieve obtain a set of PVC tee in a previously were environment it for four different faces and two types of parts found: defective and non-defective. Then image processing where we obtain the characteristic vector and using feed forward artificial neuronal network based on a multilayer perceptron mentioned images are classified account to the type expected. An n training procedure and is performance to classifi images are discussed in detail in the contect of quality control.

Keywords: Quality control · Image processing · Multilayer perceptron · Classification

1 Introduction

Polyvinyl Chloride or PVC is one of the most popular industrial thermoplastics chosen to create a variety of plastic products. These include pipes, medical tubes and connectors. In PVC pipeline industry, the inspection and testing PVC tee requires a high level of concentration of the worker to find the defects of the tee.

In this work a vision machine is implemented to detect defects in PVC connectors. The development of this technique and its use is proposed to quality control in injected parts, specifically for the detection of defects in the Tee 110×110 mm cemented.

Injection Molding Machinery injected and ejected the tee, which generates a falling process which implies a more complex design of the vision machine moreover the piece must be captured by all its faces, a total of six faces of which four are different, It begins with the capture of images in a controlled

© The Author(s), under exclusive license to Springer Nature Switzerland AG 2022
T. Guarda et al. (Eds.): ARTIIS 2022, CCIS 1675, pp. 558–571, 2022.
https://doi.org/10.1007/978-3-031-20319-0_42

environment for the realization of the database, the piece has four different faces captured for evaluation, once the images are obtained, the preprocessing is carried out to highlight the piece of the established background and thus generate the extraction of its characteristics in a data vector that is characterized by the moments of the image, since the vectors are available, these are entered into the multi-layer perceptron neural network for its training where we present the results of the classification of the two types of parts, whether they are defective or not defective.

2   Image Processing

In general an image be described as a two-dimensional array of pixels with different luminous intensity. In a mathematical form it can be functionally expressed as:

$$r = f(x, y) \tag{1}$$

where r is the luminous intensity and (x, y) the coordinates of each pixel, the color of the image is formed by three colors: red, blue and green (RGB), Additionally, images has more describing elements such as the brightness that includes the illumination of an area, the tone that refers to the similarity of an area to red, yellow, green or blue, we also find the brightness of a sector with respect to the brightness of a white [5, 6].

The RGB space is the combination of three different signals: red, green and blue. We can obtain a specific color by determining the amount of red, green and blue color that is needed to combine this by means of arithmetic operations of the signals such as: addition, subtraction, multiplication or division of channels [6, 7].

2.1   Noise in Images

Noise is the change in the pixels of an image that modifies the characteristics of the image, we can find two types of noise: uniform and impulsive [8].

Uniform noise shows changes in the image gray levels but without saturating the intensity of the pixels, its distribution is close to the shape of a Gaussian bell that has a wide exponential tail, finite momentum and variance that allows to reduce the noise [8]. The application of filters like "simple average" are very useful to remove Gaussian noise from an image with variations in brightness or color [9, 11, 17, 22].

2.2   Addition of Images

It is possible to add a scalar to an image, this results in a clarification of the image and it is done by adding the scalar to each of the pixels of the image where if the result is greater than 255 it takes 255 as the value resulting [4]. The sum of two images is executed by adding pixel plus pixel found in the same location of the images and is represented in the form [4]:

$$A(x, y) + B(x, y) = R(x, y) \tag{2}$$

2.3   Image Segmentation

Image segmentation is a technique that highlight the objects of interest from the rest in an image, where it is desired to obtain an image with a clean background without stains, shadows or excess light that separate the main object [3]. Image segmentation is based on separating the gray levels with a predetermined threshold value [13], where if the gray level is less than the threshold, the pixel is assigned the value of 0, that is, it takes the color black and if it is greater it will take the value of 1 taking the color white [6,14].

3   Image Moments

The moments of the image comprise a set of statistical values that help to measure the distribution and intensities of the pixels, these does not vary even if the image object appears in a different position or different size and are also descriptors of the shape of the objects in the image of the picture. The image momentum M_{uv} of order (u, v) for a gray scale image with pixel intensities I(x, y) can be described as

$$Muv = \sum_x \sum_y x^u y^v I(x,y) \tag{3}$$

where x, y defines the row and column index, I(x, y) corresponds to the intensity at location (x, y) [18].

3.1   Moments Invariants

Hu arrived at seven moments that are invariant with respect to changes in size, position and orientation, defines the seven functions calculated from the normalized moments up to third order, which result by replacing the central moments [10], and six of the 7 moments are presented as follows [15]

$$\mu_{20} + \mu_{02} \tag{4}$$

$$(\mu_{20} - \mu_{02})^2 + (4\mu_{11}^2) \tag{5}$$

$$(\mu_{30} - 3\mu_{12})^2 + (3\mu_{21} - \mu_{03})^2 \tag{6}$$

$$(\mu_{30} + \mu_{12})^2 + (\mu_{21} + \mu_{03})^2 \tag{7}$$

$$(\mu_{30} - 3\mu_{12})(\mu_{30} + \mu_{12})[(\mu_{30} + \mu_{12})^2 - 3(\mu_{21} + \mu_{03})^2] \\ + (3\mu_{21} - \mu_{03})(\mu_{21} + \mu_{03})[3(\mu_{30} + \mu_{12})^2 - (\mu_{21} + \mu_{03})^2] \tag{8}$$

$$(\mu_{20} - \mu_{02})[(\mu_{30} + \mu_{12})^2 - [(\mu_{21} + \mu_{03})^2] + 4\mu_{11}(\mu_{30} + \mu_{12})(\mu_{21} + \mu_{03}) \tag{9}$$

and one skew orthogonal invariants [15].

$$(3\mu_{21} - \mu_{03})(\mu_{30} + \mu_{12})[(\mu_{30} + \mu_{12})^2 - 3(\mu_{21} \\ + \mu_{03})^2] - (\mu_{30} + 3\mu_{12})^2 + (\mu_{21} + \mu_{03}) \\ [3(\mu_{30} + \mu_{12})^2 - (\mu_{21} + \mu_{03}^2)]$$
(10)

his skew invariant is useful in to distinguish mirror images [15], also where:

$$\mu_{pq} = \mu_{pq}(\Omega) = \frac{\int \int \Omega(x - x_c)^p(y - y_c)^q dxdy}{(\int \int \Omega dxdy)^{\frac{p+q+2}{2}}}$$
(11)

which is the central moment of the domain Ω and (x_c, y_c) are the coordinates of center the gravity of Ω [16]. These moments are applied for the generation of the feature vector of each image.

4   Artficial Neuronal Network

Artificial neural networks (ANN) are a subset of machine learning techniques that uses a vector of input data that feed node called neuron. These neurons have a numerical value called weight that modifies the input, neurons are grouped in layers and the results of each passes to the next layer. This procedure is repeated many times as inner layers the ANN has, until to the last layer that performs a prediction ref. [1,2].

This kind of ANN is often called Multilayer Perceptron (MLP), which is composed of the input layer, one or more intermediate or hidden layers, and an output layer [19,20]. The MLP learning process is based on finding a function that correctly represents the learning patterns as well as carrying out a generalization process that allows treating unknown individuals, This is achieved by a vector of weights W from the information of the sample. Given the set of sample patterns $(x_1, y_1), (x_2, y_2), ..., (x_p, y_{1p})$ an error function $\epsilon(W, X, Y)$ the training is based on the search for n set of weights that decrease the learning error E(W) [19,20] (Fig. 1):

$$min_W E(W) = min_W \sum_{i=1}^{p} \epsilon(W, x_i, y_i)$$
(12)

4.1   Differential Evolution

Differential evolution is an algorithm that starts with a population of NP individuals, the first population randomly distributes the individuals where an iterative process of mutation, crossing and selection is carried out, DE first applies a mutation operator that gives us a mutated vector with respect to each individual

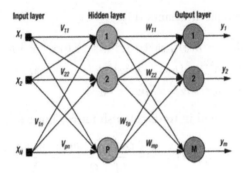

Fig. 1. Multilayer perceptron architecturecite [19].

of the current population. After the mutation phase, the crossover operator is applied to each vector of the population and its corresponding mutated vector generating a new vector which we name test vector [12,21], this is applied in union with MLP to search for the best vector of weights that would support the classification of images.

5 Methodology

It begins by taking images for the generation of the database, we proceed to the preprocessing to continue with the extraction of the vector of characteristics through the invariant moments of Hu of the image with which we can train the ANN and process to tests of classification that finally give using us the results Fig. 2.

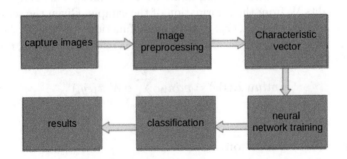

Fig. 2. Diagram of the sequence of activities.

The methodology used for image processing is shown in Fig. 3 for hollows and stains and in Fig. 4 for burr.

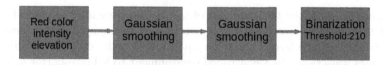

Fig. 3. Diagram of the sequence of hollows and stains processing.

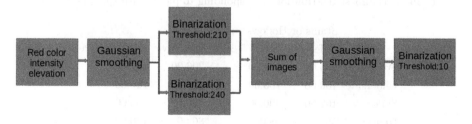

Fig. 4. Diagram of the sequence of burr processing.

5.1   Data

Injected parts could present a serie of defects as a result of different factors. These defects can be classified in terms of the piece shape as:

- Burr: Excess material
- Hollows: Material missing
- Stains: Stains that can include burns, a combination of materials or dirt.

Fig. 5. Presented in the parts: burr, stains and holes.

In Fig. 5 we can see an example of how these defects appear in the injected piece. Each piece of the population with defects contains at least one of these and even all three and is composed of eight databases, distributed as follows: four of them describe the pieces that contain spots or holes on the front, side, upper and lower, the following four for burrs on the same faces, in these we find two types of pieces those that contain the defect and those that do not in Table 1 we can find the number of individuals per class for each, this was determined through the total number of pieces that presented the defect, in the case of the non-defective ones it was determined through the total number of adequate shots of the face in the same environment as its defective counterpart. The images were taken in a controlled environment to achieve better quality.

Table 1. Database distribution corresponding to pieces with spots and holes.

	Stains or Hollows		Burr	
	Defective	Not defective	Defective	Not defective
Frontal	206.00	206.00	206.00	527.00
Underside	100.00	100.00	126.00	226.00
Sude	162.00	400.00	429.00	163.00
Higher	50.00	98.00	86.00	140.00

5.2 Image Preprocessing

A series of filters are applied to the images to enhance the respective piece image of the corresponding piece, in Fig. 6 and Fig. 13 we can see an example of the results obtained. The first processing corresponds to the enhancement of burrs and the second to the enhancement of stains or holes in the piece (Figs. 7, 8, 9, 10, 11 and 12).

Fig. 6. Non-defective part before and after front face treatment.

Fig. 7. Defective part before and after front face treatment.

Fig. 8. Non-defective part before and after treatment underside.

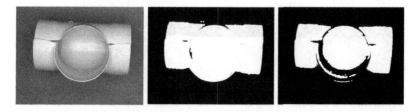

Fig. 9. Defective piece before and after the lower face treatment.

Fig. 10. Non-defective part before and after side face treatment.

Fig. 11. Defective part before and after side face treatment.

5.3   Turning Database Images into Characteristic Vectors

as we already For the training of the neural network it is necessary to have a set of vectors that describe the images, these were extracted through the invariant moments of Hu that the image presents, the databases comprise a total of 7 elements per vector.

Fig. 12. Non-defective part before and after top face treatment.

Fig. 13. Defective piece with stains before and after treatment for burrs and stains respectively upper face.

6   MLP Training

It is proposed that MLP support us in the separation of the images to achieve a classification between the parts that meet the requirements, these are labeled as non-defective and those that do not meet the requirements, which are labeled as defective. MLP is trained from the vectors obtained from the images, these vectors are labeled according to their class.

The structure of the neural network is particular for each of the databases, this includes only one hidden layer and its input values are defined according to the characteristics of the individuals in the database, that is, 7, our parameters are established as follows: NG = 1000 or error = 0.0001, experiments = 33 and 2 neurons in the output layer since they are the kinds of pieces that we have. The network will be trained with 50% of the individuals and later tested with the other 50%.

6.1   DE-MLP Training

The DE-MLP neural network is defined in the same way as MLP, however N takes the value of 20 for the vectors that subsequently enter the mutation process.

7   ANN Quality Control Prediction Assesment

For classification experiments carried out using MLP of the 110×110 mm Tee, the statistics shown in Tables 2, 3, 4 and Table 5.

For the classification experiments carried out using DE-MLP of the 110 × 110 mm Tee, the statistics shown in Tables 6, 7, 8 and Table 9.

Regarding the results obtained, the classification of both defects when it comes to the front face, if we are talking about MLP, neither is greater than 75%, that is to say that at least 3 out of 10 PVC pieces are classified in an erroneous way, in the case of De -MLP for holes and stains does not exceed 55%, that is, half of the pieces are classified incorrectly, we can only observe an advantage in the burr classified with DE-MLP, since the minimum classification is 81.88% and the maximum is 99.05%, that is, their worst classification corresponds to 2 out of 10 pieces and their best classification corresponds to 1 incorrect piece out of 10. If we talk about the lower face, the results are outstanding in most of the classifications because we only observe low classifications in MLP when it comes to burrs, where the wrongly classified pieces go from 4 to 8 out of 10 pieces, however the rest of the Results, that is, MLP for holes or stains and DE-MLP for both defects achieve up to a maximum of 90–95% of correct classifications and a minimum of 46%. Regarding the upper face, MLP gives us maximum results of 70% or a maximum of 7 pieces correctly classified in a set of 10 for both defects, DE-MLP there is no notable variation for holes or stains, since the maximum percentage is found at 68.92% however for burr it achieves an improvement with a minimum of 84% of correct classification and a maximum of 98.41% that is to say of 10 pieces less than 2 are incorrectly classified. Finally, the lateral face in MLP, both defects do not exceed 90%, their maximums are found at 79.56% and 86.83% for stains or holes and burrs respectively, again DE-MLP has a better performance, although the worst classification percentage is 54.05% most of the rest are above 70% even reaching 97.97% for holes or stains and 88.25% for burrs.

Table 2. Statistics of the percentage of classification of MLP of the front face with spots or holes and burr.

	Front face: Stains or Hollow		Front face: Burr	
	Training	Test	Training	Test
Maximium	74.03	74.03	73.43	73.98
Minimium	59.47	57.04	71.53	68.53
Average	67.69	68.62	72.38	71.93
Median	69.17	71.36	72.21	71.93
Mode	71.36	71.36	71.93	71.93

Table 3. Statistics of the percentage of classification of MLP of the inferior face with spots or holes and burr.

	Underside face: Stains or Hollow		Underside face: Burr	
	Training	Test	Training	Test
Maximium	90	95	79.55	44.03
Minimium	46	50	40.06	44.03
Average	78.52	82.85	63.41	60.49
Median	82	86	65.34	63.07
Mode	84	89	50	50

Table 4. Statistics of the percentage of classification of MLP of the upper face with burr and holes.

	Upper face: Stains or Hollow		Upper face: Burr	
	Training	Test	Training	Test
Maximium	66.89	66.89	70.80	70.80
Minimium54.05	54.05	53.38	57.52	53.10
Average	63.84	61.94	60.93	62.81
Median	65.54	63.51	61.95	61.95
Mode	66.22	66.22	61.95	61.95

Table 5. Statistics of the percentage of classification of MLP of the upper face with spots or holes and burr.

	Side face: Stains or Hollow		Side face: Burr	
	Training	Test	Training	Test
Maximium	77.87	79.56	79.54	86.83
Minimium	67.57	68.41	62.63	62.63
Average	71.40	72.50	70.68	72.45
Median	71.79	72.47	71.17	72.24
Mode	72.64	72.30	71.17	71.17

Table 6. Statistics of the percentage of classification of DE-MLP of the side face with spots or holes and burr.

	Front face: Stains or Hollow		Front face: Burr	
	Training	Test	Training	Test
Maximium	52.43	51.70	99.05	91.55
Minimium	46.12	21.84	81.88	81.34
Average	48.90	48.07	88.42	86.03
Median	49.27	49.76	88.56	85.56
Mode	50.00	50.00	99.05	82.83

Table 7. Statistics of the percentage of classification of DE-MLP of the underside face with spots or holes and burr.

	Underside face: Stains or Hollow		Underside face: Burr	
	Training	Test	Training	Test
Maximum	95.00	95.50	94.60	95.17
Minimium	80.50	53.00	65.34	84.09
Average	86.39	85.76	88.38	89.34
Median	87.00	87.50	89.20	88.64
Mode	83.00	83.50	90.34	88.35

Table 8. Statistics of the percentage of classification of DE-MLP of the upper face with spots or holes and burr.

	Upper face: Stains or Hollow		Upper face: Burr	
	Training	Test	Training	Test
Maximium	68.92	66.22	98.41	96.02
Minimium	57.43	58.11	84.07	83.19
Average	63.51	63.02	91.56	90.12
Median	63.51	63.51	92.92	90.71
Mode	64.86	64.86	94.69	85.84

Table 9. Statistics of the percentage of classification of DE-MLP of the side face with spots or hollow and burr

	Side face: Stains or Hollow		Side face: Burr	
	Training	Test	Training	Test
Maximium	97.97	66.89	88.25	88.25
Minimium	72.63	54.05	71.17	71.17
Average	83.10	85.14	72.72	78.89
Median	84.79	64.35	71.17	71.17
Mode	72.63	66.22	71.17	71.17

8   Conclusion

A database of images of 110×110 mm tees was generate. Image processing established in the methodology according to the defect that we wanted to detect. If it corresponded to a burr, the images were treated by applying an intensity of the red color of the image followed by two Gaussian filters and binarizing, in terms of spots or holes we started with an intensity of the red color, then a Gaussian filter, two binarizations of the same image to achieve an addition of both, again a Gaussian filter and the final binarization. The classification of the images processed by ANN was achieved by applying MLP and DE-MLP. In the results already described, we can conclude the following as those that achieve a better classification for the front face. MLP achieves percentages above 70%, although this is higher than the rest, it is not suitable for quality control since it indicates that there are 30% probability of error that can even increase, in the case of De-MLP for the burr with up to 99% it is more viable, however, observing the rest of the statistics, it is not certain that this percentage will be maintained, something that is not It is acceptable in quality control. The lower face achieves a great improvement when we apply DE-MLP for both defects, even classifying in some cases 9 out of 10 pieces correctly. When we talk about the upper face we could well take MLP for spots or holes and De-MLP for burr thus achieving maximum ratings of 70% and 80% respectively. The best results of the lateral face are found in DE-MLP for both defects, since it achieves up to 97.97% and 88.25% of correct classification for holes or stains and burrs, respectively. Although despite the varied results we achieved some above 90% correct classification, in a quality control system this is not enough to achieve what is desired since the number of errors must be minimal at the time of classification, so In this way, it is necessary to reduce the percentage of error when classifying.

References

1. Gil, A.: Método automático para extraer información de óredenes de compra de la ferreteria herramientas y suministros, Universidad Catolica de Colombia (2020)
2. Ladino, E., García, C., García, M.: Estimación de fugas en tuberías a presión para sistemas de agua potable mediante redes neuronales artificiales y Epanet, Scielo (2022)
3. Reyes, C.: Binarización de imágenes de texto con iluminación no uniforme, Universidad Michoacana de San Nicolás de Hidalgo (2021)
4. López, A.: Adquisición y Procesamiento de imágenes con FPGA, Universidad de la Salle Bajio (2021)
5. Masabanda, W., Moreno, H.: Desarrollo de un sistema de inspección automático de PCB'S mediante vision artificial, Universidad politécnica salesiana sede Quito (2021)
6. Esqueda, J.: Fundamentos de Procesamiento de Imágenes, Conatec (2002)
7. García, I., Caaranqui, C.: La visión artificial y los campos de aplicación, Universidad Politécnica Estatal del Carchi - Ecuador (2015)
8. Betancourt, A., Tapias, H.: Procesamiento difuso de imágenes: filtro difuso para eliminar el ruido impulsivo. Ciencia, Investigación, Academia y Desarrollo (2003)
9. Dominguez, T.: Visión artificial: Aplicaciones prácticas con OpenCV - Python, Marcombo, (2021)
10. Chávez, O.: Discriminación robusta de imágenes basada en momentos geométricos y el clasificador Gamm, Instituto Politécnico Nacional (2012)
11. Gonzales, W.: Digital Image Processing, 3nd edn. Prentice hall (2008)
12. Gutiérrez, P., Triguero, I., Herrera, F.: Algoritmos Basados en Nubes de Partículas y Evoluci on Diferencial para el Problema de Optimizaci on Continua: Un estudio experimental, VIII Congreso Español sobre Metaheurística, Algoritmos Evolutivos y Bioinspirados (MAEB12) (2012)

13. Palomino, N., Concepción, N.: Wathershed: Un algoritmo eficiente y flexible para segmentación de imágenes de geles 2-DE, Revista de investgaciónde sistemas e informática (2010)
14. Castrillon, W., Álvarez, D., López, A.: Técnicas de extracción de características en imágenes para el reconocimiento de expresiones faciales, Scientia et technica (2008)
15. Hu, M.-K.: Visual Pattern Recognition by Moment Invariants. IRE. Trans. Inf. Theory (1962)
16. Rhouma, M., Minhal, M., Khan, R.: Improving the Performance of Hu Moments for Shape Recognition, Researchgate (2015)
17. Gonzales, R., Woods, R.: Digital Image Processing. Prentice Hall (2008)
18. Escolano, F., Cazorla, M., Galipienso. I., Colomina, O., Lozano, M.: Inteligencia artificial, Modelos, Técnicas y Áreas de aplicación, Paraninfo (2003)
19. Flores, R., Fernández, J.: Las Redes Neuronales Artificiales: fundamentos teóricos y aplicaciones práctica, Netbiblo (2008)
20. Shepherd, A.J.: Second-Order Methods for Neural Networks: Fast and Reliable Training Methods For Multi-Layer Perceptrons. Springer (2012). https://doi.org/ 10.1007/978-1-4471-0953-2
21. Qing, A.: Differential Evolution: Fundamentals and Applications in Electrical Engineering. IEEE Press (2009)
22. Alpaydin, A.: Introduction to machine learning (2004)

Author Index

Printed in the United States
by Baker & Taylor Publisher Services

Printed in the United States
by Baker & Taylor Publisher Services